STORY
KEVIN EASTMAN, BOBBY CURNOW, & TOM WALTZ

SCRIPT
TOM WALTZ

LAYOUTS
KEVIN EASTMAN *(Issue #25)*

ART
MATEUS SANTOLOUCO *(Issues #25–28 and #33–36)*
and **SOPHIE CAMPBELL** *(Issues #29–32)*

ADDITIONAL ART
CHARLES PAUL WILSON III *(Issue #26)*,
MIKE HENDERSON *(Issue #35)*, **MARK TORRES** *(Issue #36)*,
and **CORY SMITH** *(Issue #36)*

COLORS
RONDA PATTISON

ADDITIONAL COLORS
IAN HERRING *(Issue #28)*

LETTERS
SHAWN LEE

SERIES EDITS
BOBBY CURNOW

"The Pied Piper of Hamelin" (1842) written by **ROBERT BROWNING**

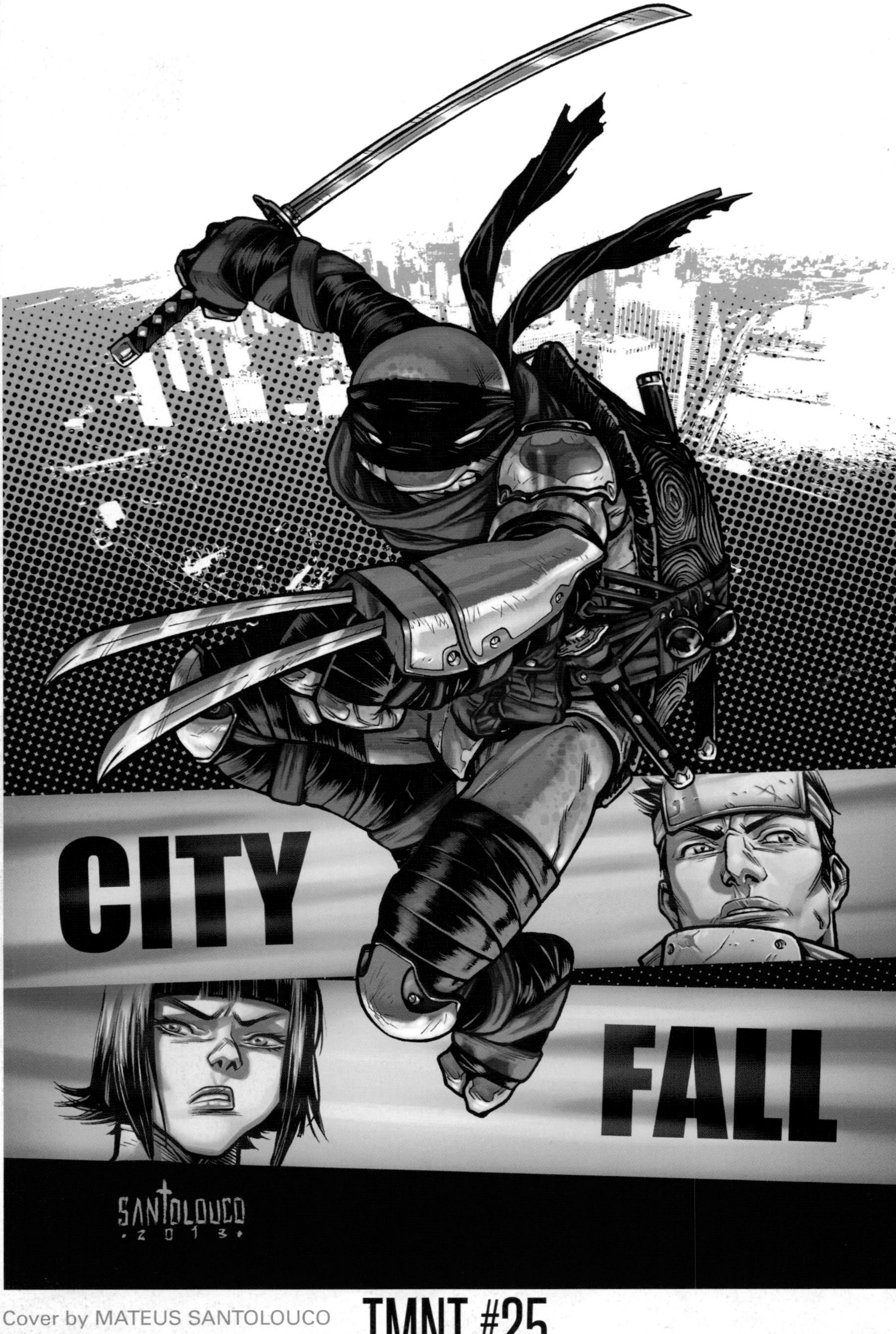
CITY
FALL
SANTOLOUCO
2013

Cover by MATEUS SANTOLOUCO

TMNT #25

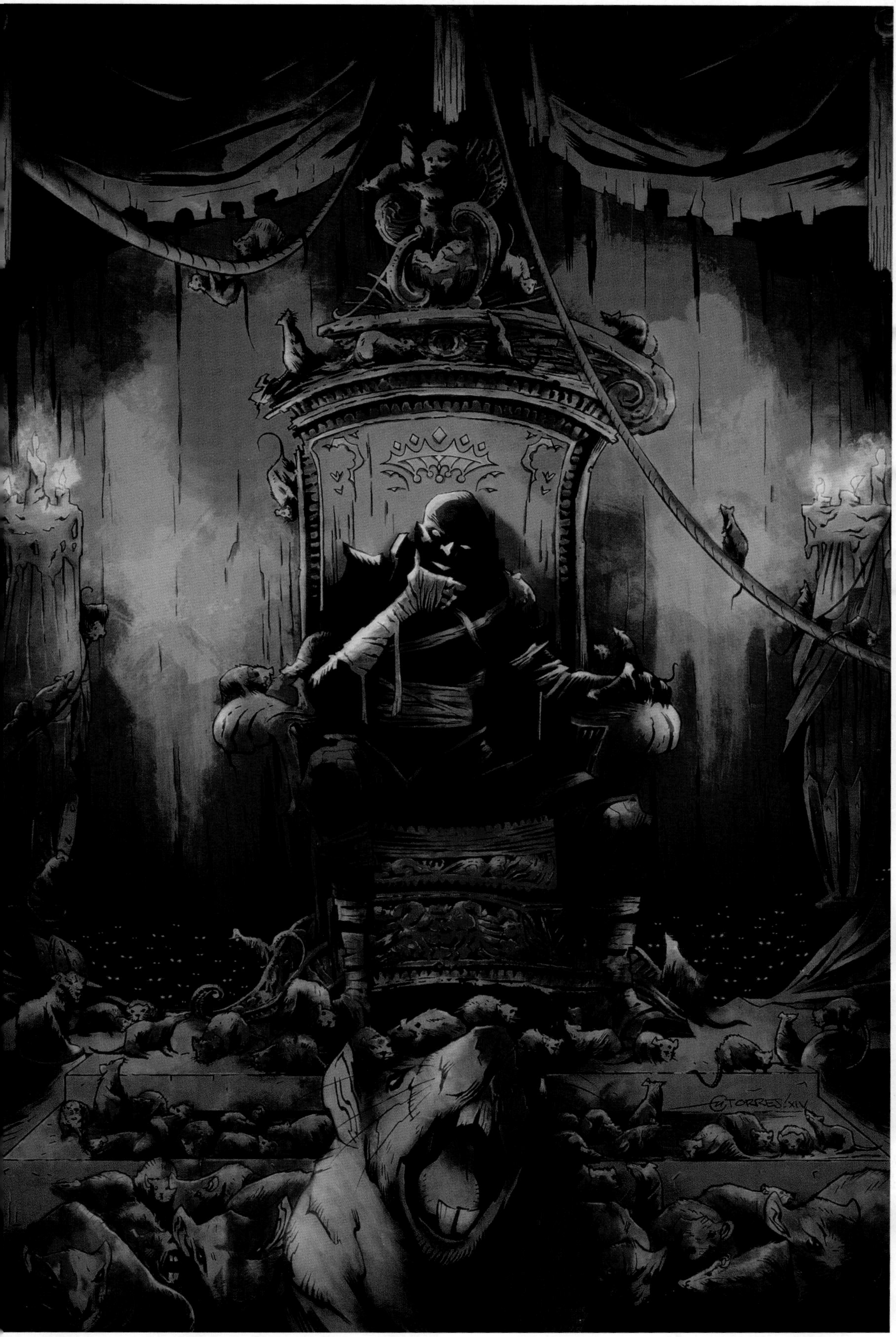
TORRES XIV

Cover by MARK TORRES

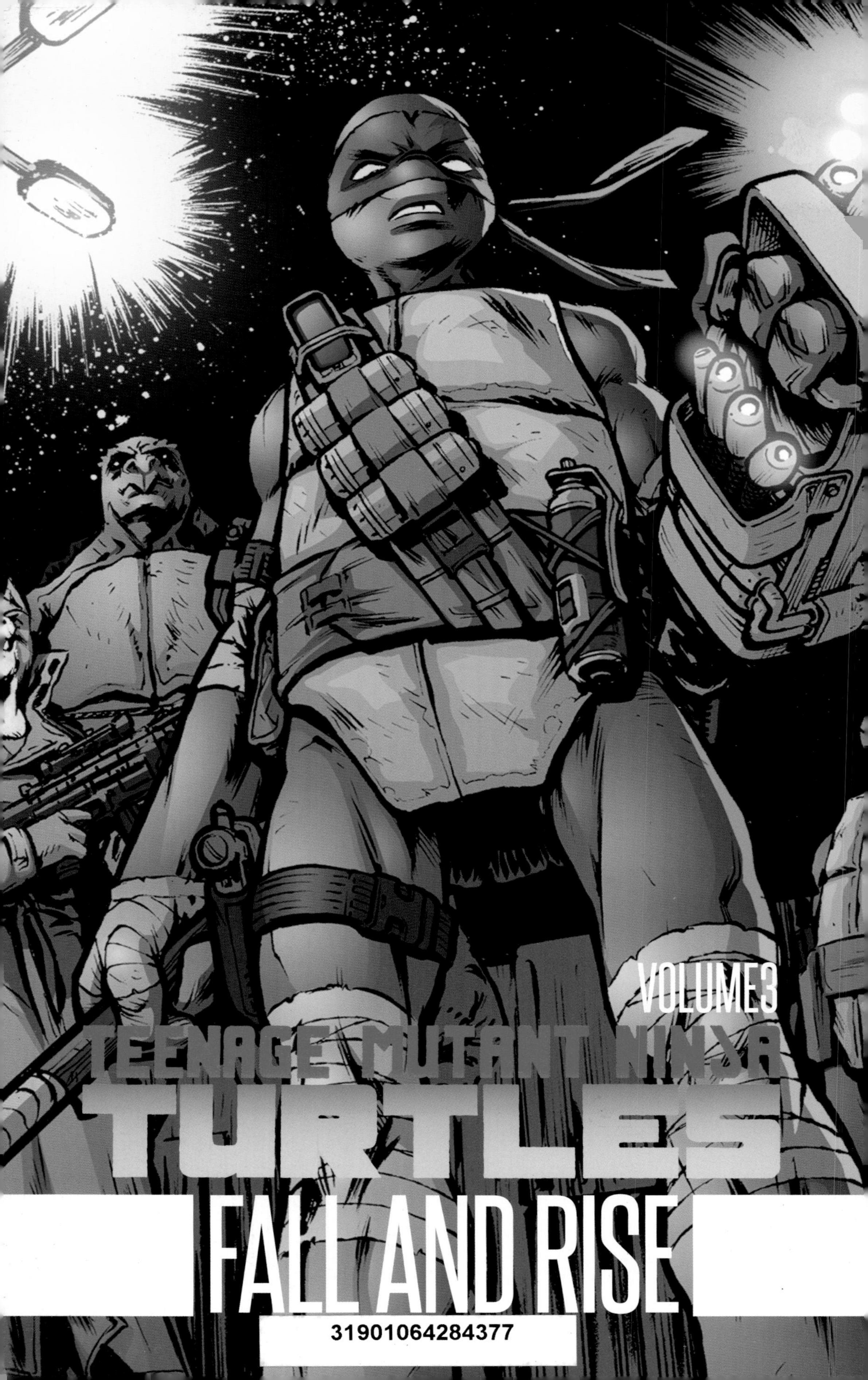
VOLUME 3
TEENAGE MUTANT NINJA
TURTLES
FALL AND RISE

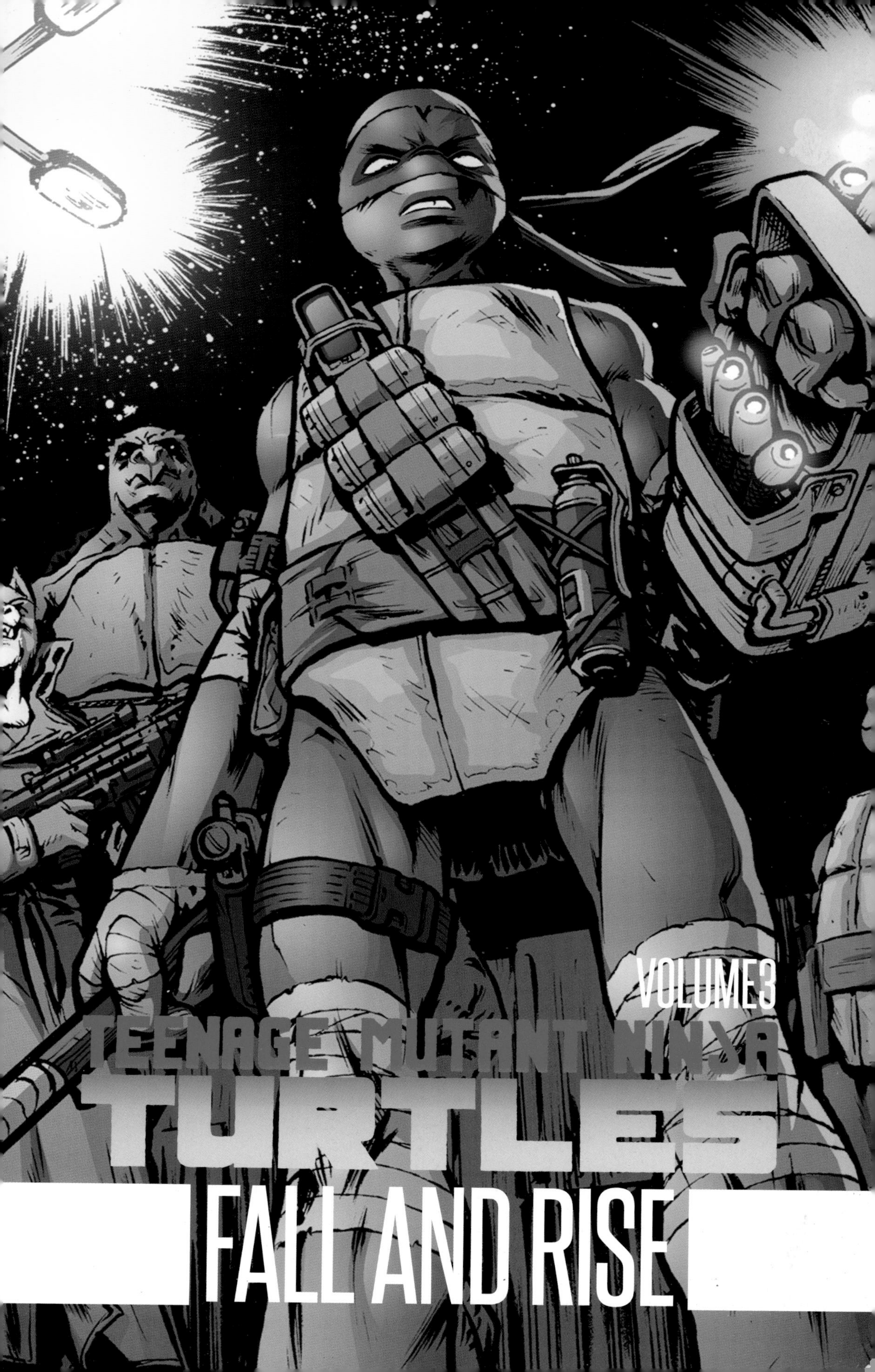
VOLUME 3
TEENAGE MUTANT NINJA
TURTLES
FALL AND RISE

Become our fan on Facebook **facebook.com/idwpublishing**
Follow us on Twitter **@idwpublishing**
Subscribe to us on YouTube **youtube.com/idwpublishing**
See what's new on Tumblr **tumblr.idwpublishing.com**
Check us out on Instagram **instagram.com/idwpublishing**

COVER ART BY
KEVIN EASTMAN

COVER COLORS BY
RONDA PATTISON

COLLECTION EDITS BY
JUSTIN EISINGER
AND ALONZO SIMON

PUBLISHER
GREG GOLDSTEIN

PRODUCTION ASSISTANCE BY
SHAWN LEE

nickelodeon

Special thanks to **Joan Hilty** and
Linda Lee for their invaluable assistance.

978-1-68405-252-3   21 20 19 18   1 2 3 4

Originally published as TEENAGE MUTANT NINJA TURTLES
issues #25–36.

Greg Goldstein, President & Publisher
Robbie Robbins, EVP & Sr. Art Director
Matthew Ruzicka, CPA, Chief Financial Officer
David Hedgecock, Associate Publisher
Laurie Windrow, Sr. VP of Sales & Marketing
Lorelei Bunjes, VP of Digital Services
Jerry Bennington, VP of New Product Development
Eric Moss, Sr. Director, Licensing & Business Development

Ted Adams, Founder & CEO of IDW Media Holdings

For international rights, please contact
licensing@idwpublishing.com

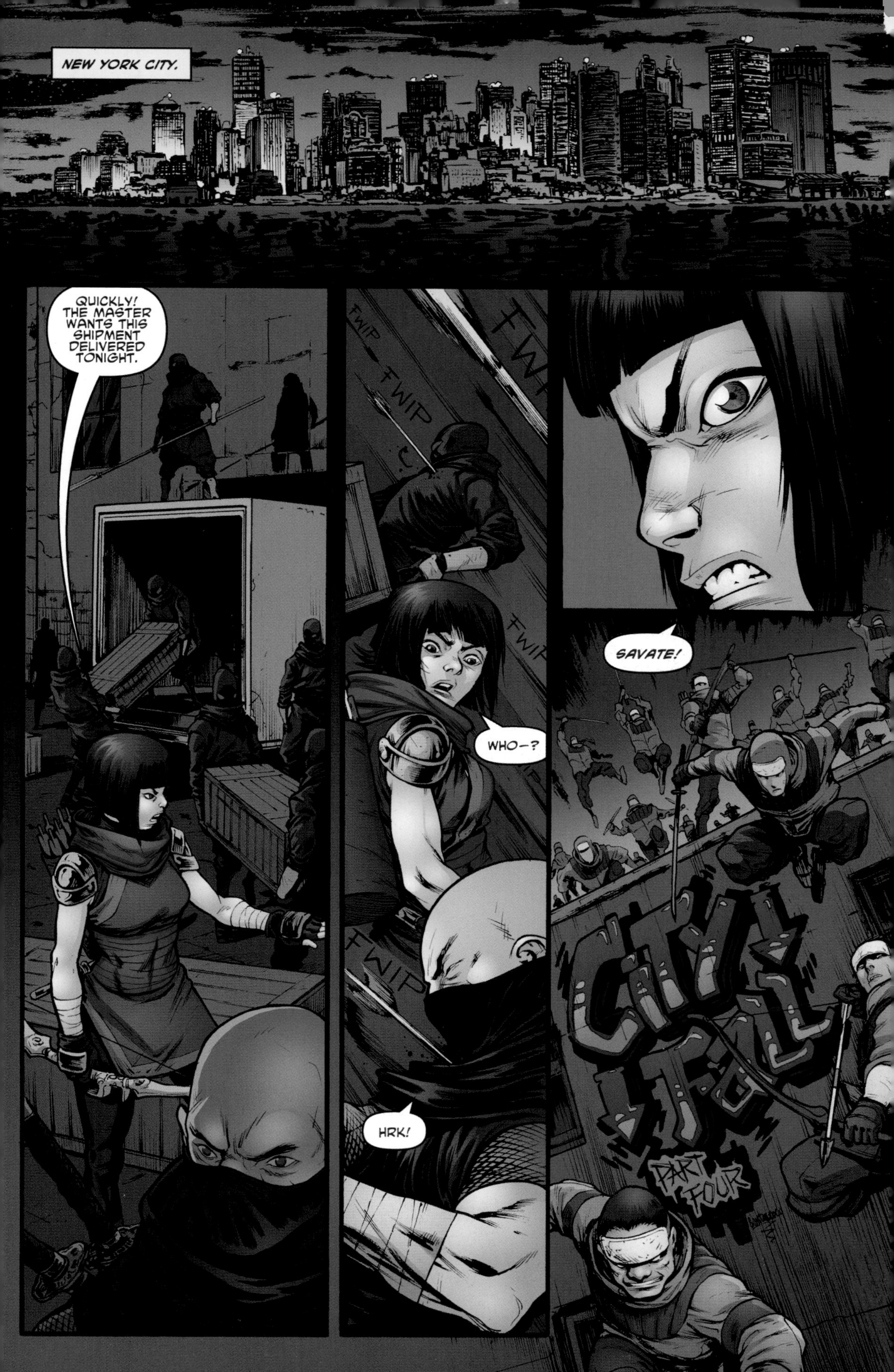
NEW YORK CITY.
QUICKLY! THE MASTER WANTS THIS SHIPMENT DELIVERED TONIGHT.
FWIP
FWIP
FWIP
FWIP
WHO–?
FWIP
HRK!
SAVATE!
PART FOUR

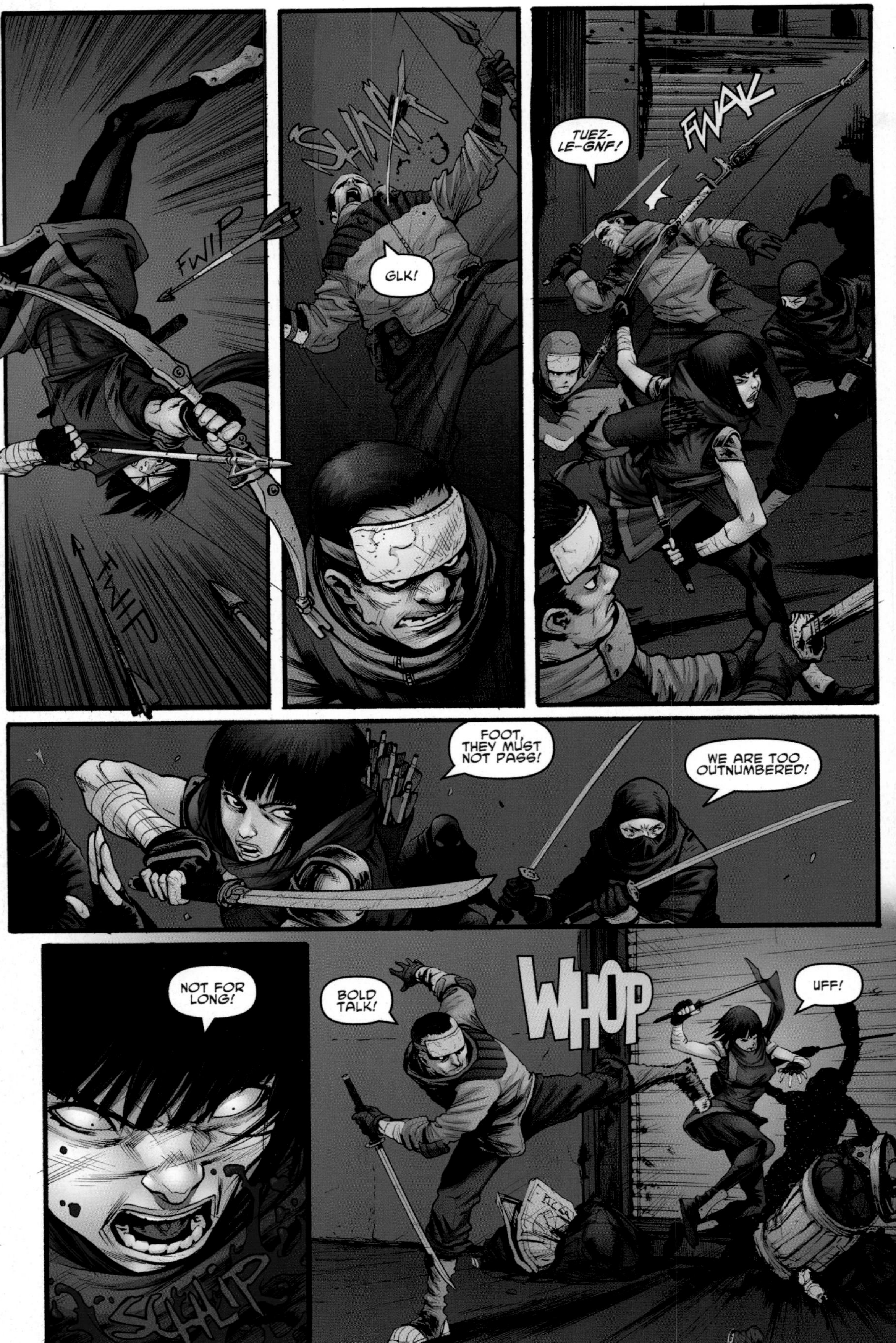
FWIP
FWIP
SHNK
GLK!
TUEZ-LE-GNF!
FWAK
FOOT, THEY MUST NOT PASS!
WE ARE TOO OUTNUMBERED!
NOT FOR LONG!
SCHLIP
BOLD TALK!
WHOP
UFF!

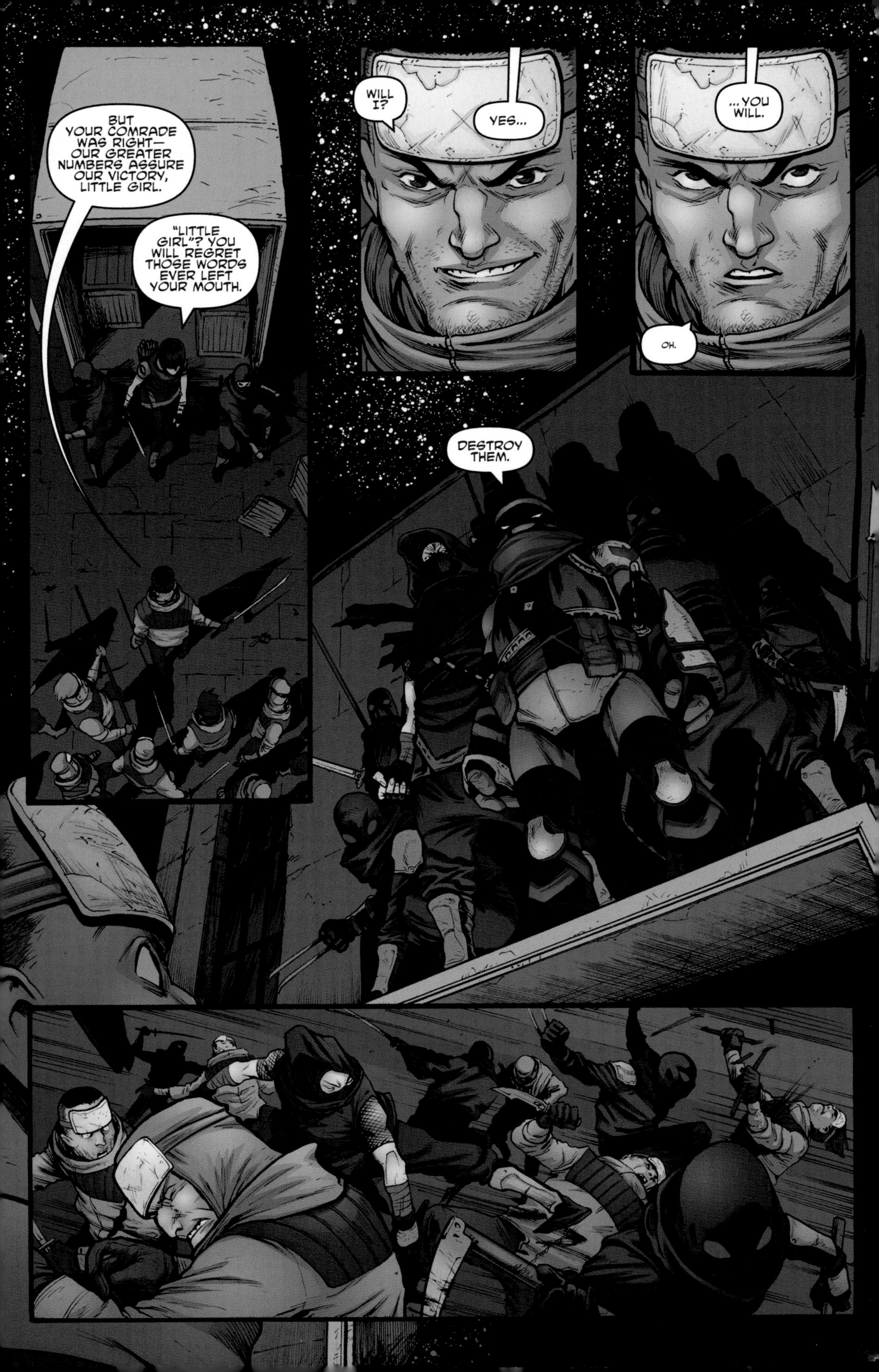
BUT YOUR COMRADE WAS RIGHT— OUR GREATER NUMBERS ASSURE OUR VICTORY, LITTLE GIRL.
"LITTLE GIRL"? YOU WILL REGRET THOSE WORDS EVER LEFT YOUR MOUTH.
WILL I?
YES...
...YOU WILL.
OH.
DESTROY THEM.

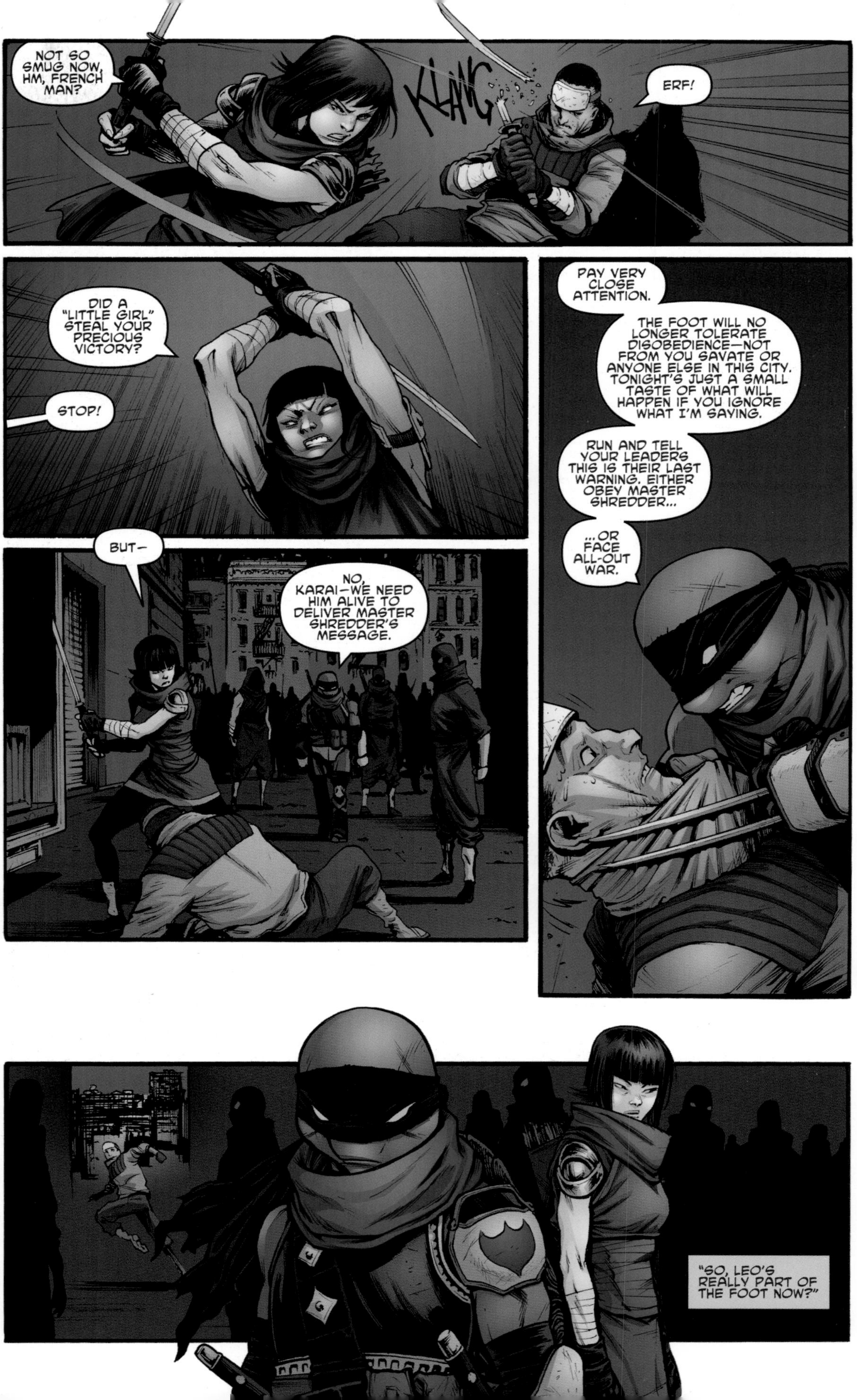
NOT SO SMUG NOW, HM, FRENCH MAN?
KLANG
ERF!
DID A "LITTLE GIRL" STEAL YOUR PRECIOUS VICTORY?
STOP!
PAY VERY CLOSE ATTENTION.
THE FOOT WILL NO LONGER TOLERATE DISOBEDIENCE—NOT FROM YOU SAVATE OR ANYONE ELSE IN THIS CITY. TONIGHT'S JUST A SMALL TASTE OF WHAT WILL HAPPEN IF YOU IGNORE WHAT I'M SAYING.
RUN AND TELL YOUR LEADERS THIS IS THEIR LAST WARNING. EITHER OBEY MASTER SHREDDER...
...OR FACE ALL-OUT WAR.
BUT—
NO, KARAI—WE NEED HIM ALIVE TO DELIVER MASTER SHREDDER'S MESSAGE.
"SO, LEO'S REALLY PART OF THE FOOT NOW?"

"MAN, THAT... THAT'S A HARD ONE TO SWALLOW, DONNIE."

EMERGENCY

IT'S BEEN ALMOST TWO WEEKS SINCE WE SAW HIM LAST. THINGS HAVEN'T BEEN SO GOOD AROUND HERE.

YEAH, APRIL TOLD ME RAPH TOOK IT PRETTY HARD.

WE *ALL* HAVE. BUT YOU KNOW RAPH—HE DOESN'T ALWAYS DEAL WITH STRESS IN... *CONSTRUCTIVE* WAYS. HE'S OFF ON HIS OWN DOING GOD KNOWS WHAT RIGHT NOW.

AND IT'S NOT JUST HIM—MASTER SPLINTER'S GONE, TOO, TAKING CARE OF SOME KIND OF "URGENT MATTER" WITH OLD HOB AND SLASH.

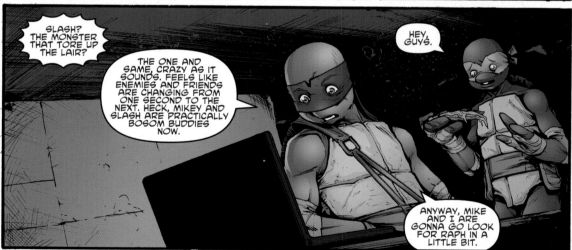

SLASH? THE MONSTER THAT TORE UP THE LAIR?

THE ONE AND SAME, CRAZY AS IT SOUNDS. FEELS LIKE ENEMIES AND FRIENDS ARE CHANGING FROM ONE SECOND TO THE NEXT. HECK, MIKEY AND SLASH ARE PRACTICALLY BOSOM BUDDIES NOW.

HEY, GUYS.

ANYWAY, MIKE AND I ARE GONNA GO LOOK FOR RAPH IN A LITTLE BIT.

ANYTHING'S BETTER THAN SITTING AROUND HERE DOING NOTHING, YOU KNOW?

I HEAR YA. I'M GONNA GO NUTSO IF I GOTTA STAY IN THIS STUPID BED MUCH LONGER.

OKAY, WE BETTER RUN. REALLY GOOD TALKING TO YOU, CASEY. HOPEFULLY WE'LL HAVE BETTER NEWS FOR YOU NEXT TIME.

YEAH—HANG IN THERE, GUYS.

SEE YA.

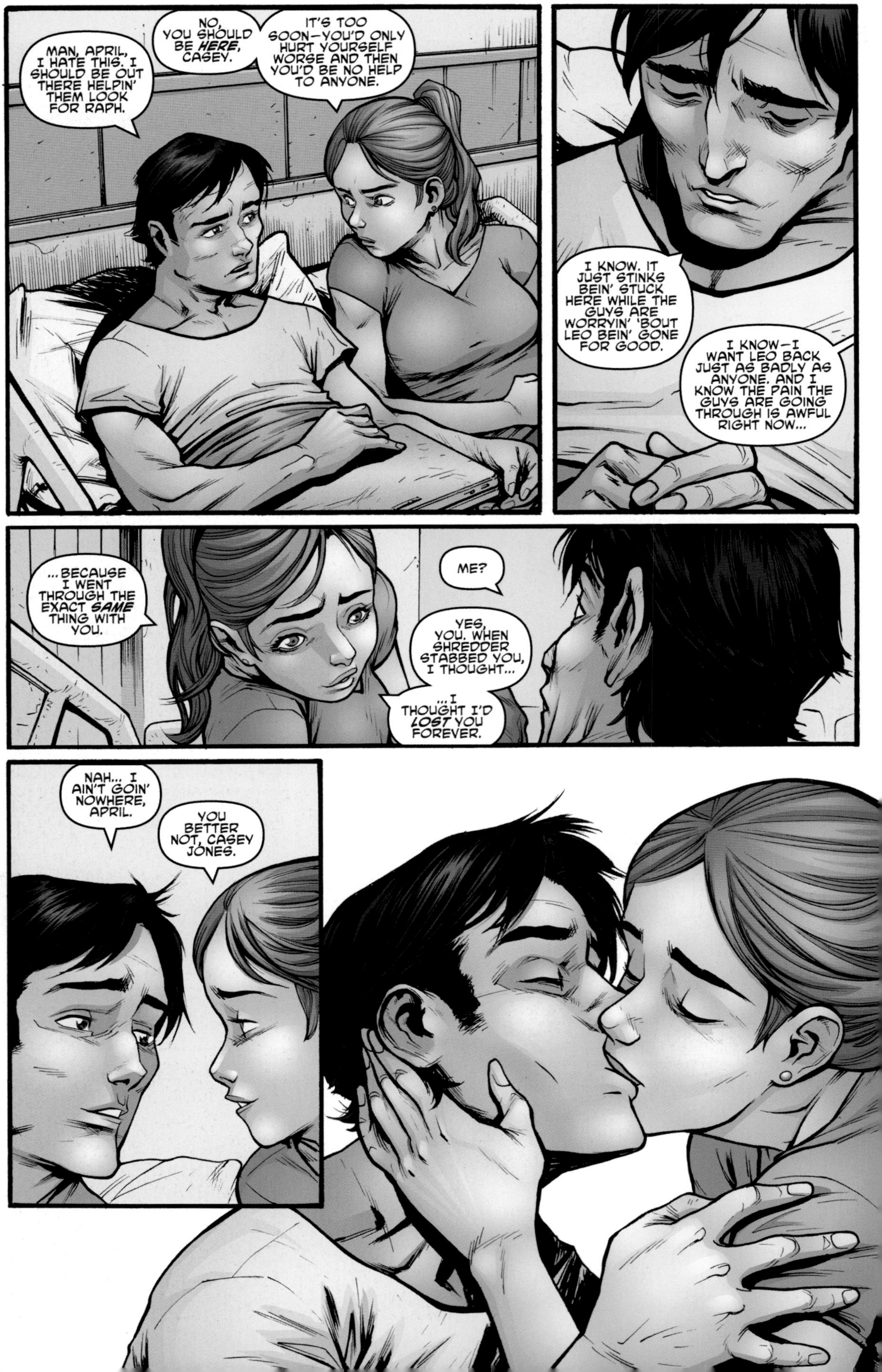
MAN, APRIL, I HATE THIS. I SHOULD BE OUT THERE HELPIN' THEM LOOK FOR RAPH.
NO, YOU SHOULD BE HERE, CASEY.
IT'S TOO SOON—YOU'D ONLY HURT YOURSELF WORSE AND THEN YOU'D BE NO HELP TO ANYONE.
I KNOW. IT JUST STINKS BEIN' STUCK HERE WHILE THE GUYS ARE WORRYIN' 'BOUT LEO BEIN' GONE FOR GOOD.
I KNOW—I WANT LEO BACK JUST AS BADLY AS ANYONE. AND I KNOW THE PAIN THE GUYS ARE GOING THROUGH IS AWFUL RIGHT NOW...
...BECAUSE I WENT THROUGH THE EXACT SAME THING WITH YOU.
ME?
YES, YOU. WHEN SHREDDER STABBED YOU, I THOUGHT...
...I THOUGHT I'D LOST YOU FOREVER.
NAH... I AIN'T GOIN' NOWHERE, APRIL.
YOU BETTER NOT, CASEY JONES.

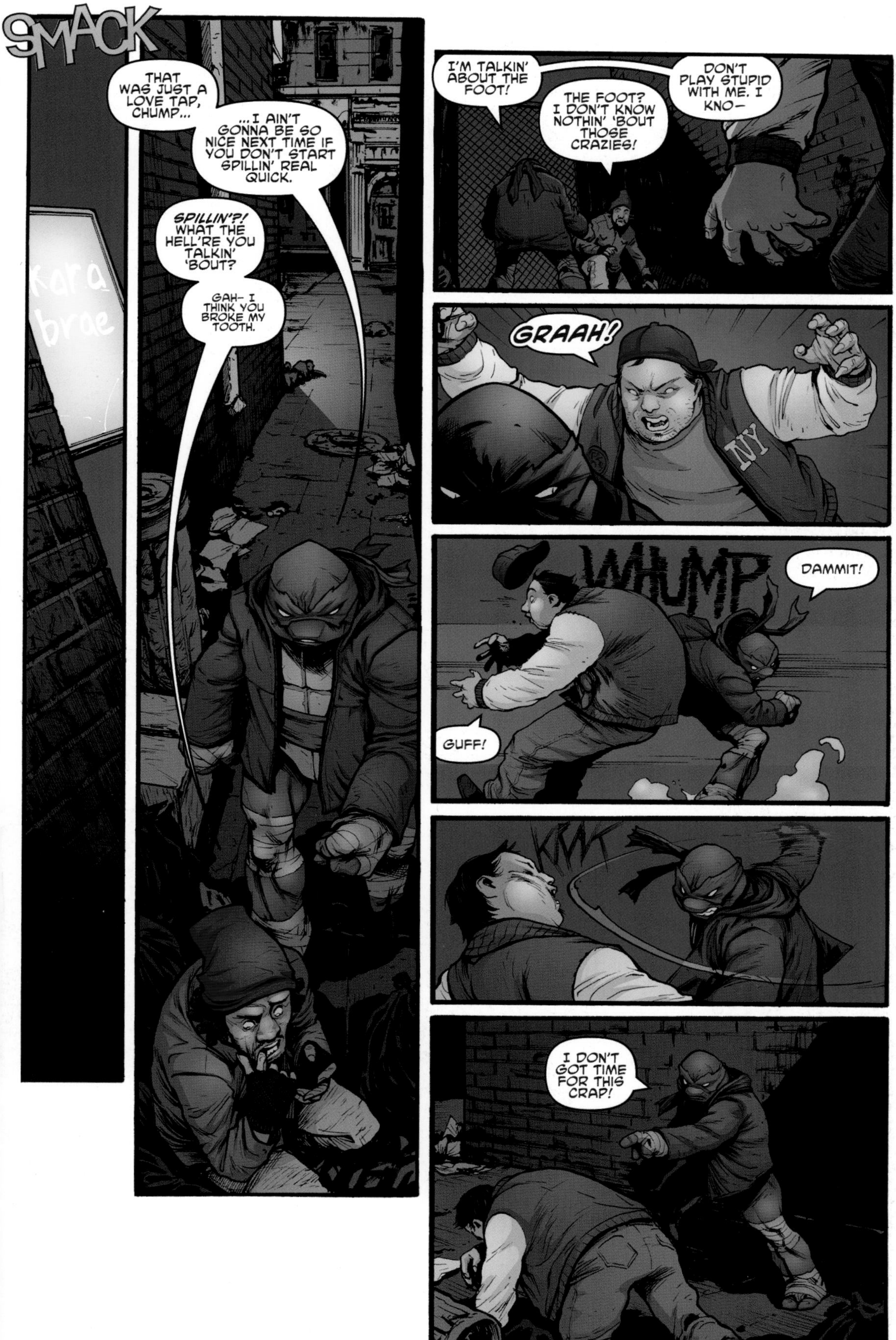
SMACK
THAT WAS JUST A LOVE TAP, CHUMP...
...I AIN'T GONNA BE SO NICE NEXT TIME IF YOU DON'T START SPILLIN' REAL QUICK.
SPILLIN'?! WHAT THE HELL'RE YOU TALKIN' 'BOUT?
GAH- I THINK YOU BROKE MY TOOTH.
I'M TALKIN' ABOUT THE FOOT!
THE FOOT? I DON'T KNOW NOTHIN' 'BOUT THOSE CRAZIES!
DON'T PLAY STUPID WITH ME. I KNO—
GRAAH!
WHUMP
DAMMIT!
GUFF!
KRAK
I DON'T GOT TIME FOR THIS CRAP!

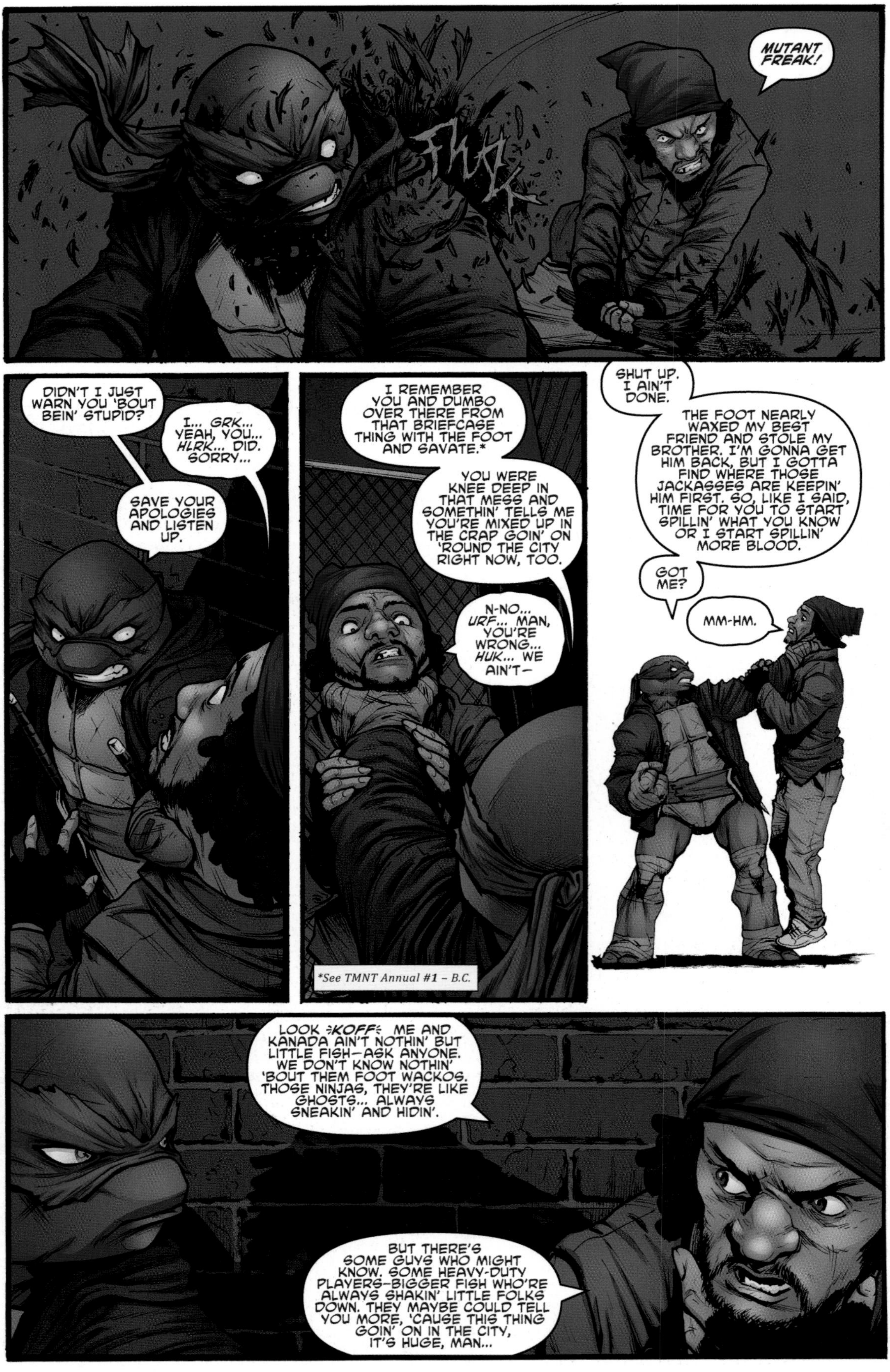
MUTANT FREAK!
FTHAK
DIDN'T I JUST WARN YOU 'BOUT BEIN' STUPID?
I... GRK... YEAH, YOU... HLRK... DID. SORRY...
SAVE YOUR APOLOGIES AND LISTEN UP.
I REMEMBER YOU AND DUMBO OVER THERE FROM THAT BRIEFCASE THING WITH THE FOOT AND SAVATE.*
YOU WERE KNEE DEEP IN THAT MESS AND SOMETHIN' TELLS ME YOU'RE MIXED UP IN THE CRAP GOIN' ON 'ROUND THE CITY RIGHT NOW, TOO.
N-NO... URF... MAN, YOU'RE WRONG... HUK... WE AIN'T—
*See TMNT Annual #1 – B.C.
SHUT UP. I AIN'T DONE.
THE FOOT NEARLY WAXED MY BEST FRIEND AND STOLE MY BROTHER. I'M GONNA GET HIM BACK, BUT I GOTTA FIND WHERE THOSE JACKASSES ARE KEEPIN' HIM FIRST. SO, LIKE I SAID, TIME FOR YOU TO START SPILLIN' WHAT YOU KNOW OR I START SPILLIN' MORE BLOOD.
GOT ME?
MM-HM.
LOOK -KOFF- ME AND KANADA AIN'T NOTHIN' BUT LITTLE FISH—ASK ANYONE. WE DON'T KNOW NOTHIN' 'BOUT THEM FOOT WACKOS. THOSE NINJAS, THEY'RE LIKE GHOSTS... ALWAYS SNEAKIN' AND HIDIN'.
BUT THERE'S SOME GUYS WHO MIGHT KNOW. SOME HEAVY-DUTY PLAYERS—BIGGER FISH WHO'RE ALWAYS SHAKIN' LITTLE FOLKS DOWN. THEY MAYBE COULD TELL YOU MORE, 'CAUSE THIS THING GOIN' ON IN THE CITY, IT'S HUGE, MAN...

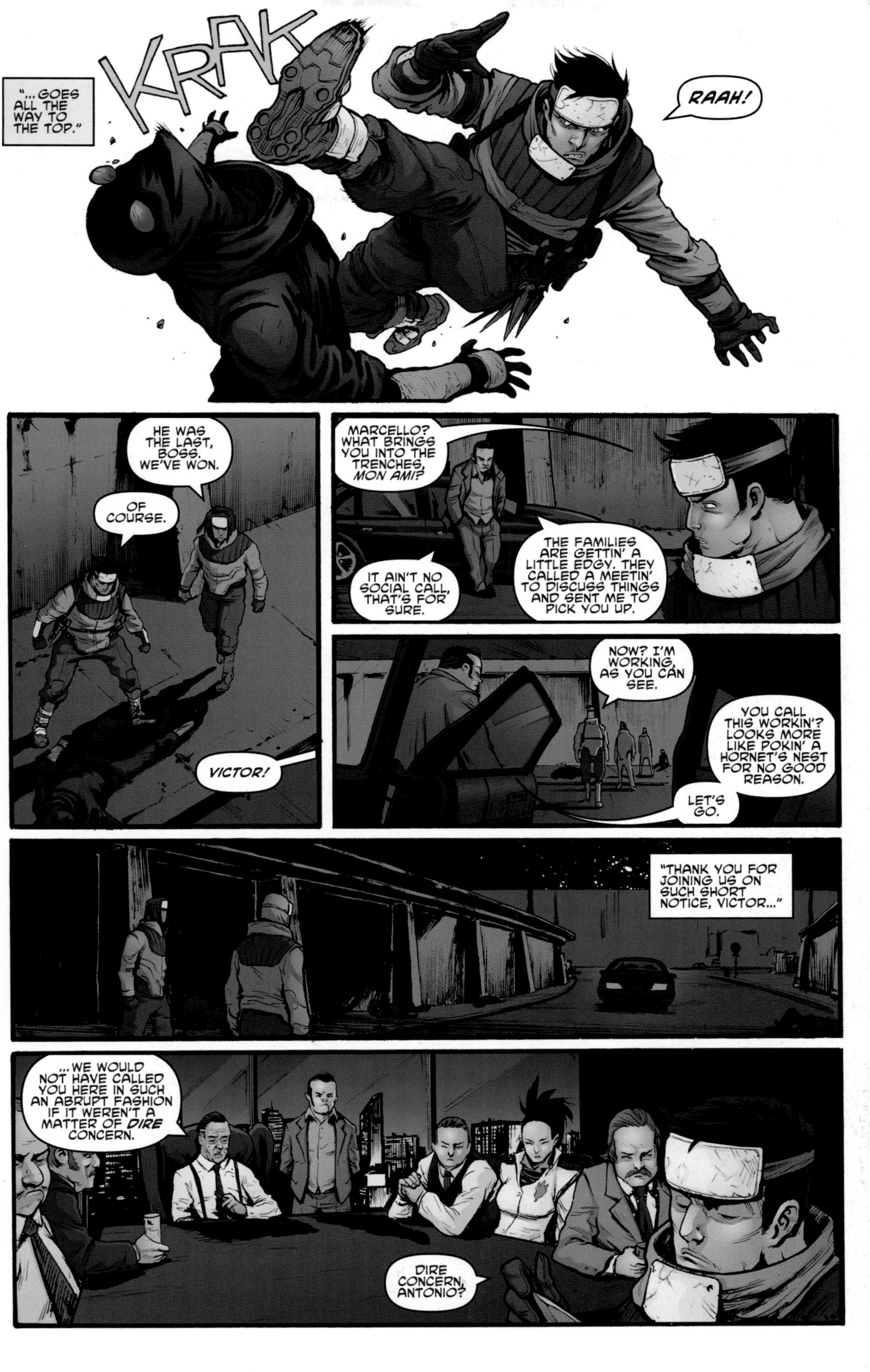
"...GOES ALL THE WAY TO THE TOP."
KRAK
RAAH!
HE WAS THE LAST, BOSS. WE'VE WON.
OF COURSE.
VICTOR!
MARCELLO? WHAT BRINGS YOU INTO THE TRENCHES, MON AMI?
IT AIN'T NO SOCIAL CALL, THAT'S FOR SURE.
THE FAMILIES ARE GETTIN' A LITTLE EDGY. THEY CALLED A MEETIN' TO DISCUSS THINGS AND SENT ME TO PICK YOU UP.
NOW? I'M WORKING, AS YOU CAN SEE.
YOU CALL THIS WORKIN'? LOOKS MORE LIKE POKIN' A HORNET'S NEST FOR NO GOOD REASON.
LET'S GO.
"THANK YOU FOR JOINING US ON SUCH SHORT NOTICE, VICTOR..."
...WE WOULD NOT HAVE CALLED YOU HERE IN SUCH AN ABRUPT FASHION IF IT WEREN'T A MATTER OF DIRE CONCERN.
DIRE CONCERN, ANTONIO?

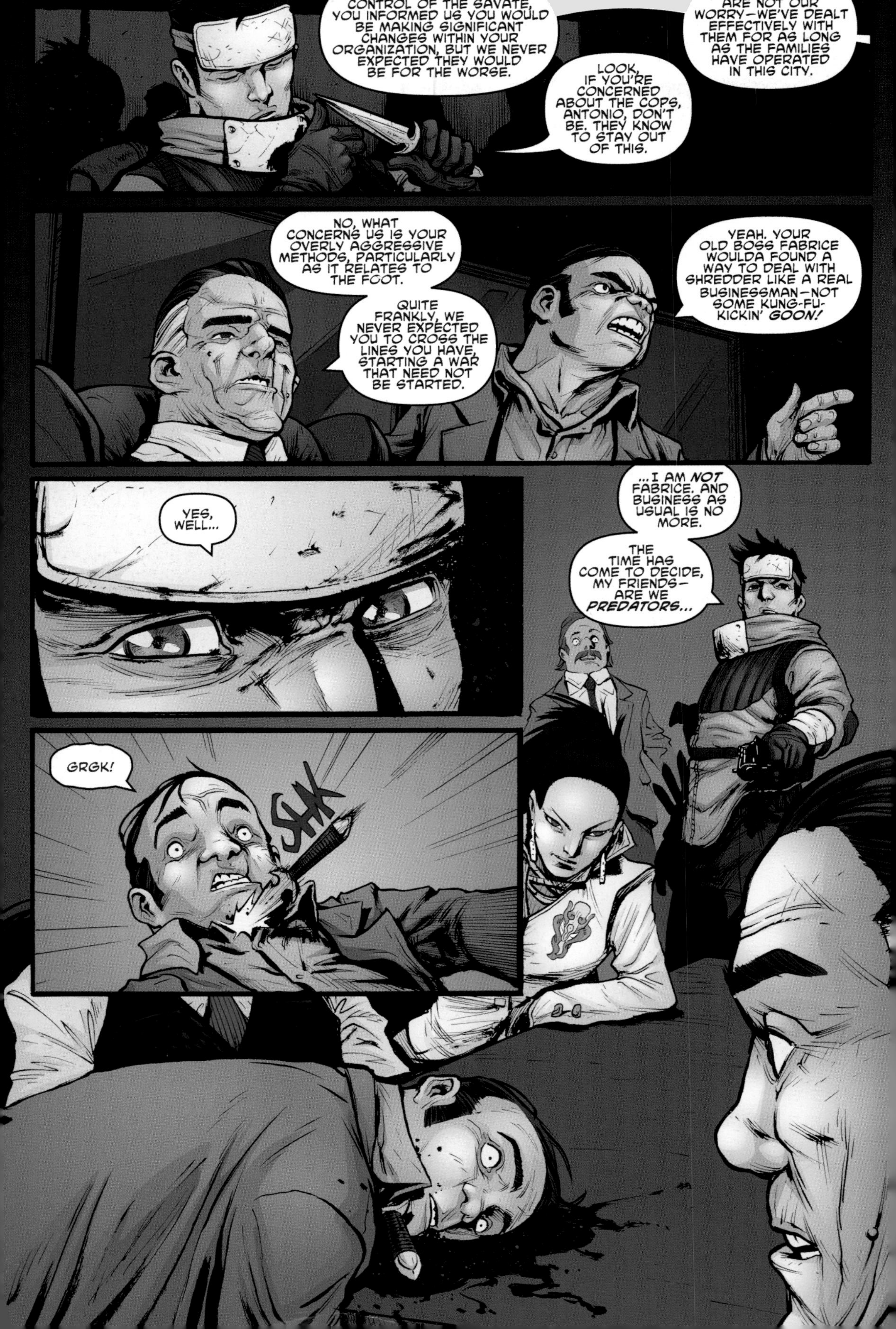
YES. WHEN YOU TOOK CONTROL OF THE SAVATE, YOU INFORMED US YOU WOULD BE MAKING SIGNIFICANT CHANGES WITHIN YOUR ORGANIZATION, BUT WE NEVER EXPECTED THEY WOULD BE FOR THE WORSE.
LOOK, IF YOU'RE CONCERNED ABOUT THE COPS, ANTONIO, DON'T BE. THEY KNOW TO STAY OUT OF THIS.
THE POLICE ARE NOT OUR WORRY—WE'VE DEALT EFFECTIVELY WITH THEM FOR AS LONG AS THE FAMILIES HAVE OPERATED IN THIS CITY.
NO, WHAT CONCERNS US IS YOUR OVERLY AGGRESSIVE METHODS, PARTICULARLY AS IT RELATES TO THE FOOT.
QUITE FRANKLY, WE NEVER EXPECTED YOU TO CROSS THE LINES YOU HAVE, STARTING A WAR THAT NEED NOT BE STARTED.
YEAH. YOUR OLD BOSS FABRICE WOULDA FOUND A WAY TO DEAL WITH SHREDDER LIKE A REAL BUSINESSMAN—NOT SOME KUNG-FU-KICKIN' *GOON!*
YES, WELL...
...I AM *NOT* FABRICE. AND BUSINESS AS USUAL IS NO MORE.
THE TIME HAS COME TO DECIDE, MY FRIENDS—ARE WE *PREDATORS...*
GRGK!
SHK

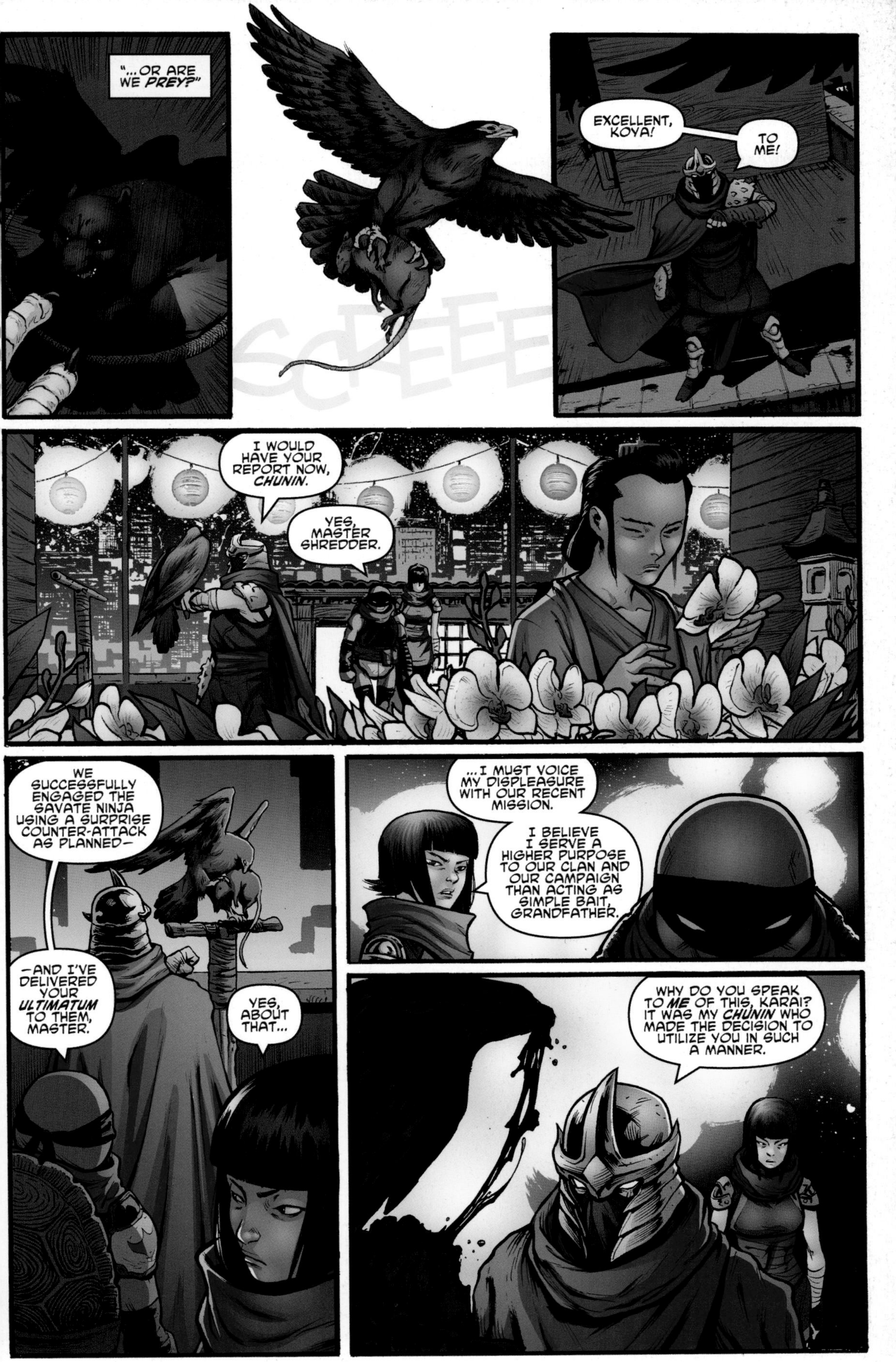
"...OR ARE WE *PREY?*"
SCREEE
EXCELLENT, KOYA!
TO ME!
I WOULD HAVE YOUR REPORT NOW, *CHUNIN*.
YES, MASTER SHREDDER.
WE SUCCESSFULLY ENGAGED THE SAVATE NINJA USING A SURPRISE COUNTER-ATTACK AS PLANNED—
—AND I'VE DELIVERED YOUR *ULTIMATUM* TO THEM, MASTER.
YES, ABOUT THAT...
...I MUST VOICE MY DISPLEASURE WITH OUR RECENT MISSION.
I BELIEVE I SERVE A HIGHER PURPOSE TO OUR CLAN AND OUR CAMPAIGN THAN ACTING AS SIMPLE BAIT, GRANDFATHER.
WHY DO YOU SPEAK TO *ME* OF THIS, KARAI? IT WAS MY *CHUNIN* WHO MADE THE DECISION TO UTILIZE YOU IN SUCH A MANNER.

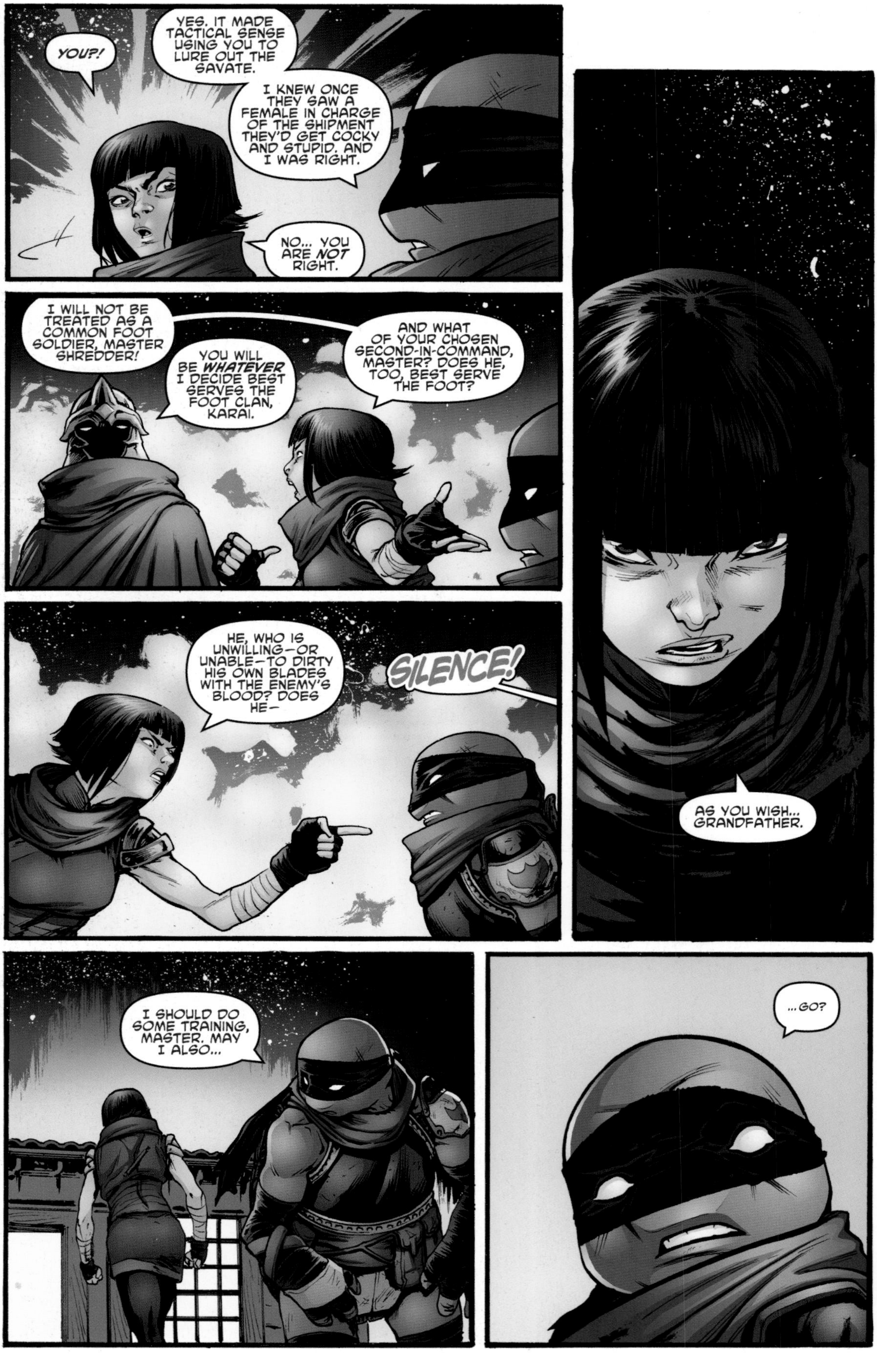
YOU?!
YES. IT MADE TACTICAL SENSE USING YOU TO LURE OUT THE SAVATE.
I KNEW ONCE THEY SAW A FEMALE IN CHARGE OF THE SHIPMENT THEY'D GET COCKY AND STUPID. AND I WAS RIGHT.
NO... YOU ARE NOT RIGHT.
I WILL NOT BE TREATED AS A COMMON FOOT SOLDIER, MASTER SHREDDER!
YOU WILL BE WHATEVER I DECIDE BEST SERVES THE FOOT CLAN, KARAI.
AND WHAT OF YOUR CHOSEN SECOND-IN-COMMAND, MASTER? DOES HE, TOO, BEST SERVE THE FOOT?
HE, WHO IS UNWILLING—OR UNABLE—TO DIRTY HIS OWN BLADES WITH THE ENEMY'S BLOOD? DOES HE—
SILENCE!
AS YOU WISH... GRANDFATHER.
I SHOULD DO SOME TRAINING, MASTER. MAY I ALSO...
...GO?

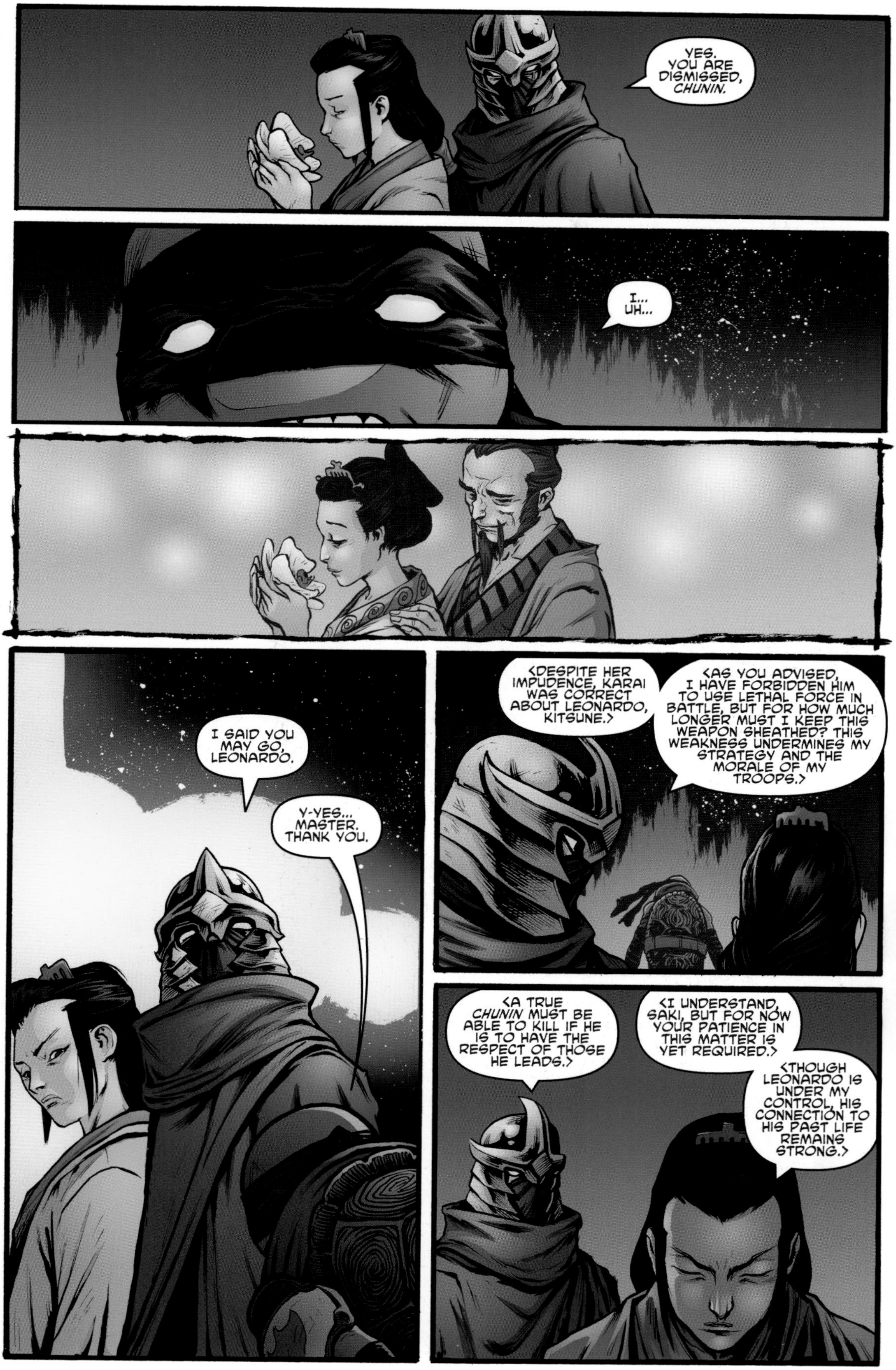
YES. YOU ARE DISMISSED, *CHUNIN.*
I... UH...
I SAID YOU MAY GO, LEONARDO.
Y-YES... MASTER. THANK YOU.
<DESPITE HER IMPUDENCE, KARAI WAS CORRECT ABOUT LEONARDO, KITSUNE.>
<AS YOU ADVISED, I HAVE FORBIDDEN HIM TO USE LETHAL FORCE IN BATTLE, BUT FOR HOW MUCH LONGER MUST I KEEP THIS WEAPON SHEATHED? THIS WEAKNESS UNDERMINES MY STRATEGY AND THE MORALE OF MY TROOPS.>
<A TRUE *CHUNIN* MUST BE ABLE TO KILL IF HE IS TO HAVE THE RESPECT OF THOSE HE LEADS.>
<I UNDERSTAND, SAKI, BUT FOR NOW YOUR PATIENCE IN THIS MATTER IS YET REQUIRED.>
<THOUGH LEONARDO IS UNDER MY CONTROL, HIS CONNECTION TO HIS PAST LIFE REMAINS STRONG.>

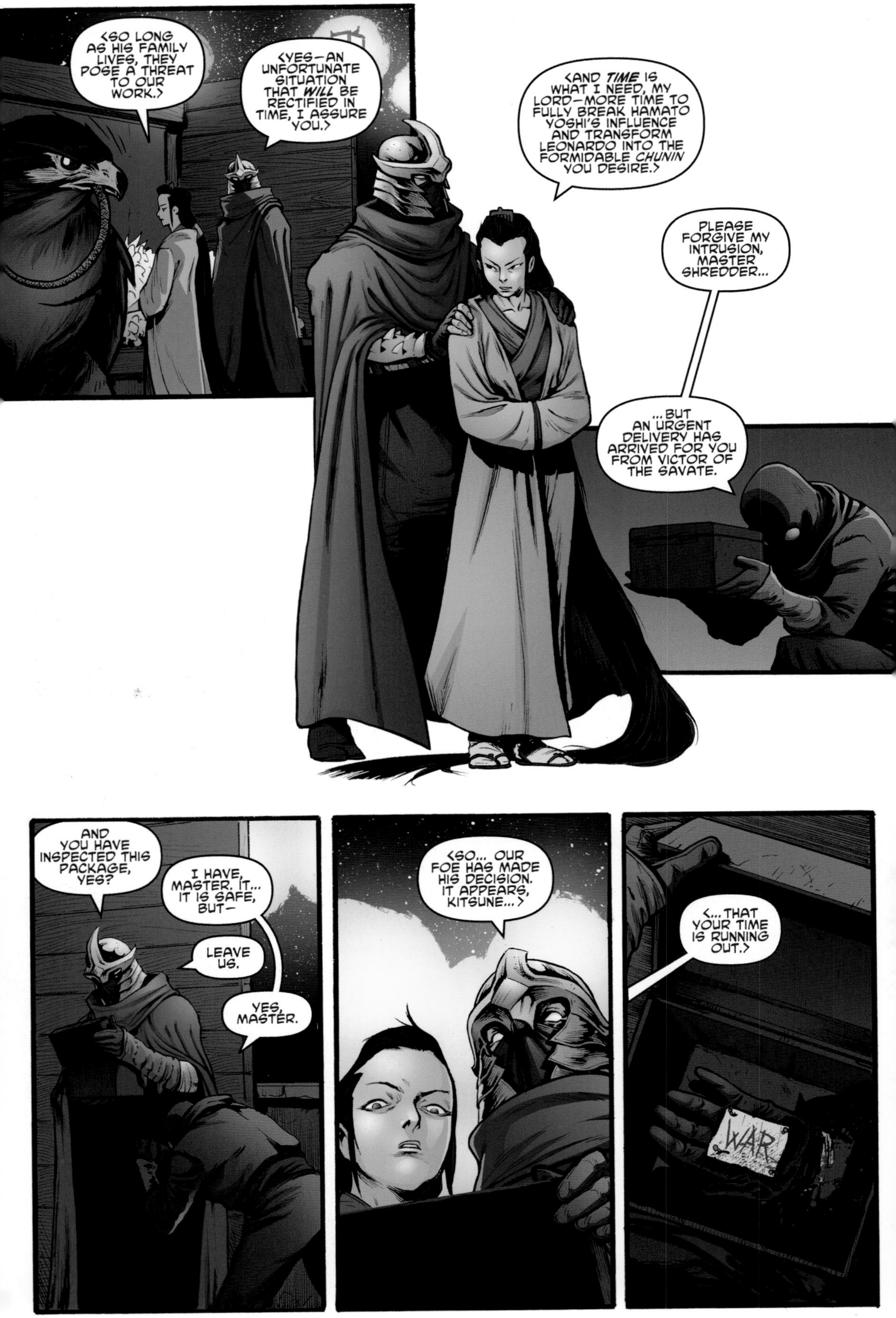
<SO LONG AS HIS FAMILY LIVES, THEY POSE A THREAT TO OUR WORK.>
<YES—AN UNFORTUNATE SITUATION THAT *WILL* BE RECTIFIED IN TIME, I ASSURE YOU.>
<AND *TIME* IS WHAT I NEED, MY LORD—MORE TIME TO FULLY BREAK HAMATO YOSHI'S INFLUENCE AND TRANSFORM LEONARDO INTO THE FORMIDABLE *CHUNIN* YOU DESIRE.>
PLEASE FORGIVE MY INTRUSION, MASTER SHREDDER...
...BUT AN URGENT DELIVERY HAS ARRIVED FOR YOU FROM VICTOR OF THE SAVATE.
AND YOU HAVE INSPECTED THIS PACKAGE, YES?
I HAVE, MASTER. IT... IT IS SAFE, BUT—
LEAVE US.
YES, MASTER.
<SO... OUR FOE HAS MADE HIS DECISION. IT APPEARS, KITSUNE...>
<...THAT YOUR TIME IS RUNNING OUT.>
WAR

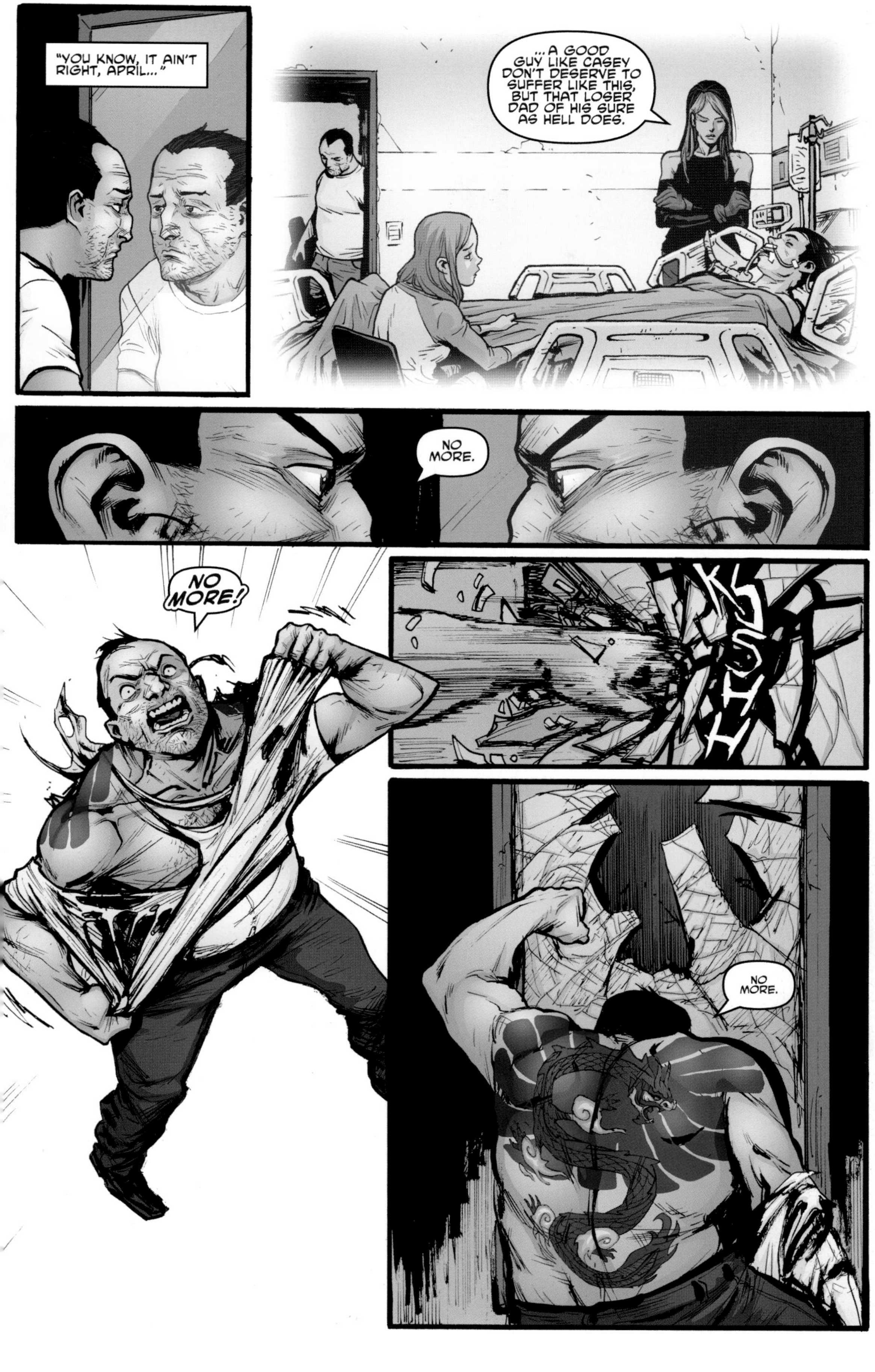
"YOU KNOW, IT AIN'T RIGHT, APRIL..."
...A GOOD GUY LIKE CASEY DON'T DESERVE TO SUFFER LIKE THIS, BUT THAT LOSER DAD OF HIS SURE AS HELL DOES.
NO MORE.
NO MORE!
KSSHH
NO MORE.

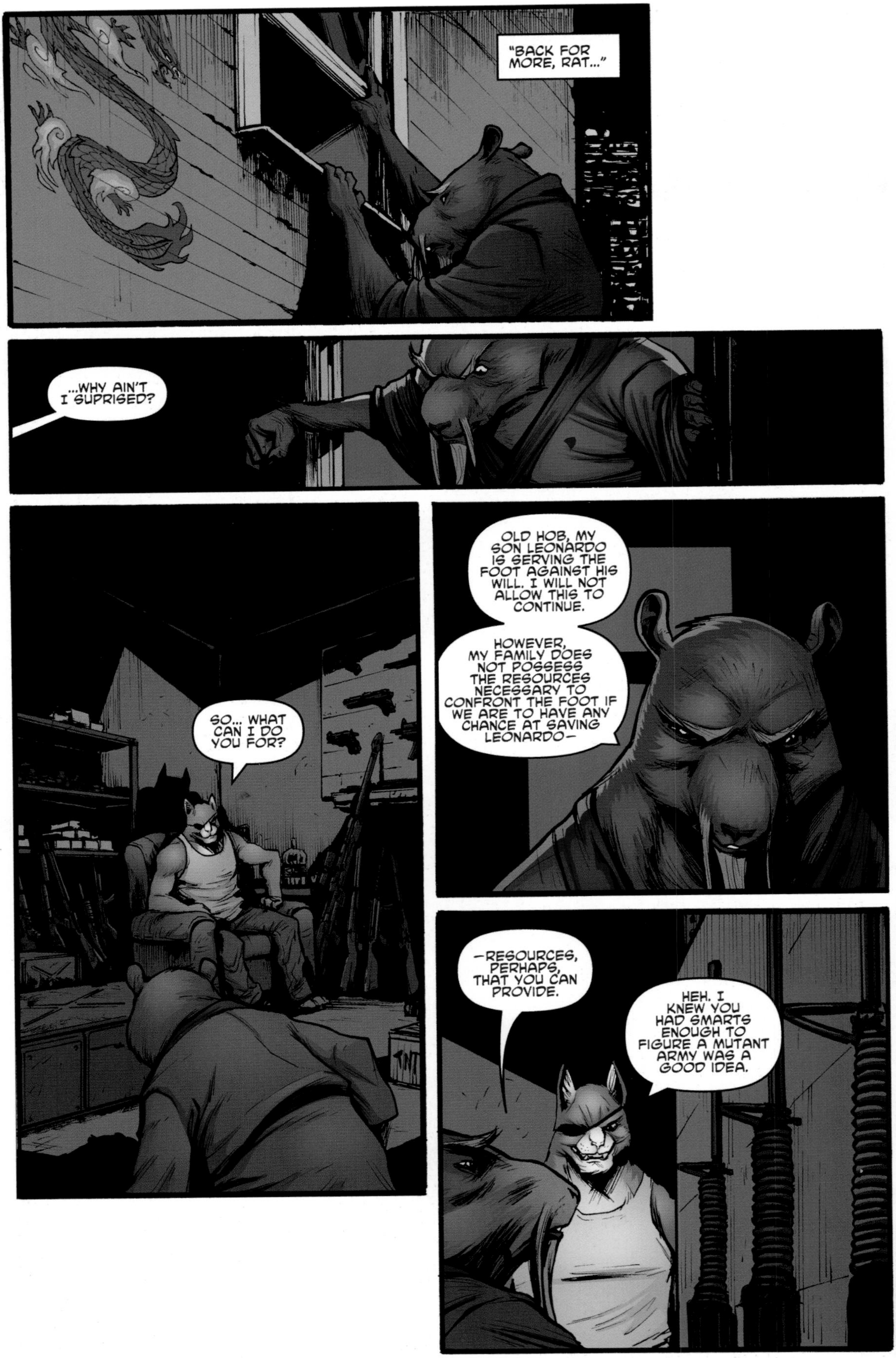
"BACK FOR MORE, RAT..."
...WHY AIN'T I SUPRISED?
SO... WHAT CAN I DO YOU FOR?
OLD HOB, MY SON LEONARDO IS SERVING THE FOOT AGAINST HIS WILL. I WILL NOT ALLOW THIS TO CONTINUE.
HOWEVER, MY FAMILY DOES NOT POSSESS THE RESOURCES NECESSARY TO CONFRONT THE FOOT IF WE ARE TO HAVE ANY CHANCE AT SAVING LEONARDO—
—RESOURCES, PERHAPS, THAT YOU CAN PROVIDE.
HEH. I KNEW YOU HAD SMARTS ENOUGH TO FIGURE A MUTANT ARMY WAS A GOOD IDEA.

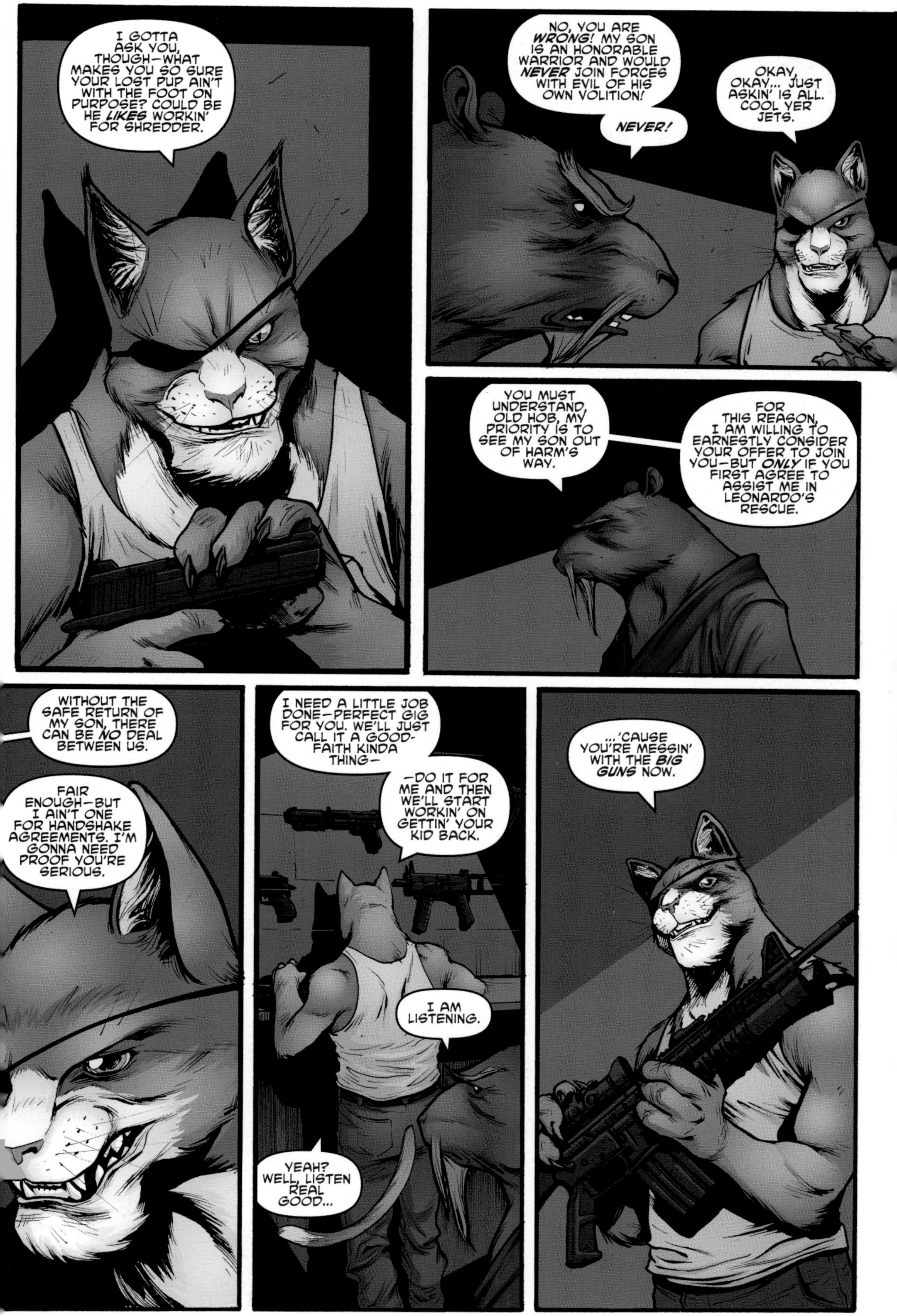
I GOTTA ASK YOU, THOUGH—WHAT MAKES YOU SO SURE YOUR LOST PUP AIN'T WITH THE FOOT ON PURPOSE? COULD BE HE LIKES WORKIN' FOR SHREDDER.
NO, YOU ARE WRONG! MY SON IS AN HONORABLE WARRIOR AND WOULD NEVER JOIN FORCES WITH EVIL OF HIS OWN VOLITION!
NEVER!
OKAY, OKAY... JUST ASKIN' IS ALL. COOL YER JETS.
YOU MUST UNDERSTAND, OLD HOB, MY PRIORITY IS TO SEE MY SON OUT OF HARM'S WAY.
FOR THIS REASON, I AM WILLING TO EARNESTLY CONSIDER YOUR OFFER TO JOIN YOU—BUT ONLY IF YOU FIRST AGREE TO ASSIST ME IN LEONARDO'S RESCUE.
WITHOUT THE SAFE RETURN OF MY SON, THERE CAN BE NO DEAL BETWEEN US.
FAIR ENOUGH—BUT I AIN'T ONE FOR HANDSHAKE AGREEMENTS. I'M GONNA NEED PROOF YOU'RE SERIOUS.
I NEED A LITTLE JOB DONE—PERFECT GIG FOR YOU. WE'LL JUST CALL IT A GOOD-FAITH KINDA THING—
—DO IT FOR ME AND THEN WE'LL START WORKIN' ON GETTIN' YOUR KID BACK.
I AM LISTENING.
YEAH? WELL, LISTEN REAL GOOD...
...'CAUSE YOU'RE MESSIN' WITH THE BIG GUNS NOW.

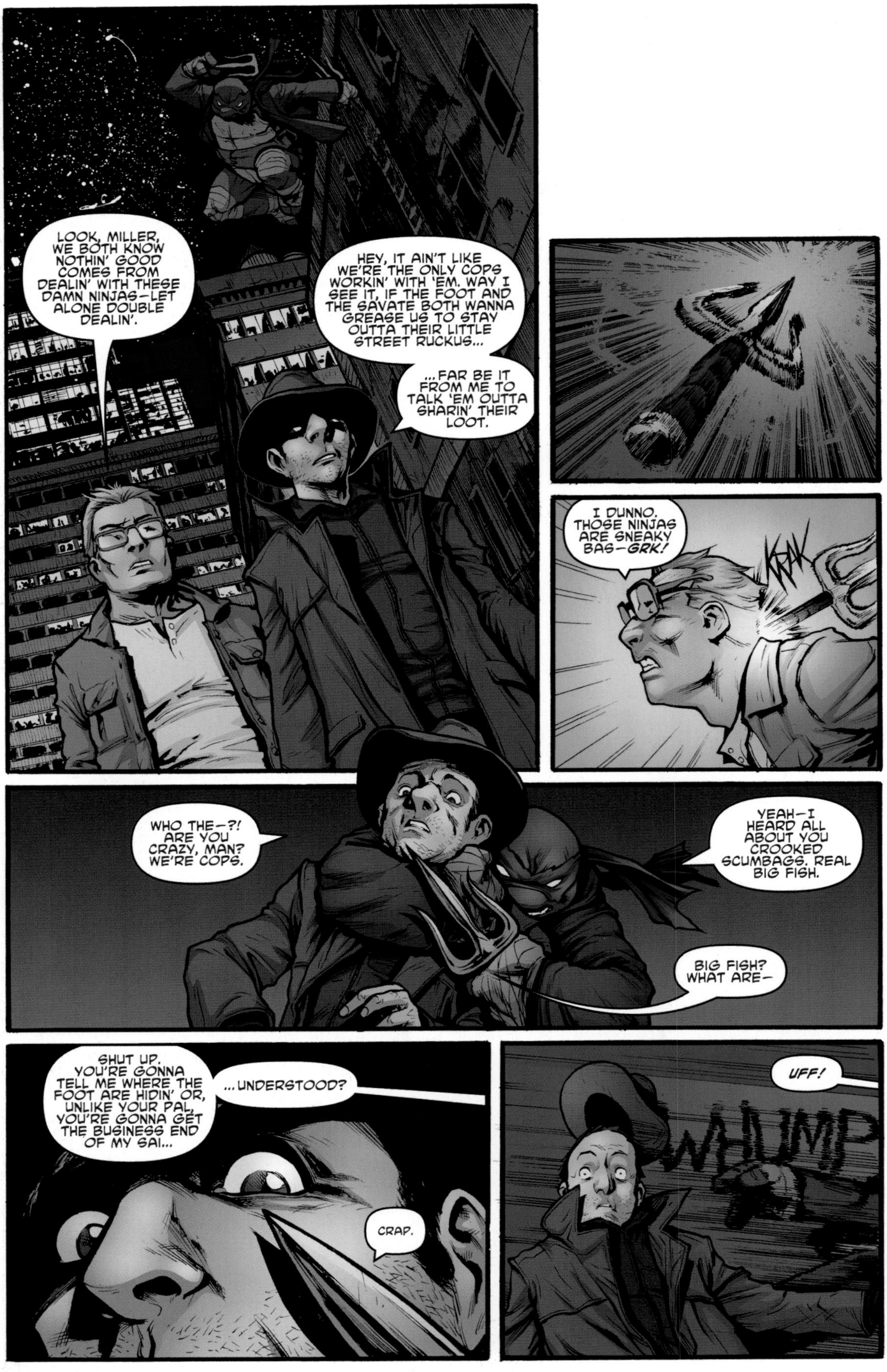
LOOK, MILLER, WE BOTH KNOW NOTHIN' GOOD COMES FROM DEALIN' WITH THESE DAMN NINJAS—LET ALONE DOUBLE DEALIN'.
HEY, IT AIN'T LIKE WE'RE THE ONLY COPS WORKIN' WITH 'EM. WAY I SEE IT, IF THE FOOT AND THE SAVATE BOTH WANNA GREASE US TO STAY OUTTA THEIR LITTLE STREET RUCKUS...
...FAR BE IT FROM ME TO TALK 'EM OUTTA SHARIN' THEIR LOOT.
I DUNNO. THOSE NINJAS ARE SNEAKY BAS—GRK!
KRAK
WHO THE—?! ARE YOU CRAZY, MAN? WE'RE COPS.
YEAH—I HEARD ALL ABOUT YOU CROOKED SCUMBAGS. REAL BIG FISH.
BIG FISH? WHAT ARE—
SHUT UP. YOU'RE GONNA TELL ME WHERE THE FOOT ARE HIDIN' OR, UNLIKE YOUR PAL, YOU'RE GONNA GET THE BUSINESS END OF MY SAI...
...UNDERSTOOD?
CRAP.
UFF!
WHUMP

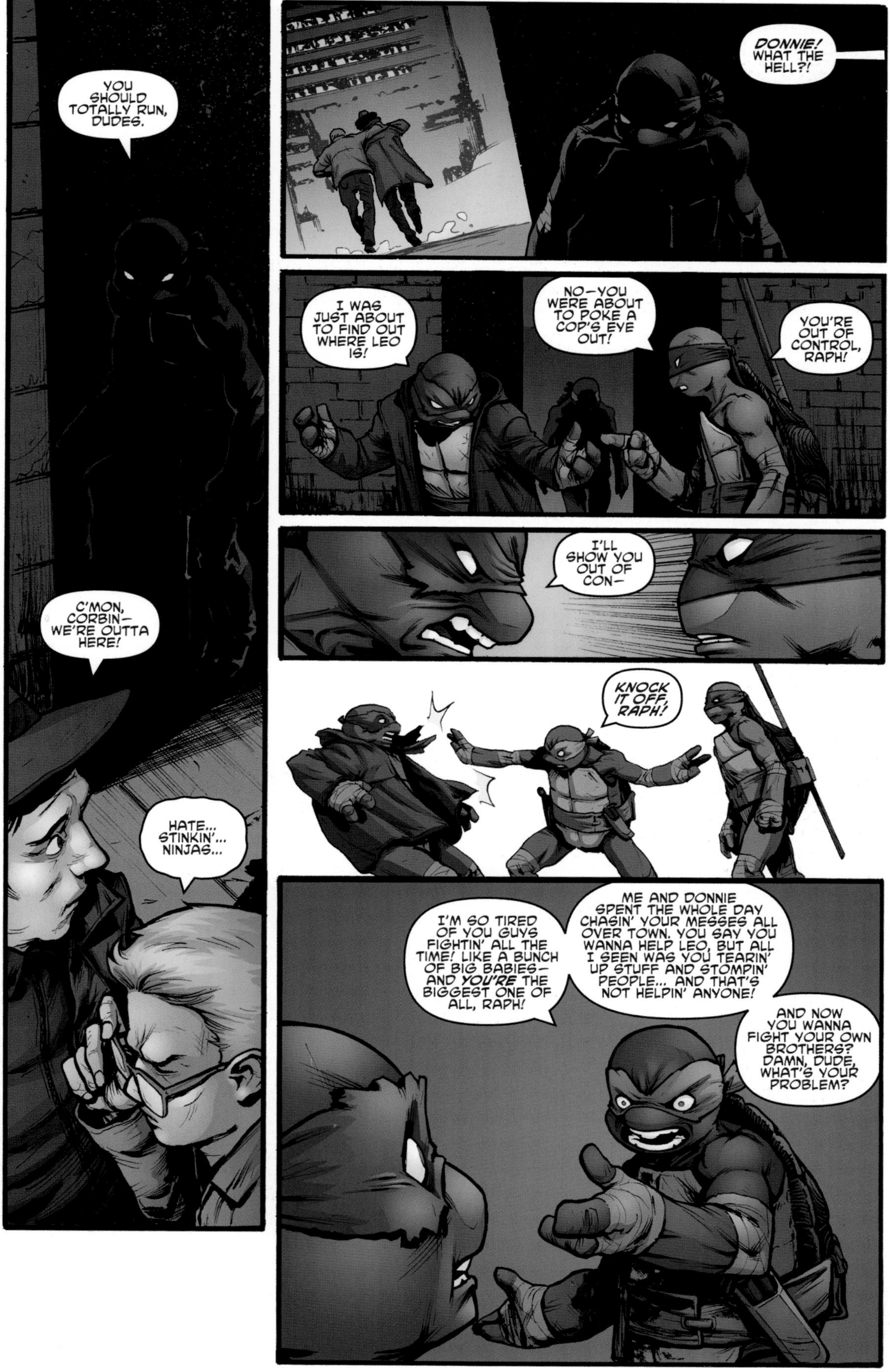
YOU SHOULD TOTALLY RUN, DUDES.
C'MON, CORBIN— WE'RE OUTTA HERE!
HATE... STINKIN'... NINJAS...
DONNIE! WHAT THE HELL?!
I WAS JUST ABOUT TO FIND OUT WHERE LEO IS!
NO—YOU WERE ABOUT TO POKE A COP'S EYE OUT!
YOU'RE OUT OF CONTROL, RAPH!
I'LL SHOW YOU OUT OF CON—
KNOCK IT OFF, RAPH!
I'M SO TIRED OF YOU GUYS FIGHTIN' ALL THE TIME! LIKE A BUNCH OF BIG BABIES— AND YOU'RE THE BIGGEST ONE OF ALL, RAPH!
ME AND DONNIE SPENT THE WHOLE DAY CHASIN' YOUR MESSES ALL OVER TOWN. YOU SAY YOU WANNA HELP LEO, BUT ALL I SEEN WAS YOU TEARIN' UP STUFF AND STOMPIN' PEOPLE... AND THAT'S NOT HELPIN' ANYONE!
AND NOW YOU WANNA FIGHT YOUR OWN BROTHERS? DAMN, DUDE, WHAT'S YOUR PROBLEM?

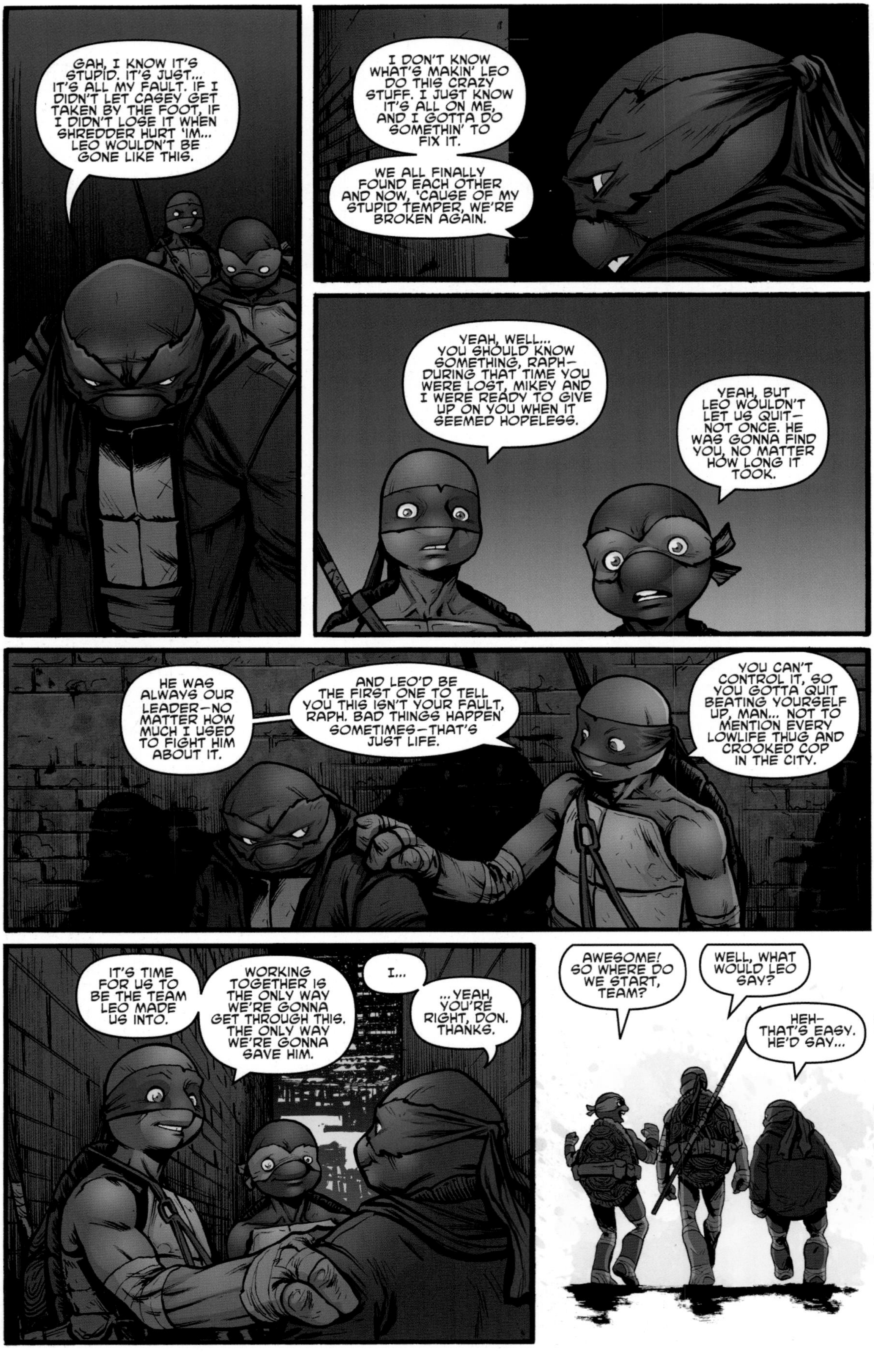

GAH, I KNOW IT'S STUPID. IT'S JUST... IT'S ALL MY FAULT. IF I DIDN'T LET CASEY GET TAKEN BY THE FOOT, IF I DIDN'T LOSE IT WHEN SHREDDER HURT 'IM... LEO WOULDN'T BE GONE LIKE THIS.

I DON'T KNOW WHAT'S MAKIN' LEO DO THIS CRAZY STUFF. I JUST KNOW IT'S ALL ON ME, AND I GOTTA DO SOMETHIN' TO FIX IT.

WE ALL FINALLY FOUND EACH OTHER AND NOW, 'CAUSE OF MY STUPID TEMPER, WE'RE BROKEN AGAIN.

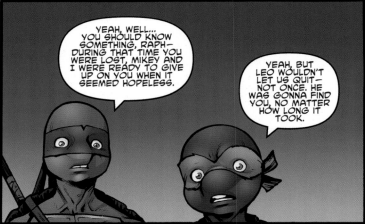

YEAH, WELL... YOU SHOULD KNOW SOMETHING, RAPH— DURING THAT TIME YOU WERE LOST, MIKEY AND I WERE READY TO GIVE UP ON YOU WHEN IT SEEMED HOPELESS.

YEAH, BUT LEO WOULDN'T LET US QUIT— NOT ONCE. HE WAS GONNA FIND YOU, NO MATTER HOW LONG IT TOOK.

HE WAS ALWAYS OUR LEADER—NO MATTER HOW MUCH I USED TO FIGHT HIM ABOUT IT.

AND LEO'D BE THE FIRST ONE TO TELL YOU THIS ISN'T YOUR FAULT, RAPH. BAD THINGS HAPPEN SOMETIMES—THAT'S JUST LIFE.

YOU CAN'T CONTROL IT, SO YOU GOTTA QUIT BEATING YOURSELF UP, MAN... NOT TO MENTION EVERY LOWLIFE THUG AND CROOKED COP IN THE CITY.

IT'S TIME FOR US TO BE THE TEAM LEO MADE US INTO.

WORKING TOGETHER IS THE ONLY WAY WE'RE GONNA GET THROUGH THIS. THE ONLY WAY WE'RE GONNA SAVE HIM.

I...

...YEAH, YOU'RE RIGHT, DON. THANKS.

AWESOME! SO WHERE DO WE START, TEAM?

WELL, WHAT WOULD LEO SAY?

HEH— THAT'S EASY. HE'D SAY...

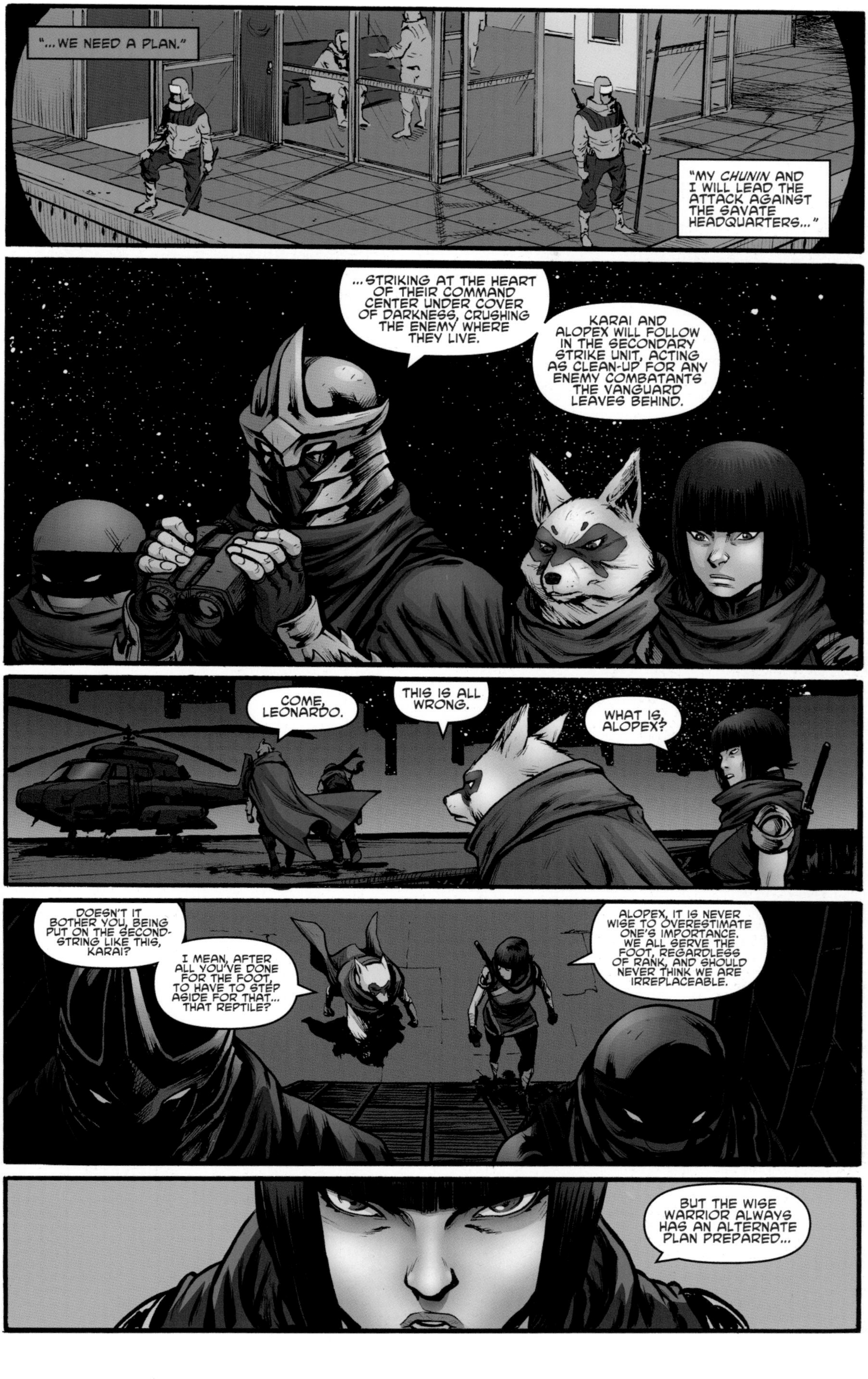
"...WE NEED A PLAN."
"MY CHUNIN AND I WILL LEAD THE ATTACK AGAINST THE SAVATE HEADQUARTERS..."
...STRIKING AT THE HEART OF THEIR COMMAND CENTER UNDER COVER OF DARKNESS, CRUSHING THE ENEMY WHERE THEY LIVE.
KARAI AND ALOPEX WILL FOLLOW IN THE SECONDARY STRIKE UNIT, ACTING AS CLEAN-UP FOR ANY ENEMY COMBATANTS THE VANGUARD LEAVES BEHIND.
COME, LEONARDO.
THIS IS ALL WRONG.
WHAT IS, ALOPEX?
DOESN'T IT BOTHER YOU, BEING PUT ON THE SECOND-STRING LIKE THIS, KARAI?
I MEAN, AFTER ALL YOU'VE DONE FOR THE FOOT, TO HAVE TO STEP ASIDE FOR THAT... THAT REPTILE?
ALOPEX, IT IS NEVER WISE TO OVERESTIMATE ONE'S IMPORTANCE. WE ALL SERVE THE FOOT, REGARDLESS OF RANK, AND SHOULD NEVER THINK WE ARE IRREPLACEABLE.
BUT THE WISE WARRIOR ALWAYS HAS AN ALTERNATE PLAN PREPARED...

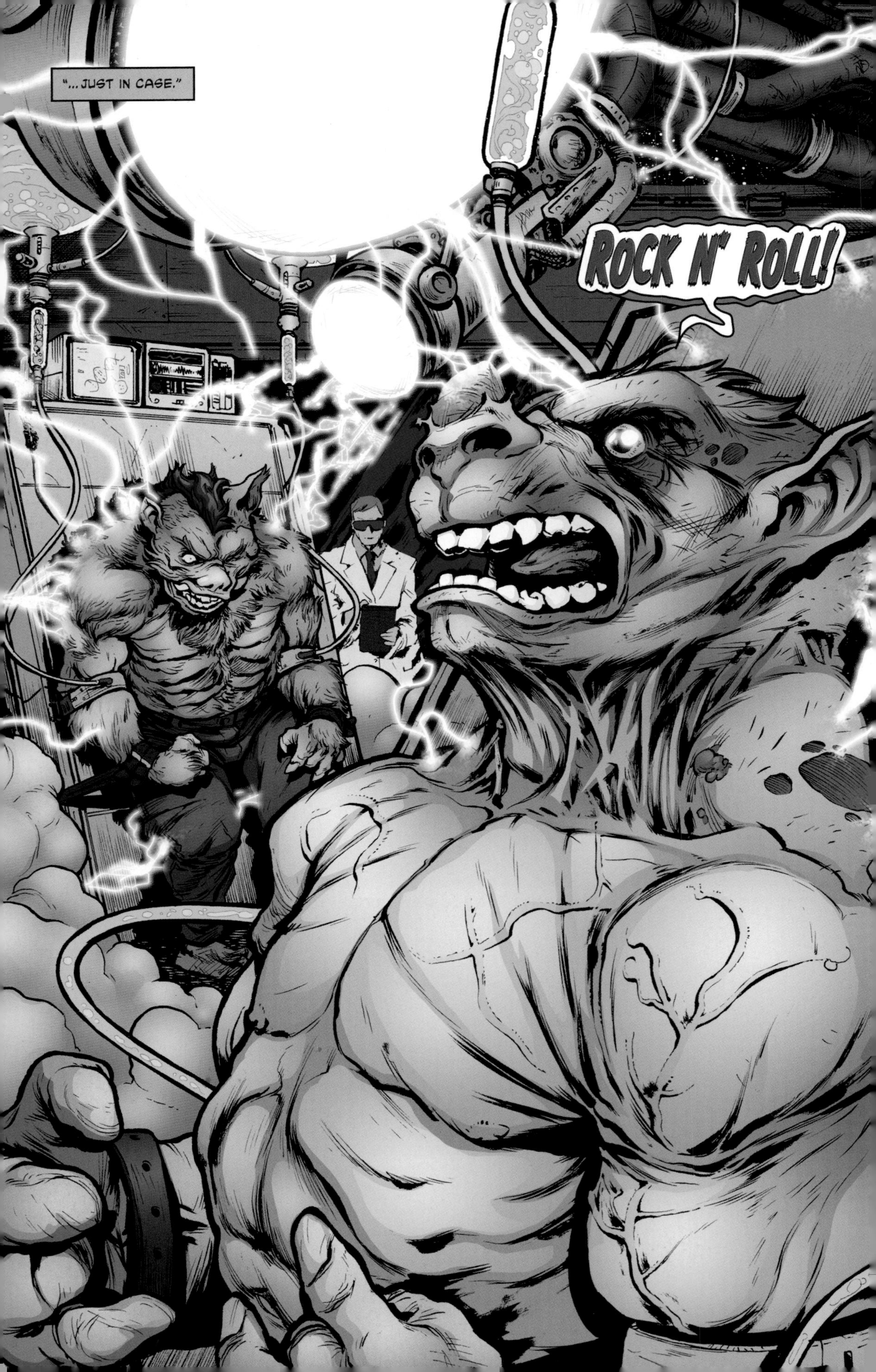
"...JUST IN CASE."
ROCK N' ROLL!

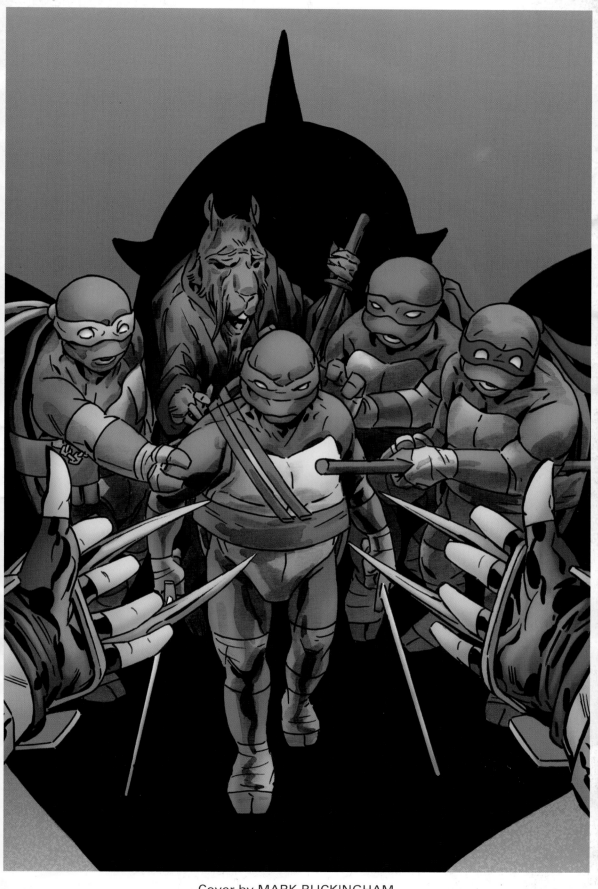

Cover by MARK BUCKINGHAM
Colors by CHARLIE KIRCHOFF

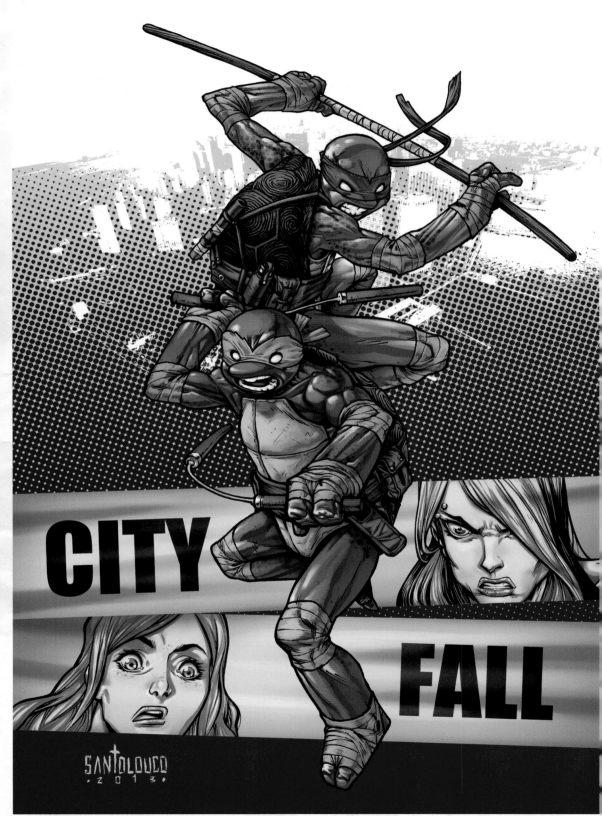

CITY FALL

SANTOLOUCO
·2013·

Cover by MATEUS SANTOLOUCO   TMNT #26

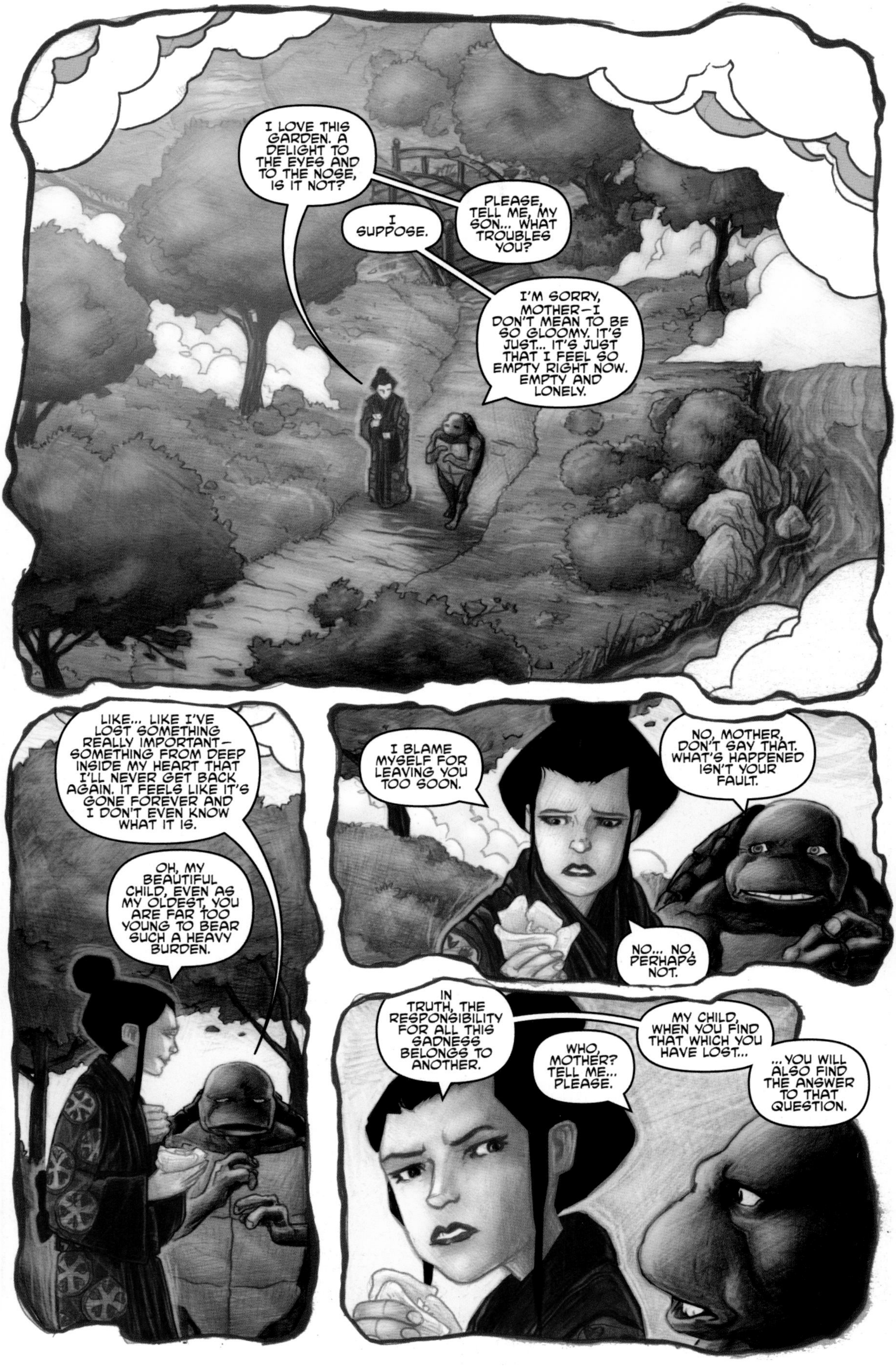
I LOVE THIS GARDEN. A DELIGHT TO THE EYES AND TO THE NOSE, IS IT NOT?
I SUPPOSE.
PLEASE, TELL ME, MY SON... WHAT TROUBLES YOU?
I'M SORRY, MOTHER—I DON'T MEAN TO BE SO GLOOMY. IT'S JUST... IT'S JUST THAT I FEEL SO EMPTY RIGHT NOW. EMPTY AND LONELY.
LIKE... LIKE I'VE LOST SOMETHING REALLY IMPORTANT—SOMETHING FROM DEEP INSIDE MY HEART THAT I'LL NEVER GET BACK AGAIN. IT FEELS LIKE IT'S GONE FOREVER AND I DON'T EVEN KNOW WHAT IT IS.
OH, MY BEAUTIFUL CHILD, EVEN AS MY OLDEST, YOU ARE FAR TOO YOUNG TO BEAR SUCH A HEAVY BURDEN.
I BLAME MYSELF FOR LEAVING YOU TOO SOON.
NO, MOTHER, DON'T SAY THAT. WHAT'S HAPPENED ISN'T YOUR FAULT.
NO... NO, PERHAPS NOT.
IN TRUTH, THE RESPONSIBILITY FOR ALL THIS SADNESS BELONGS TO ANOTHER.
WHO, MOTHER? TELL ME... PLEASE.
MY CHILD, WHEN YOU FIND THAT WHICH YOU HAVE LOST...
...YOU WILL ALSO FIND THE ANSWER TO THAT QUESTION.

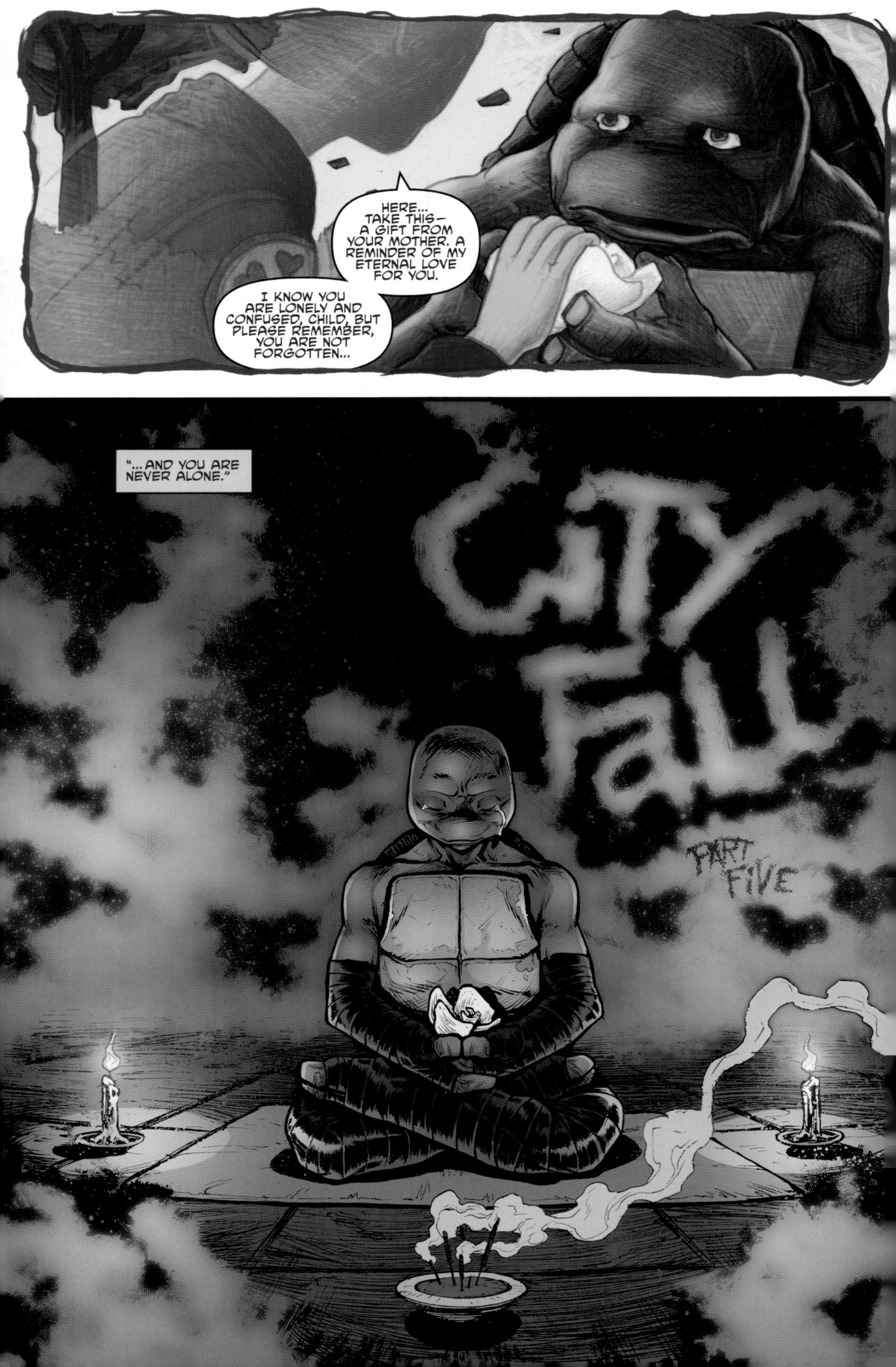
HERE... TAKE THIS— A GIFT FROM YOUR MOTHER. A REMINDER OF MY ETERNAL LOVE FOR YOU.
I KNOW YOU ARE LONELY AND CONFUSED, CHILD, BUT PLEASE REMEMBER, YOU ARE NOT FORGOTTEN...
"...AND YOU ARE NEVER ALONE."
CITY FALL
PART FIVE

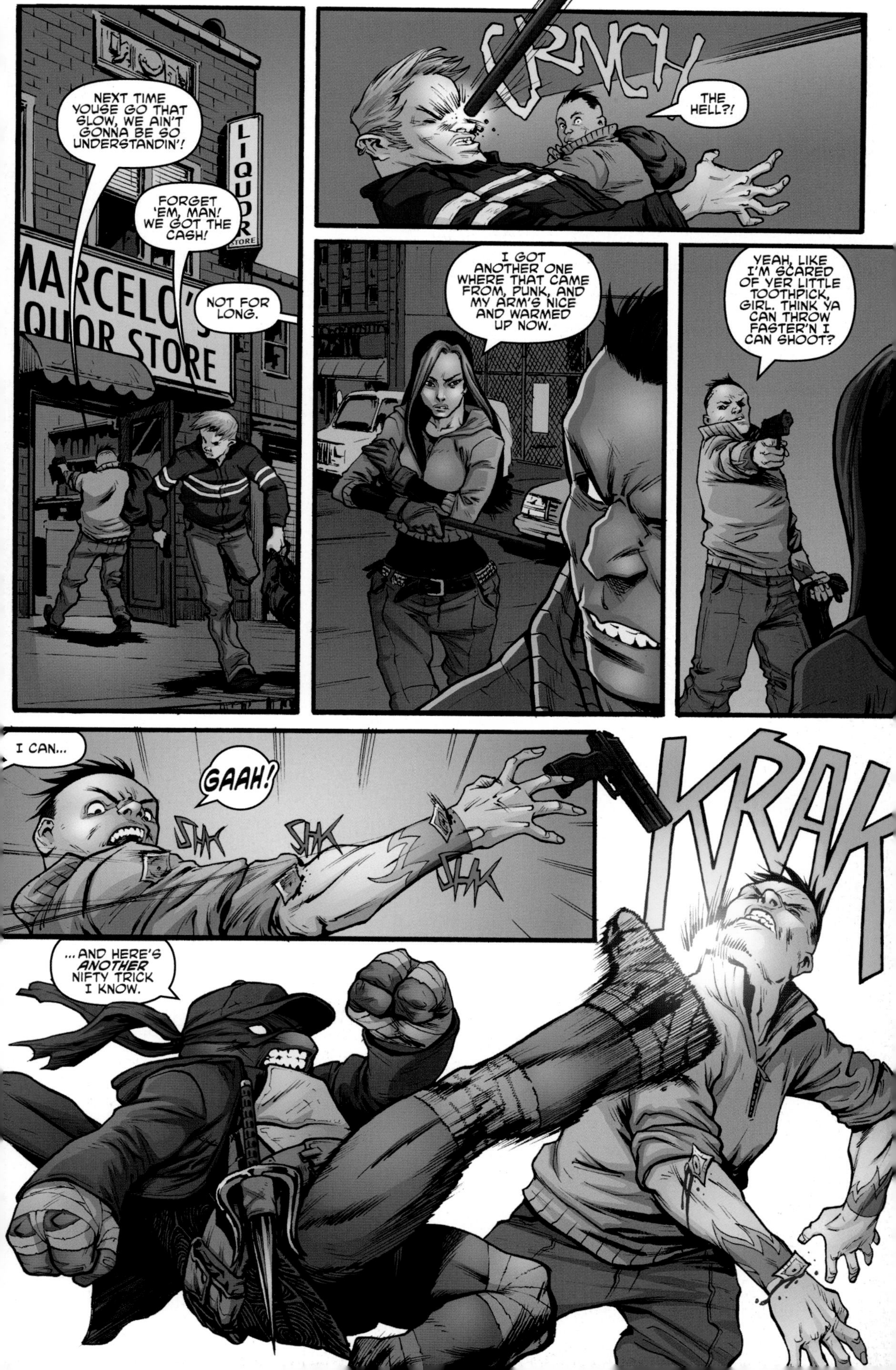

NEXT TIME YOUSE GO THAT SLOW, WE AIN'T GONNA BE SO UNDERSTANDIN'!
FORGET 'EM, MAN! WE GOT THE CASH!
NOT FOR LONG.
LIQUOR STORE
MARCELO'S LIQUOR STORE
SKRNCH
THE HELL?!
I GOT ANOTHER ONE WHERE THAT CAME FROM, PUNK, AND MY ARM'S NICE AND WARMED UP NOW.
YEAH, LIKE I'M SCARED OF YER LITTLE TOOTHPICK, GIRL. THINK YA CAN THROW FASTER'N I CAN SHOOT?
I CAN...
GAAH!
SHK
SHK
SHK
KRAK
...AND HERE'S ANOTHER NIFTY TRICK I KNOW.

ANGEL, YOU GOT TIME TO TALK?

I DO NOW. THANKS FOR THE ASSIST.

NO BIGGIE. WHY AIN'T THE OTHER PURPLE DRAGONS WITH YOU?

UH... THE DRAGONS ARE DEALIN' WITH SOME, UM... *FUNNY BUSINESS* RIGHT NOW. WHAT YOU MIGHT CALL A FAMILY SQUABBLE.*

THAT SEEMS TO BE GOIN' 'ROUND THESE DAYS. MUST BE SOMETHIN' IN THE WATER.

*See the **HUN** micro-series for more info. – B.C.

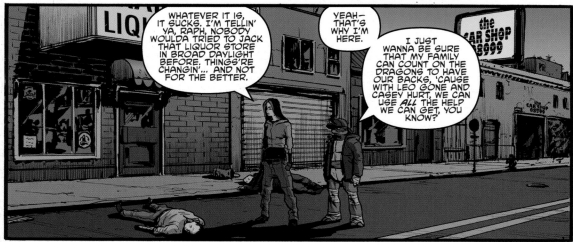

WHATEVER IT IS, IT SUCKS. I'M TELLIN' YA, RAPH, NOBODY WOULDA TRIED TO JACK THAT LIQUOR STORE IN BROAD DAYLIGHT BEFORE. THINGS'RE CHANGIN'... AND NOT FOR THE BETTER.

YEAH— THAT'S WHY I'M HERE.

I JUST WANNA BE SURE THAT MY FAMILY CAN COUNT ON THE DRAGONS TO HAVE OUR BACKS, 'CAUSE WITH LEO GONE AND CASEY HURT, WE CAN USE *ALL* THE HELP WE CAN GET, YOU KNOW?

YEAH, I KNOW. BUT SINCE THINGS IN THE DRAGONS AIN'T EXACTLY WHAT YOU'D CALL COPACETIC RIGHT NOW, I CAN'T GUARANTEE THE OTHERS WILL HELP YOU GUYS.

BUT YOU KNOW *I* GOT ALL YOUR BACKS...

...NO MATTER WHAT.

THANKS, ANGEL—THAT MEANS A LOT. REALLY.

OKAY, I'M OUTTA HERE. GOTTA MAKE ONE MORE STOP...

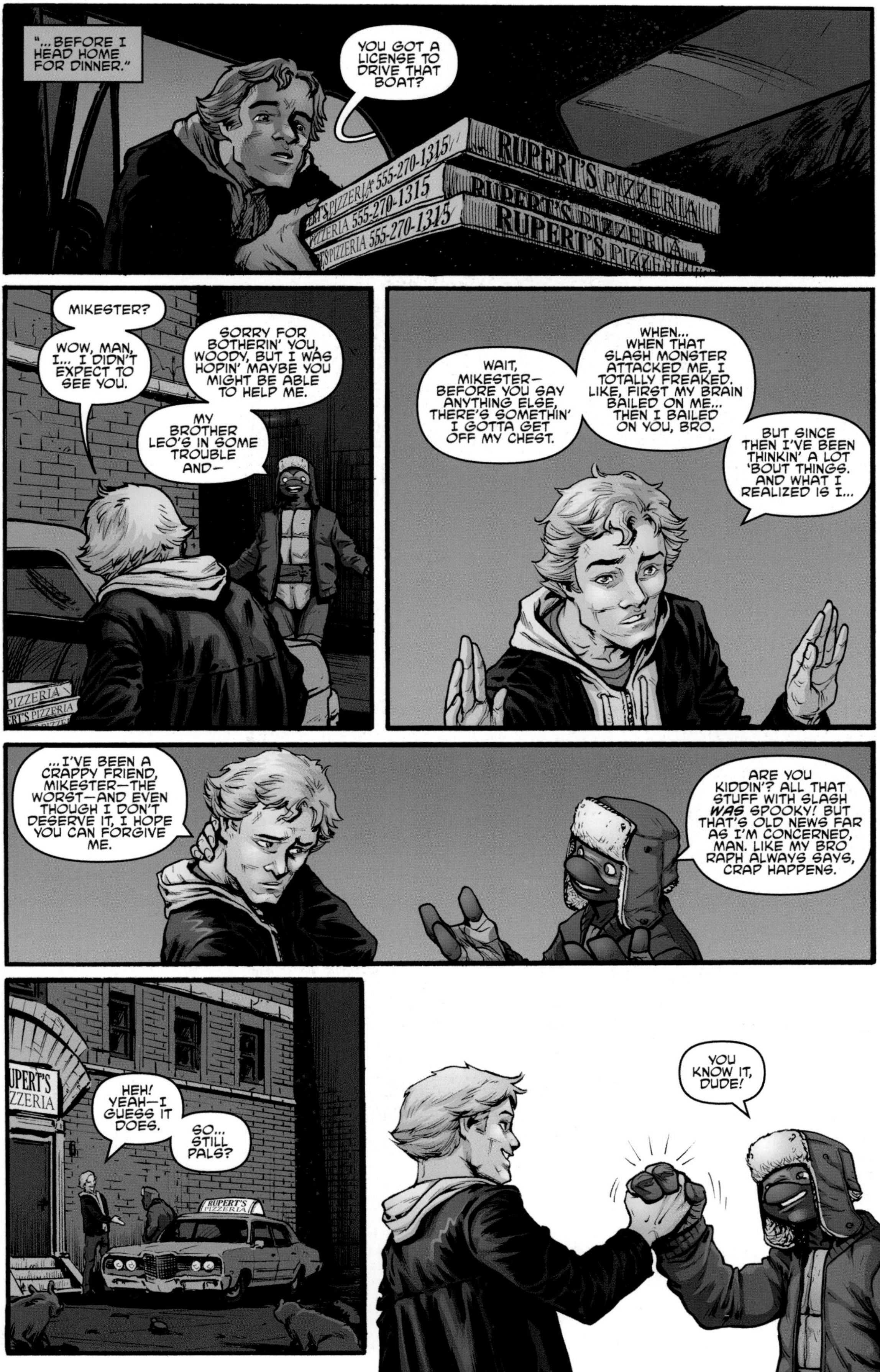
"...BEFORE I HEAD HOME FOR DINNER."
YOU GOT A LICENSE TO DRIVE THAT BOAT?
RUPERT'S PIZZERIA 555-270-1315
MIKESTER?
WOW, MAN, I... I DIDN'T EXPECT TO SEE YOU.
SORRY FOR BOTHERIN' YOU, WOODY, BUT I WAS HOPIN' MAYBE YOU MIGHT BE ABLE TO HELP ME.
MY BROTHER LEO'S IN SOME TROUBLE AND—
WAIT, MIKESTER—BEFORE YOU SAY ANYTHING ELSE, THERE'S SOMETHIN' I GOTTA GET OFF MY CHEST.
WHEN... WHEN THAT SLASH MONSTER ATTACKED ME, I TOTALLY FREAKED. LIKE, FIRST MY BRAIN BAILED ON ME... THEN I BAILED ON YOU, BRO.
BUT SINCE THEN I'VE BEEN THINKIN' A LOT 'BOUT THINGS. AND WHAT I REALIZED IS I...
...I'VE BEEN A CRAPPY FRIEND, MIKESTER—THE WORST—AND EVEN THOUGH I DON'T DESERVE IT, I HOPE YOU CAN FORGIVE ME.
ARE YOU KIDDIN'? ALL THAT STUFF WITH SLASH *WAS* SPOOKY! BUT THAT'S OLD NEWS FAR AS I'M CONCERNED, MAN. LIKE MY BRO RAPH ALWAYS SAYS, CRAP HAPPENS.
RUPERT'S PIZZERIA
HEH! YEAH—I GUESS IT DOES.
SO... STILL PALS?
YOU KNOW IT, DUDE!

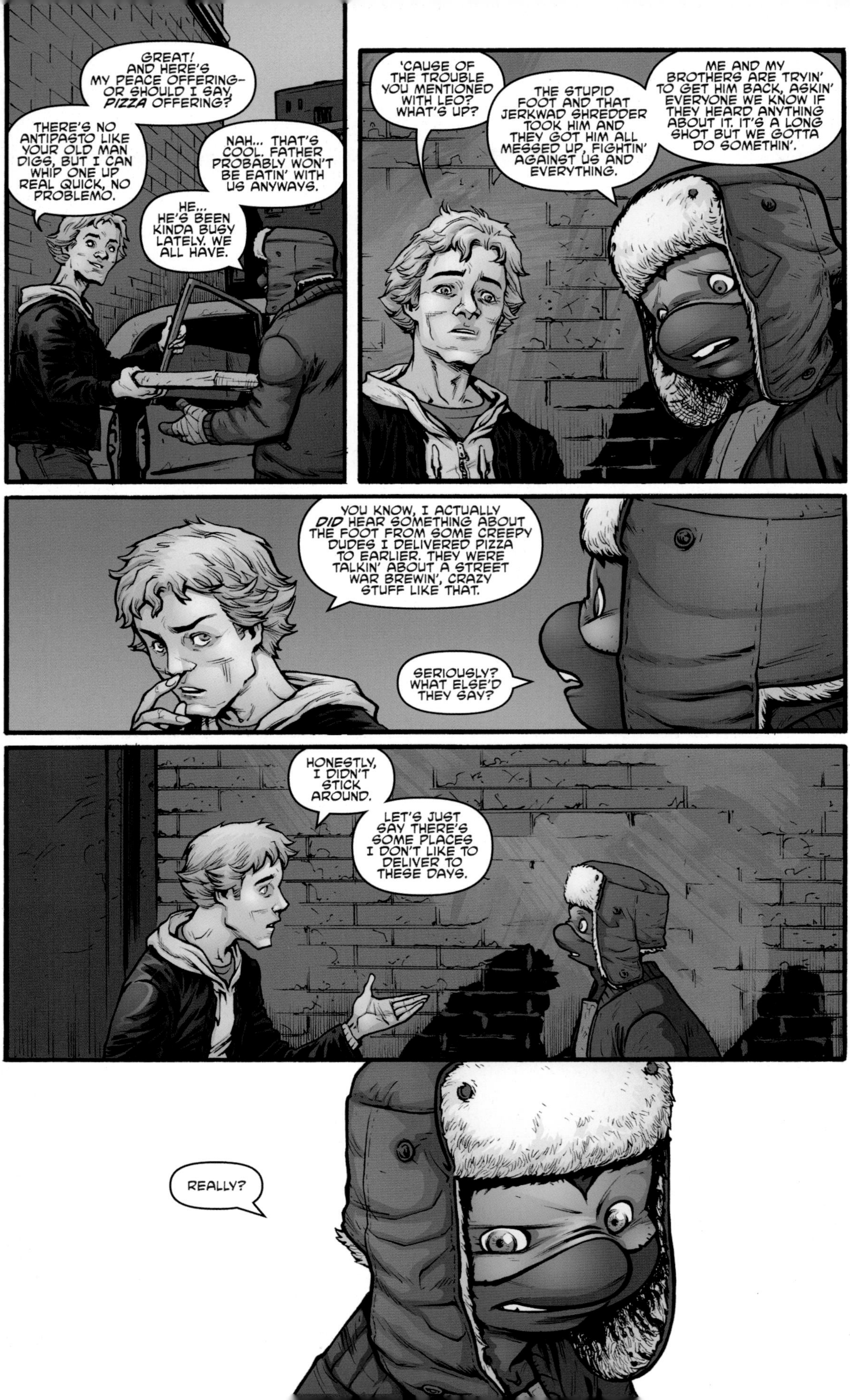
GREAT! AND HERE'S MY PEACE OFFERING-- OR SHOULD I SAY, PIZZA OFFERING?
THERE'S NO ANTIPASTO LIKE YOUR OLD MAN DIGS, BUT I CAN WHIP ONE UP REAL QUICK, NO PROBLEMO.
NAH... THAT'S COOL. FATHER PROBABLY WON'T BE EATIN' WITH US ANYWAYS.
HE... HE'S BEEN KINDA BUSY LATELY. WE ALL HAVE.
'CAUSE OF THE TROUBLE YOU MENTIONED WITH LEO? WHAT'S UP?
THE STUPID FOOT AND THAT JERKWAD SHREDDER TOOK HIM AND THEY GOT HIM ALL MESSED UP, FIGHTIN' AGAINST US AND EVERYTHING.
ME AND MY BROTHERS ARE TRYIN' TO GET HIM BACK, ASKIN' EVERYONE WE KNOW IF THEY HEARD ANYTHING ABOUT IT. IT'S A LONG SHOT BUT WE GOTTA DO SOMETHIN'.
YOU KNOW, I ACTUALLY DID HEAR SOMETHING ABOUT THE FOOT FROM SOME CREEPY DUDES I DELIVERED PIZZA TO EARLIER. THEY WERE TALKIN' ABOUT A STREET WAR BREWIN', CRAZY STUFF LIKE THAT.
SERIOUSLY? WHAT ELSE'D THEY SAY?
HONESTLY, I DIDN'T STICK AROUND.
LET'S JUST SAY THERE'S SOME PLACES I DON'T LIKE TO DELIVER TO THESE DAYS.
REALLY?

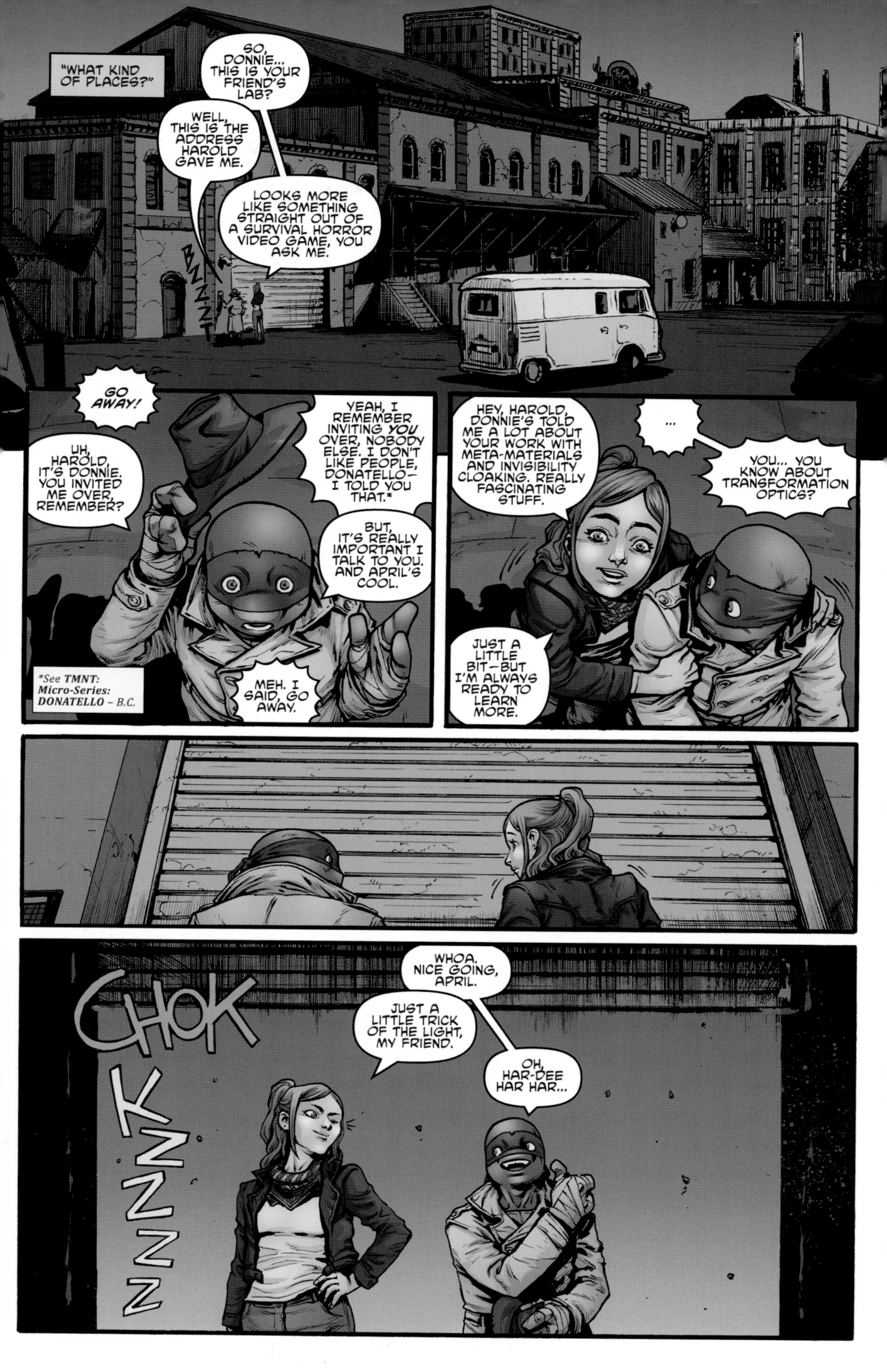
"WHAT KIND OF PLACES?"
SO, DONNIE... THIS IS YOUR FRIEND'S LAB?
WELL, THIS IS THE ADDRESS HAROLD GAVE ME.
LOOKS MORE LIKE SOMETHING STRAIGHT OUT OF A SURVIVAL HORROR VIDEO GAME, YOU ASK ME.
BZZZT
GO AWAY!
UH, HAROLD, IT'S DONNIE. YOU INVITED ME OVER, REMEMBER?
YEAH, I REMEMBER INVITING *YOU* OVER, NOBODY ELSE. I DON'T LIKE PEOPLE, DONATELLO— I TOLD YOU THAT.*
BUT, IT'S REALLY IMPORTANT I TALK TO YOU. AND APRIL'S COOL.
MEH. I SAID, GO AWAY.
*See **TMNT: Micro-Series: DONATELLO** – B.C.
HEY, HAROLD, DONNIE'S TOLD ME A LOT ABOUT YOUR WORK WITH META-MATERIALS AND INVISIBILITY CLOAKING. REALLY FASCINATING STUFF.
...
YOU... YOU KNOW ABOUT TRANSFORMATION OPTICS?
JUST A LITTLE BIT—BUT I'M ALWAYS READY TO LEARN MORE.
CHOK
KZZZZ
WHOA. NICE GOING, APRIL.
JUST A LITTLE TRICK OF THE LIGHT, MY FRIEND.
OH, HAR-DEE HAR HAR...

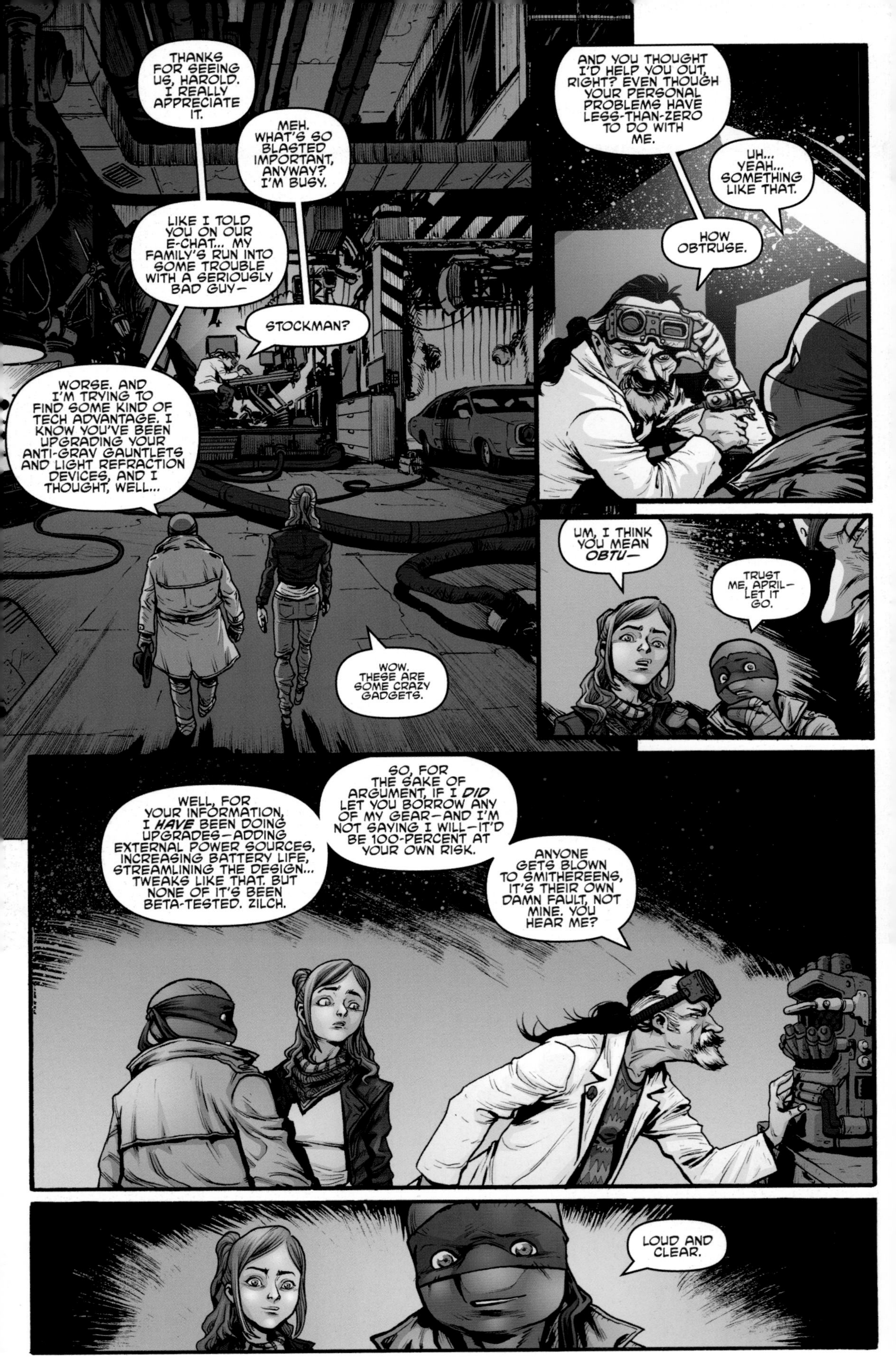
THANKS FOR SEEING US, HAROLD. I REALLY APPRECIATE IT.
MEH. WHAT'S SO BLASTED IMPORTANT, ANYWAY? I'M BUSY.
LIKE I TOLD YOU ON OUR E-CHAT... MY FAMILY'S RUN INTO SOME TROUBLE WITH A SERIOUSLY BAD GUY—
STOCKMAN?
WORSE. AND I'M TRYING TO FIND SOME KIND OF TECH ADVANTAGE. I KNOW YOU'VE BEEN UPGRADING YOUR ANTI-GRAV GAUNTLETS AND LIGHT REFRACTION DEVICES, AND I THOUGHT, WELL...
WOW. THESE ARE SOME CRAZY GADGETS.
AND YOU THOUGHT I'D HELP YOU OUT, RIGHT? EVEN THOUGH YOUR PERSONAL PROBLEMS HAVE LESS-THAN-ZERO TO DO WITH ME.
UH... YEAH... SOMETHING LIKE THAT.
HOW OBTRUSE.
UM, I THINK YOU MEAN *OBTU*—
TRUST ME, APRIL—LET IT GO.
WELL, FOR YOUR INFORMATION, I ***HAVE*** BEEN DOING UPGRADES—ADDING EXTERNAL POWER SOURCES, INCREASING BATTERY LIFE, STREAMLINING THE DESIGN... TWEAKS LIKE THAT. BUT NONE OF IT'S BEEN BETA-TESTED. ZILCH.
SO, FOR THE SAKE OF ARGUMENT, IF I *DID* LET YOU BORROW ANY OF MY GEAR—AND I'M NOT SAYING I WILL—IT'D BE 100-PERCENT AT YOUR OWN RISK.
ANYONE GETS BLOWN TO SMITHEREENS, IT'S THEIR OWN DAMN FAULT, NOT MINE. YOU HEAR ME?
LOUD AND CLEAR.

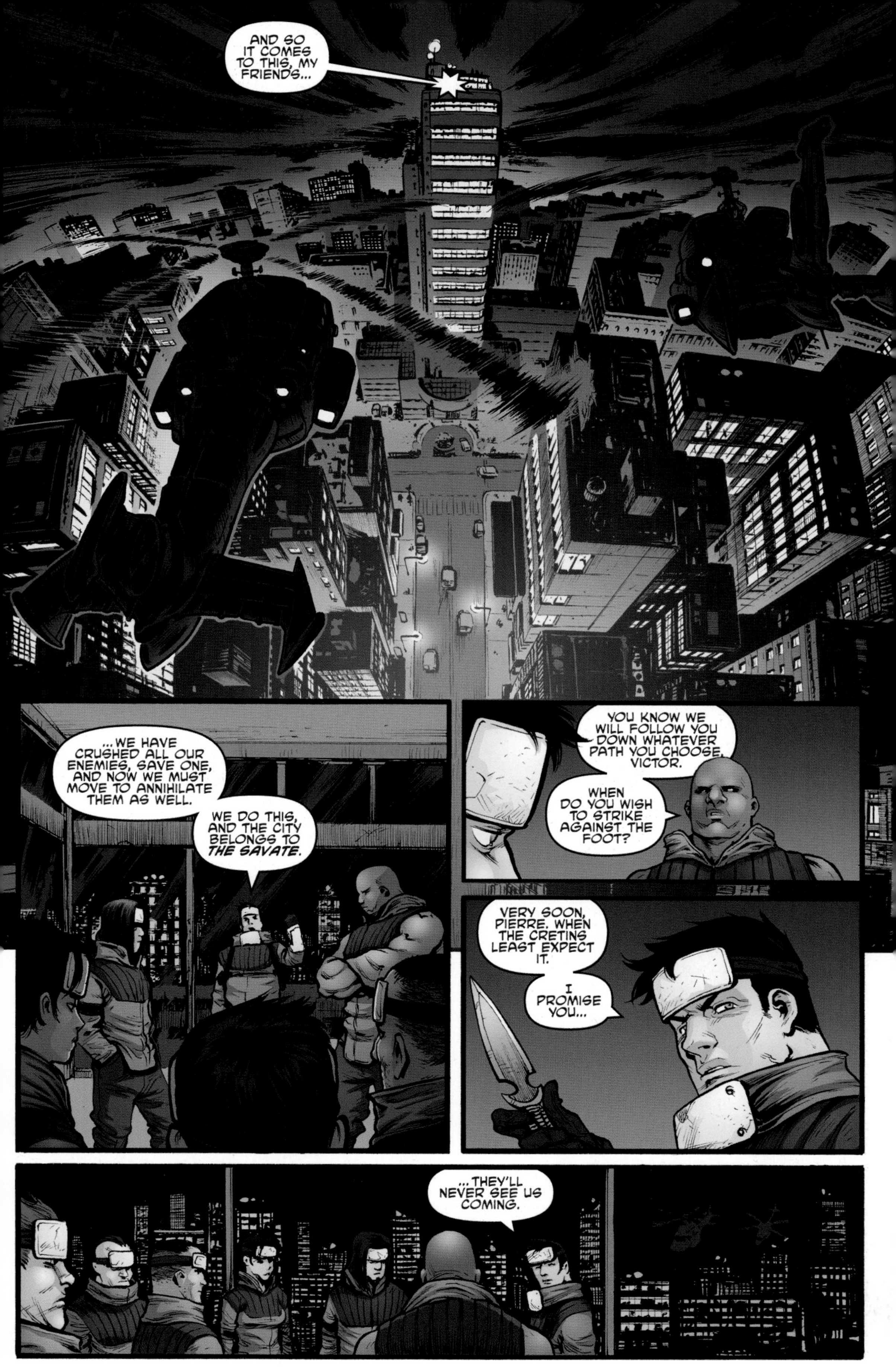
AND SO IT COMES TO THIS, MY FRIENDS...
...WE HAVE CRUSHED ALL OUR ENEMIES, SAVE ONE, AND NOW WE MUST MOVE TO ANNIHILATE THEM AS WELL.
WE DO THIS, AND THE CITY BELONGS TO THE SAVATE.
YOU KNOW WE WILL FOLLOW YOU DOWN WHATEVER PATH YOU CHOOSE, VICTOR.
WHEN DO YOU WISH TO STRIKE AGAINST THE FOOT?
VERY SOON, PIERRE. WHEN THE CRETINS LEAST EXPECT IT.
I PROMISE YOU...
...THEY'LL NEVER SEE US COMING.

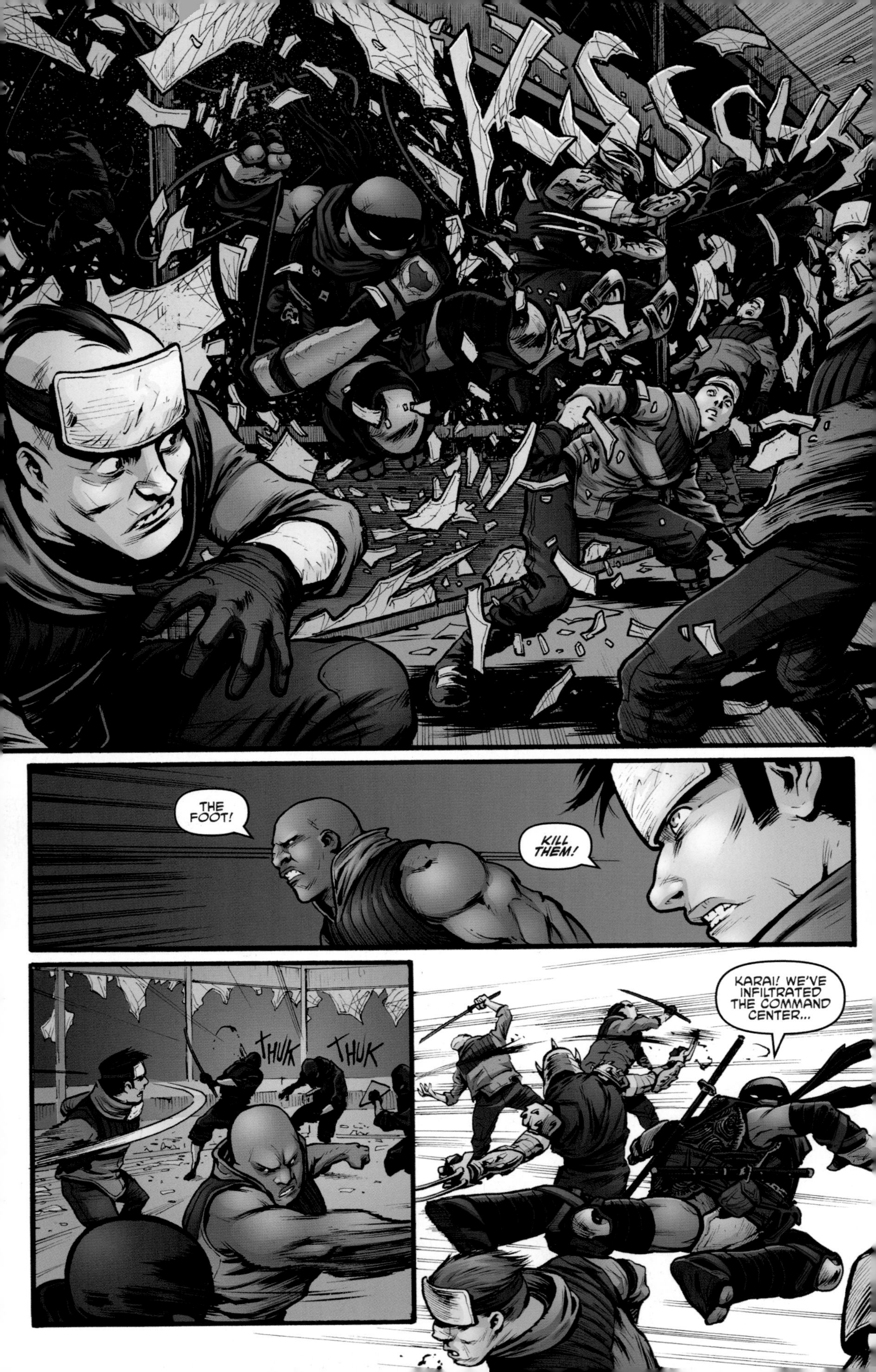

THE FOOT!
KILL THEM!
THUK
THUK
KARAI! WE'VE INFILTRATED THE COMMAND CENTER...

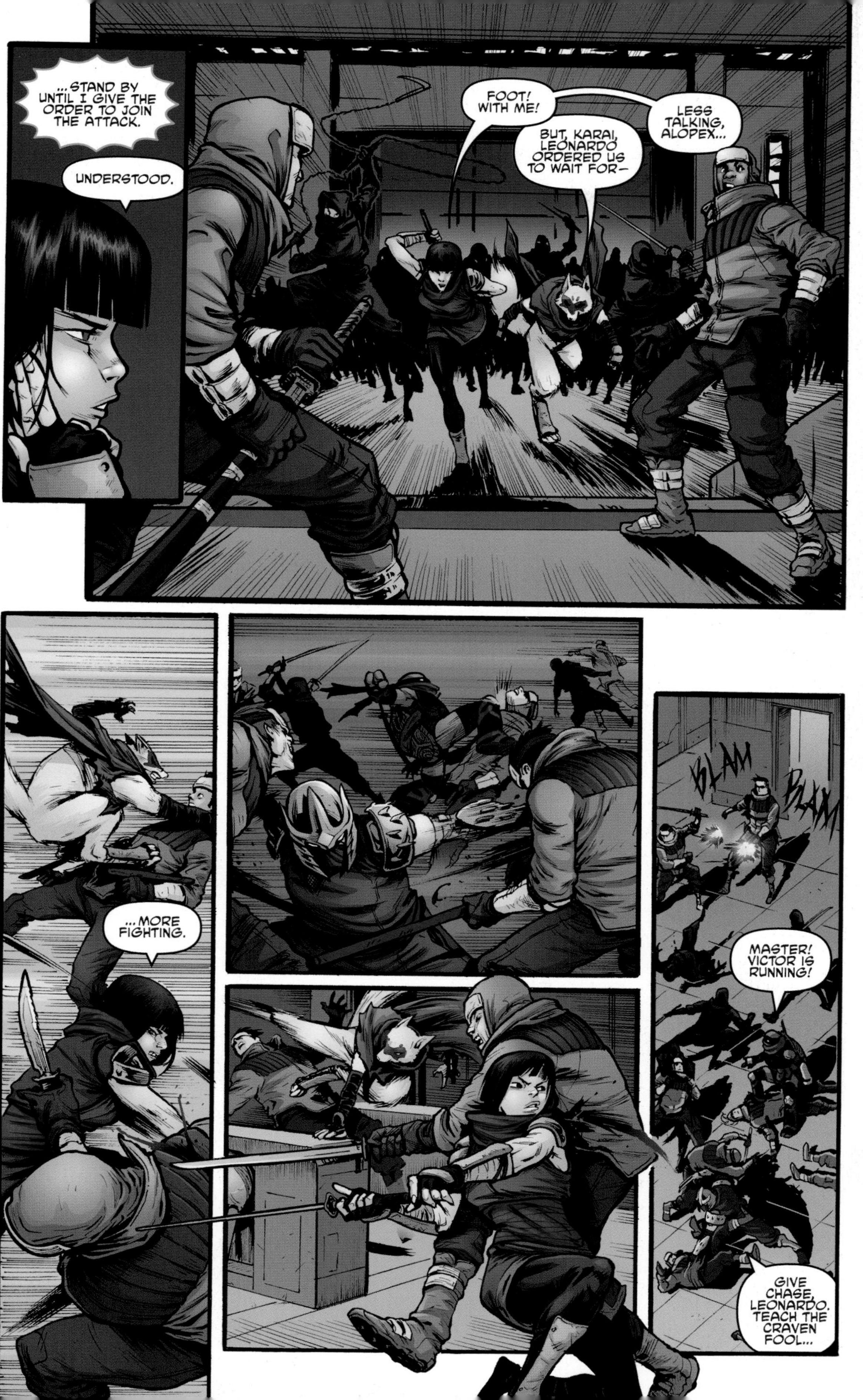
...STAND BY UNTIL I GIVE THE ORDER TO JOIN THE ATTACK.
UNDERSTOOD.
FOOT! WITH ME!
BUT, KARAI, LEONARDO ORDERED US TO WAIT FOR—
LESS TALKING, ALOPEX...
...MORE FIGHTING.
BLAM
BLAM
MASTER! VICTOR IS RUNNING!
GIVE CHASE, LEONARDO. TEACH THE CRAVEN FOOL...

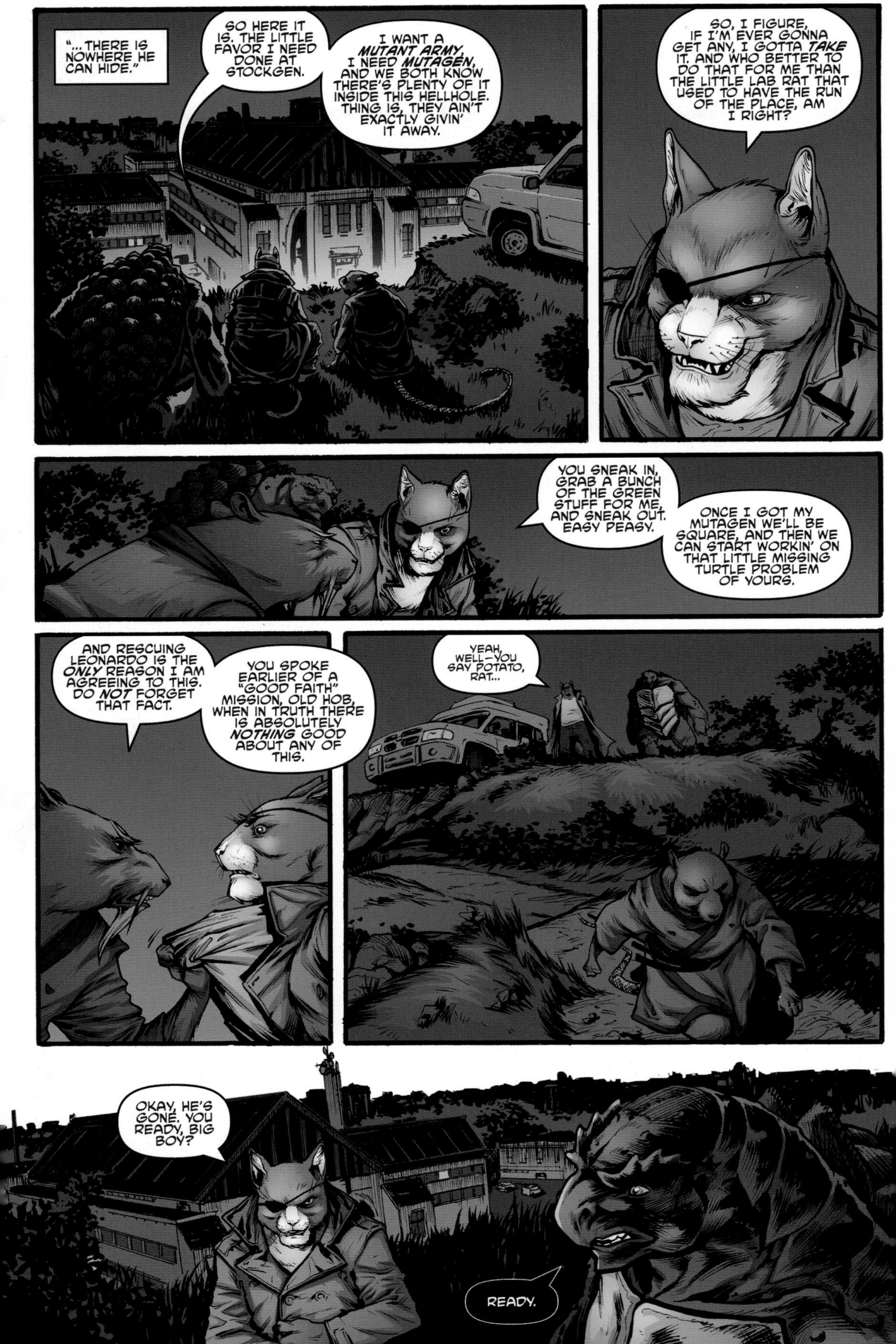
"...THERE IS NOWHERE HE CAN HIDE."
SO HERE IT IS. THE LITTLE FAVOR I NEED DONE AT STOCKGEN.
I WANT A MUTANT ARMY, I NEED MUTAGEN, AND WE BOTH KNOW THERE'S PLENTY OF IT INSIDE THIS HELLHOLE. THING IS, THEY AIN'T EXACTLY GIVIN' IT AWAY.
SO, I FIGURE, IF I'M EVER GONNA GET ANY, I GOTTA TAKE IT. AND WHO BETTER TO DO THAT FOR ME THAN THE LITTLE LAB RAT THAT USED TO HAVE THE RUN OF THE PLACE, AM I RIGHT?
YOU SNEAK IN, GRAB A BUNCH OF THE GREEN STUFF FOR ME, AND SNEAK OUT. EASY PEASY.
ONCE I GOT MY MUTAGEN WE'LL BE SQUARE, AND THEN WE CAN START WORKIN' ON THAT LITTLE MISSING TURTLE PROBLEM OF YOURS.
AND RESCUING LEONARDO IS THE ONLY REASON I AM AGREEING TO THIS. DO NOT FORGET THAT FACT.
YOU SPOKE EARLIER OF A "GOOD FAITH" MISSION, OLD HOB, WHEN IN TRUTH THERE IS ABSOLUTELY NOTHING GOOD ABOUT ANY OF THIS.
YEAH, WELL—YOU SAY POTATO, RAT...
OKAY, HE'S GONE. YOU READY, BIG BOY?
READY.

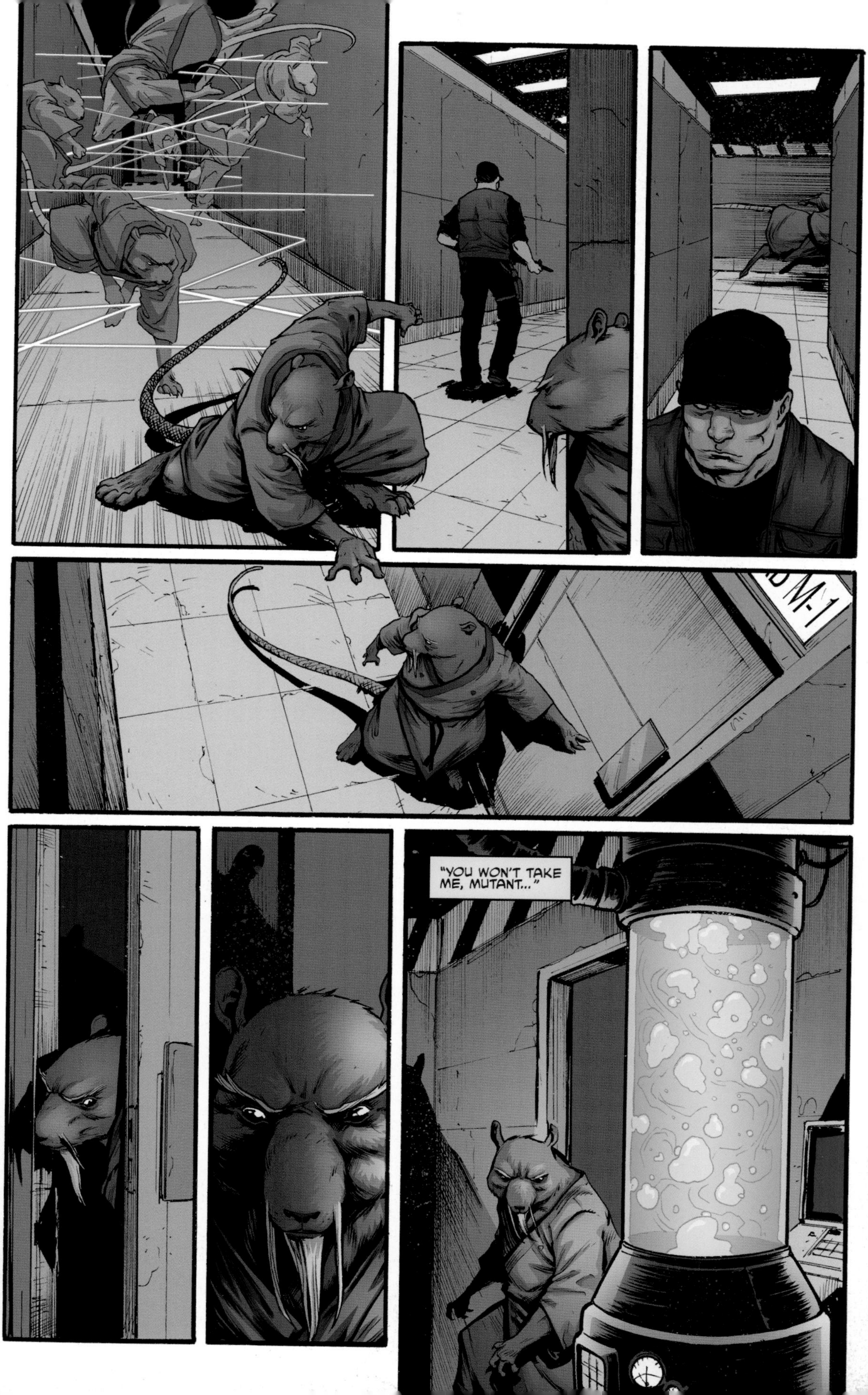
M-1
"YOU WON'T TAKE ME, MUTANT..."

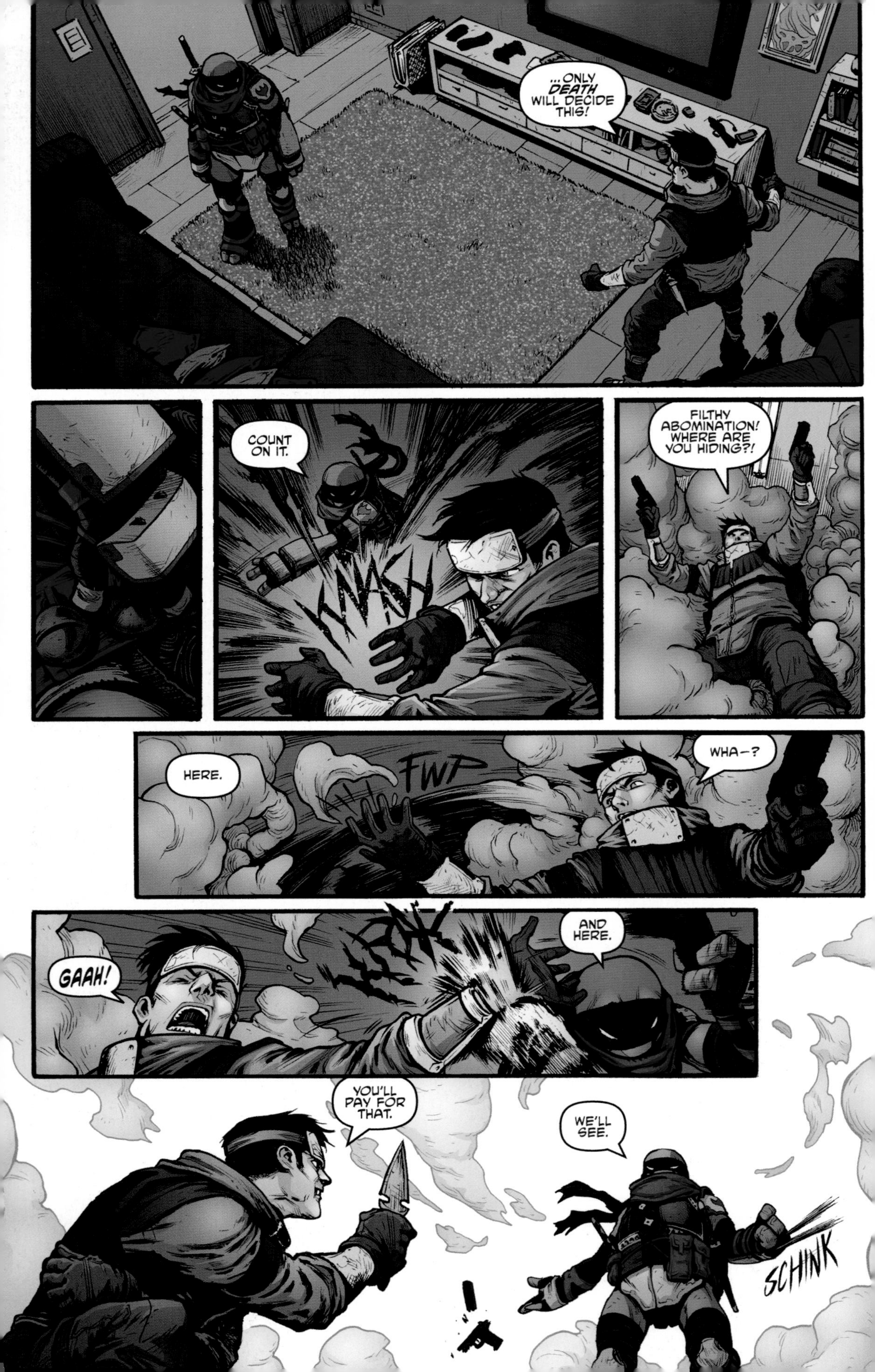
...ONLY *DEATH* WILL DECIDE THIS!
COUNT ON IT.
KNASH
FILTHY ABOMINATION! WHERE ARE YOU HIDING?!
HERE.
FWP
WHA–?
GAAH!
AND HERE.
YOU'LL PAY FOR THAT.
WE'LL SEE.
SCHINK

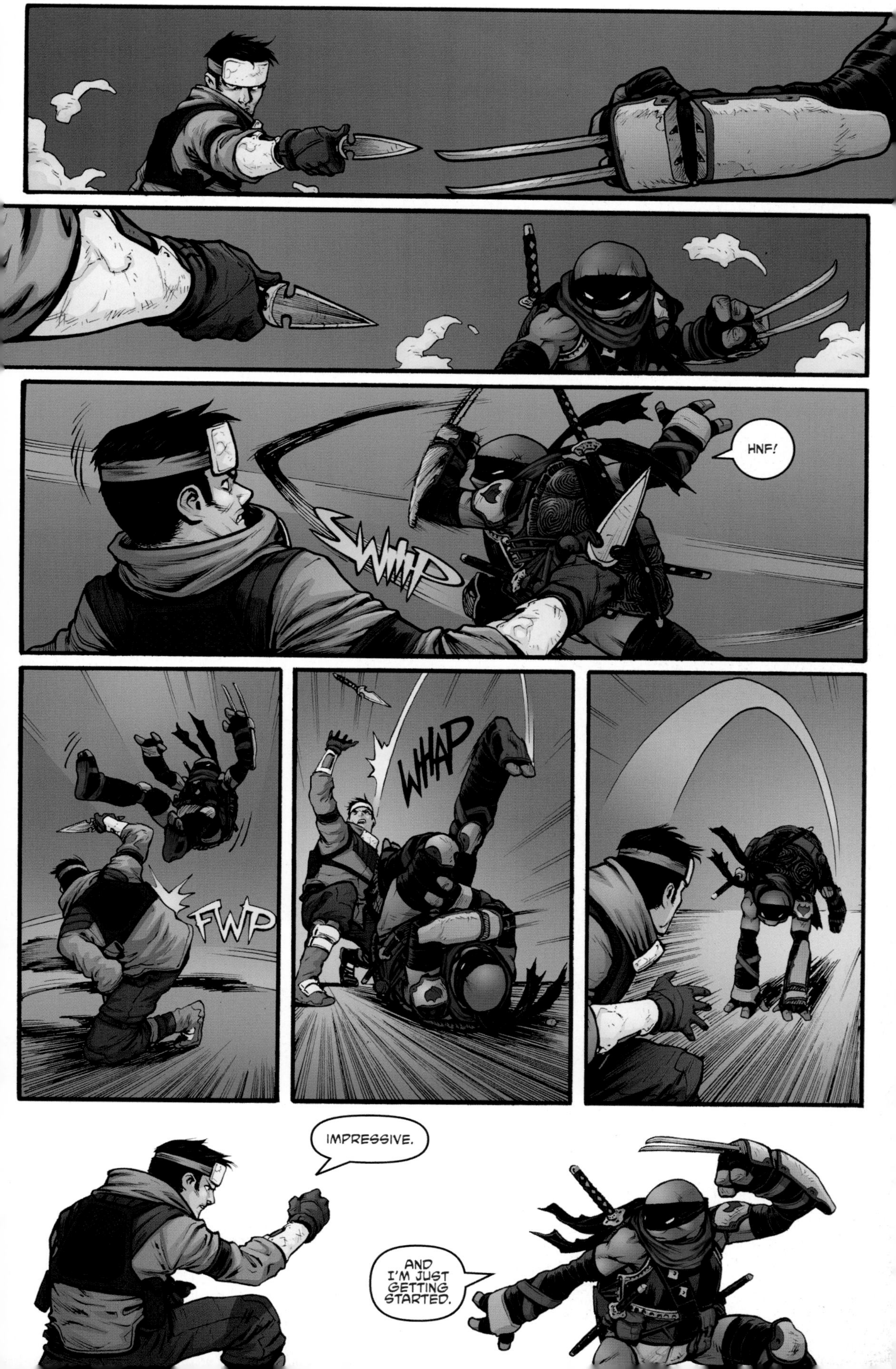
HNF!
SWHIP
FWP
WHAP
IMPRESSIVE.
AND I'M JUST GETTING STARTED.

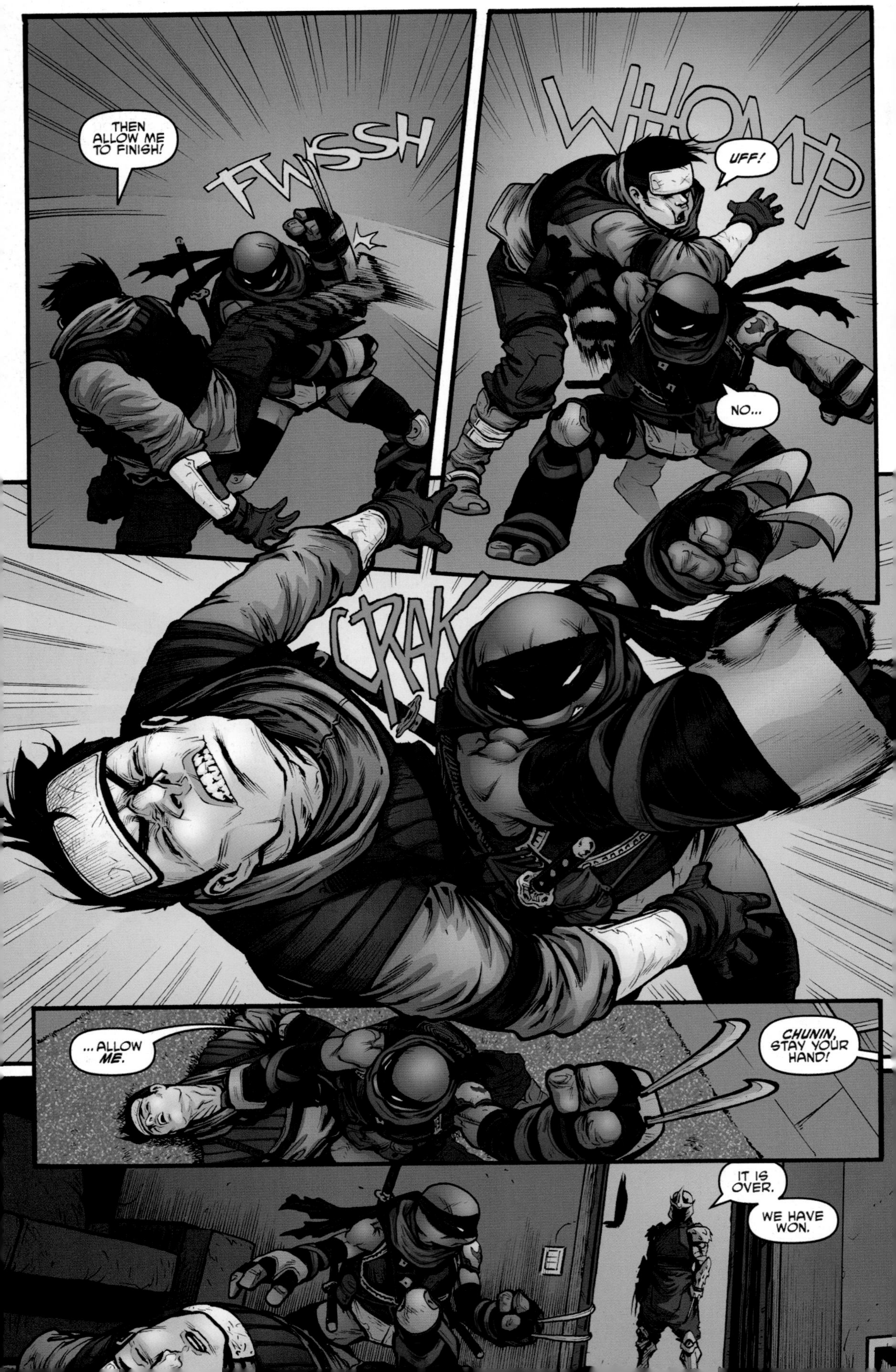
THEN ALLOW ME TO FINISH!
FWSSH
WHOAMP
UFF!
NO...
CRAK
...ALLOW ME.
CHUNIN, STAY YOUR HAND!
IT IS OVER.
WE HAVE WON.

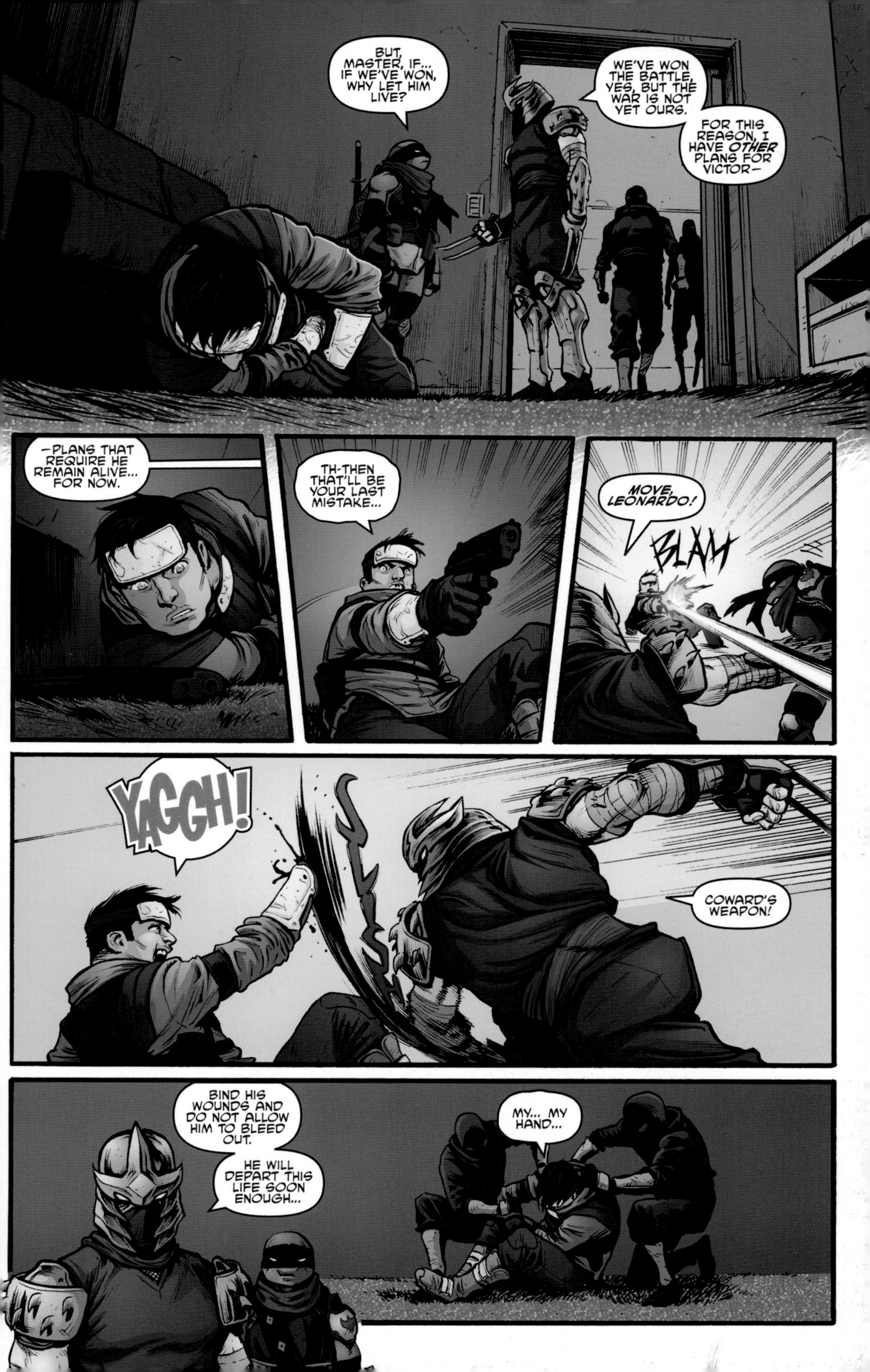
BUT, MASTER, IF... IF WE'VE WON, WHY LET HIM LIVE?
WE'VE WON THE BATTLE, YES, BUT THE WAR IS NOT YET OURS.
FOR THIS REASON, I HAVE OTHER PLANS FOR VICTOR—
—PLANS THAT REQUIRE HE REMAIN ALIVE... FOR NOW.
TH-THEN THAT'LL BE YOUR LAST MISTAKE...
MOVE, LEONARDO!
BLAM
YAGGH!
COWARD'S WEAPON!
BIND HIS WOUNDS AND DO NOT ALLOW HIM TO BLEED OUT.
HE WILL DEPART THIS LIFE SOON ENOUGH...
MY... MY HAND...

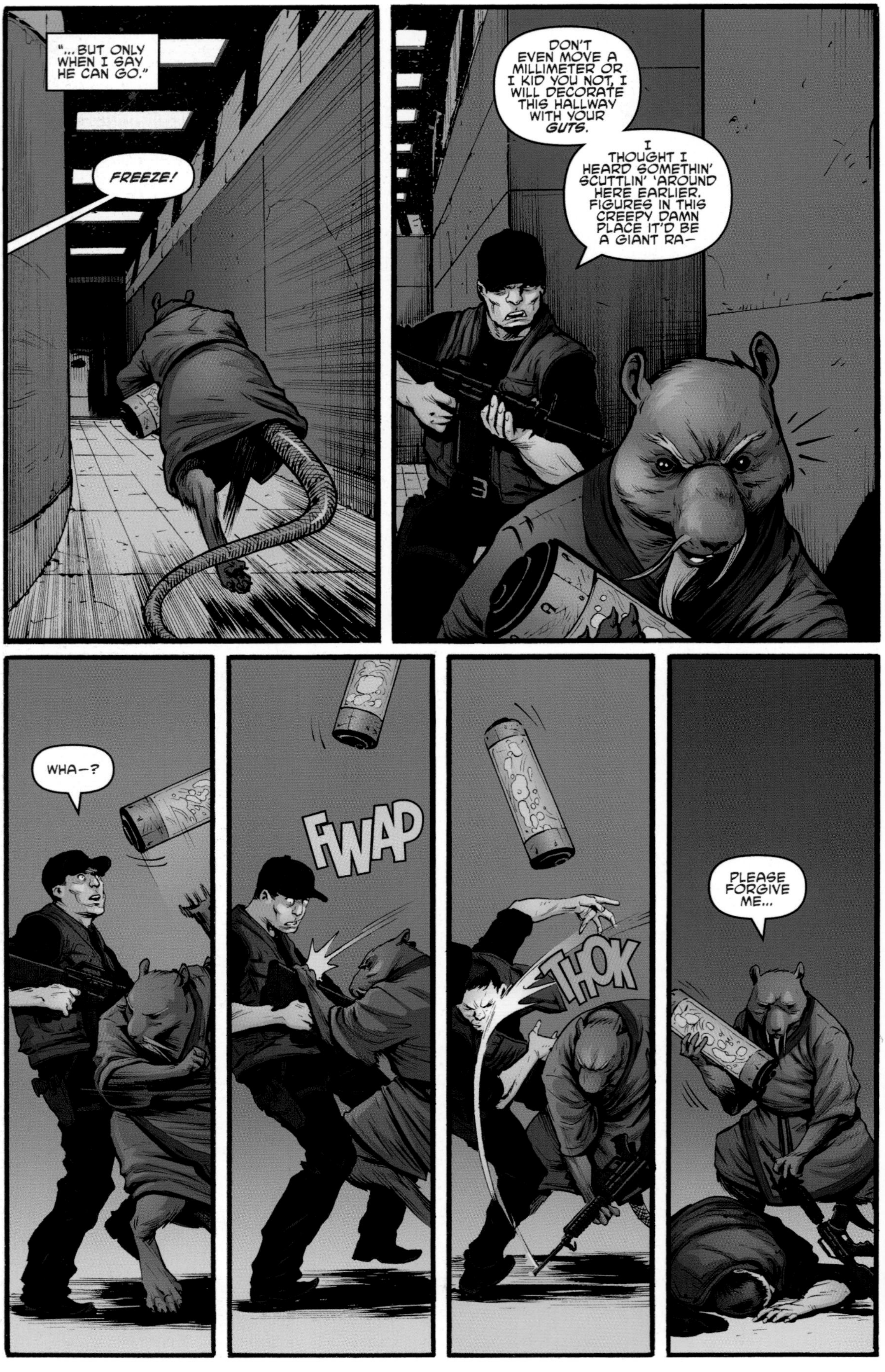
"...BUT ONLY WHEN I SAY HE CAN GO."
FREEZE!
DON'T EVEN MOVE A MILLIMETER OR I KID YOU NOT, I WILL DECORATE THIS HALLWAY WITH YOUR GUTS.
I THOUGHT I HEARD SOMETHIN' SCUTTLIN' 'AROUND HERE EARLIER. FIGURES IN THIS CREEPY DAMN PLACE IT'D BE A GIANT RA—
WHA—?
FWAP
THOK
PLEASE FORGIVE ME...

"...I DID NOT WISH FOR THIS TO HAPPEN."

SO, YOU GONNA MOPE IN THAT WINDOW ALL NIGHT, OR YOU GONNA COME IN ALREADY?

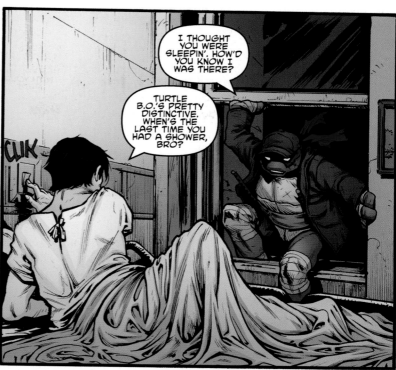

I THOUGHT YOU WERE SLEEPIN'. HOW'D YOU KNOW I WAS THERE?

TURTLE B.O.'S PRETTY DISTINCTIVE. WHEN'S THE LAST TIME YOU HAD A SHOWER, BRO?

GOTTA SAY, WITH ALL I'M HEARIN' 'BOUT LEO, I'M SURPRISED TO SEE YOU HERE.

UM... YEAH, I BEEN PRETTY BUSY, BUT I... I WANTED TO STOP BY AND...

...AND TELL YOU I'M SORRY, MAN—SORRY FOR GETTIN' YOU HURT AND ALL THE BAD STUFF THAT'S HAPPENED.

IF... IF I COULD CHANGE PLACES WITH YOU, I'D DO IT IN A SECOND—I SWEAR I WOULD.

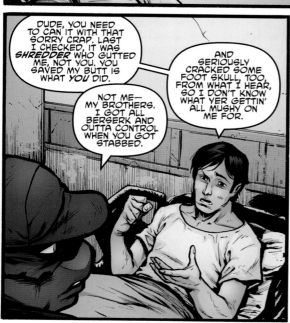

DUDE, YOU NEED TO CAN IT WITH THAT SORRY CRAP. LAST I CHECKED, IT WAS SHREDDER WHO GUTTED ME, NOT YOU. YOU SAVED MY BUTT IS WHAT YOU DID.

AND SERIOUSLY CRACKED SOME FOOT SKULL, TOO, FROM WHAT I HEAR, SO I DON'T KNOW WHAT YER GETTIN' ALL MUSHY ON ME FOR.

NOT ME— MY BROTHERS. I GOT ALL BERSERK AND OUTTA CONTROL WHEN YOU GOT STABBED.

THANKS, CASE.

AIN'T NOTHIN' TO THANK—WE'RE FAMILY AND WE GOT EACH OTHER'S BACKS, NO MATTER WHAT.

THAT'S WHAT LEO ALWAYS SAYS. OR... SAID.

WE'RE ALL TRYIN' TO FIGURE OUT HOW TO GET HIM BACK. MIKEY'S OUT TALKIN' TO ANYONE ON THE STREET WHO MIGHT KNOW SOMETHIN' AND DONNIE'S TRYIN' TO HOOK US UP WITH SOME HIGH-TECH GEAR FOR... WHO KNOWS WHAT.

HELL, I EVEN TALKED TO ANGEL TODAY, HOPIN' SHE COULD HELP. SHE PROMISED TO DO HER BEST.

AIN'T SURPRISED— ANGEL'S GOOD PEOPLE. AND SPLINTER? HOW'S HE HOLDIN' UP?

YEAH, FATHER...

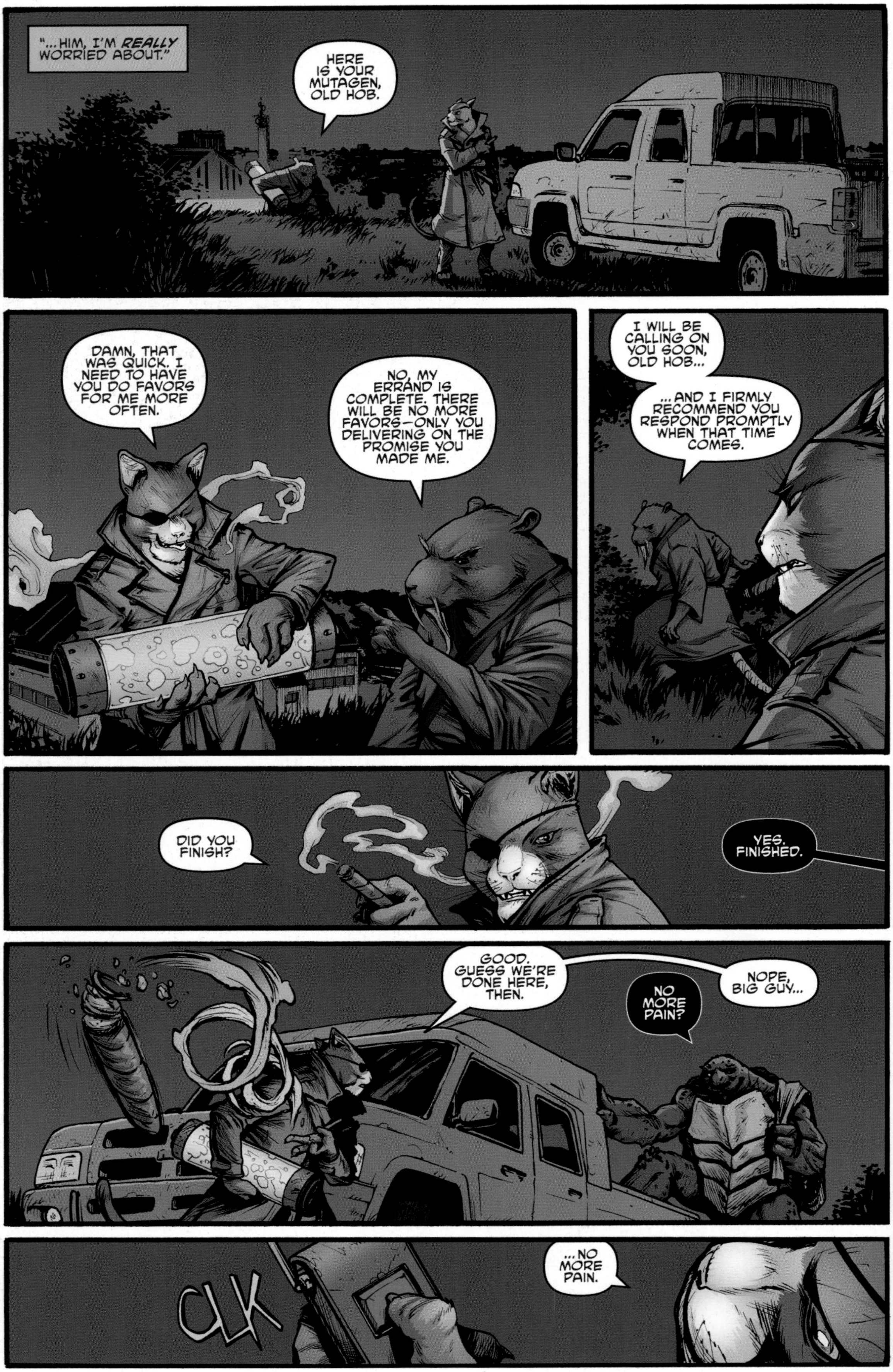
"...HIM, I'M *REALLY* WORRIED ABOUT."
HERE IS YOUR MUTAGEN, OLD HOB.
DAMN, THAT WAS QUICK. I NEED TO HAVE YOU DO FAVORS FOR ME MORE OFTEN.
NO, MY ERRAND IS COMPLETE. THERE WILL BE NO MORE FAVORS—ONLY YOU DELIVERING ON THE PROMISE YOU MADE ME.
I WILL BE CALLING ON YOU SOON, OLD HOB...
...AND I FIRMLY RECOMMEND YOU RESPOND PROMPTLY WHEN THAT TIME COMES.
DID YOU FINISH?
YES. FINISHED.
GOOD. GUESS WE'RE DONE HERE, THEN.
NO MORE PAIN?
NOPE, BIG GUY...
CLK
...NO MORE PAIN.

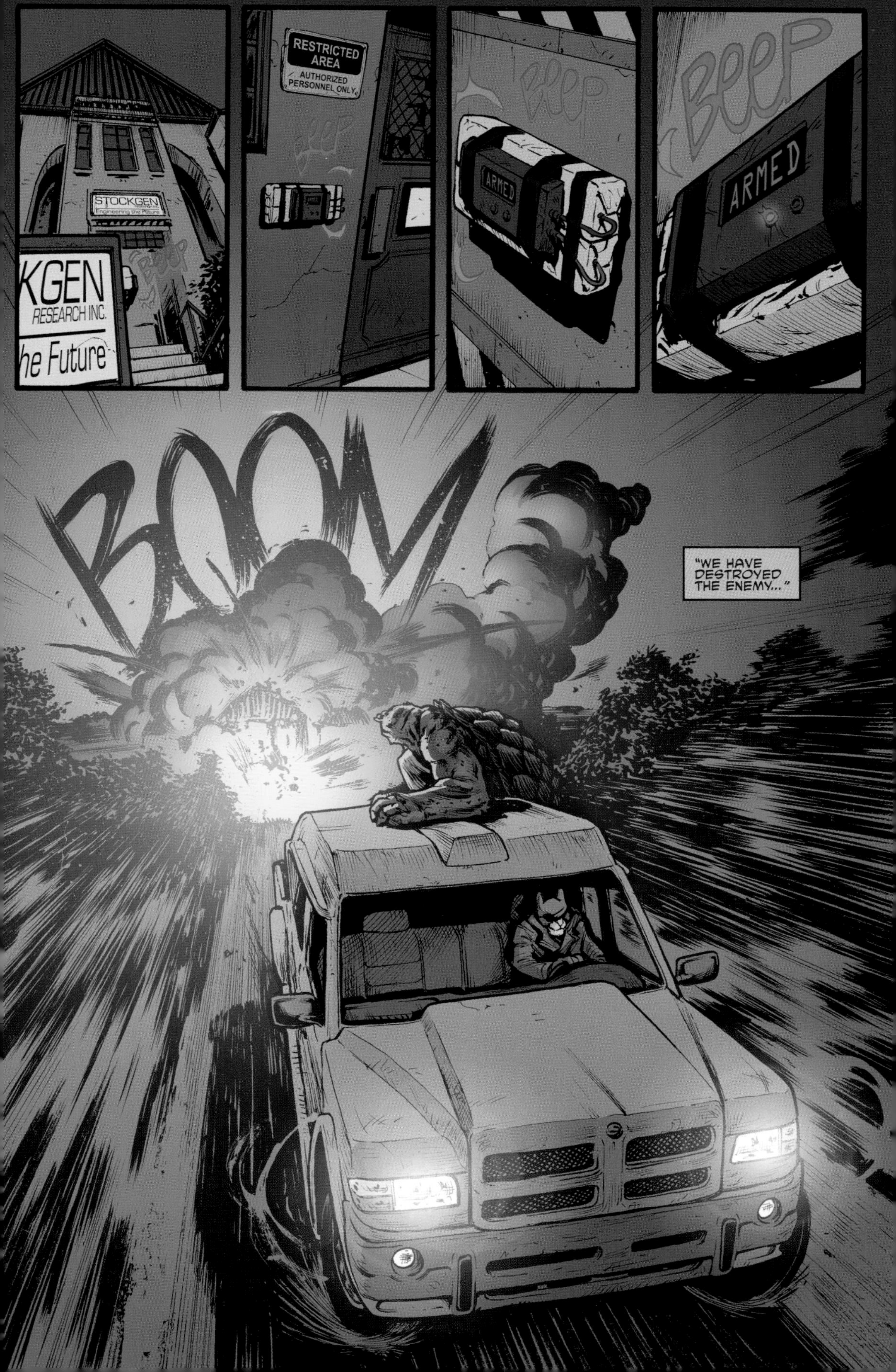
STOCKGEN
Engineering the Future
KGEN
RESEARCH INC.
he Future
BEEP
RESTRICTED AREA
AUTHORIZED PERSONNEL ONLY
BEEP
BEEP
ARMED
BEEP
ARMED
BOOM
"WE HAVE DESTROYED THE ENEMY..."

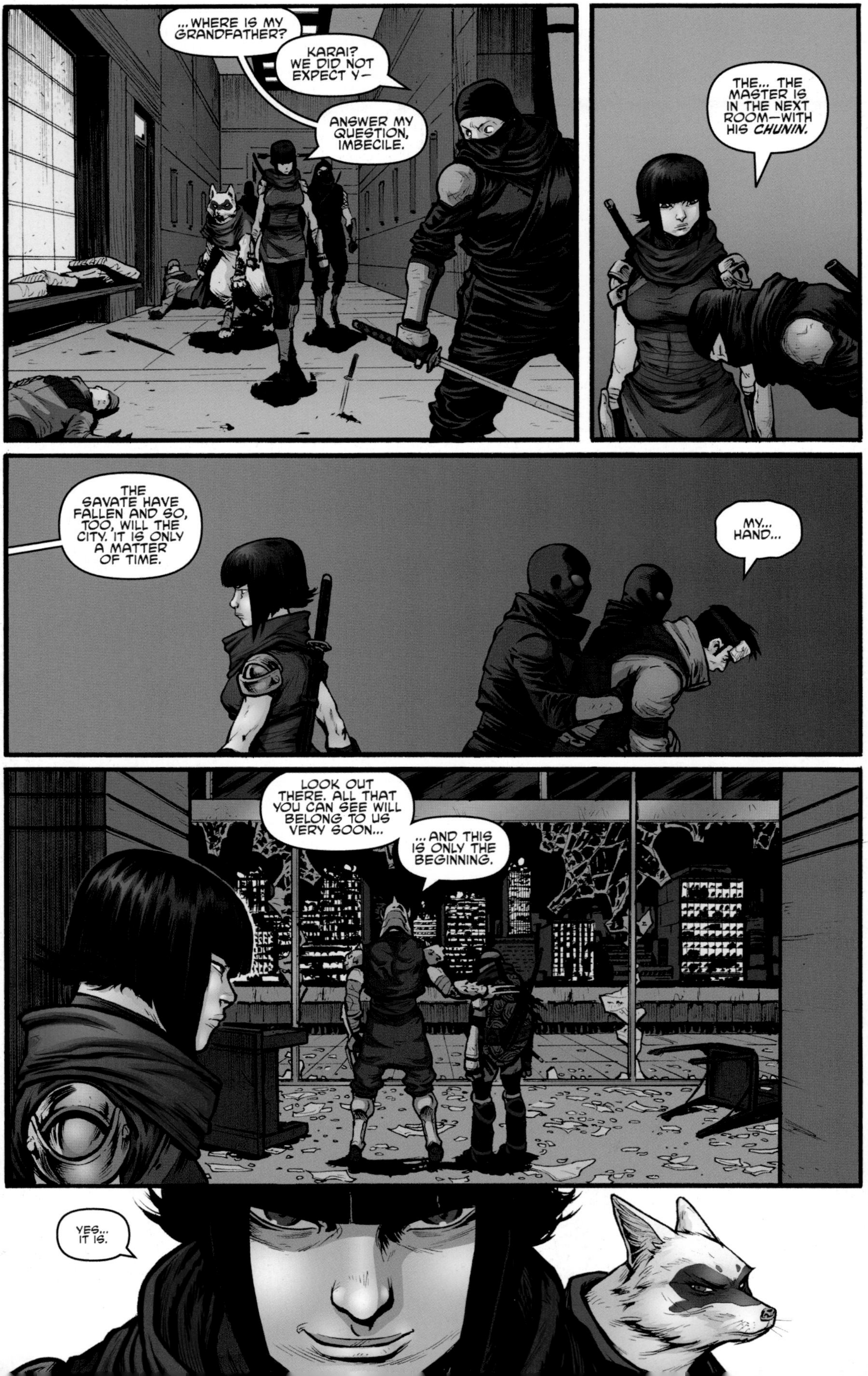
...WHERE IS MY GRANDFATHER?
KARAI? WE DID NOT EXPECT Y—
ANSWER MY QUESTION, IMBECILE.
THE... THE MASTER IS IN THE NEXT ROOM—WITH HIS CHUNIN.
THE SAVATE HAVE FALLEN AND SO, TOO, WILL THE CITY. IT IS ONLY A MATTER OF TIME.
MY... HAND...
LOOK OUT THERE. ALL THAT YOU CAN SEE WILL BELONG TO US VERY SOON...
...AND THIS IS ONLY THE BEGINNING.
YES... IT IS.

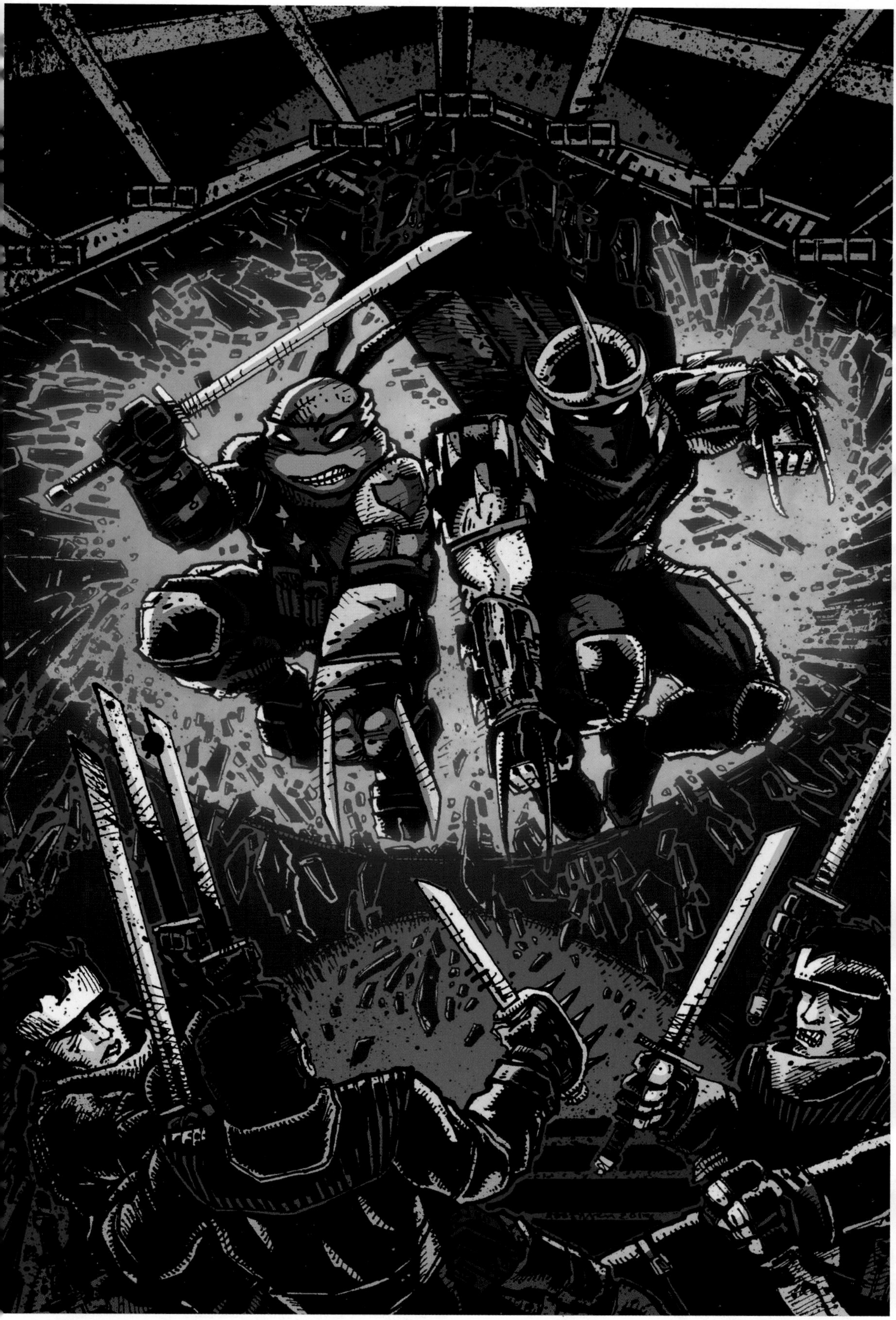

Cover by KEVIN EASTMAN
Colors by RONDA PATTISON

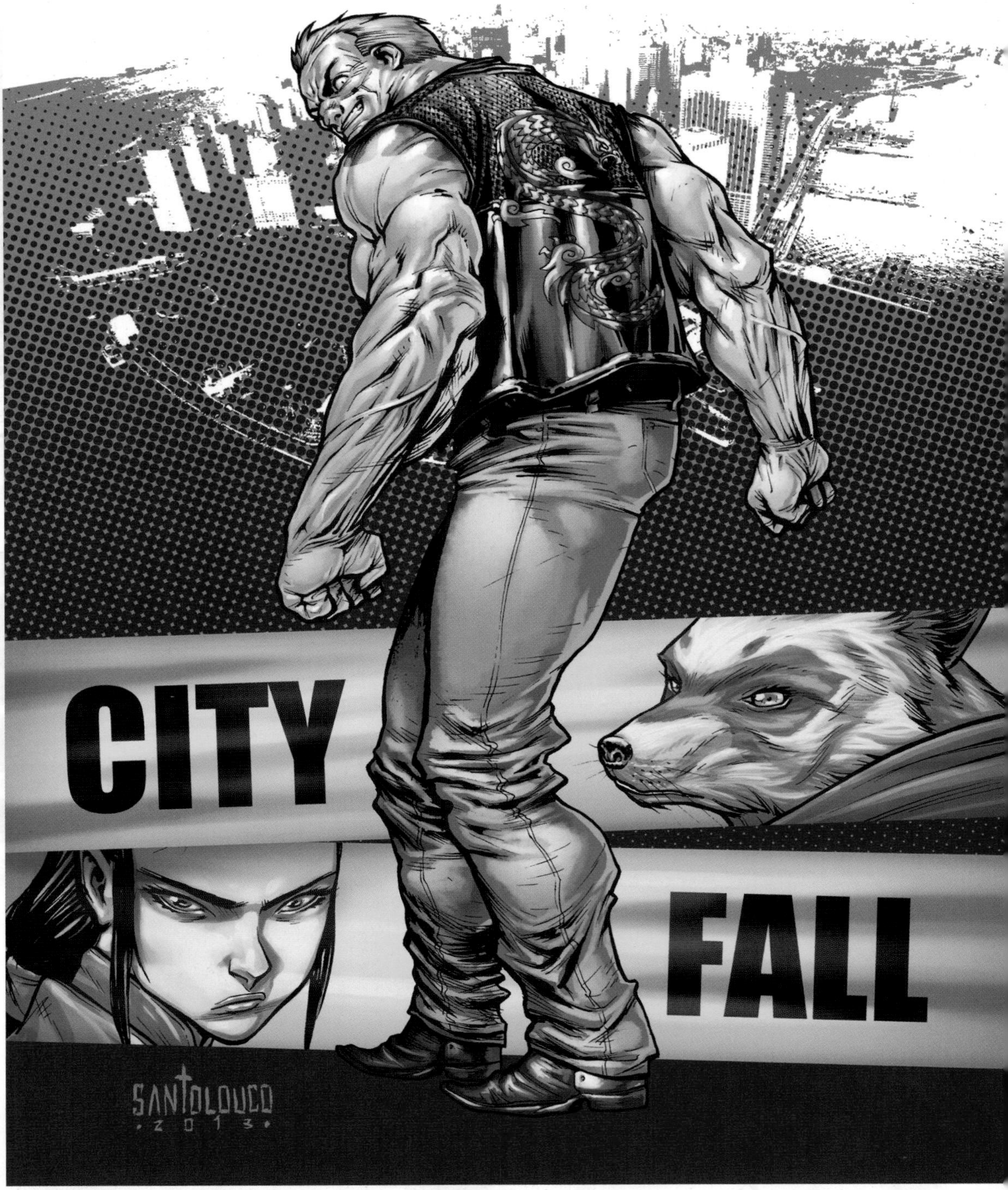
CITY
FALL
SANTOLOUCO
2013

Cover by MATEUS SANTOLOUCO

TMNT #27

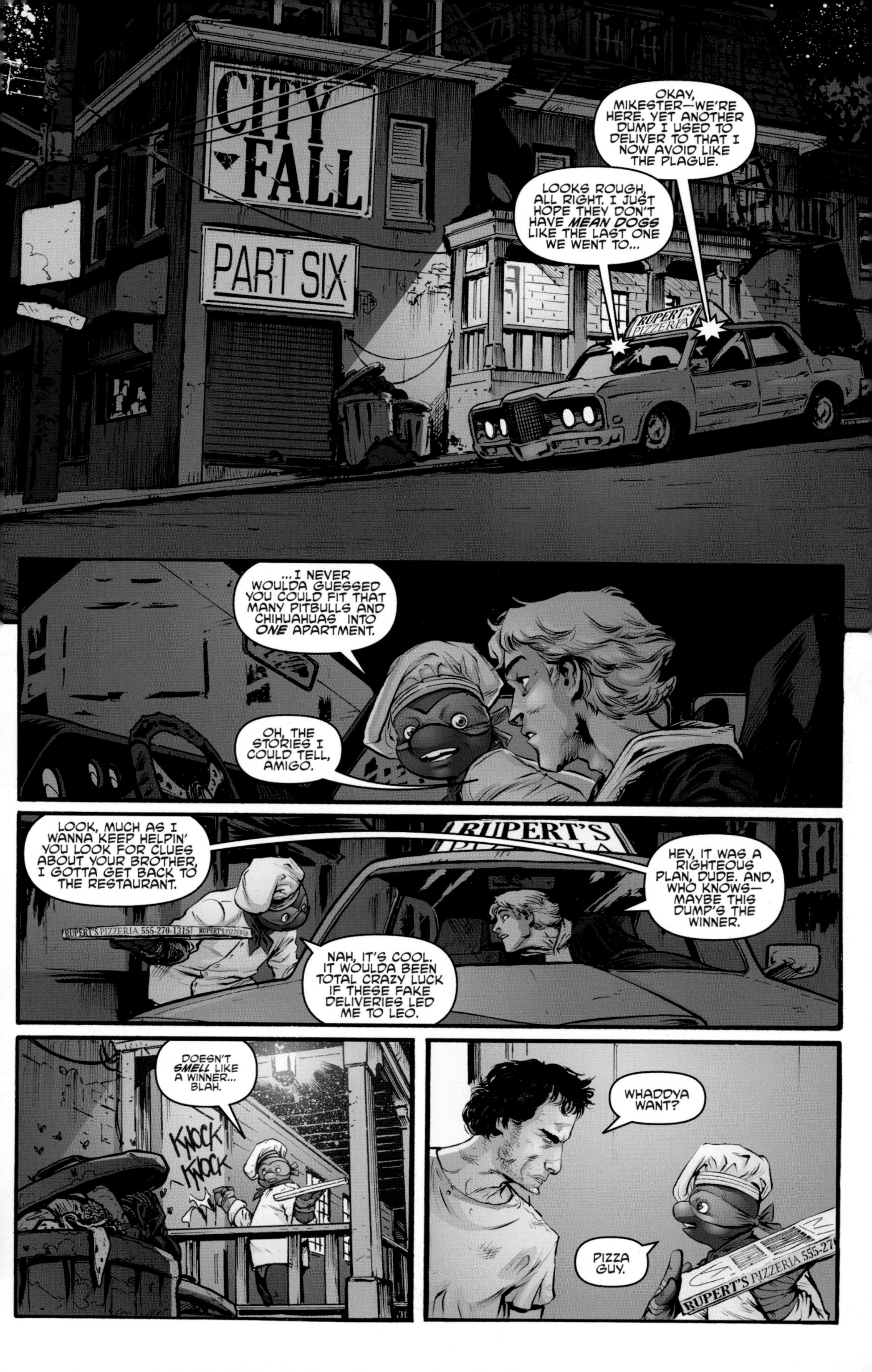
CITY FALL
PART SIX
OKAY, MIKESTER—WE'RE HERE. YET ANOTHER DUMP I USED TO DELIVER TO THAT I NOW AVOID LIKE THE PLAGUE.
LOOKS ROUGH, ALL RIGHT. I JUST HOPE THEY DON'T HAVE MEAN DOGS LIKE THE LAST ONE WE WENT TO...
RUPERT'S PIZZERIA
...I NEVER WOULDA GUESSED YOU COULD FIT THAT MANY PITBULLS AND CHIHUAHUAS INTO ONE APARTMENT.
OH, THE STORIES I COULD TELL, AMIGO.
RUPERT'S PIZZERIA
LOOK, MUCH AS I WANNA KEEP HELPIN' YOU LOOK FOR CLUES ABOUT YOUR BROTHER, I GOTTA GET BACK TO THE RESTAURANT.
HEY, IT WAS A RIGHTEOUS PLAN, DUDE. AND, WHO KNOWS— MAYBE THIS DUMP'S THE WINNER.
RUPERT'S PIZZERIA 555-270-1315 RUPERT'S PIZZERIA
NAH, IT'S COOL. IT WOULDA BEEN TOTAL CRAZY LUCK IF THESE FAKE DELIVERIES LED ME TO LEO.
DOESN'T SMELL LIKE A WINNER... BLAH.
KNOCK KNOCK
WHADDYA WANT?
PIZZA GUY.
RUPERT'S PIZZERIA 555-27

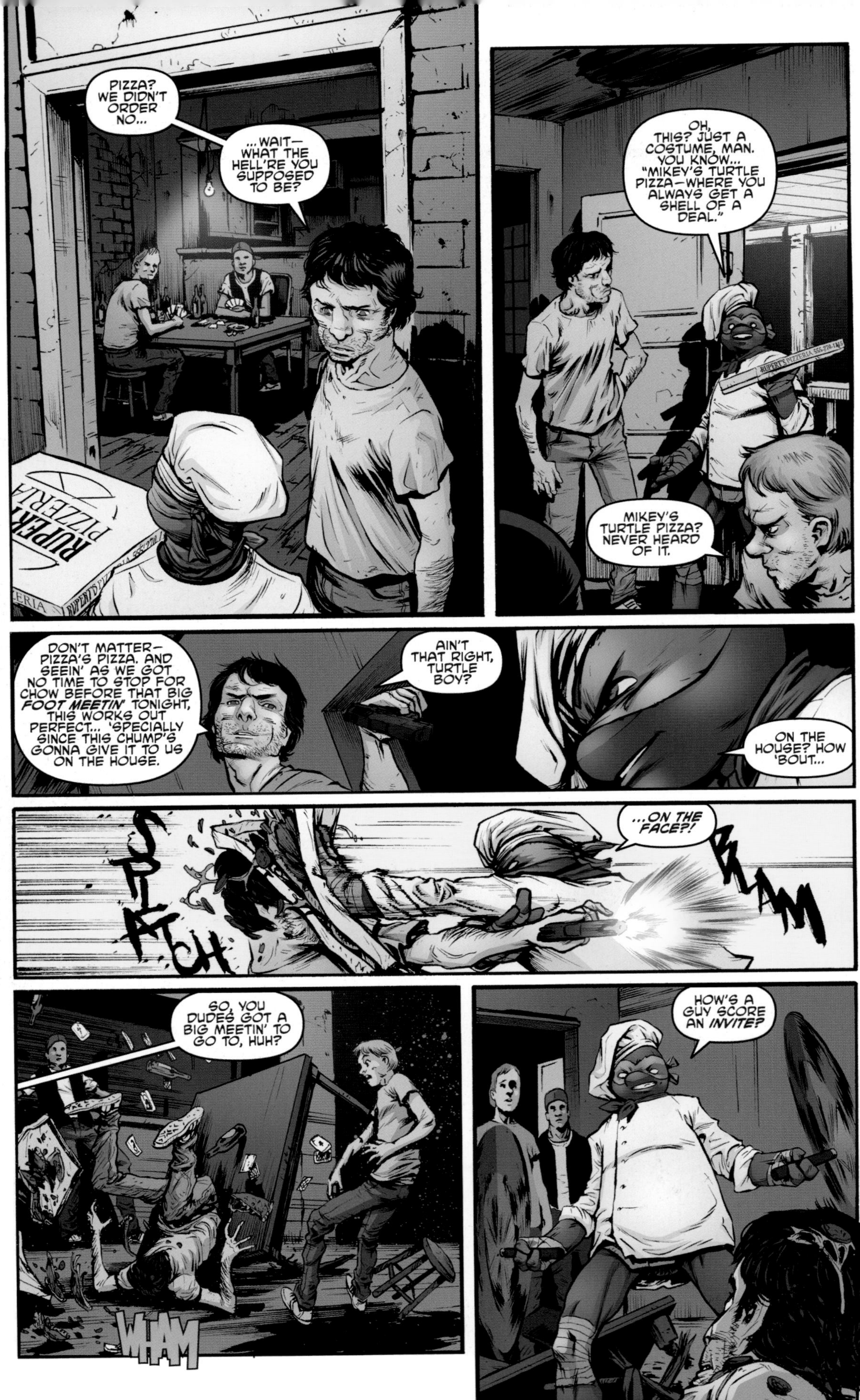
PIZZA? WE DIDN'T ORDER NO...
...WAIT—WHAT THE HELL'RE YOU SUPPOSED TO BE?
RUPERT'S PIZZERIA
OH, THIS? JUST A COSTUME, MAN. YOU KNOW... "MIKEY'S TURTLE PIZZA—WHERE YOU ALWAYS GET A SHELL OF A DEAL."
MIKEY'S TURTLE PIZZA? NEVER HEARD OF IT.
DON'T MATTER—PIZZA'S PIZZA. AND SEEIN' AS WE GOT NO TIME TO STOP FOR CHOW BEFORE THAT BIG *FOOT MEETIN'* TONIGHT, THIS WORKS OUT PERFECT... 'SPECIALLY SINCE THIS CHUMP'S GONNA GIVE IT TO US ON THE HOUSE.
AIN'T THAT RIGHT, TURTLE BOY?
ON THE HOUSE? HOW 'BOUT...
...*ON THE FACE?!*
SPLATCH
BLAM
SO, YOU DUDES GOT A BIG MEETIN' TO GO TO, HUH?
WHAM
HOW'S A GUY SCORE AN *INVITE?*

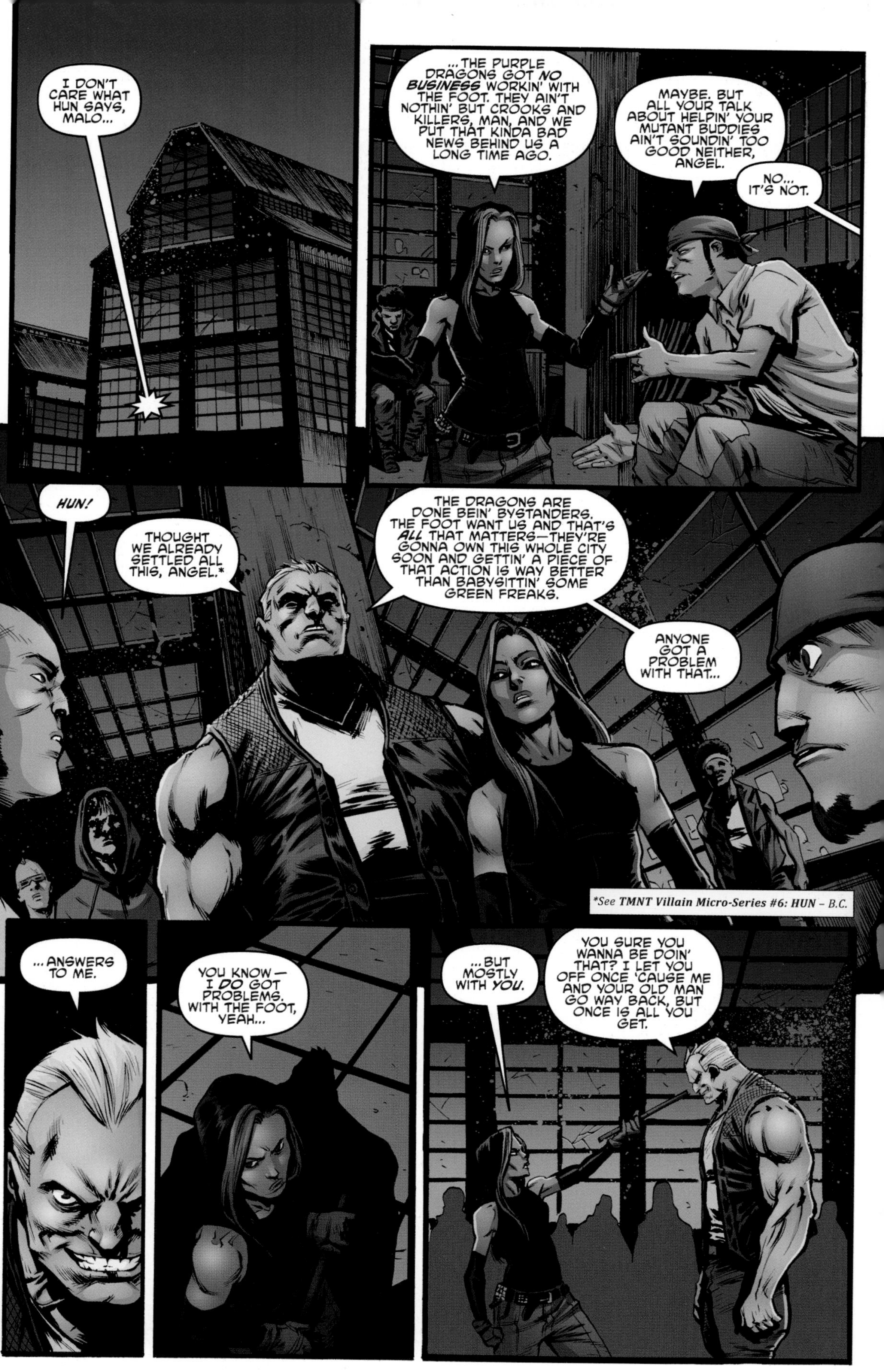
I DON'T CARE WHAT HUN SAYS, MALO...
...THE PURPLE DRAGONS GOT NO BUSINESS WORKIN' WITH THE FOOT. THEY AIN'T NOTHIN' BUT CROOKS AND KILLERS, MAN, AND WE PUT THAT KINDA BAD NEWS BEHIND US A LONG TIME AGO.
MAYBE. BUT ALL YOUR TALK ABOUT HELPIN' YOUR MUTANT BUDDIES AIN'T SOUNDIN' TOO GOOD NEITHER, ANGEL.
NO... IT'S NOT.
HUN!
THOUGHT WE ALREADY SETTLED ALL THIS, ANGEL.*
THE DRAGONS ARE DONE BEIN' BYSTANDERS. THE FOOT WANT US AND THAT'S ALL THAT MATTERS—THEY'RE GONNA OWN THIS WHOLE CITY SOON AND GETTIN' A PIECE OF THAT ACTION IS WAY BETTER THAN BABYSITTIN' SOME GREEN FREAKS.
ANYONE GOT A PROBLEM WITH THAT...
*See TMNT Villain Micro-Series #6: HUN – B.C.
...ANSWERS TO ME.
YOU KNOW— I DO GOT PROBLEMS. WITH THE FOOT, YEAH...
...BUT MOSTLY WITH YOU.
YOU SURE YOU WANNA BE DOIN' THAT? I LET YOU OFF ONCE 'CAUSE ME AND YOUR OLD MAN GO WAY BACK, BUT ONCE IS ALL YOU GET.

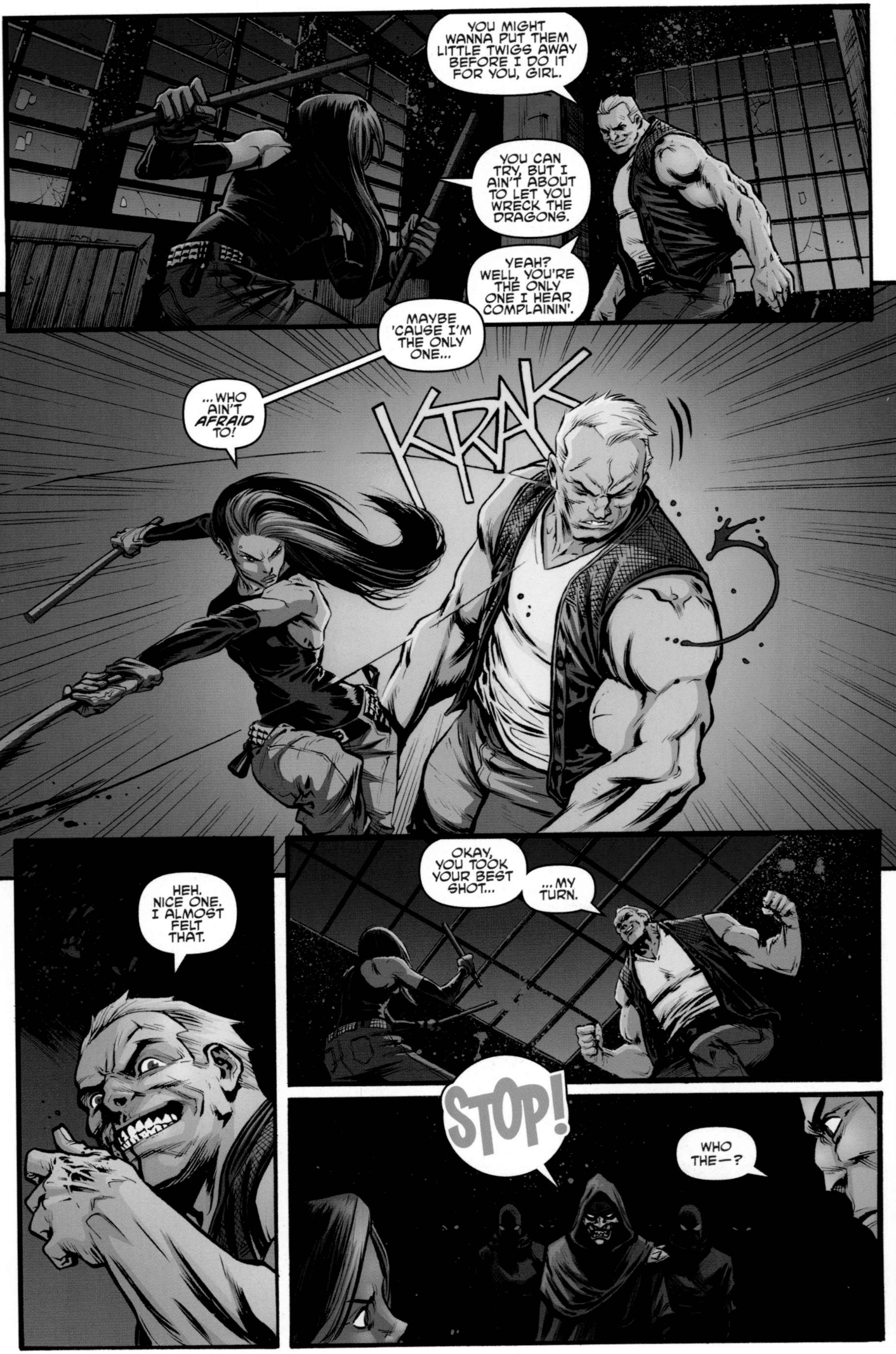

YOU MIGHT WANNA PUT THEM LITTLE TWIGS AWAY BEFORE I DO IT FOR YOU, GIRL.
YOU CAN TRY, BUT I AIN'T ABOUT TO LET YOU WRECK THE DRAGONS.
YEAH? WELL, YOU'RE THE ONLY ONE I HEAR COMPLAININ'.
MAYBE 'CAUSE I'M THE ONLY ONE...
...WHO AIN'T AFRAID TO!
KTRAK
HEH. NICE ONE. I ALMOST FELT THAT.
OKAY, YOU TOOK YOUR BEST SHOT...
...MY TURN.
STOP!
WHO THE—?

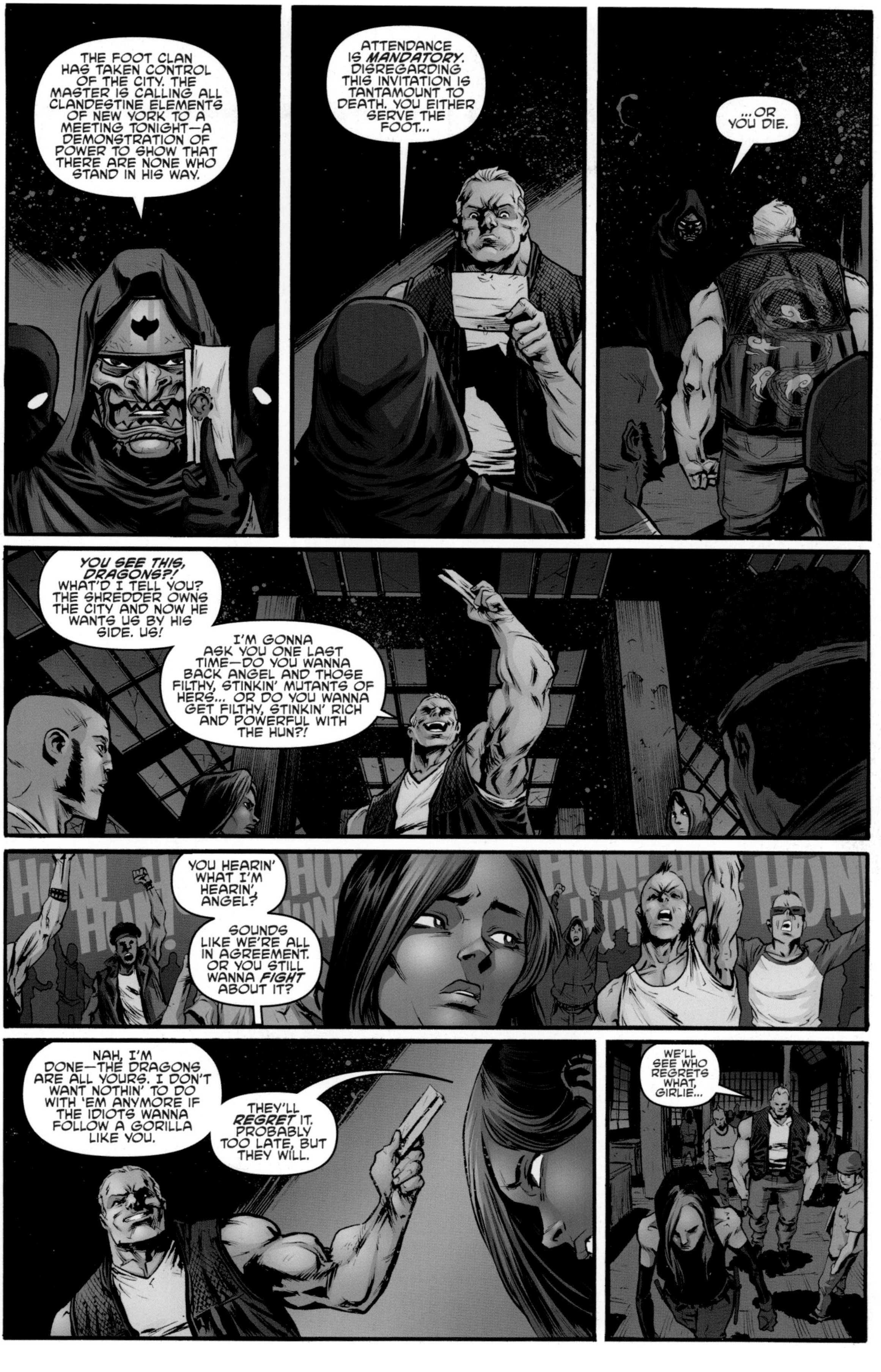
THE FOOT CLAN HAS TAKEN CONTROL OF THE CITY. THE MASTER IS CALLING ALL CLANDESTINE ELEMENTS OF NEW YORK TO A MEETING TONIGHT—A DEMONSTRATION OF POWER TO SHOW THAT THERE ARE NONE WHO STAND IN HIS WAY.
ATTENDANCE IS *MANDATORY*. DISREGARDING THIS INVITATION IS TANTAMOUNT TO DEATH. YOU EITHER SERVE THE FOOT...
...OR YOU DIE.
YOU SEE THIS, DRAGONS?! WHAT'D I TELL YOU? THE SHREDDER OWNS THE CITY AND NOW HE WANTS US BY HIS SIDE. US!
I'M GONNA ASK YOU ONE LAST TIME—DO YOU WANNA BACK ANGEL AND THOSE FILTHY, STINKIN' MUTANTS OF HERS... OR DO YOU WANNA GET FILTHY, STINKIN' RICH AND POWERFUL WITH THE HUN?!
HUN! HUN!
YOU HEARIN' WHAT I'M HEARIN', ANGEL?
SOUNDS LIKE WE'RE ALL IN AGREEMENT. OR YOU STILL WANNA *FIGHT* ABOUT IT?
NAH, I'M DONE—THE DRAGONS ARE ALL YOURS. I DON'T WANT NOTHIN' TO DO WITH 'EM ANYMORE IF THE IDIOTS WANNA FOLLOW A GORILLA LIKE YOU.
THEY'LL *REGRET* IT. PROBABLY TOO LATE, BUT THEY WILL.
WE'LL SEE WHO REGRETS WHAT, GIRLIE...

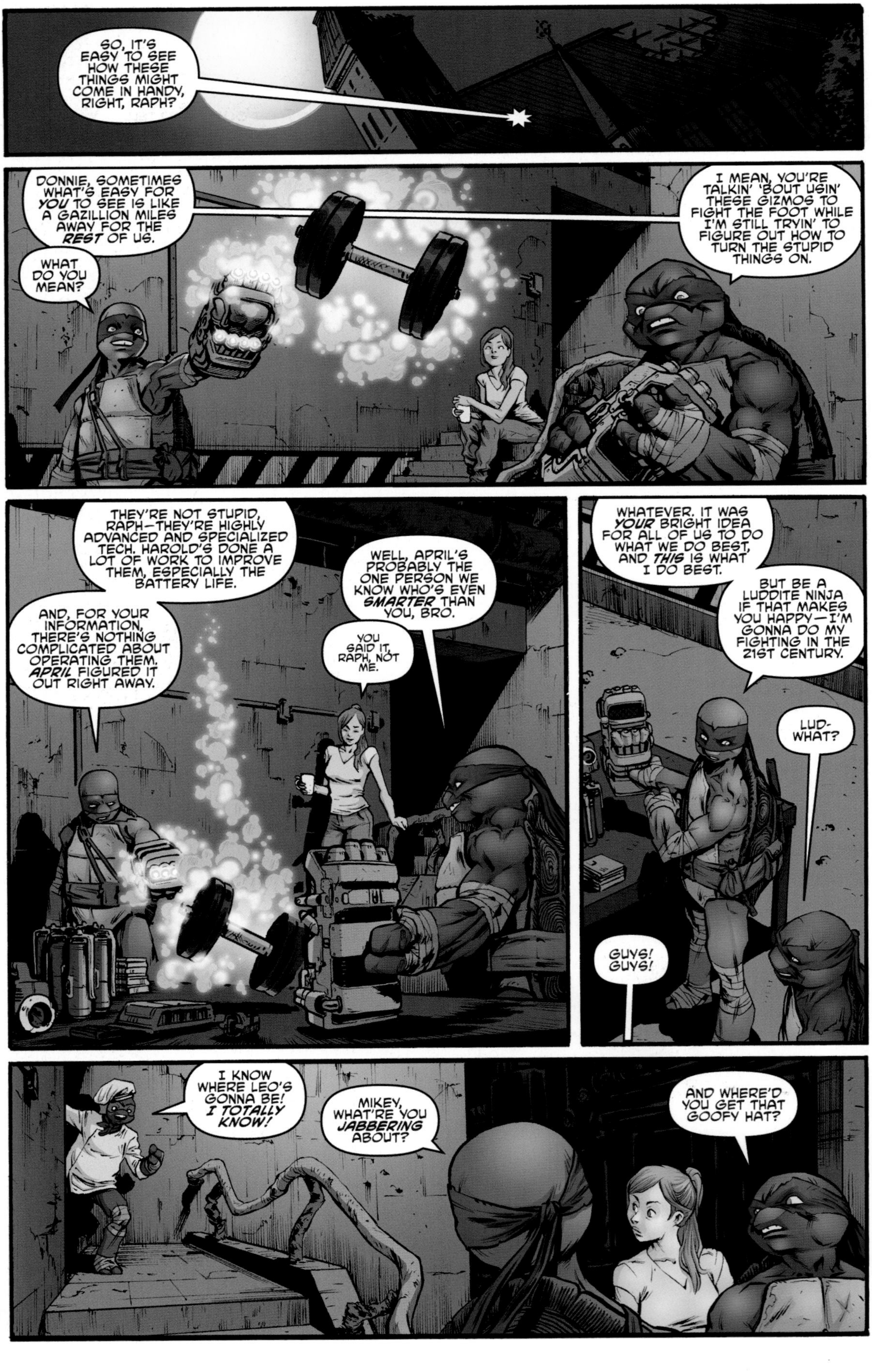
SO, IT'S EASY TO SEE HOW THESE THINGS MIGHT COME IN HANDY, RIGHT, RAPH?
DONNIE, SOMETIMES WHAT'S EASY FOR YOU TO SEE IS LIKE A GAZILLION MILES AWAY FOR THE REST OF US.
I MEAN, YOU'RE TALKIN' 'BOUT USIN' THESE GIZMOS TO FIGHT THE FOOT WHILE I'M STILL TRYIN' TO FIGURE OUT HOW TO TURN THE STUPID THINGS ON.
WHAT DO YOU MEAN?
THEY'RE NOT STUPID, RAPH—THEY'RE HIGHLY ADVANCED AND SPECIALIZED TECH. HAROLD'S DONE A LOT OF WORK TO IMPROVE THEM, ESPECIALLY THE BATTERY LIFE.
AND, FOR YOUR INFORMATION, THERE'S NOTHING COMPLICATED ABOUT OPERATING THEM. APRIL FIGURED IT OUT RIGHT AWAY.
WELL, APRIL'S PROBABLY THE ONE PERSON WE KNOW WHO'S EVEN SMARTER THAN YOU, BRO.
YOU SAID IT, RAPH, NOT ME.
WHATEVER. IT WAS YOUR BRIGHT IDEA FOR ALL OF US TO DO WHAT WE DO BEST, AND THIS IS WHAT I DO BEST.
BUT BE A LUDDITE NINJA IF THAT MAKES YOU HAPPY—I'M GONNA DO MY FIGHTING IN THE 21ST CENTURY.
LUD-WHAT?
GUYS! GUYS!
I KNOW WHERE LEO'S GONNA BE! I TOTALLY KNOW!
MIKEY, WHAT'RE YOU JABBERING ABOUT?
AND WHERE'D YOU GET THAT GOOFY HAT?

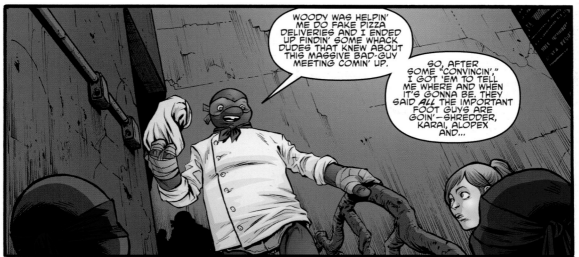

WOODY WAS HELPIN' ME DO FAKE PIZZA DELIVERIES AND I ENDED UP FINDIN' SOME WHACK DUDES THAT KNEW ABOUT THIS MASSIVE BAD-GUY MEETING COMIN' UP.

SO, AFTER SOME "CONVINCIN'," I GOT 'EM TO TELL ME WHERE AND WHEN IT'S GONNA BE. THEY SAID *ALL* THE IMPORTANT FOOT GUYS ARE GOIN'—SHREDDER, KARAI, ALOPEX AND...

...LEONARDO.

YOU ARE TO BE *COMMENDED*, MY SONS—YOU HAVE BONDED TOGETHER IN THE FACE OF ADVERSITY, AND IT APPEARS YOUR COMBINED EFFORTS HAVE PAID OFF.

AND NOW THE TIME HAS COME TO CALL ON OUR ALLIES FOR THE ADVERSITY TO COME—

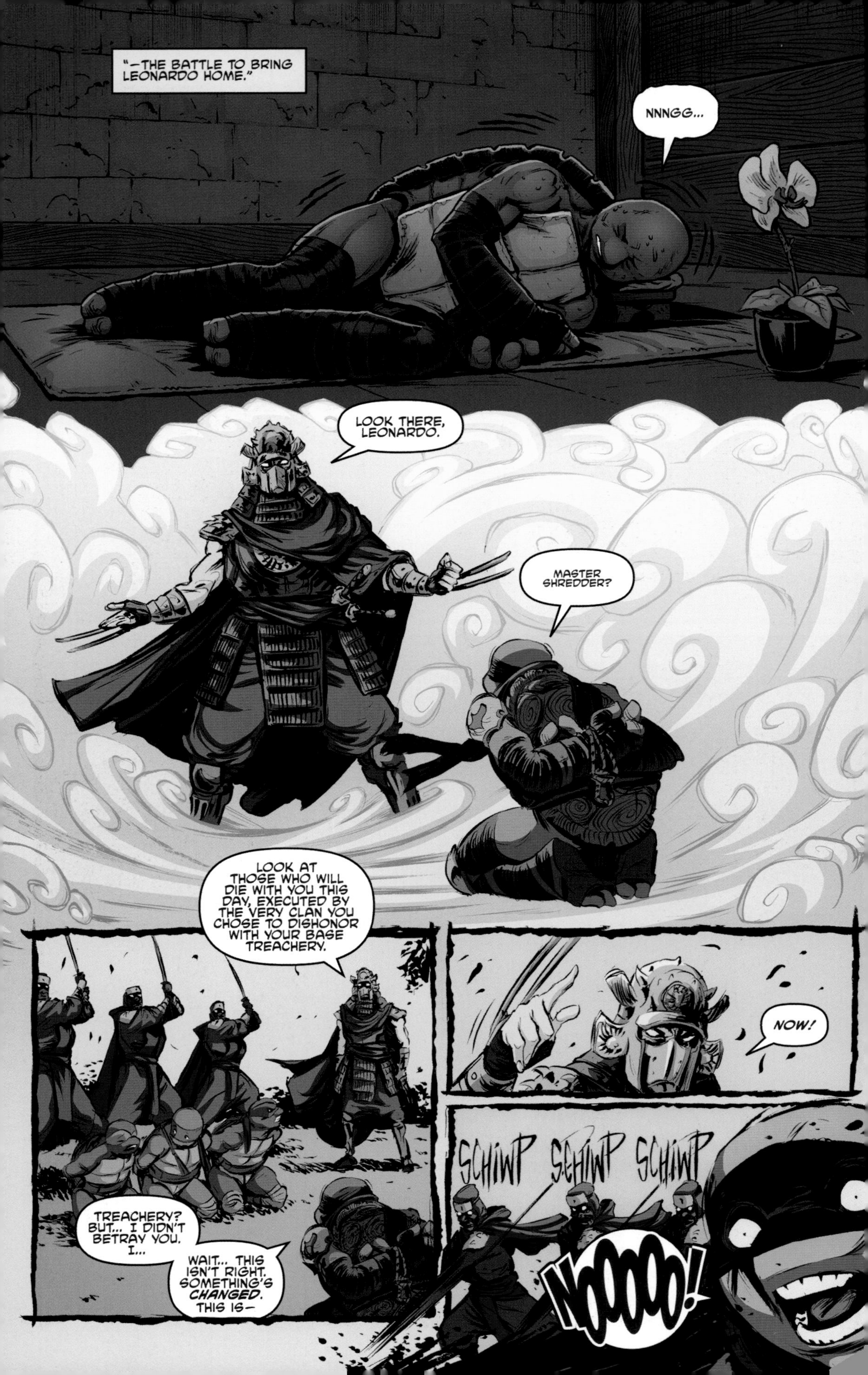
"—THE BATTLE TO BRING LEONARDO HOME."
NNNGG...
LOOK THERE, LEONARDO.
MASTER SHREDDER?
LOOK AT THOSE WHO WILL DIE WITH YOU THIS DAY, EXECUTED BY THE VERY CLAN YOU CHOSE TO DISHONOR WITH YOUR BASE TREACHERY.
TREACHERY? BUT... I DIDN'T BETRAY YOU. I...
WAIT... THIS ISN'T RIGHT. SOMETHING'S *CHANGED*. THIS IS—
NOW!
SCHIWP SCHIWP SCHIWP
NOOOOO!

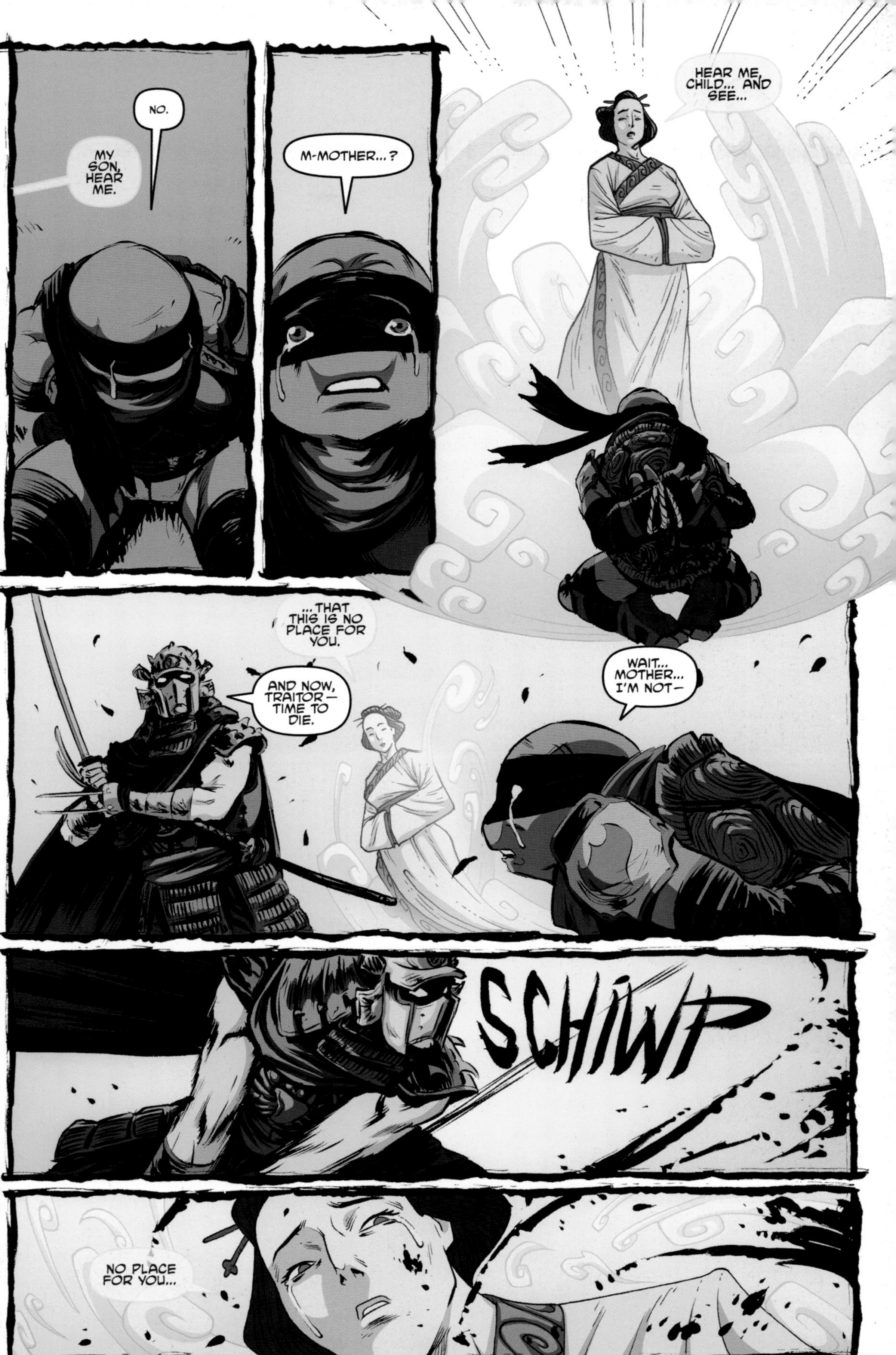
NO.
MY SON, HEAR ME.
M-MOTHER...?
HEAR ME, CHILD... AND SEE...
...THAT THIS IS NO PLACE FOR YOU.
AND NOW, TRAITOR— TIME TO DIE.
WAIT... MOTHER... I'M NOT—
SCHIWP
NO PLACE FOR YOU...

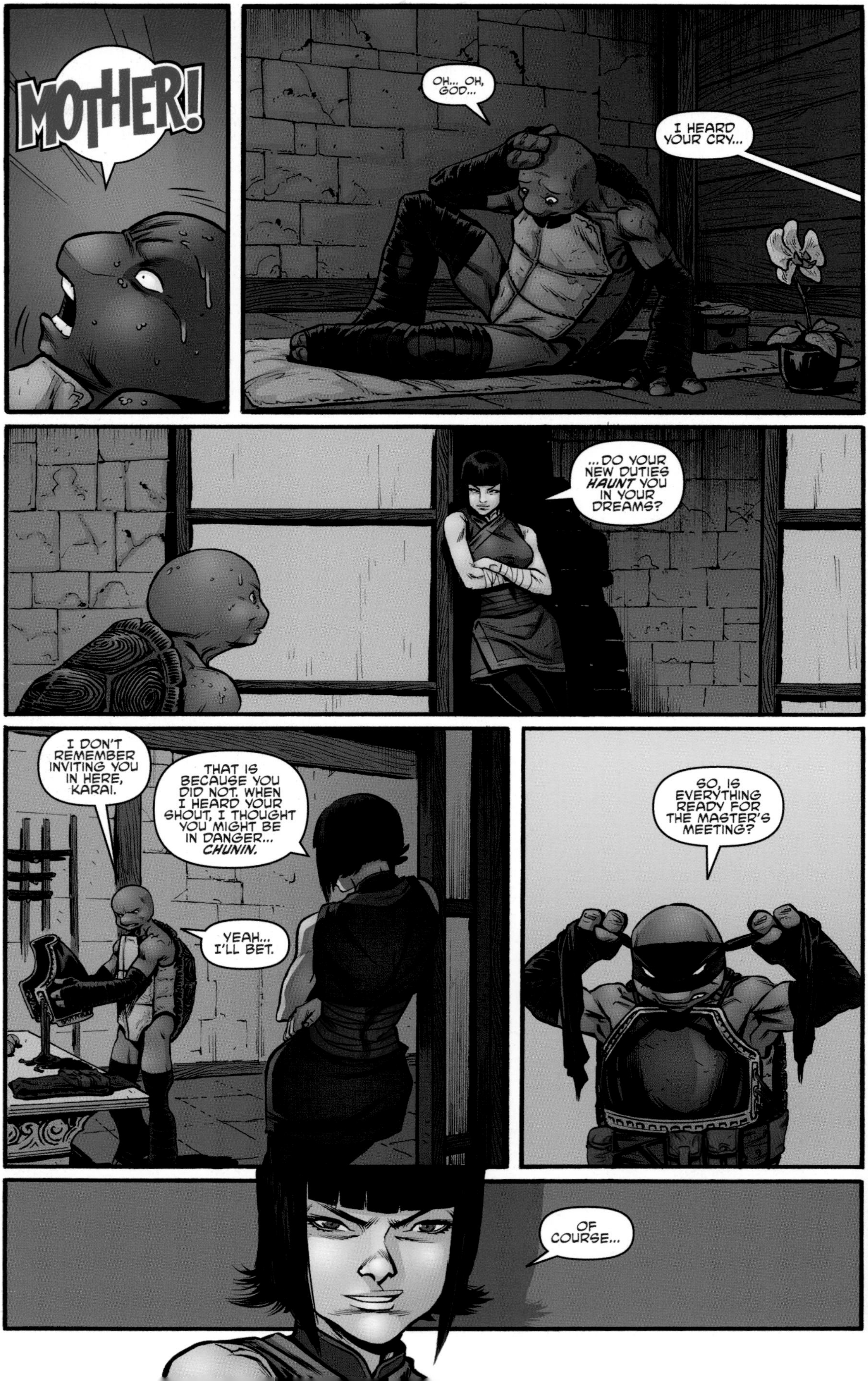
MOTHER!
OH... OH, GOD...
I HEARD YOUR CRY...
...DO YOUR NEW DUTIES HAUNT YOU IN YOUR DREAMS?
I DON'T REMEMBER INVITING YOU IN HERE, KARAI.
THAT IS BECAUSE YOU DID NOT. WHEN I HEARD YOUR SHOUT, I THOUGHT YOU MIGHT BE IN DANGER... CHUNIN.
YEAH... I'LL BET.
SO, IS EVERYTHING READY FOR THE MASTER'S MEETING?
OF COURSE...

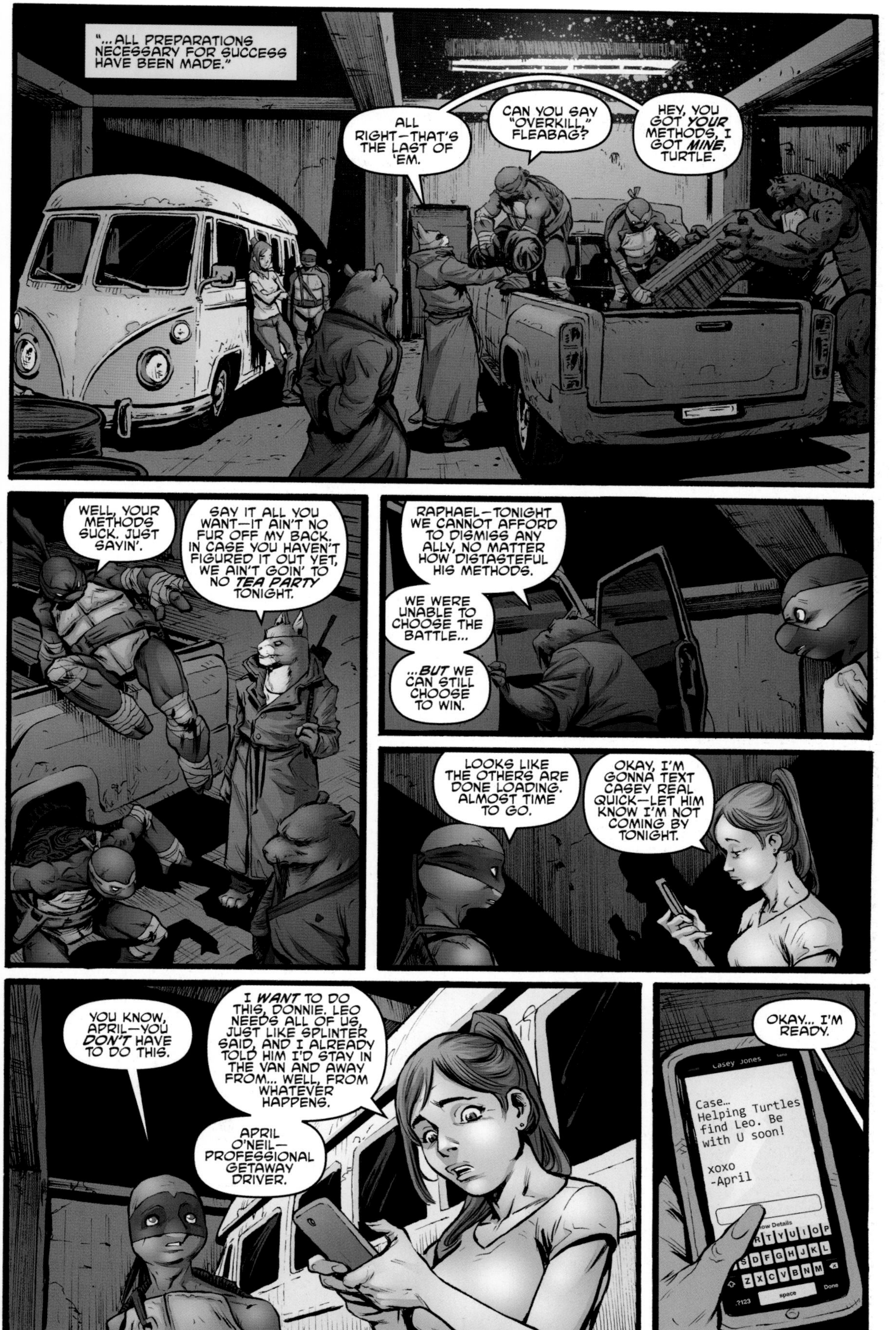
"...ALL PREPARATIONS NECESSARY FOR SUCCESS HAVE BEEN MADE."
ALL RIGHT—THAT'S THE LAST OF 'EM.
CAN YOU SAY "OVERKILL," FLEABAG?
HEY, YOU GOT YOUR METHODS, I GOT MINE, TURTLE.
WELL, YOUR METHODS SUCK. JUST SAYIN'.
SAY IT ALL YOU WANT—IT AIN'T NO FUR OFF MY BACK. IN CASE YOU HAVEN'T FIGURED IT OUT YET, WE AIN'T GOIN' TO NO TEA PARTY TONIGHT.
RAPHAEL—TONIGHT WE CANNOT AFFORD TO DISMISS ANY ALLY, NO MATTER HOW DISTASTEFUL HIS METHODS.
WE WERE UNABLE TO CHOOSE THE BATTLE...
...BUT WE CAN STILL CHOOSE TO WIN.
LOOKS LIKE THE OTHERS ARE DONE LOADING. ALMOST TIME TO GO.
OKAY, I'M GONNA TEXT CASEY REAL QUICK—LET HIM KNOW I'M NOT COMING BY TONIGHT.
YOU KNOW, APRIL—YOU DON'T HAVE TO DO THIS.
I WANT TO DO THIS, DONNIE. LEO NEEDS ALL OF US, JUST LIKE SPLINTER SAID, AND I ALREADY TOLD HIM I'D STAY IN THE VAN AND AWAY FROM... WELL, FROM WHATEVER HAPPENS.
APRIL O'NEIL—PROFESSIONAL GETAWAY DRIVER.
OKAY... I'M READY.
Casey Jones
Case... Helping Turtles find Leo. Be with U soon!
xoxo
-April

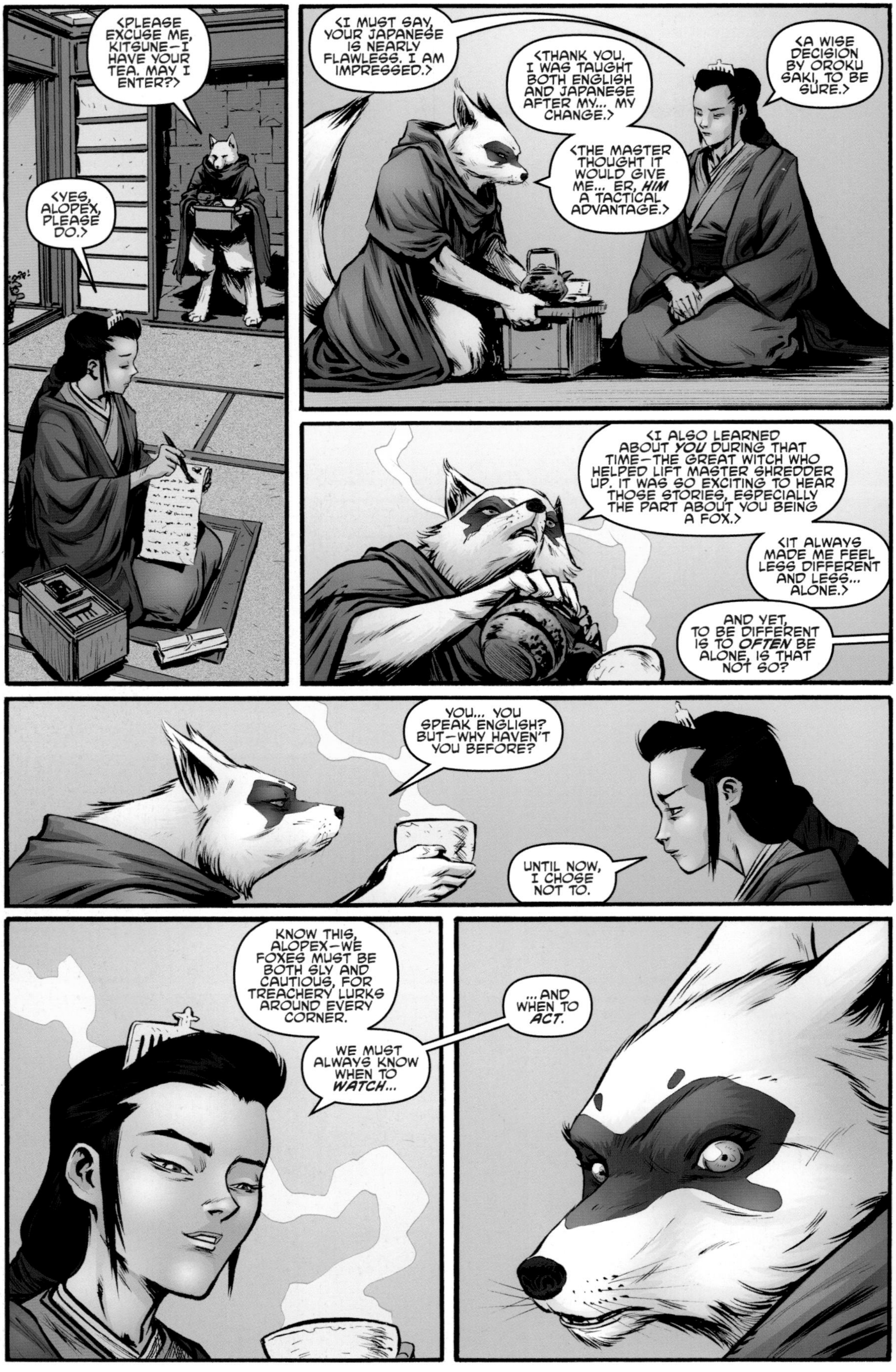
<PLEASE EXCUSE ME, KITSUNE—I HAVE YOUR TEA. MAY I ENTER?>
<YES, ALOPEX, PLEASE DO.>
<I MUST SAY, YOUR JAPANESE IS NEARLY FLAWLESS. I AM IMPRESSED.>
<THANK YOU. I WAS TAUGHT BOTH ENGLISH AND JAPANESE AFTER MY... MY CHANGE.>
<THE MASTER THOUGHT IT WOULD GIVE ME... ER, *HIM* A TACTICAL ADVANTAGE.>
<A WISE DECISION BY OROKU SAKI, TO BE SURE.>
<I ALSO LEARNED ABOUT *YOU* DURING THAT TIME—THE GREAT WITCH WHO HELPED LIFT MASTER SHREDDER UP. IT WAS SO EXCITING TO HEAR THOSE STORIES, ESPECIALLY THE PART ABOUT YOU BEING A FOX.>
<IT ALWAYS MADE ME FEEL LESS DIFFERENT AND LESS... ALONE.>
AND YET, TO BE DIFFERENT IS TO *OFTEN* BE ALONE, IS THAT NOT SO?
YOU... YOU SPEAK ENGLISH? BUT—WHY HAVEN'T YOU BEFORE?
UNTIL NOW, I CHOSE NOT TO.
KNOW THIS, ALOPEX—WE FOXES MUST BE BOTH SLY AND CAUTIOUS, FOR TREACHERY LURKS AROUND EVERY CORNER.
WE MUST ALWAYS KNOW WHEN TO *WATCH*...
...AND WHEN TO *ACT*.

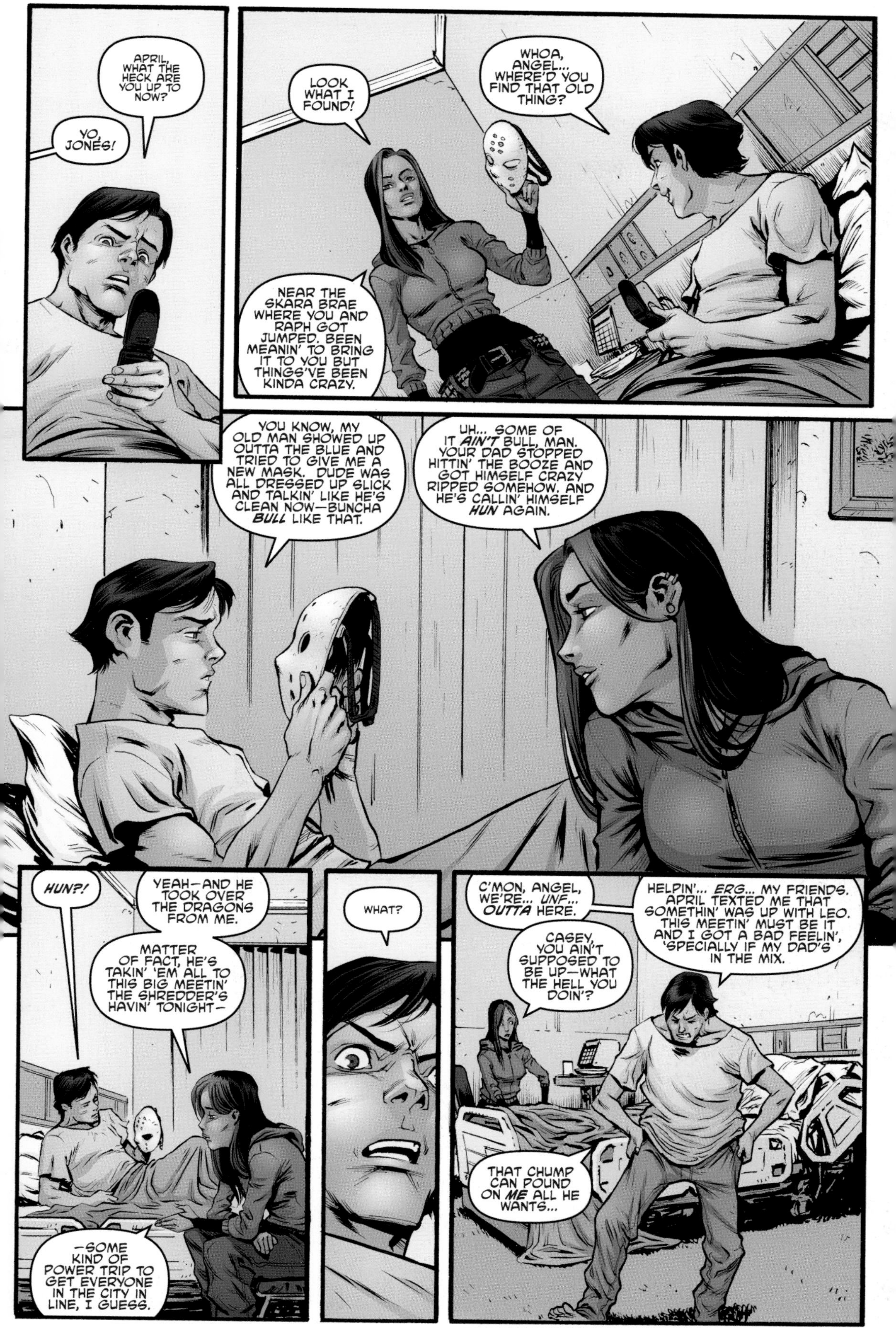
APRIL, WHAT THE HECK ARE YOU UP TO NOW?
YO, JONES!
LOOK WHAT I FOUND!
WHOA, ANGEL... WHERE'D YOU FIND THAT OLD THING?
NEAR THE SKARA BRAE WHERE YOU AND RAPH GOT JUMPED. BEEN MEANIN' TO BRING IT TO YOU BUT THINGS'VE BEEN KINDA CRAZY.
YOU KNOW, MY OLD MAN SHOWED UP OUTTA THE BLUE AND TRIED TO GIVE ME A NEW MASK. DUDE WAS ALL DRESSED UP SLICK AND TALKIN' LIKE HE'S CLEAN NOW—BUNCHA BULL LIKE THAT.
UH... SOME OF IT AIN'T BULL, MAN. YOUR DAD STOPPED HITTIN' THE BOOZE AND GOT HIMSELF CRAZY RIPPED SOMEHOW. AND HE'S CALLIN' HIMSELF HUN AGAIN.
HUN?!
YEAH—AND HE TOOK OVER THE DRAGONS FROM ME.
MATTER OF FACT, HE'S TAKIN' 'EM ALL TO THIS BIG MEETIN' THE SHREDDER'S HAVIN' TONIGHT—
—SOME KIND OF POWER TRIP TO GET EVERYONE IN THE CITY IN LINE, I GUESS.
WHAT?
C'MON, ANGEL, WE'RE... UNF... OUTTA HERE.
CASEY, YOU AIN'T SUPPOSED TO BE UP—WHAT THE HELL YOU DOIN'?
HELPIN'... ERG... MY FRIENDS. APRIL TEXTED ME THAT SOMETHIN' WAS UP WITH LEO. THIS MEETIN' MUST BE IT AND I GOT A BAD FEELIN', 'SPECIALLY IF MY DAD'S IN THE MIX.
THAT CHUMP CAN POUND ON ME ALL HE WANTS...

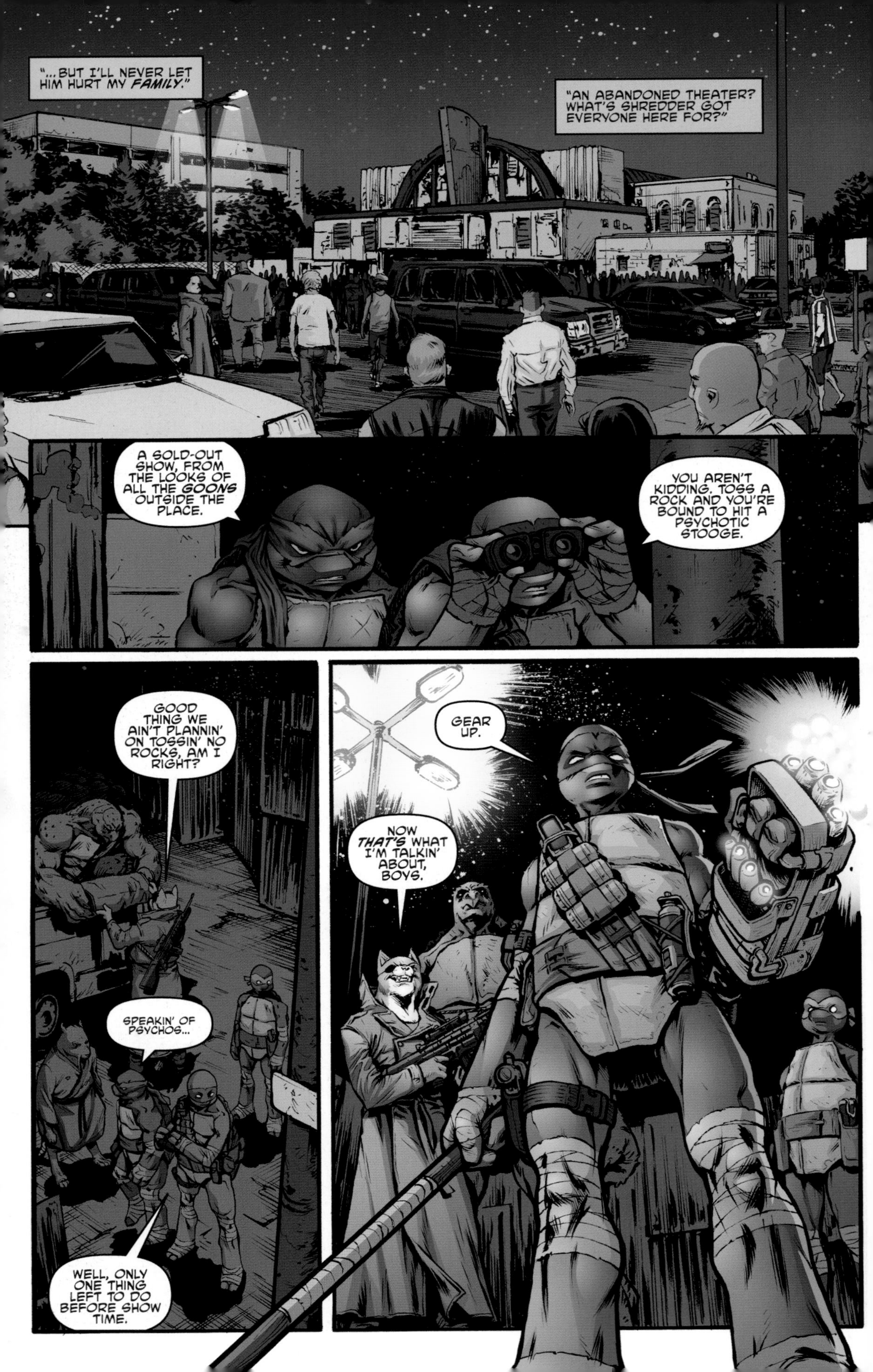
"...BUT I'LL NEVER LET HIM HURT MY *FAMILY*."
"AN ABANDONED THEATER? WHAT'S SHREDDER GOT EVERYONE HERE FOR?"
A SOLD-OUT SHOW, FROM THE LOOKS OF ALL THE *GOONS* OUTSIDE THE PLACE.
YOU AREN'T KIDDING. TOSS A ROCK AND YOU'RE BOUND TO HIT A PSYCHOTIC STOOGE.
GOOD THING WE AIN'T PLANNIN' ON TOSSIN' NO ROCKS, AM I RIGHT?
SPEAKIN' OF PSYCHOS...
WELL, ONLY ONE THING LEFT TO DO BEFORE SHOW TIME.
GEAR UP.
NOW *THAT'S* WHAT I'M TALKIN' ABOUT, BOYS.

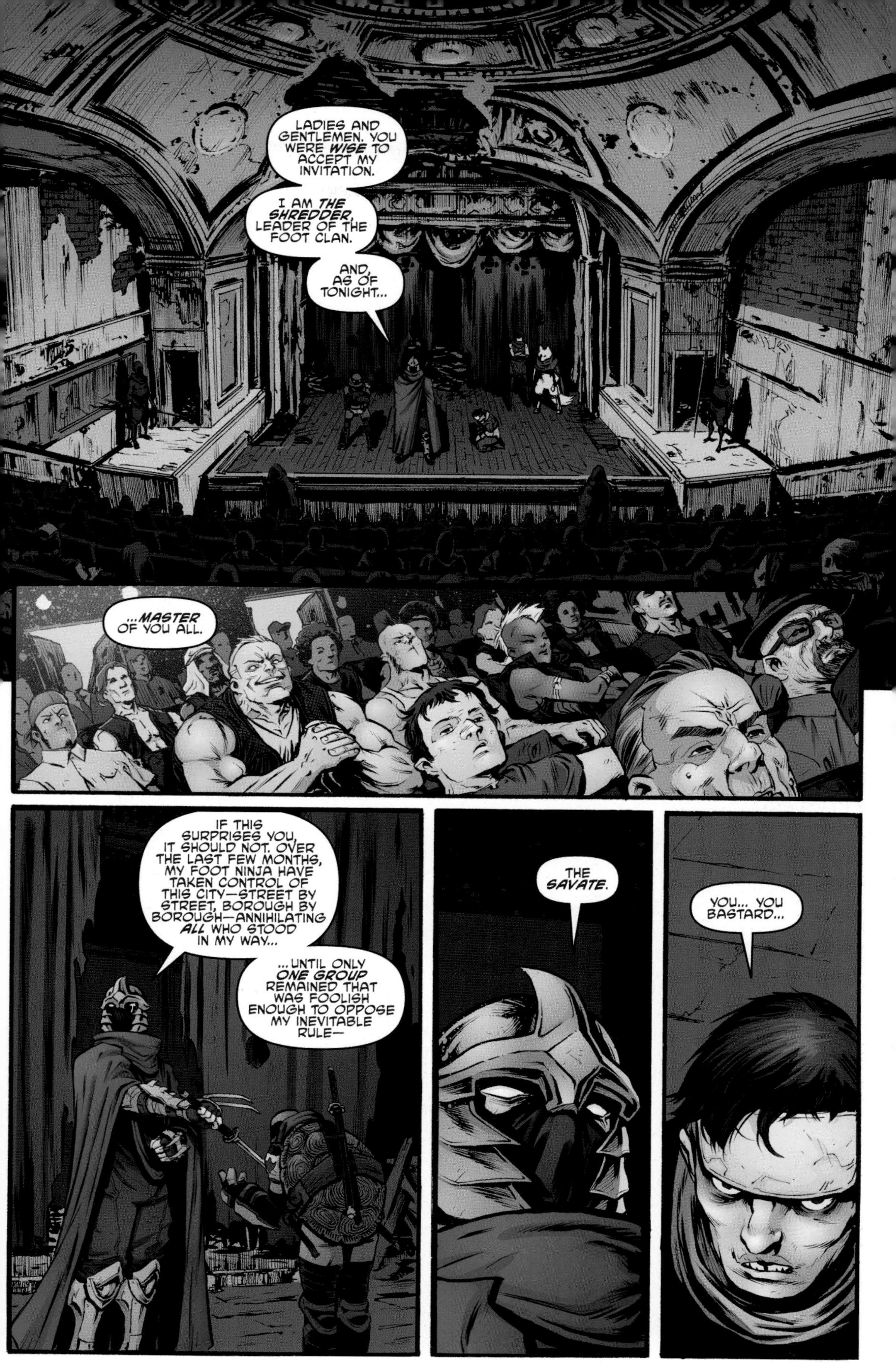
LADIES AND GENTLEMEN. YOU WERE *WISE* TO ACCEPT MY INVITATION.
I AM *THE SHREDDER*, LEADER OF THE FOOT CLAN.
AND, AS OF TONIGHT...
...*MASTER* OF YOU ALL.
IF THIS SURPRISES YOU, IT SHOULD NOT. OVER THE LAST FEW MONTHS, MY FOOT NINJA HAVE TAKEN CONTROL OF THIS CITY—STREET BY STREET, BOROUGH BY BOROUGH—ANNIHILATING *ALL* WHO STOOD IN MY WAY...
...UNTIL ONLY *ONE GROUP* REMAINED THAT WAS FOOLISH ENOUGH TO OPPOSE MY INEVITABLE RULE—
THE *SAVATE*.
YOU... YOU BASTARD...

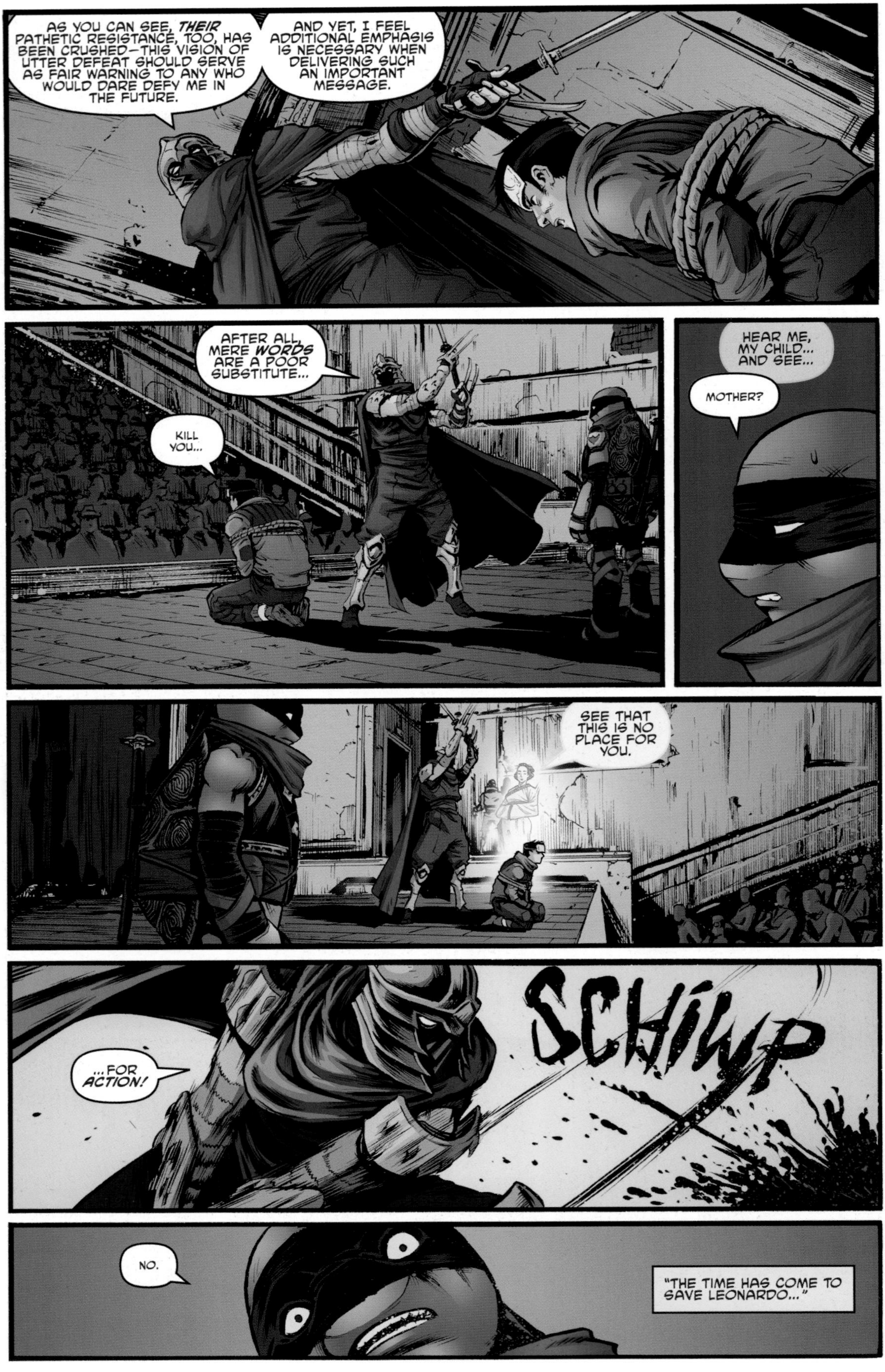
AS YOU CAN SEE, THEIR PATHETIC RESISTANCE, TOO, HAS BEEN CRUSHED—THIS VISION OF UTTER DEFEAT SHOULD SERVE AS FAIR WARNING TO ANY WHO WOULD DARE DEFY ME IN THE FUTURE.
AND YET, I FEEL ADDITIONAL EMPHASIS IS NECESSARY WHEN DELIVERING SUCH AN IMPORTANT MESSAGE.
AFTER ALL, MERE WORDS ARE A POOR SUBSTITUTE...
KILL YOU...
HEAR ME, MY CHILD... AND SEE...
MOTHER?
SEE THAT THIS IS NO PLACE FOR YOU.
...FOR ACTION!
SCHWP
NO.
"THE TIME HAS COME TO SAVE LEONARDO..."

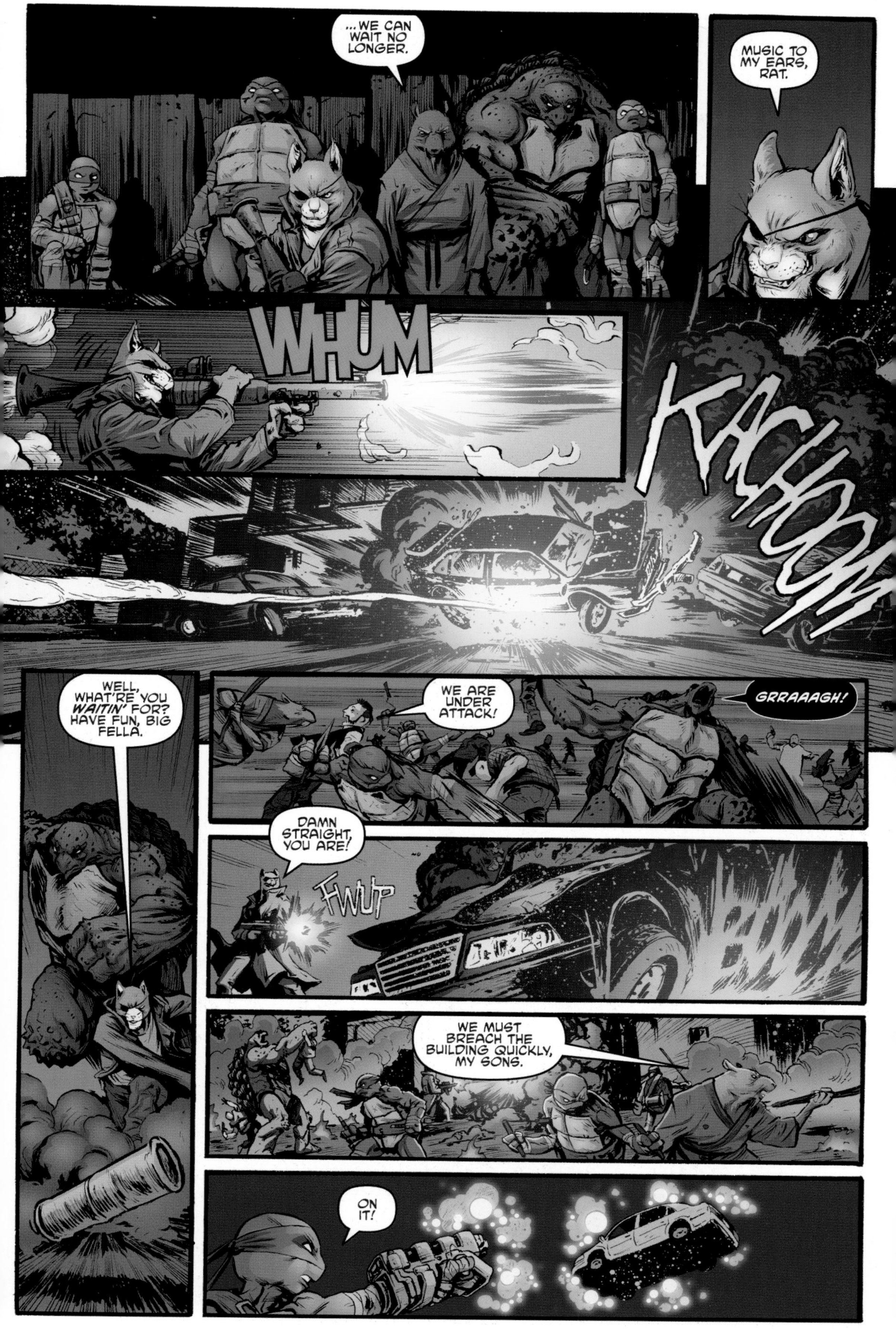
...WE CAN WAIT NO LONGER.
MUSIC TO MY EARS, RAT.
WHUM
KACHOOM
WELL, WHAT'RE YOU *WAITIN'* FOR? HAVE FUN, BIG FELLA.
WE ARE UNDER ATTACK!
GRRAAAGH!
DAMN STRAIGHT, YOU ARE!
FWUP
WE MUST BREACH THE BUILDING QUICKLY, MY SONS.
ON IT!

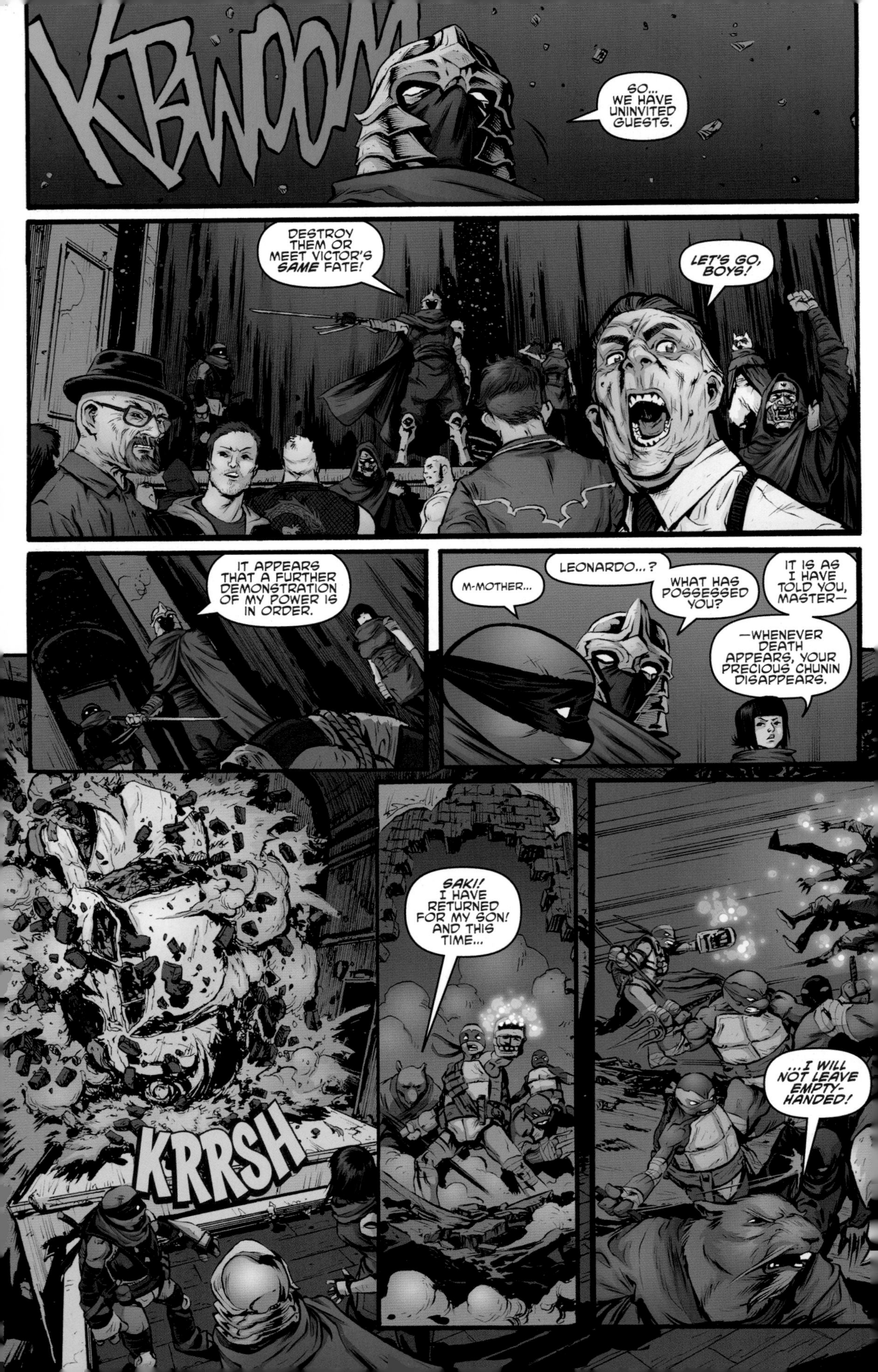
KRAWOOM
SO... WE HAVE UNINVITED GUESTS.
DESTROY THEM OR MEET VICTOR'S SAME FATE!
LET'S GO, BOYS!
IT APPEARS THAT A FURTHER DEMONSTRATION OF MY POWER IS IN ORDER.
M-MOTHER...
LEONARDO...?
WHAT HAS POSSESSED YOU?
IT IS AS I HAVE TOLD YOU, MASTER—
—WHENEVER DEATH APPEARS, YOUR PRECIOUS CHUNIN DISAPPEARS.
KRRSH
SAKI! I HAVE RETURNED FOR MY SON! AND THIS TIME...
...I WILL NOT LEAVE EMPTY-HANDED!

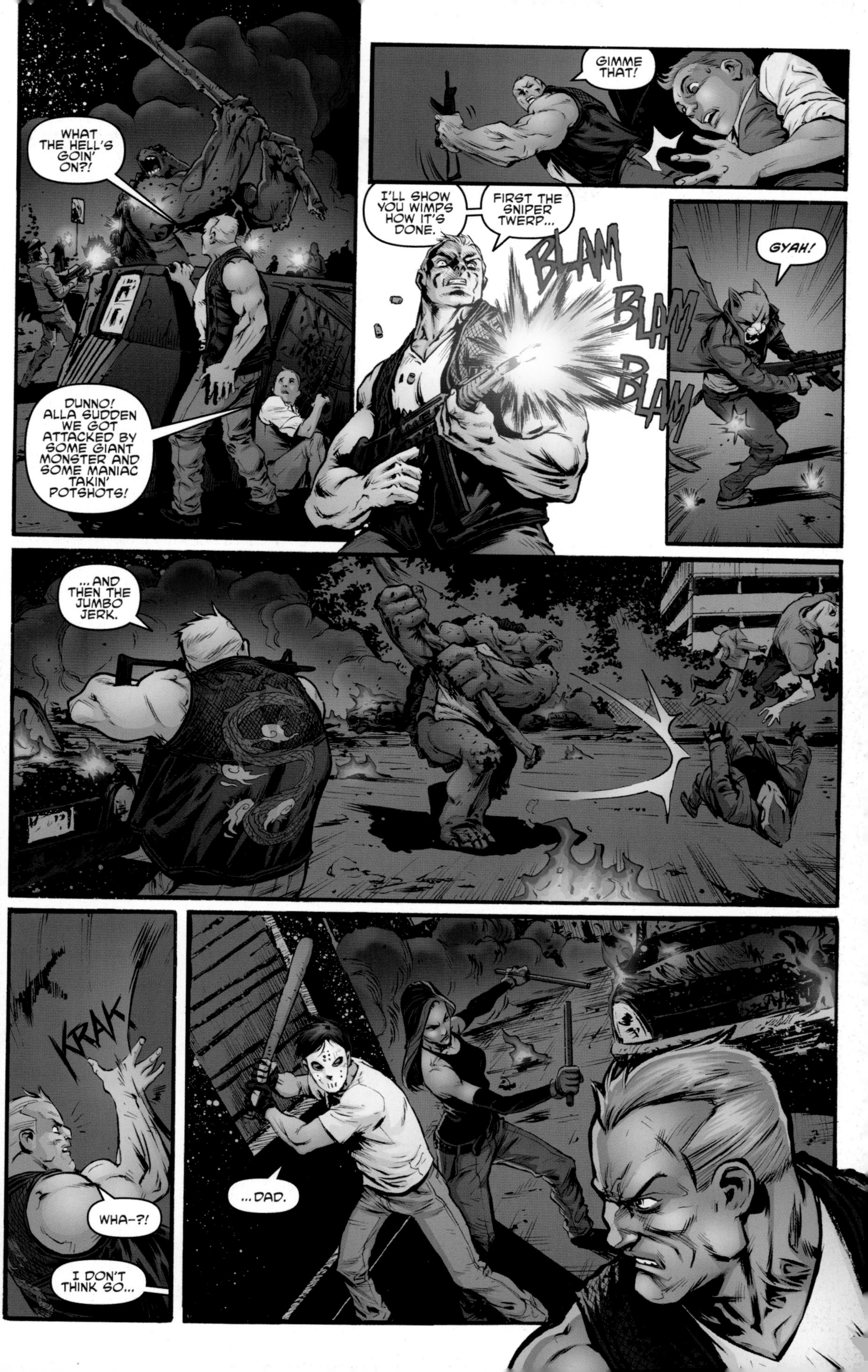
WHAT THE HELL'S GOIN' ON?!
DUNNO! ALLA SUDDEN WE GOT ATTACKED BY SOME GIANT MONSTER AND SOME MANIAC TAKIN' POTSHOTS!
GIMME THAT!
I'LL SHOW YOU WIMPS HOW IT'S DONE.
FIRST THE SNIPER TWERP...
BLAM
BLAM
BLAM
GYAH!
...AND THEN THE JUMBO JERK.
KRAK
WHA-?!
I DON'T THINK SO...
...DAD.

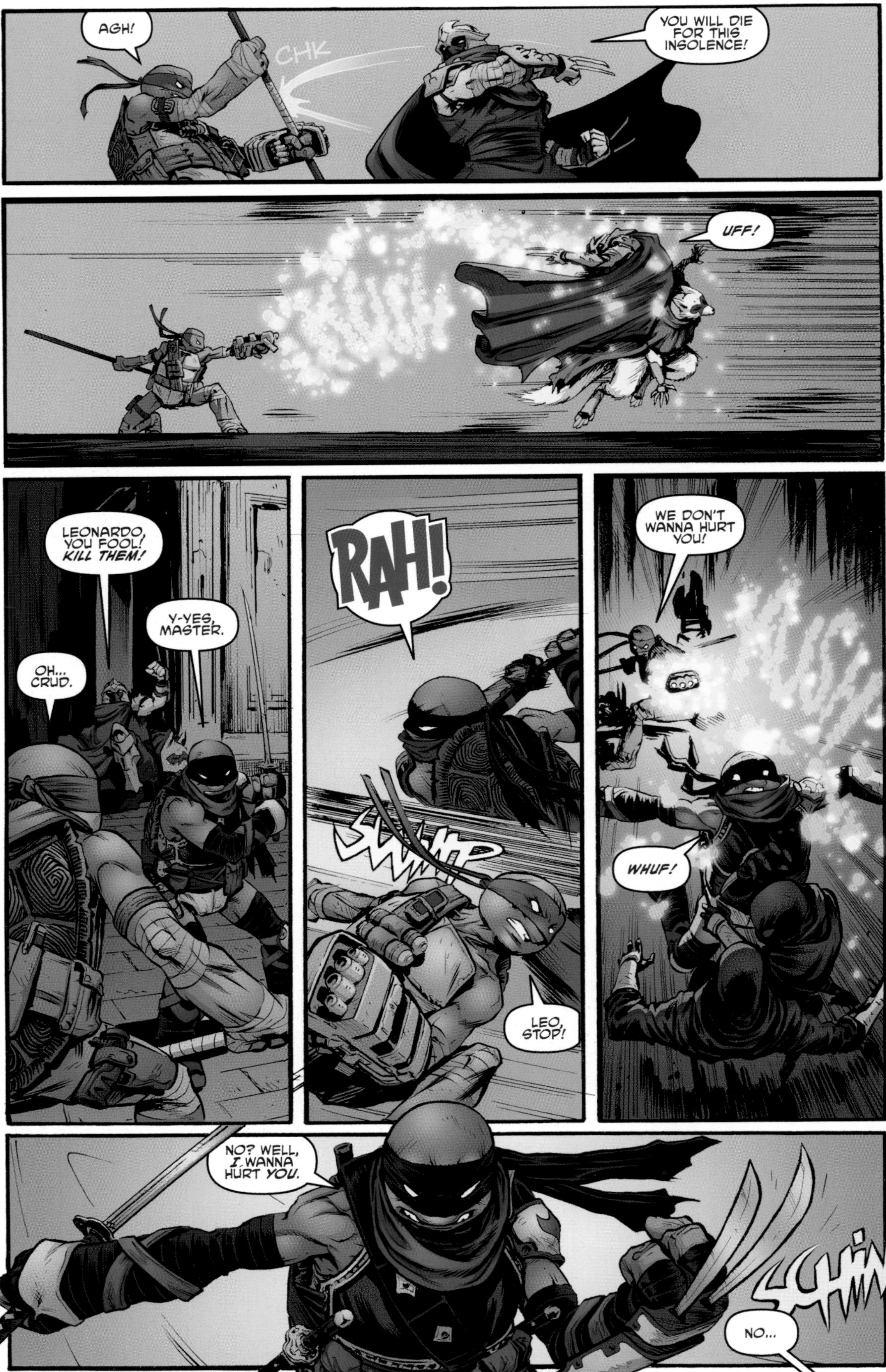
AGH!
CHK
YOU WILL DIE FOR THIS INSOLENCE!
UFF!
LEONARDO, YOU FOOL! *KILL THEM!*
Y-YES, MASTER.
OH... CRUD.
RAH!
LEO, STOP!
WE DON'T WANNA HURT YOU!
WHUF!
NO? WELL, *I* WANNA HURT *YOU*.
NO...

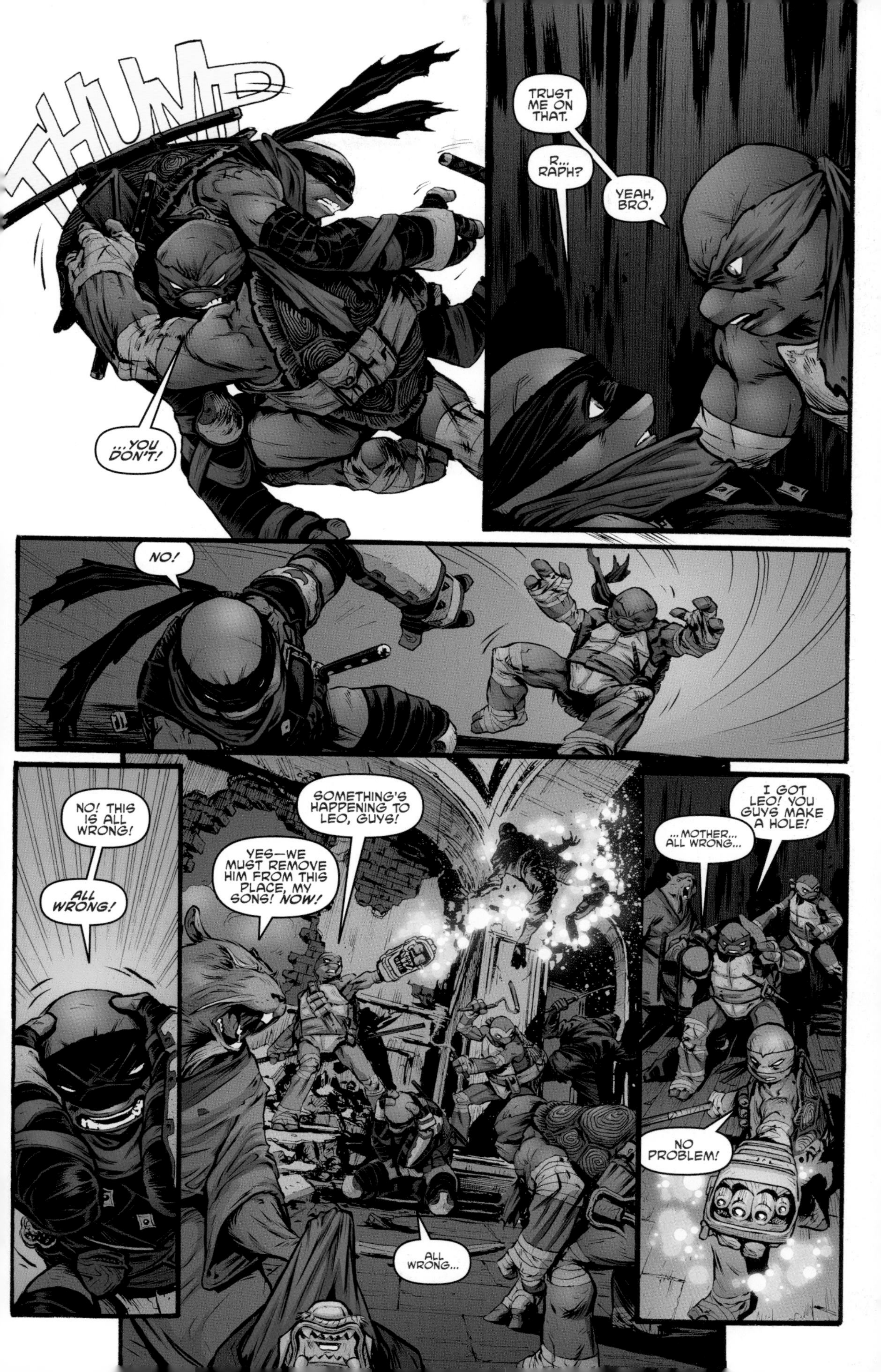
THUMP
...YOU DON'T!
TRUST ME ON THAT.
R... RAPH?
YEAH, BRO.
NO!
NO! THIS IS ALL WRONG!
ALL WRONG!
SOMETHING'S HAPPENING TO LEO, GUYS!
YES—WE MUST REMOVE HIM FROM THIS PLACE, MY SONS! NOW!
ALL WRONG...
I GOT LEO! YOU GUYS MAKE A HOLE!
...MOTHER... ALL WRONG...
NO PROBLEM!

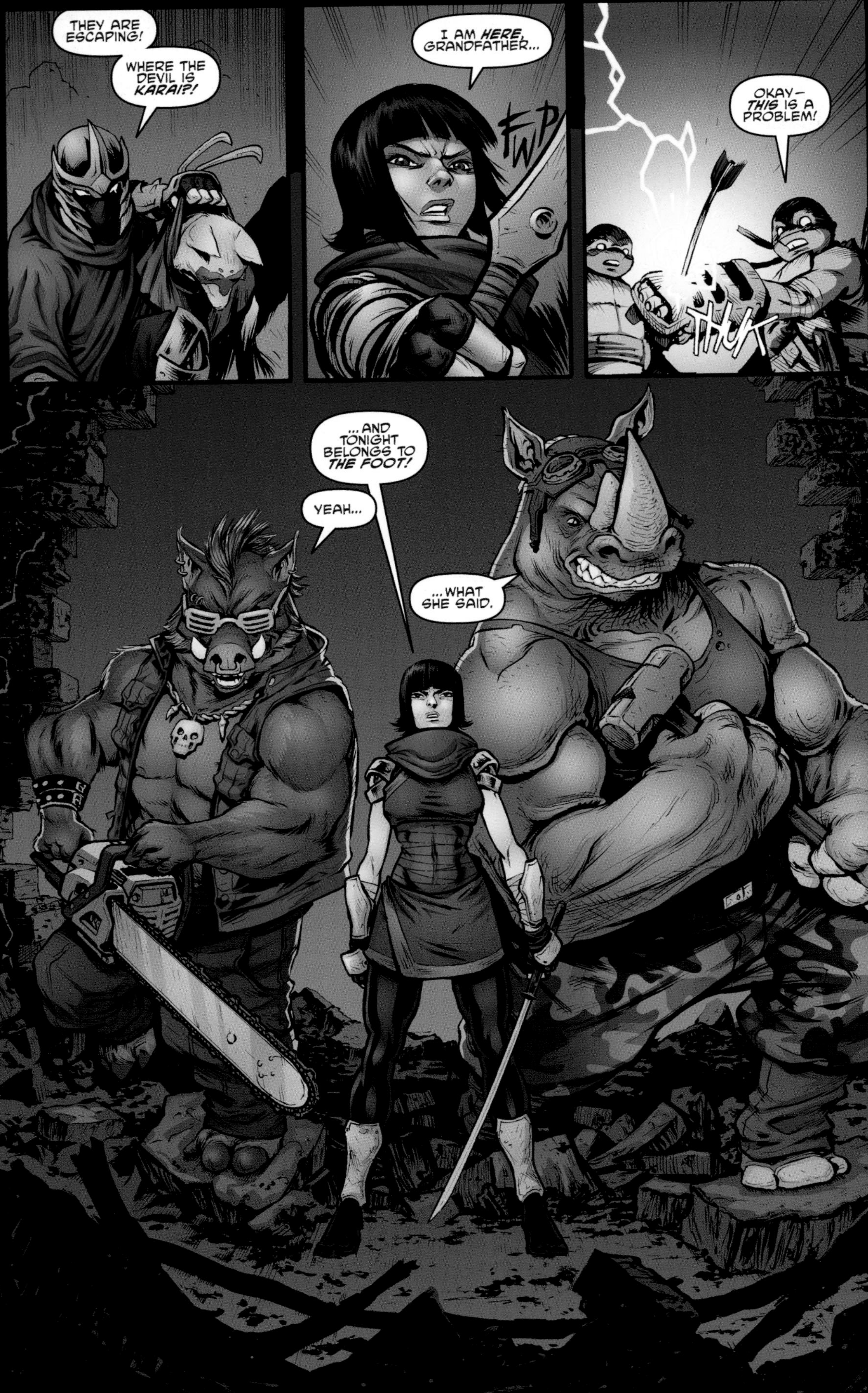
THEY ARE ESCAPING!
WHERE THE DEVIL IS KARAI?!
I AM HERE, GRANDFATHER...
FWP
OKAY— THIS IS A PROBLEM!
THUK
...AND TONIGHT BELONGS TO THE FOOT!
YEAH...
...WHAT SHE SAID.

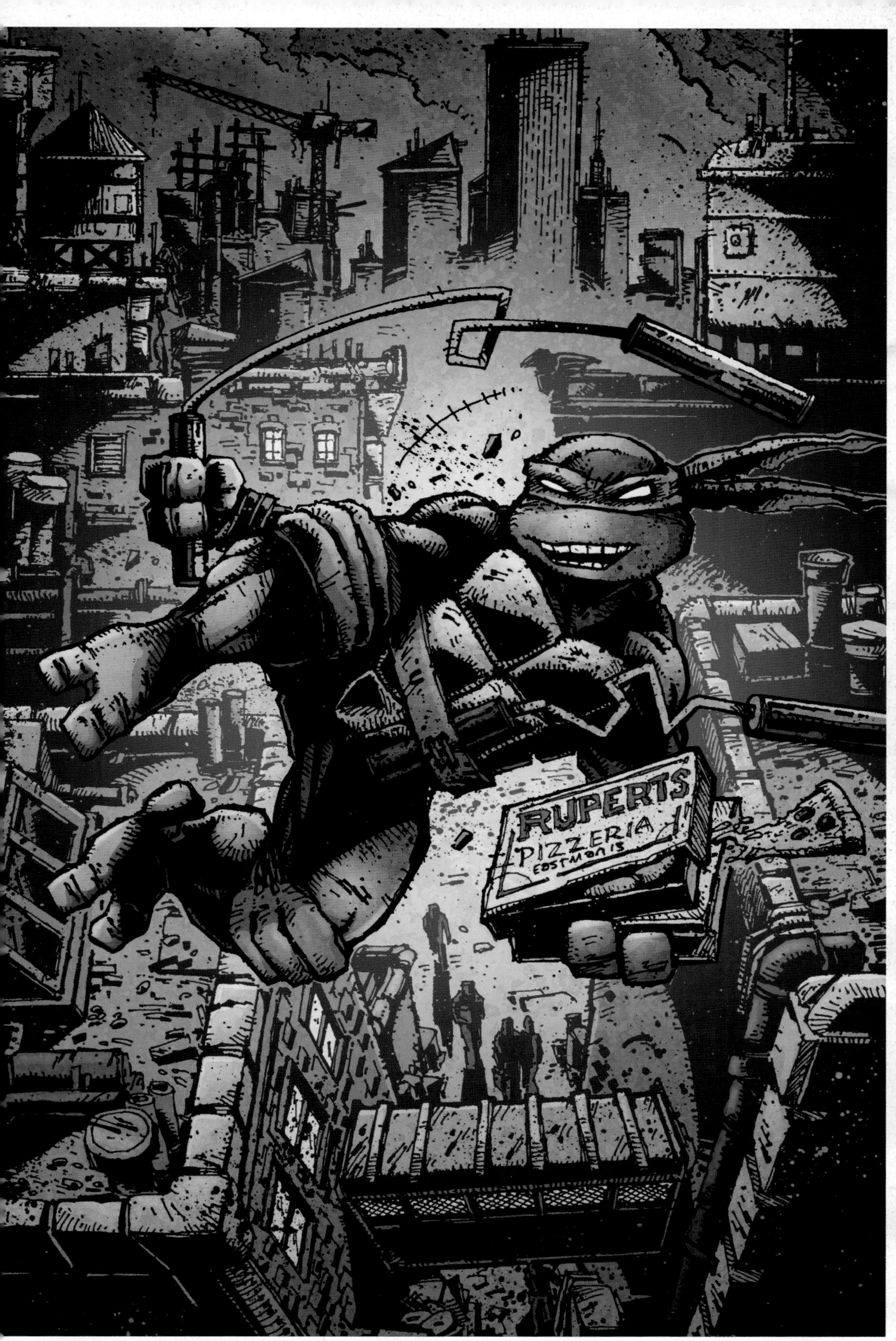
RUPERTS
PIZZERIA

Cover by KEVIN EASTMAN
Colors by RONDA PATTISON

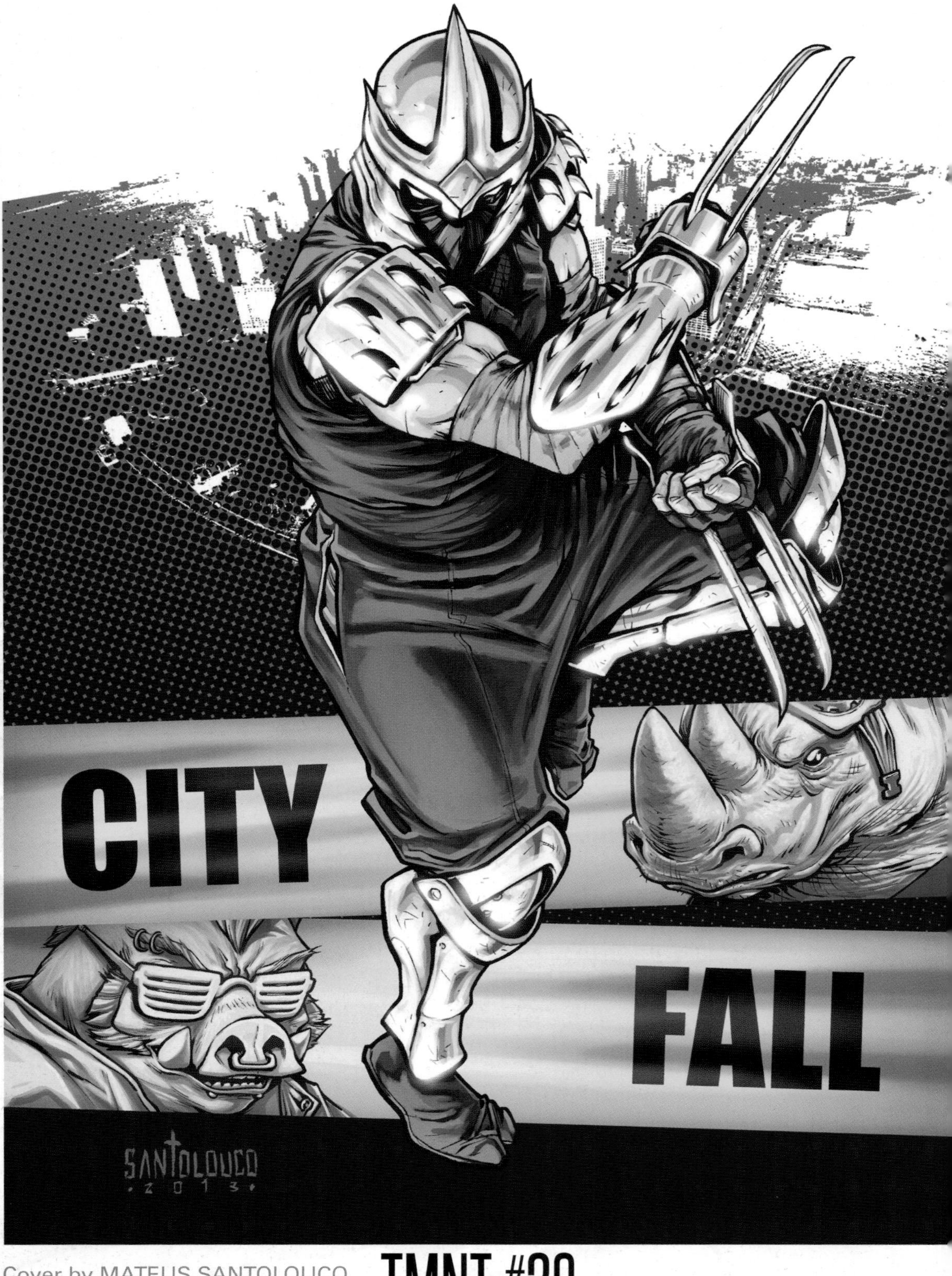
CITY
FALL
SANTOLOUCO
2013

Cover by MATEUS SANTOLOUCO

TMNT #28

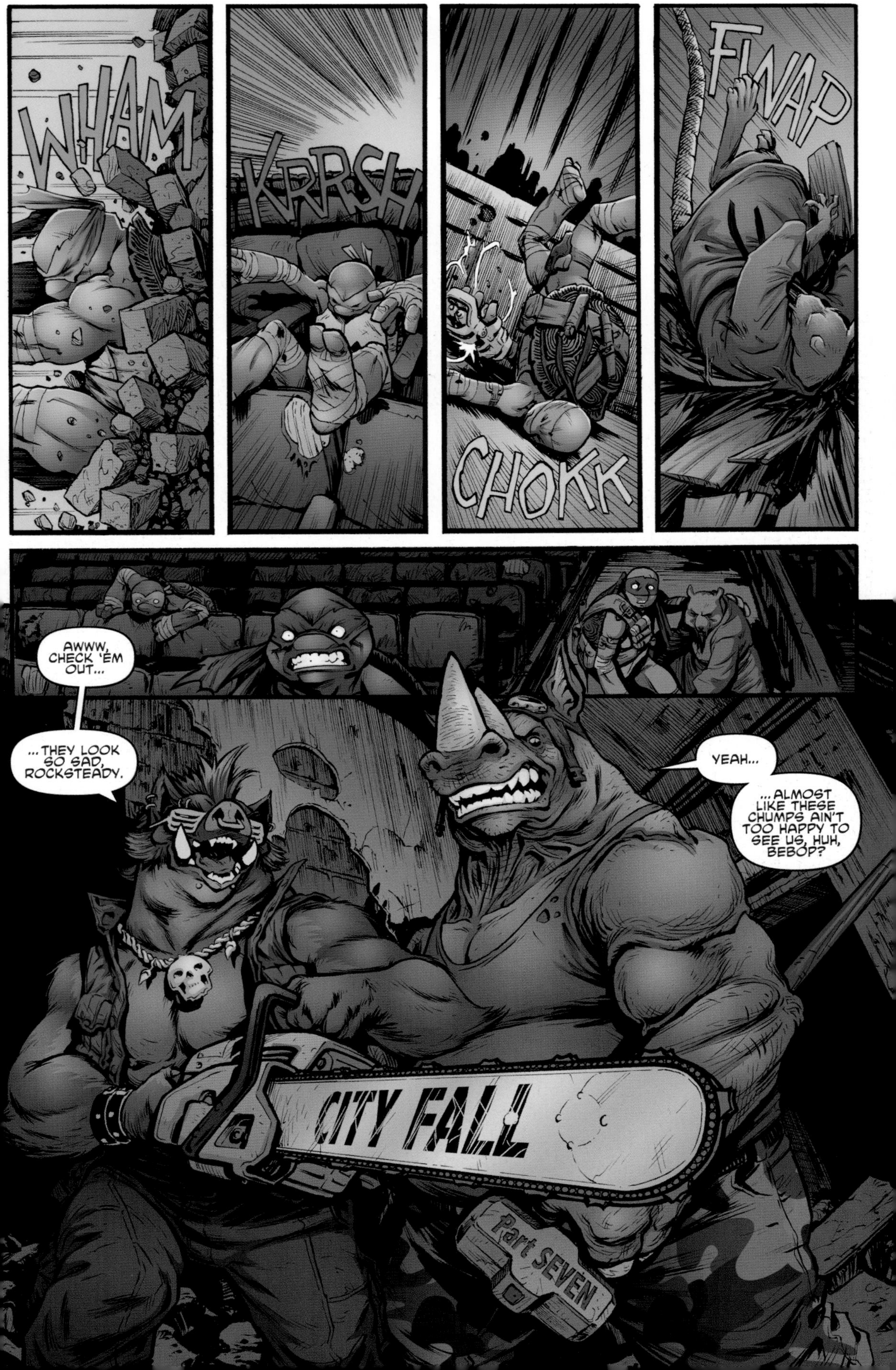
WHAM
KRRSH
CHOKK
FWAP
AWWW, CHECK 'EM OUT...
...THEY LOOK SO SAD, ROCKSTEADY.
YEAH...
...ALMOST LIKE THESE CHUMPS AIN'T TOO HAPPY TO SEE US, HUH, BEBOP?
CITY FALL
Part SEVEN

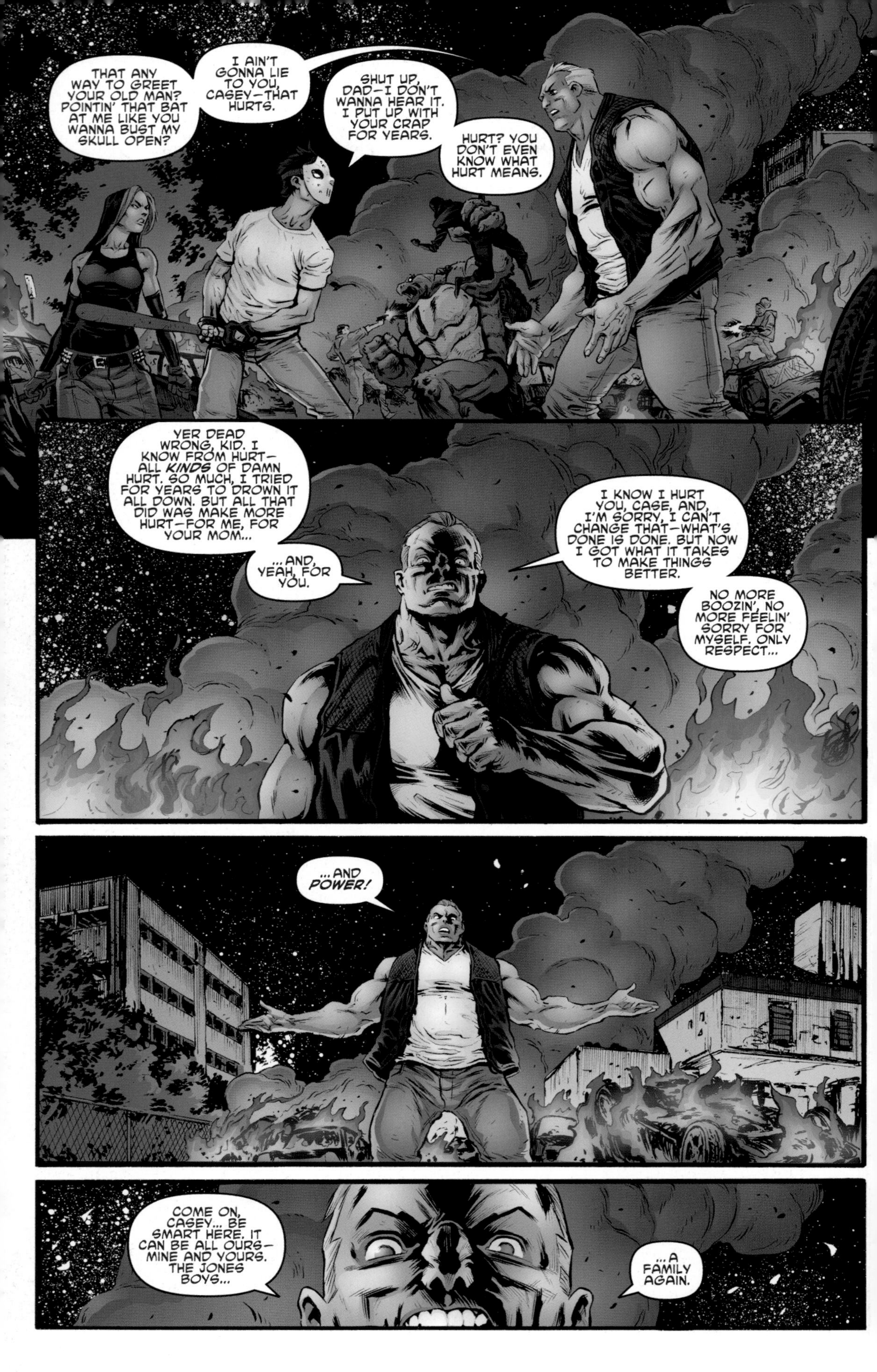
THAT ANY WAY TO GREET YOUR OLD MAN? POINTIN' THAT BAT AT ME LIKE YOU WANNA BUST MY SKULL OPEN?
I AIN'T GONNA LIE TO YOU, CASEY—THAT HURTS.
SHUT UP, DAD—I DON'T WANNA HEAR IT. I PUT UP WITH YOUR CRAP FOR YEARS.
HURT? YOU DON'T EVEN KNOW WHAT HURT MEANS.
YER DEAD WRONG, KID. I KNOW FROM HURT—ALL KINDS OF DAMN HURT. SO MUCH, I TRIED FOR YEARS TO DROWN IT ALL DOWN. BUT ALL THAT DID WAS MAKE MORE HURT—FOR ME, FOR YOUR MOM...
...AND, YEAH, FOR YOU.
I KNOW I HURT YOU, CASE, AND, I'M SORRY, I CAN'T CHANGE THAT—WHAT'S DONE IS DONE. BUT NOW I GOT WHAT IT TAKES TO MAKE THINGS BETTER.
NO MORE BOOZIN', NO MORE FEELIN' SORRY FOR MYSELF. ONLY RESPECT...
...AND POWER!
COME ON, CASEY... BE SMART HERE. IT CAN BE ALL OURS—MINE AND YOURS. THE JONES BOYS...
...A FAMILY AGAIN.

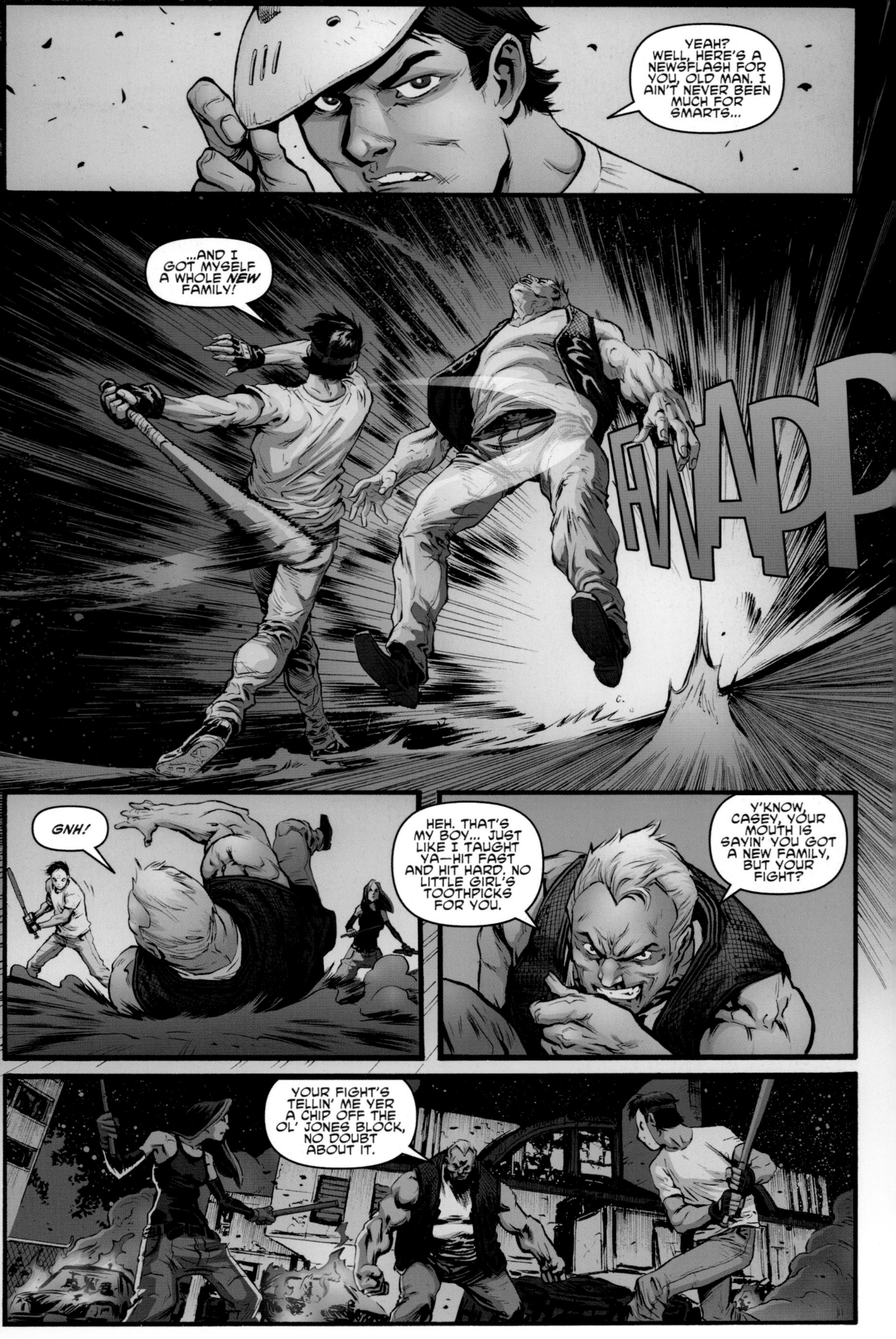
YEAH? WELL, HERE'S A NEWSFLASH FOR YOU, OLD MAN. I AIN'T NEVER BEEN MUCH FOR SMARTS...
...AND I GOT MYSELF A WHOLE NEW FAMILY!
FWAPP
GNH!
HEH. THAT'S MY BOY... JUST LIKE I TAUGHT YA--HIT FAST AND HIT HARD. NO LITTLE GIRL'S TOOTHPICKS FOR YOU.
Y'KNOW, CASEY, YOUR MOUTH IS SAYIN' YOU GOT A NEW FAMILY, BUT YOUR FIGHT?
YOUR FIGHT'S TELLIN' ME YER A CHIP OFF THE OL' JONES BLOCK, NO DOUBT ABOUT IT.

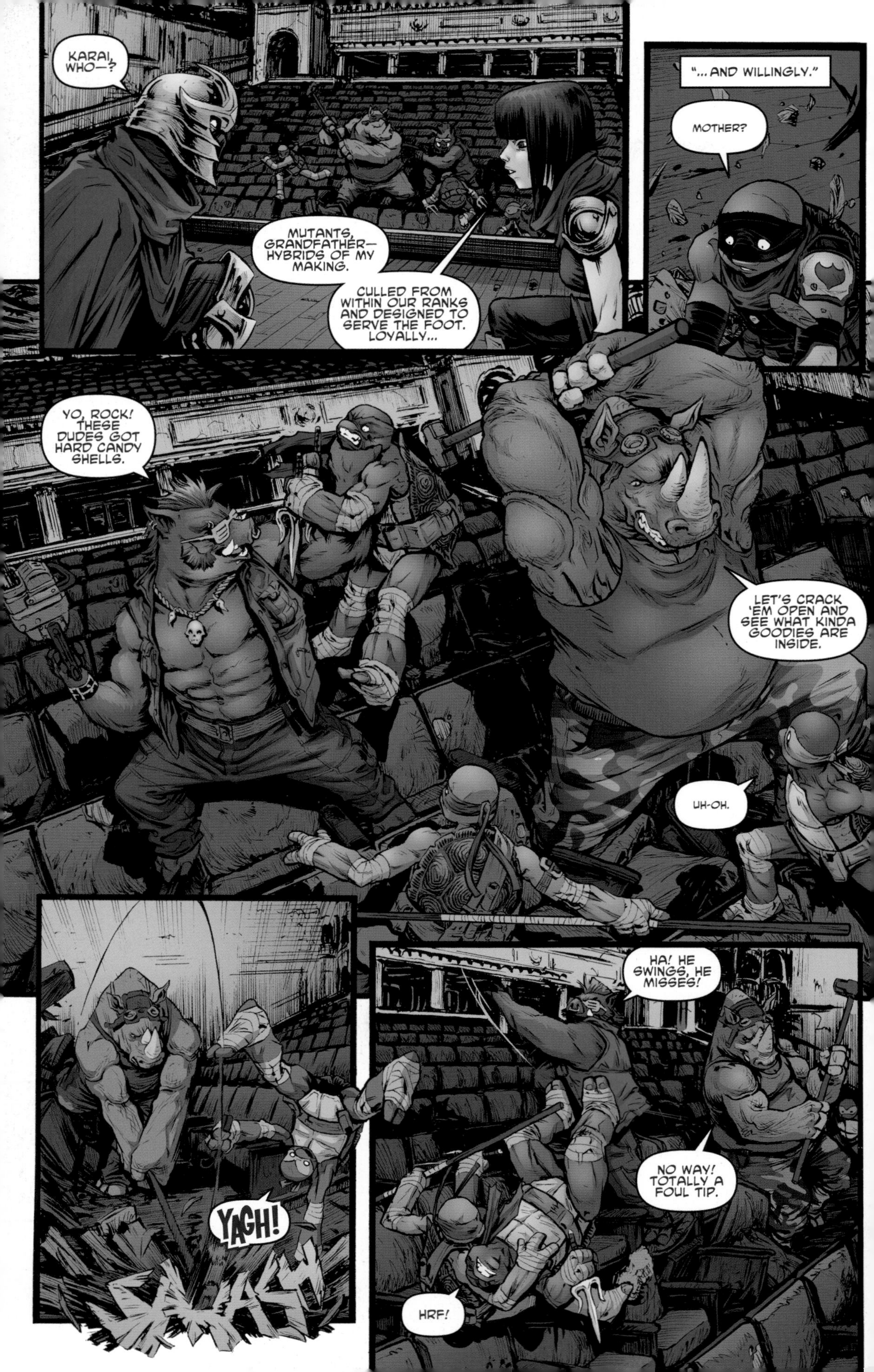
KARAI, WHO—?
MUTANTS, GRANDFATHER— HYBRIDS OF MY MAKING.
CULLED FROM WITHIN OUR RANKS AND DESIGNED TO SERVE THE FOOT. LOYALLY...
"... AND WILLINGLY."
MOTHER?
YO, ROCK! THESE DUDES GOT HARD CANDY SHELLS.
LET'S CRACK 'EM OPEN AND SEE WHAT KINDA GOODIES ARE INSIDE.
UH-OH.
YAGH!
SMASH
HA! HE SWINGS, HE MISSES!
NO WAY! TOTALLY A FOUL TIP.
HRF!

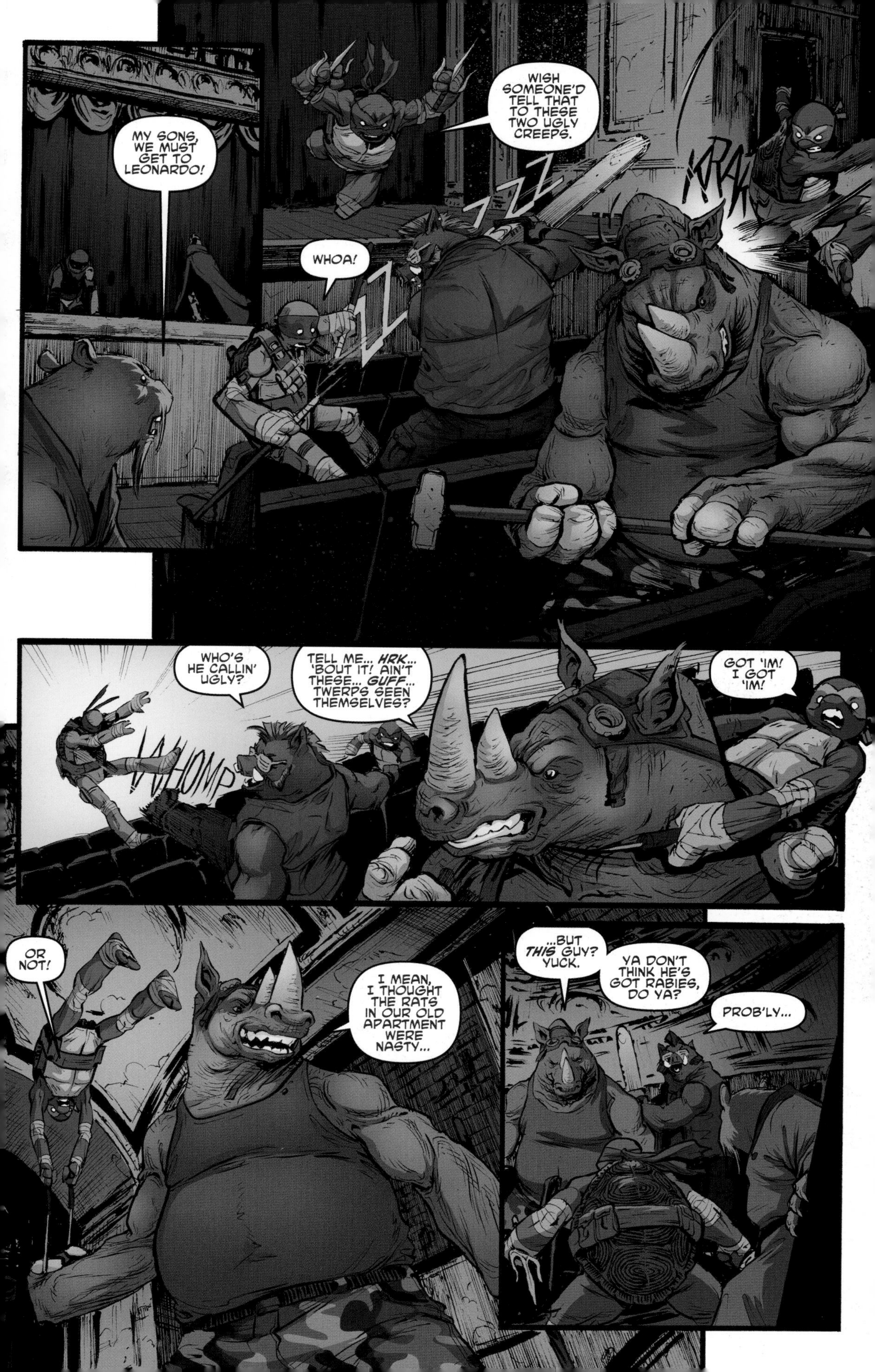
MY SONS, WE MUST GET TO LEONARDO!
WISH SOMEONE'D TELL THAT TO THESE TWO UGLY CREEPS.
ZZZZ
KRAK
WHOA!
WHO'S HE CALLIN' UGLY?
TELL ME... HRK... 'BOUT IT! AIN'T THESE... GUFF... TWERPS SEEN THEMSELVES?
GOT 'IM! I GOT 'IM!
WHOMP
OR NOT!
I MEAN, I THOUGHT THE RATS IN OUR OLD APARTMENT WERE NASTY...
...BUT THIS GUY? YUCK.
YA DON'T THINK HE'S GOT RABIES, DO YA?
PROB'LY...

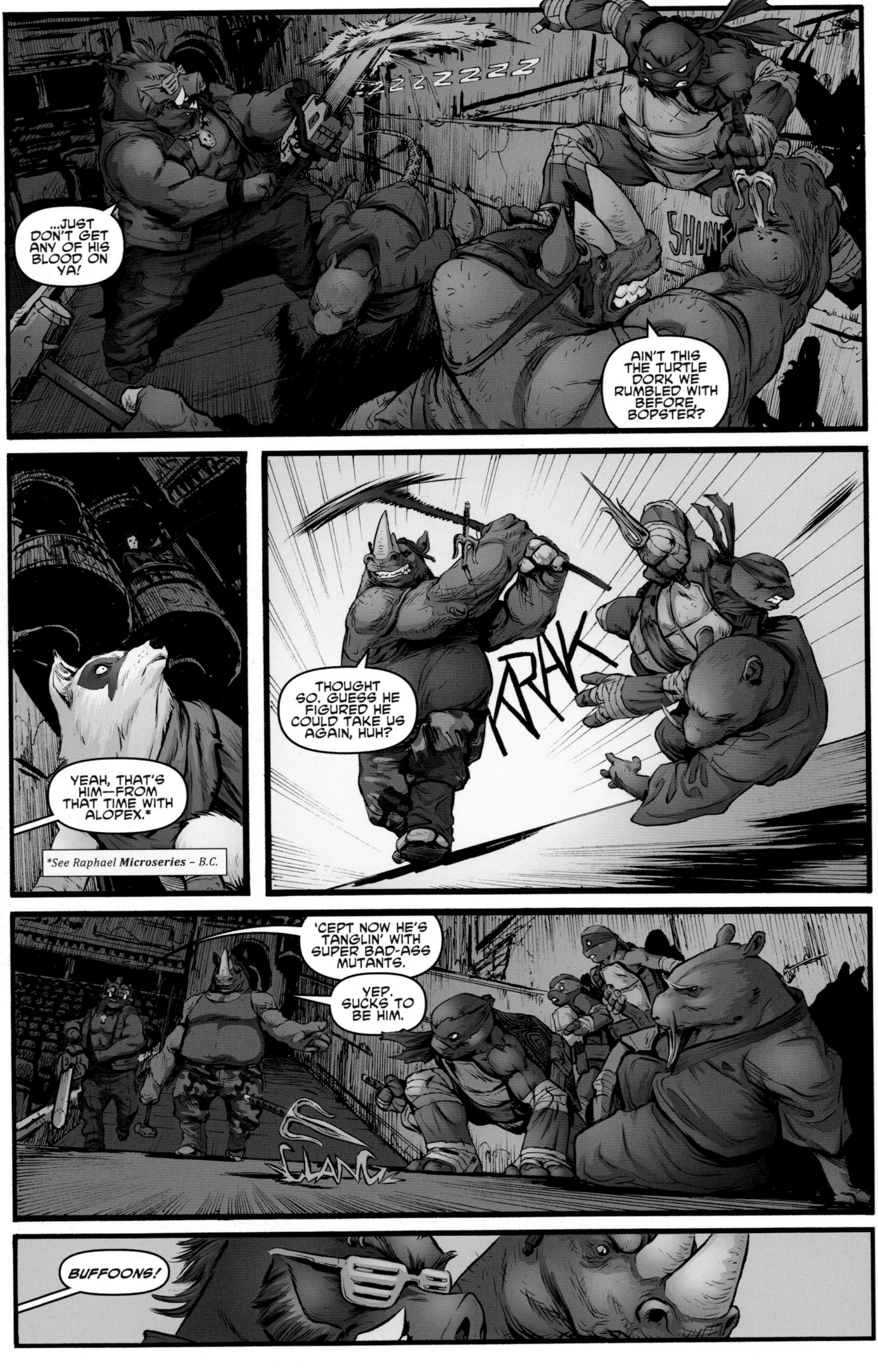

ZZZZZZZZZZ
...JUST DON'T GET ANY OF HIS BLOOD ON YA!
SHUNK
AIN'T THIS THE TURTLE DORK WE RUMBLED WITH BEFORE, BOPSTER?
YEAH, THAT'S HIM—FROM THAT TIME WITH ALOPEX.*
*See Raphael Microseries – B.C.
THOUGHT SO. GUESS HE FIGURED HE COULD TAKE US AGAIN, HUH?
KRAK
'CEPT NOW HE'S TANGLIN' WITH SUPER BAD-ASS MUTANTS.
YEP. SUCKS TO BE HIM.
CLANG
BUFFOONS!

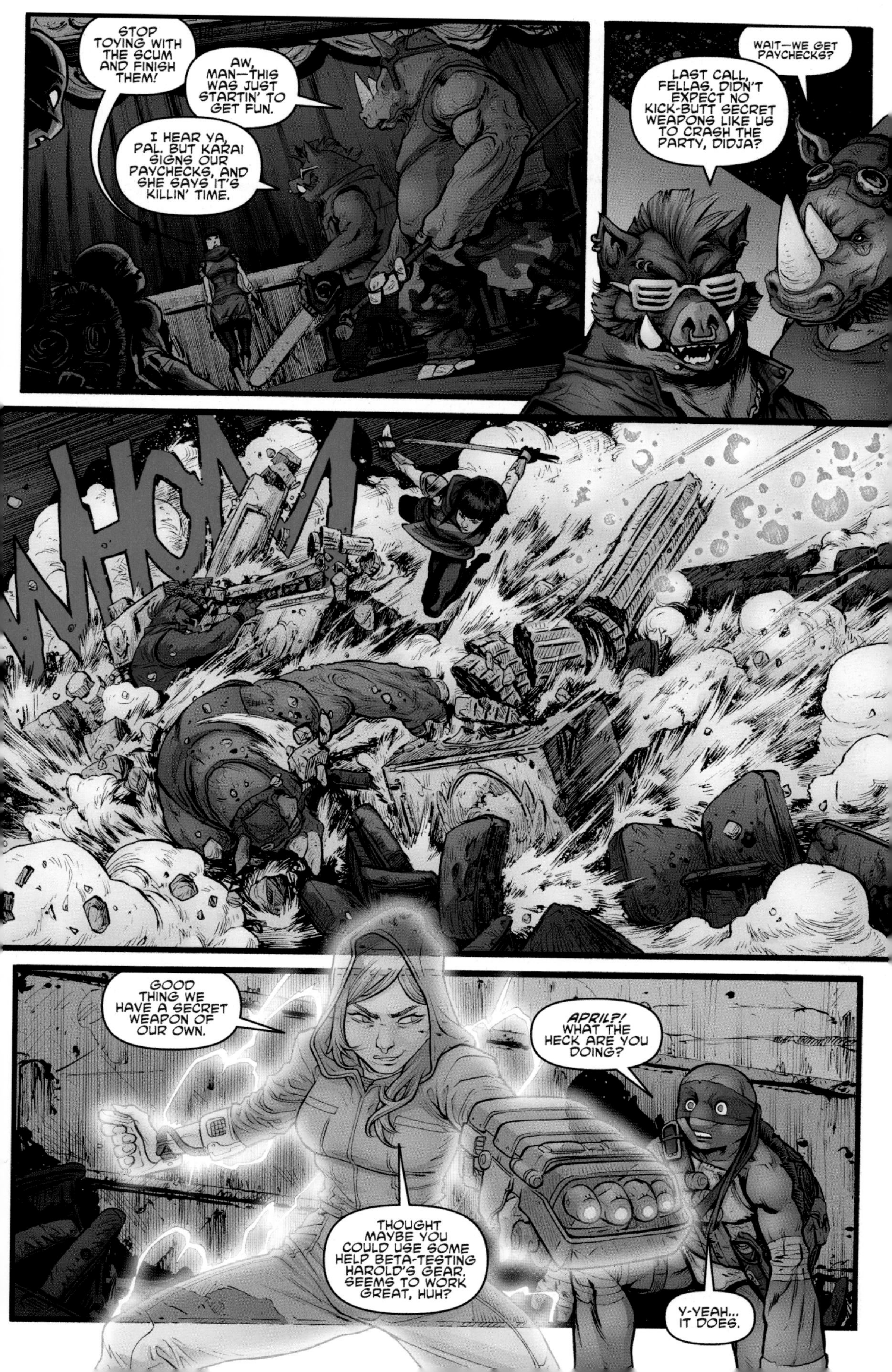
STOP TOYING WITH THE SCUM AND FINISH THEM!
AW, MAN—THIS WAS JUST STARTIN' TO GET FUN.
I HEAR YA, PAL. BUT KARAI SIGNS OUR PAYCHECKS, AND SHE SAYS IT'S KILLIN' TIME.
LAST CALL, FELLAS. DIDN'T EXPECT NO KICK-BUTT SECRET WEAPONS LIKE US TO CRASH THE PARTY, DIDJA?
WAIT—WE GET PAYCHECKS?
WHOM
GOOD THING WE HAVE A SECRET WEAPON OF OUR OWN.
APRIL?! WHAT THE HECK ARE YOU DOING?
THOUGHT MAYBE YOU COULD USE SOME HELP BETA-TESTING HAROLD'S GEAR. SEEMS TO WORK GREAT, HUH?
Y-YEAH... IT DOES.

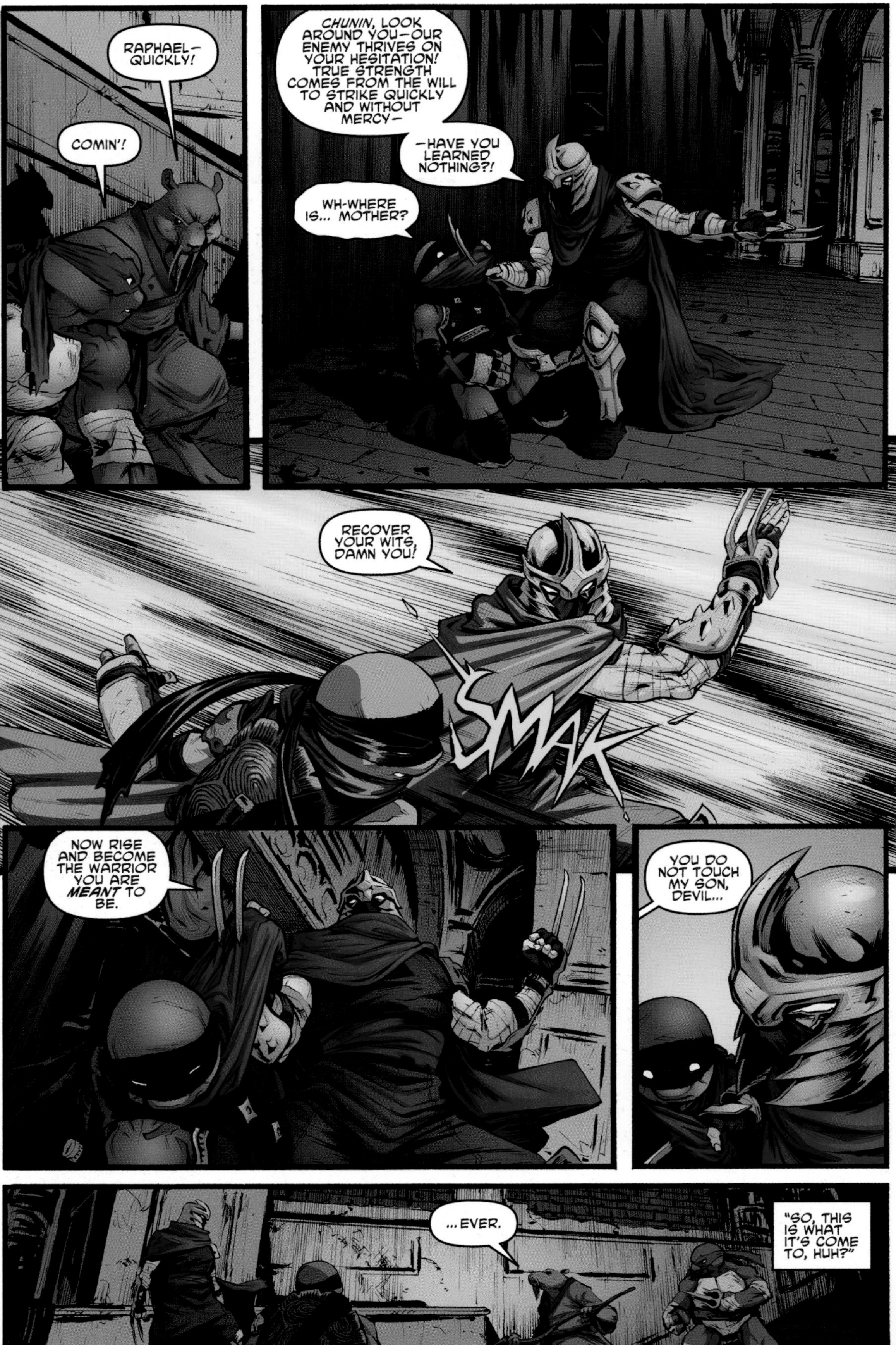
RAPHAEL—
QUICKLY!
COMIN'!
CHUNIN, LOOK AROUND YOU—OUR ENEMY THRIVES ON YOUR HESITATION! TRUE STRENGTH COMES FROM THE WILL TO STRIKE QUICKLY AND WITHOUT MERCY—
—HAVE YOU LEARNED NOTHING?!
WH-WHERE IS... MOTHER?
RECOVER YOUR WITS, DAMN YOU!
SMAK
NOW RISE AND BECOME THE WARRIOR YOU ARE *MEANT* TO BE.
YOU DO NOT TOUCH MY SON, DEVIL...
...EVER.
"SO, THIS IS WHAT IT'S COME TO, HUH?"

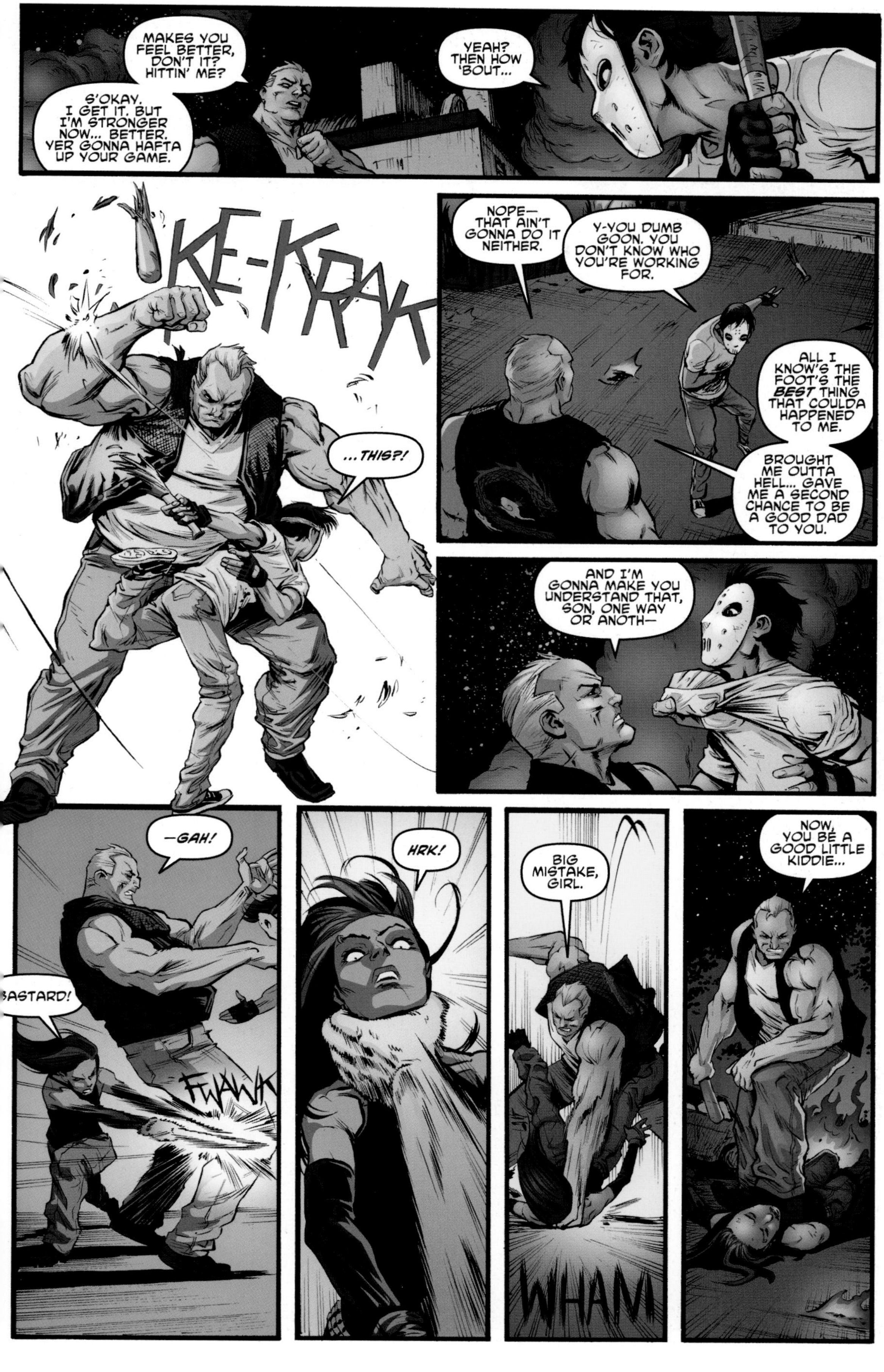
MAKES YOU FEEL BETTER, DON'T IT? HITTIN' ME?
S'OKAY. I GET IT. BUT I'M STRONGER NOW... BETTER. YER GONNA HAFTA UP YOUR GAME.
YEAH? THEN HOW 'BOUT...
KE-KRAK
...THIS?!
NOPE— THAT AIN'T GONNA DO IT NEITHER.
Y-YOU DUMB GOON. YOU DON'T KNOW WHO YOU'RE WORKING FOR.
ALL I KNOW'S THE FOOT'S THE BEST THING THAT COULDA HAPPENED TO ME.
BROUGHT ME OUTTA HELL... GAVE ME A SECOND CHANCE TO BE A GOOD DAD TO YOU.
AND I'M GONNA MAKE YOU UNDERSTAND THAT, SON, ONE WAY OR ANOTH—
—GAH!
BASTARD!
FWAWK
HRK!
BIG MISTAKE, GIRL.
WHAM
NOW, YOU BE A GOOD LITTLE KIDDIE...

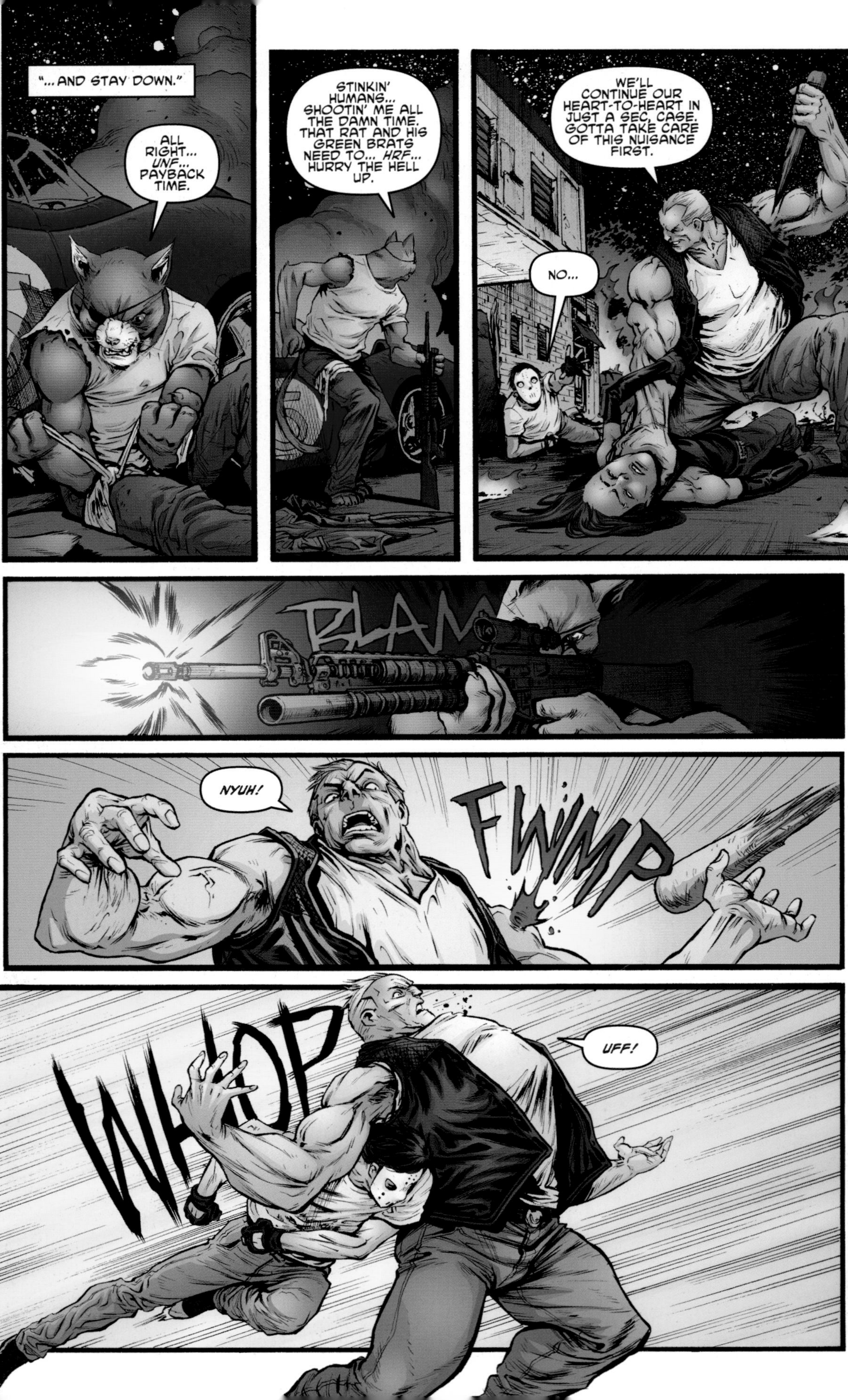
"...AND STAY DOWN."
ALL RIGHT... UNF... PAYBACK TIME.
STINKIN' HUMANS... SHOOTIN' ME ALL THE DAMN TIME. THAT RAT AND HIS GREEN BRATS NEED TO... HRF... HURRY THE HELL UP.
WE'LL CONTINUE OUR HEART-TO-HEART IN JUST A SEC, CASE. GOTTA TAKE CARE OF THIS NUISANCE FIRST.
NO...
BLAM
NYUH!
FWIMP
WHOP
UFF!

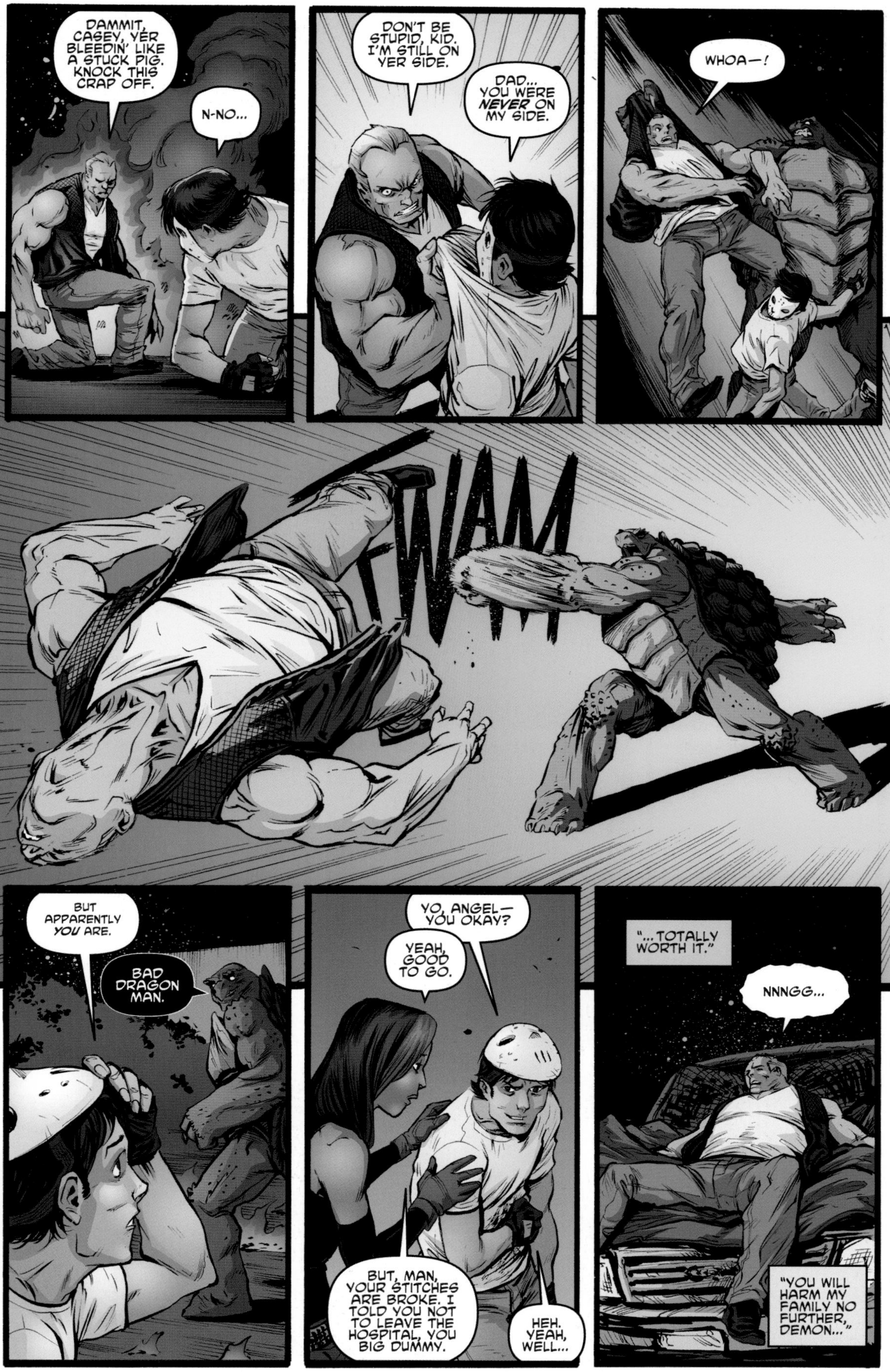
DAMMIT, CASEY, YER BLEEDIN' LIKE A STUCK PIG. KNOCK THIS CRAP OFF.
N-NO...
DON'T BE STUPID, KID. I'M STILL ON YER SIDE.
DAD... YOU WERE NEVER ON MY SIDE.
WHOA—!
TWAM
BUT APPARENTLY YOU ARE.
BAD DRAGON MAN.
YO, ANGEL— YOU OKAY?
YEAH, GOOD TO GO.
BUT, MAN, YOUR STITCHES ARE BROKE. I TOLD YOU NOT TO LEAVE THE HOSPITAL, YOU BIG DUMMY.
HEH. YEAH, WELL...
"...TOTALLY WORTH IT."
NNNGG...
"YOU WILL HARM MY FAMILY NO FURTHER, DEMON..."

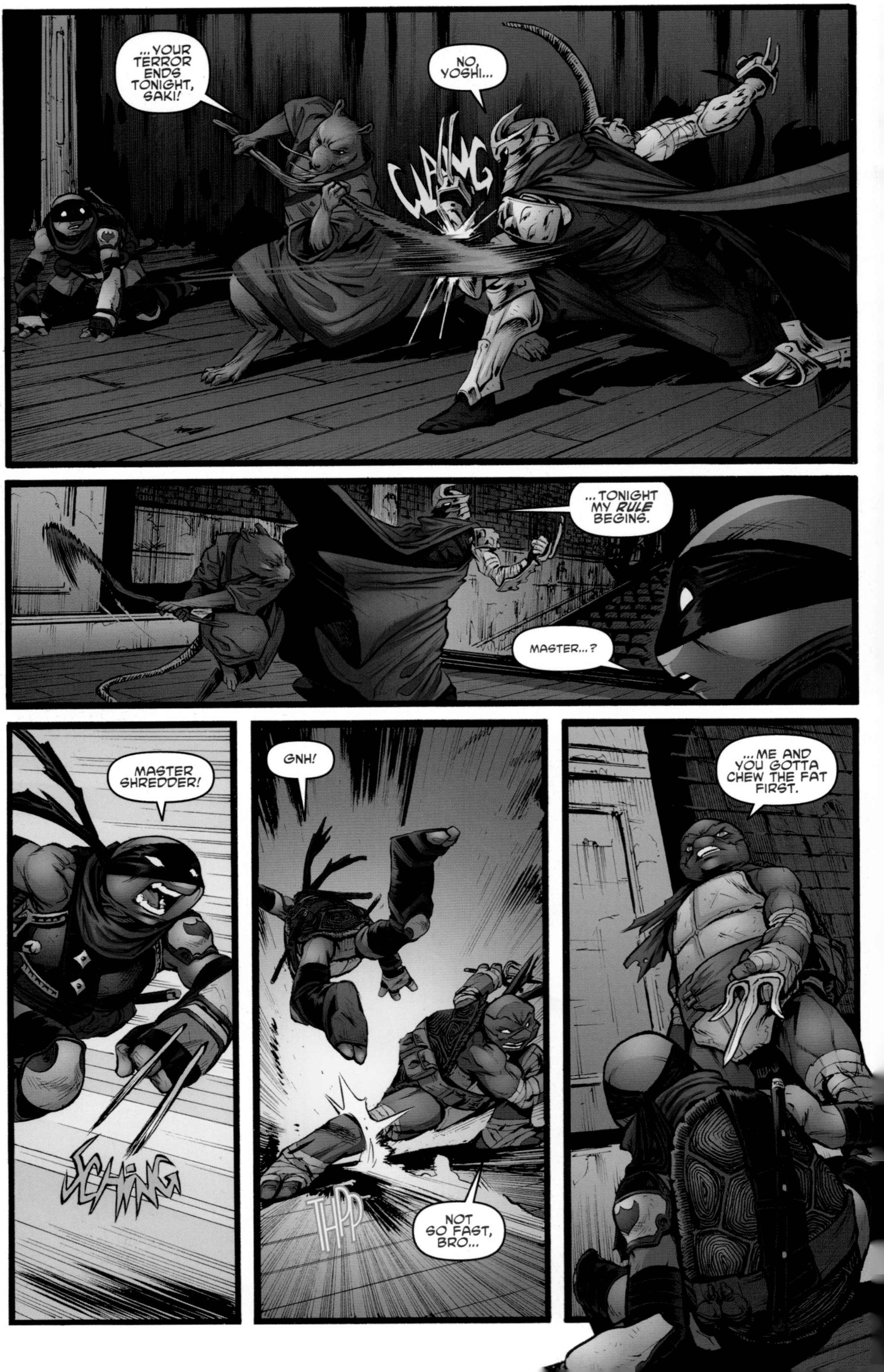
...YOUR TERROR ENDS TONIGHT, SAKI!
NO, YOSHI...
CLANG
...TONIGHT MY RULE BEGINS.
MASTER...?
MASTER SHREDDER!
SCHING
GNH!
THPP
NOT SO FAST, BRO...
...ME AND YOU GOTTA CHEW THE FAT FIRST.

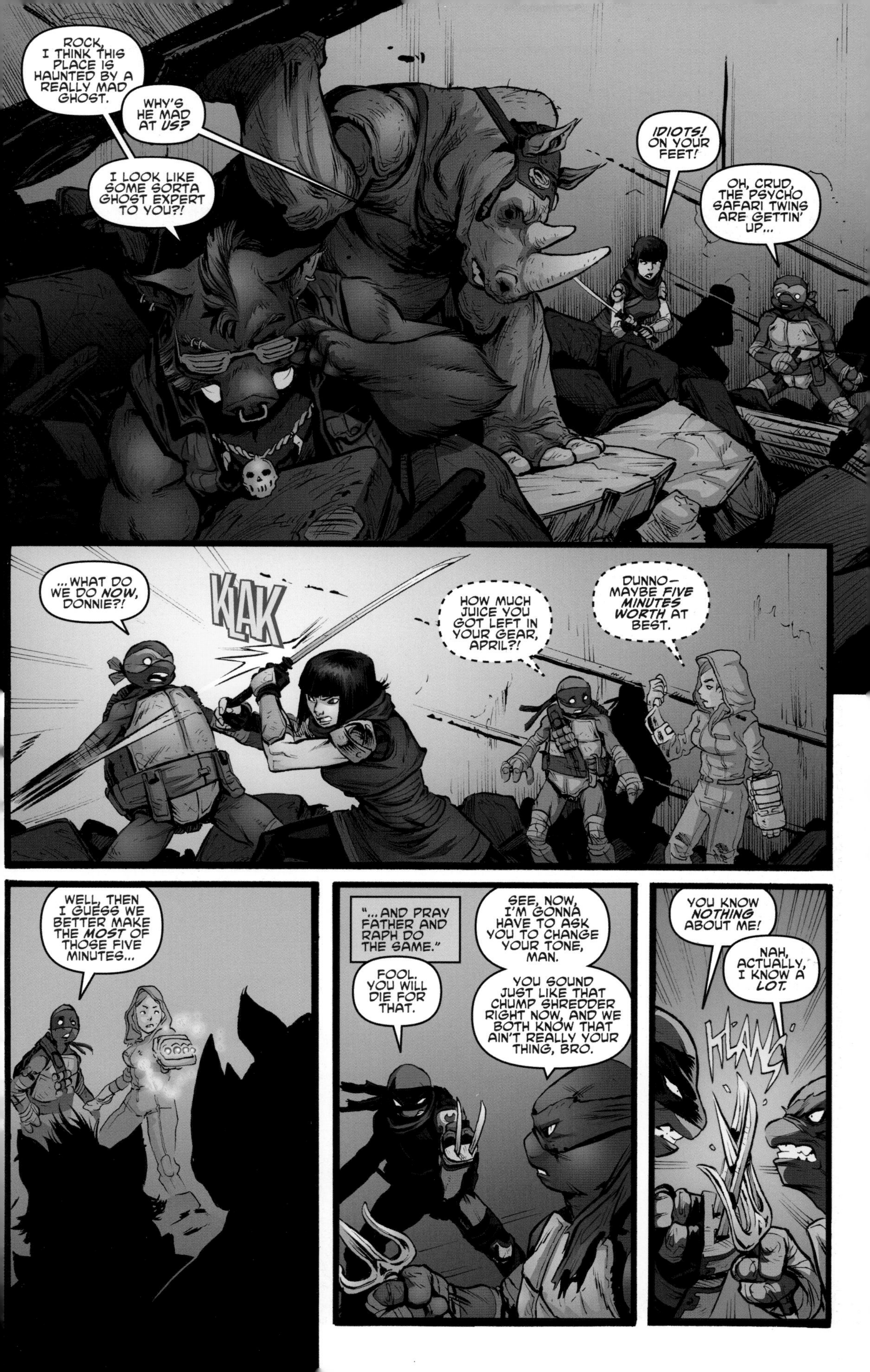

ROCK, I THINK THIS PLACE IS HAUNTED BY A REALLY MAD GHOST.
WHY'S HE MAD AT *US?*
I LOOK LIKE SOME SORTA GHOST EXPERT TO YOU?!
IDIOTS! ON YOUR FEET!
OH, CRUD, THE PSYCHO SAFARI TWINS ARE GETTIN' UP...
...WHAT DO WE DO *NOW*, DONNIE?!
KLAK
HOW MUCH JUICE YOU GOT LEFT IN YOUR GEAR, APRIL?!
DUNNO— MAYBE *FIVE MINUTES WORTH* AT BEST.
WELL, THEN I GUESS WE BETTER MAKE THE *MOST* OF THOSE FIVE MINUTES...
"...AND PRAY FATHER AND RAPH DO THE SAME."
FOOL. YOU WILL DIE FOR THAT.
SEE, NOW, I'M GONNA HAVE TO ASK YOU TO CHANGE YOUR TONE, MAN.
YOU SOUND JUST LIKE THAT CHUMP SHREDDER RIGHT NOW, AND WE BOTH KNOW THAT AIN'T REALLY YOUR THING, BRO.
YOU KNOW *NOTHING* ABOUT ME!
NAH, ACTUALLY, I KNOW A *LOT.*

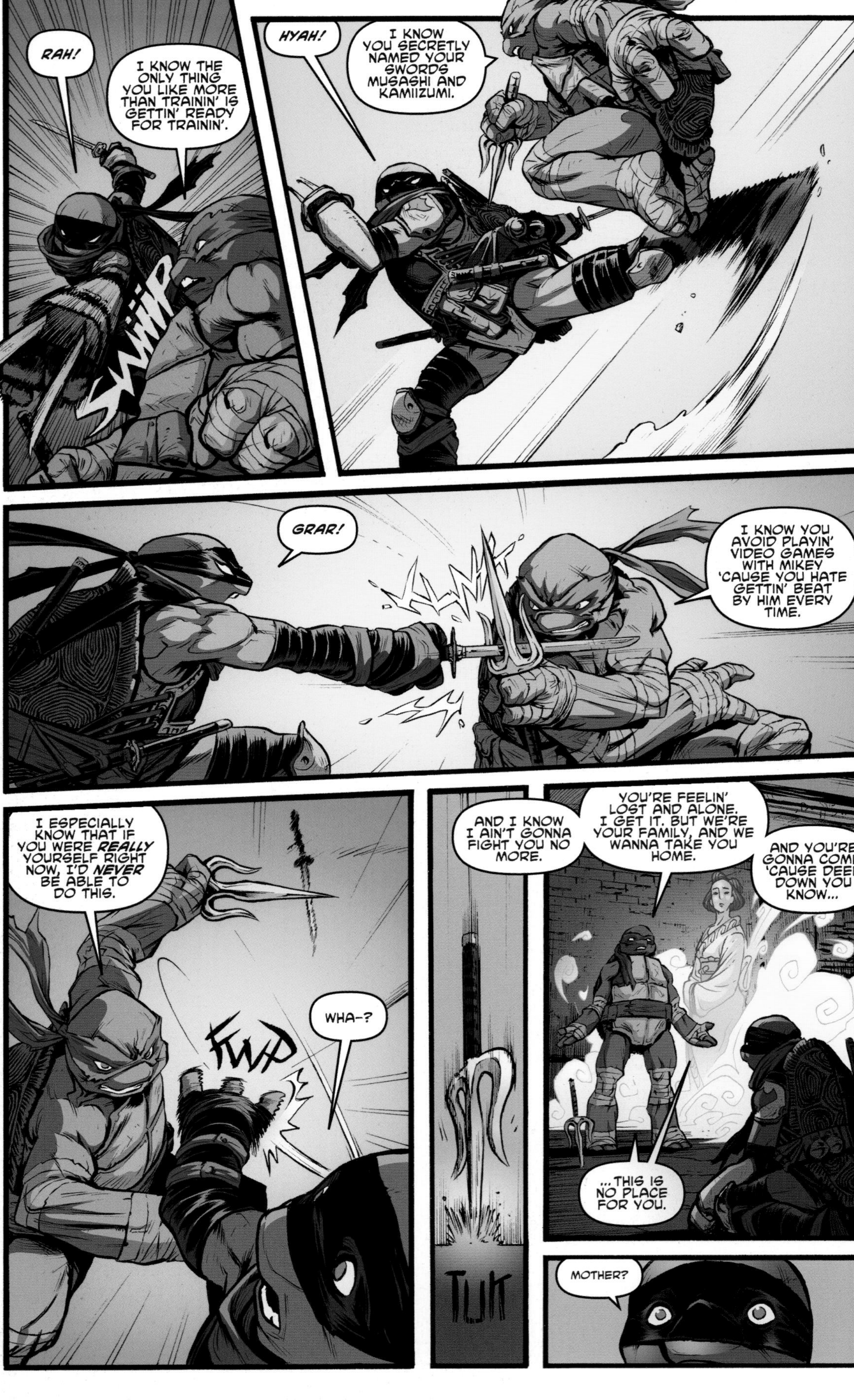
RAH!
I KNOW THE ONLY THING YOU LIKE MORE THAN TRAININ' IS GETTIN' READY FOR TRAININ'.
HYAH!
I KNOW YOU SECRETLY NAMED YOUR SWORDS MUSASHI AND KAMIIZUMI.
GRAR!
I KNOW YOU AVOID PLAYIN' VIDEO GAMES WITH MIKEY 'CAUSE YOU HATE GETTIN' BEAT BY HIM EVERY TIME.
I ESPECIALLY KNOW THAT IF YOU WERE REALLY YOURSELF RIGHT NOW, I'D NEVER BE ABLE TO DO THIS.
FWP
WHA-?
AND I KNOW I AIN'T GONNA FIGHT YOU NO MORE.
TUK
YOU'RE FEELIN' LOST AND ALONE. I GET IT. BUT WE'RE YOUR FAMILY, AND WE WANNA TAKE YOU HOME.
AND YOU'RE GONNA COME, 'CAUSE DEEP DOWN YOU KNOW...
...THIS IS NO PLACE FOR YOU.
MOTHER?

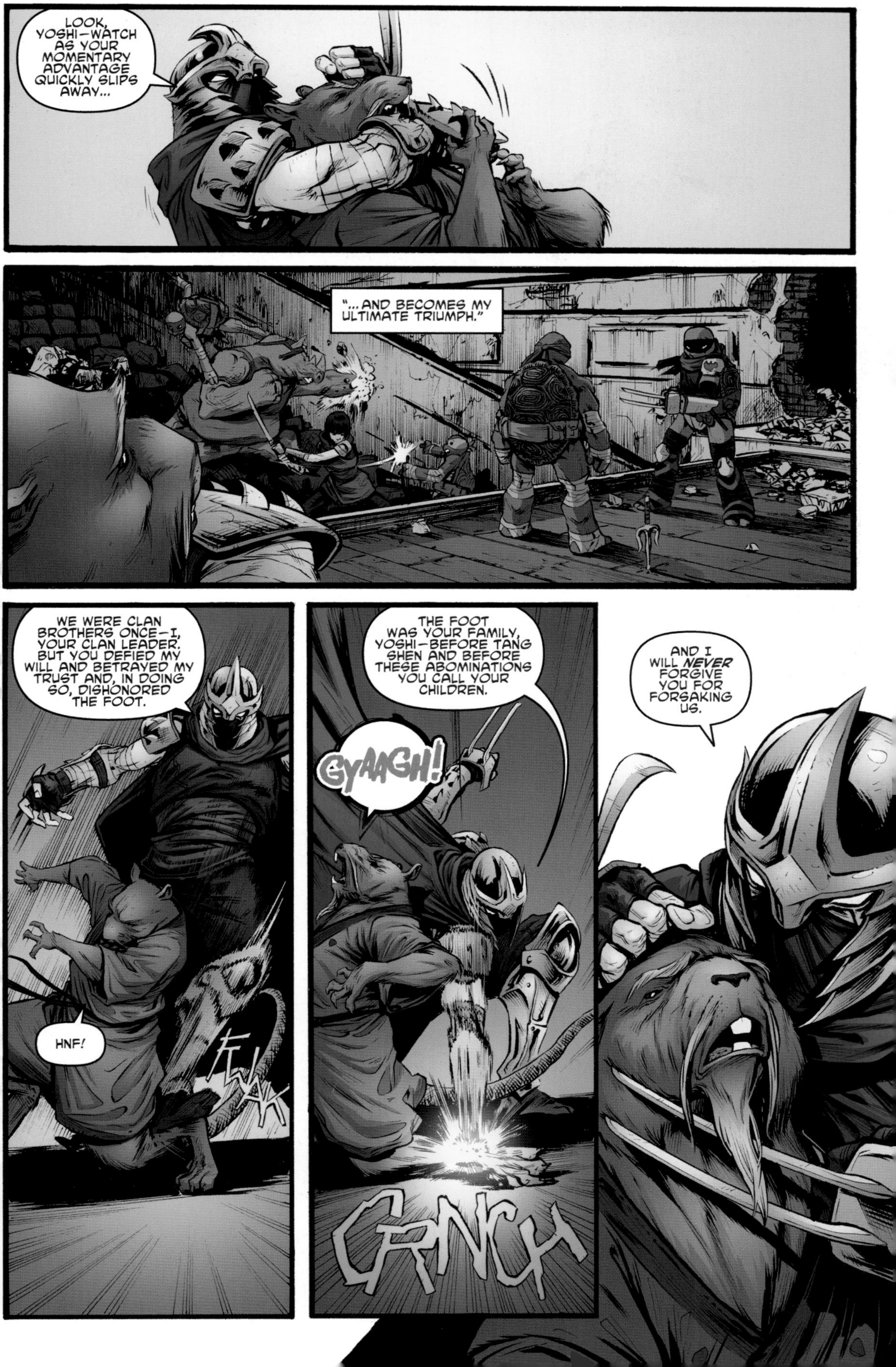
LOOK, YOSHI—WATCH AS YOUR MOMENTARY ADVANTAGE QUICKLY SLIPS AWAY...
"...AND BECOMES MY ULTIMATE TRIUMPH."
WE WERE CLAN BROTHERS ONCE—I, YOUR CLAN LEADER. BUT YOU DEFIED MY WILL AND BETRAYED MY TRUST AND, IN DOING SO, DISHONORED THE FOOT.
HNF!
THE FOOT WAS YOUR FAMILY, YOSHI—BEFORE TANG SHEN AND BEFORE THESE ABOMINATIONS YOU CALL YOUR CHILDREN.
GYAAGH!
CRNCH
AND I WILL *NEVER* FORGIVE YOU FOR FORSAKING US.

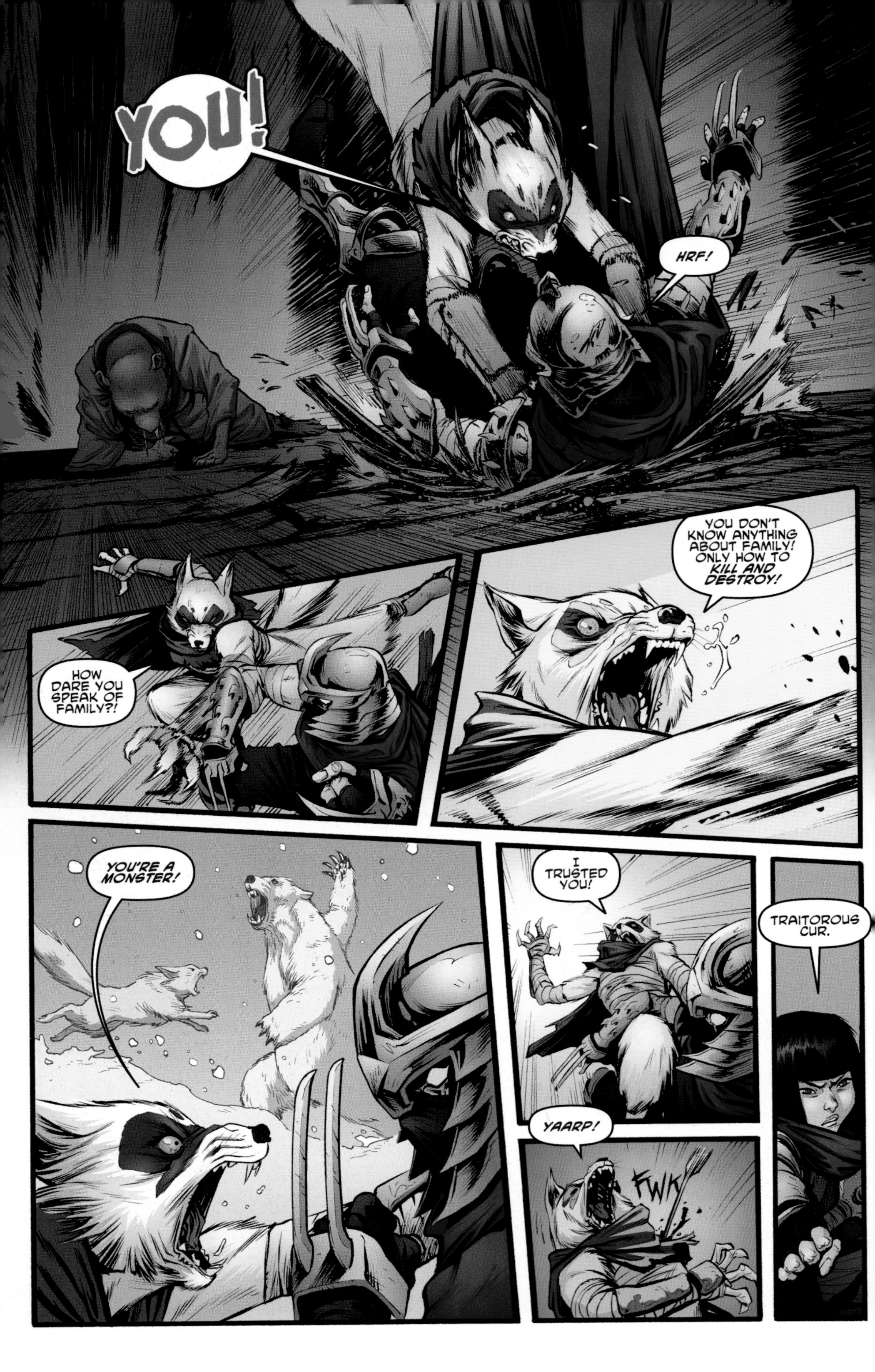
YOU!
HRF!
HOW DARE YOU SPEAK OF FAMILY?!
YOU DON'T KNOW ANYTHING ABOUT FAMILY! ONLY HOW TO KILL AND DESTROY!
YOU'RE A MONSTER!
I TRUSTED YOU!
YAARP!
FWK
TRAITOROUS CUR.

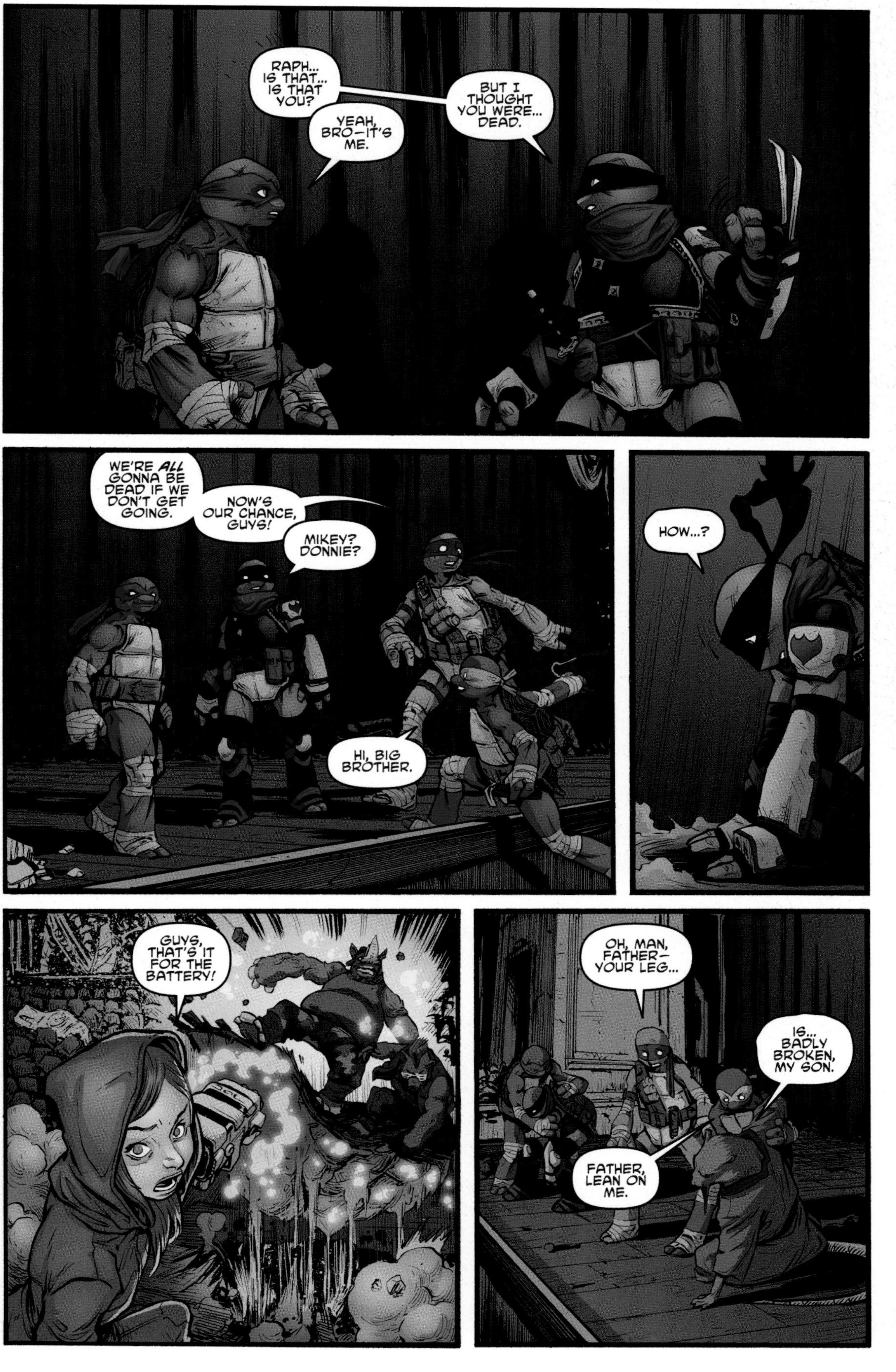
RAPH... IS THAT... IS THAT YOU?
BUT I THOUGHT YOU WERE... DEAD.
YEAH, BRO—IT'S ME.
WE'RE ALL GONNA BE DEAD IF WE DON'T GET GOING.
NOW'S OUR CHANCE, GUYS!
MIKEY? DONNIE?
HI, BIG BROTHER.
HOW...?
GUYS, THAT'S IT FOR THE BATTERY!
OH, MAN, FATHER—YOUR LEG...
IS... BADLY BROKEN, MY SON.
FATHER, LEAN ON ME.

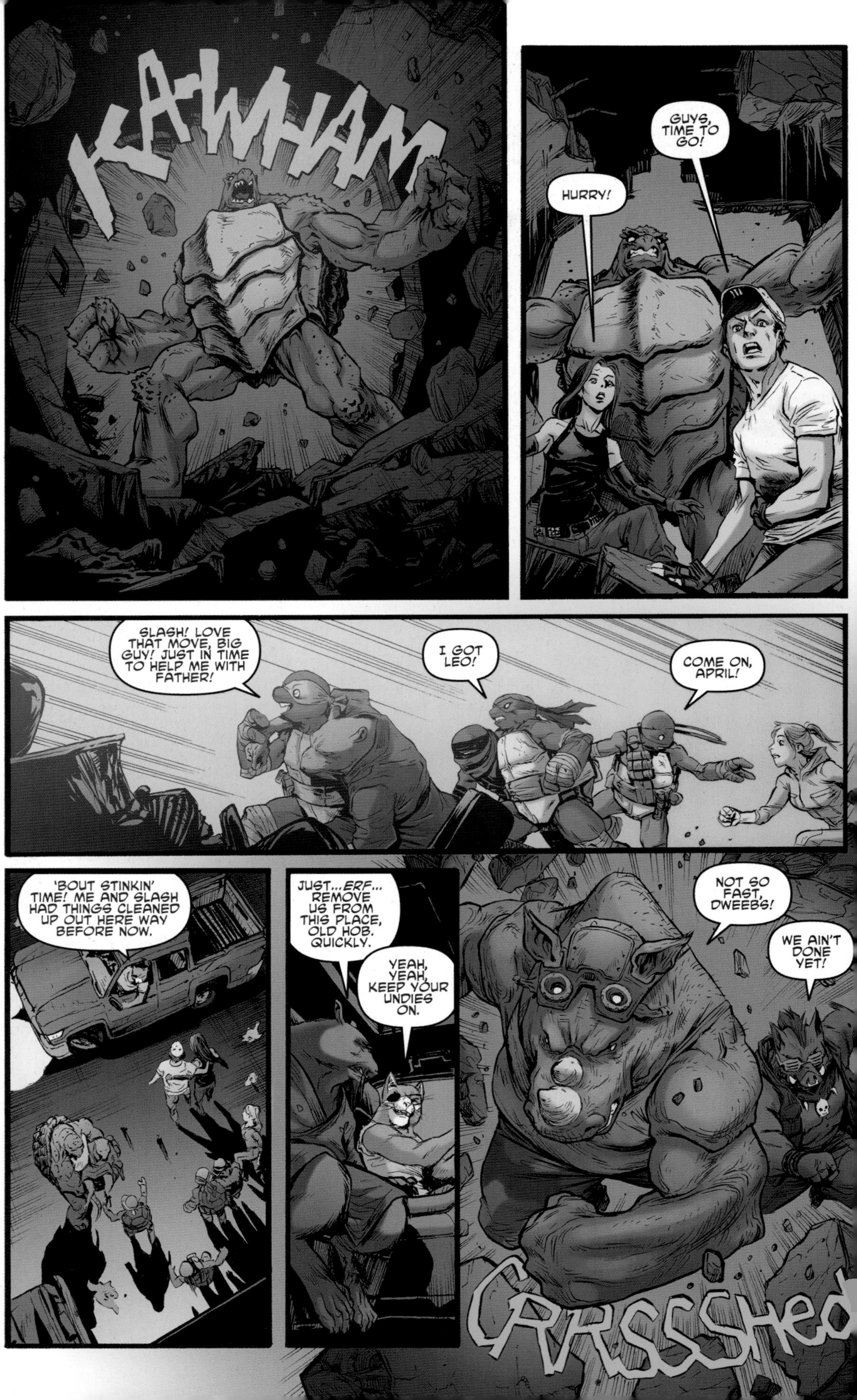
KA-WHAM
GUYS, TIME TO GO!
HURRY!
SLASH! LOVE THAT MOVE, BIG GUY! JUST IN TIME TO HELP ME WITH FATHER!
I GOT LEO!
COME ON, APRIL!
'BOUT STINKIN' TIME! ME AND SLASH HAD THINGS CLEANED UP OUT HERE WAY BEFORE NOW.
JUST...ERF... REMOVE US FROM THIS PLACE, OLD HOB. QUICKLY.
YEAH, YEAH, KEEP YOUR UNDIES ON.
NOT SO FAST, DWEEBS!
WE AIN'T DONE YET!
CRRSSSHED

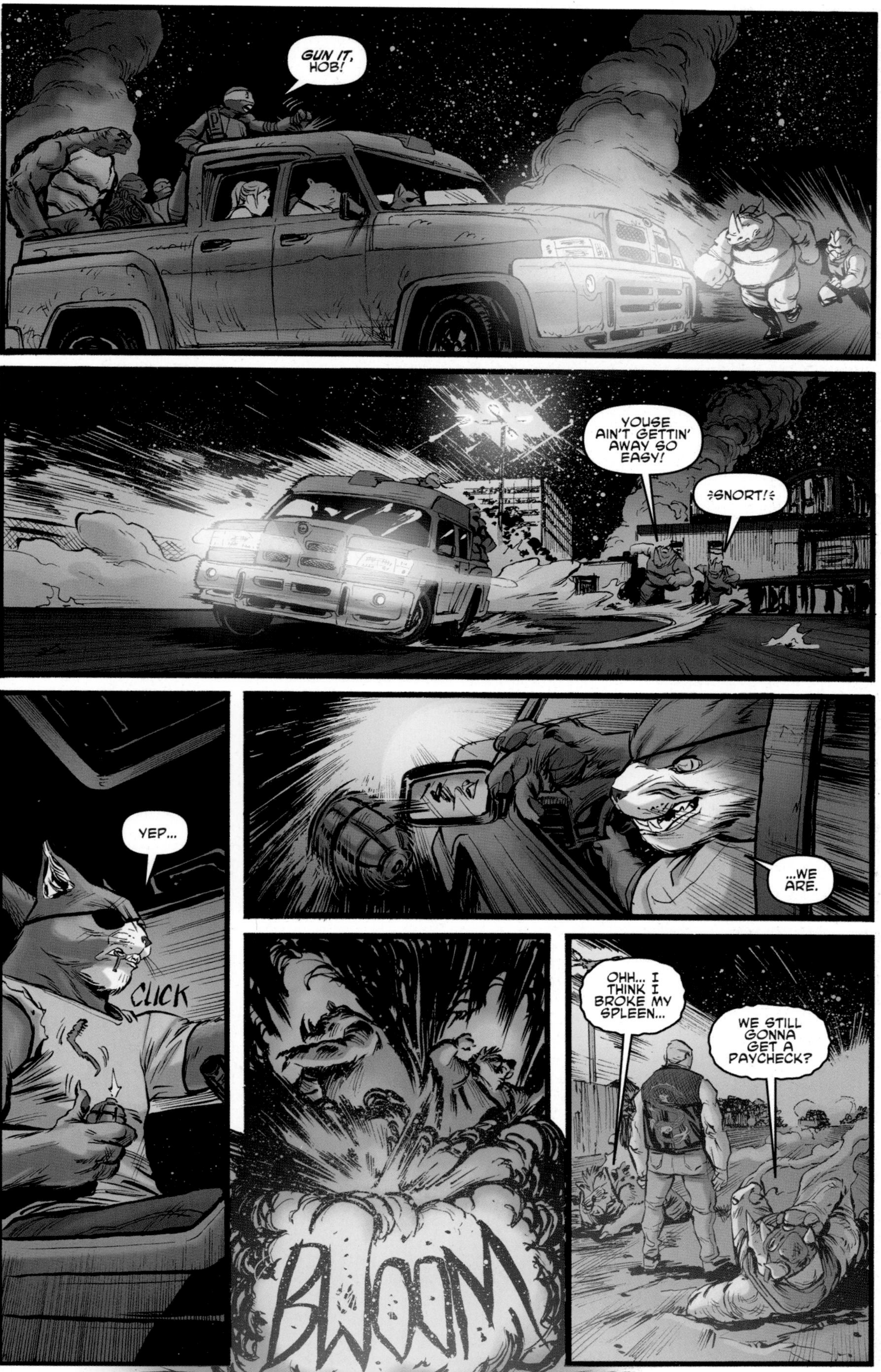
GUN IT, HOB!
YOUSE AIN'T GETTIN' AWAY SO EASY!
≈SNORT!≈
YEP...
CLICK
...WE ARE.
BWOOM
OHH... I THINK I BROKE MY SPLEEN...
WE STILL GONNA GET A PAYCHECK?

LATER.

HERE IS OUR TRIBUTE TO YOU, SHREDDER, AS YOU REQUESTED. WE HOPE WE CAN PUT THE SAVATE FIASCO BEHIND US AND MOVE FORWARD IN A MORE COOPERATIVE FASHION.

EXCELLENT. IN TIME, I'M CONFIDENT YOU WILL FIND THIS TO BE A MUTUALLY BENEFICIAL ARRANGEMENT FOR ALL INVOLVED, ANTONIO.

YOU ARE DISMISSED.

KARAI, I WOULD SPEAK WITH YOU NOW.

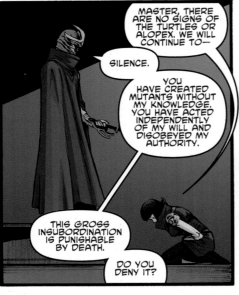

MASTER, THERE ARE NO SIGNS OF THE TURTLES OR ALOPEX. WE WILL CONTINUE TO—

SILENCE.

YOU HAVE CREATED MUTANTS WITHOUT MY KNOWLEDGE. YOU HAVE ACTED INDEPENDENTLY OF MY WILL AND DISOBEYED MY AUTHORITY.

THIS GROSS INSUBORDINATION IS PUNISHABLE BY DEATH.

DO YOU DENY IT?

I... I DO NOT.

BUT ALL I DID, I DID IN THE NAME OF THE FOOT.

EVERYTHING I DO... I DO TO HONOR THE CLAN.

I ACCEPT MY FATE.

VERY WELL.

RISE...

...CHUNIN.

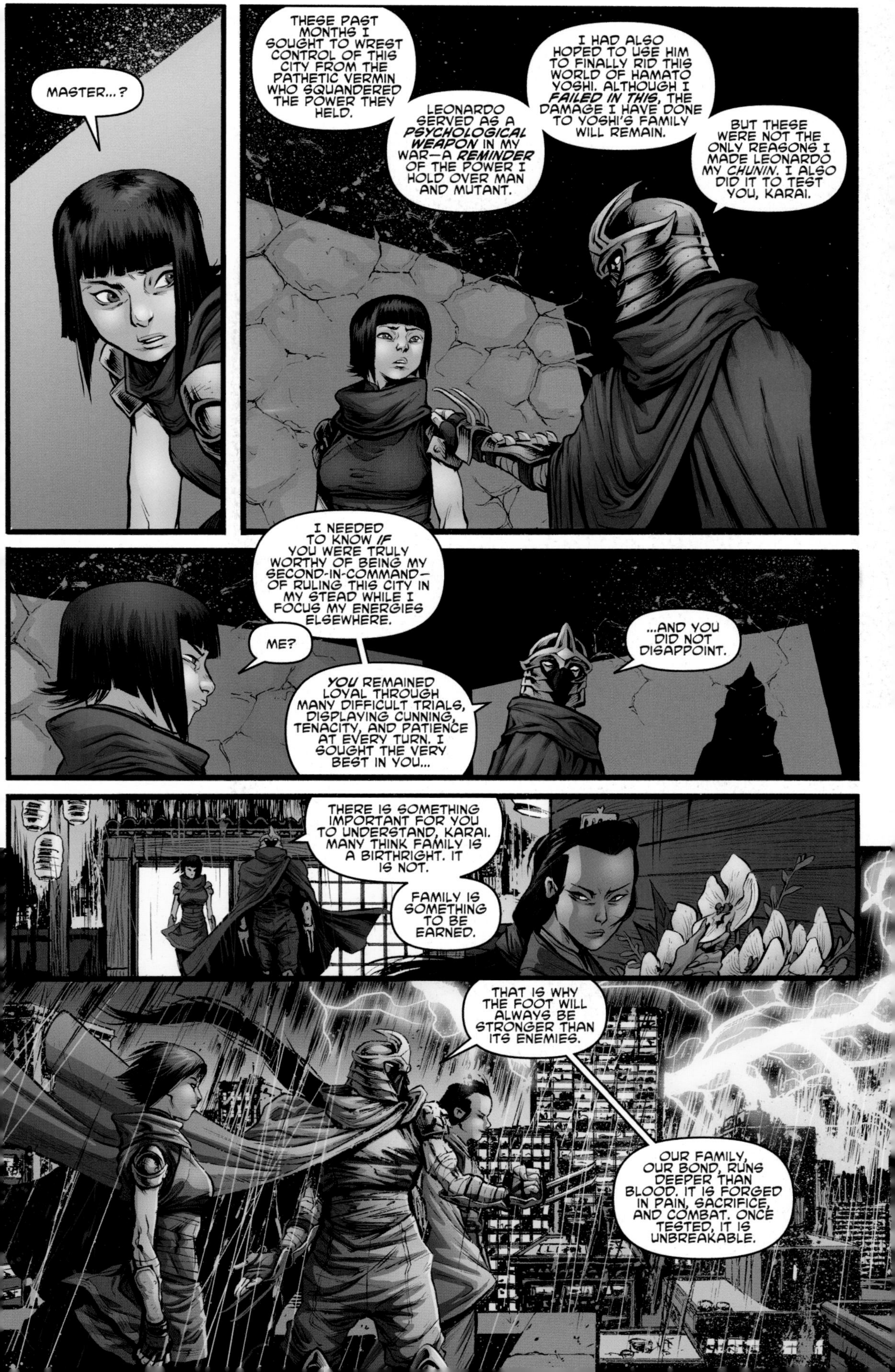
MASTER...?
THESE PAST MONTHS I SOUGHT TO WREST CONTROL OF THIS CITY FROM THE PATHETIC VERMIN WHO SQUANDERED THE POWER THEY HELD.
LEONARDO SERVED AS A PSYCHOLOGICAL WEAPON IN MY WAR—A REMINDER OF THE POWER I HOLD OVER MAN AND MUTANT.
I HAD ALSO HOPED TO USE HIM TO FINALLY RID THIS WORLD OF HAMATO YOSHI. ALTHOUGH I FAILED IN THIS, THE DAMAGE I HAVE DONE TO YOSHI'S FAMILY WILL REMAIN.
BUT THESE WERE NOT THE ONLY REASONS I MADE LEONARDO MY CHUNIN. I ALSO DID IT TO TEST YOU, KARAI.
I NEEDED TO KNOW IF YOU WERE TRULY WORTHY OF BEING MY SECOND-IN-COMMAND—OF RULING THIS CITY IN MY STEAD WHILE I FOCUS MY ENERGIES ELSEWHERE.
ME?
YOU REMAINED LOYAL THROUGH MANY DIFFICULT TRIALS, DISPLAYING CUNNING, TENACITY, AND PATIENCE AT EVERY TURN. I SOUGHT THE VERY BEST IN YOU...
...AND YOU DID NOT DISAPPOINT.
THERE IS SOMETHING IMPORTANT FOR YOU TO UNDERSTAND, KARAI. MANY THINK FAMILY IS A BIRTHRIGHT. IT IS NOT.
FAMILY IS SOMETHING TO BE EARNED.
THAT IS WHY THE FOOT WILL ALWAYS BE STRONGER THAN ITS ENEMIES.
OUR FAMILY, OUR BOND, RUNS DEEPER THAN BLOOD. IT IS FORGED IN PAIN, SACRIFICE, AND COMBAT. ONCE TESTED, IT IS UNBREAKABLE.

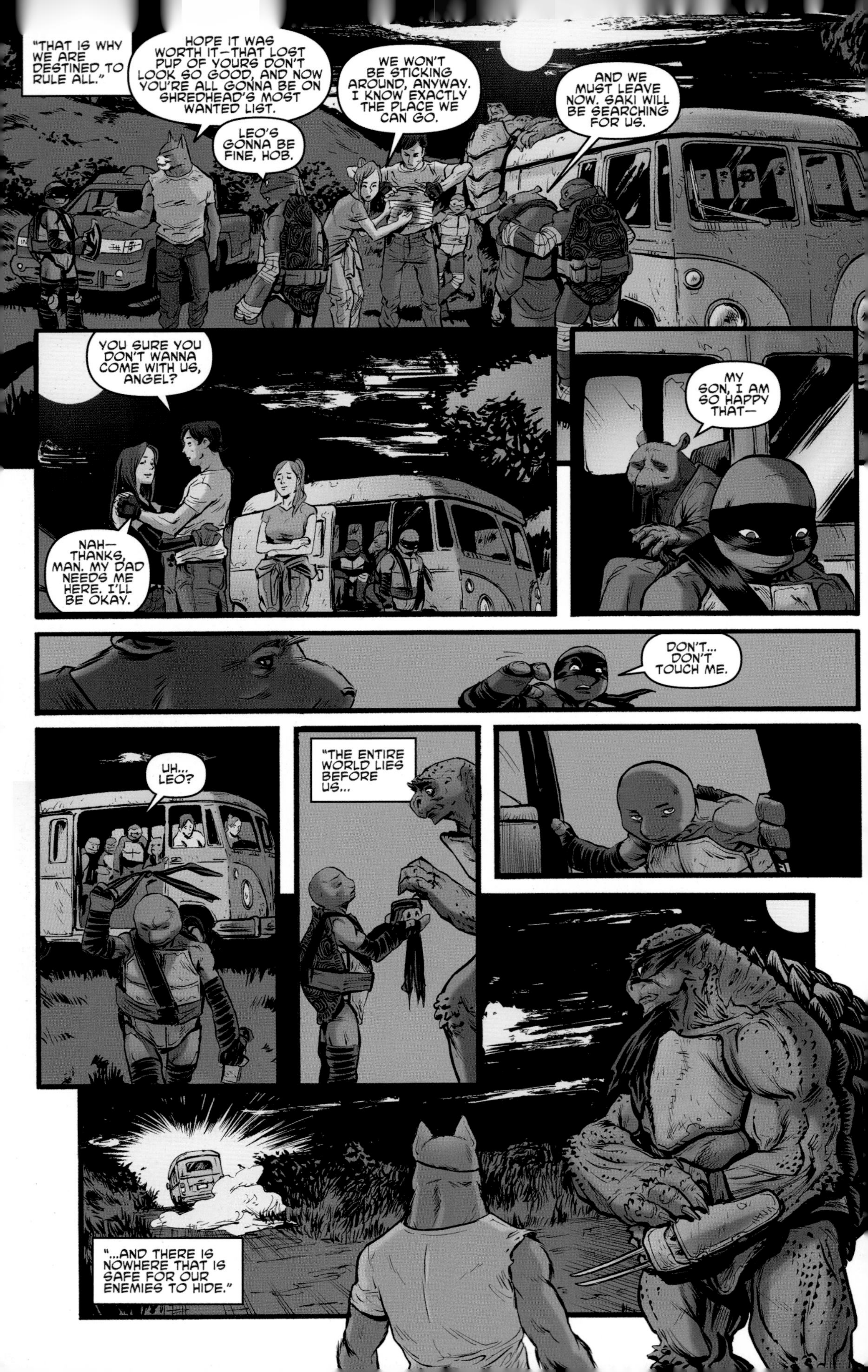
"THAT IS WHY WE ARE DESTINED TO RULE ALL."
HOPE IT WAS WORTH IT—THAT LOST PUP OF YOURS DON'T LOOK SO GOOD, AND NOW YOU'RE ALL GONNA BE ON SHREDHEAD'S MOST WANTED LIST.
LEO'S GONNA BE FINE, HOB.
WE WON'T BE STICKING AROUND, ANYWAY. I KNOW EXACTLY THE PLACE WE CAN GO.
AND WE MUST LEAVE NOW. SAKI WILL BE SEARCHING FOR US.
YOU SURE YOU DON'T WANNA COME WITH US, ANGEL?
NAH— THANKS, MAN. MY DAD NEEDS ME HERE. I'LL BE OKAY.
MY SON, I AM SO HAPPY THAT—
DON'T... DON'T TOUCH ME.
UH... LEO?
"THE ENTIRE WORLD LIES BEFORE US...
"...AND THERE IS NOWHERE THAT IS SAFE FOR OUR ENEMIES TO HIDE."

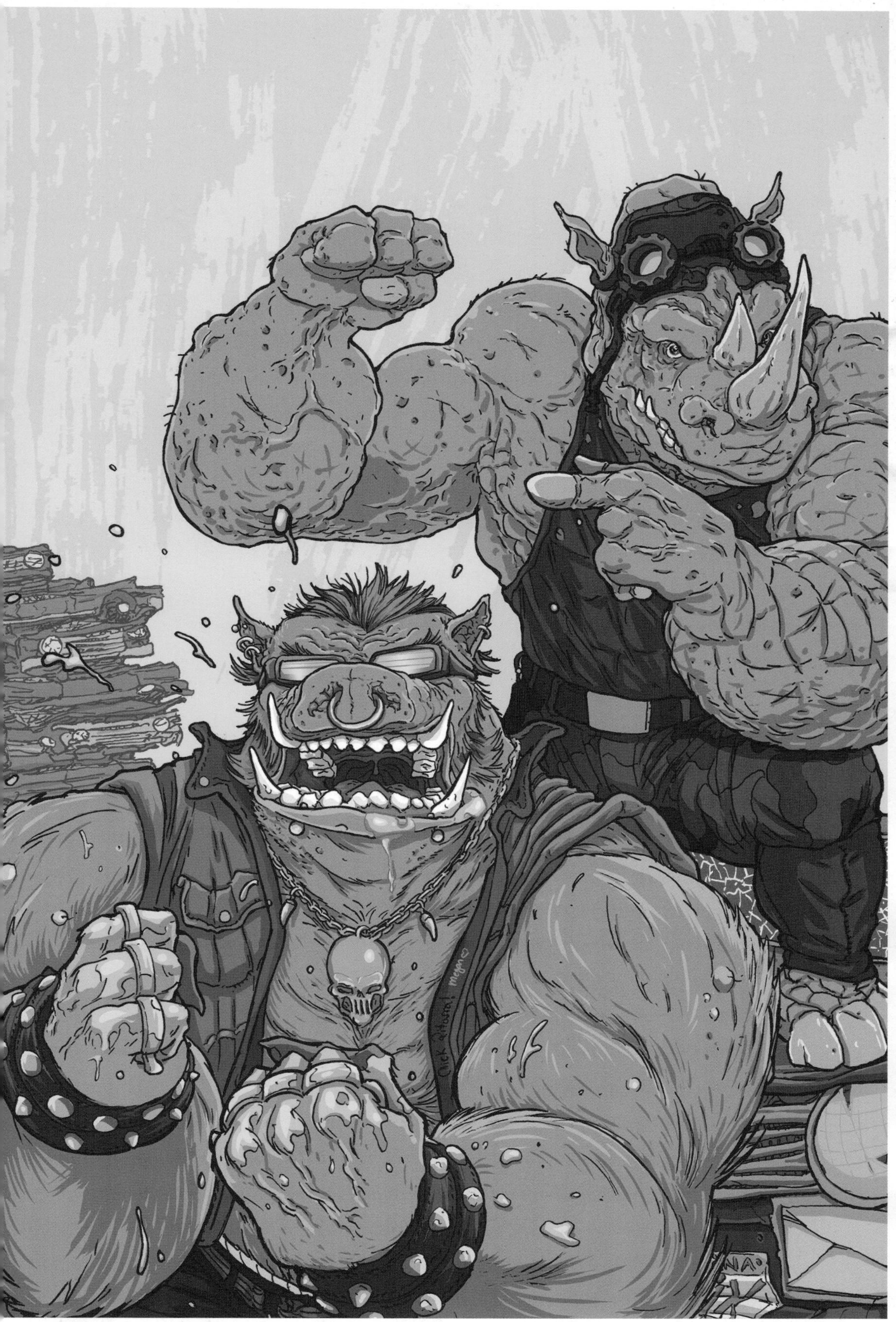

Cover by NICK PITARRA
Colors by MEGAN WILSON

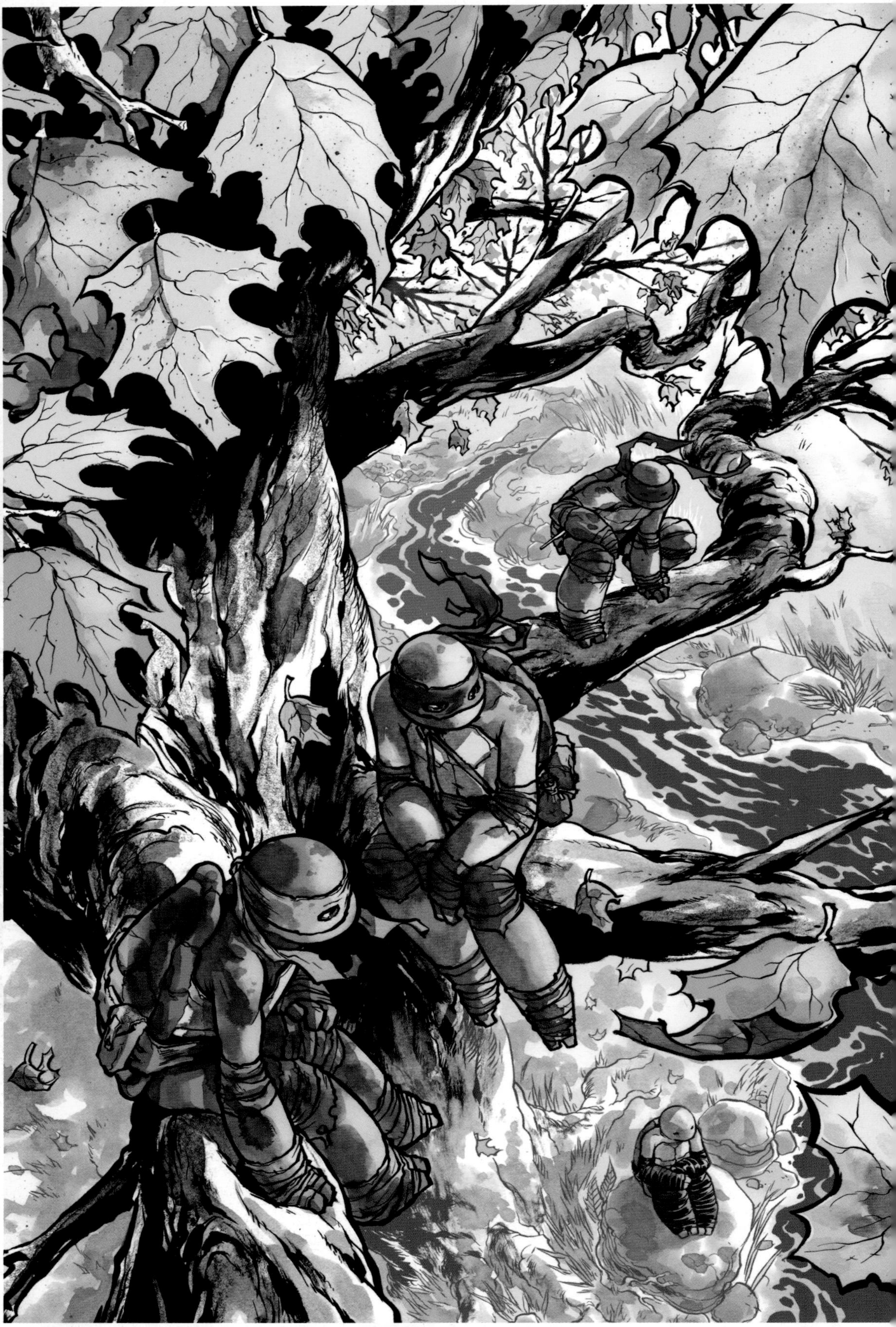

Cover by SOPHIE CAMPBELL

TMNT #29

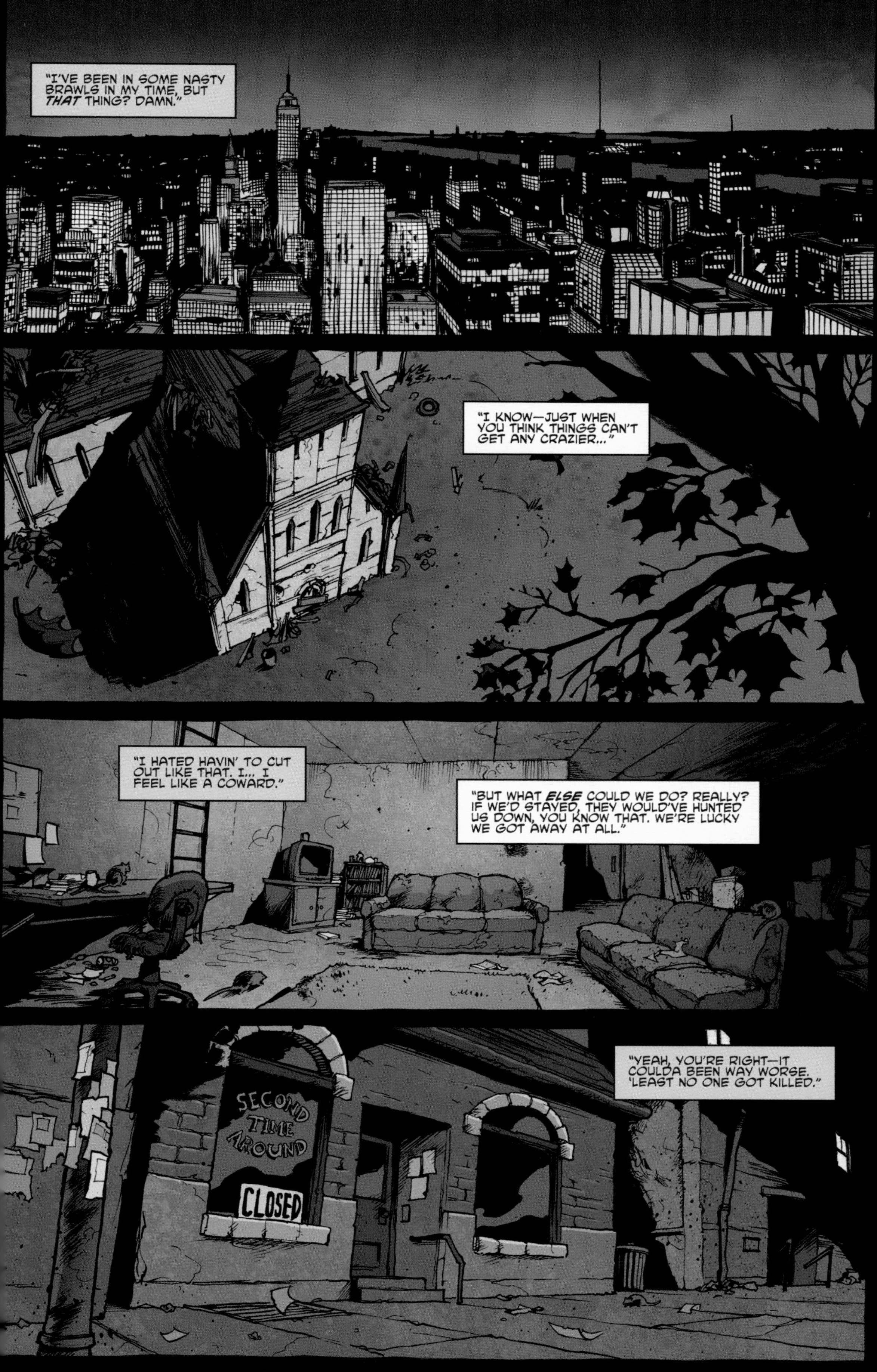
"I'VE BEEN IN SOME NASTY BRAWLS IN MY TIME, BUT *THAT* THING? DAMN."
"I KNOW—JUST WHEN YOU THINK THINGS CAN'T GET ANY CRAZIER..."
"I HATED HAVIN' TO CUT OUT LIKE THAT. I... I FEEL LIKE A COWARD."
"BUT WHAT *ELSE* COULD WE DO? REALLY? IF WE'D STAYED, THEY WOULD'VE HUNTED US DOWN, YOU KNOW THAT. WE'RE LUCKY WE GOT AWAY AT ALL."
SECOND TIME AROUND
CLOSED
"YEAH, YOU'RE RIGHT—IT COULDA BEEN WAY WORSE. 'LEAST NO ONE GOT KILLED."

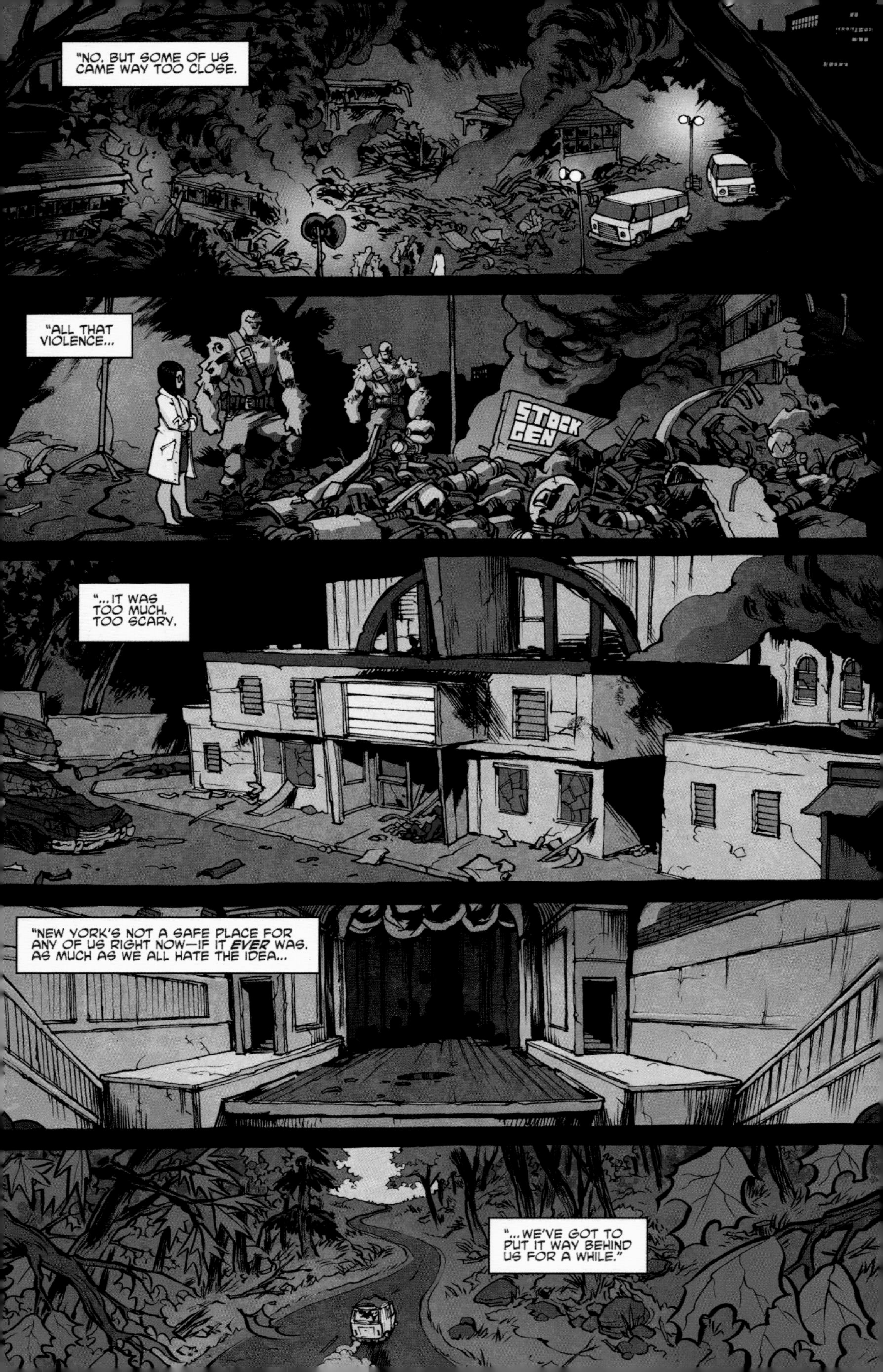
"NO. BUT SOME OF US CAME WAY TOO CLOSE.
"ALL THAT VIOLENCE...
STOCK GEN
"...IT WAS TOO MUCH. TOO SCARY.
"NEW YORK'S NOT A SAFE PLACE FOR ANY OF US RIGHT NOW—IF IT *EVER* WAS. AS MUCH AS WE ALL HATE THE IDEA...
"...WE'VE GOT TO PUT IT WAY BEHIND US FOR A WHILE."

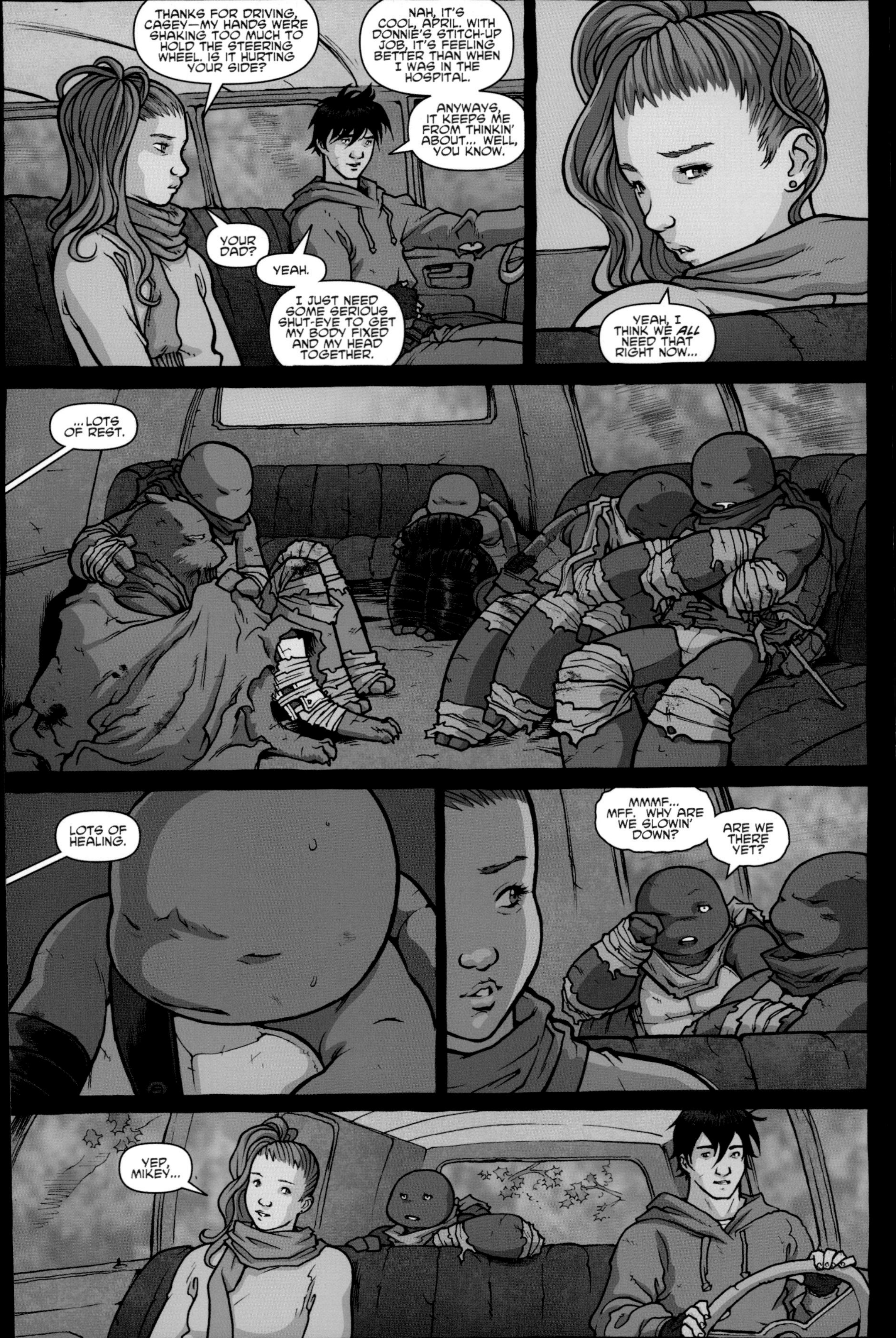
THANKS FOR DRIVING, CASEY—MY HANDS WERE SHAKING TOO MUCH TO HOLD THE STEERING WHEEL. IS IT HURTING YOUR SIDE?
NAH, IT'S COOL, APRIL. WITH DONNIE'S STITCH-UP JOB, IT'S FEELING BETTER THAN WHEN I WAS IN THE HOSPITAL.
ANYWAYS, IT KEEPS ME FROM THINKIN' ABOUT... WELL, YOU KNOW.
YOUR DAD?
YEAH.
I JUST NEED SOME SERIOUS SHUT-EYE TO GET MY BODY FIXED AND MY HEAD TOGETHER.
YEAH, I THINK WE *ALL* NEED THAT RIGHT NOW...
...LOTS OF REST.
LOTS OF HEALING.
MMMF... MFF. WHY ARE WE SLOWIN' DOWN?
ARE WE THERE YET?
YEP, MIKEY...

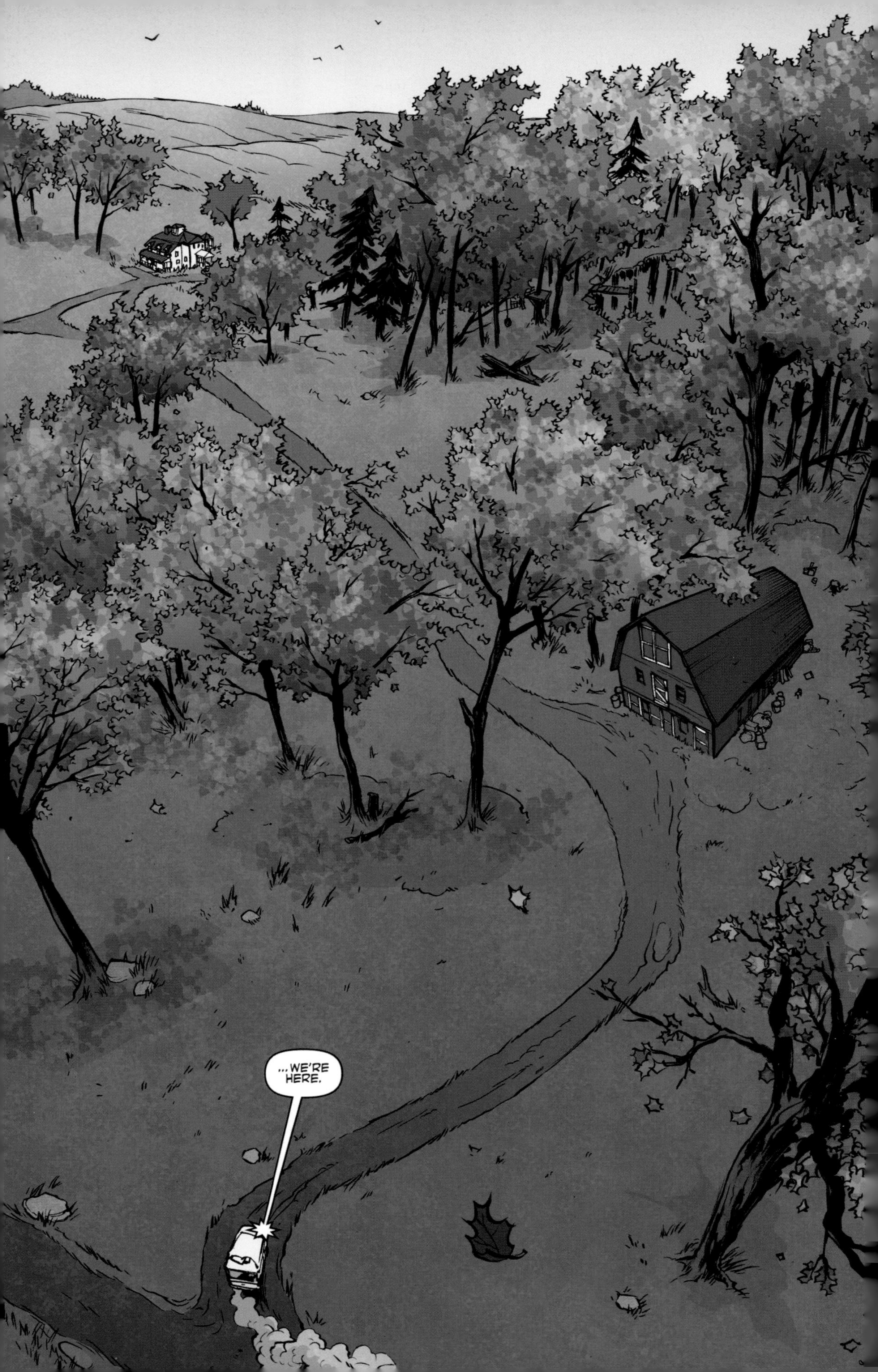
...WE'RE HERE.

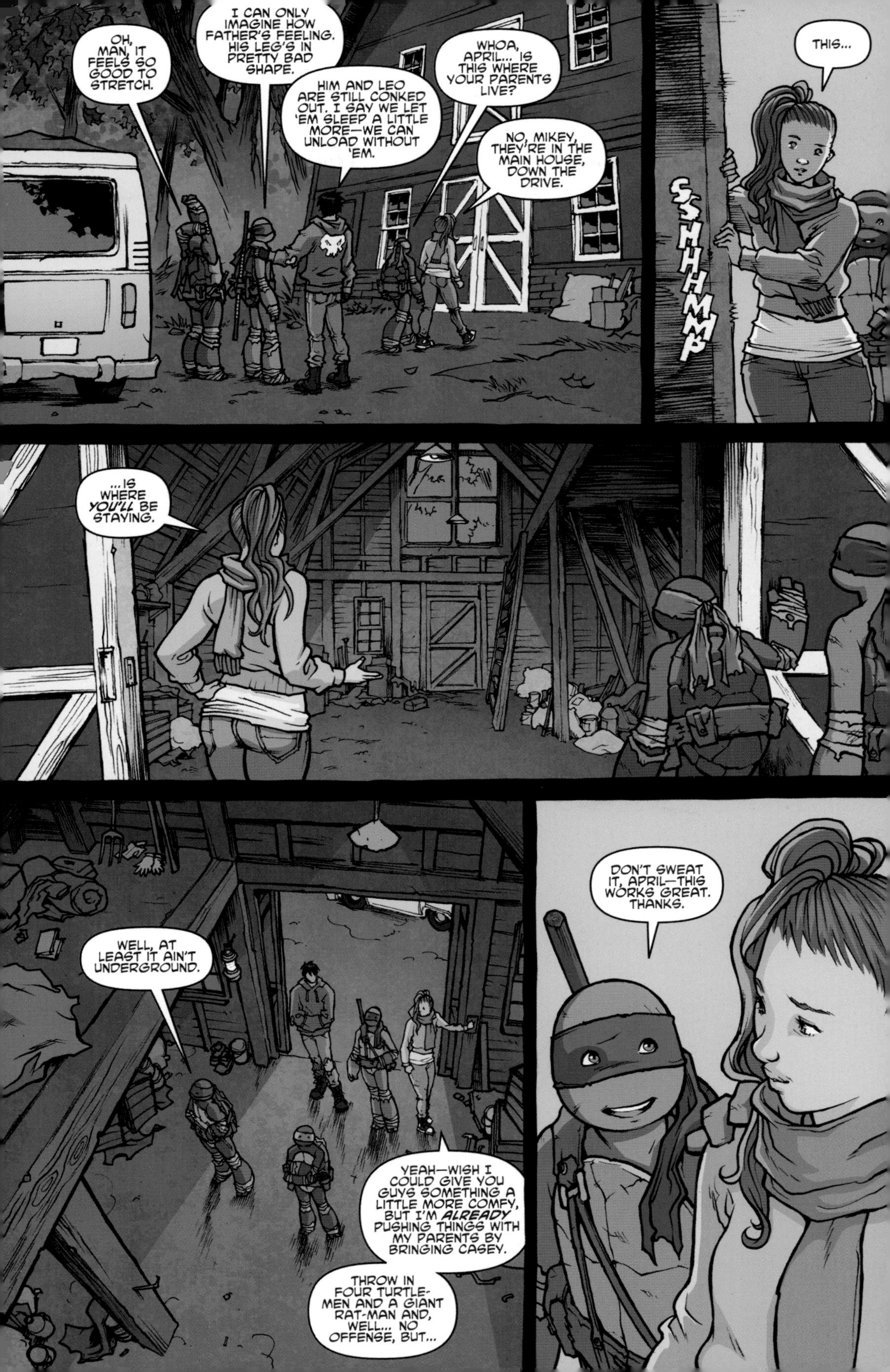
OH, MAN, IT FEELS SO GOOD TO STRETCH.
I CAN ONLY IMAGINE HOW FATHER'S FEELING. HIS LEG'S IN PRETTY BAD SHAPE.
HIM AND LEO ARE STILL CONKED OUT. I SAY WE LET 'EM SLEEP A LITTLE MORE—WE CAN UNLOAD WITHOUT 'EM.
WHOA, APRIL... IS THIS WHERE YOUR PARENTS LIVE?
NO, MIKEY, THEY'RE IN THE MAIN HOUSE, DOWN THE DRIVE.
THIS...
SSHHHMMP
...IS WHERE YOU'LL BE STAYING.
WELL, AT LEAST IT AIN'T UNDERGROUND.
YEAH—WISH I COULD GIVE YOU GUYS SOMETHING A LITTLE MORE COMFY, BUT I'M ALREADY PUSHING THINGS WITH MY PARENTS BY BRINGING CASEY.
THROW IN FOUR TURTLE-MEN AND A GIANT RAT-MAN AND, WELL... NO OFFENSE, BUT...
DON'T SWEAT IT, APRIL—THIS WORKS GREAT. THANKS.

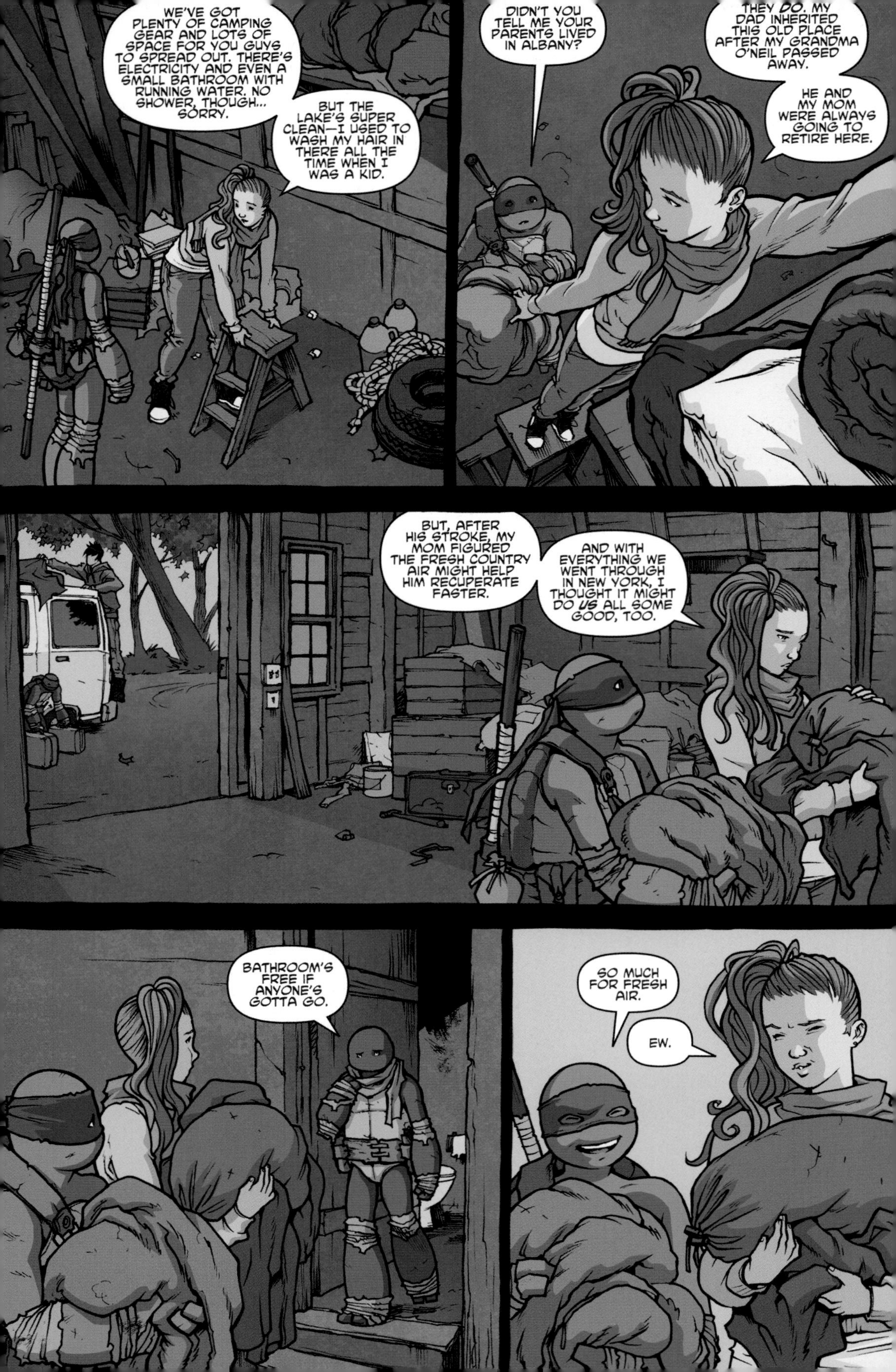
WE'VE GOT PLENTY OF CAMPING GEAR AND LOTS OF SPACE FOR YOU GUYS TO SPREAD OUT. THERE'S ELECTRICITY AND EVEN A SMALL BATHROOM WITH RUNNING WATER. NO SHOWER, THOUGH... SORRY.
BUT THE LAKE'S SUPER CLEAN—I USED TO WASH MY HAIR IN THERE ALL THE TIME WHEN I WAS A KID.
DIDN'T YOU TELL ME YOUR PARENTS LIVED IN ALBANY?
THEY DO. MY DAD INHERITED THIS OLD PLACE AFTER MY GRANDMA O'NEIL PASSED AWAY.
HE AND MY MOM WERE ALWAYS GOING TO RETIRE HERE.
BUT, AFTER HIS STROKE, MY MOM FIGURED THE FRESH COUNTRY AIR MIGHT HELP HIM RECUPERATE FASTER.
AND WITH EVERYTHING WE WENT THROUGH IN NEW YORK, I THOUGHT IT MIGHT DO US ALL SOME GOOD, TOO.
BATHROOM'S FREE IF ANYONE'S GOTTA GO.
SO MUCH FOR FRESH AIR.
EW.

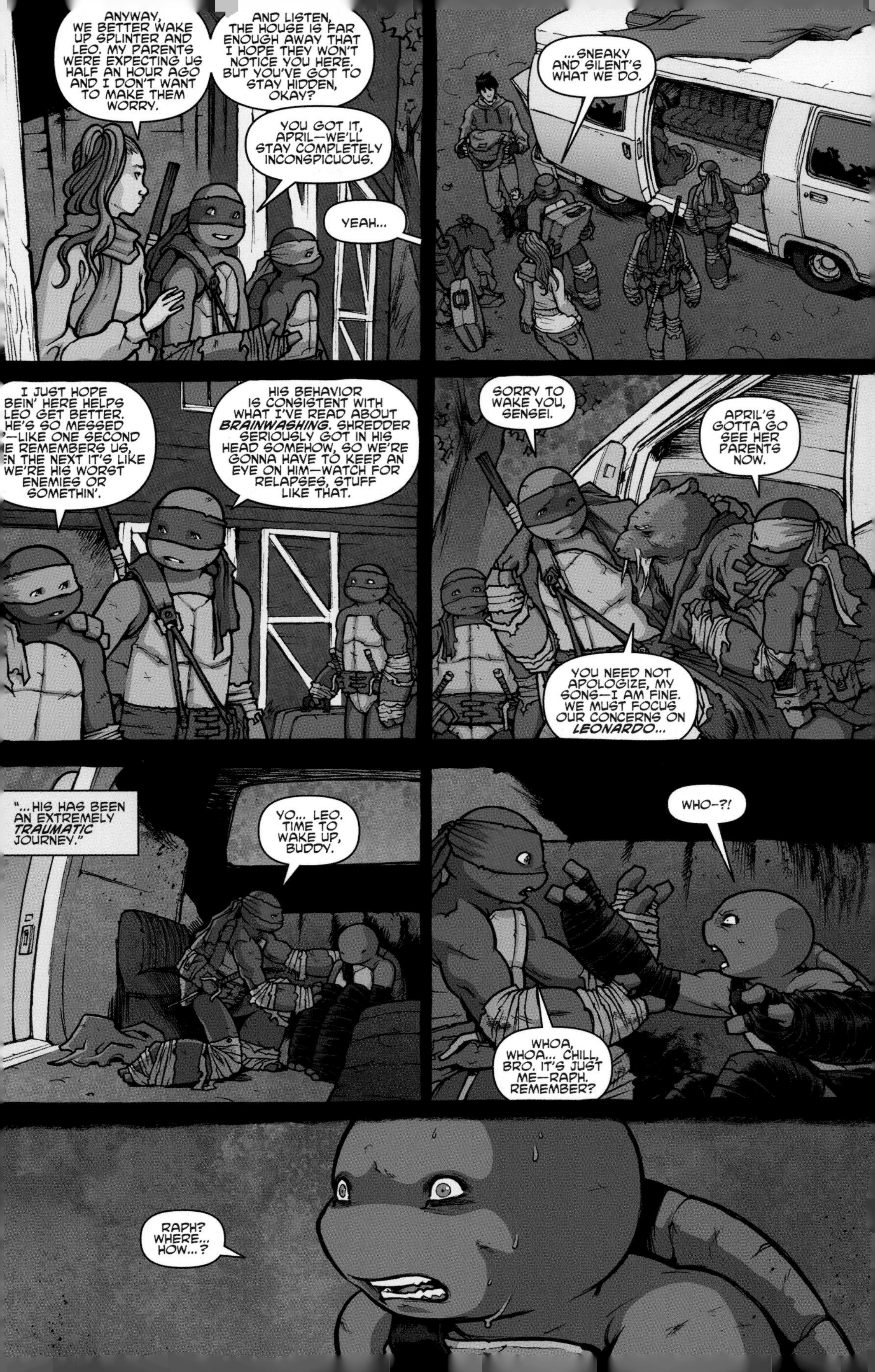
ANYWAY, WE BETTER WAKE UP SPLINTER AND LEO. MY PARENTS WERE EXPECTING US HALF AN HOUR AGO AND I DON'T WANT TO MAKE THEM WORRY.
AND LISTEN, THE HOUSE IS FAR ENOUGH AWAY THAT I HOPE THEY WON'T NOTICE YOU HERE. BUT YOU'VE GOT TO STAY HIDDEN, OKAY?
YOU GOT IT, APRIL—WE'LL STAY COMPLETELY INCONSPICUOUS.
YEAH...
...SNEAKY AND SILENT'S WHAT WE DO.
I JUST HOPE BEIN' HERE HELPS LEO GET BETTER. HE'S SO MESSED '—LIKE ONE SECOND E REMEMBERS US, EN THE NEXT IT'S LIKE WE'RE HIS WORST ENEMIES OR SOMETHIN'.
HIS BEHAVIOR IS CONSISTENT WITH WHAT I'VE READ ABOUT BRAINWASHING. SHREDDER SERIOUSLY GOT IN HIS HEAD SOMEHOW, SO WE'RE GONNA HAVE TO KEEP AN EYE ON HIM—WATCH FOR RELAPSES, STUFF LIKE THAT.
SORRY TO WAKE YOU, SENSEI.
APRIL'S GOTTA GO SEE HER PARENTS NOW.
YOU NEED NOT APOLOGIZE, MY SONS—I AM FINE. WE MUST FOCUS OUR CONCERNS ON LEONARDO...
"...HIS HAS BEEN AN EXTREMELY TRAUMATIC JOURNEY."
YO... LEO. TIME TO WAKE UP, BUDDY.
WHO-?!
WHOA, WHOA... CHILL, BRO. IT'S JUST ME—RAPH. REMEMBER?
RAPH? WHERE... HOW...?

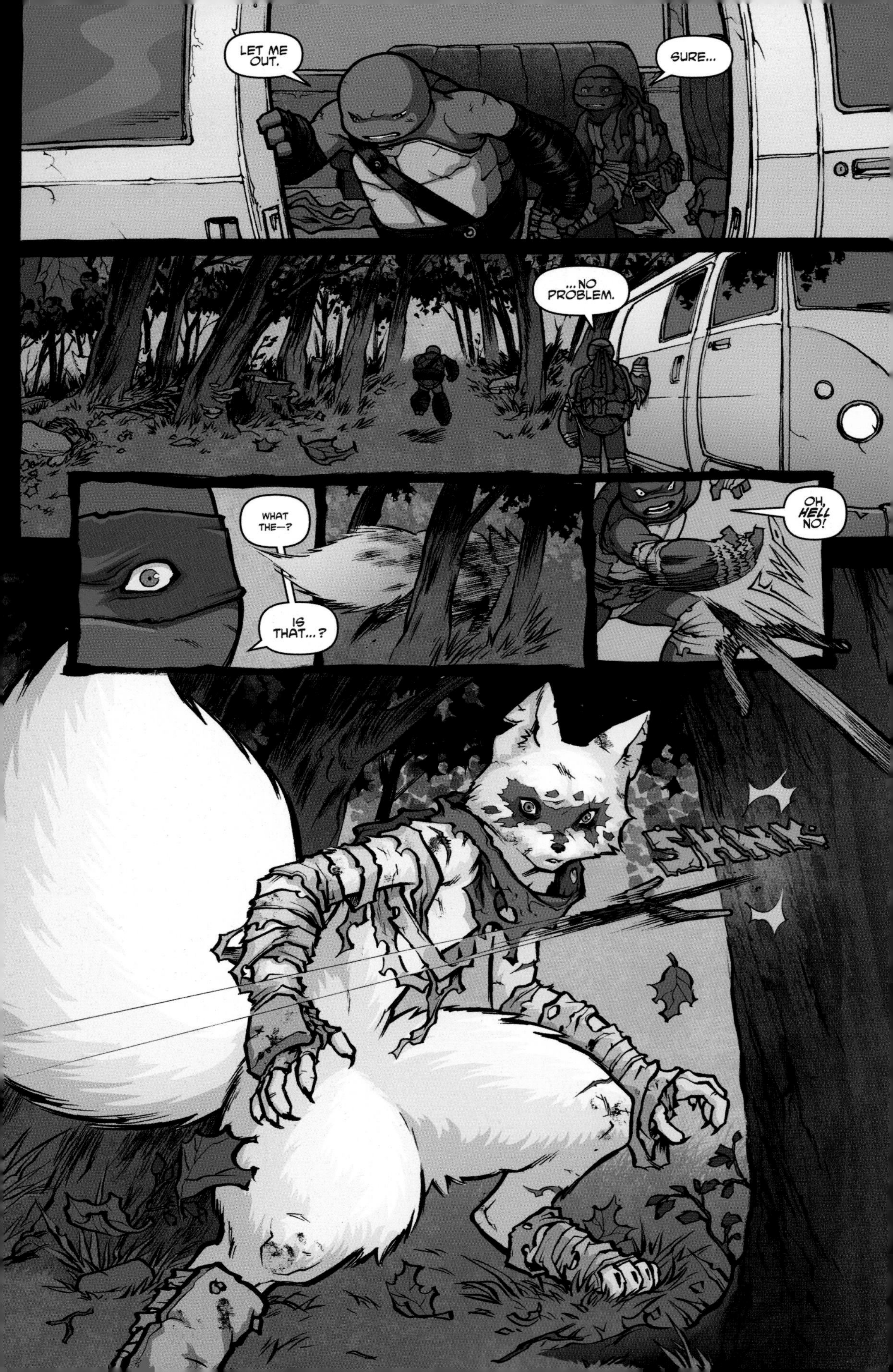
LET ME OUT.
SURE...
...NO PROBLEM.
WHAT THE--?
IS THAT...?
OH, HELL NO!
SHNK!

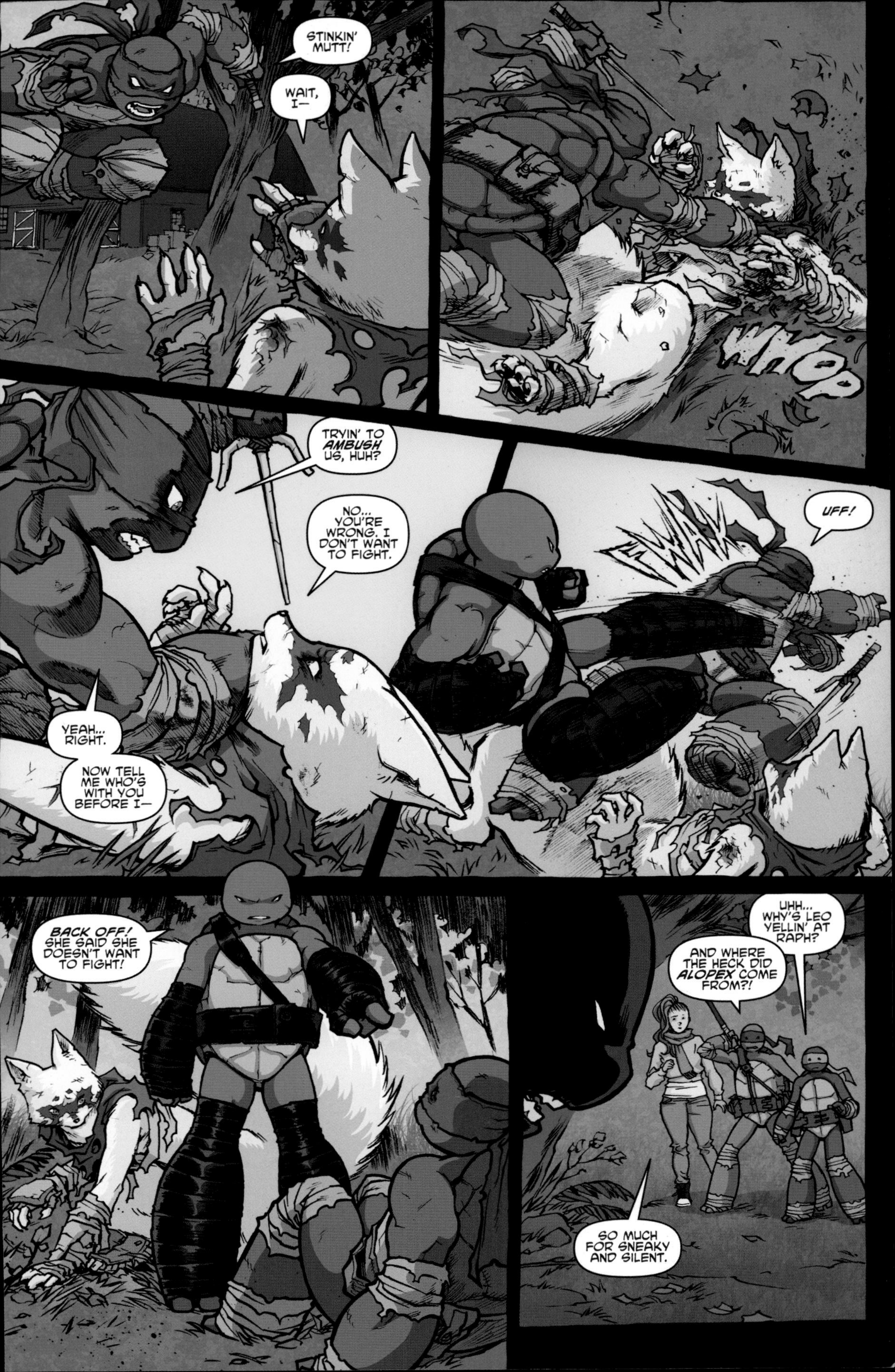
STINKIN' MUTT!
WAIT, I—
WHOP
TRYIN' TO AMBUSH US, HUH?
NO... YOU'RE WRONG. I DON'T WANT TO FIGHT.
YEAH... RIGHT.
NOW TELL ME WHO'S WITH YOU BEFORE I—
WAK
UFF!
BACK OFF! SHE SAID SHE DOESN'T WANT TO FIGHT!
UHH... WHY'S LEO YELLIN' AT RAPH?
AND WHERE THE HECK DID ALOPEX COME FROM?!
SO MUCH FOR SNEAKY AND SILENT.

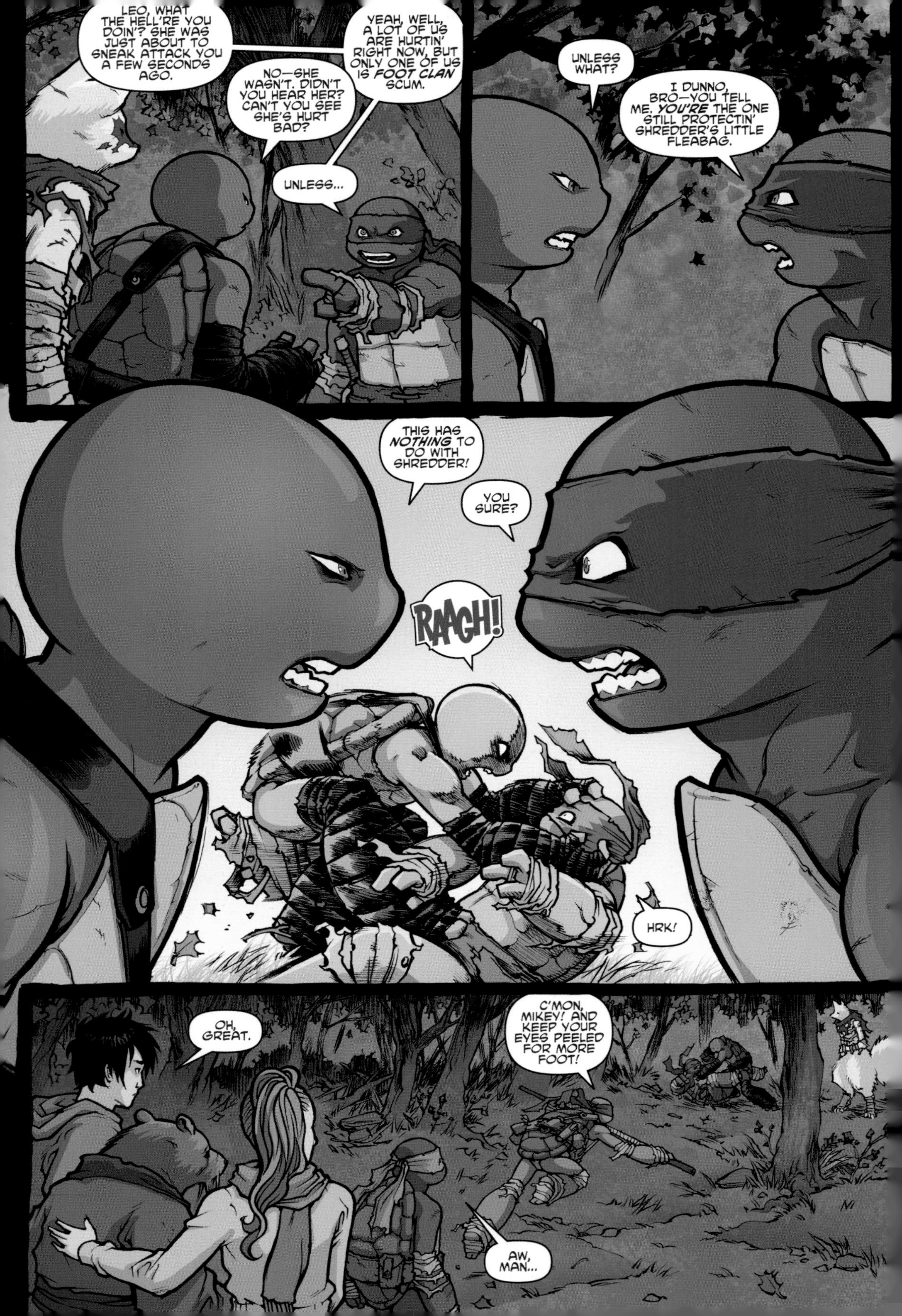
LEO, WHAT THE HELL'RE YOU DOIN'? SHE WAS JUST ABOUT TO SNEAK ATTACK YOU A FEW SECONDS AGO.
NO—SHE WASN'T. DIDN'T YOU HEAR HER? CAN'T YOU SEE SHE'S HURT BAD?
YEAH, WELL, A LOT OF US ARE HURTIN' RIGHT NOW, BUT ONLY ONE OF US IS FOOT CLAN SCUM.
UNLESS...
UNLESS WHAT?
I DUNNO, BRO—YOU TELL ME, YOU'RE THE ONE STILL PROTECTIN' SHREDDER'S LITTLE FLEABAG.
THIS HAS NOTHING TO DO WITH SHREDDER!
YOU SURE?
RAAGH!
HRK!
OH, GREAT.
C'MON, MIKEY! AND KEEP YOUR EYES PEELED FOR MORE FOOT!
AW, MAN...

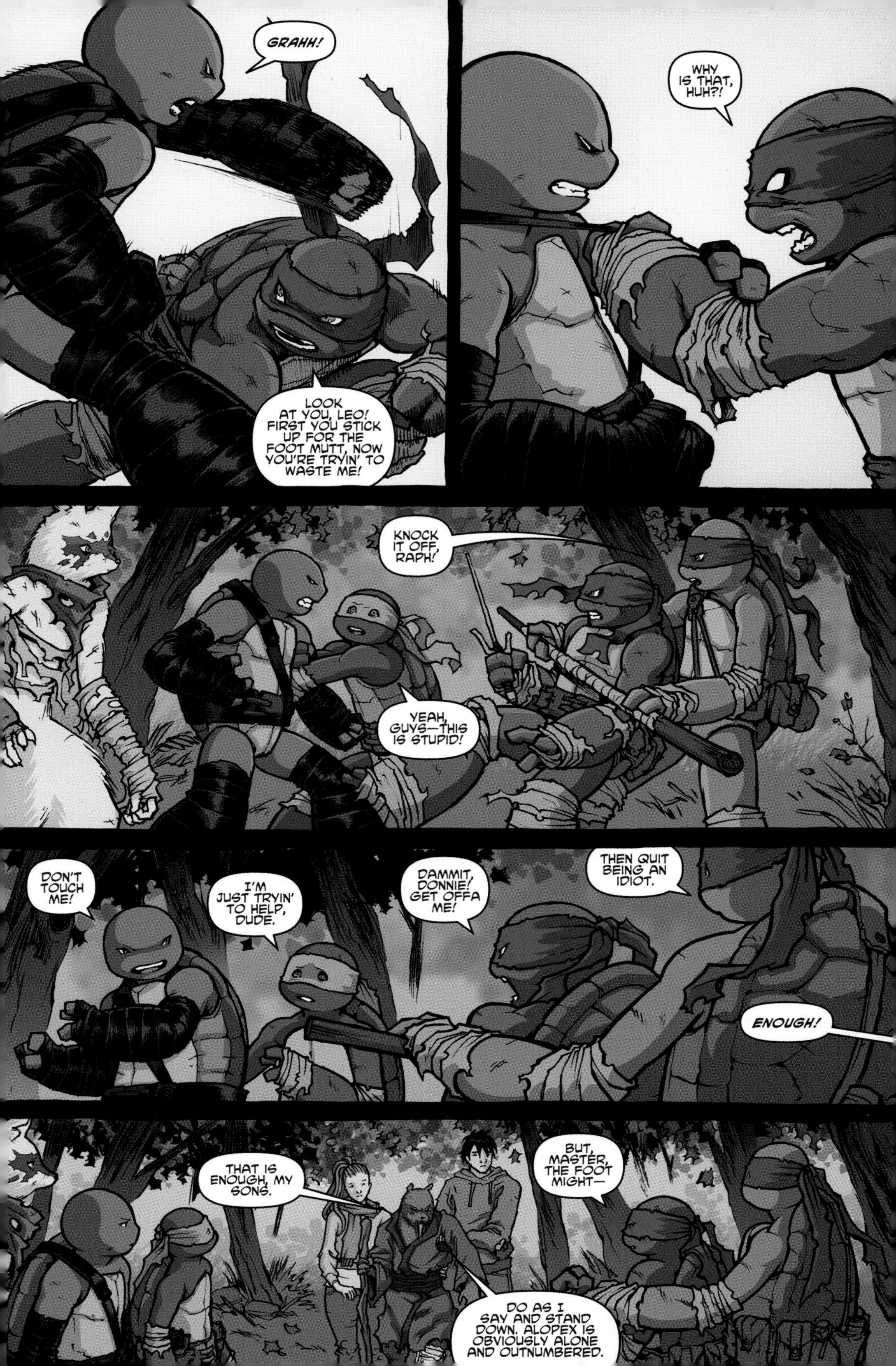
GRAHH!
LOOK AT YOU, LEO! FIRST YOU STICK UP FOR THE FOOT MUTT, NOW YOU'RE TRYIN' TO WASTE ME!
WHY IS THAT, HUH?!
KNOCK IT OFF, RAPH!
YEAH, GUYS—THIS IS STUPID!
DON'T TOUCH ME!
I'M JUST TRYIN' TO HELP, DUDE.
DAMMIT, DONNIE! GET OFFA ME!
THEN QUIT BEING AN IDIOT.
ENOUGH!
THAT IS ENOUGH, MY SONS.
BUT, MASTER, THE FOOT MIGHT—
DO AS I SAY AND STAND DOWN. ALOPEX IS OBVIOUSLY ALONE AND OUTNUMBERED.

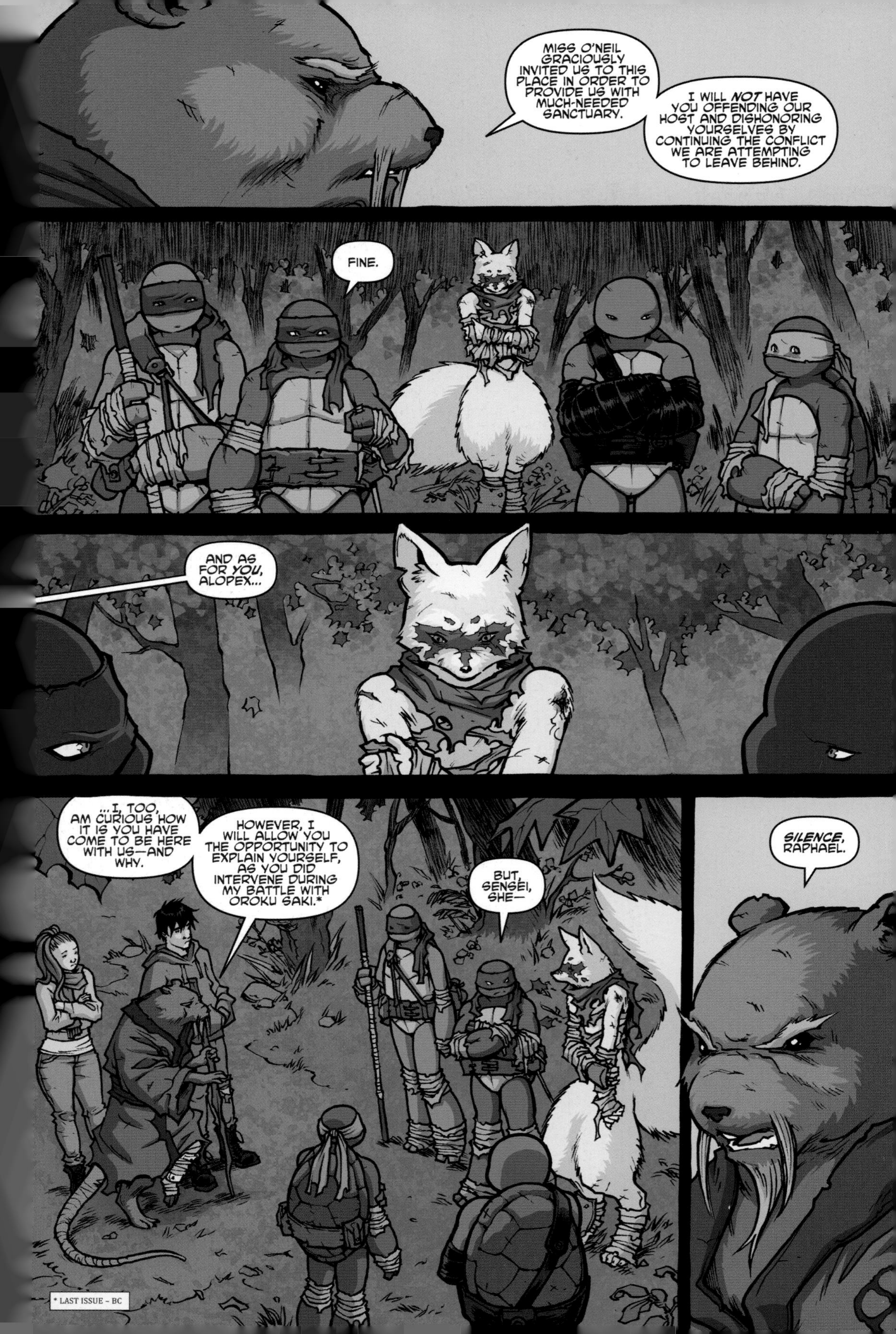
MISS O'NEIL GRACIOUSLY INVITED US TO THIS PLACE IN ORDER TO PROVIDE US WITH MUCH-NEEDED SANCTUARY.
I WILL *NOT* HAVE YOU OFFENDING OUR HOST AND DISHONORING YOURSELVES BY CONTINUING THE CONFLICT WE ARE ATTEMPTING TO LEAVE BEHIND.
FINE.
AND AS FOR *YOU*, ALOPEX...
...I, TOO, AM CURIOUS HOW IT IS YOU HAVE COME TO BE HERE WITH US—AND WHY.
HOWEVER, I WILL ALLOW YOU THE OPPORTUNITY TO EXPLAIN YOURSELF, AS YOU DID INTERVENE DURING MY BATTLE WITH OROKU SAKI.*
BUT, SENSEI, SHE—
SILENCE, RAPHAEL.
* LAST ISSUE – BC

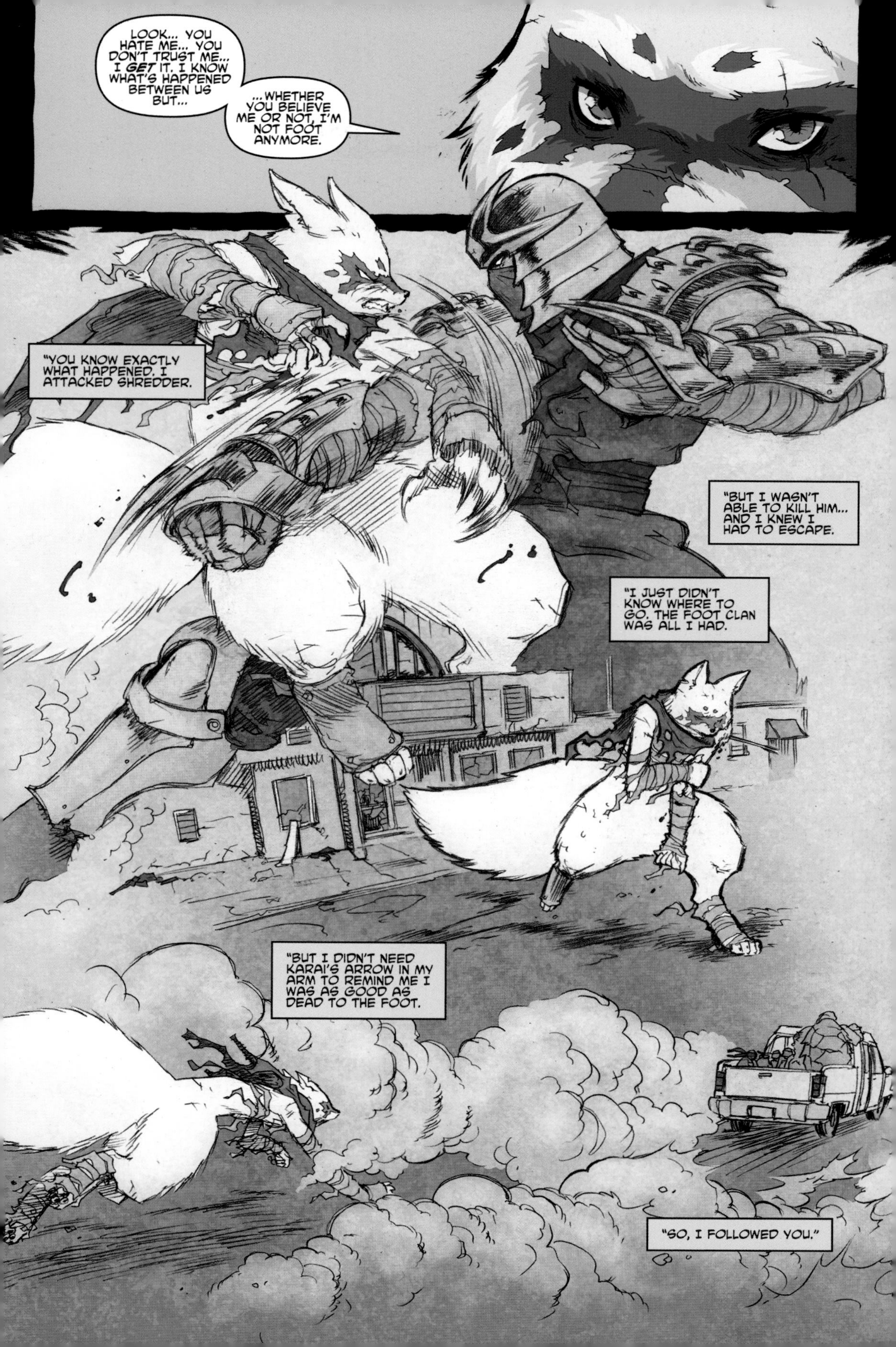
LOOK... YOU HATE ME... YOU DON'T TRUST ME... I *GET* IT. I KNOW WHAT'S HAPPENED BETWEEN US BUT...
...WHETHER YOU BELIEVE ME OR NOT, I'M NOT FOOT ANYMORE.
"YOU KNOW EXACTLY WHAT HAPPENED. I ATTACKED SHREDDER.
"BUT I WASN'T ABLE TO KILL HIM... AND I KNEW I HAD TO ESCAPE.
"I JUST DIDN'T KNOW WHERE TO GO. THE FOOT CLAN WAS ALL I HAD.
"BUT I DIDN'T NEED KARAI'S ARROW IN MY ARM TO REMIND ME I WAS AS GOOD AS DEAD TO THE FOOT.
"SO, I FOLLOWED YOU."

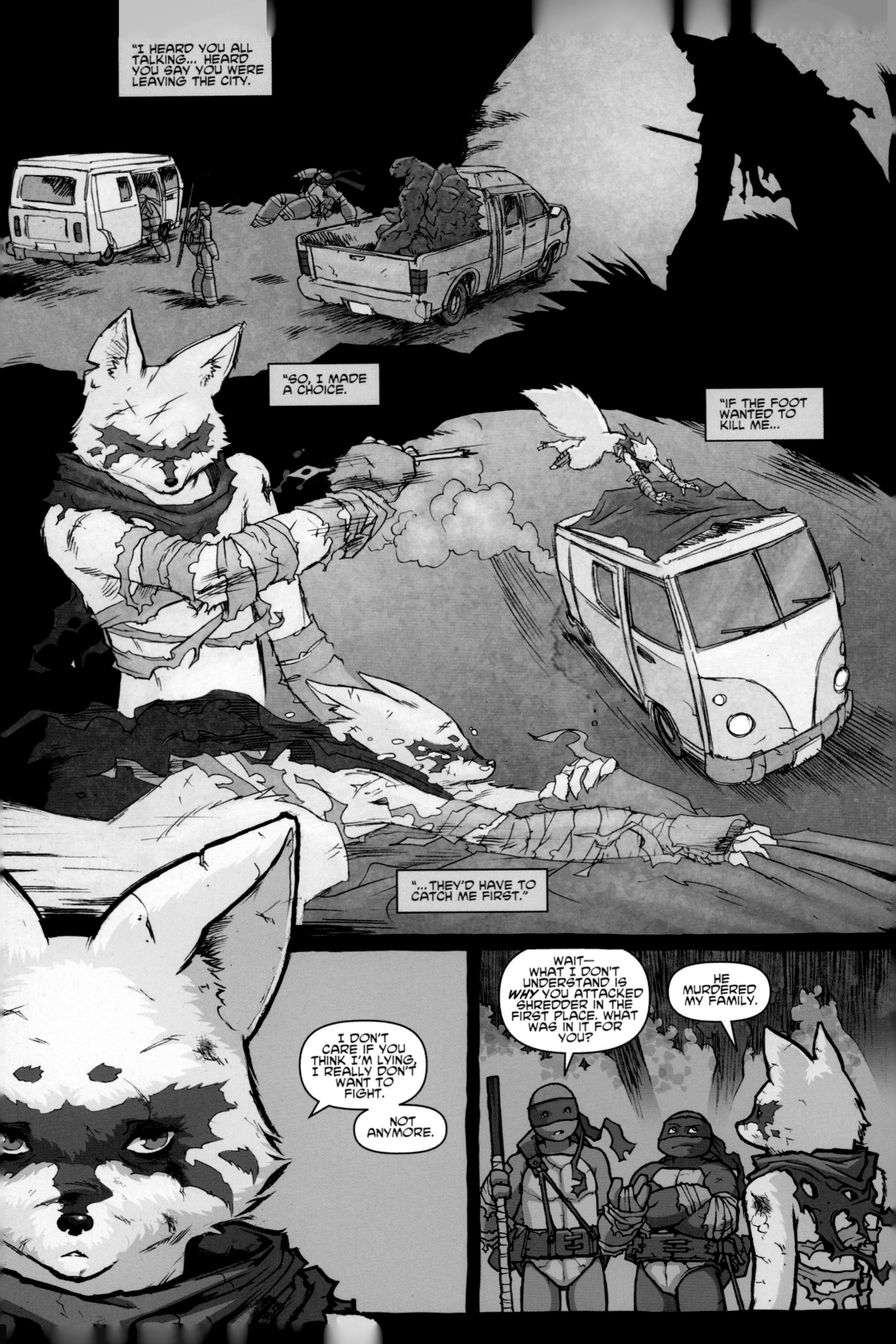
"I HEARD YOU ALL TALKING... HEARD YOU SAY YOU WERE LEAVING THE CITY.
"SO, I MADE A CHOICE.
"IF THE FOOT WANTED TO KILL ME...
"...THEY'D HAVE TO CATCH ME FIRST."
I DON'T CARE IF YOU THINK I'M LYING, I REALLY DON'T WANT TO FIGHT.
NOT ANYMORE.
WAIT— WHAT I DON'T UNDERSTAND IS *WHY* YOU ATTACKED SHREDDER IN THE FIRST PLACE. WHAT WAS IN IT FOR YOU?
HE MURDERED MY FAMILY.

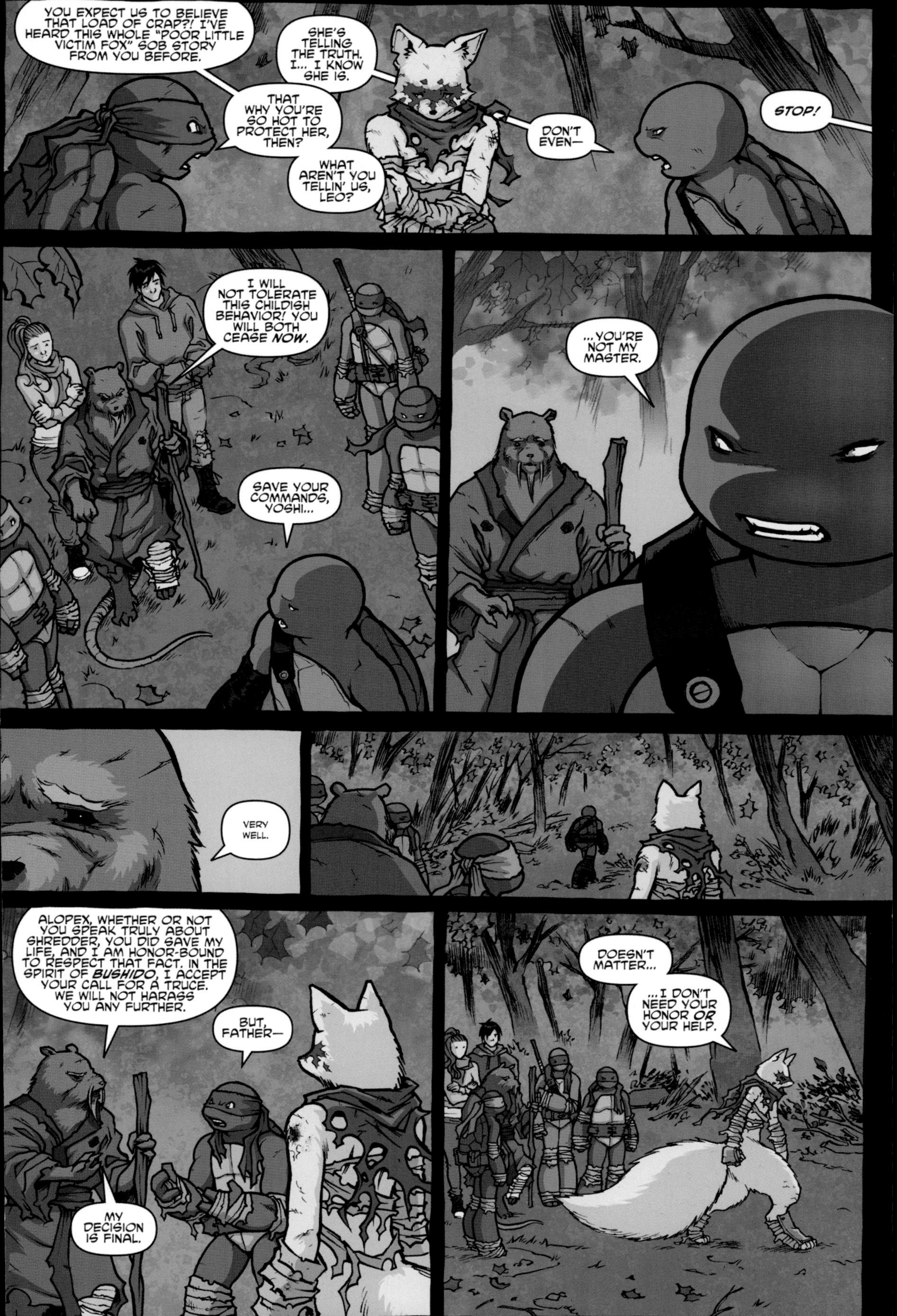

YOU EXPECT US TO BELIEVE THAT LOAD OF CRAP?! I'VE HEARD THIS WHOLE "POOR LITTLE VICTIM FOX" SOB STORY FROM YOU BEFORE.
SHE'S TELLING THE TRUTH. I... I KNOW SHE IS.
THAT WHY YOU'RE SO HOT TO PROTECT HER, THEN?
WHAT AREN'T YOU TELLIN' US, LEO?
DON'T EVEN—
STOP!
I WILL NOT TOLERATE THIS CHILDISH BEHAVIOR! YOU WILL BOTH CEASE *NOW*.
SAVE YOUR COMMANDS, YOSHI...
...YOU'RE NOT MY MASTER.
VERY WELL.
ALOPEX, WHETHER OR NOT YOU SPEAK TRULY ABOUT SHREDDER, YOU DID SAVE MY LIFE, AND I AM HONOR-BOUND TO RESPECT THAT FACT. IN THE SPIRIT OF *BUSHIDO*, I ACCEPT YOUR CALL FOR A TRUCE. WE WILL NOT HARASS YOU ANY FURTHER.
BUT, FATHER—
MY DECISION IS FINAL.
DOESN'T MATTER...
...I DON'T NEED YOUR HONOR *OR* YOUR HELP.

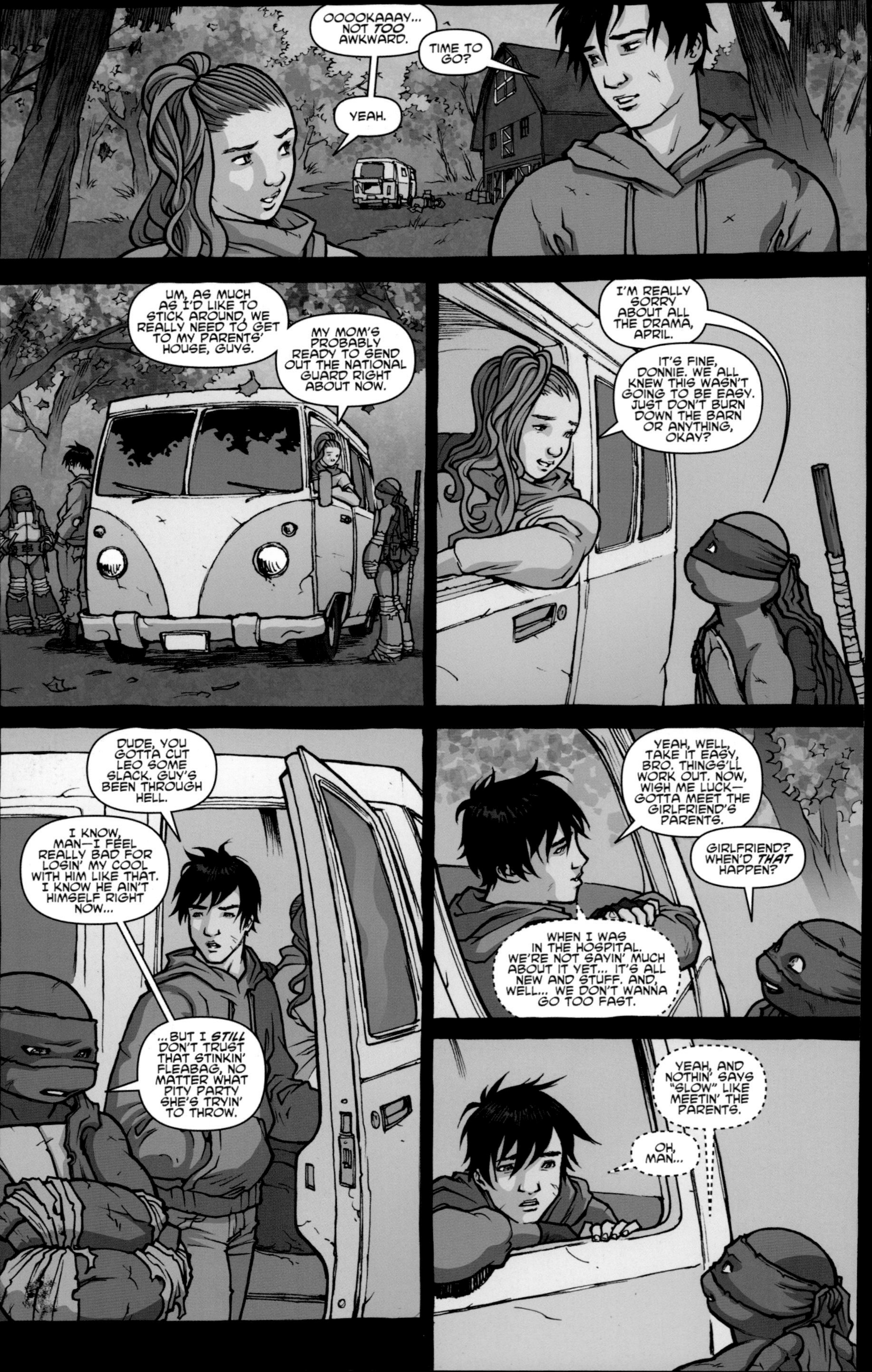
OOOOKAAAY... NOT *TOO* AWKWARD.
TIME TO GO?
YEAH.
UM, AS MUCH AS I'D LIKE TO STICK AROUND, WE REALLY NEED TO GET TO MY PARENTS' HOUSE, GUYS.
MY MOM'S PROBABLY READY TO SEND OUT THE NATIONAL GUARD RIGHT ABOUT NOW.
I'M REALLY SORRY ABOUT ALL THE DRAMA, APRIL.
IT'S FINE, DONNIE. WE ALL KNEW THIS WASN'T GOING TO BE EASY. JUST DON'T BURN DOWN THE BARN OR ANYTHING, OKAY?
DUDE, YOU GOTTA CUT LEO SOME SLACK. GUY'S BEEN THROUGH HELL.
I KNOW, MAN—I FEEL REALLY BAD FOR LOSIN' MY COOL WITH HIM LIKE THAT. I KNOW HE AIN'T HIMSELF RIGHT NOW...
...BUT I *STILL* DON'T TRUST THAT STINKIN' FLEABAG, NO MATTER WHAT PITY PARTY SHE'S TRYIN' TO THROW.
YEAH, WELL, TAKE IT EASY, BRO. THINGS'LL WORK OUT. NOW, WISH ME LUCK—GOTTA MEET THE GIRLFRIEND'S PARENTS.
GIRLFRIEND? WHEN'D *THAT* HAPPEN?
WHEN I WAS IN THE HOSPITAL. WE'RE NOT SAYIN' MUCH ABOUT IT YET... IT'S ALL NEW AND STUFF. AND, WELL... WE DON'T WANNA GO TOO FAST.
YEAH, AND NOTHIN' SAYS "SLOW" LIKE MEETIN' THE PARENTS.
OH, MAN...

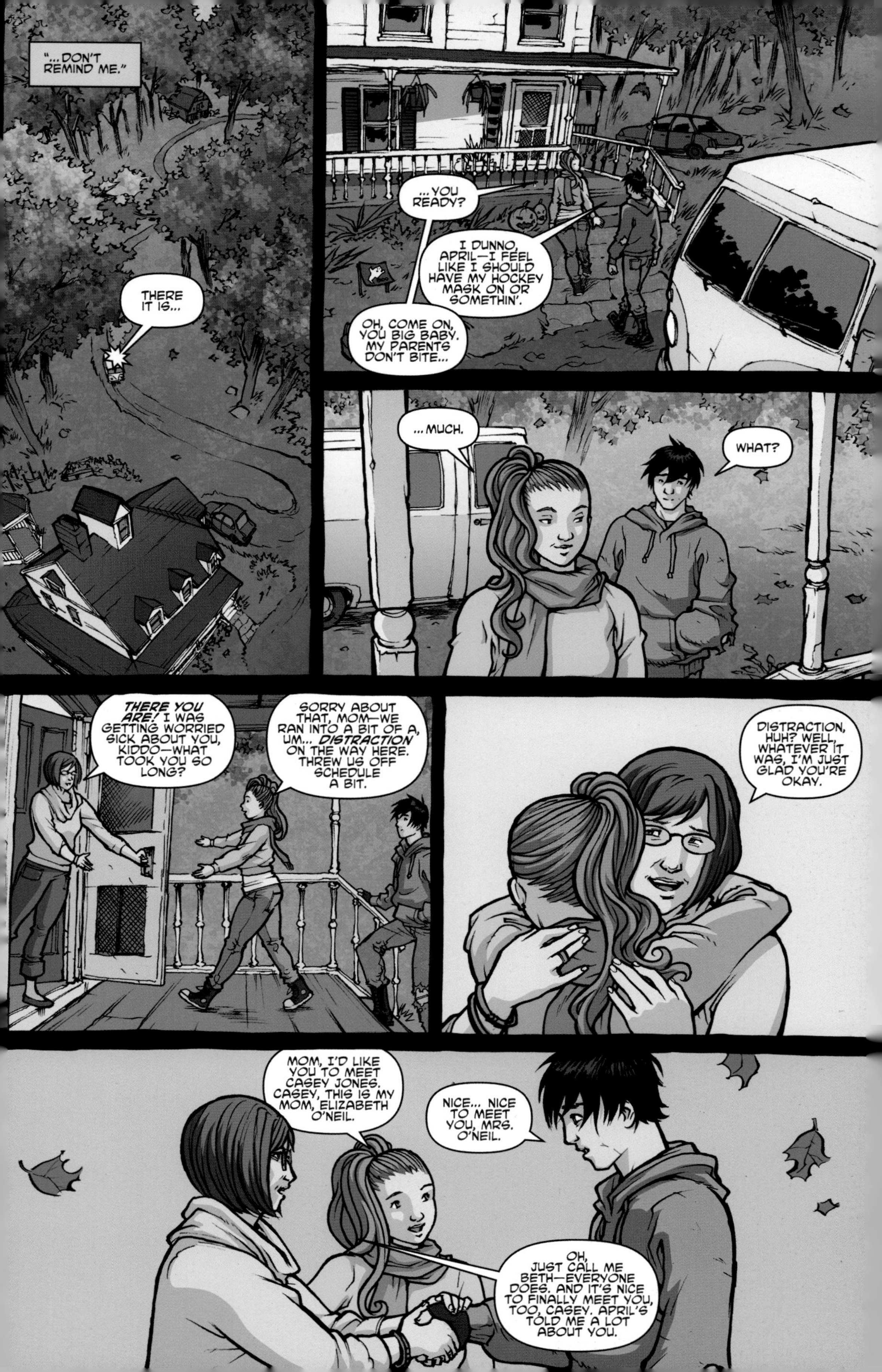
"...DON'T REMIND ME."
THERE IT IS...
...YOU READY?
I DUNNO, APRIL—I FEEL LIKE I SHOULD HAVE MY HOCKEY MASK ON OR SOMETHIN'.
OH, COME ON, YOU BIG BABY. MY PARENTS DON'T BITE...
...MUCH.
WHAT?
THERE YOU ARE! I WAS GETTING WORRIED SICK ABOUT YOU, KIDDO—WHAT TOOK YOU SO LONG?
SORRY ABOUT THAT, MOM—WE RAN INTO A BIT OF A, UM... DISTRACTION ON THE WAY HERE. THREW US OFF SCHEDULE A BIT.
DISTRACTION, HUH? WELL, WHATEVER IT WAS, I'M JUST GLAD YOU'RE OKAY.
MOM, I'D LIKE YOU TO MEET CASEY JONES. CASEY, THIS IS MY MOM, ELIZABETH O'NEIL.
NICE... NICE TO MEET YOU, MRS. O'NEIL.
OH, JUST CALL ME BETH—EVERYONE DOES. AND IT'S NICE TO FINALLY MEET YOU, TOO, CASEY. APRIL'S TOLD ME A LOT ABOUT YOU.

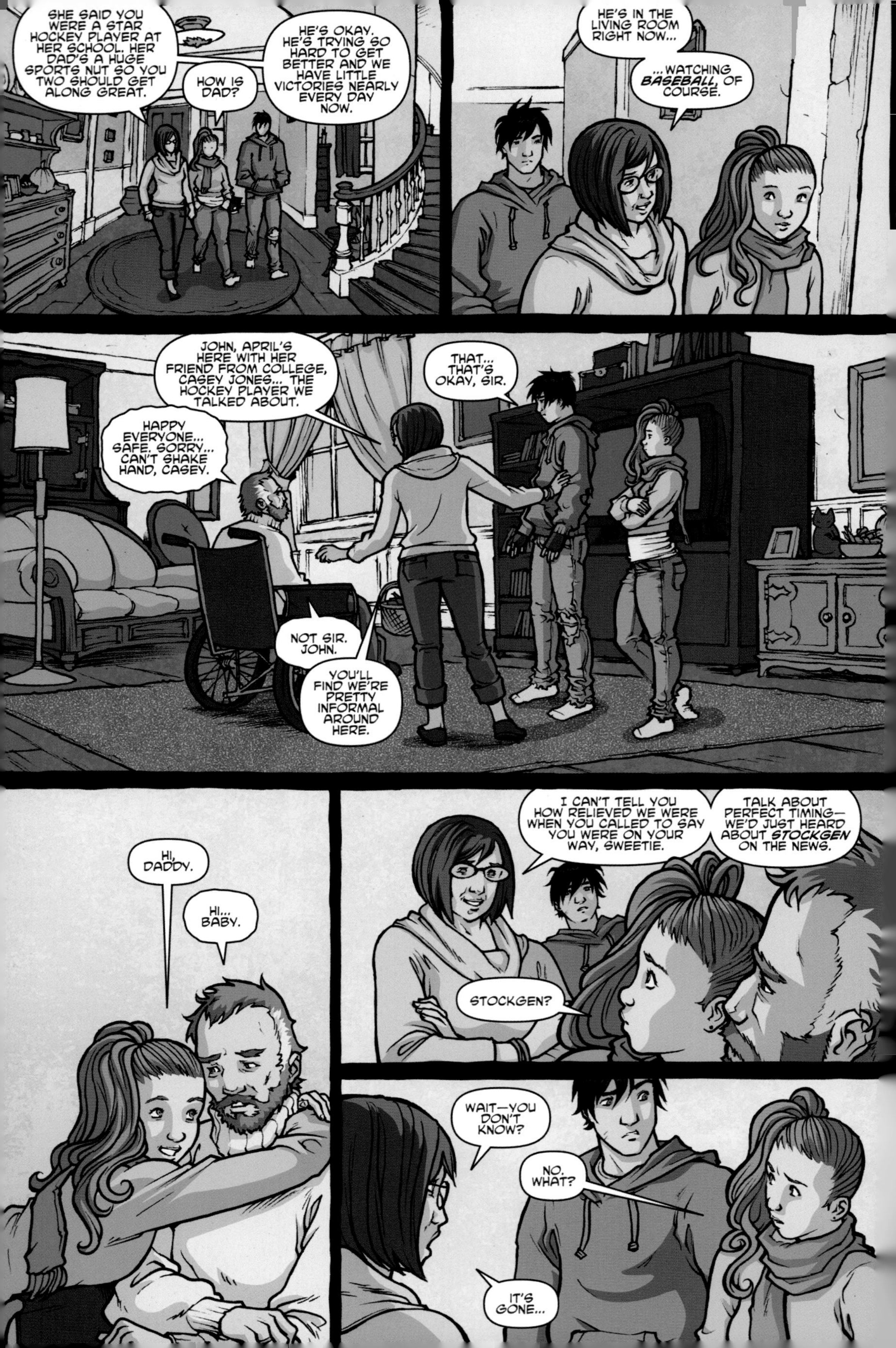
SHE SAID YOU WERE A STAR HOCKEY PLAYER AT HER SCHOOL. HER DAD'S A HUGE SPORTS NUT SO YOU TWO SHOULD GET ALONG GREAT.
HOW IS DAD?
HE'S OKAY. HE'S TRYING SO HARD TO GET BETTER AND WE HAVE LITTLE VICTORIES NEARLY EVERY DAY NOW.
HE'S IN THE LIVING ROOM RIGHT NOW...
...WATCHING BASEBALL, OF COURSE.
JOHN, APRIL'S HERE WITH HER FRIEND FROM COLLEGE, CASEY JONES... THE HOCKEY PLAYER WE TALKED ABOUT.
HAPPY EVERYONE... SAFE. SORRY... CAN'T SHAKE HAND, CASEY.
THAT... THAT'S OKAY, SIR.
NOT SIR. JOHN.
YOU'LL FIND WE'RE PRETTY INFORMAL AROUND HERE.
HI, DADDY.
HI... BABY.
I CAN'T TELL YOU HOW RELIEVED WE WERE WHEN YOU CALLED TO SAY YOU WERE ON YOUR WAY, SWEETIE.
TALK ABOUT PERFECT TIMING— WE'D JUST HEARD ABOUT STOCKGEN ON THE NEWS.
STOCKGEN?
WAIT—YOU DON'T KNOW?
NO. WHAT?
IT'S GONE...

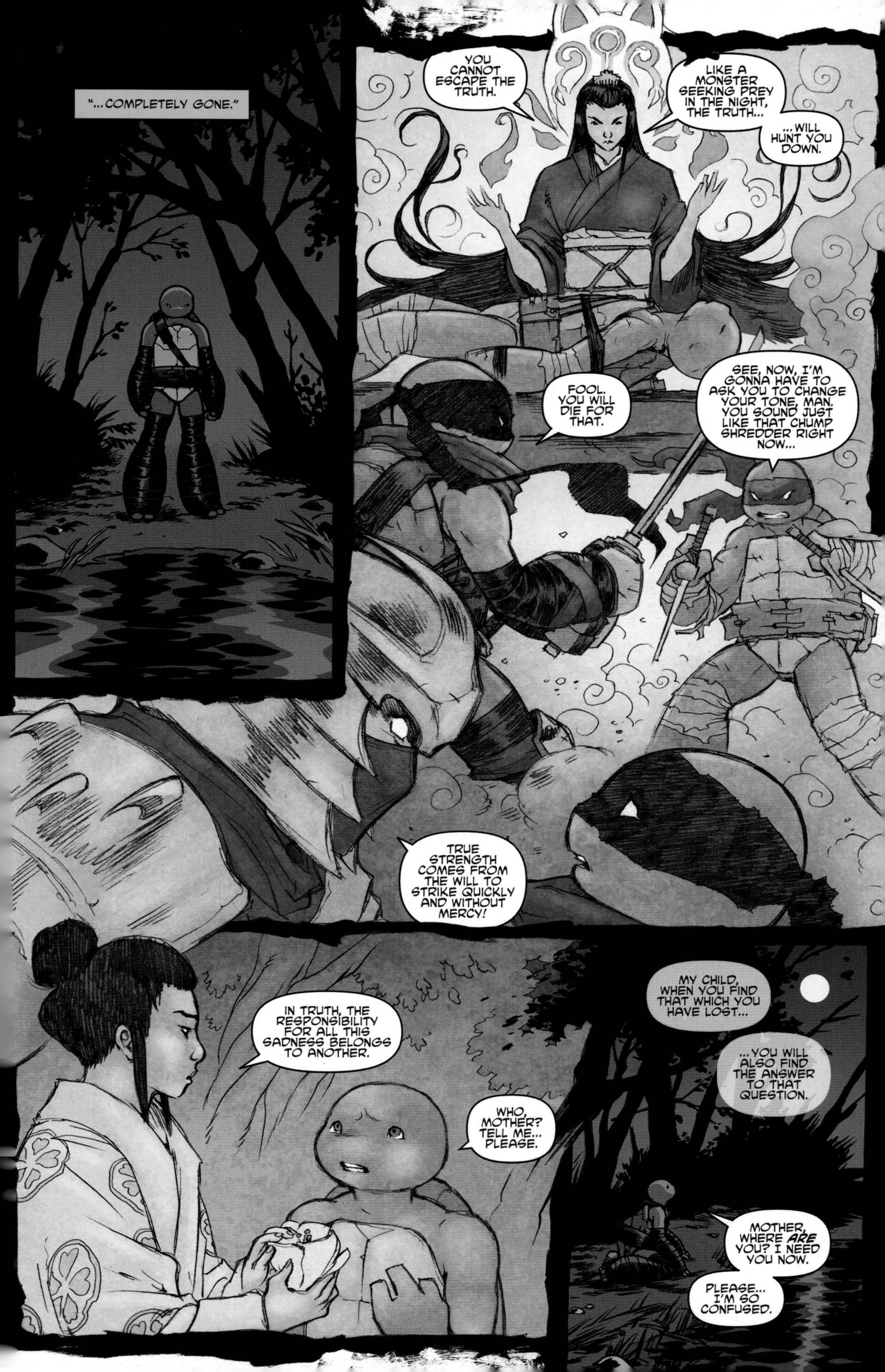
"...COMPLETELY GONE."
YOU CANNOT ESCAPE THE TRUTH.
LIKE A MONSTER SEEKING PREY IN THE NIGHT, THE TRUTH...
...WILL HUNT YOU DOWN.
FOOL. YOU WILL DIE FOR THAT.
SEE, NOW, I'M GONNA HAVE TO ASK YOU TO CHANGE YOUR TONE, MAN. YOU SOUND JUST LIKE THAT CHUMP SHREDDER RIGHT NOW...
TRUE STRENGTH COMES FROM THE WILL TO STRIKE QUICKLY AND WITHOUT MERCY!
IN TRUTH, THE RESPONSIBILITY FOR ALL THIS SADNESS BELONGS TO ANOTHER.
WHO, MOTHER? TELL ME... PLEASE.
MY CHILD, WHEN YOU FIND THAT WHICH YOU HAVE LOST...
...YOU WILL ALSO FIND THE ANSWER TO THAT QUESTION.
MOTHER, WHERE *ARE* YOU? I NEED YOU NOW.
PLEASE... I'M SO CONFUSED.

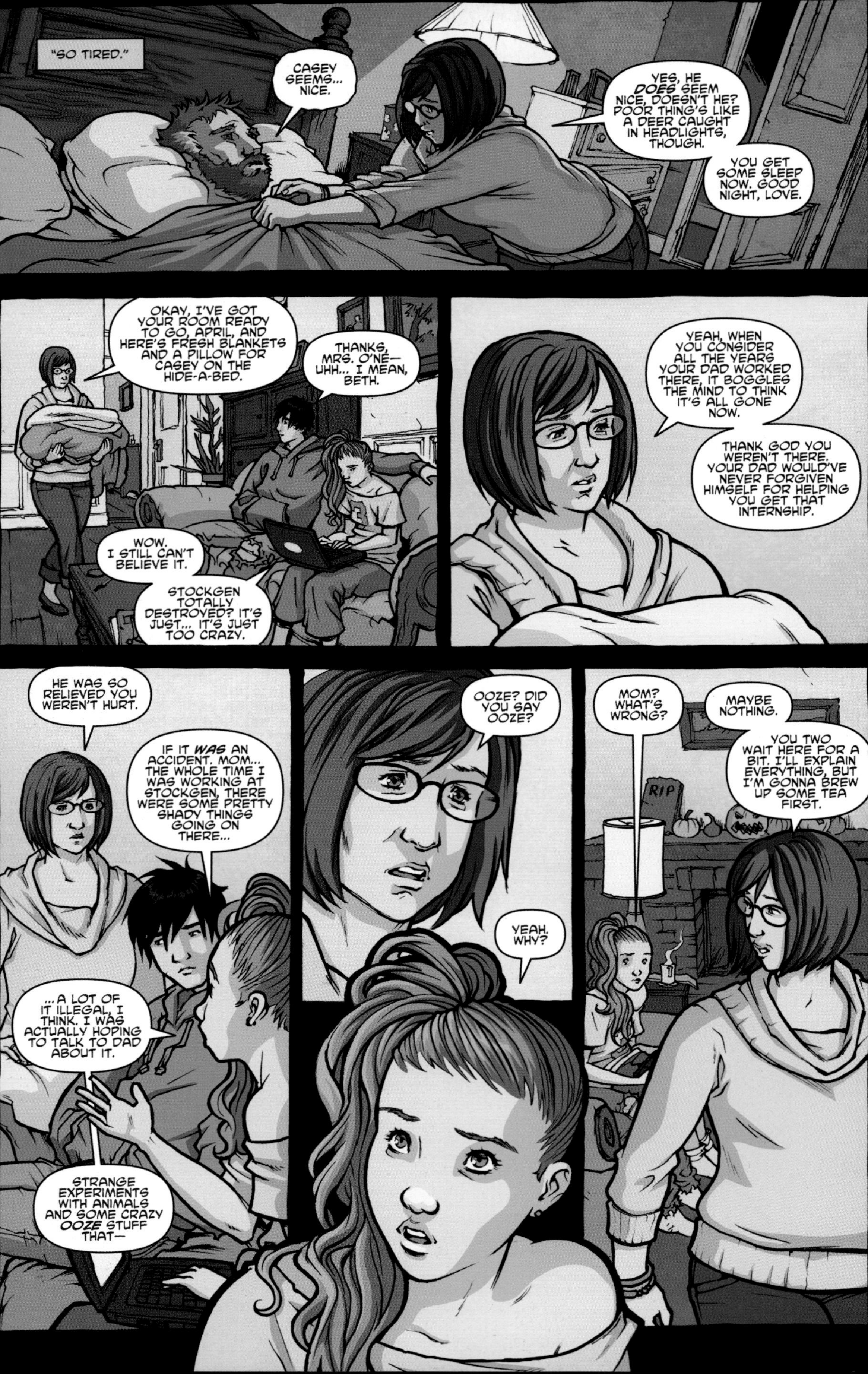

"SO TIRED."
CASEY SEEMS... NICE.
YES, HE DOES SEEM NICE, DOESN'T HE? POOR THING'S LIKE A DEER CAUGHT IN HEADLIGHTS, THOUGH.
YOU GET SOME SLEEP NOW. GOOD NIGHT, LOVE.
OKAY, I'VE GOT YOUR ROOM READY TO GO, APRIL, AND HERE'S FRESH BLANKETS AND A PILLOW FOR CASEY ON THE HIDE-A-BED.
THANKS, MRS. O'NE— UHH... I MEAN, BETH.
WOW. I STILL CAN'T BELIEVE IT.
STOCKGEN TOTALLY DESTROYED? IT'S JUST... IT'S JUST TOO CRAZY.
YEAH, WHEN YOU CONSIDER ALL THE YEARS YOUR DAD WORKED THERE, IT BOGGLES THE MIND TO THINK IT'S ALL GONE NOW.
THANK GOD YOU WEREN'T THERE. YOUR DAD WOULD'VE NEVER FORGIVEN HIMSELF FOR HELPING YOU GET THAT INTERNSHIP.
HE WAS SO RELIEVED YOU WEREN'T HURT.
IF IT WAS AN ACCIDENT. MOM... THE WHOLE TIME I WAS WORKING AT STOCKGEN, THERE WERE SOME PRETTY SHADY THINGS GOING ON THERE...
...A LOT OF IT ILLEGAL, I THINK. I WAS ACTUALLY HOPING TO TALK TO DAD ABOUT IT.
STRANGE EXPERIMENTS WITH ANIMALS AND SOME CRAZY OOZE STUFF THAT—
OOZE? DID YOU SAY OOZE?
YEAH. WHY?
MOM? WHAT'S WRONG?
MAYBE NOTHING.
YOU TWO WAIT HERE FOR A BIT. I'LL EXPLAIN EVERYTHING, BUT I'M GONNA BREW UP SOME TEA FIRST.
RIP

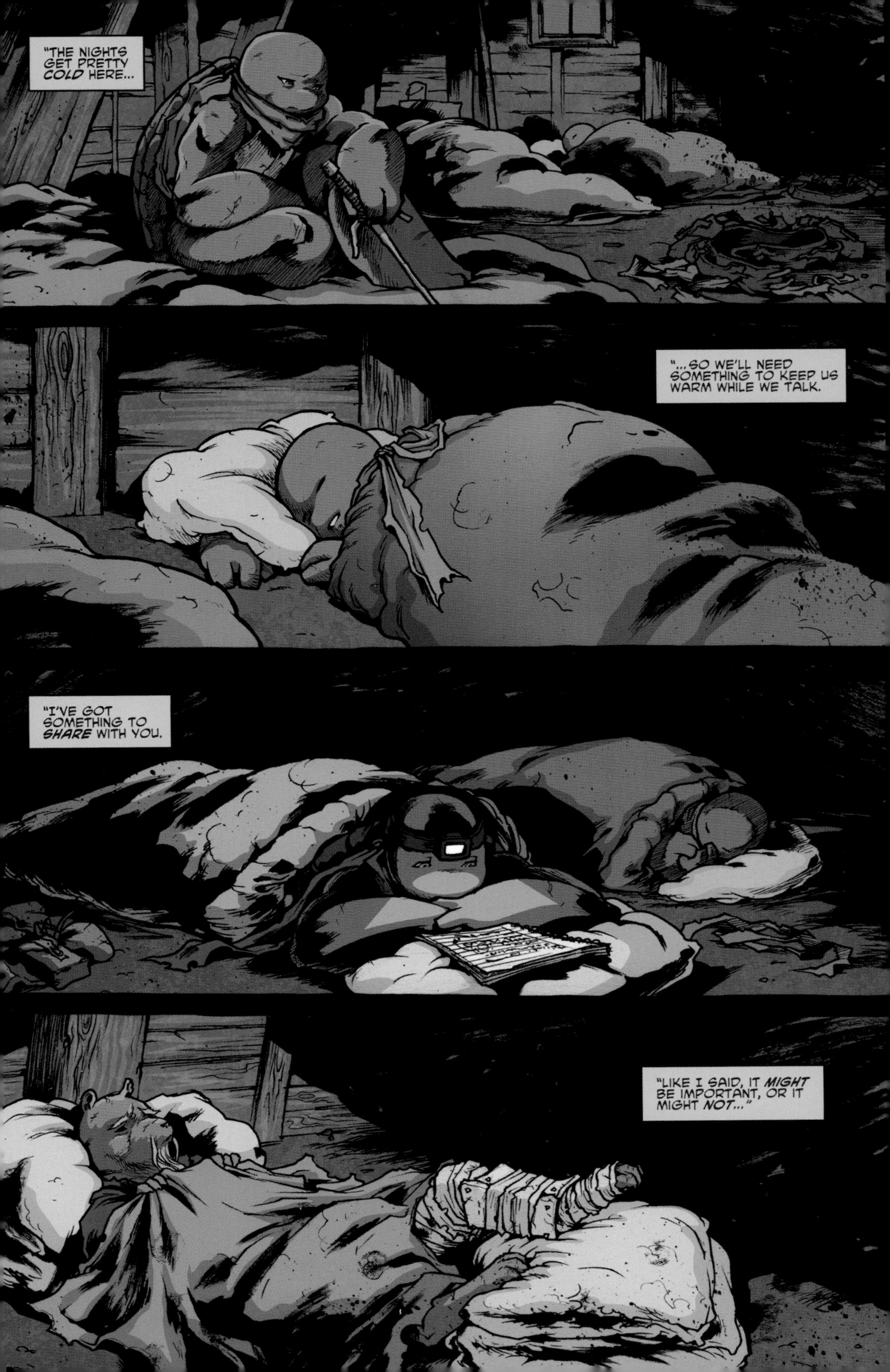
"THE NIGHTS GET PRETTY COLD HERE...
"...SO WE'LL NEED SOMETHING TO KEEP US WARM WHILE WE TALK.
"I'VE GOT SOMETHING TO SHARE WITH YOU.
"LIKE I SAID, IT MIGHT BE IMPORTANT, OR IT MIGHT NOT..."

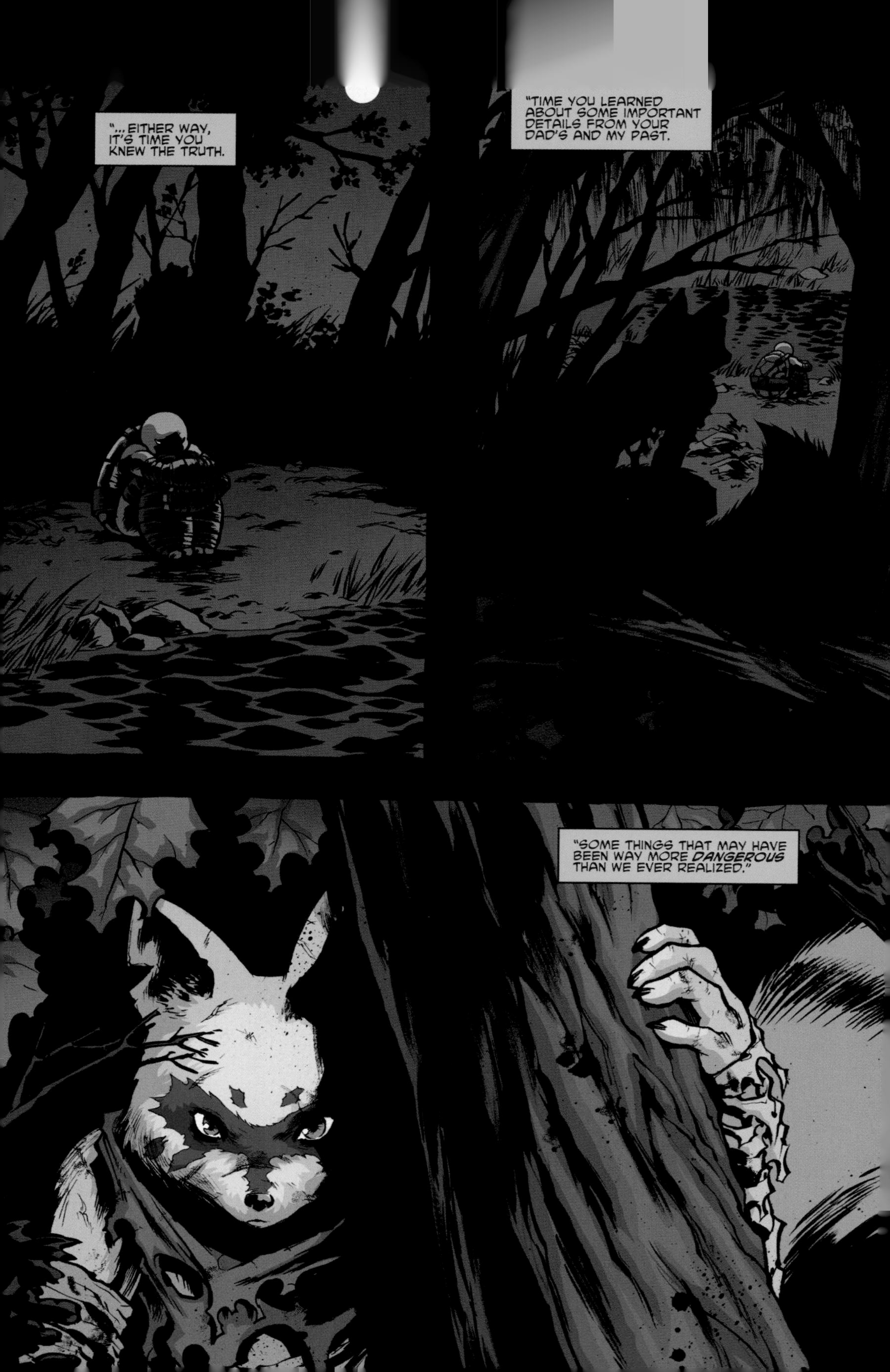
"...EITHER WAY, IT'S TIME YOU KNEW THE TRUTH.
"TIME YOU LEARNED ABOUT SOME IMPORTANT DETAILS FROM YOUR DAD'S AND MY PAST.
"SOME THINGS THAT MAY HAVE BEEN WAY MORE *DANGEROUS* THAN WE EVER REALIZED."

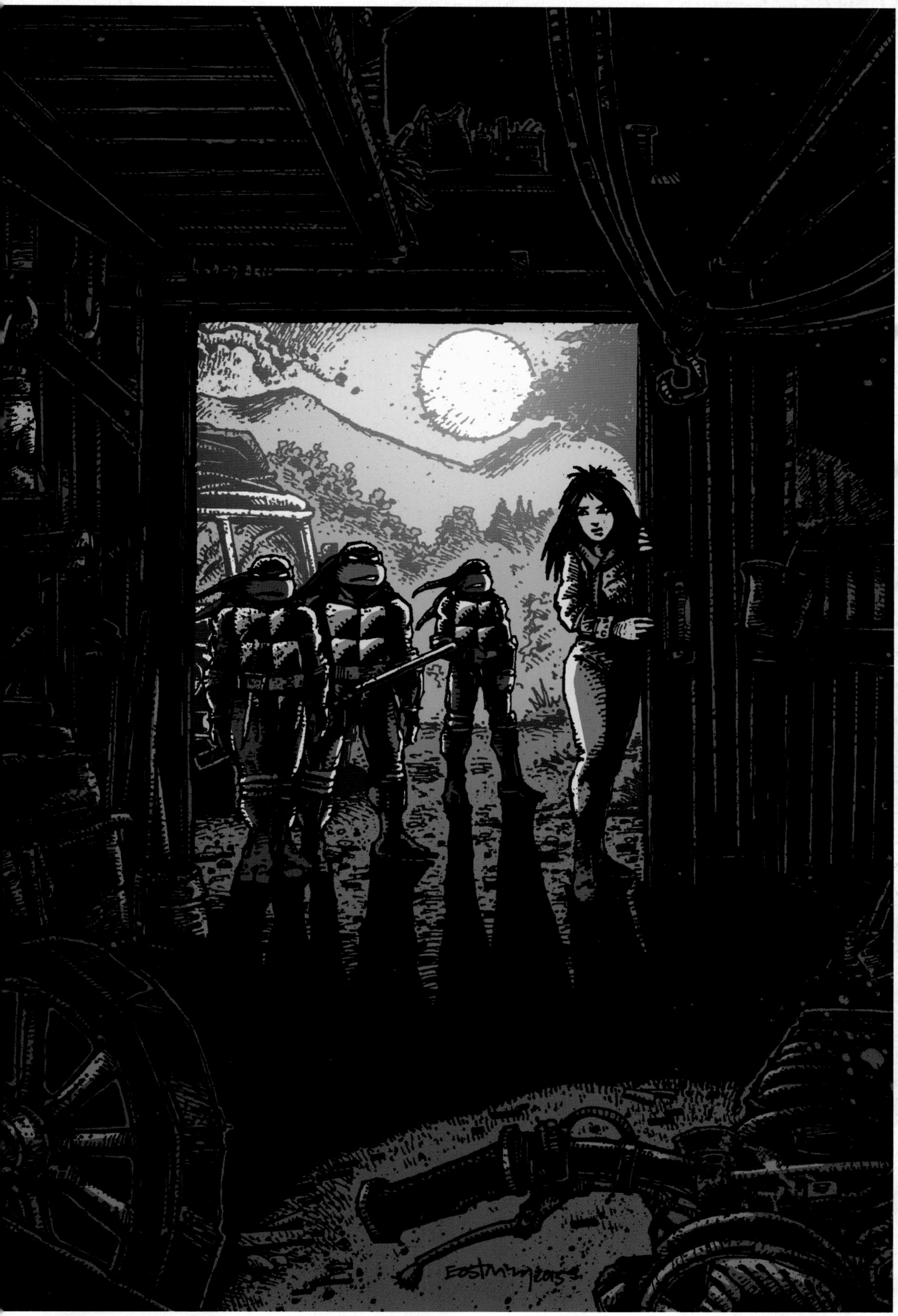

Cover by KEVIN EASTMAN
Colors by RONDA PATTISON

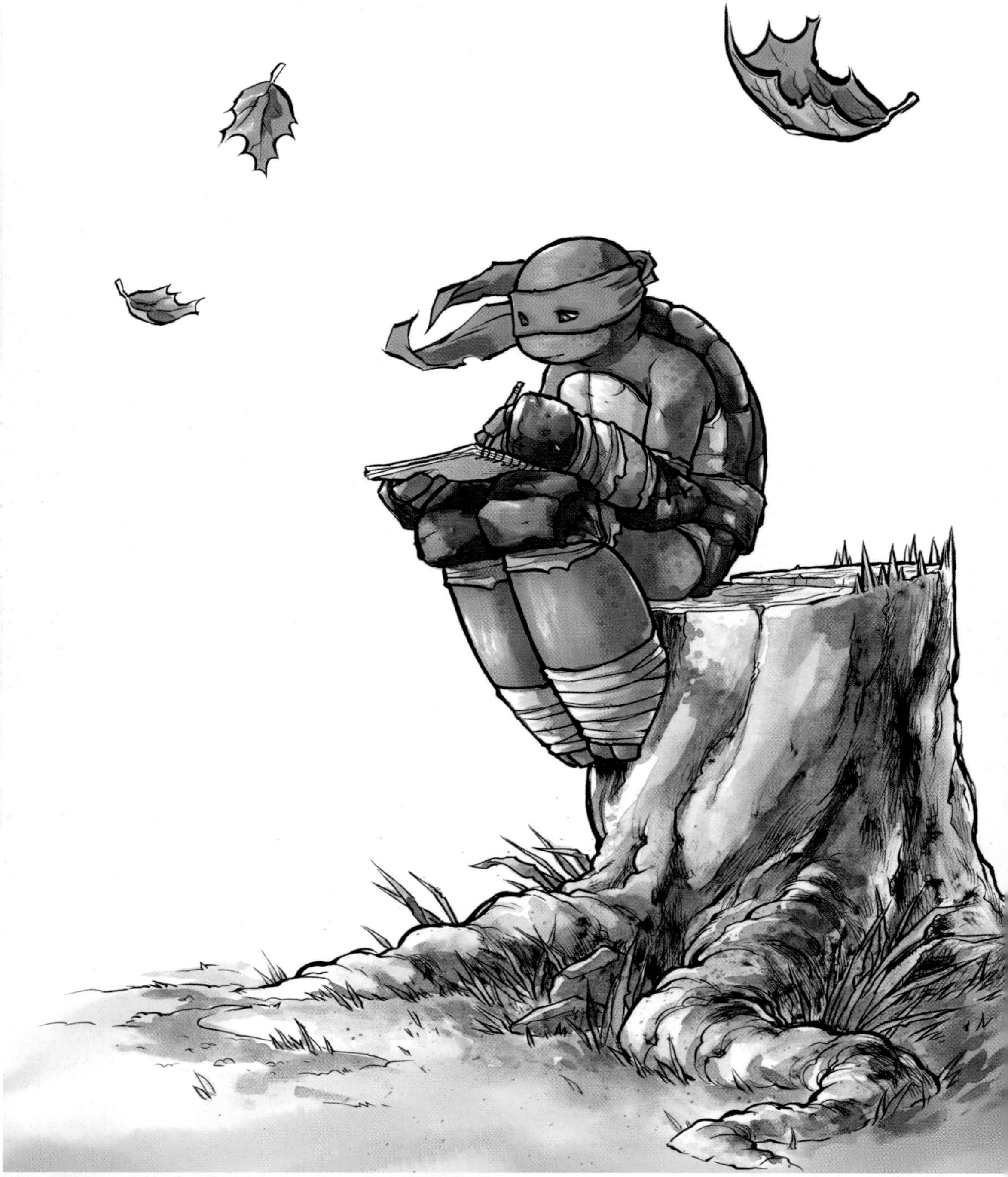

Cover by SOPHIE CAMPBELL

TMNT #30

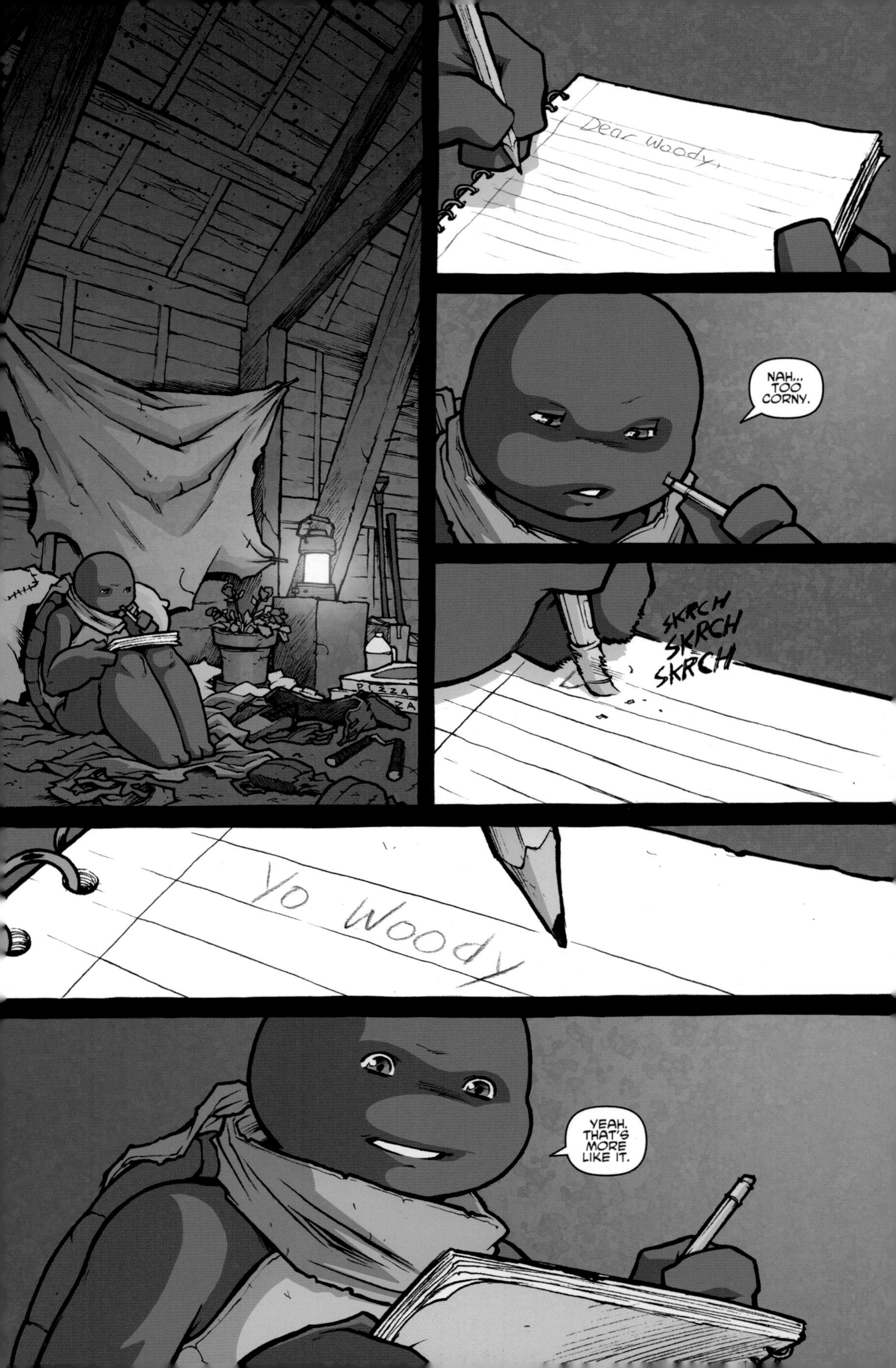
Dear Woody,
NAH... TOO CORNY.
SKRCH SKRCH SKRCH
Yo Woody
YEAH. THAT'S MORE LIKE IT.

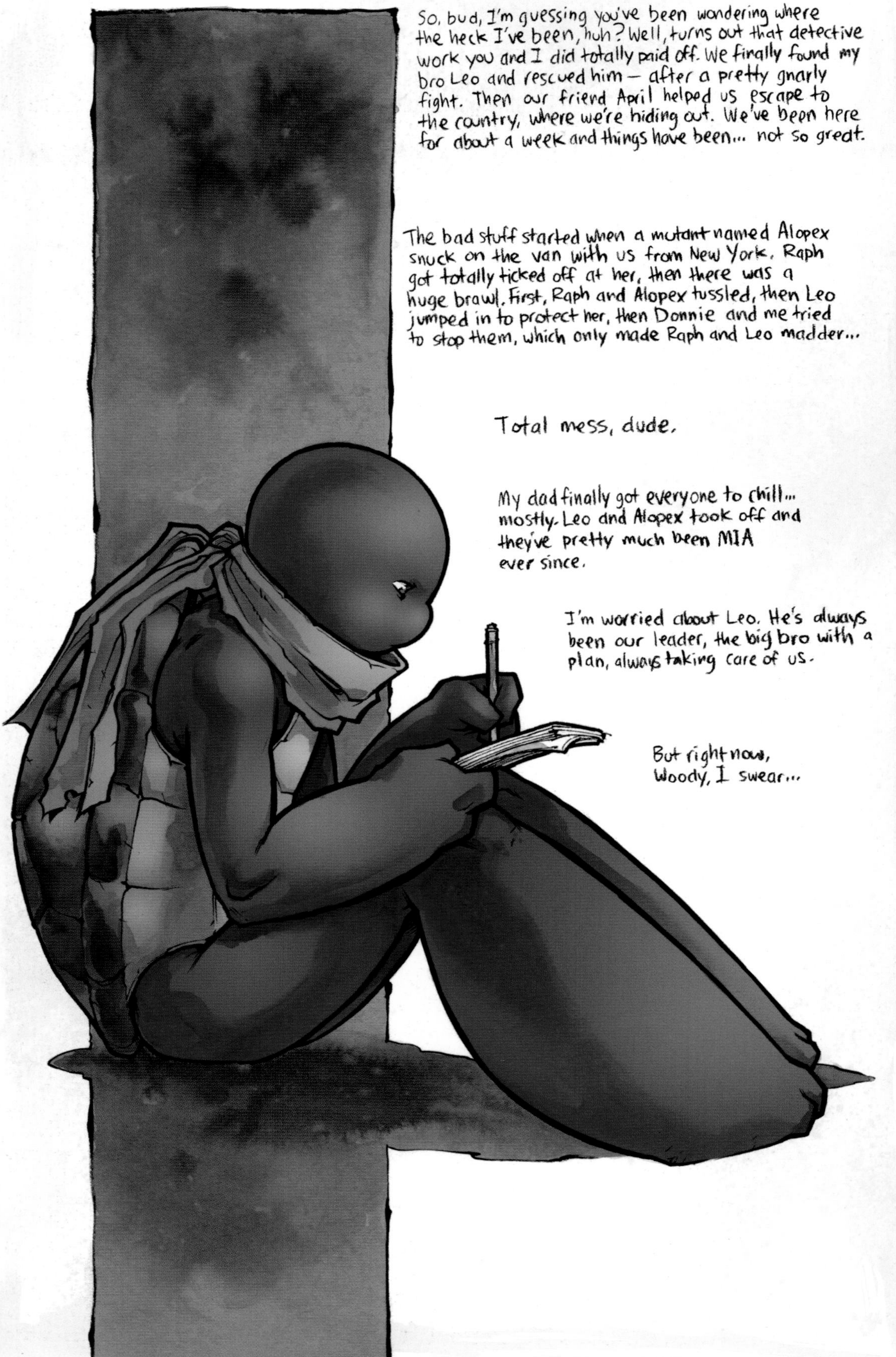
So, bud, I'm guessing you've been wondering where the heck I've been, huh? Well, turns out that detective work you and I did totally paid off. We finally found my bro Leo and rescued him — after a pretty gnarly fight. Then our friend April helped us escape to the country, where we're hiding out. We've been here for about a week and things have been... not so great.
The bad stuff started when a mutant named Alopex snuck on the van with us from New York. Raph got totally ticked off at her, then there was a huge brawl. First, Raph and Alopex tussled, then Leo jumped in to protect her, then Donnie and me tried to stop them, which only made Raph and Leo madder...
Total mess, dude.
My dad finally got everyone to chill... mostly. Leo and Alopex took off and they've pretty much been MIA ever since.
I'm worried about Leo. He's always been our leader, the big bro with a plan, always taking care of us.
But right now, Woody, I swear...

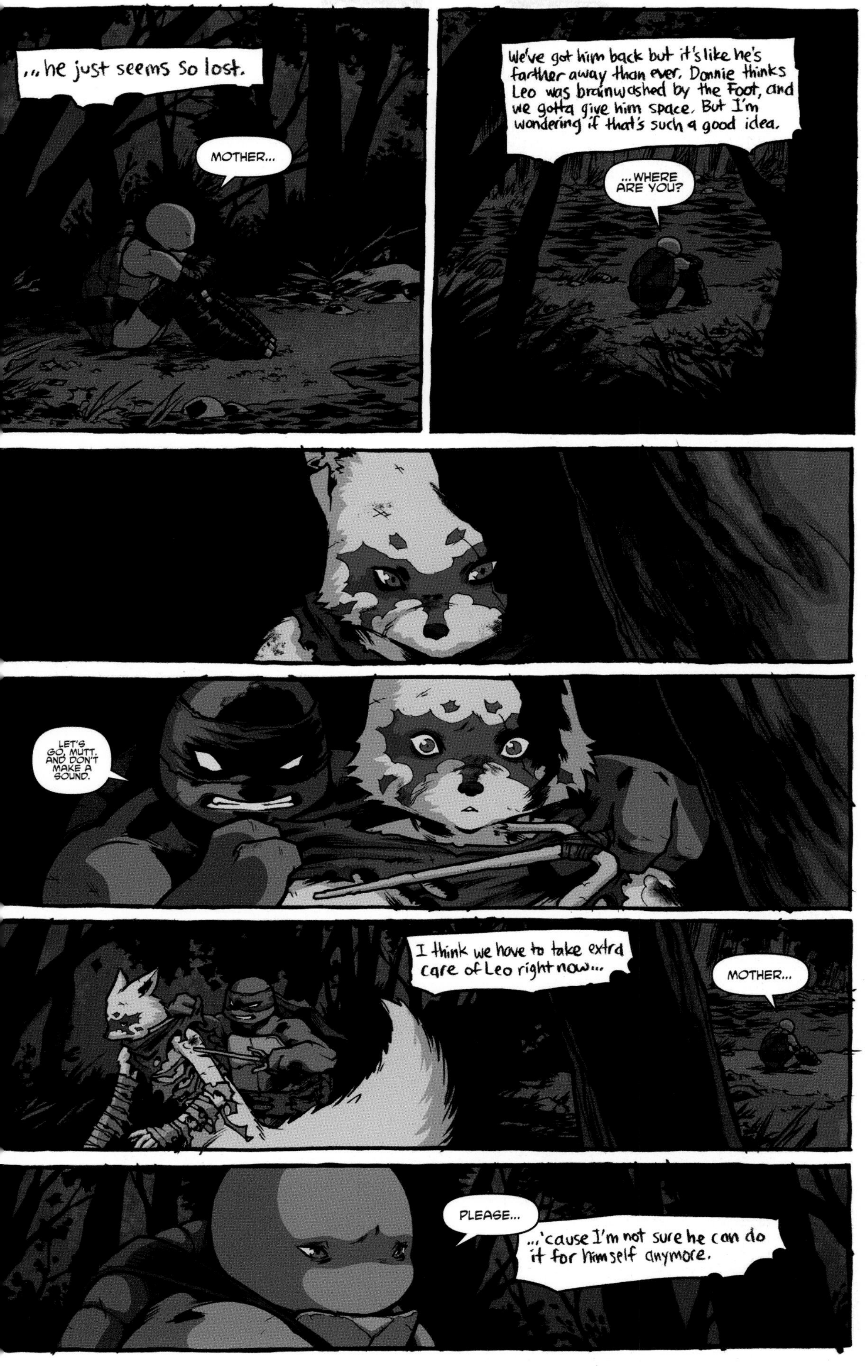
...he just seems so lost.
MOTHER...
We've got him back but it's like he's farther away than ever. Donnie thinks Leo was brainwashed by the Foot, and we gotta give him space. But I'm wondering if that's such a good idea.
...WHERE ARE YOU?
LET'S GO, MUTT. AND DON'T MAKE A SOUND.
I think we have to take extra care of Leo right now...
MOTHER...
PLEASE...
...'cause I'm not sure he can do it for himself anymore.

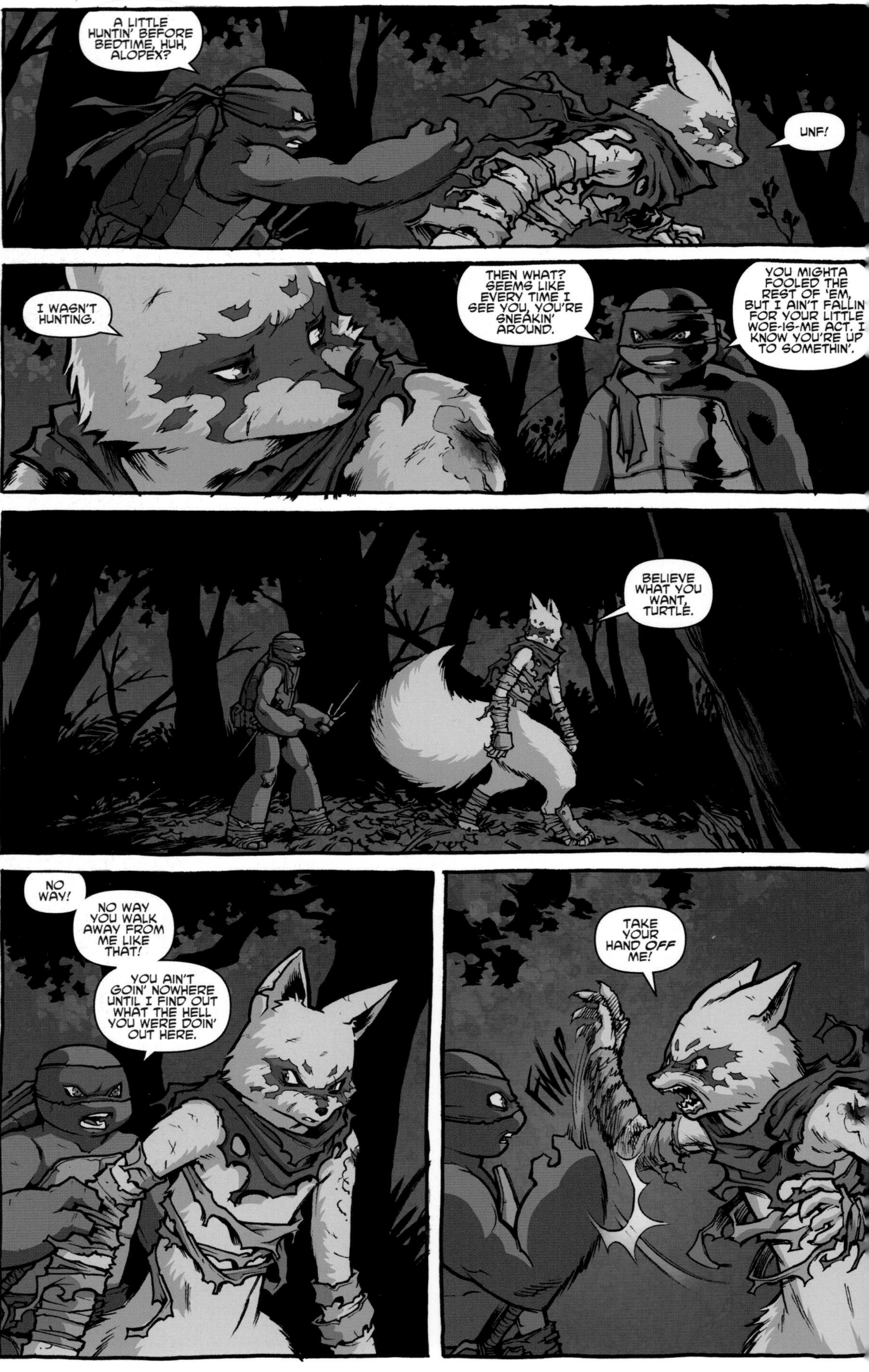
A LITTLE HUNTIN' BEFORE BEDTIME, HUH, ALOPEX?
UNF!
I WASN'T HUNTING.
THEN WHAT? SEEMS LIKE EVERY TIME I SEE YOU, YOU'RE SNEAKIN' AROUND.
YOU MIGHTA FOOLED THE REST OF 'EM, BUT I AIN'T FALLIN FOR YOUR LITTLE WOE-IS-ME ACT. I KNOW YOU'RE UP TO SOMETHIN'.
BELIEVE WHAT YOU WANT, TURTLE.
NO WAY!
NO WAY YOU WALK AWAY FROM ME LIKE THAT!
YOU AIN'T GOIN' NOWHERE UNTIL I FIND OUT WHAT THE HELL YOU WERE DOIN' OUT HERE.
TAKE YOUR HAND OFF ME!

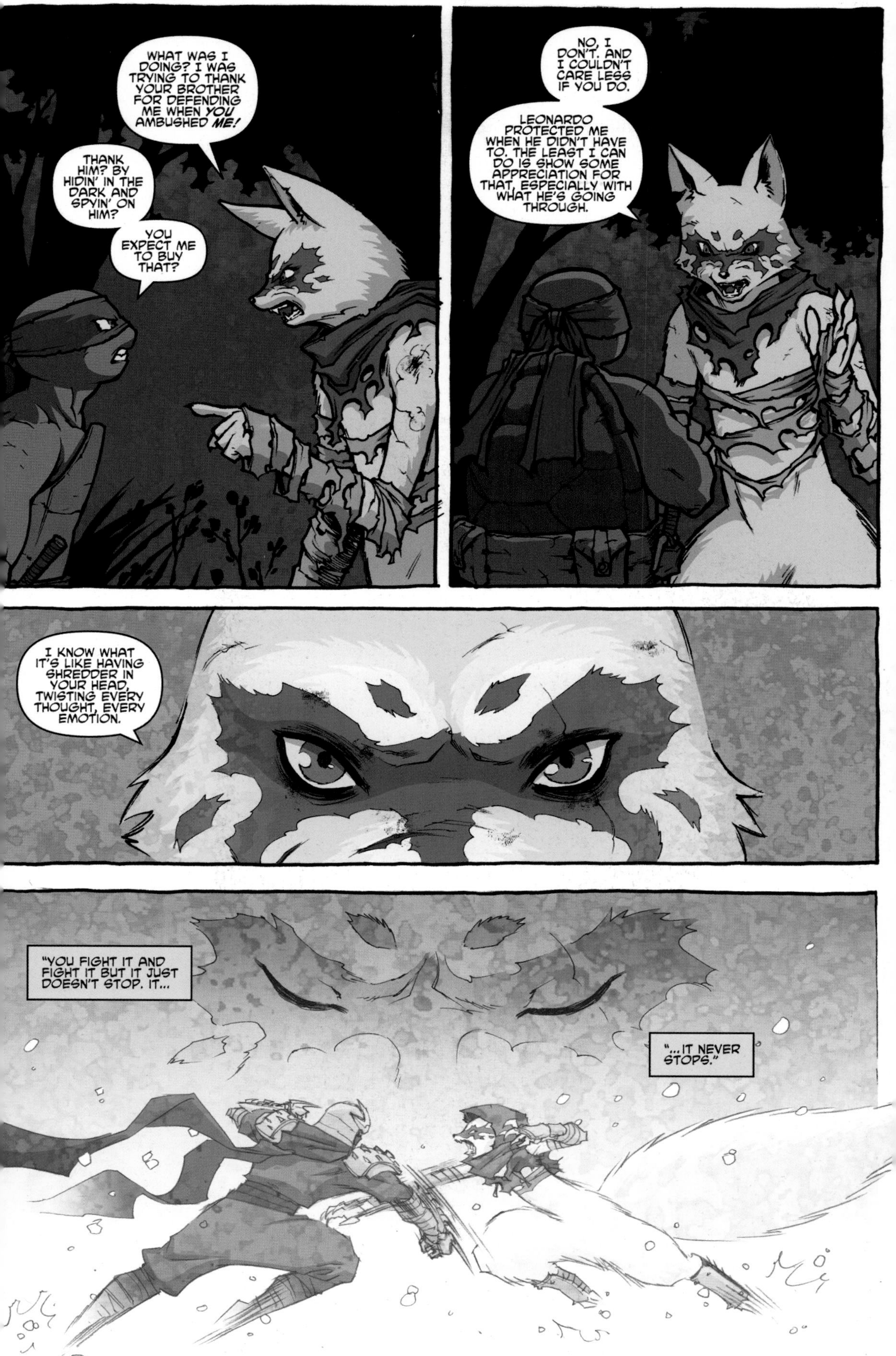
WHAT WAS I DOING? I WAS TRYING TO THANK YOUR BROTHER FOR DEFENDING ME WHEN *YOU* AMBUSHED *ME!*
THANK HIM? BY HIDIN' IN THE DARK AND SPYIN' ON HIM?
YOU EXPECT ME TO BUY THAT?
NO, I DON'T. AND I COULDN'T CARE LESS IF YOU DO.
LEONARDO PROTECTED ME WHEN HE DIDN'T HAVE TO. THE LEAST I CAN DO IS SHOW SOME APPRECIATION FOR THAT, ESPECIALLY WITH WHAT HE'S GOING THROUGH.
I KNOW WHAT IT'S LIKE HAVING SHREDDER IN YOUR HEAD, TWISTING EVERY THOUGHT, EVERY EMOTION.
"YOU FIGHT IT AND FIGHT IT BUT IT JUST DOESN'T STOP. IT...
"...IT NEVER STOPS."

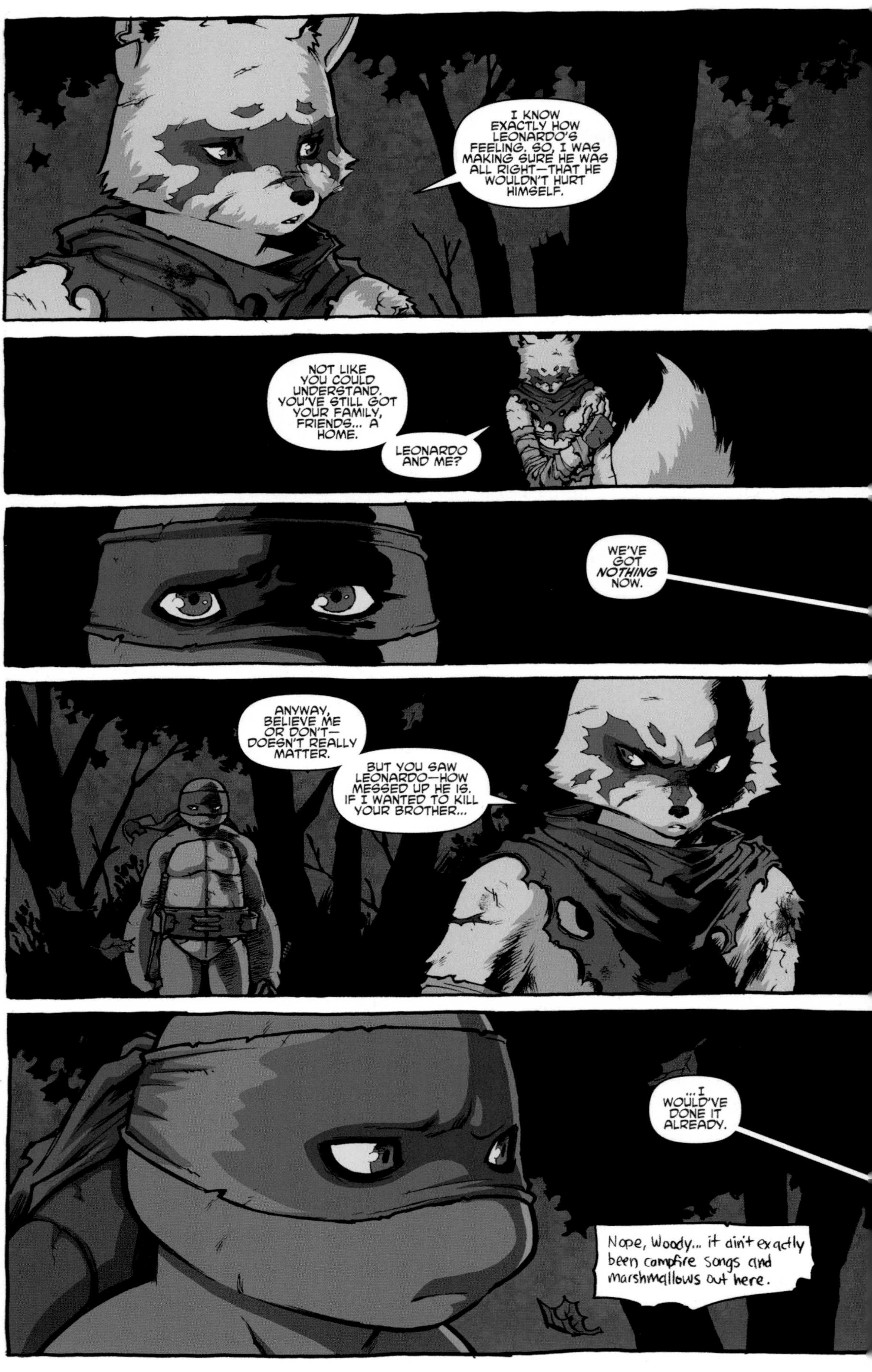
I KNOW EXACTLY HOW LEONARDO'S FEELING. SO, I WAS MAKING SURE HE WAS ALL RIGHT—THAT HE WOULDN'T HURT HIMSELF.
NOT LIKE YOU COULD UNDERSTAND. YOU'VE STILL GOT YOUR FAMILY, FRIENDS... A HOME.
LEONARDO AND ME?
WE'VE GOT *NOTHING* NOW.
ANYWAY, BELIEVE ME OR DON'T— DOESN'T REALLY MATTER.
BUT YOU SAW LEONARDO—HOW MESSED UP HE IS. IF I WANTED TO KILL YOUR BROTHER...
...I WOULD'VE DONE IT ALREADY.
Nope, Woody... it ain't exactly been campfire songs and marshmallows out here.

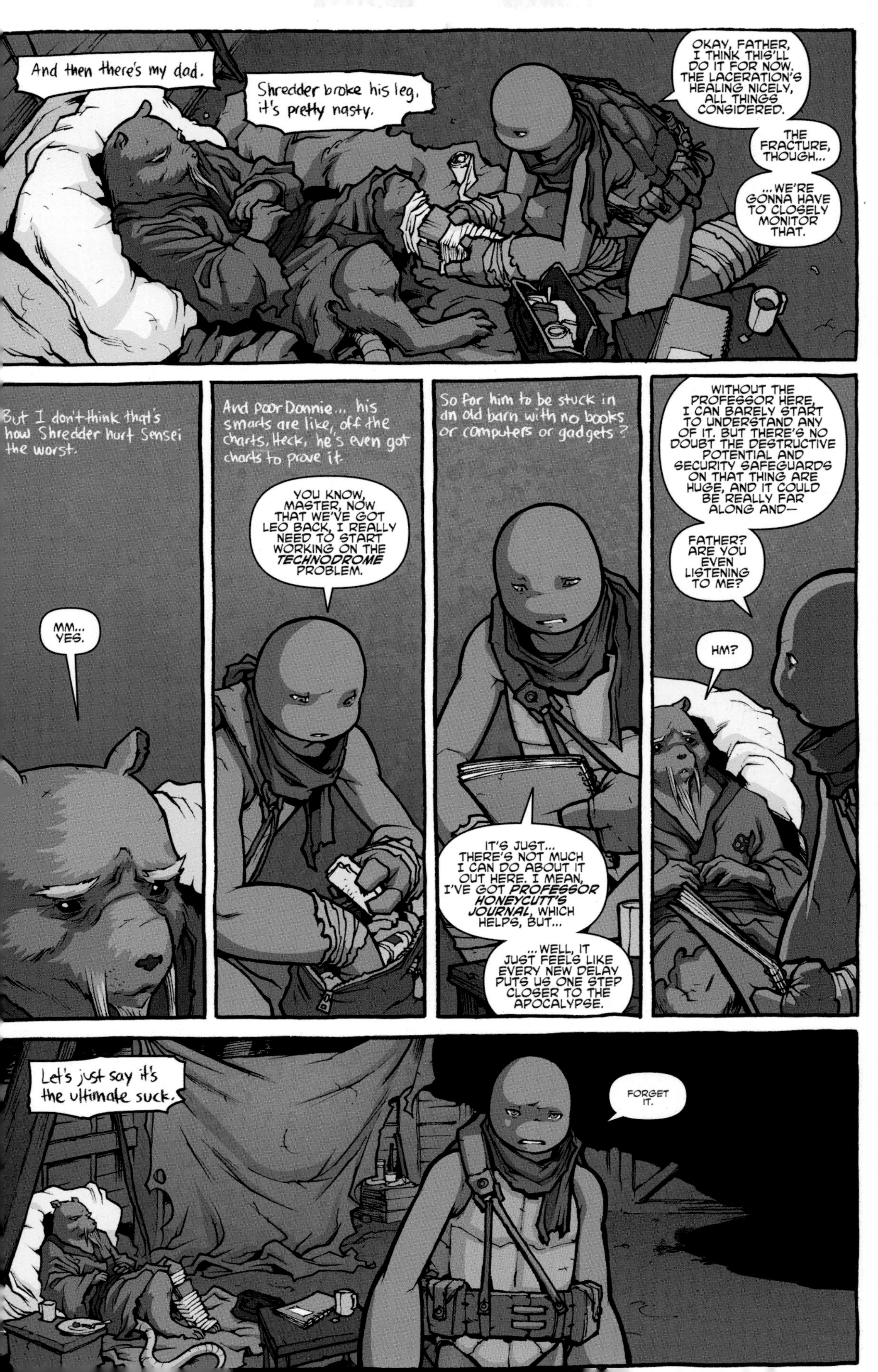

And then there's my dad.
Shredder broke his leg, it's pretty nasty.
OKAY, FATHER, I THINK THIS'LL DO IT FOR NOW. THE LACERATION'S HEALING NICELY, ALL THINGS CONSIDERED.
THE FRACTURE, THOUGH...
...WE'RE GONNA HAVE TO CLOSELY MONITOR THAT.
But I don't think that's how Shredder hurt Sensei the worst.
MM... YES.
And poor Donnie... his smarts are like, off the charts. Heck, he's even got charts to prove it.
YOU KNOW, MASTER, NOW THAT WE'VE GOT LEO BACK, I REALLY NEED TO START WORKING ON THE TECHNODROME PROBLEM.
So for him to be stuck in an old barn with no books or computers or gadgets?
IT'S JUST... THERE'S NOT MUCH I CAN DO ABOUT IT OUT HERE. I MEAN, I'VE GOT PROFESSOR HONEYCUTT'S JOURNAL, WHICH HELPS, BUT...
...WELL, IT JUST FEELS LIKE EVERY NEW DELAY PUTS US ONE STEP CLOSER TO THE APOCALYPSE.
WITHOUT THE PROFESSOR HERE, I CAN BARELY START TO UNDERSTAND ANY OF IT. BUT THERE'S NO DOUBT THE DESTRUCTIVE POTENTIAL AND SECURITY SAFEGUARDS ON THAT THING ARE HUGE, AND IT COULD BE REALLY FAR ALONG AND—
FATHER? ARE YOU EVEN LISTENING TO ME?
HM?
Let's just say it's the ultimate suck.
FORGET IT.

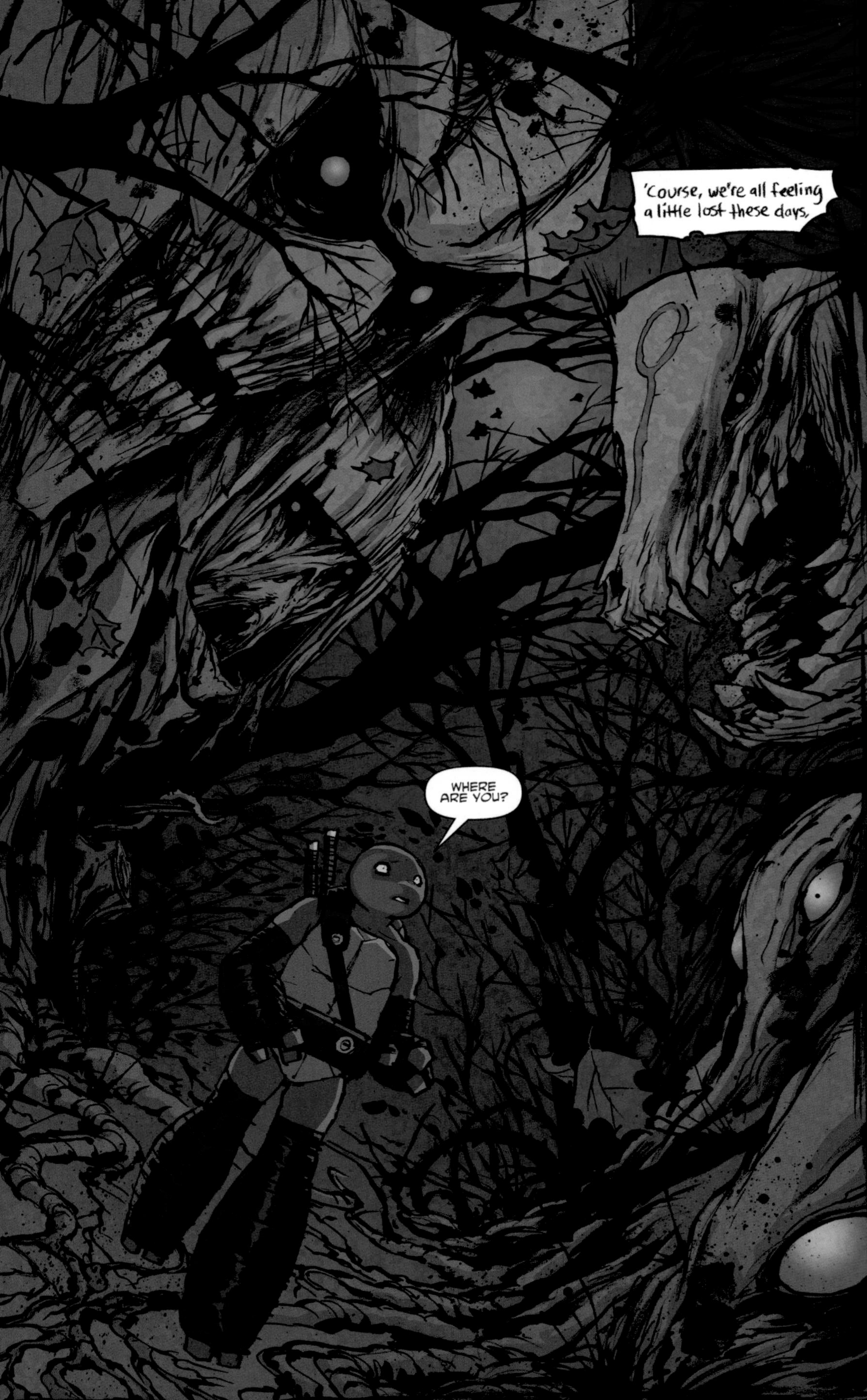
'Course, we're all feeling a little lost these days,
WHERE ARE YOU?

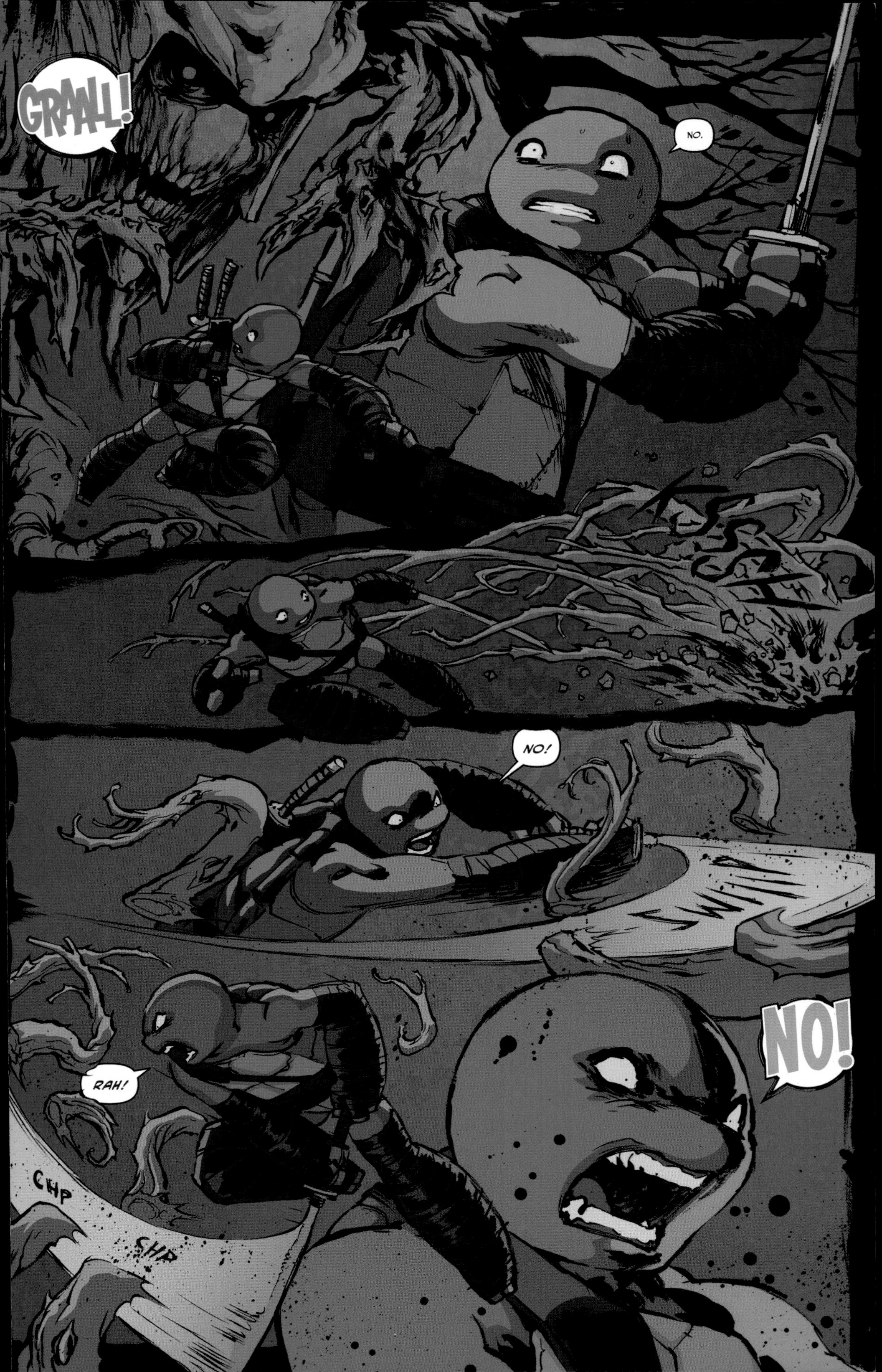
GRAALL!
NO.
NO!
RAH!
NO!
CHP
CHP

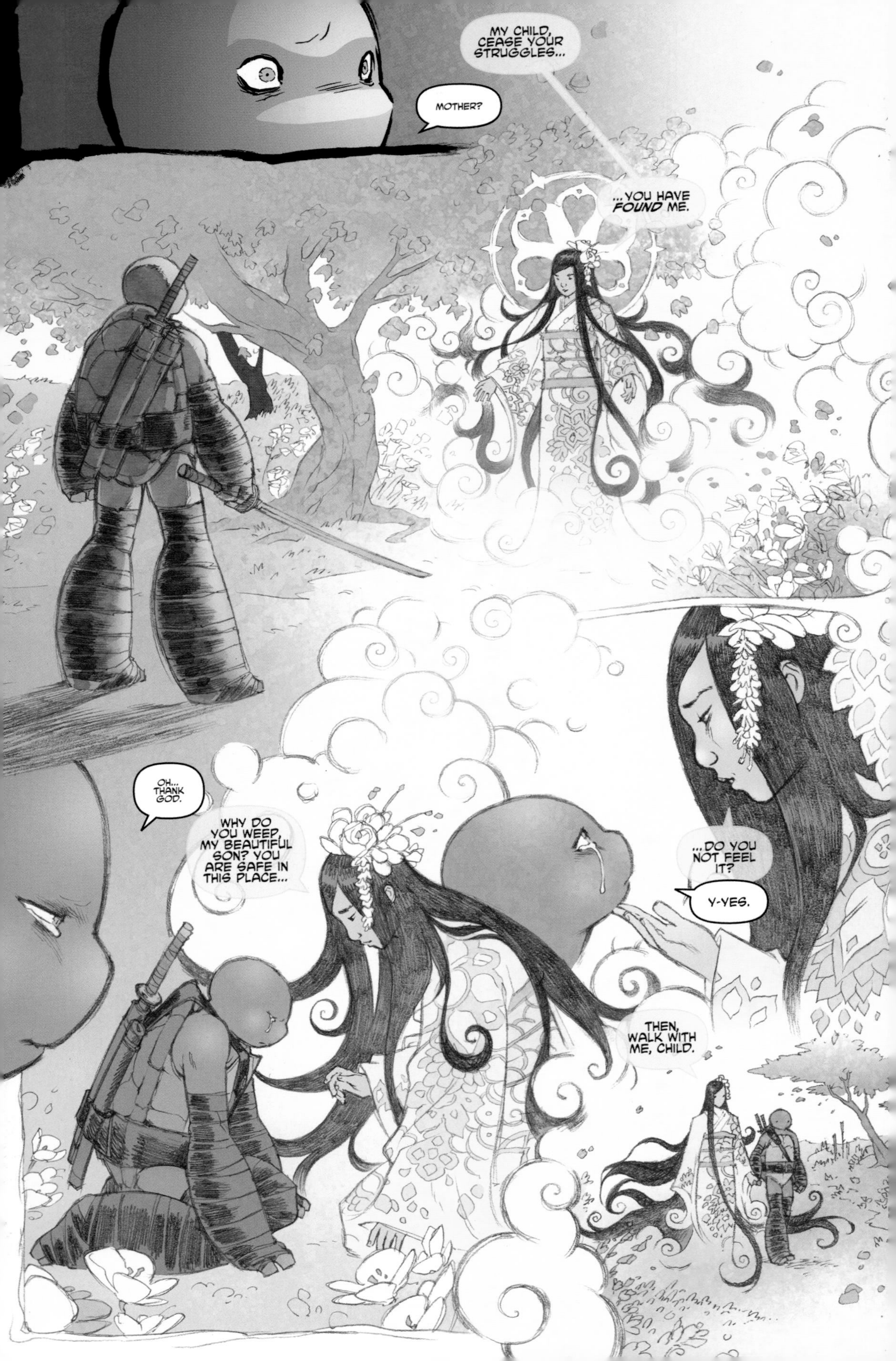
MY CHILD, CEASE YOUR STRUGGLES...
MOTHER?
...YOU HAVE FOUND ME.
OH... THANK GOD.
WHY DO YOU WEEP, MY BEAUTIFUL SON? YOU ARE SAFE IN THIS PLACE...
...DO YOU NOT FEEL IT?
Y-YES.
THEN, WALK WITH ME, CHILD.

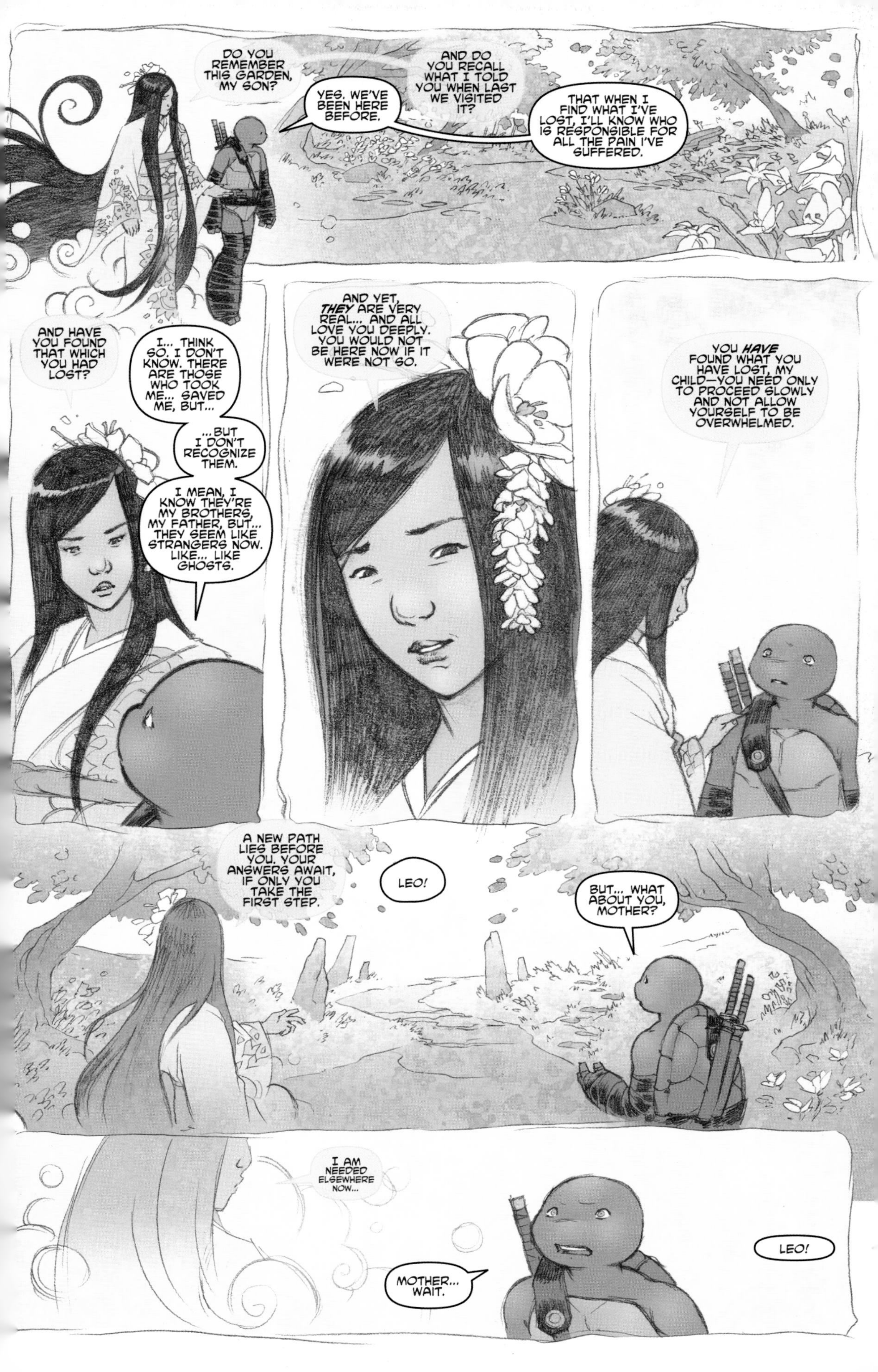
DO YOU REMEMBER THIS GARDEN, MY SON?
YES. WE'VE BEEN HERE BEFORE.
AND DO YOU RECALL WHAT I TOLD YOU WHEN LAST WE VISITED IT?
THAT WHEN I FIND WHAT I'VE LOST, I'LL KNOW WHO IS RESPONSIBLE FOR ALL THE PAIN I'VE SUFFERED.
AND HAVE YOU FOUND THAT WHICH YOU HAD LOST?
I... THINK SO. I DON'T KNOW. THERE ARE THOSE WHO TOOK ME... SAVED ME, BUT...
...BUT I DON'T RECOGNIZE THEM.
I MEAN, I KNOW THEY'RE MY BROTHERS, MY FATHER, BUT... THEY SEEM LIKE STRANGERS NOW. LIKE... LIKE GHOSTS.
AND YET, THEY ARE VERY REAL... AND ALL LOVE YOU DEEPLY. YOU WOULD NOT BE HERE NOW IF IT WERE NOT SO.
YOU HAVE FOUND WHAT YOU HAVE LOST, MY CHILD—YOU NEED ONLY TO PROCEED SLOWLY AND NOT ALLOW YOURSELF TO BE OVERWHELMED.
A NEW PATH LIES BEFORE YOU. YOUR ANSWERS AWAIT, IF ONLY YOU TAKE THE FIRST STEP.
LEO!
BUT... WHAT ABOUT YOU, MOTHER?
I AM NEEDED ELSEWHERE NOW...
MOTHER... WAIT.
LEO!

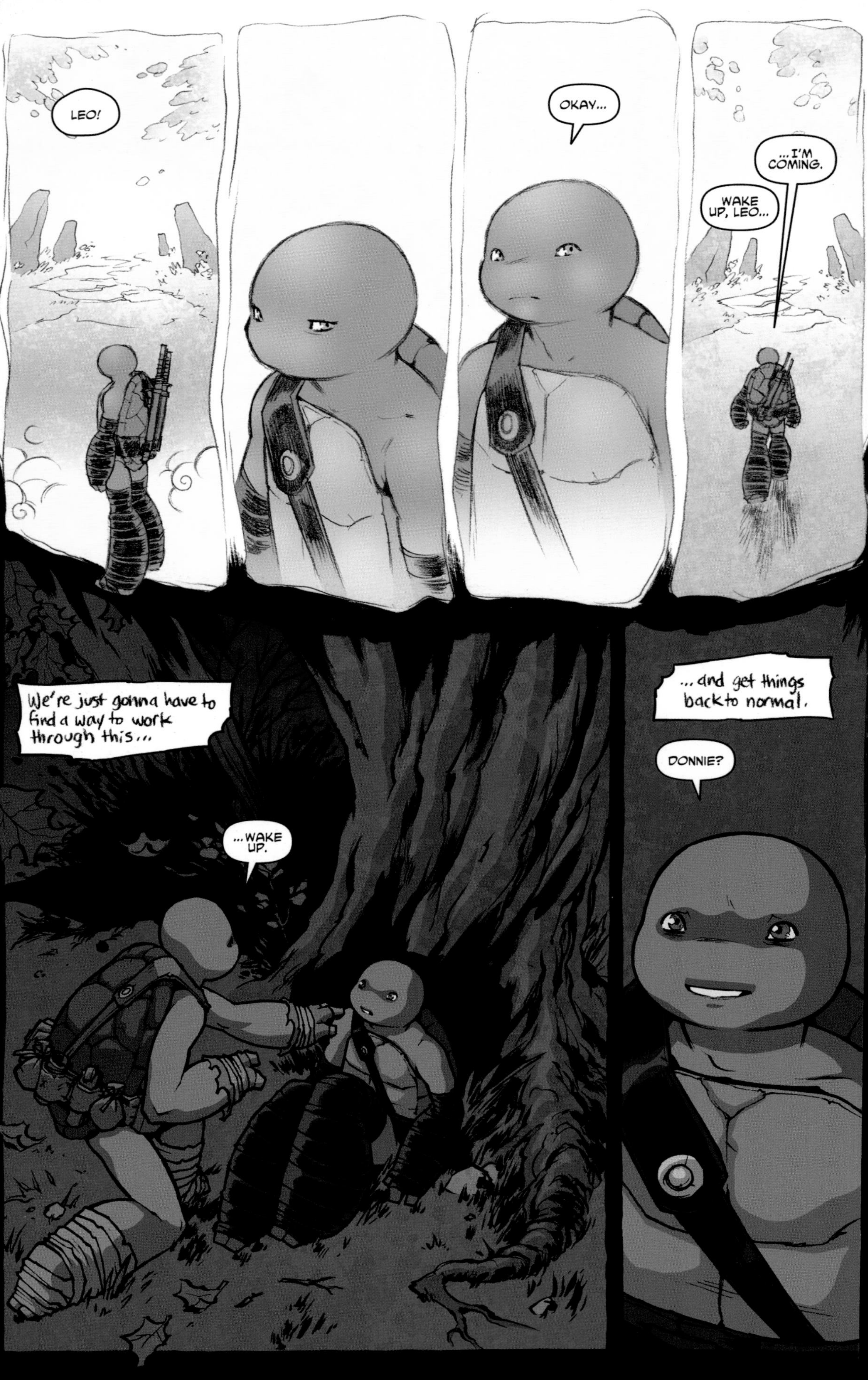

LEO!
OKAY...
WAKE UP, LEO...
...I'M COMING.
We're just gonna have to find a way to work through this...
...WAKE UP.
...and get things back to normal.
DONNIE?

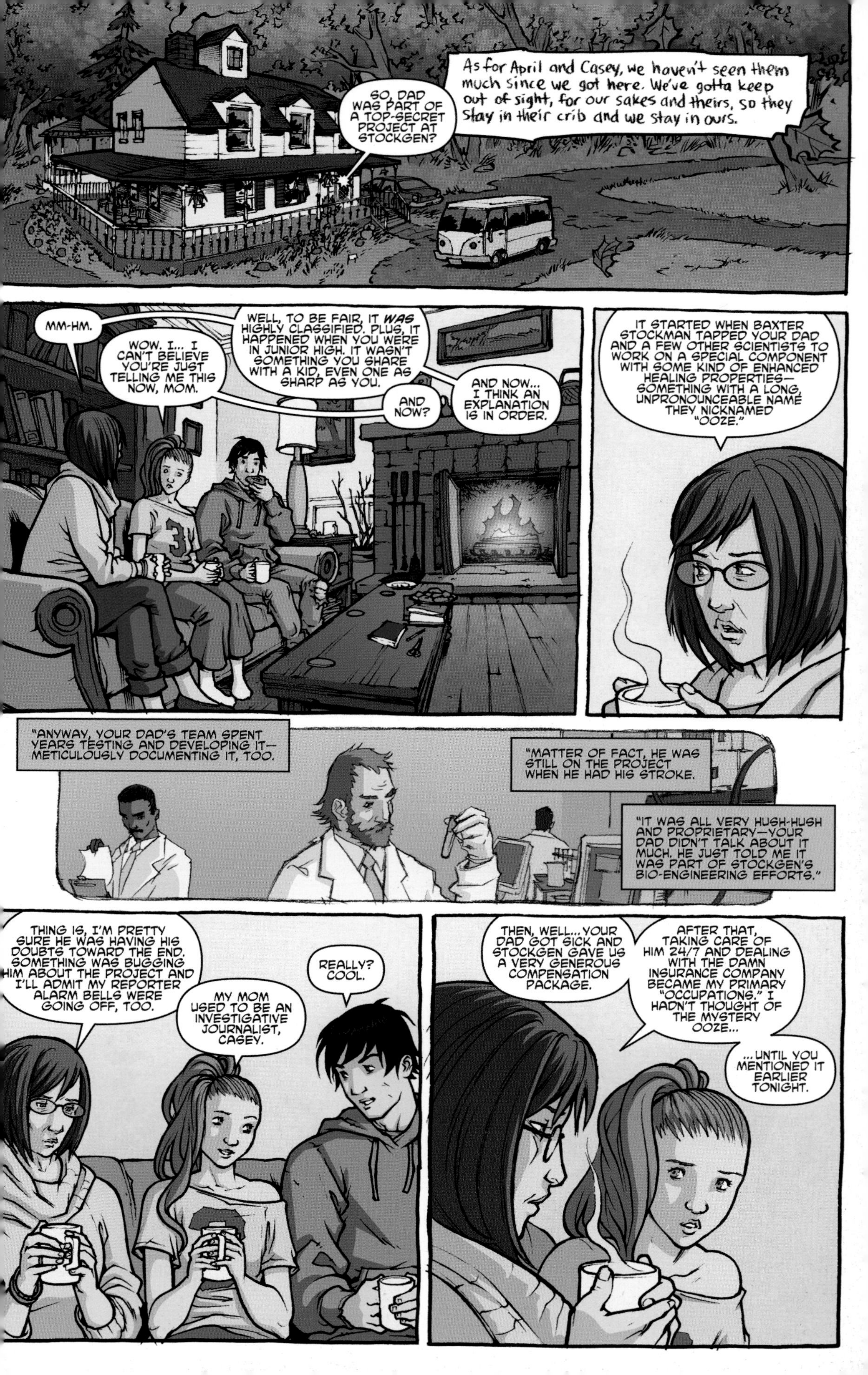

SO, DAD WAS PART OF A TOP-SECRET PROJECT AT STOCKGEN?
As for April and Casey, we haven't seen them much since we got here. We've gotta keep out of sight, for our sakes and theirs, so they stay in their crib and we stay in ours.
MM-HM.
WOW. I... I CAN'T BELIEVE YOU'RE JUST TELLING ME THIS NOW, MOM.
WELL, TO BE FAIR, IT WAS HIGHLY CLASSIFIED. PLUS, IT HAPPENED WHEN YOU WERE IN JUNIOR HIGH. IT WASN'T SOMETHING YOU SHARE WITH A KID, EVEN ONE AS SHARP AS YOU.
AND NOW?
AND NOW... I THINK AN EXPLANATION IS IN ORDER.
IT STARTED WHEN BAXTER STOCKMAN TAPPED YOUR DAD AND A FEW OTHER SCIENTISTS TO WORK ON A SPECIAL COMPONENT WITH SOME KIND OF ENHANCED HEALING PROPERTIES—SOMETHING WITH A LONG, UNPRONOUNCEABLE NAME THEY NICKNAMED "OOZE."
"ANYWAY, YOUR DAD'S TEAM SPENT YEARS TESTING AND DEVELOPING IT—METICULOUSLY DOCUMENTING IT, TOO.
"MATTER OF FACT, HE WAS STILL ON THE PROJECT WHEN HE HAD HIS STROKE.
"IT WAS ALL VERY HUSH-HUSH AND PROPRIETARY—YOUR DAD DIDN'T TALK ABOUT IT MUCH. HE JUST TOLD ME IT WAS PART OF STOCKGEN'S BIO-ENGINEERING EFFORTS."
THING IS, I'M PRETTY SURE HE WAS HAVING HIS DOUBTS TOWARD THE END. SOMETHING WAS BUGGING HIM ABOUT THE PROJECT AND I'LL ADMIT MY REPORTER ALARM BELLS WERE GOING OFF, TOO.
MY MOM USED TO BE AN INVESTIGATIVE JOURNALIST, CASEY.
REALLY? COOL.
THEN, WELL... YOUR DAD GOT SICK AND STOCKGEN GAVE US A VERY GENEROUS COMPENSATION PACKAGE.
AFTER THAT, TAKING CARE OF HIM 24/7 AND DEALING WITH THE DAMN INSURANCE COMPANY BECAME MY PRIMARY "OCCUPATIONS." I HADN'T THOUGHT OF THE MYSTERY OOZE...
...UNTIL YOU MENTIONED IT EARLIER TONIGHT.

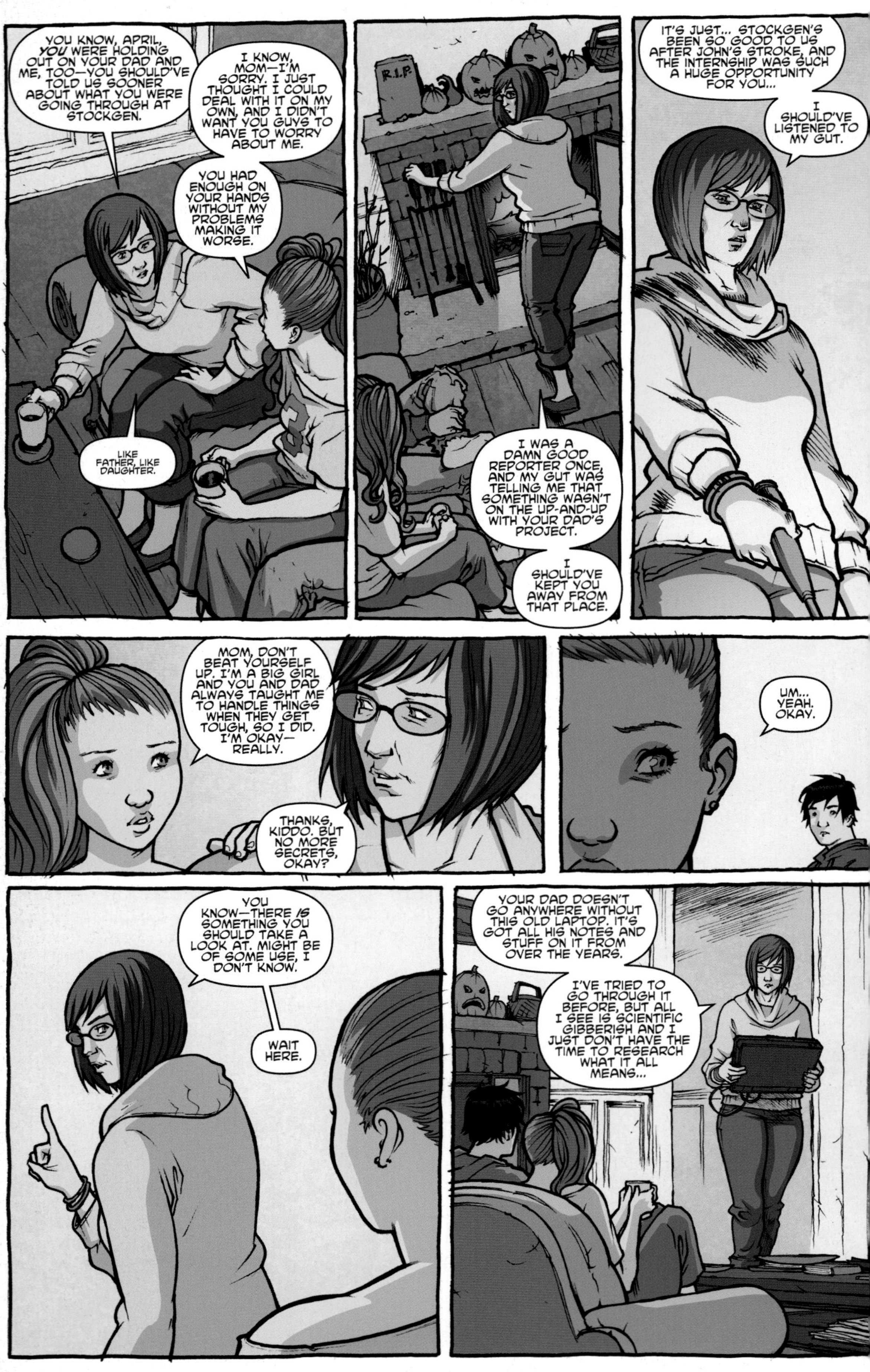
YOU KNOW, APRIL, *YOU* WERE HOLDING OUT ON YOUR DAD AND ME, TOO—YOU SHOULD'VE TOLD US SOONER ABOUT WHAT YOU WERE GOING THROUGH AT STOCKGEN.
I KNOW, MOM—I'M SORRY. I JUST THOUGHT I COULD DEAL WITH IT ON MY OWN, AND I DIDN'T WANT YOU GUYS TO HAVE TO WORRY ABOUT ME.
YOU HAD ENOUGH ON YOUR HANDS WITHOUT MY PROBLEMS MAKING IT WORSE.
LIKE FATHER, LIKE DAUGHTER.
I WAS A DAMN GOOD REPORTER ONCE, AND MY GUT WAS TELLING ME THAT SOMETHING WASN'T ON THE UP-AND-UP WITH YOUR DAD'S PROJECT.
I SHOULD'VE KEPT YOU AWAY FROM THAT PLACE.
R.I.P.
IT'S JUST... STOCKGEN'S BEEN SO GOOD TO US AFTER JOHN'S STROKE, AND THE INTERNSHIP WAS SUCH A HUGE OPPORTUNITY FOR YOU...
I SHOULD'VE LISTENED TO MY GUT.
MOM, DON'T BEAT YOURSELF UP. I'M A BIG GIRL AND YOU AND DAD ALWAYS TAUGHT ME TO HANDLE THINGS WHEN THEY GET TOUGH, SO I DID. I'M OKAY—REALLY.
THANKS, KIDDO. BUT NO MORE SECRETS, OKAY?
UM... YEAH. OKAY.
YOU KNOW—THERE *IS* SOMETHING YOU SHOULD TAKE A LOOK AT. MIGHT BE OF SOME USE, I DON'T KNOW.
WAIT HERE.
YOUR DAD DOESN'T GO ANYWHERE WITHOUT THIS OLD LAPTOP. IT'S GOT ALL HIS NOTES AND STUFF ON IT FROM OVER THE YEARS.
I'VE TRIED TO GO THROUGH IT BEFORE, BUT ALL I SEE IS SCIENTIFIC GIBBERISH AND I JUST DON'T HAVE THE TIME TO RESEARCH WHAT IT ALL MEANS...

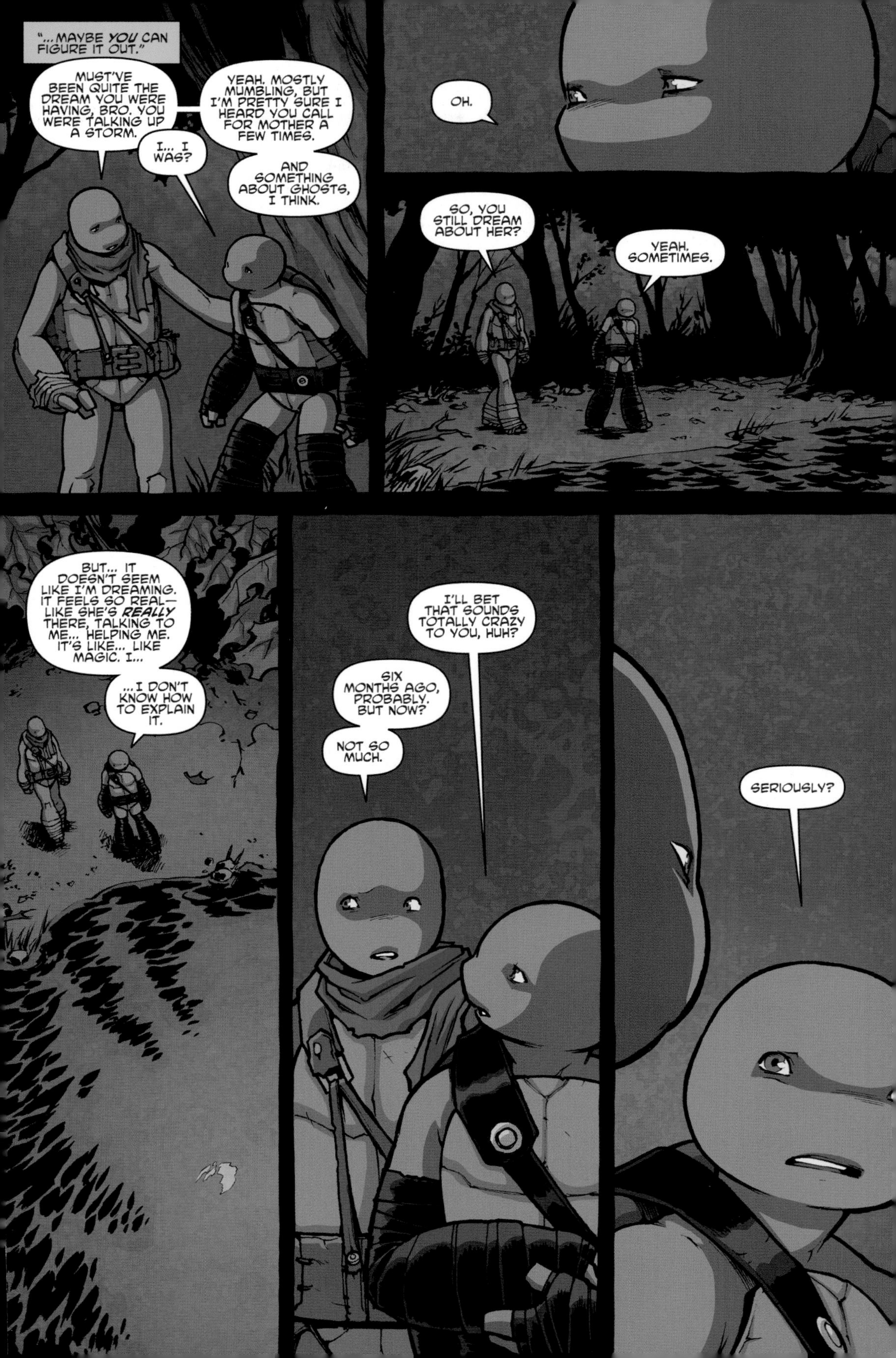
"...MAYBE *YOU* CAN FIGURE IT OUT."
MUST'VE BEEN QUITE THE DREAM YOU WERE HAVING, BRO. YOU WERE TALKING UP A STORM.
YEAH. MOSTLY MUMBLING, BUT I'M PRETTY SURE I HEARD YOU CALL FOR MOTHER A FEW TIMES.
I... I WAS?
AND SOMETHING ABOUT GHOSTS, I THINK.
OH.
SO, YOU STILL DREAM ABOUT HER?
YEAH. SOMETIMES.
BUT... IT DOESN'T SEEM LIKE I'M DREAMING. IT FEELS SO REAL— LIKE SHE'S ***REALLY*** THERE, TALKING TO ME... HELPING ME. IT'S LIKE... LIKE MAGIC. I...
...I DON'T KNOW HOW TO EXPLAIN IT.
I'LL BET THAT SOUNDS TOTALLY CRAZY TO YOU, HUH?
SIX MONTHS AGO, PROBABLY. BUT NOW?
NOT SO MUCH.
SERIOUSLY?

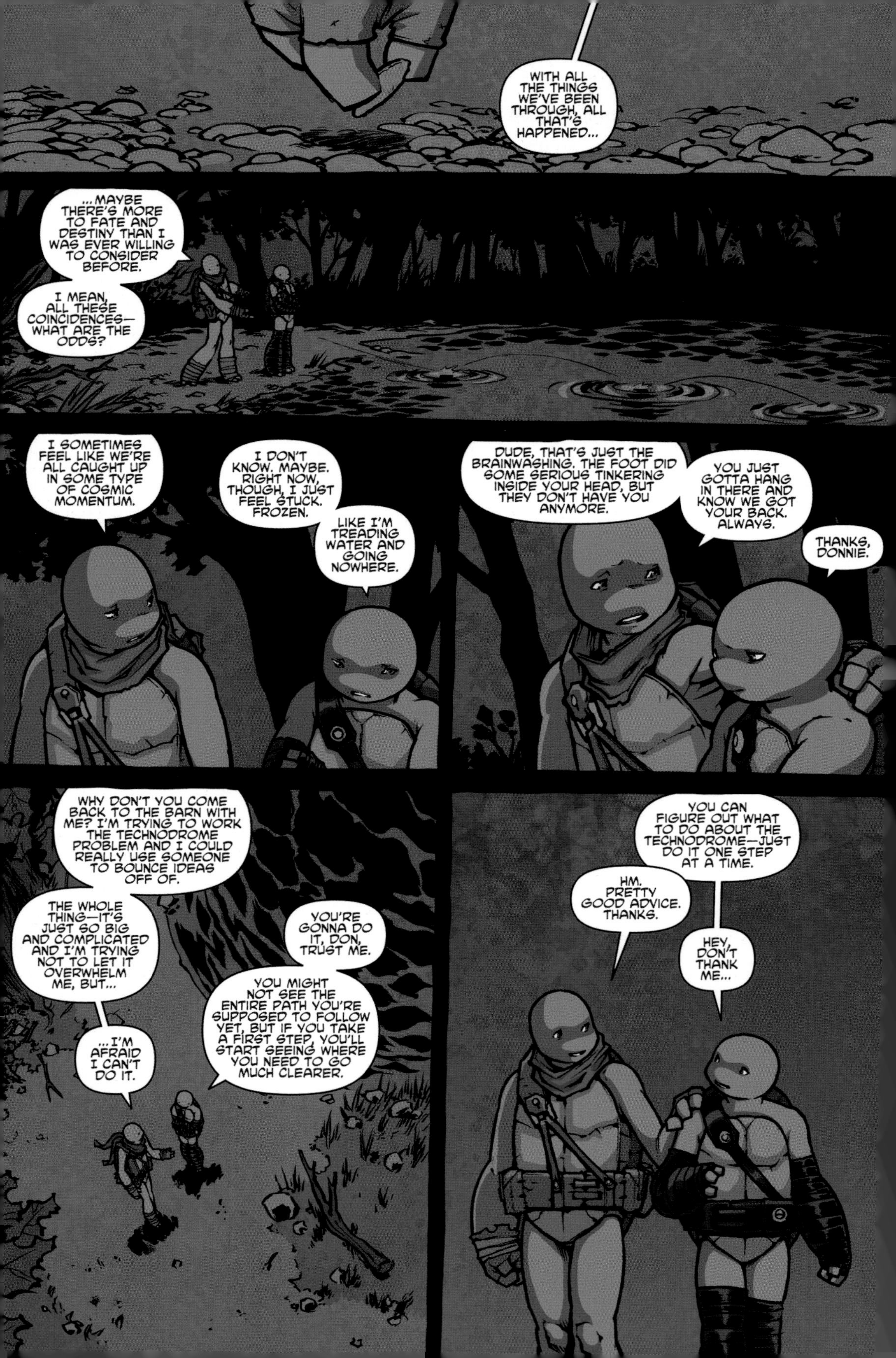

WITH ALL THE THINGS WE'VE BEEN THROUGH, ALL THAT'S HAPPENED...
...MAYBE THERE'S MORE TO FATE AND DESTINY THAN I WAS EVER WILLING TO CONSIDER BEFORE.
I MEAN, ALL THESE COINCIDENCES— WHAT ARE THE ODDS?
I SOMETIMES FEEL LIKE WE'RE ALL CAUGHT UP IN SOME TYPE OF COSMIC MOMENTUM.
I DON'T KNOW. MAYBE. RIGHT NOW, THOUGH, I JUST FEEL STUCK. FROZEN.
LIKE I'M TREADING WATER AND GOING NOWHERE.
DUDE, THAT'S JUST THE BRAINWASHING. THE FOOT DID SOME SERIOUS TINKERING INSIDE YOUR HEAD, BUT THEY DON'T HAVE YOU ANYMORE.
YOU JUST GOTTA HANG IN THERE AND KNOW WE GOT YOUR BACK. ALWAYS.
THANKS, DONNIE.
WHY DON'T YOU COME BACK TO THE BARN WITH ME? I'M TRYING TO WORK THE TECHNODROME PROBLEM AND I COULD REALLY USE SOMEONE TO BOUNCE IDEAS OFF OF.
THE WHOLE THING—IT'S JUST SO BIG AND COMPLICATED AND I'M TRYING NOT TO LET IT OVERWHELM ME, BUT...
...I'M AFRAID I CAN'T DO IT.
YOU'RE GONNA DO IT, DON, TRUST ME.
YOU MIGHT NOT SEE THE ENTIRE PATH YOU'RE SUPPOSED TO FOLLOW YET, BUT IF YOU TAKE A FIRST STEP, YOU'LL START SEEING WHERE YOU NEED TO GO MUCH CLEARER.
YOU CAN FIGURE OUT WHAT TO DO ABOUT THE TECHNODROME—JUST DO IT ONE STEP AT A TIME.
HM. PRETTY GOOD ADVICE. THANKS.
HEY, DON'T THANK ME...

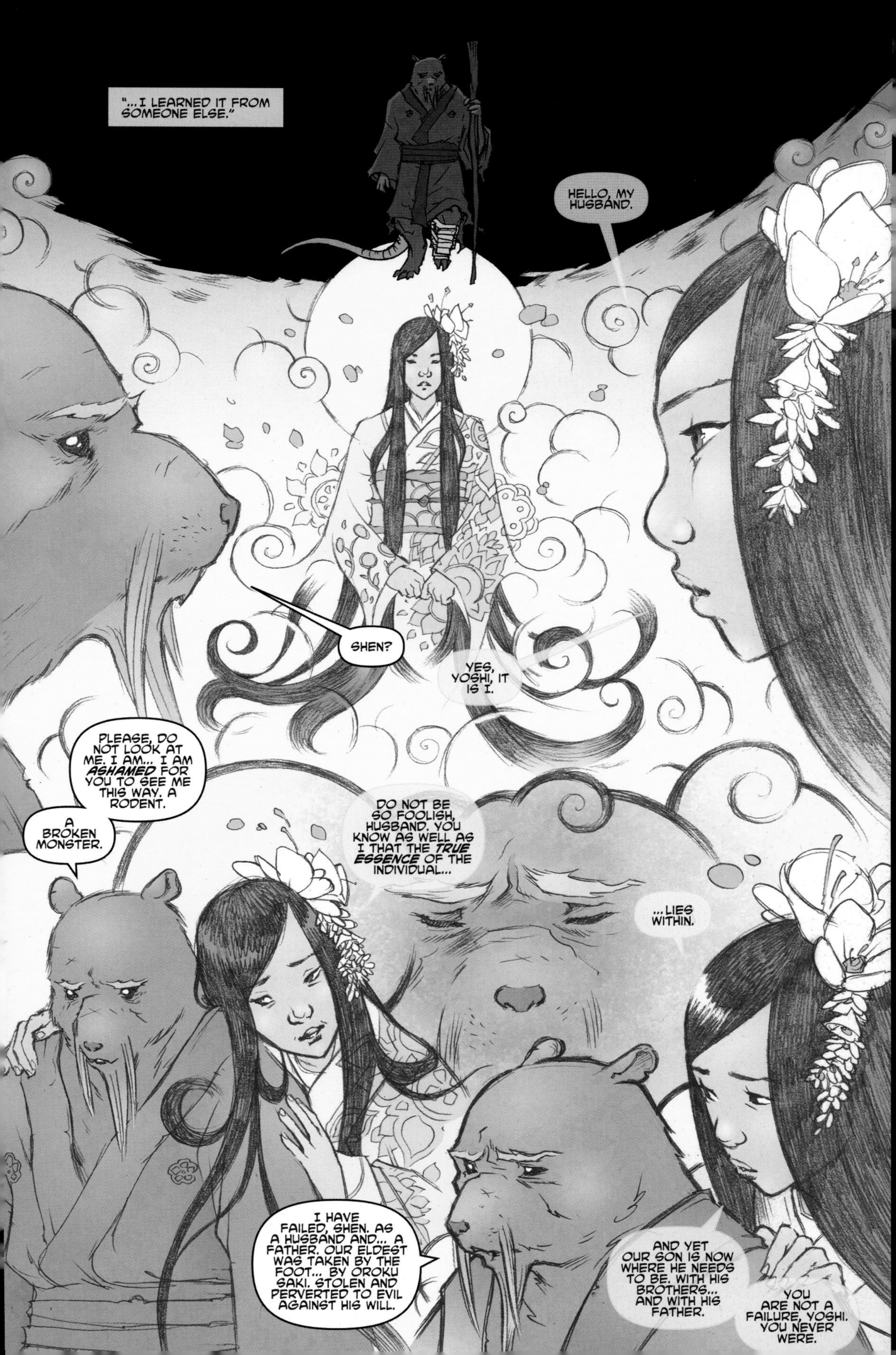
"...I LEARNED IT FROM SOMEONE ELSE."
HELLO, MY HUSBAND.
SHEN?
YES, YOSHI, IT IS I.
PLEASE, DO NOT LOOK AT ME. I AM... I AM ASHAMED FOR YOU TO SEE ME THIS WAY. A RODENT.
A BROKEN MONSTER.
DO NOT BE SO FOOLISH, HUSBAND. YOU KNOW AS WELL AS I THAT THE TRUE ESSENCE OF THE INDIVIDUAL...
...LIES WITHIN.
I HAVE FAILED, SHEN. AS A HUSBAND AND... A FATHER. OUR ELDEST WAS TAKEN BY THE FOOT... BY OROKU SAKI. STOLEN AND PERVERTED TO EVIL AGAINST HIS WILL.
AND YET OUR SON IS NOW WHERE HE NEEDS TO BE. WITH HIS BROTHERS... AND WITH HIS FATHER.
YOU ARE NOT A FAILURE, YOSHI. YOU NEVER WERE.

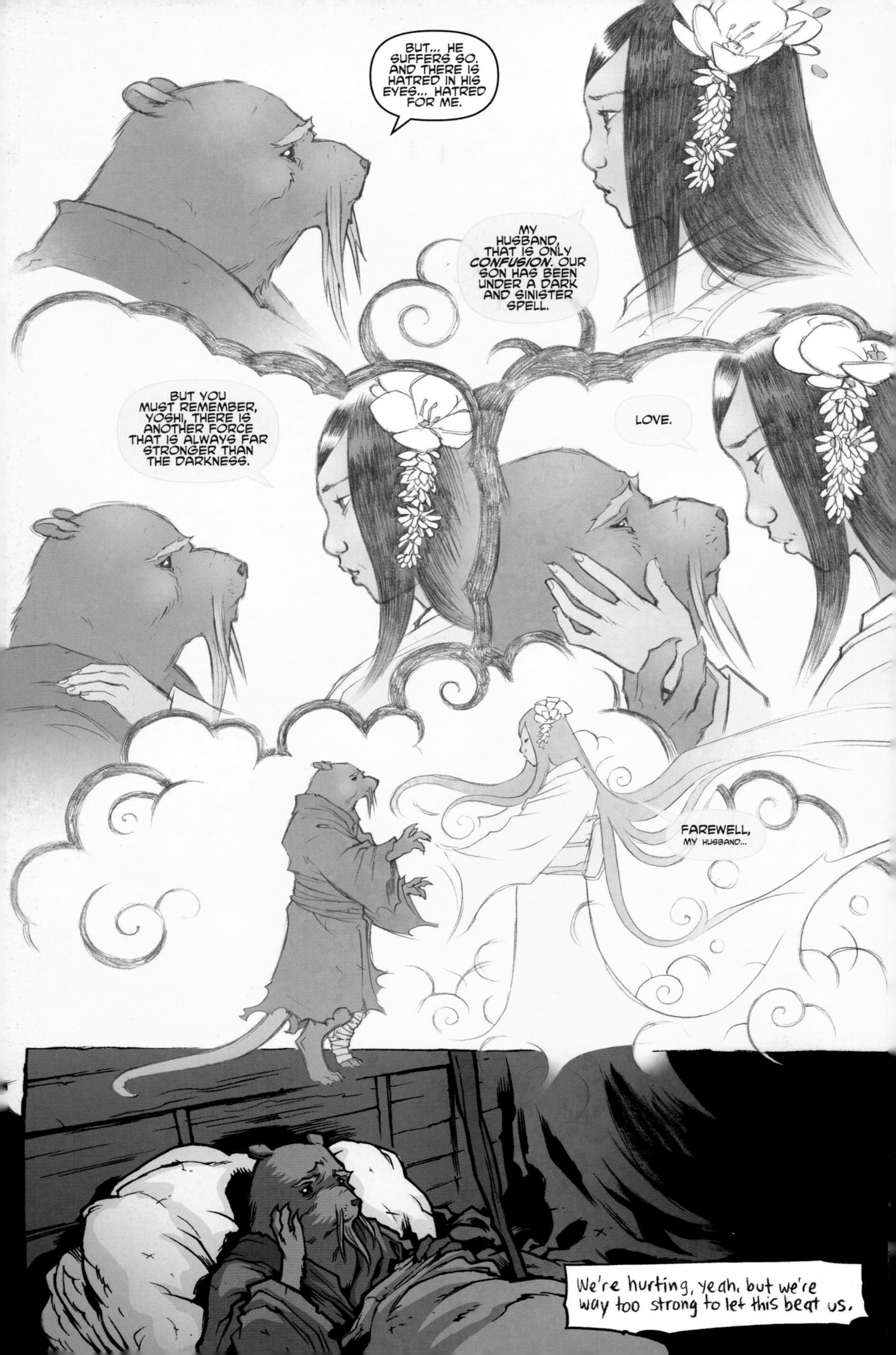
BUT... HE SUFFERS SO. AND THERE IS HATRED IN HIS EYES... HATRED FOR ME.
MY HUSBAND, THAT IS ONLY *CONFUSION*. OUR SON HAS BEEN UNDER A DARK AND SINISTER SPELL.
BUT YOU MUST REMEMBER, YOSHI, THERE IS ANOTHER FORCE THAT IS ALWAYS FAR STRONGER THAN THE DARKNESS.
LOVE.
FAREWELL, MY HUSBAND...
We're hurting, yeah, but we're way too strong to let this beat us.

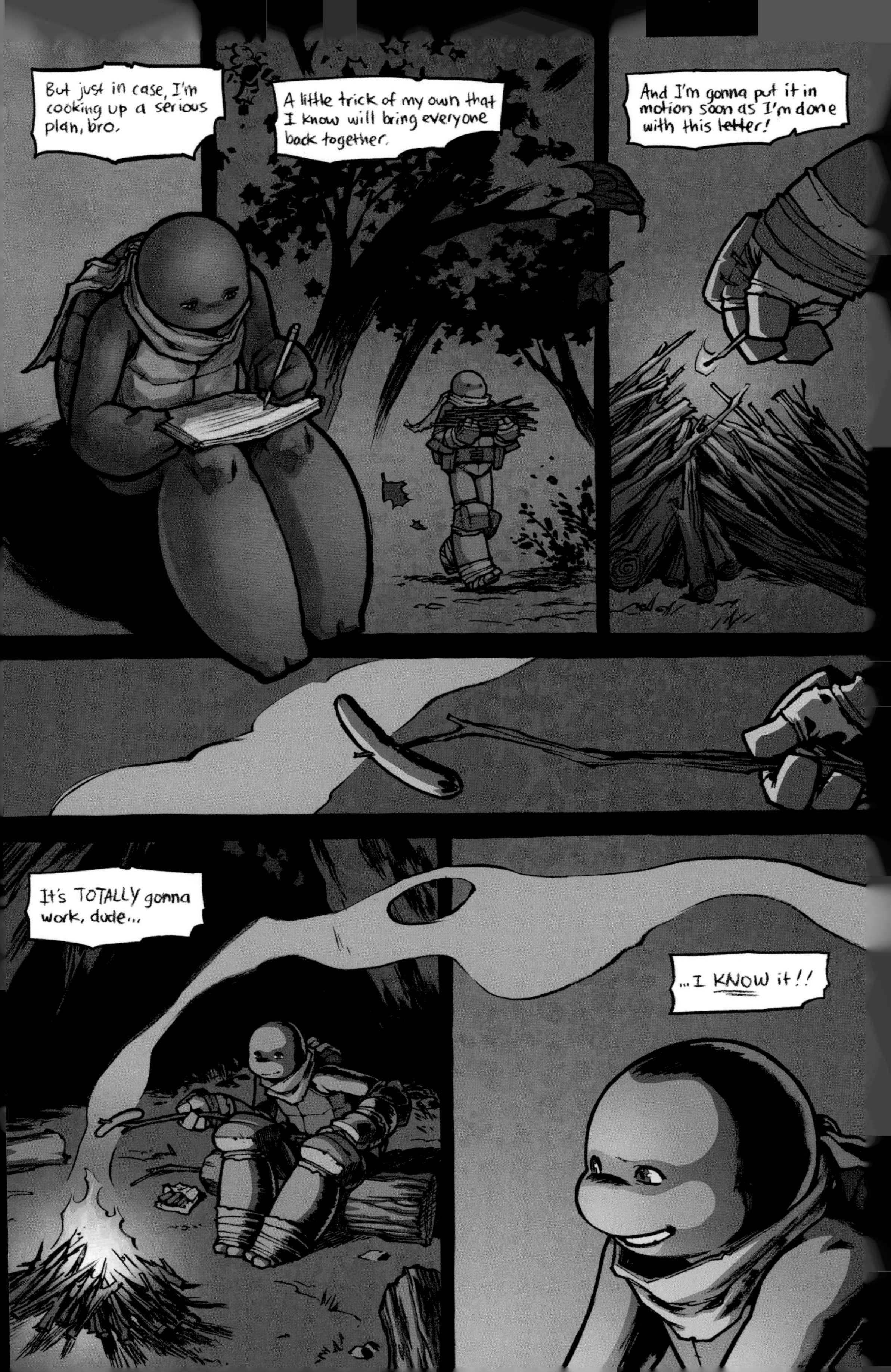
But just in case, I'm cooking up a serious plan, bro.
A little trick of my own that I know will bring everyone back together.
And I'm gonna put it in motion soon as I'm done with this letter!
It's TOTALLY gonna work, dude...
...I KNOW it!!

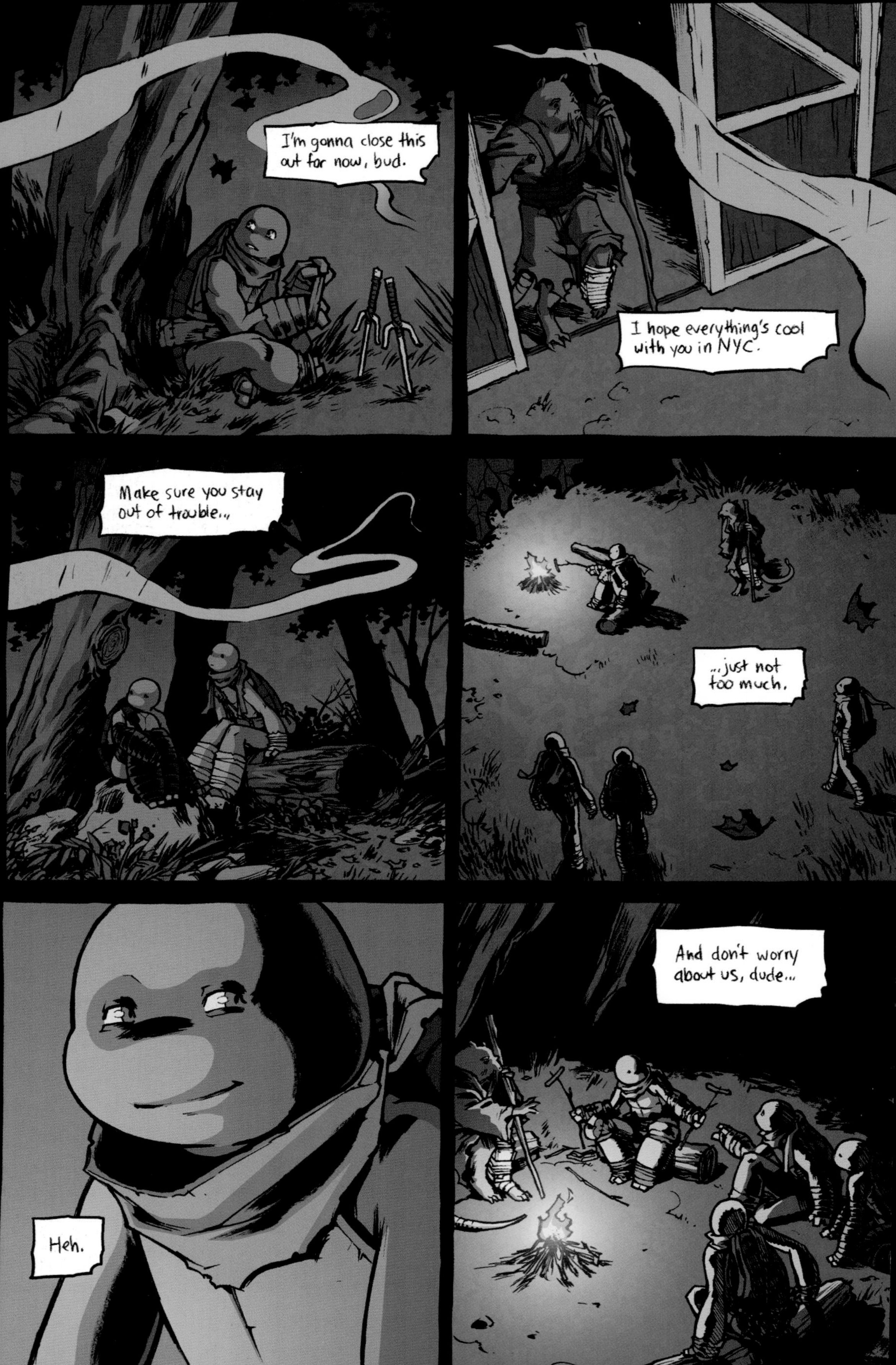

I'm gonna close this out for now, bud.
I hope everything's cool with you in NYC.
Make sure you stay out of trouble...
...just not too much.
Heh.
And don't worry about us, dude...

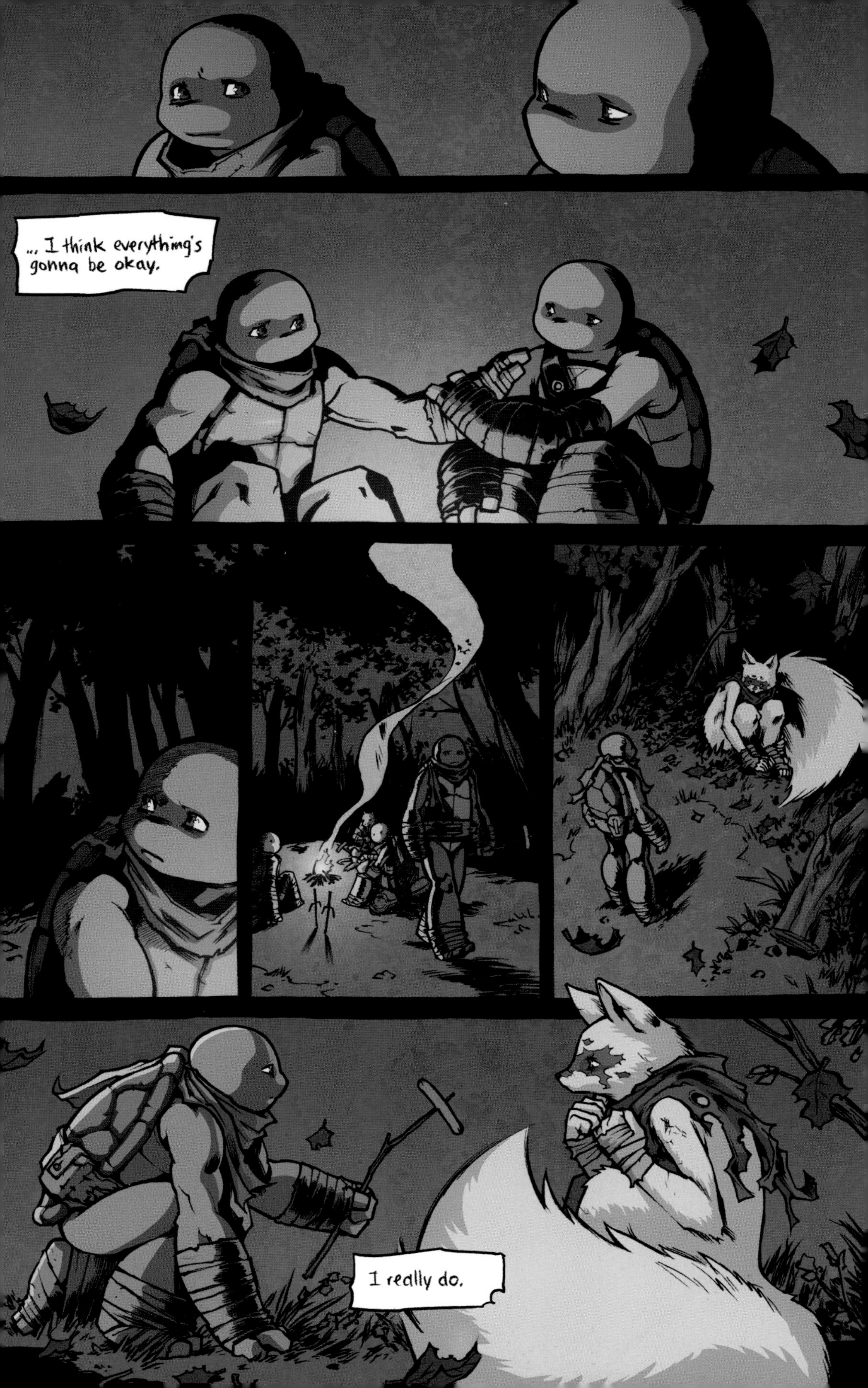
... I think everything's gonna be okay.
I really do.

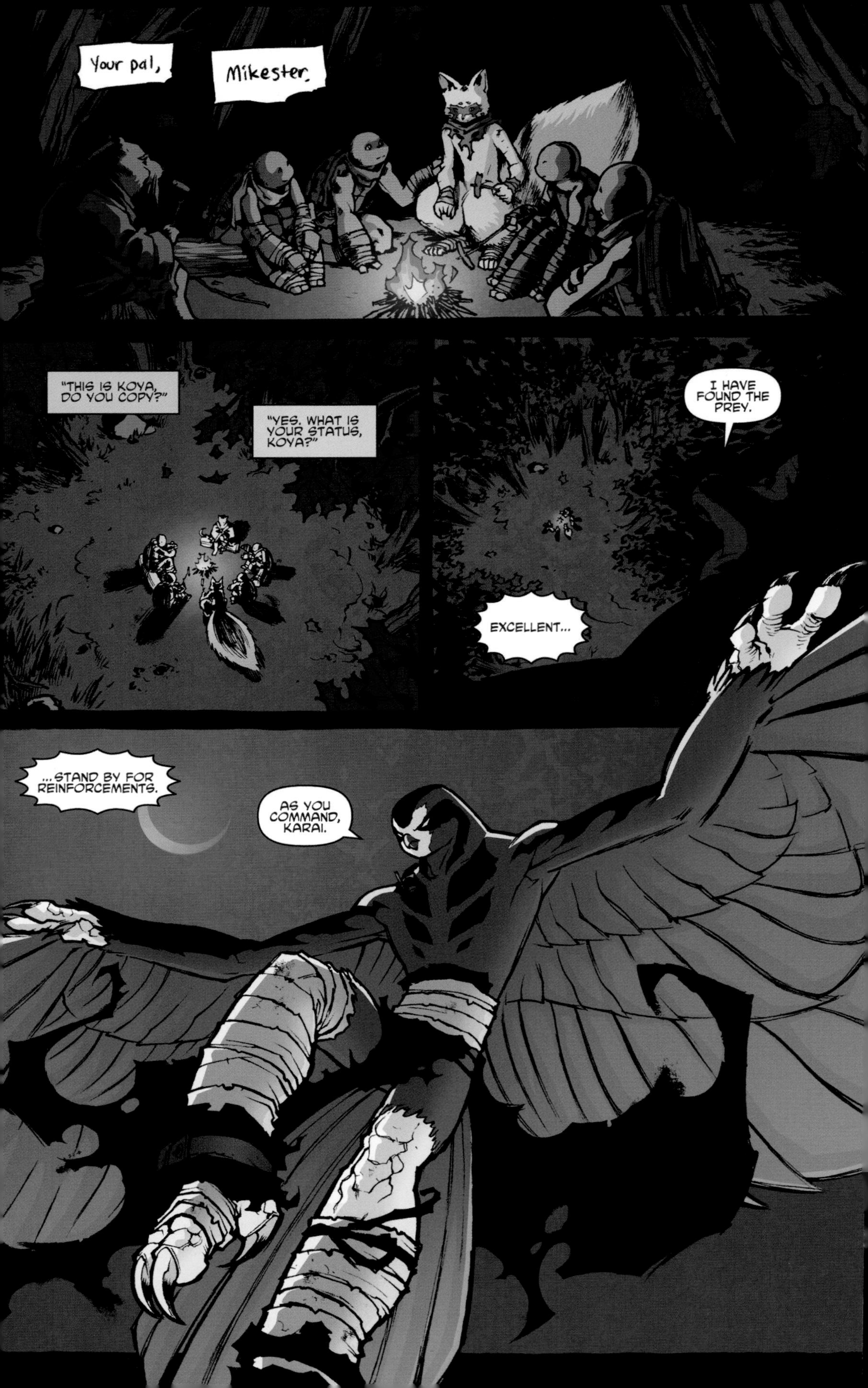
Your pal,
Mikester.
"THIS IS KOYA, DO YOU COPY?"
"YES. WHAT IS YOUR STATUS, KOYA?"
I HAVE FOUND THE PREY.
EXCELLENT...
...STAND BY FOR REINFORCEMENTS.
AS YOU COMMAND, KARAI.

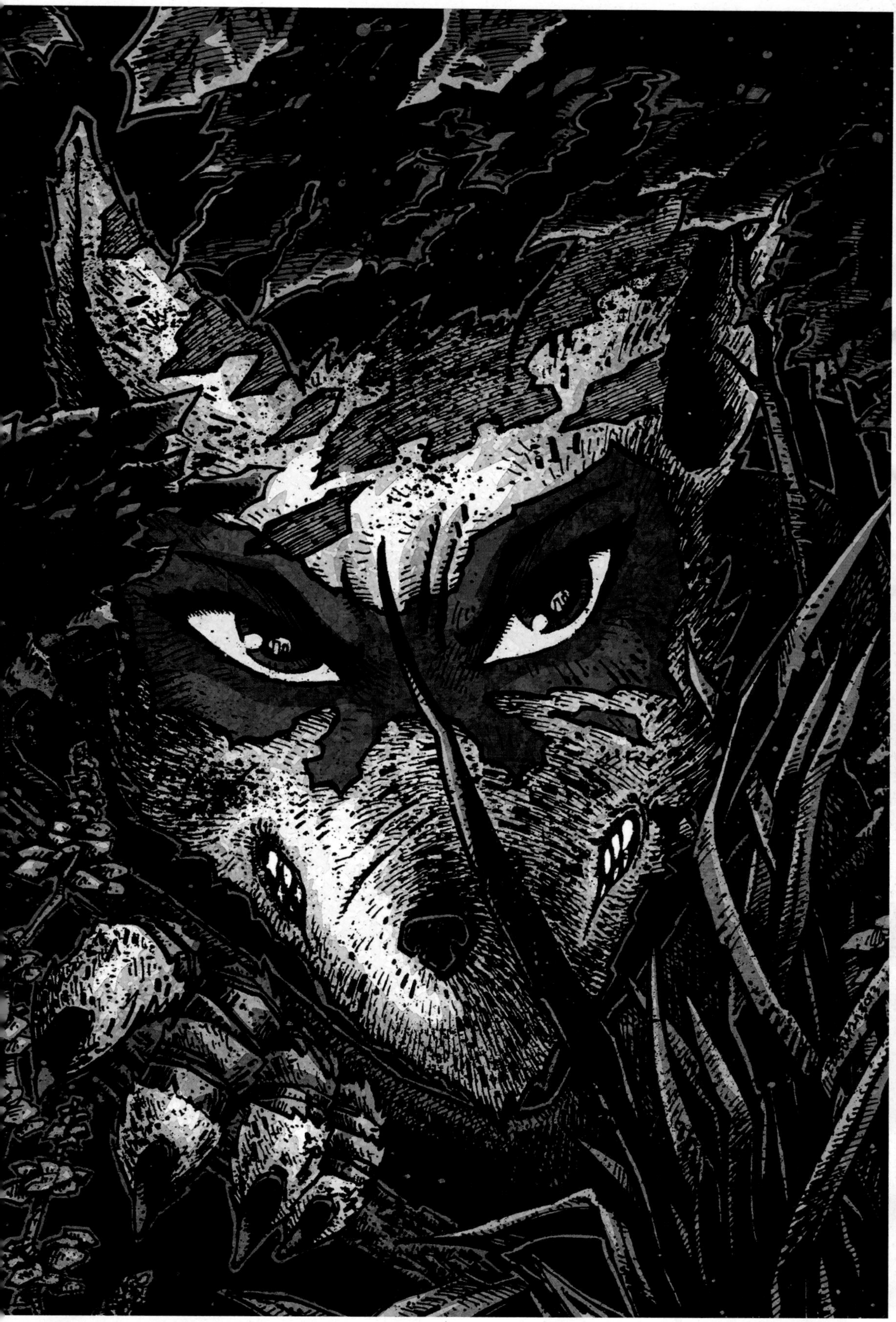

Cover by KEVIN EASTMAN
Colors by RONDA PATTISON

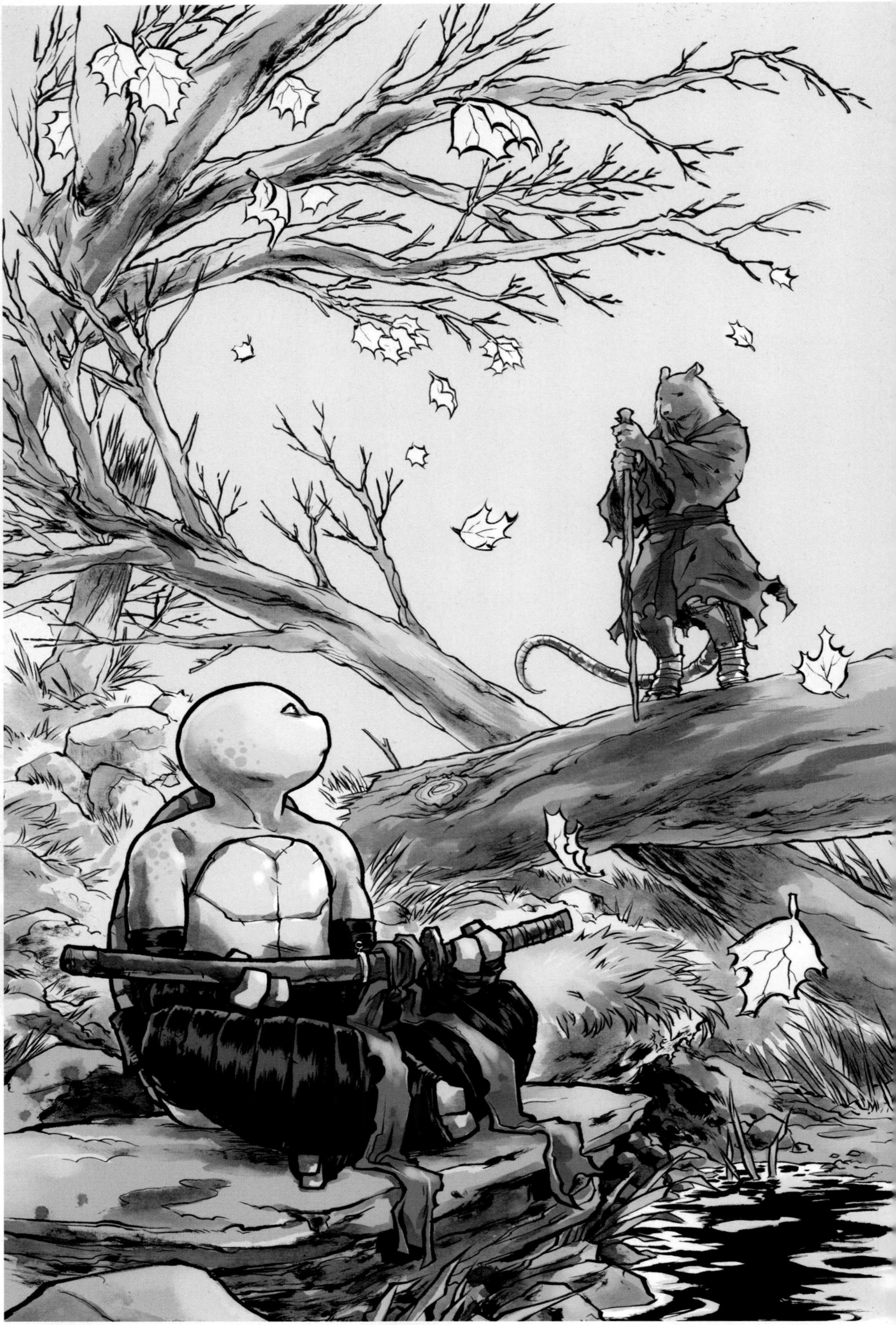

Cover by SOPHIE CAMPBELL

TMNT #31

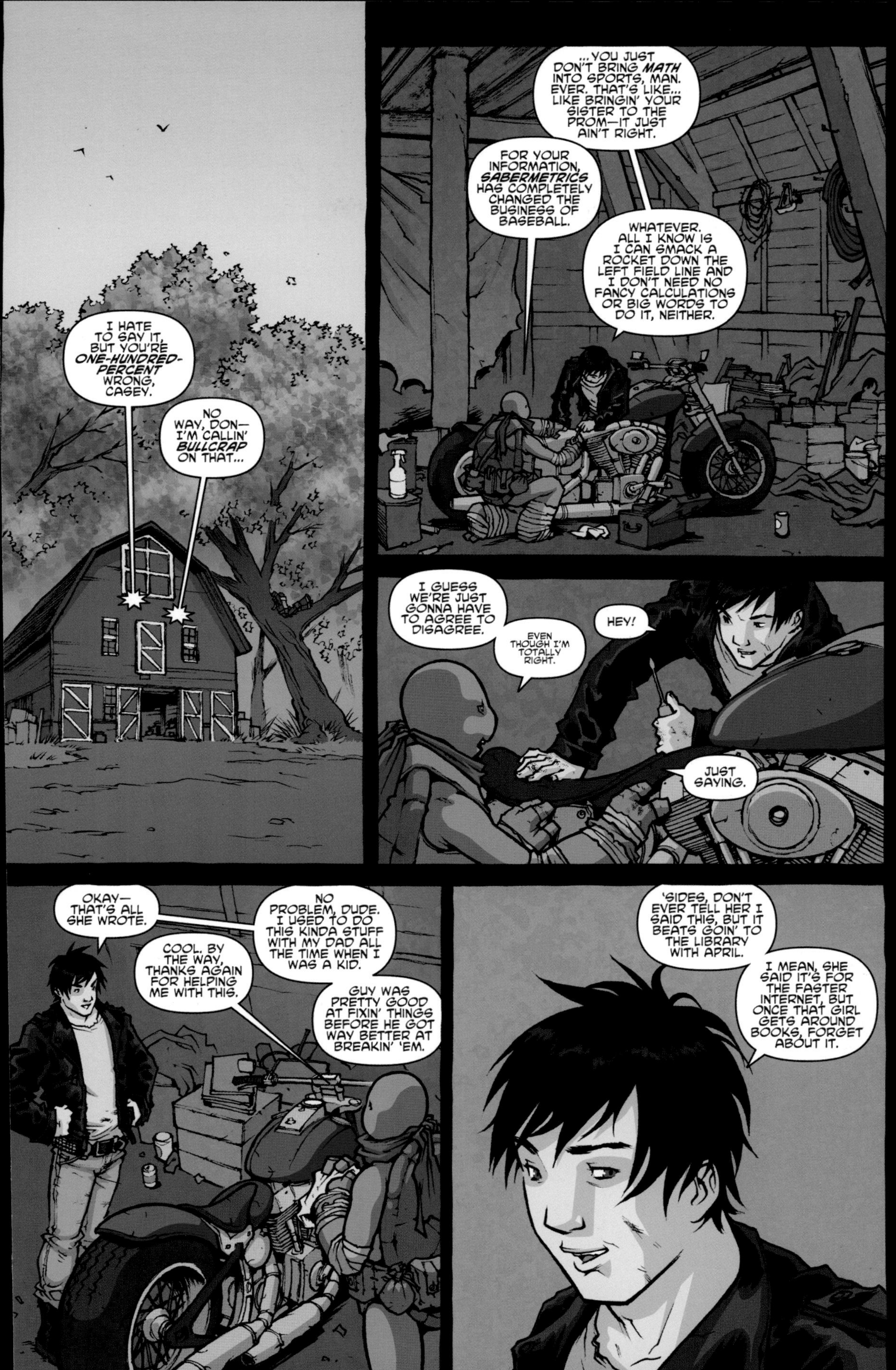
I HATE TO SAY IT, BUT YOU'RE ONE-HUNDRED-PERCENT WRONG, CASEY.
NO WAY, DON— I'M CALLIN' BULLCRAP ON THAT...
...YOU JUST DON'T BRING MATH INTO SPORTS, MAN. EVER. THAT'S LIKE... LIKE BRINGIN' YOUR SISTER TO THE PROM—IT JUST AIN'T RIGHT.
FOR YOUR INFORMATION, SABERMETRICS HAS COMPLETELY CHANGED THE BUSINESS OF BASEBALL.
WHATEVER. ALL I KNOW IS I CAN SMACK A ROCKET DOWN THE LEFT FIELD LINE AND I DON'T NEED NO FANCY CALCULATIONS OR BIG WORDS TO DO IT, NEITHER.
I GUESS WE'RE JUST GONNA HAVE TO AGREE TO DISAGREE.
EVEN THOUGH I'M TOTALLY RIGHT.
HEY!
JUST SAYING.
OKAY— THAT'S ALL SHE WROTE.
NO PROBLEM, DUDE. I USED TO DO THIS KINDA STUFF WITH MY DAD ALL THE TIME WHEN I WAS A KID.
COOL. BY THE WAY, THANKS AGAIN FOR HELPING ME WITH THIS.
GUY WAS PRETTY GOOD AT FIXIN' THINGS BEFORE HE GOT WAY BETTER AT BREAKIN' 'EM.
'SIDES, DON'T EVER TELL HER I SAID THIS, BUT IT BEATS GOIN' TO THE LIBRARY WITH APRIL.
I MEAN, SHE SAID IT'S FOR THE FASTER INTERNET, BUT ONCE THAT GIRL GETS AROUND BOOKS, FORGET ABOUT IT.

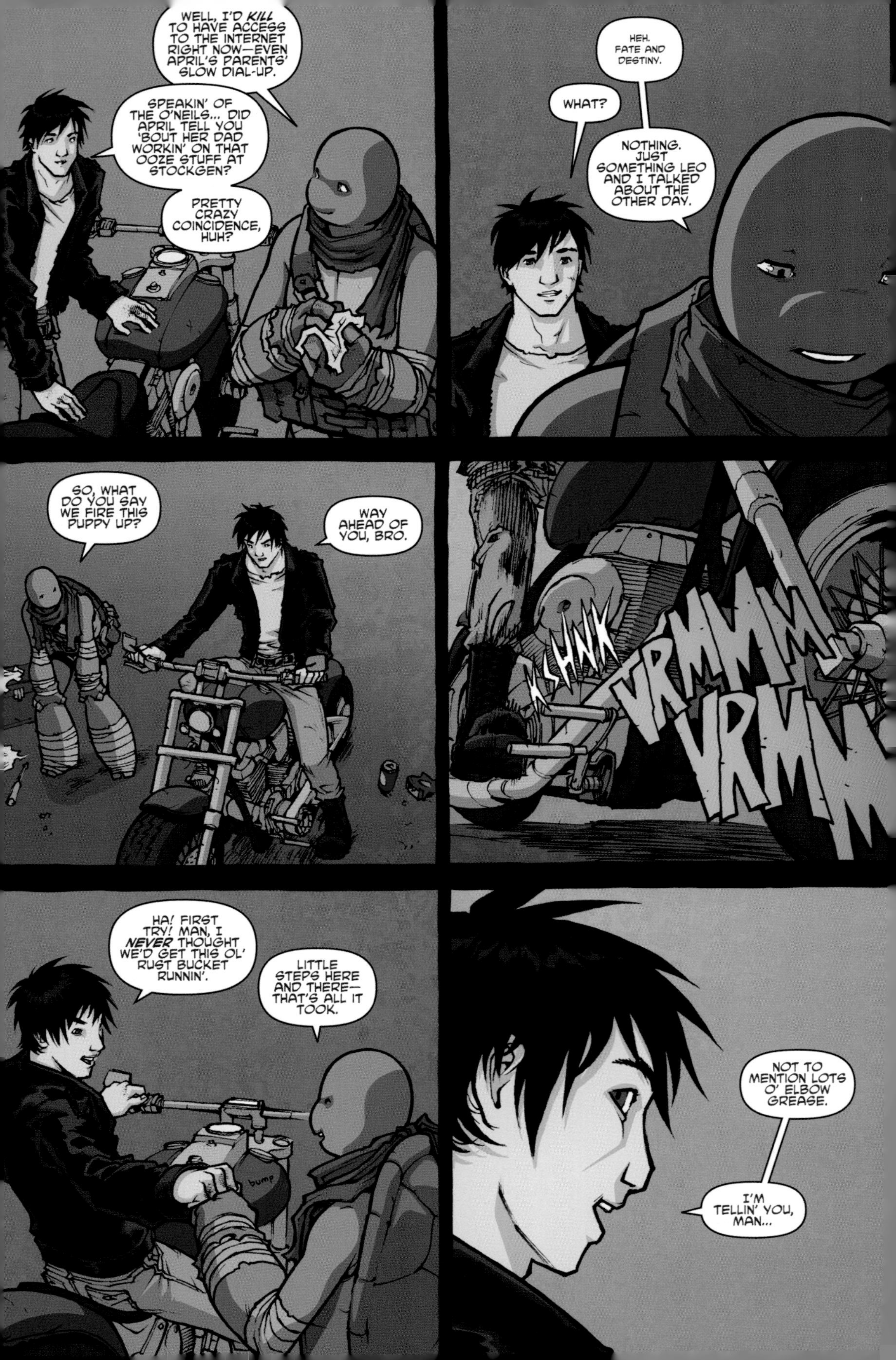
WELL, I'D KILL TO HAVE ACCESS TO THE INTERNET RIGHT NOW—EVEN APRIL'S PARENTS' SLOW DIAL-UP.
SPEAKIN' OF THE O'NEILS... DID APRIL TELL YOU 'BOUT HER DAD WORKIN' ON THAT OOZE STUFF AT STOCKGEN?
PRETTY CRAZY COINCIDENCE, HUH?
HEH. FATE AND DESTINY.
WHAT?
NOTHING. JUST SOMETHING LEO AND I TALKED ABOUT THE OTHER DAY.
SO, WHAT DO YOU SAY WE FIRE THIS PUPPY UP?
WAY AHEAD OF YOU, BRO.
KLSHNK
VRMMM
VRMM
HA! FIRST TRY! MAN, I NEVER THOUGHT WE'D GET THIS OL' RUST BUCKET RUNNIN'.
LITTLE STEPS HERE AND THERE—THAT'S ALL IT TOOK.
bump
NOT TO MENTION LOTS O' ELBOW GREASE.
I'M TELLIN' YOU, MAN...

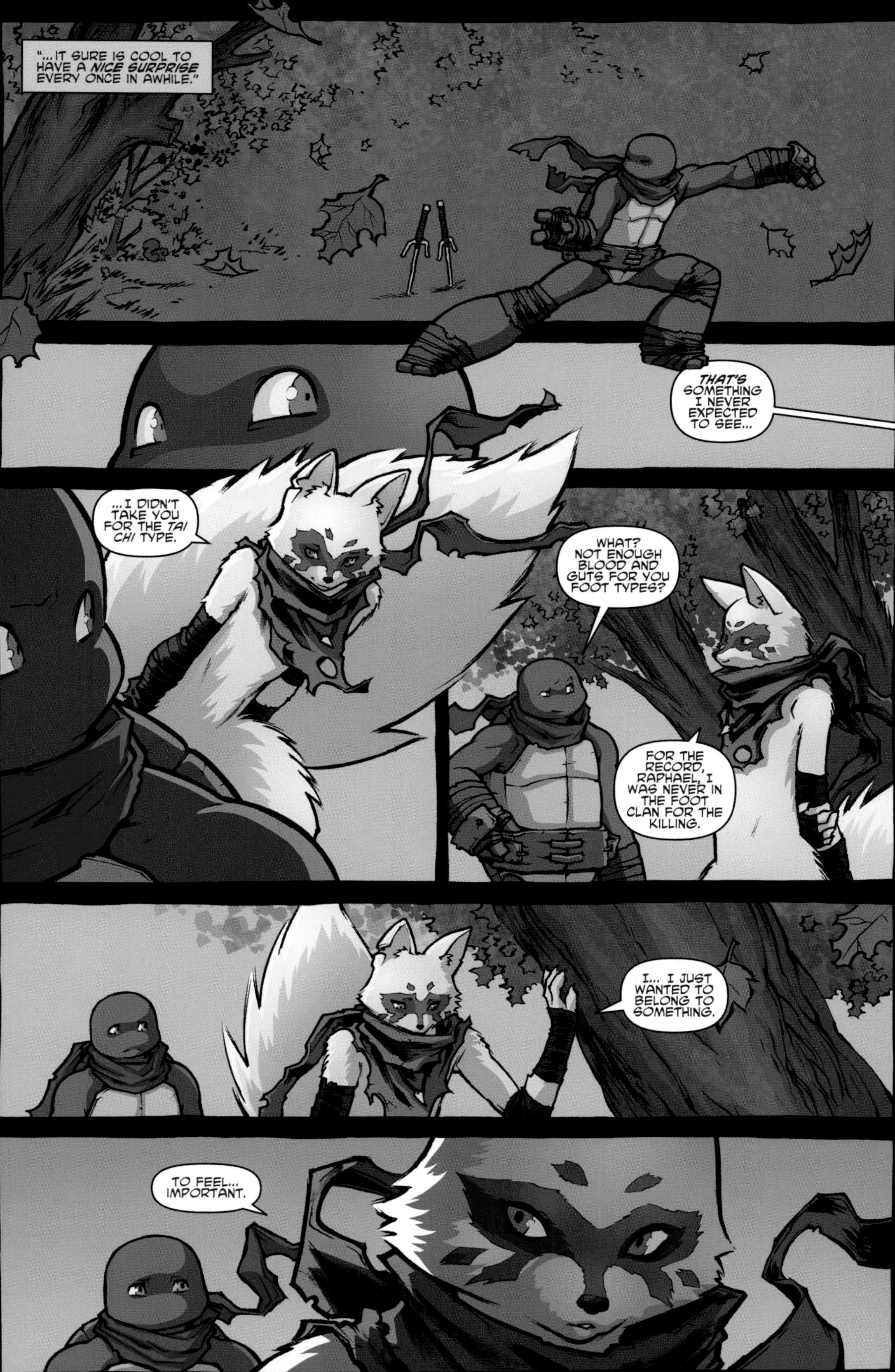
"...IT SURE IS COOL TO HAVE A *NICE SURPRISE* EVERY ONCE IN AWHILE."
THAT'S SOMETHING I NEVER EXPECTED TO SEE...
...I DIDN'T TAKE YOU FOR THE *TAI CHI* TYPE.
WHAT? NOT ENOUGH BLOOD AND GUTS FOR YOU FOOT TYPES?
FOR THE RECORD, RAPHAEL, I WAS NEVER IN THE FOOT CLAN FOR THE KILLING.
I... I JUST WANTED TO BELONG TO SOMETHING.
TO FEEL... IMPORTANT.

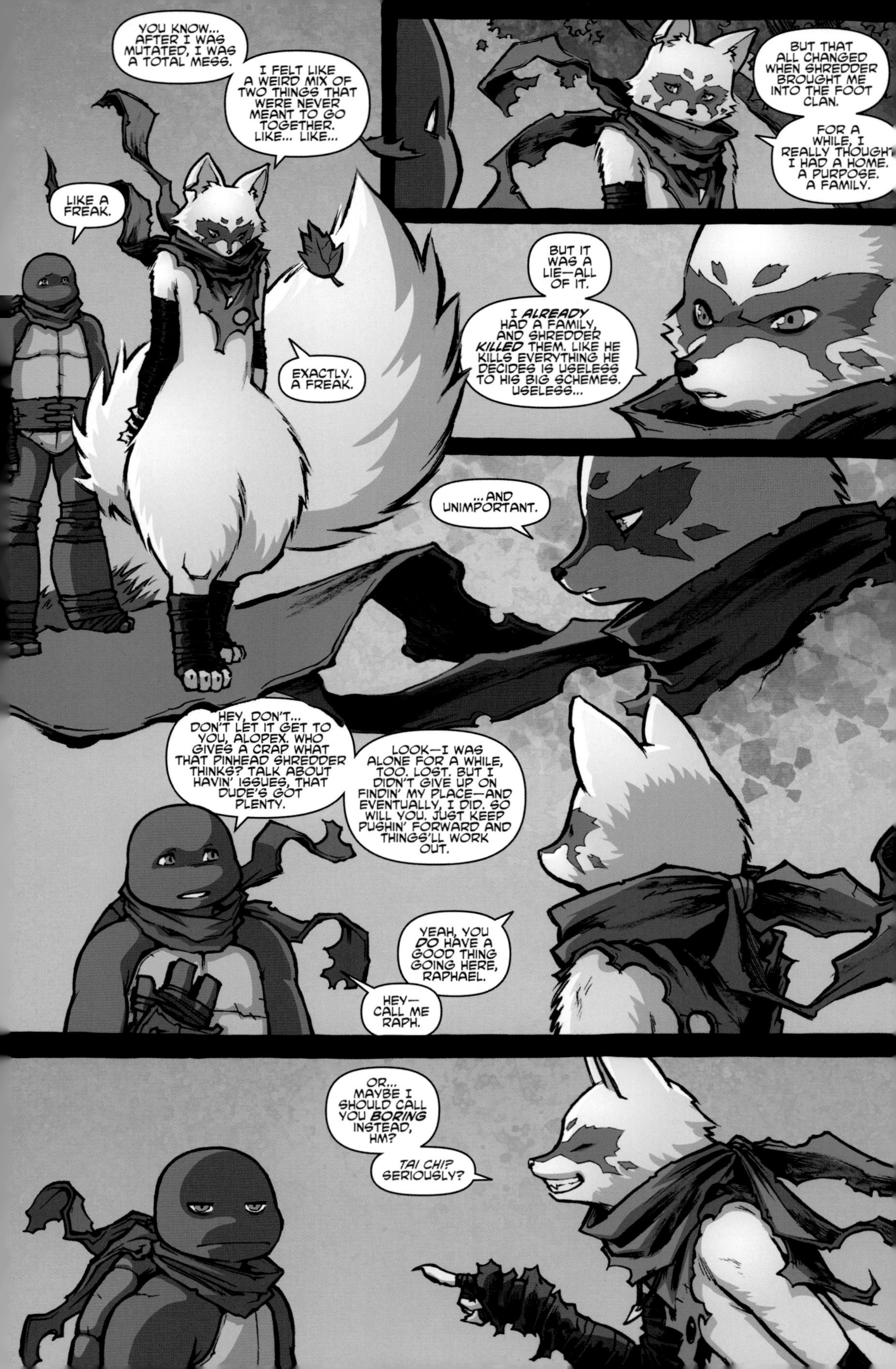
YOU KNOW... AFTER I WAS MUTATED, I WAS A TOTAL MESS.
I FELT LIKE A WEIRD MIX OF TWO THINGS THAT WERE NEVER MEANT TO GO TOGETHER. LIKE... LIKE...
LIKE A FREAK.
EXACTLY. A FREAK.
BUT THAT ALL CHANGED WHEN SHREDDER BROUGHT ME INTO THE FOOT CLAN.
FOR A WHILE, I REALLY THOUGHT I HAD A HOME. A PURPOSE. A FAMILY.
BUT IT WAS A LIE—ALL OF IT.
I ALREADY HAD A FAMILY, AND SHREDDER KILLED THEM. LIKE HE KILLS EVERYTHING HE DECIDES IS USELESS TO HIS BIG SCHEMES. USELESS...
...AND UNIMPORTANT.
HEY, DON'T... DON'T LET IT GET TO YOU, ALOPEX. WHO GIVES A CRAP WHAT THAT PINHEAD SHREDDER THINKS? TALK ABOUT HAVIN' ISSUES, THAT DUDE'S GOT PLENTY.
LOOK—I WAS ALONE FOR A WHILE, TOO. LOST. BUT I DIDN'T GIVE UP ON FINDIN' MY PLACE—AND EVENTUALLY, I DID. SO WILL YOU. JUST KEEP PUSHIN' FORWARD AND THINGS'LL WORK OUT.
YEAH, YOU DO HAVE A GOOD THING GOING HERE, RAPHAEL.
HEY— CALL ME RAPH.
OR... MAYBE I SHOULD CALL YOU BORING INSTEAD, HM?
TAI CHI? SERIOUSLY?

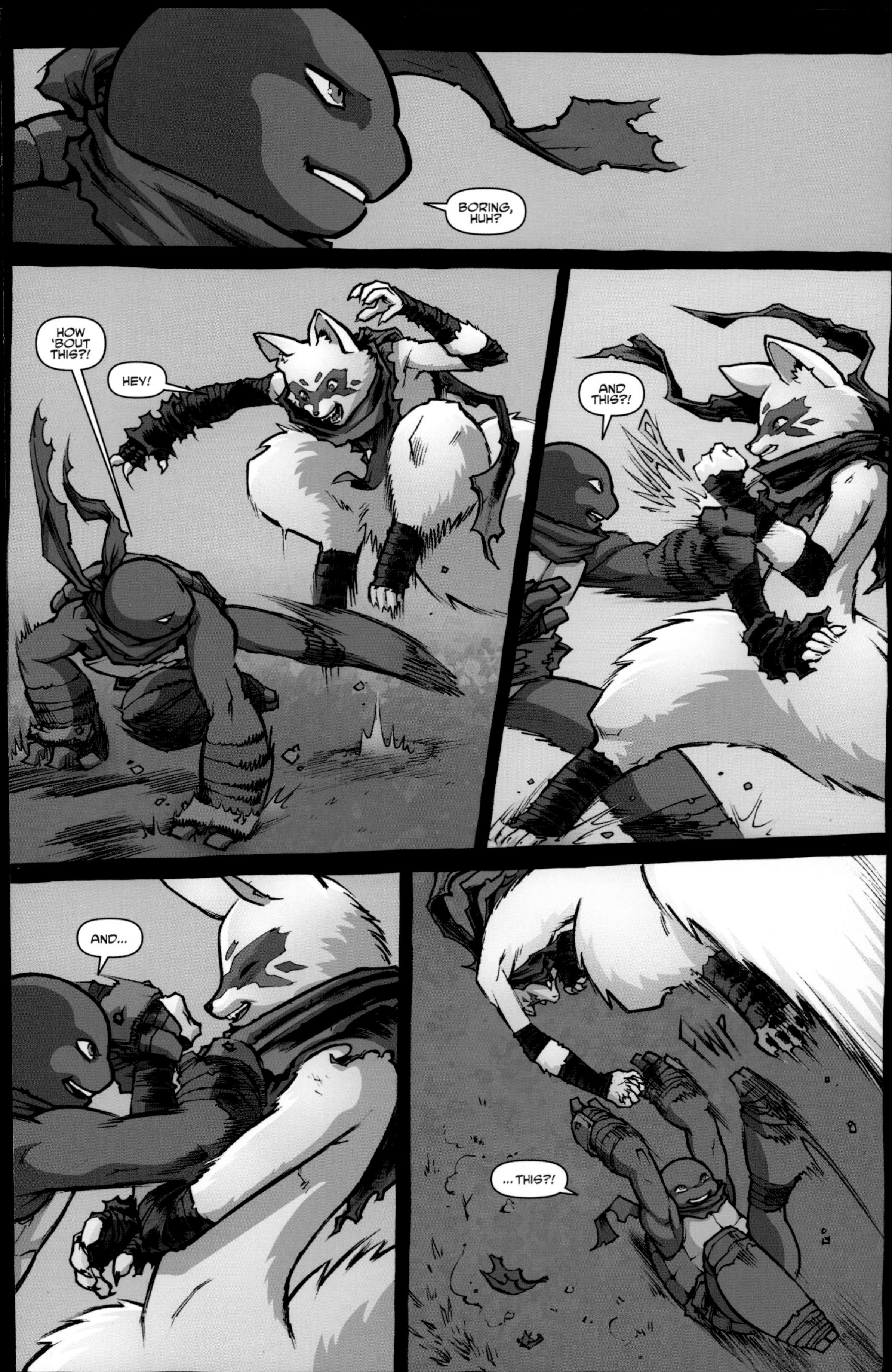
BORING, HUH?
HOW 'BOUT THIS?!
HEY!
AND THIS?!
AND...
...THIS?!

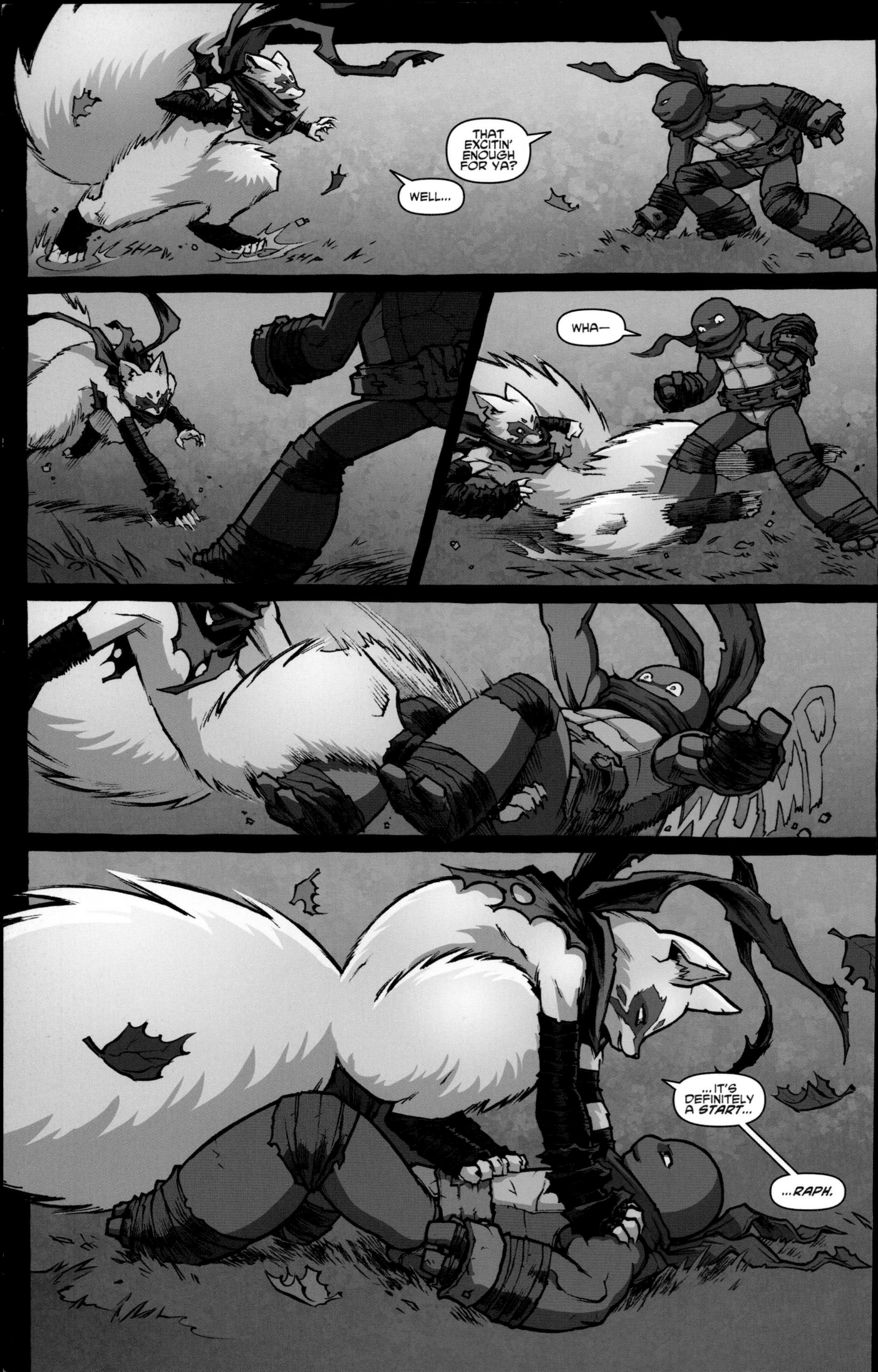

THAT EXCITIN' ENOUGH FOR YA?
WELL...
WHA—
...IT'S DEFINITELY A *START*...
...*RAPH.*

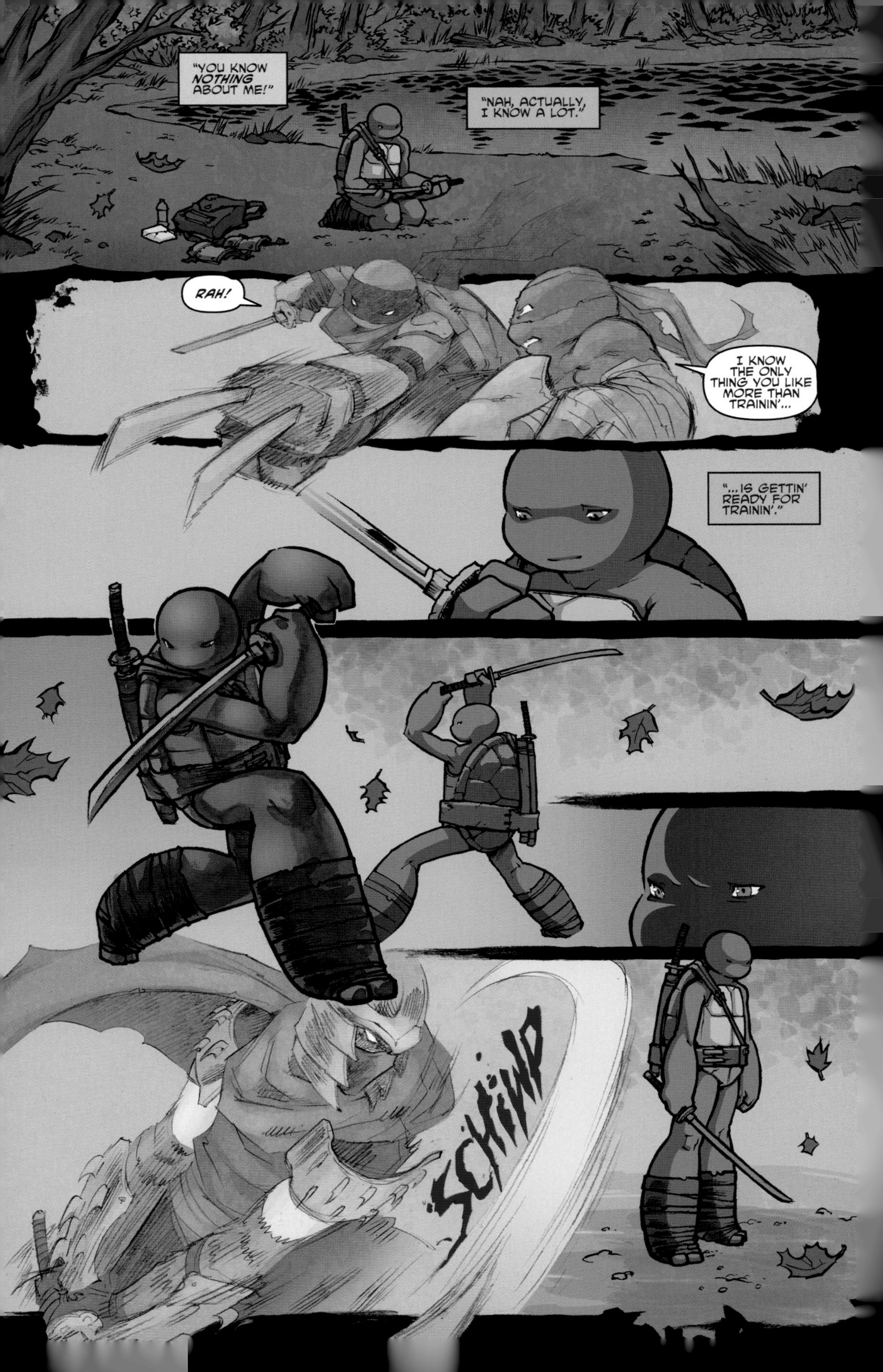
"YOU KNOW NOTHING ABOUT ME!"
"NAH, ACTUALLY, I KNOW A LOT."
RAH!
I KNOW THE ONLY THING YOU LIKE MORE THAN TRAININ'...
"...IS GETTIN' READY FOR TRAININ'."
SCHWP

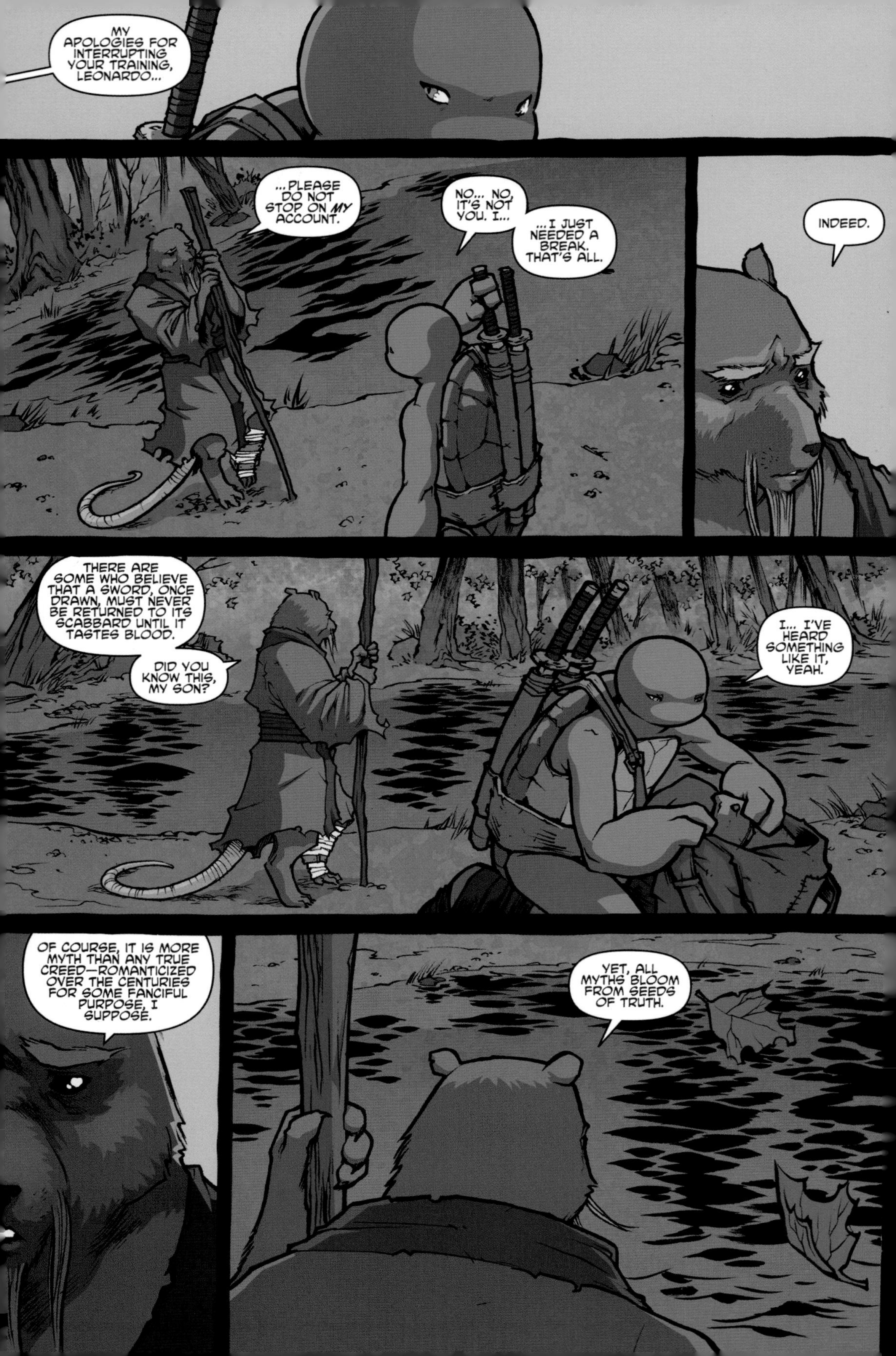
MY APOLOGIES FOR INTERRUPTING YOUR TRAINING, LEONARDO...
...PLEASE DO NOT STOP ON MY ACCOUNT.
NO... NO, IT'S NOT YOU. I...
...I JUST NEEDED A BREAK. THAT'S ALL.
INDEED.
THERE ARE SOME WHO BELIEVE THAT A SWORD, ONCE DRAWN, MUST NEVER BE RETURNED TO ITS SCABBARD UNTIL IT TASTES BLOOD.
DID YOU KNOW THIS, MY SON?
I... I'VE HEARD SOMETHING LIKE IT, YEAH.
OF COURSE, IT IS MORE MYTH THAN ANY TRUE CREED—ROMANTICIZED OVER THE CENTURIES FOR SOME FANCIFUL PURPOSE, I SUPPOSE.
YET, ALL MYTHS BLOOM FROM SEEDS OF TRUTH.

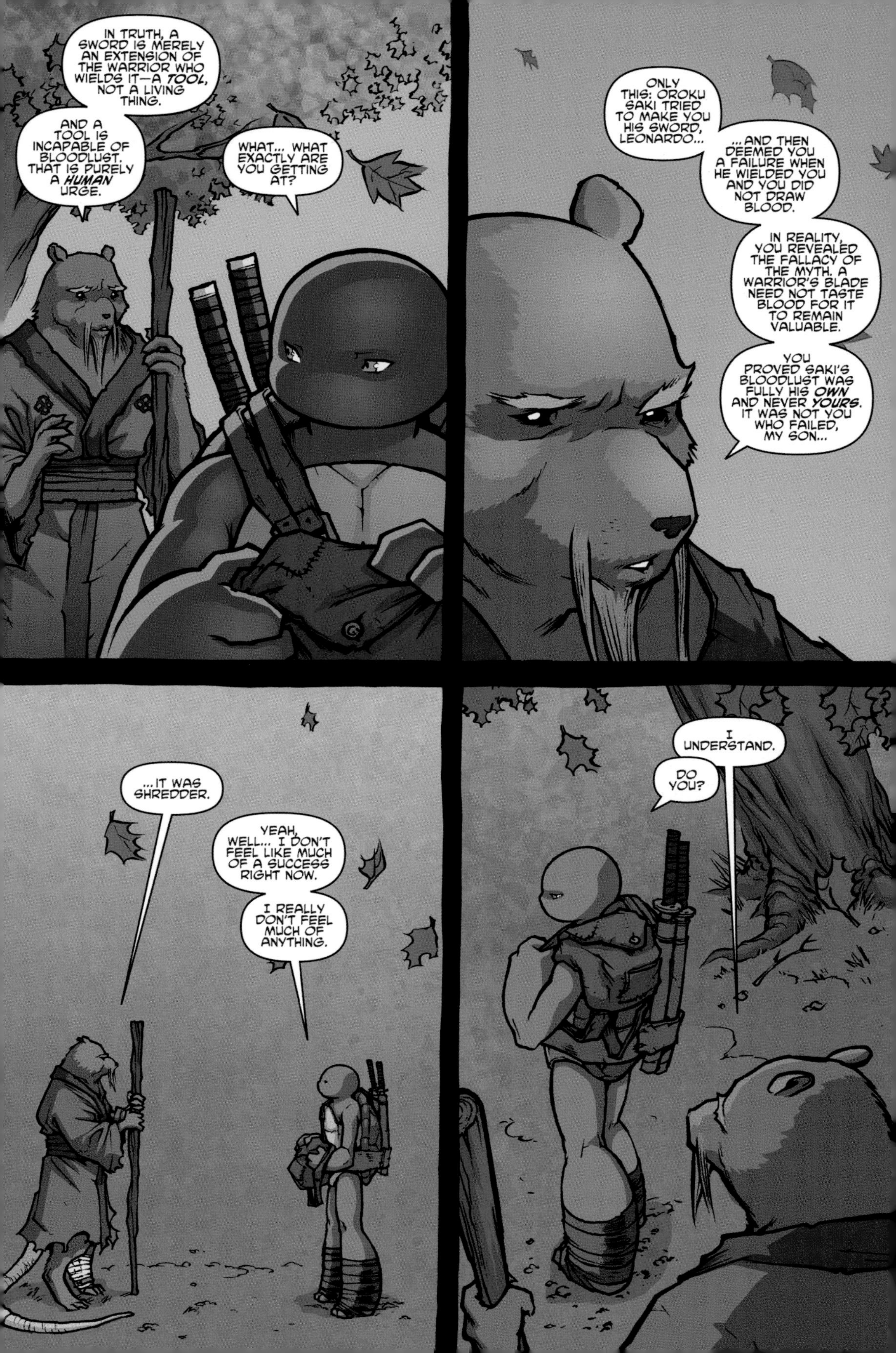
IN TRUTH, A SWORD IS MERELY AN EXTENSION OF THE WARRIOR WHO WIELDS IT—A TOOL, NOT A LIVING THING.
AND A TOOL IS INCAPABLE OF BLOODLUST. THAT IS PURELY A HUMAN URGE.
WHAT... WHAT EXACTLY ARE YOU GETTING AT?
ONLY THIS: OROKU SAKI TRIED TO MAKE YOU HIS SWORD, LEONARDO...
...AND THEN DEEMED YOU A FAILURE WHEN HE WIELDED YOU AND YOU DID NOT DRAW BLOOD.
IN REALITY, YOU REVEALED THE FALLACY OF THE MYTH. A WARRIOR'S BLADE NEED NOT TASTE BLOOD FOR IT TO REMAIN VALUABLE.
YOU PROVED SAKI'S BLOODLUST WAS FULLY HIS OWN AND NEVER YOURS. IT WAS NOT YOU WHO FAILED, MY SON...
...IT WAS SHREDDER.
YEAH, WELL... I DON'T FEEL LIKE MUCH OF A SUCCESS RIGHT NOW.
I REALLY DON'T FEEL MUCH OF ANYTHING.
I UNDERSTAND.
DO YOU?

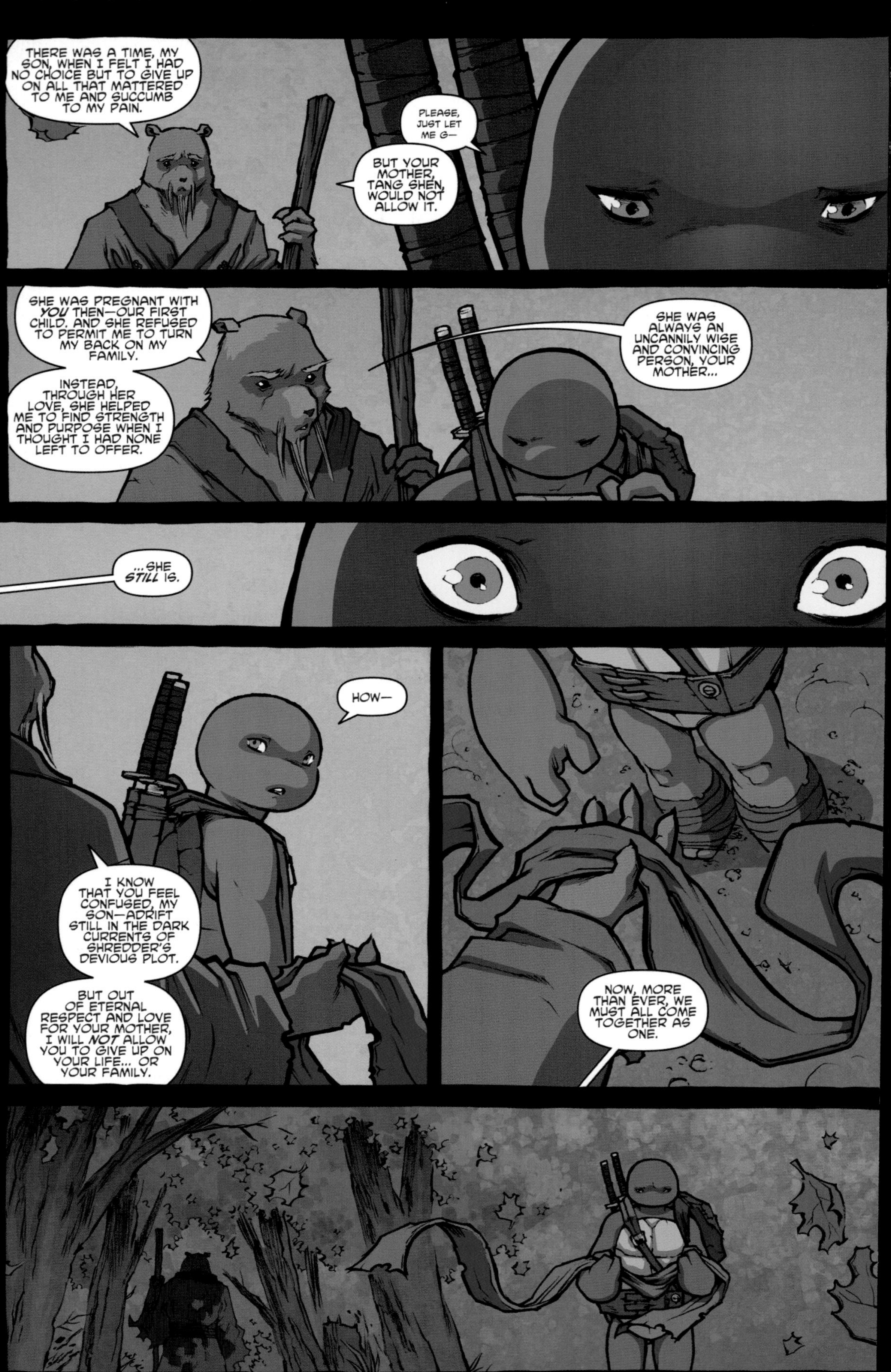
THERE WAS A TIME, MY SON, WHEN I FELT I HAD NO CHOICE BUT TO GIVE UP ON ALL THAT MATTERED TO ME AND SUCCUMB TO MY PAIN.
PLEASE, JUST LET ME G—
BUT YOUR MOTHER, TANG SHEN, WOULD NOT ALLOW IT.
SHE WAS PREGNANT WITH *YOU* THEN—OUR FIRST CHILD. AND SHE REFUSED TO PERMIT ME TO TURN MY BACK ON MY FAMILY.
INSTEAD, THROUGH HER LOVE, SHE HELPED ME TO FIND STRENGTH AND PURPOSE WHEN I THOUGHT I HAD NONE LEFT TO OFFER.
SHE WAS ALWAYS AN UNCANNILY WISE AND CONVINCING PERSON, YOUR MOTHER...
...SHE *STILL* IS.
HOW—
I KNOW THAT YOU FEEL CONFUSED, MY SON—ADRIFT STILL IN THE DARK CURRENTS OF SHREDDER'S DEVIOUS PLOT.
BUT OUT OF ETERNAL RESPECT AND LOVE FOR YOUR MOTHER, I WILL *NOT* ALLOW YOU TO GIVE UP ON YOUR LIFE... OR YOUR FAMILY.
NOW, MORE THAN EVER, WE MUST ALL COME TOGETHER AS ONE.

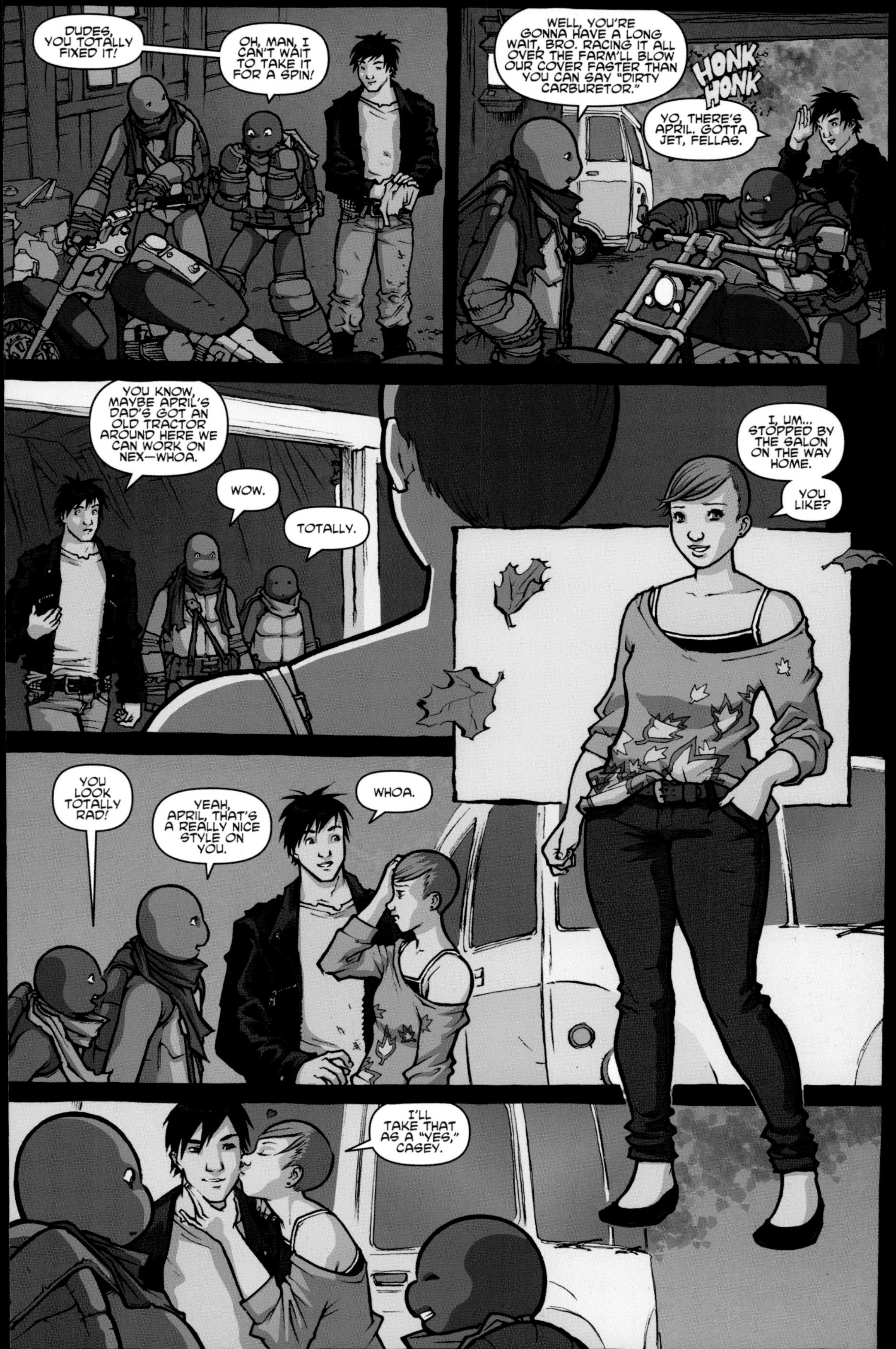
DUDES, YOU TOTALLY FIXED IT!
OH, MAN, I CAN'T WAIT TO TAKE IT FOR A SPIN!
WELL, YOU'RE GONNA HAVE A LONG WAIT, BRO. RACING IT ALL OVER THE FARM'LL BLOW OUR COVER FASTER THAN YOU CAN SAY "DIRTY CARBURETOR."
HONK HONK
YO, THERE'S APRIL. GOTTA JET, FELLAS.
YOU KNOW, MAYBE APRIL'S DAD'S GOT AN OLD TRACTOR AROUND HERE WE CAN WORK ON NEX—WHOA.
WOW.
TOTALLY.
I, UM... STOPPED BY THE SALON ON THE WAY HOME.
YOU LIKE?
YOU LOOK TOTALLY RAD!
YEAH, APRIL, THAT'S A REALLY NICE STYLE ON YOU.
WHOA.
I'LL TAKE THAT AS A "YES," CASEY.

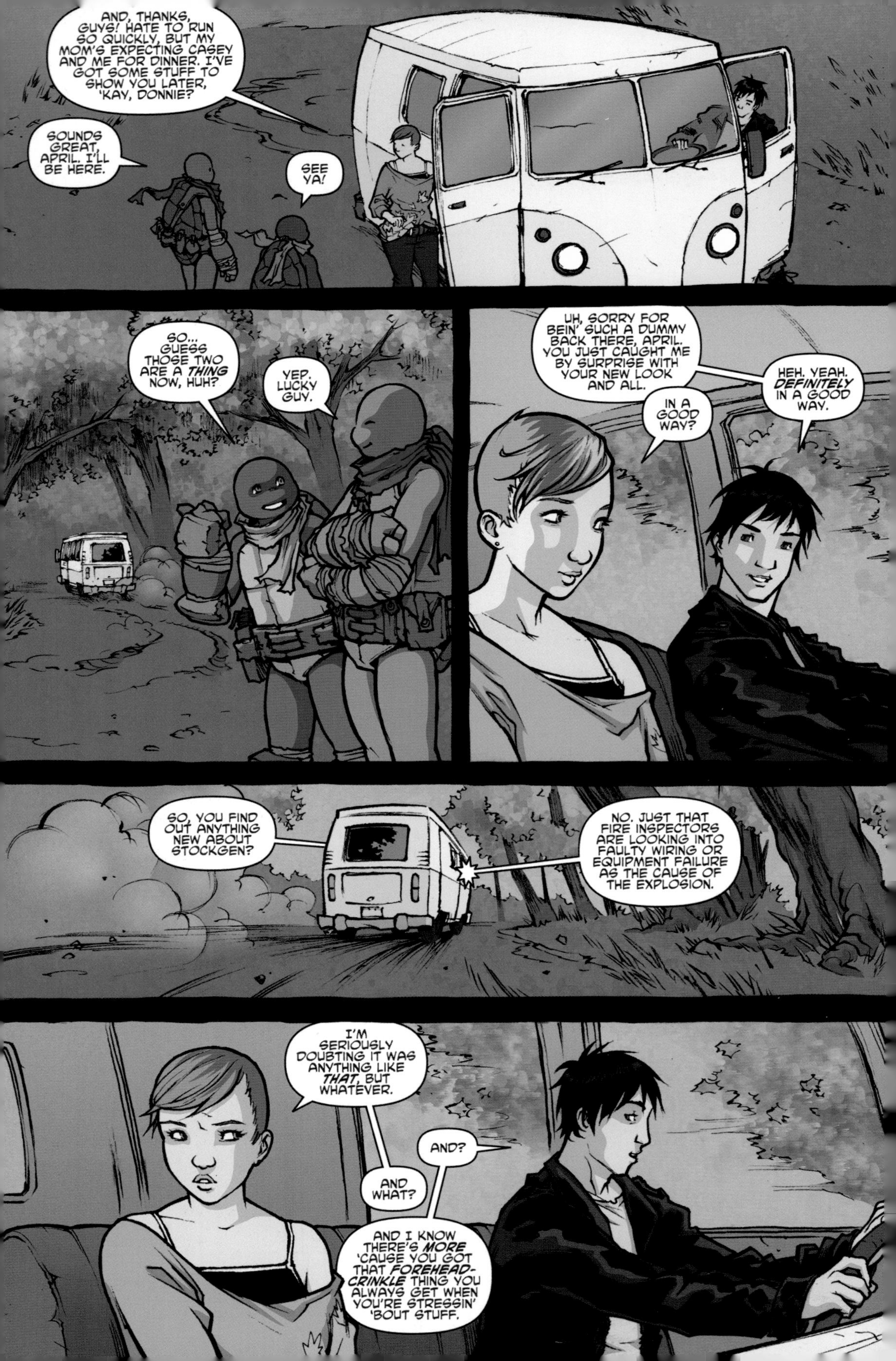
AND, THANKS, GUYS! HATE TO RUN SO QUICKLY, BUT MY MOM'S EXPECTING CASEY AND ME FOR DINNER. I'VE GOT SOME STUFF TO SHOW YOU LATER, 'KAY, DONNIE?
SOUNDS GREAT, APRIL. I'LL BE HERE.
SEE YA!
SO... GUESS THOSE TWO ARE A *THING* NOW, HUH?
YEP. LUCKY GUY.
UH, SORRY FOR BEIN' SUCH A DUMMY BACK THERE, APRIL. YOU JUST CAUGHT ME BY SURPRISE WITH YOUR NEW LOOK AND ALL.
IN A GOOD WAY?
HEH. YEAH. *DEFINITELY* IN A GOOD WAY.
SO, YOU FIND OUT ANYTHING NEW ABOUT STOCKGEN?
NO. JUST THAT FIRE INSPECTORS ARE LOOKING INTO FAULTY WIRING OR EQUIPMENT FAILURE AS THE CAUSE OF THE EXPLOSION.
I'M SERIOUSLY DOUBTING IT WAS ANYTHING LIKE *THAT*, BUT WHATEVER.
AND?
AND WHAT?
AND I KNOW THERE'S *MORE* 'CAUSE YOU GOT THAT *FOREHEAD-CRINKLE* THING YOU ALWAYS GET WHEN YOU'RE STRESSIN' 'BOUT STUFF.

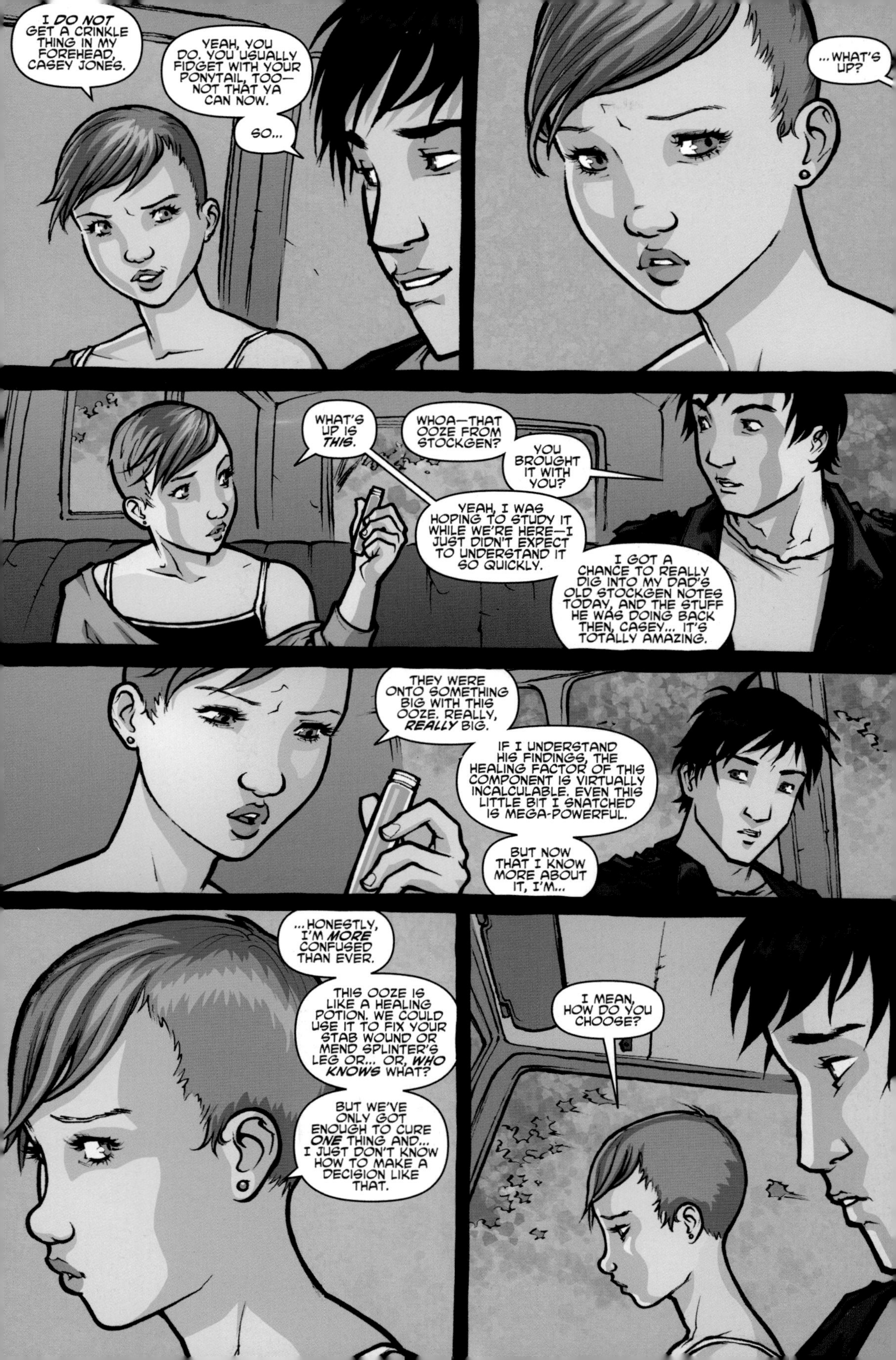
I DO NOT GET A CRINKLE THING IN MY FOREHEAD, CASEY JONES.
YEAH, YOU DO. YOU USUALLY FIDGET WITH YOUR PONYTAIL, TOO—NOT THAT YA CAN NOW.
SO...
...WHAT'S UP?
WHAT'S UP IS THIS.
WHOA—THAT OOZE FROM STOCKGEN?
YOU BROUGHT IT WITH YOU?
YEAH, I WAS HOPING TO STUDY IT WHILE WE'RE HERE—I JUST DIDN'T EXPECT TO UNDERSTAND IT SO QUICKLY.
I GOT A CHANCE TO REALLY DIG INTO MY DAD'S OLD STOCKGEN NOTES TODAY, AND THE STUFF HE WAS DOING BACK THEN, CASEY... IT'S TOTALLY AMAZING.
THEY WERE ONTO SOMETHING BIG WITH THIS OOZE. REALLY, REALLY BIG.
IF I UNDERSTAND HIS FINDINGS, THE HEALING FACTOR OF THIS COMPONENT IS VIRTUALLY INCALCULABLE. EVEN THIS LITTLE BIT I SNATCHED IS MEGA-POWERFUL.
BUT NOW THAT I KNOW MORE ABOUT IT, I'M...
...HONESTLY, I'M MORE CONFUSED THAN EVER.
THIS OOZE IS LIKE A HEALING POTION. WE COULD USE IT TO FIX YOUR STAB WOUND OR MEND SPLINTER'S LEG OR... OR, WHO KNOWS WHAT?
BUT WE'VE ONLY GOT ENOUGH TO CURE ONE THING AND... I JUST DON'T KNOW HOW TO MAKE A DECISION LIKE THAT.
I MEAN, HOW DO YOU CHOOSE?

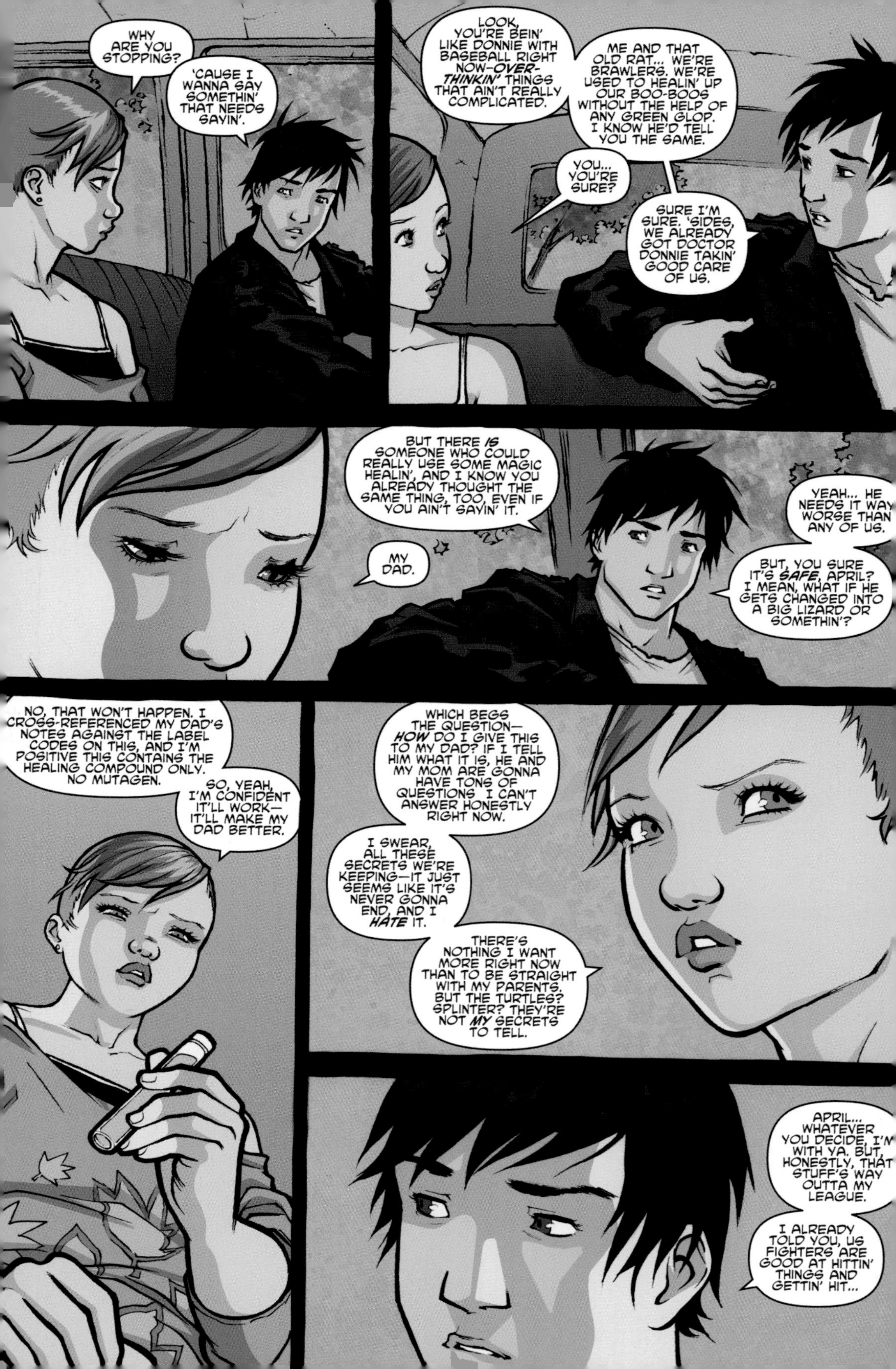
WHY ARE YOU STOPPING?
'CAUSE I WANNA SAY SOMETHIN' THAT NEEDS SAYIN'.
LOOK, YOU'RE BEIN' LIKE DONNIE WITH BASEBALL RIGHT NOW—OVER-THINKIN' THINGS THAT AIN'T REALLY COMPLICATED.
ME AND THAT OLD RAT... WE'RE BRAWLERS. WE'RE USED TO HEALIN' UP OUR BOO-BOOS WITHOUT THE HELP OF ANY GREEN GLOP. I KNOW HE'D TELL YOU THE SAME.
YOU... YOU'RE SURE?
SURE I'M SURE. 'SIDES, WE ALREADY GOT DOCTOR DONNIE TAKIN' GOOD CARE OF US.
BUT THERE IS SOMEONE WHO COULD REALLY USE SOME MAGIC HEALIN', AND I KNOW YOU ALREADY THOUGHT THE SAME THING, TOO, EVEN IF YOU AIN'T SAYIN' IT.
MY DAD.
YEAH... HE NEEDS IT WAY WORSE THAN ANY OF US.
BUT, YOU SURE IT'S SAFE, APRIL? I MEAN, WHAT IF HE GETS CHANGED INTO A BIG LIZARD OR SOMETHIN'?
NO, THAT WON'T HAPPEN. I CROSS-REFERENCED MY DAD'S NOTES AGAINST THE LABEL CODES ON THIS, AND I'M POSITIVE THIS CONTAINS THE HEALING COMPOUND ONLY. NO MUTAGEN.
SO, YEAH, I'M CONFIDENT IT'LL WORK—IT'LL MAKE MY DAD BETTER.
WHICH BEGS THE QUESTION—HOW DO I GIVE THIS TO MY DAD? IF I TELL HIM WHAT IT IS, HE AND MY MOM ARE GONNA HAVE TONS OF QUESTIONS I CAN'T ANSWER HONESTLY RIGHT NOW.
I SWEAR, ALL THESE SECRETS WE'RE KEEPING—IT JUST SEEMS LIKE IT'S NEVER GONNA END, AND I HATE IT.
THERE'S NOTHING I WANT MORE RIGHT NOW THAN TO BE STRAIGHT WITH MY PARENTS. BUT THE TURTLES? SPLINTER? THEY'RE NOT MY SECRETS TO TELL.
APRIL... WHATEVER YOU DECIDE, I'M WITH YA. BUT, HONESTLY, THAT STUFF'S WAY OUTTA MY LEAGUE.
I ALREADY TOLD YOU, US FIGHTERS ARE GOOD AT HITTIN' THINGS AND GETTIN' HIT...

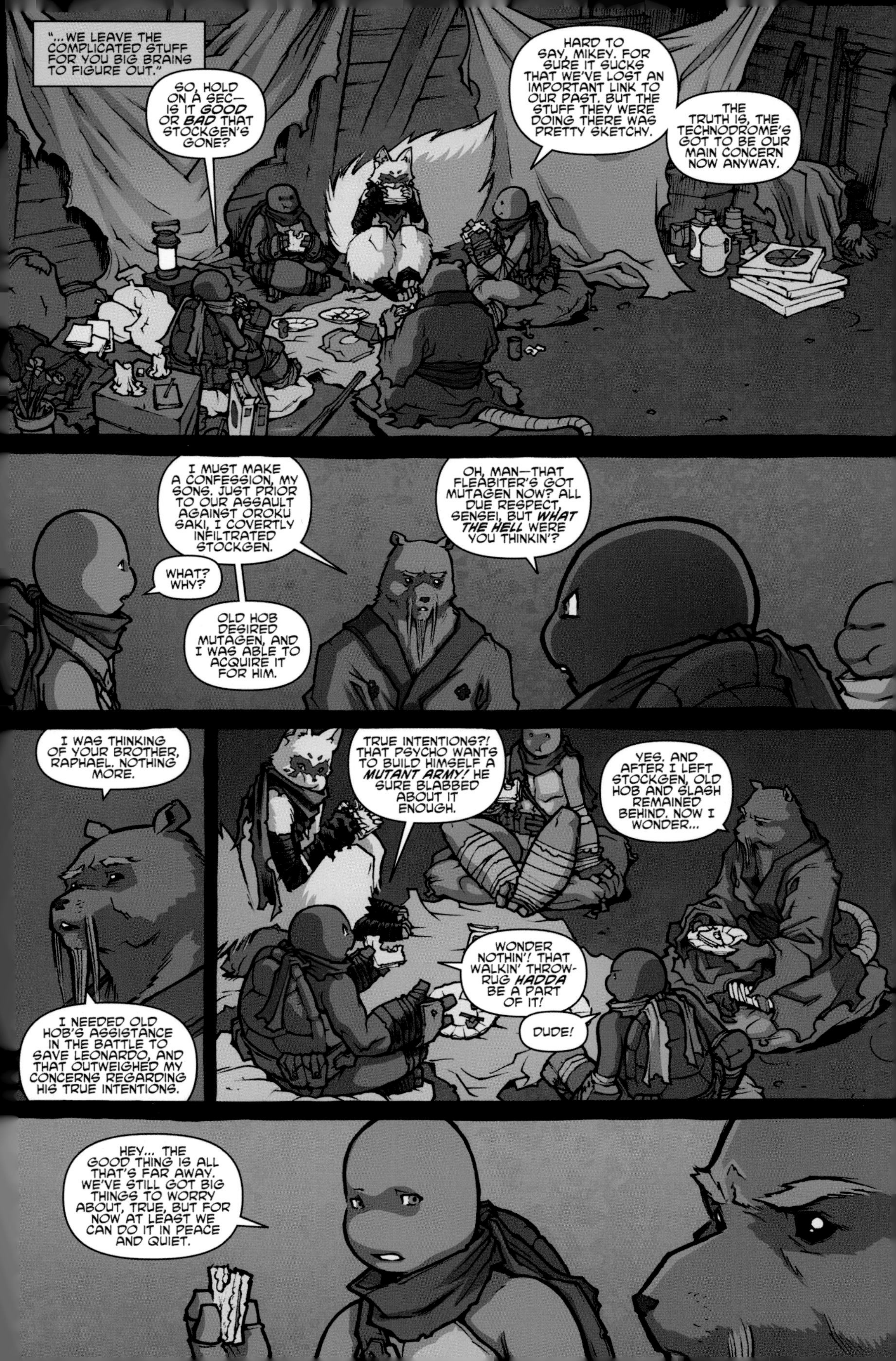
"...WE LEAVE THE COMPLICATED STUFF FOR YOU BIG BRAINS TO FIGURE OUT."
SO, HOLD ON A SEC— IS IT GOOD OR BAD THAT STOCKGEN'S GONE?
HARD TO SAY, MIKEY. FOR SURE IT SUCKS THAT WE'VE LOST AN IMPORTANT LINK TO OUR PAST. BUT THE STUFF THEY WERE DOING THERE WAS PRETTY SKETCHY.
THE TRUTH IS, THE TECHNODROME'S GOT TO BE OUR MAIN CONCERN NOW ANYWAY.
I MUST MAKE A CONFESSION, MY SONS. JUST PRIOR TO OUR ASSAULT AGAINST OROKU SAKI, I COVERTLY INFILTRATED STOCKGEN.
WHAT? WHY?
OLD HOB DESIRED MUTAGEN, AND I WAS ABLE TO ACQUIRE IT FOR HIM.
OH, MAN—THAT FLEABITER'S GOT MUTAGEN NOW? ALL DUE RESPECT, SENSEI, BUT WHAT THE HELL WERE YOU THINKIN'?
I WAS THINKING OF YOUR BROTHER, RAPHAEL. NOTHING MORE.
I NEEDED OLD HOB'S ASSISTANCE IN THE BATTLE TO SAVE LEONARDO, AND THAT OUTWEIGHED MY CONCERNS REGARDING HIS TRUE INTENTIONS.
TRUE INTENTIONS?! THAT PSYCHO WANTS TO BUILD HIMSELF A MUTANT ARMY! HE SURE BLABBED ABOUT IT ENOUGH.
YES. AND AFTER I LEFT STOCKGEN, OLD HOB AND SLASH REMAINED BEHIND. NOW I WONDER...
WONDER NOTHIN'! THAT WALKIN' THROW-RUG HADDA BE A PART OF IT!
DUDE!
HEY... THE GOOD THING IS ALL THAT'S FAR AWAY. WE'VE STILL GOT BIG THINGS TO WORRY ABOUT, TRUE, BUT FOR NOW AT LEAST WE CAN DO IT IN PEACE AND QUIET.

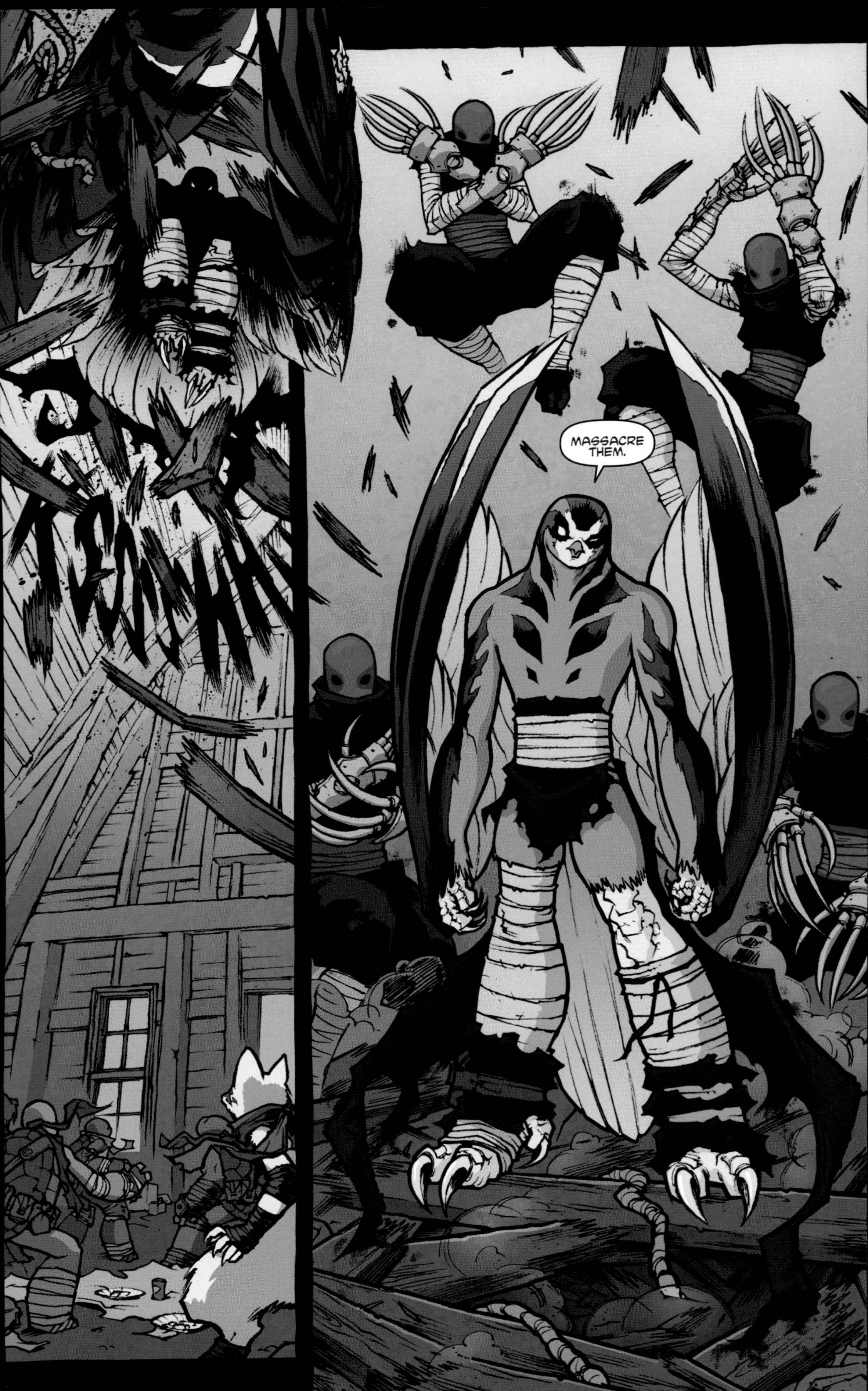
MASSACRE THEM.

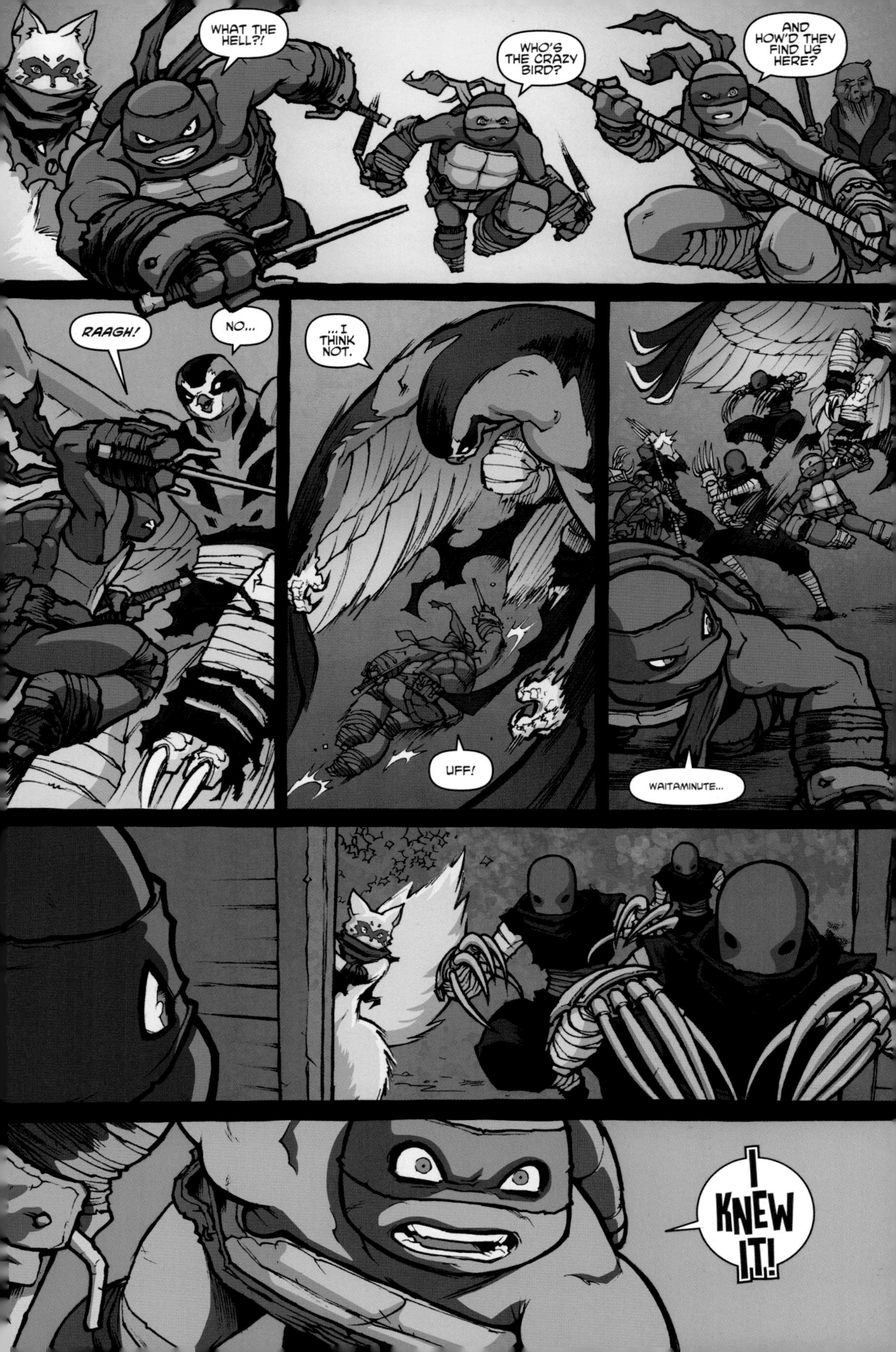
WHAT THE HELL?!
WHO'S THE CRAZY BIRD?
AND HOW'D THEY FIND US HERE?
RAAGH!
NO...
... I THINK NOT.
UFF!
WAITAMINUTE...
I KNEW IT!

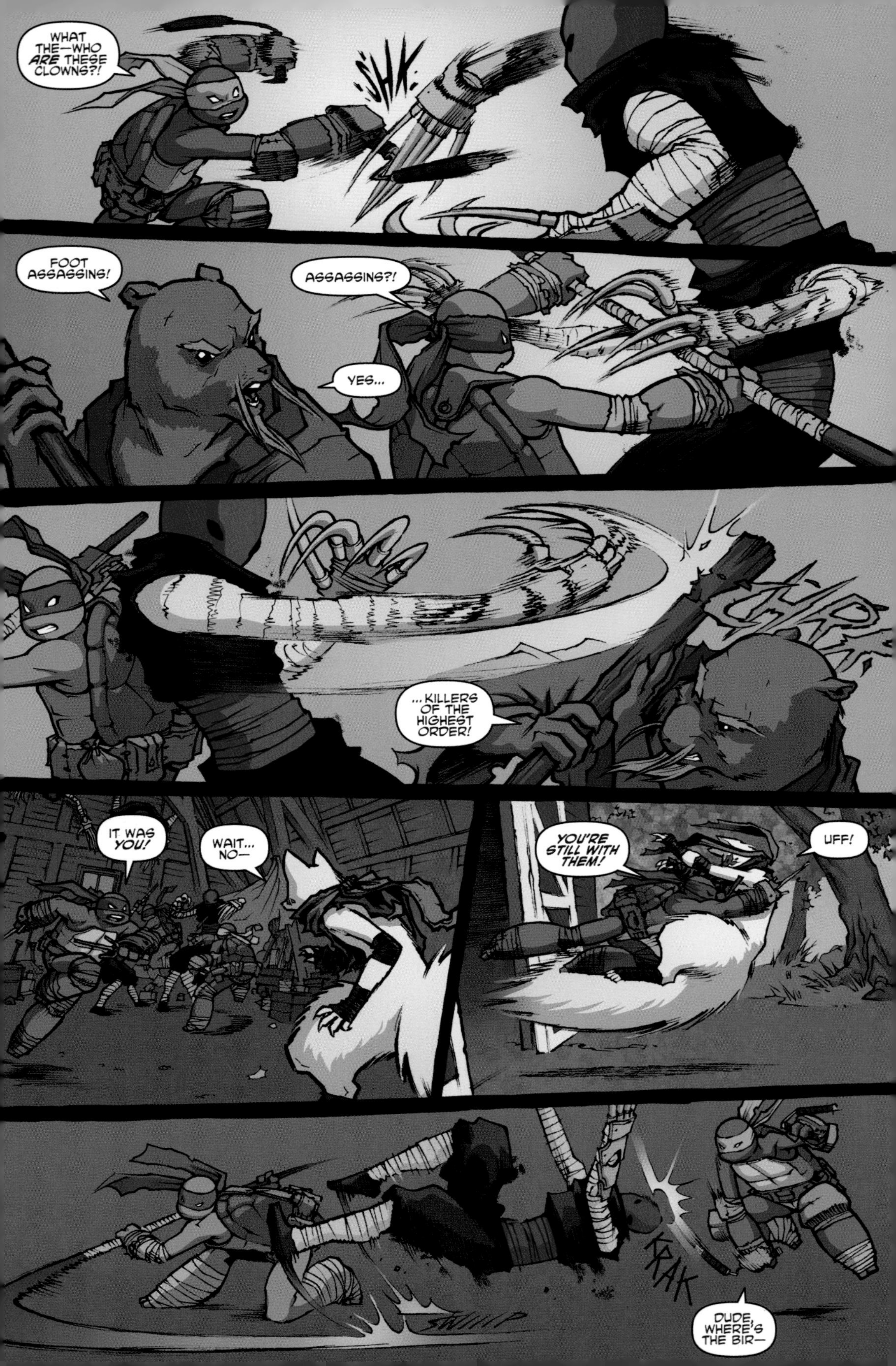
WHAT THE—WHO *ARE* THESE CLOWNS?!
SHK
FOOT ASSASSINS!
ASSASSINS?!
YES...
...KILLERS OF THE HIGHEST ORDER!
IT WAS *YOU!*
WAIT... NO—
YOU'RE STILL WITH THEM!
UFF!
KRAK
SWIIIP
DUDE, WHERE'S THE BIR—

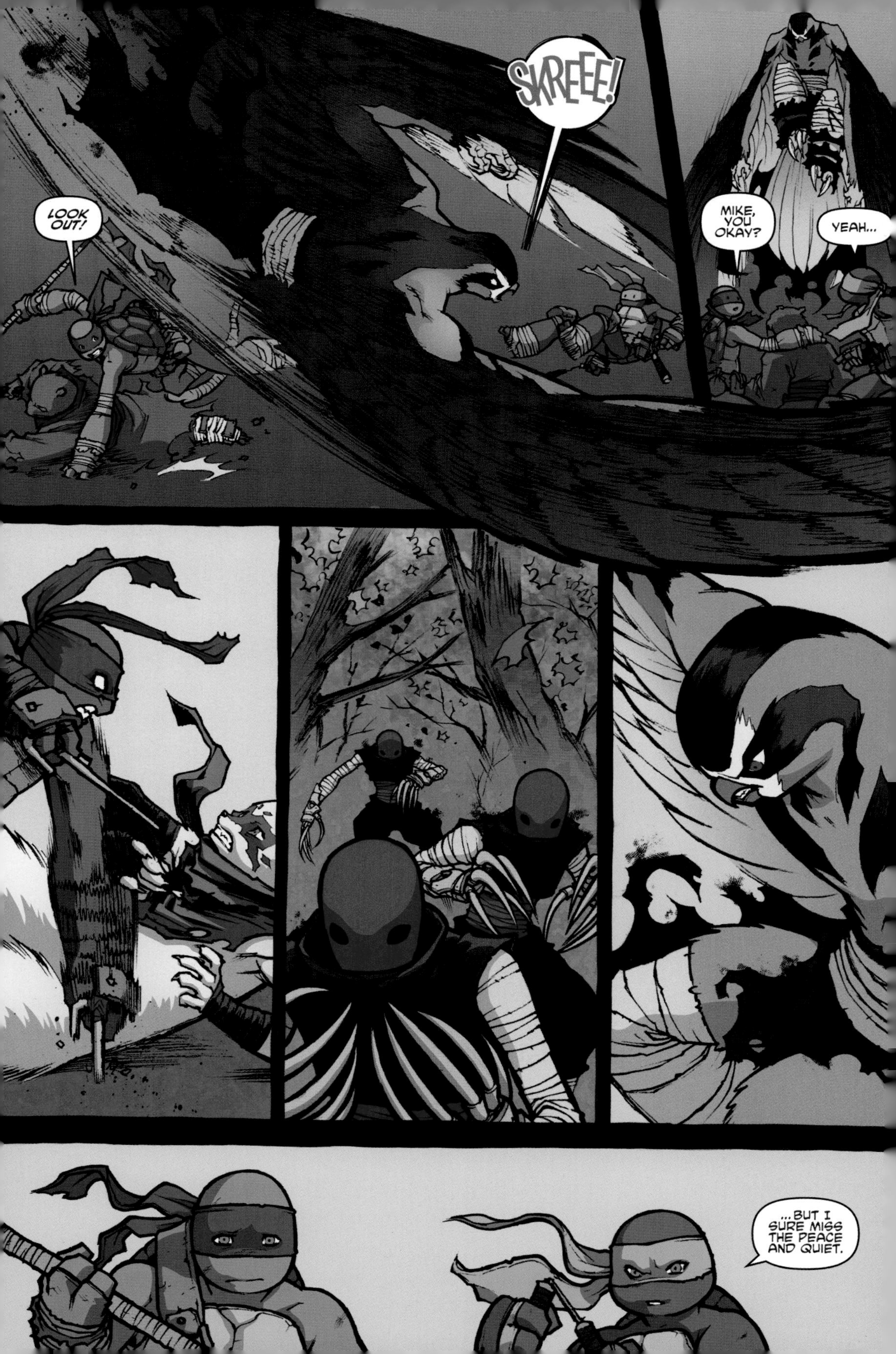
SKREEE!
LOOK OUT!
MIKE, YOU OKAY?
YEAH...
...BUT I SURE MISS THE PEACE AND QUIET.

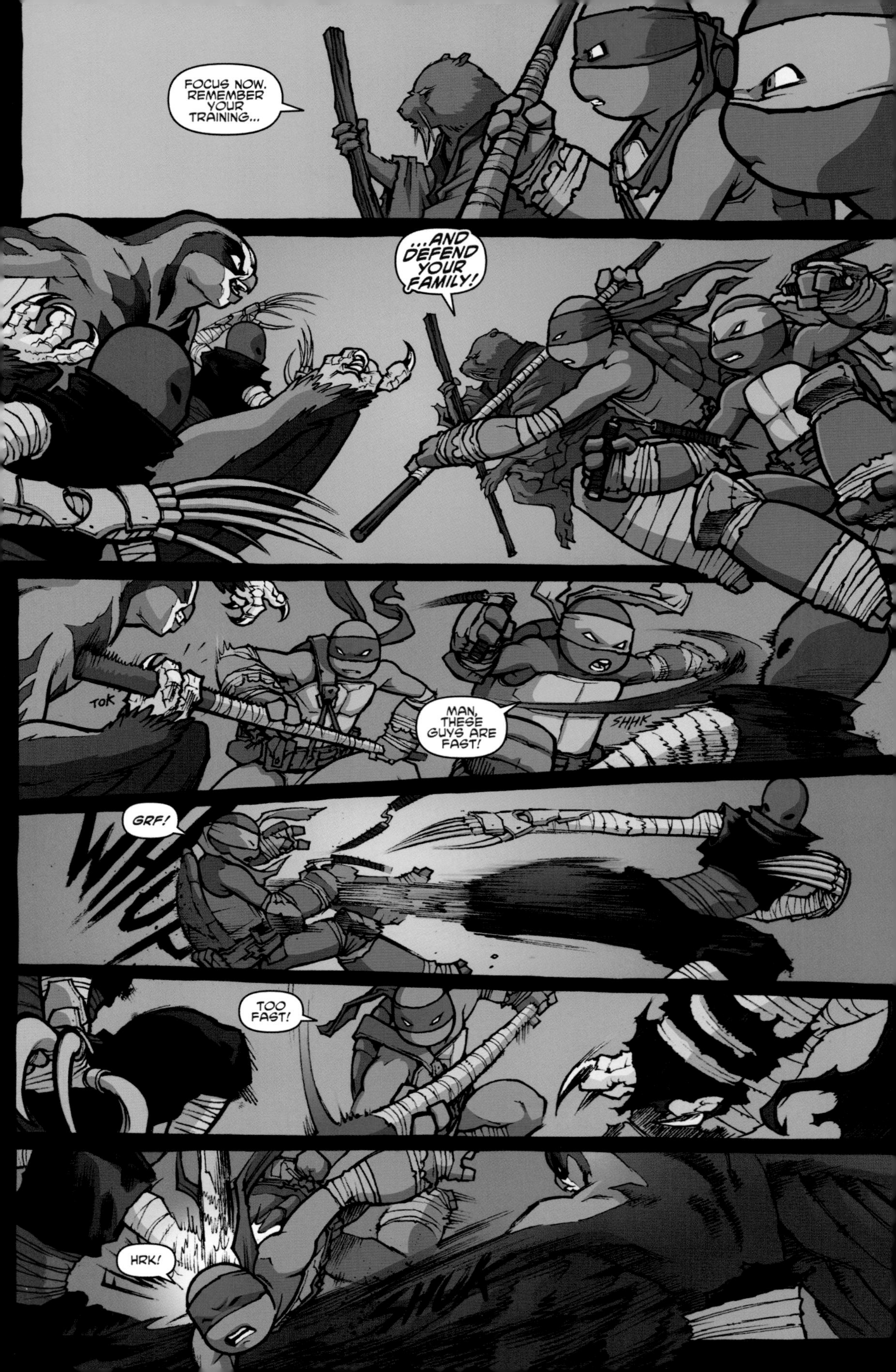

FOCUS NOW. REMEMBER YOUR TRAINING...
...AND DEFEND YOUR FAMILY!
TOK
MAN, THESE GUYS ARE FAST!
SHHK
GRF!
TOO FAST!
HRK!
SHUK

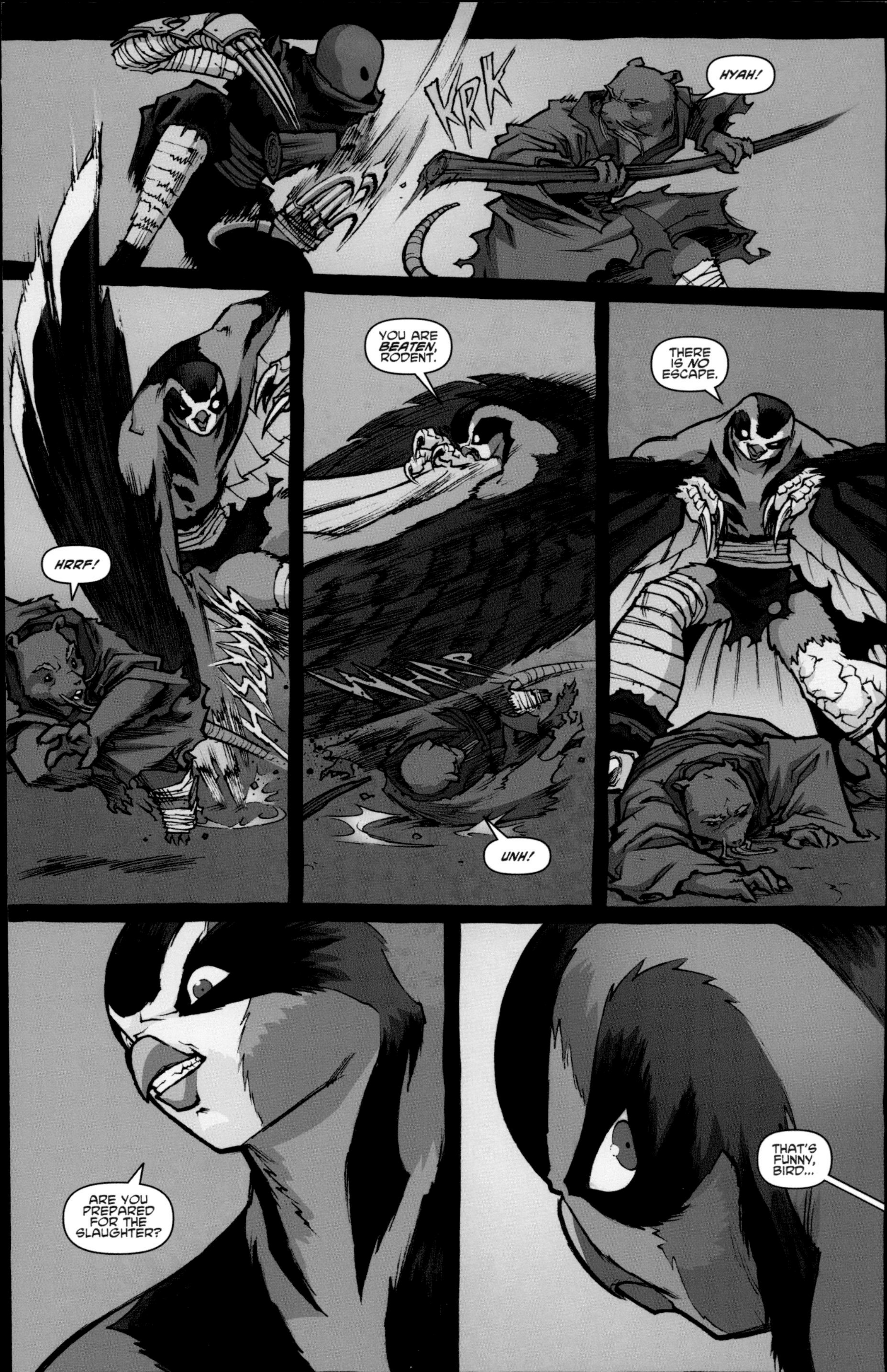
KRK
HYAH!
HRRF!
YOU ARE BEATEN, RODENT.
UNH!
THERE IS NO ESCAPE.
ARE YOU PREPARED FOR THE SLAUGHTER?
THAT'S FUNNY, BIRD...

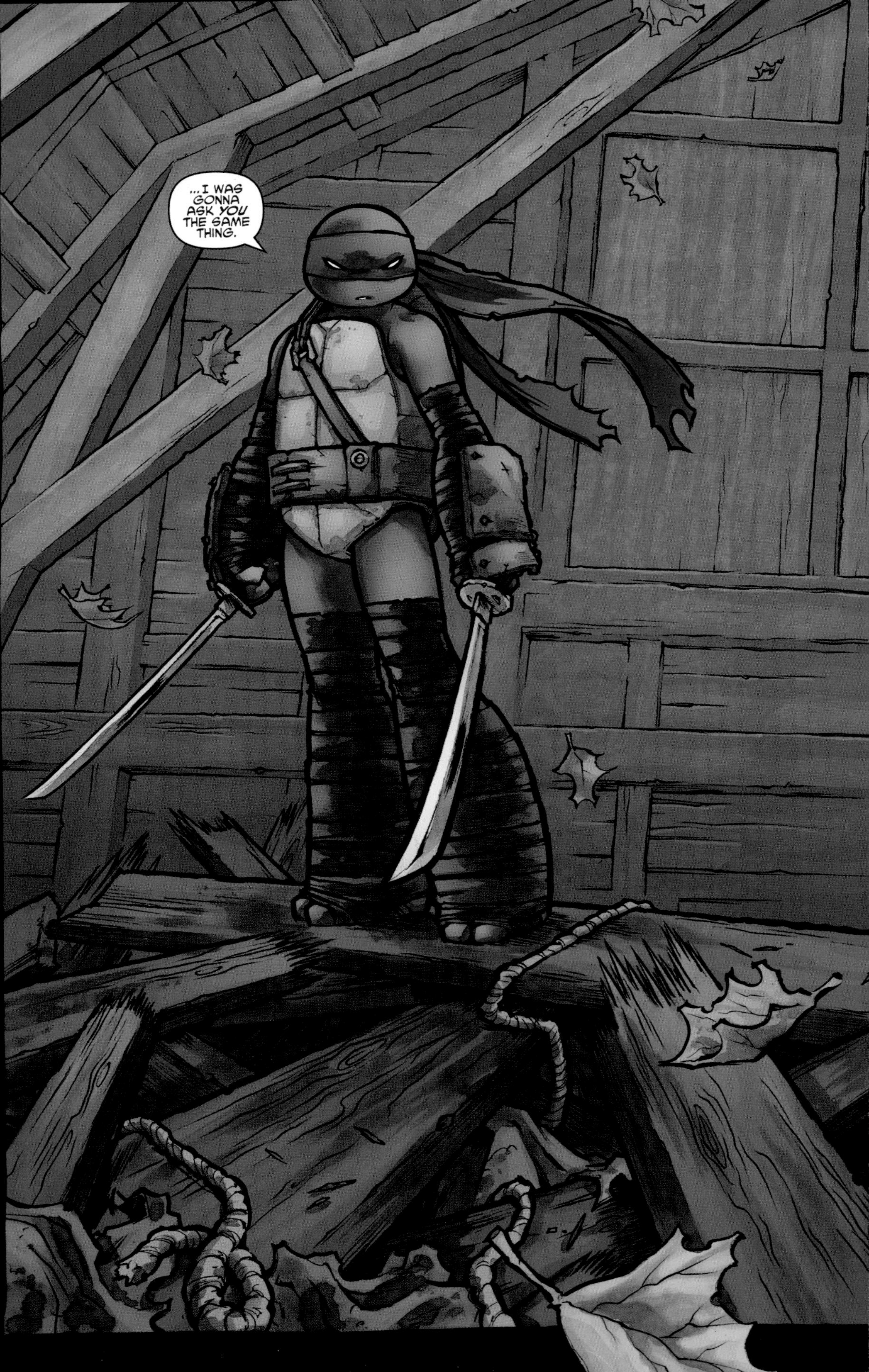
...I WAS GONNA ASK YOU THE SAME THING.

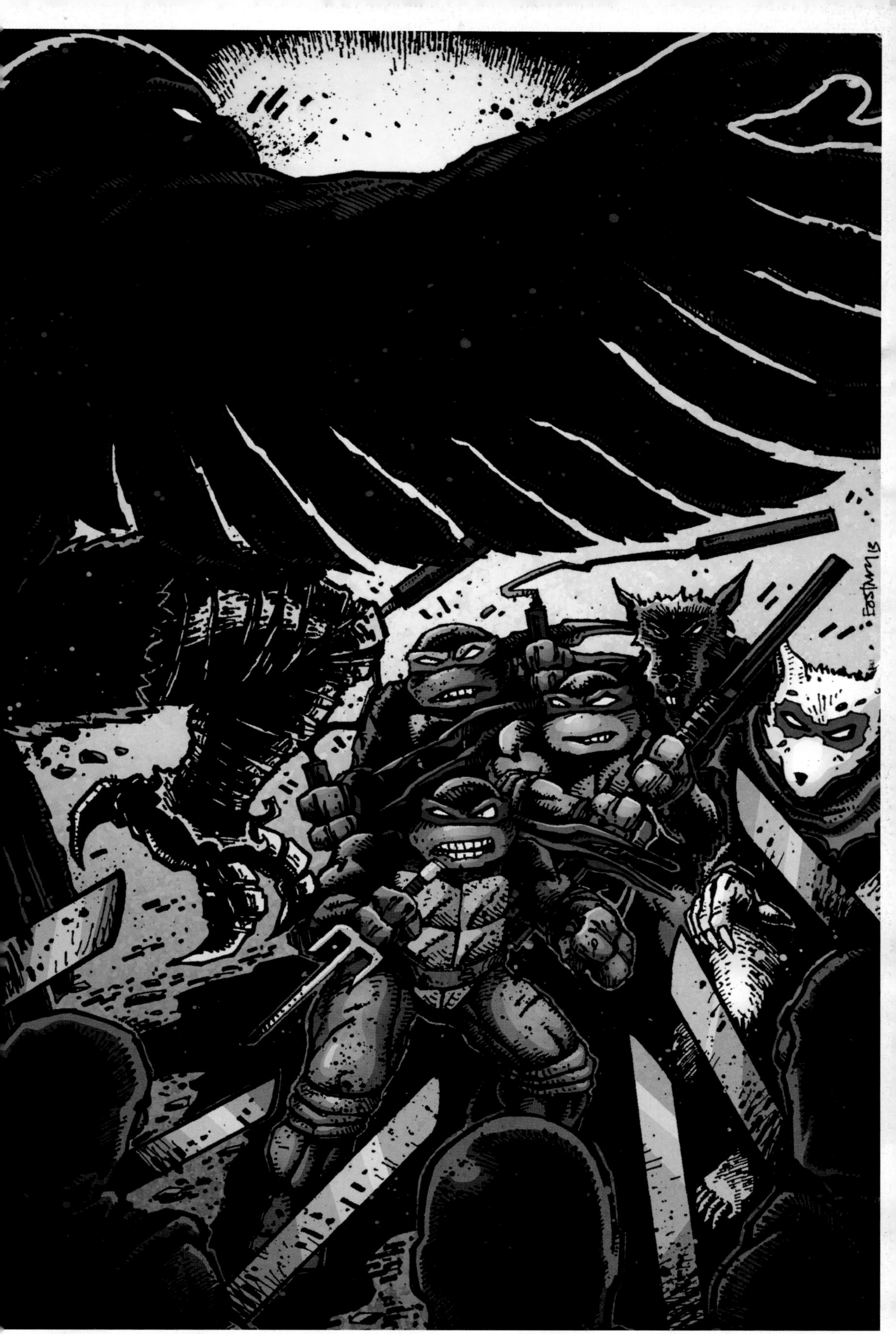

Cover by KEVIN EASTMAN
Colors by RONDA PATTISON

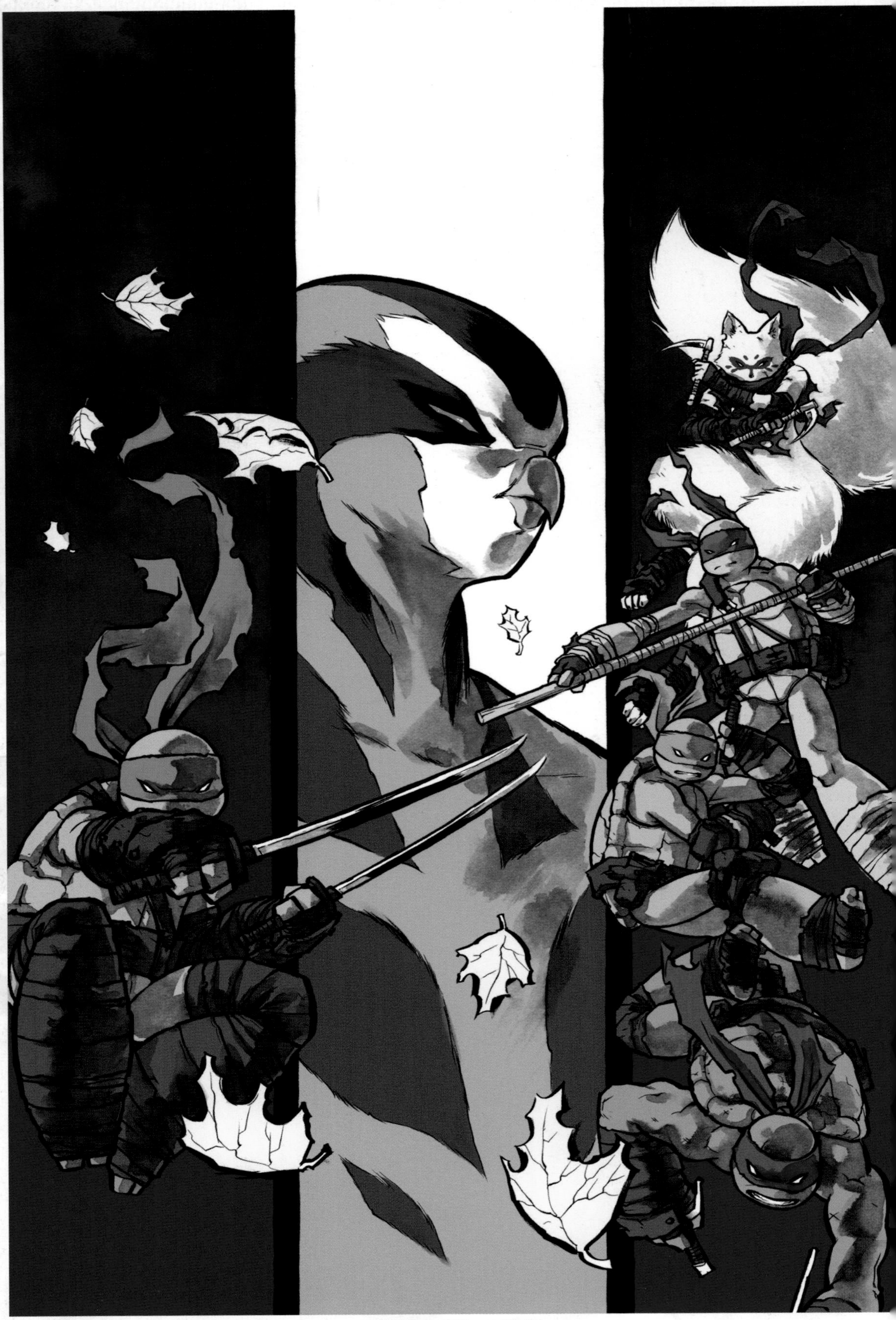

Cover by SOPHIE CAMPBELL

TMNT #32

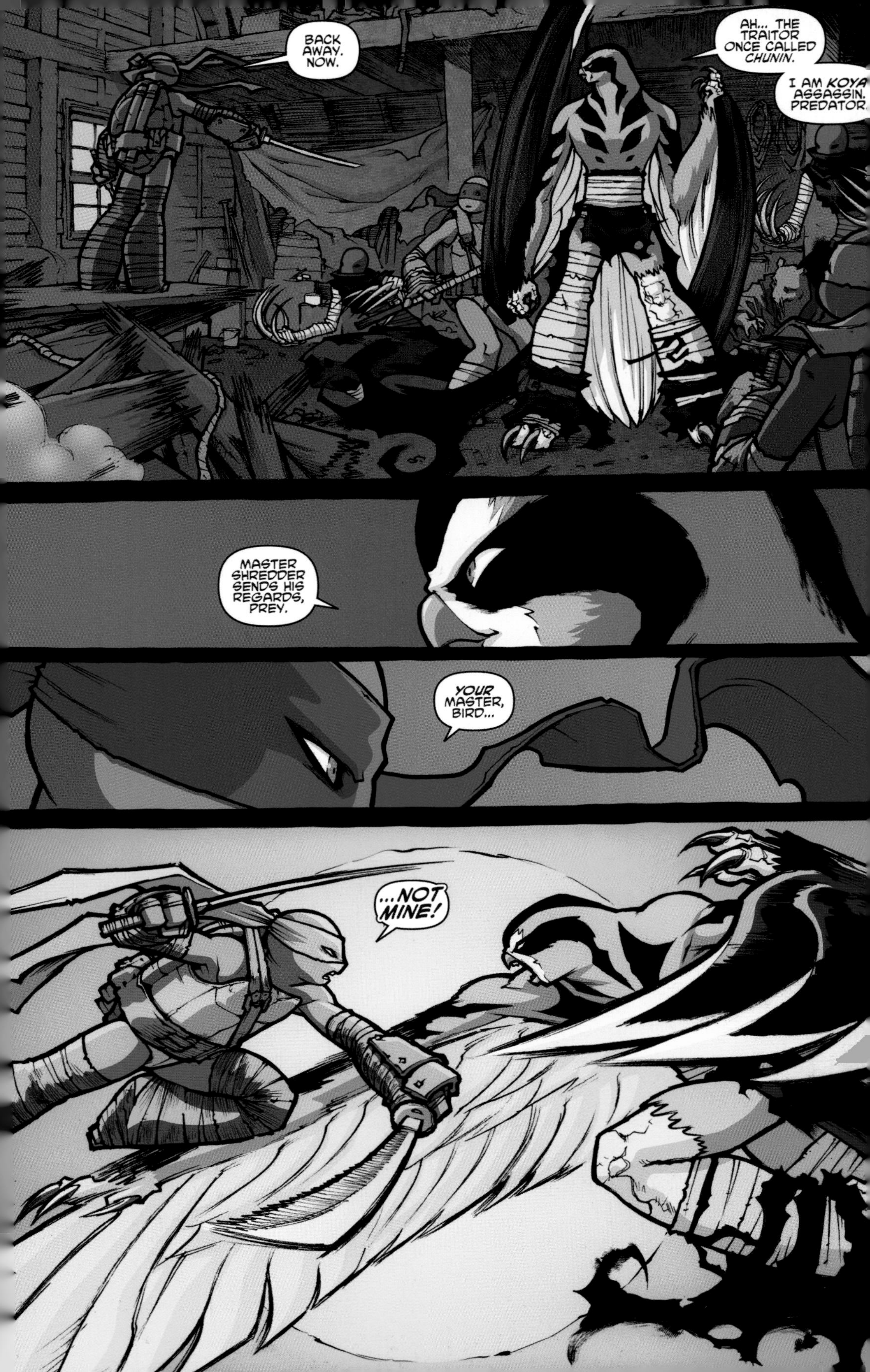
BACK AWAY. NOW.
AH... THE TRAITOR ONCE CALLED CHUNIN.
I AM KOYA. ASSASSIN. PREDATOR.
MASTER SHREDDER SENDS HIS REGARDS, PREY.
YOUR MASTER, BIRD...
...NOT MINE!

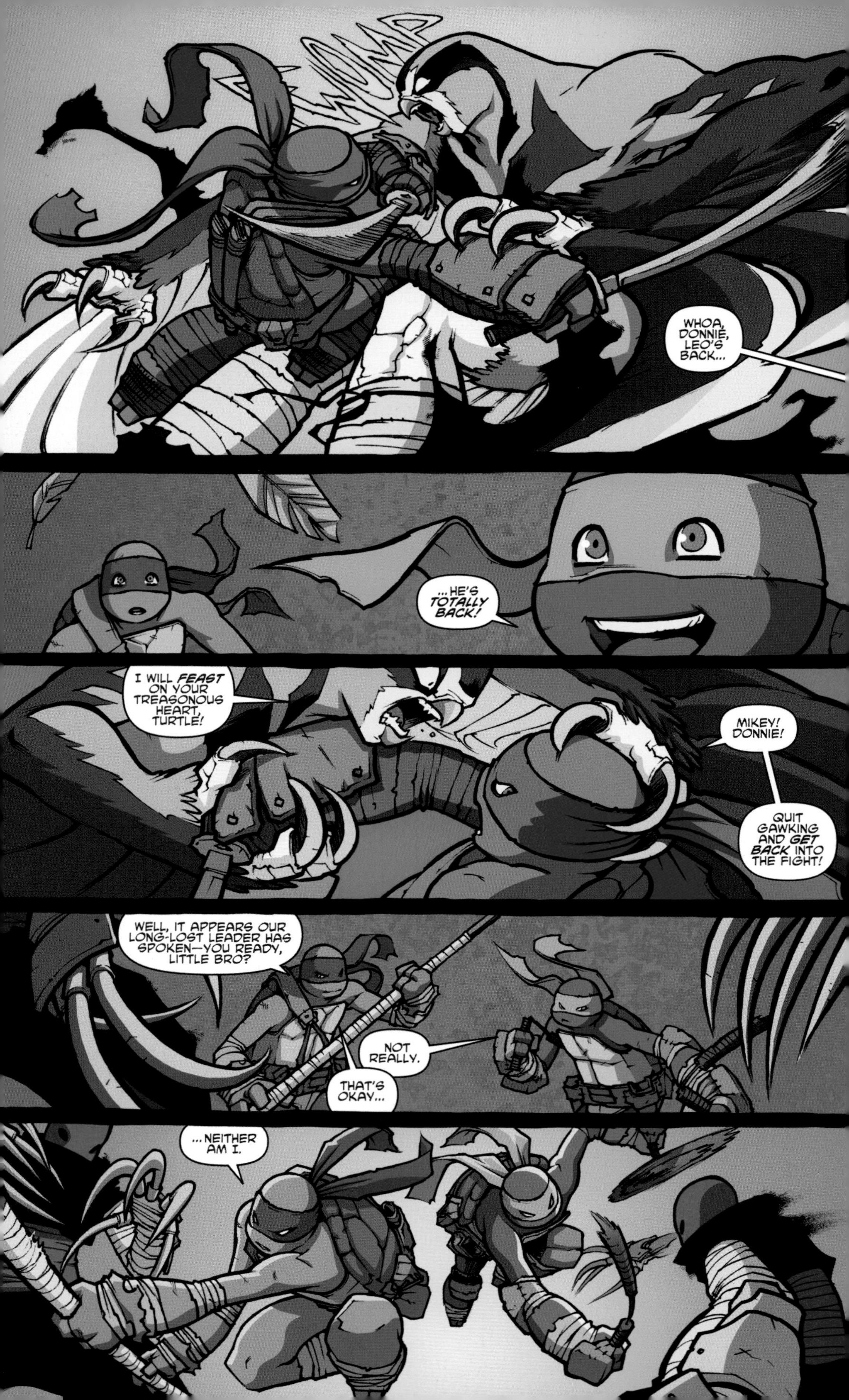
WHOA, DONNIE, LEO'S BACK...
...HE'S *TOTALLY* BACK!
I WILL *FEAST* ON YOUR TREASONOUS HEART, TURTLE!
MIKEY! DONNIE!
QUIT GAWKING AND *GET BACK* INTO THE FIGHT!
WELL, IT APPEARS OUR LONG-LOST LEADER HAS SPOKEN—YOU READY, LITTLE BRO?
NOT REALLY.
THAT'S OKAY...
...NEITHER AM I.

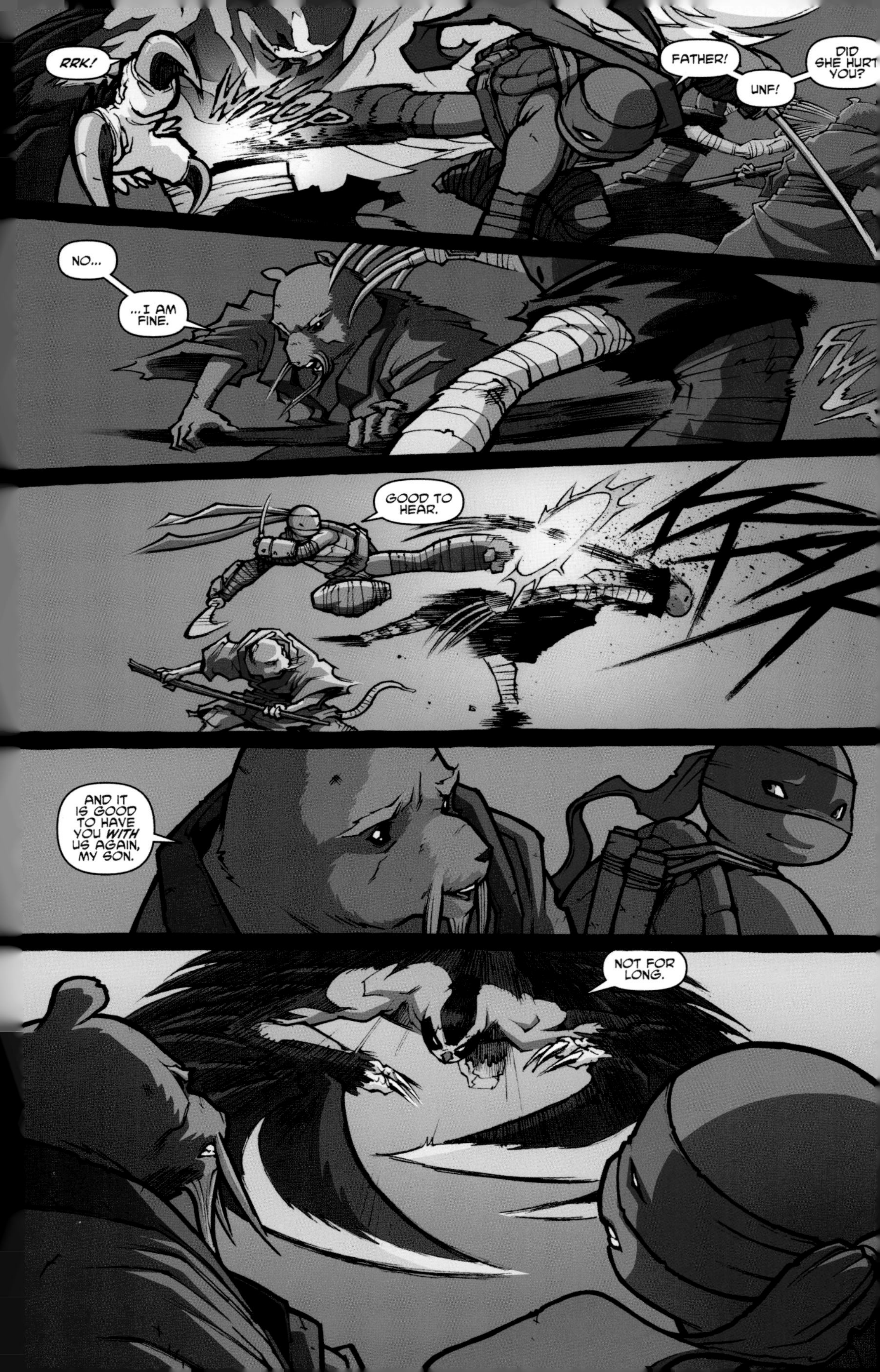
RRK!
FATHER!
UNF!
DID SHE HURT YOU?
NO...
...I AM FINE.
GOOD TO HEAR.
AND IT IS GOOD TO HAVE YOU *WITH* US AGAIN, MY SON.
NOT FOR LONG.

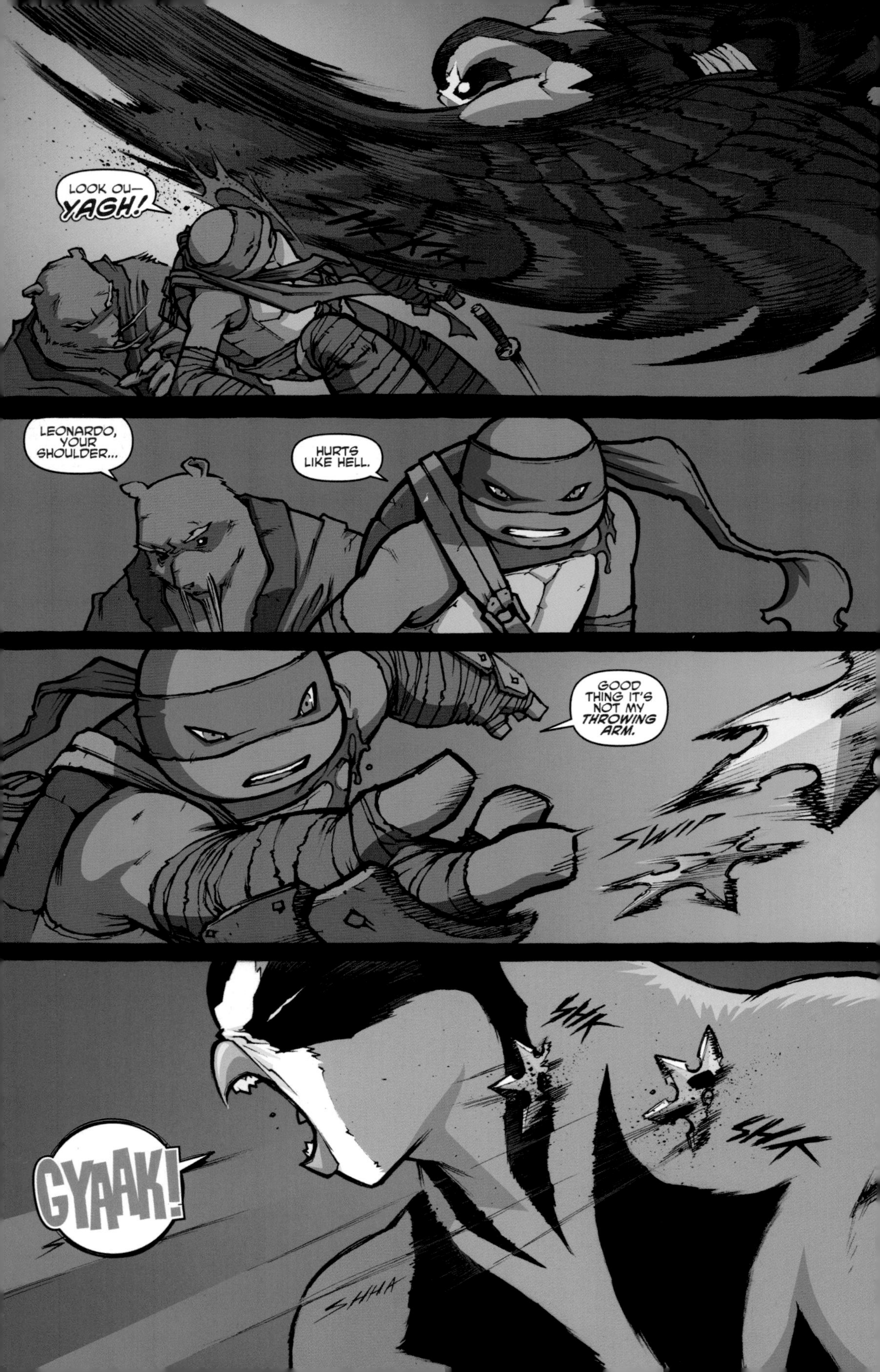
LOOK OU— YAGH!
SHKKKK
LEONARDO, YOUR SHOULDER...
HURTS LIKE HELL.
GOOD THING IT'S NOT MY THROWING ARM.
SWIP
SHK
SHK
GYAAK!
SHHA

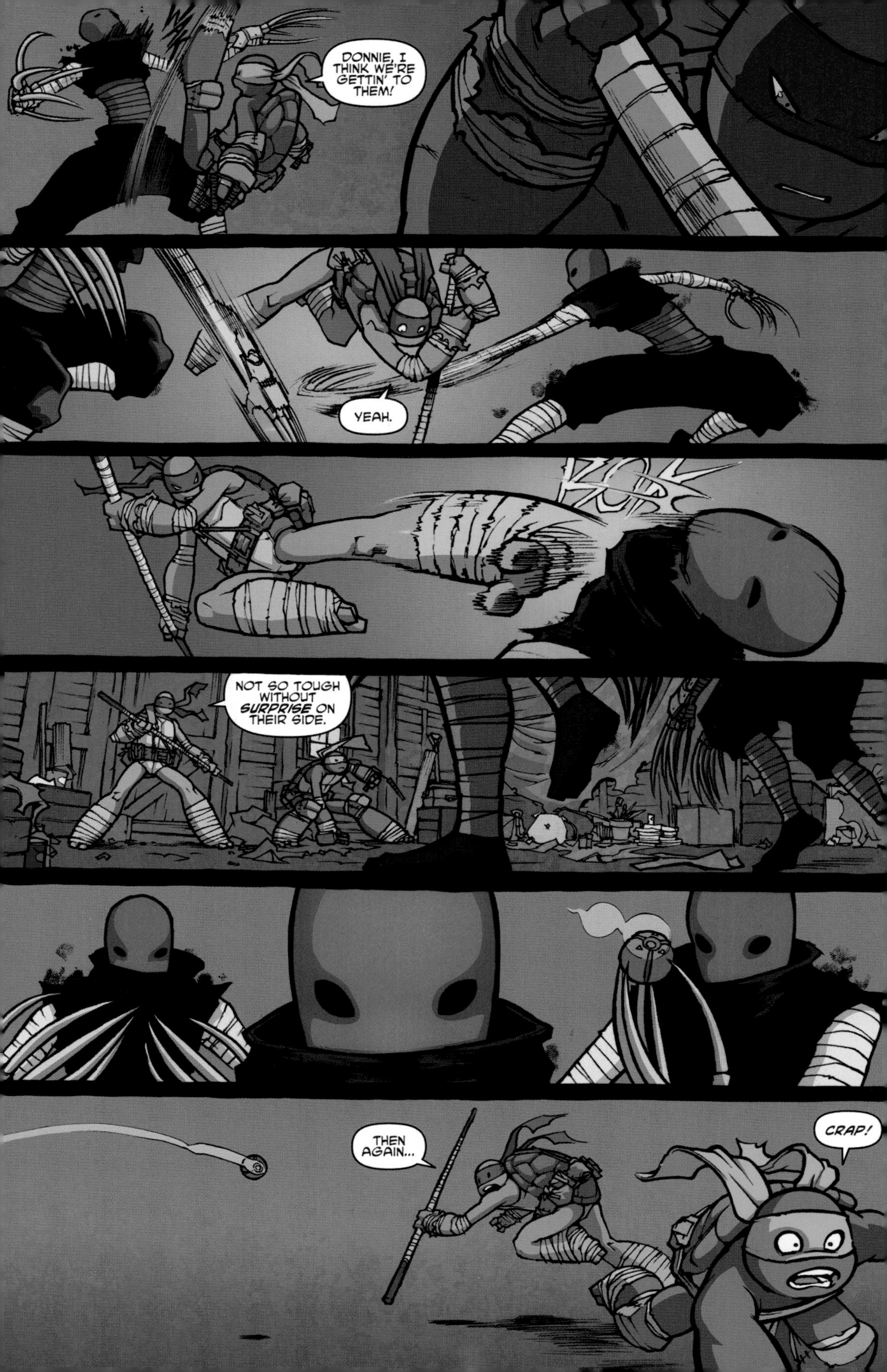
DONNIE, I THINK WE'RE GETTIN' TO THEM!
YEAH.
NOT SO TOUGH WITHOUT SURPRISE ON THEIR SIDE.
THEN AGAIN...
CRAP!

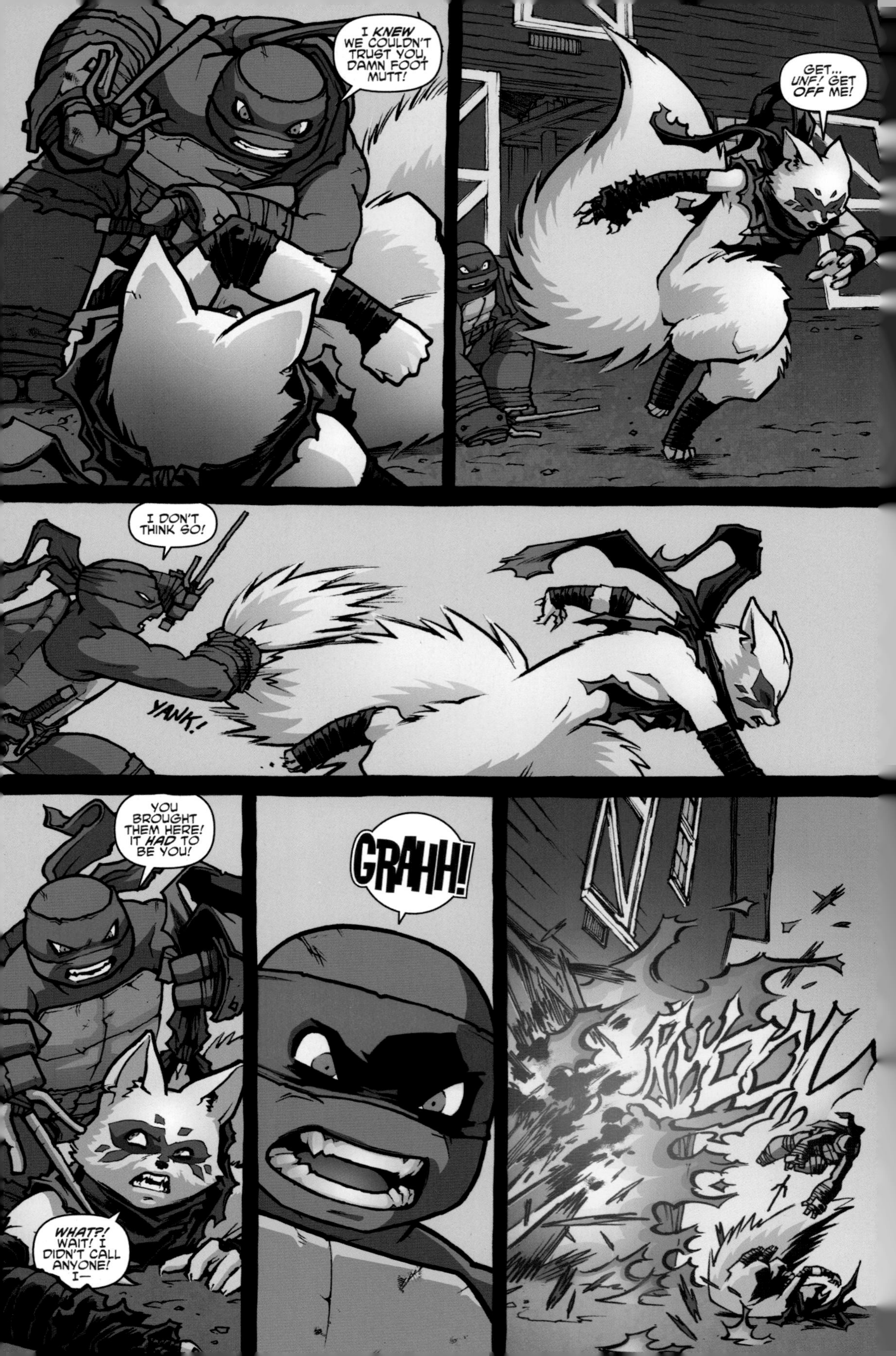
I KNEW WE COULDN'T TRUST YOU, DAMN FOOT MUTT!
GET... UNF! GET OFF ME!
I DON'T THINK SO!
YANK!
YOU BROUGHT THEM HERE! IT HAD TO BE YOU!
WHAT?! WAIT! I DIDN'T CALL ANYONE! I—
GRAHH!

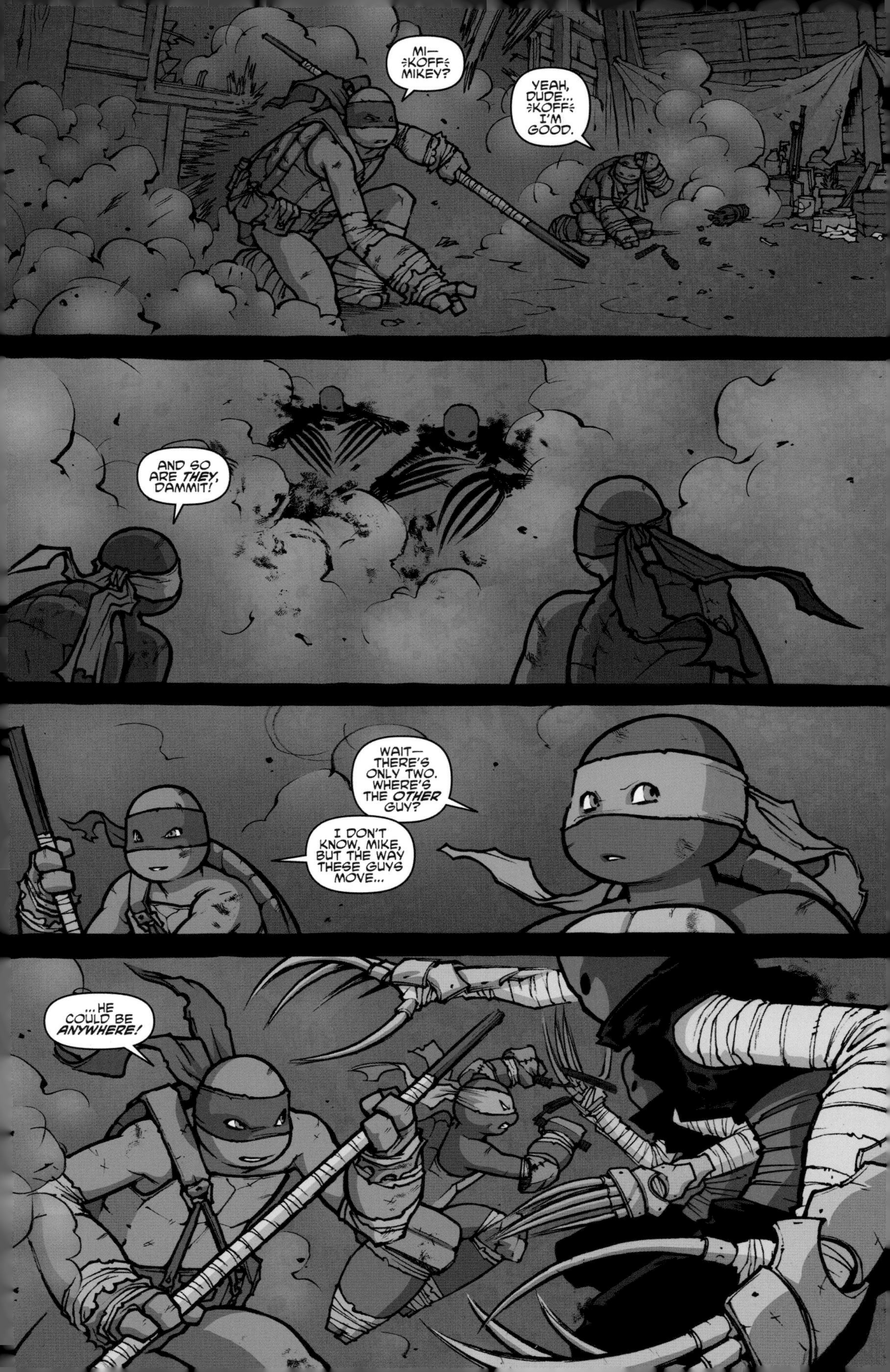
MI— *KOFF* MIKEY?
YEAH, DUDE... *KOFF* I'M GOOD.
AND SO ARE *THEY*, DAMMIT!
WAIT— THERE'S ONLY TWO. WHERE'S THE *OTHER* GUY?
I DON'T KNOW, MIKE, BUT THE WAY THESE GUYS MOVE...
...HE COULD BE ***ANYWHERE!***

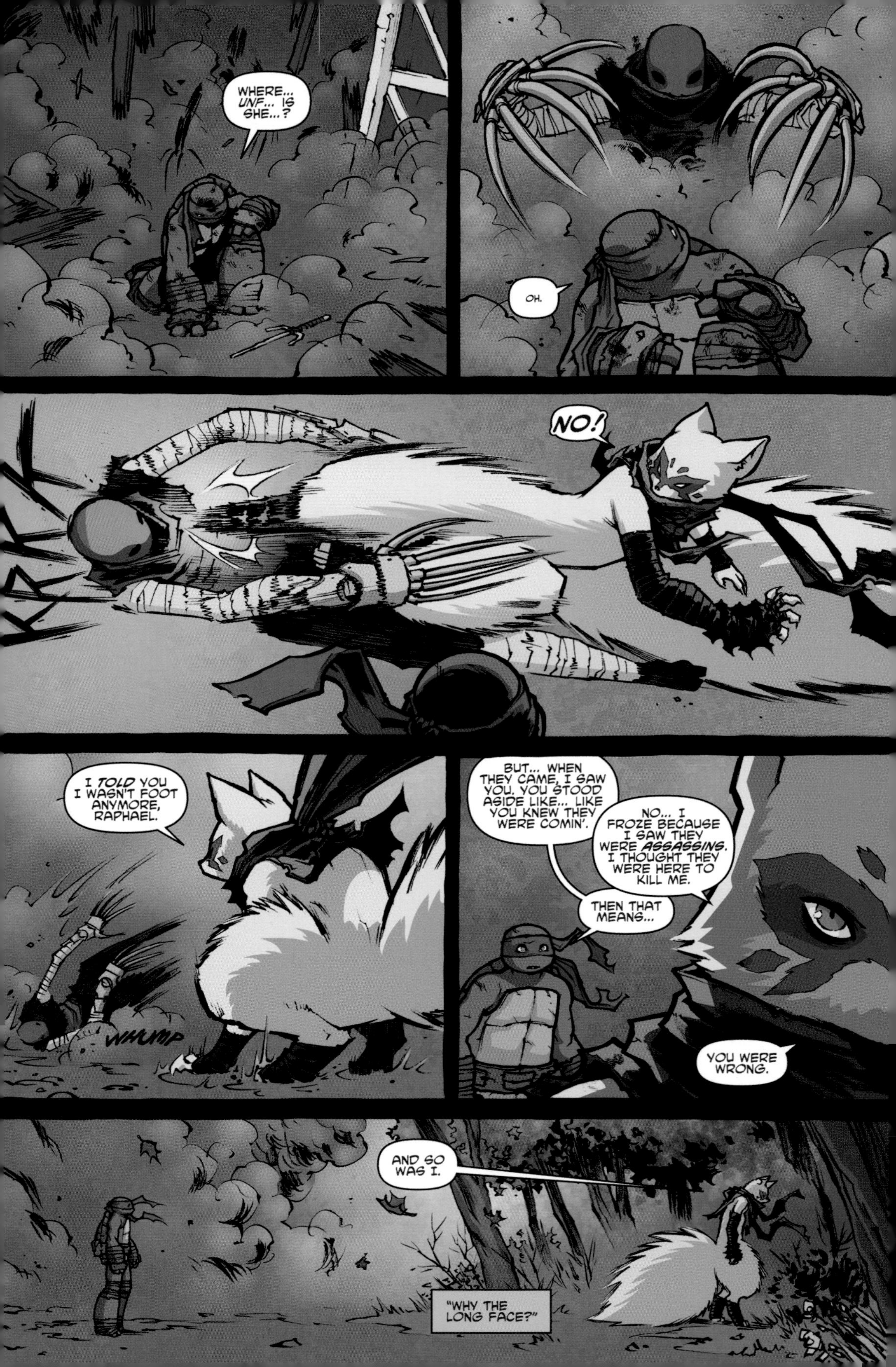
WHERE... UNF... IS SHE...?
OH.
NO!
I TOLD YOU I WASN'T FOOT ANYMORE, RAPHAEL.
WHUMP
BUT... WHEN THEY CAME, I SAW YOU. YOU STOOD ASIDE LIKE... LIKE YOU KNEW THEY WERE COMIN'.
NO... I FROZE BECAUSE I SAW THEY WERE ASSASSINS. I THOUGHT THEY WERE HERE TO KILL ME.
THEN THAT MEANS...
YOU WERE WRONG.
AND SO WAS I.
"WHY THE LONG FACE?"

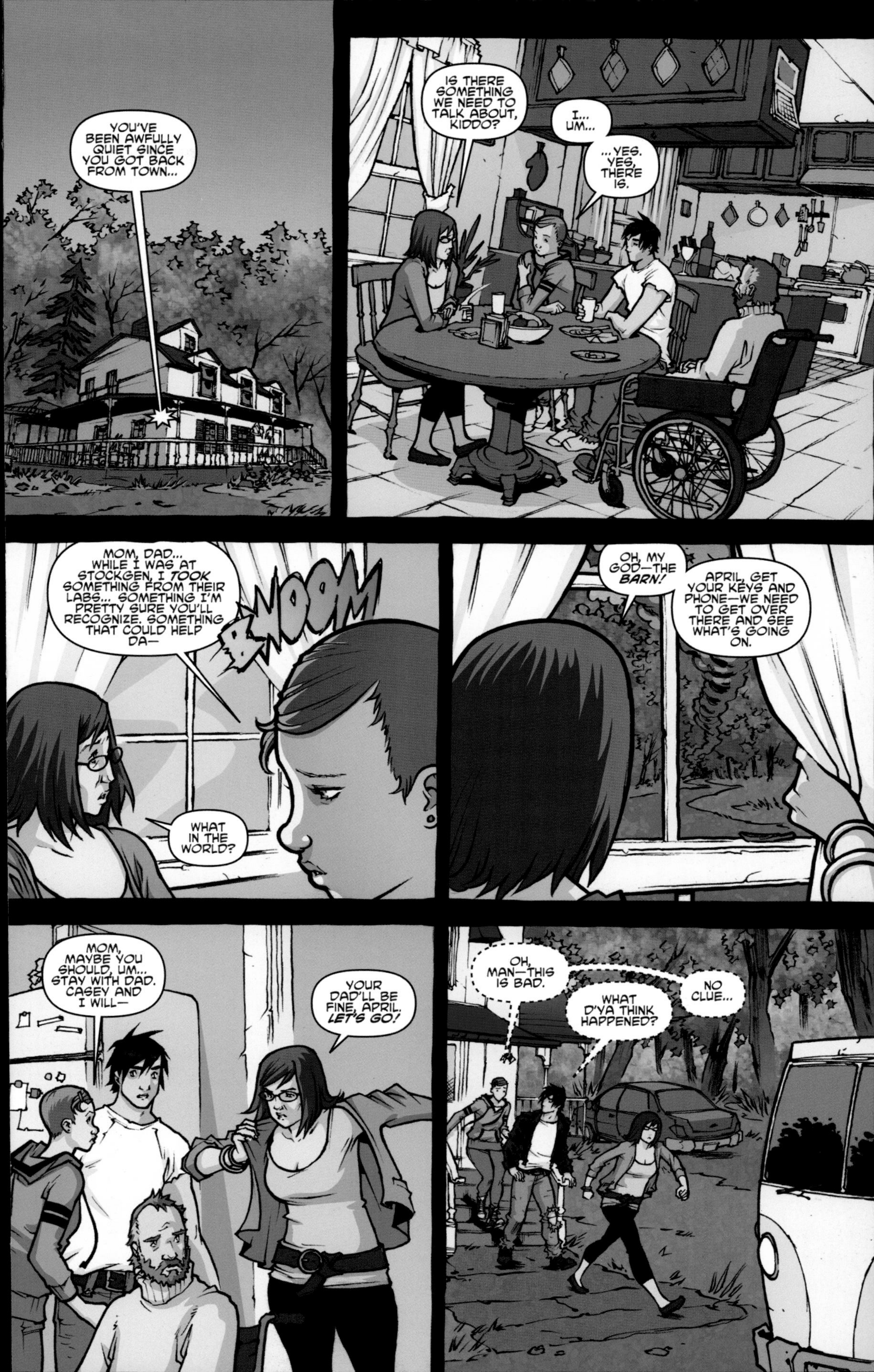
YOU'VE BEEN AWFULLY QUIET SINCE YOU GOT BACK FROM TOWN...
IS THERE SOMETHING WE NEED TO TALK ABOUT, KIDDO?
I... UM...
...YES. YES, THERE IS.
MOM, DAD... WHILE I WAS AT STOCKGEN, I *TOOK* SOMETHING FROM THEIR LABS... SOMETHING I'M PRETTY SURE YOU'LL RECOGNIZE. SOMETHING THAT COULD HELP DA—
BWOOM
WHAT IN THE WORLD?
OH, MY GOD—THE *BARN!*
APRIL, GET YOUR KEYS AND PHONE—WE NEED TO GET OVER THERE AND SEE WHAT'S GOING ON.
MOM, MAYBE YOU SHOULD, UM... STAY WITH DAD. CASEY AND I WILL—
YOUR DAD'LL BE FINE, APRIL. *LET'S GO!*
OH, MAN—THIS IS BAD.
WHAT D'YA THINK HAPPENED?
NO CLUE...

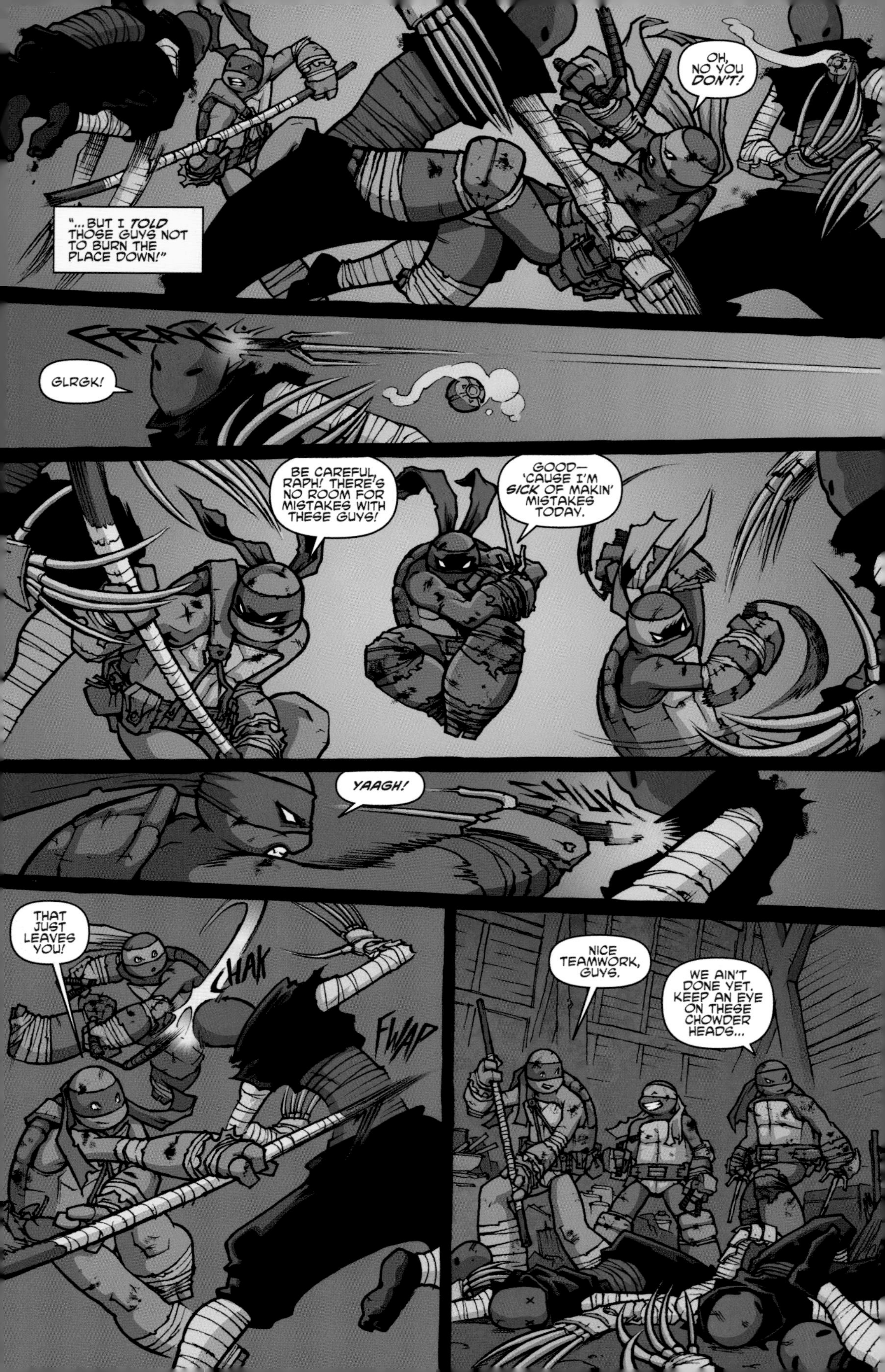

"...BUT I *TOLD* THOSE GUYS NOT TO BURN THE PLACE DOWN!"
OH, NO YOU *DON'T!*
GLRGK!
BE CAREFUL, RAPH! THERE'S NO ROOM FOR MISTAKES WITH THESE GUYS!
GOOD— 'CAUSE I'M *SICK* OF MAKIN' MISTAKES TODAY.
YAAGH!
SHUK
THAT JUST LEAVES YOU!
CHAK
FWAP
NICE TEAMWORK, GUYS.
WE AIN'T DONE YET. KEEP AN EYE ON THESE CHOWDER HEADS...

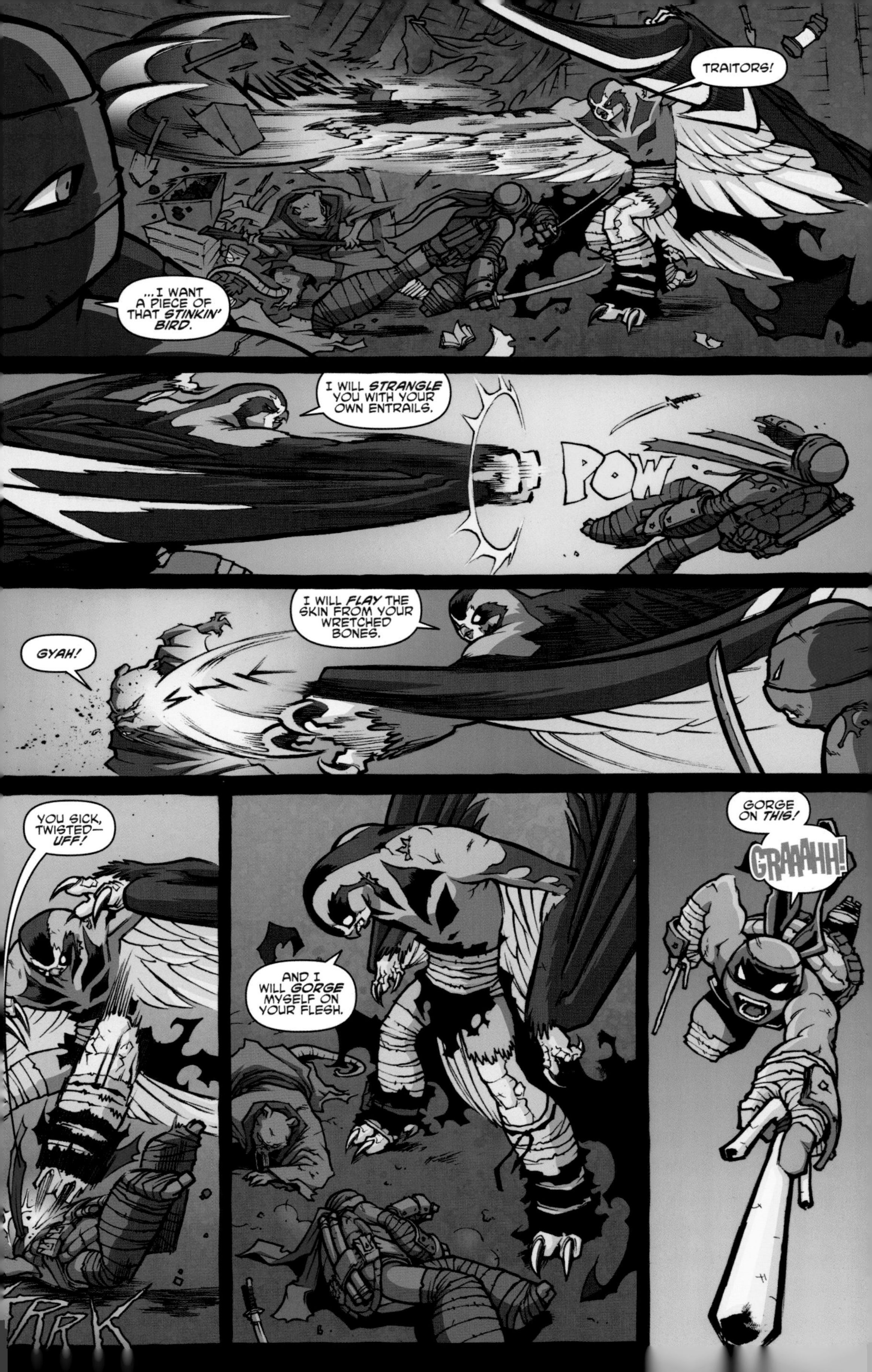
...I WANT A PIECE OF THAT STINKIN' BIRD.
TRAITORS!
I WILL STRANGLE YOU WITH YOUR OWN ENTRAILS.
POW
I WILL FLAY THE SKIN FROM YOUR WRETCHED BONES.
GYAH!
YOU SICK, TWISTED— UFF!
TRRK
AND I WILL GORGE MYSELF ON YOUR FLESH.
GORGE ON THIS!
GRAAAHH!

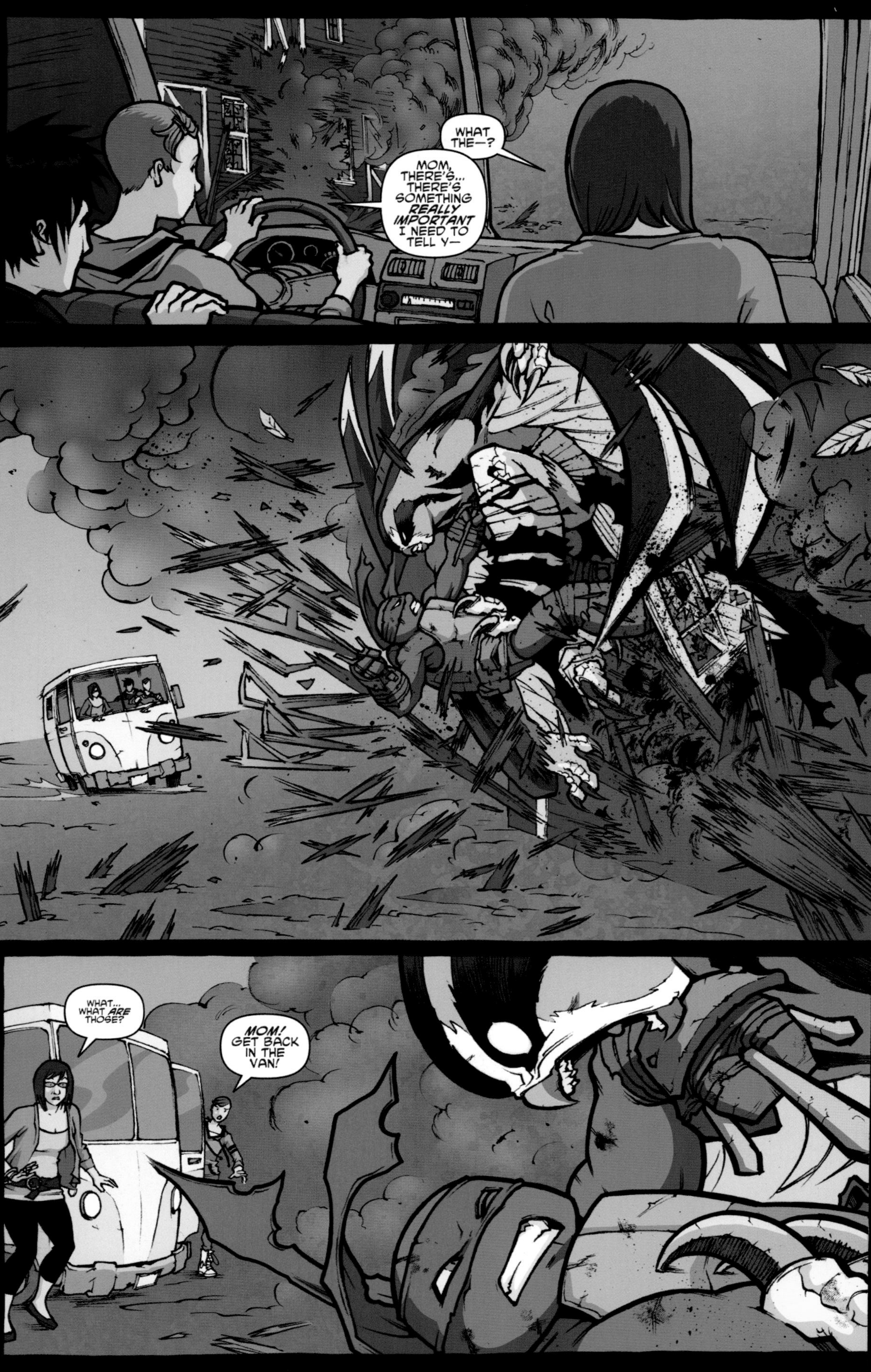
WHAT THE—?
MOM, THERE'S... THERE'S SOMETHING *REALLY IMPORTANT* I NEED TO TELL Y—
WHAT... WHAT *ARE* THOSE?
MOM! GET BACK IN THE VAN!

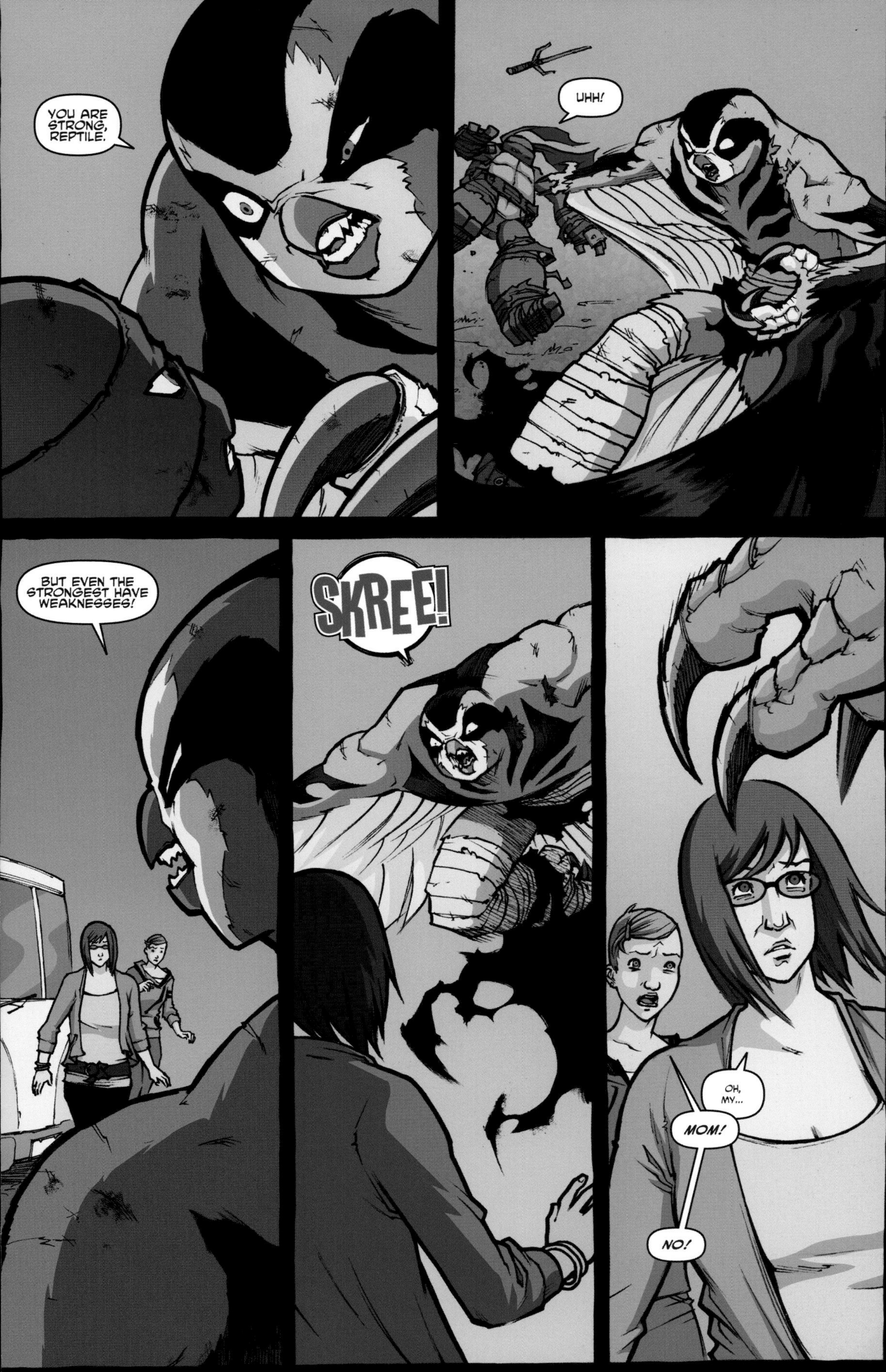

YOU ARE STRONG, REPTILE.
UHH!
BUT EVEN THE STRONGEST HAVE WEAKNESSES!
SKREE!
OH, MY...
MOM!
NO!

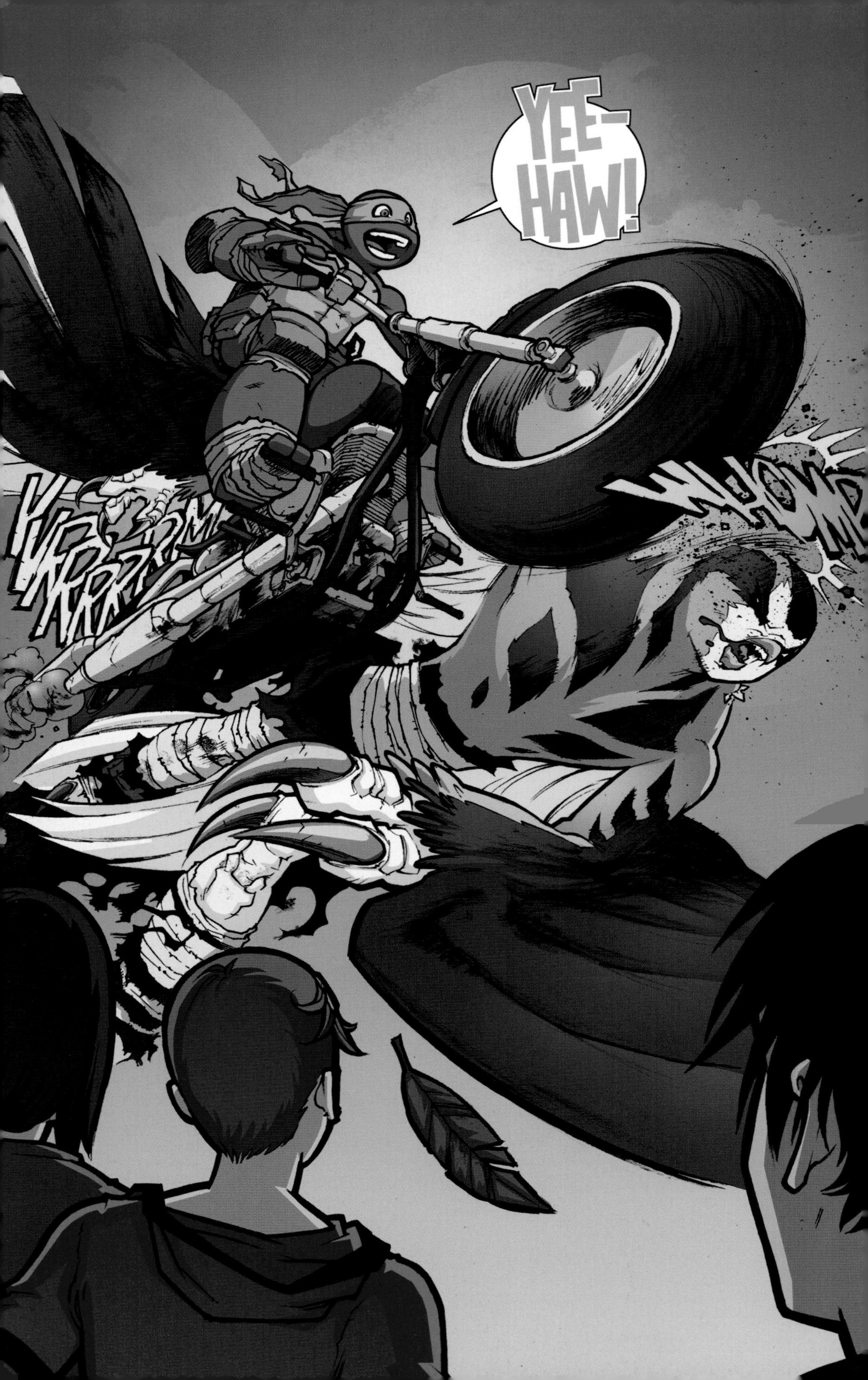
YEE-HAW!

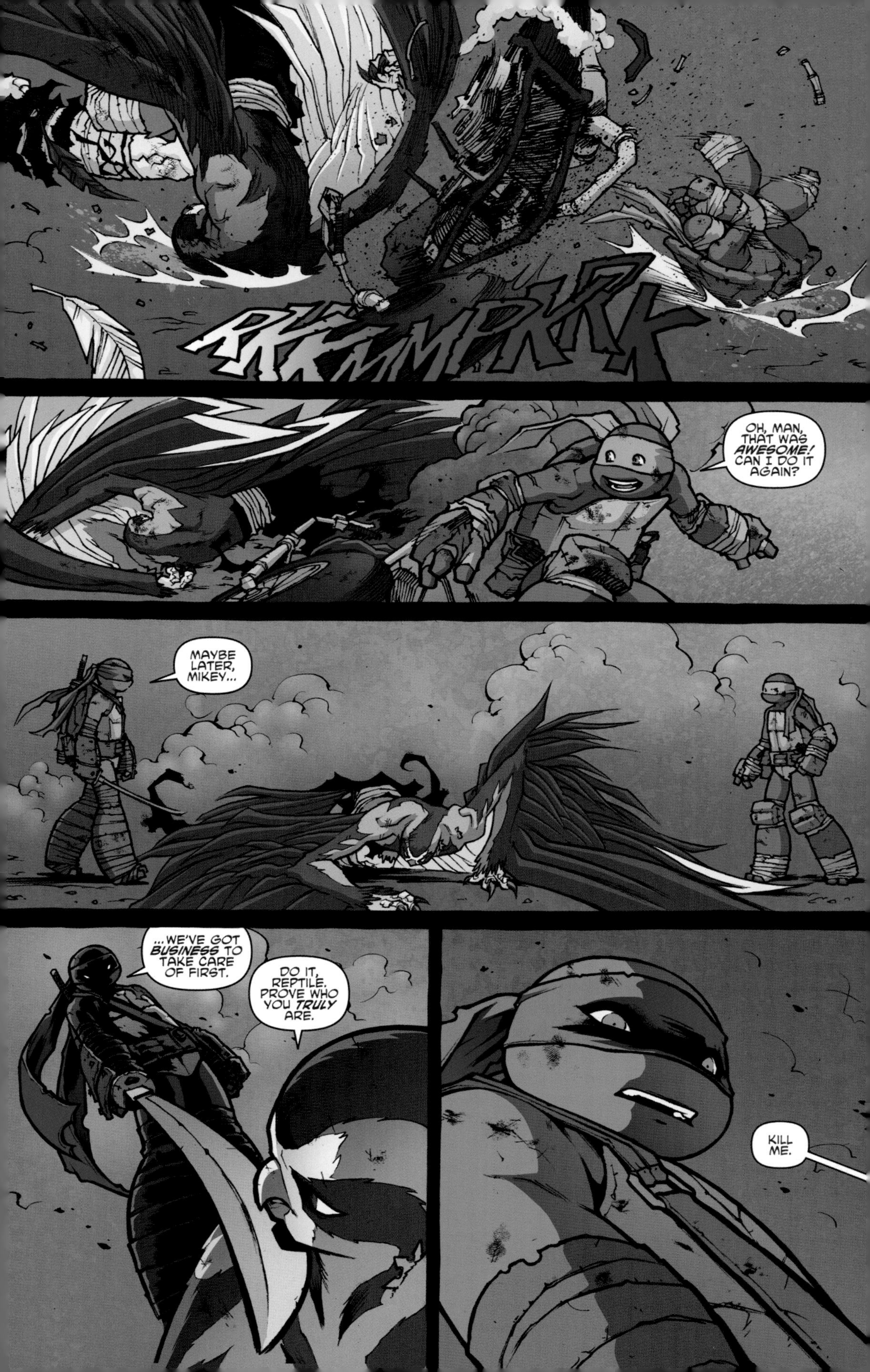
RRKKMMPKKK
OH, MAN, THAT WAS AWESOME! CAN I DO IT AGAIN?
MAYBE LATER, MIKEY...
...WE'VE GOT BUSINESS TO TAKE CARE OF FIRST.
DO IT, REPTILE. PROVE WHO YOU TRULY ARE.
KILL ME.

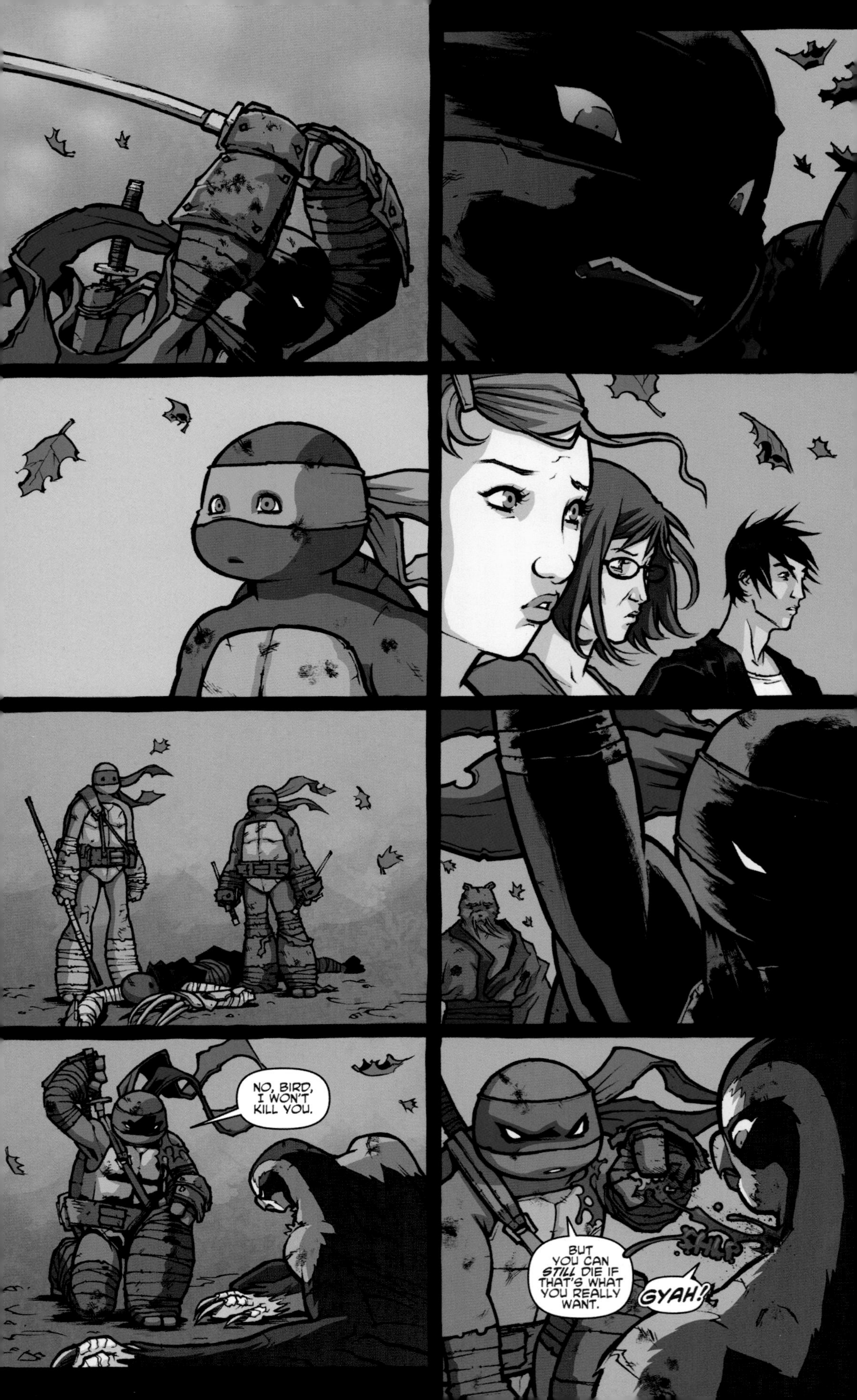
NO, BIRD, I WON'T KILL YOU.
BUT YOU CAN STILL DIE IF THAT'S WHAT YOU REALLY WANT.
GYAH!

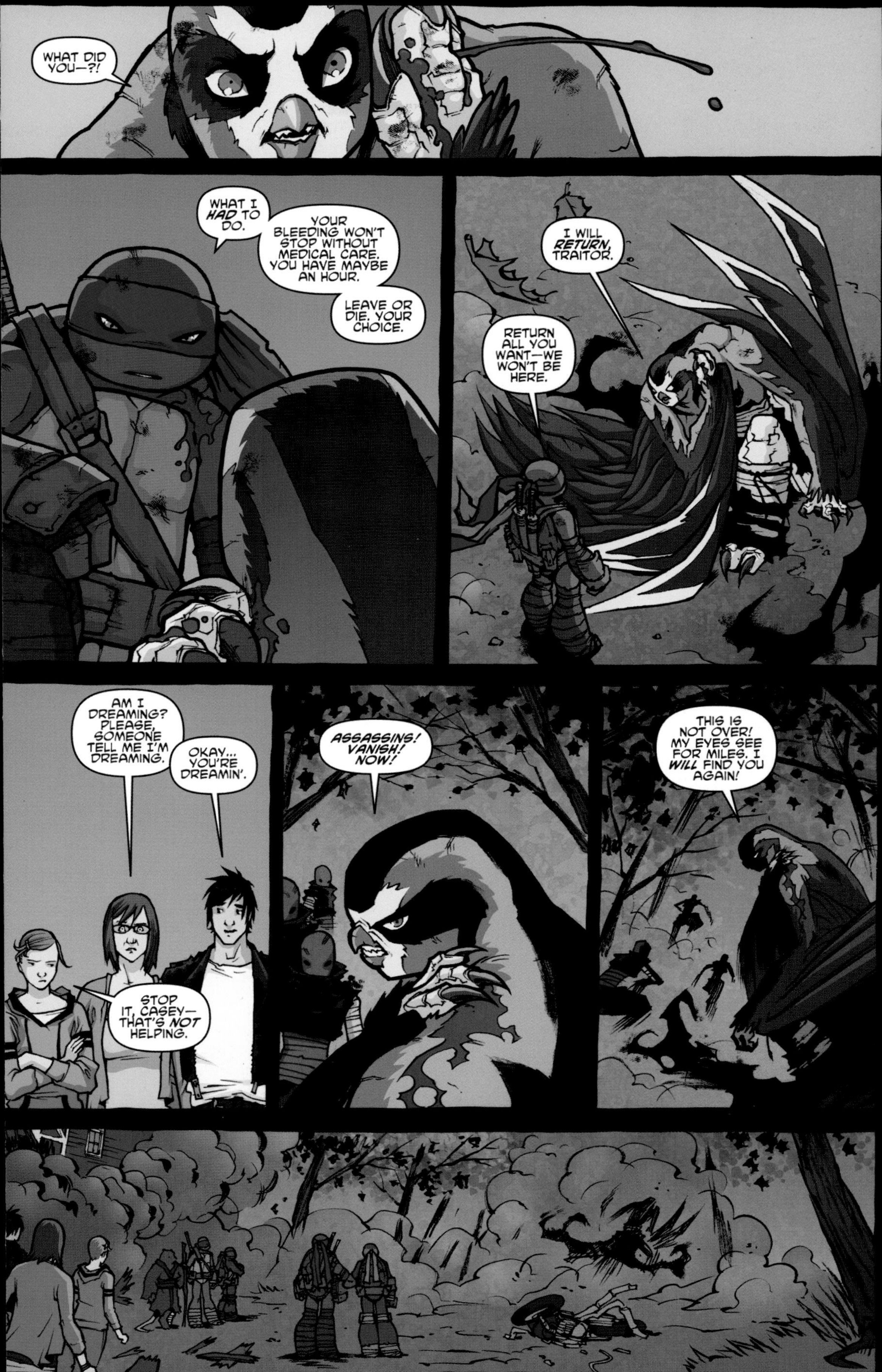
WHAT DID YOU—?!
WHAT I HAD TO DO.
YOUR BLEEDING WON'T STOP WITHOUT MEDICAL CARE. YOU HAVE MAYBE AN HOUR.
LEAVE OR DIE. YOUR CHOICE.
I WILL RETURN, TRAITOR.
RETURN ALL YOU WANT—WE WON'T BE HERE.
AM I DREAMING? PLEASE, SOMEONE TELL ME I'M DREAMING.
OKAY... YOU'RE DREAMIN'.
STOP IT, CASEY—THAT'S NOT HELPING.
ASSASSINS! VANISH! NOW!
THIS IS NOT OVER! MY EYES SEE FOR MILES. I WILL FIND YOU AGAIN!

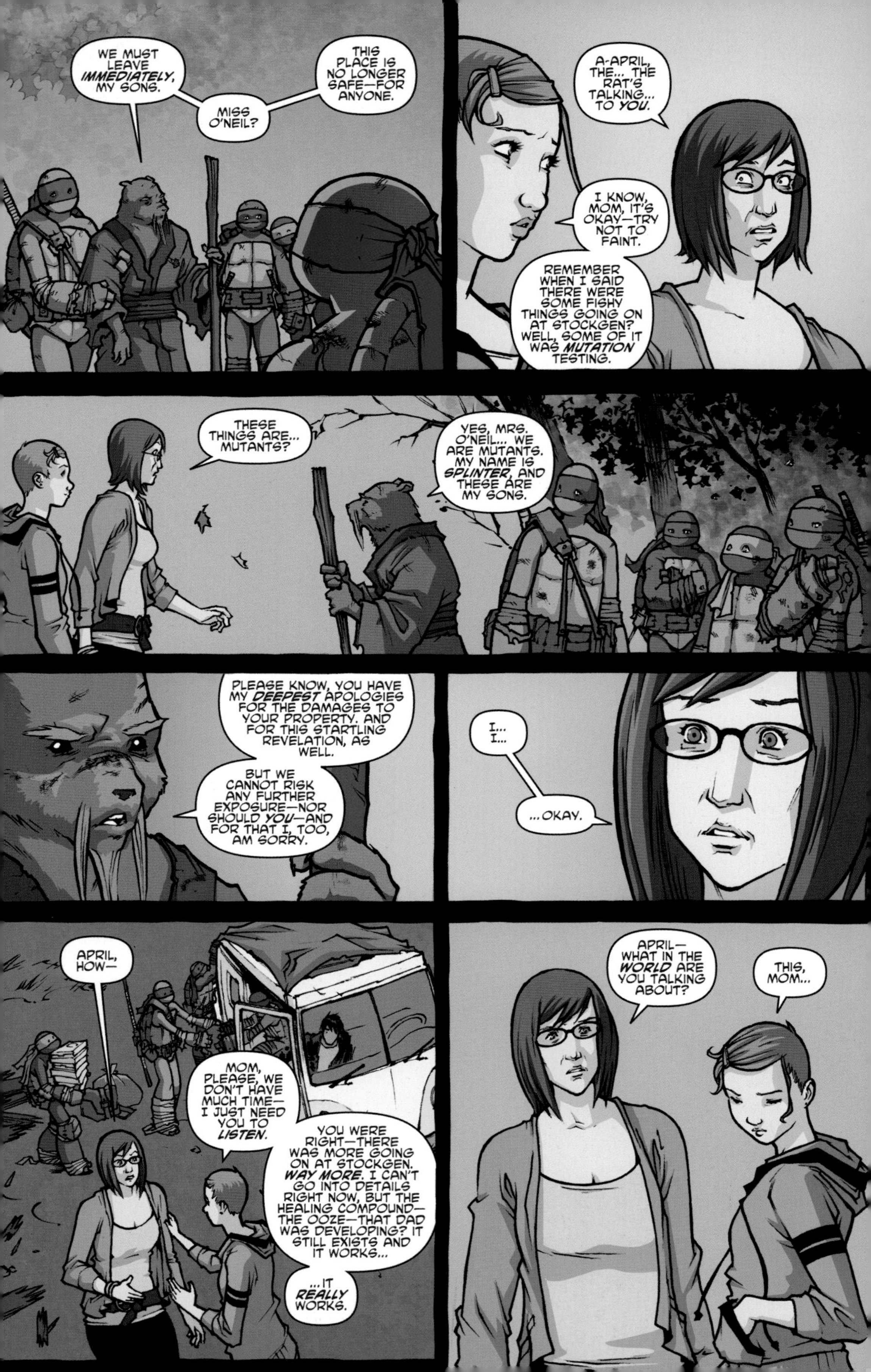
WE MUST LEAVE *IMMEDIATELY*, MY SONS.
MISS O'NEIL?
THIS PLACE IS NO LONGER SAFE—FOR ANYONE.
A-APRIL, THE... THE RAT'S TALKING... TO *YOU*.
I KNOW, MOM, IT'S OKAY—TRY NOT TO FAINT.
REMEMBER WHEN I SAID THERE WERE SOME FISHY THINGS GOING ON AT STOCKGEN? WELL, SOME OF IT WAS *MUTATION* TESTING.
THESE THINGS ARE... MUTANTS?
YES, MRS. O'NEIL... WE ARE MUTANTS. MY NAME IS *SPLINTER*, AND THESE ARE MY SONS.
PLEASE KNOW, YOU HAVE MY *DEEPEST* APOLOGIES FOR THE DAMAGES TO YOUR PROPERTY. AND FOR THIS STARTLING REVELATION, AS WELL.
BUT WE CANNOT RISK ANY FURTHER EXPOSURE—NOR SHOULD *YOU*—AND FOR THAT I, TOO, AM SORRY.
I... I...
...OKAY.
APRIL, HOW—
MOM, PLEASE, WE DON'T HAVE MUCH TIME—I JUST NEED YOU TO *LISTEN*.
YOU WERE RIGHT—THERE WAS MORE GOING ON AT STOCKGEN. *WAY MORE*. I CAN'T GO INTO DETAILS RIGHT NOW, BUT THE HEALING COMPOUND—THE OOZE—THAT DAD WAS DEVELOPING? IT STILL EXISTS AND IT WORKS...
...IT *REALLY* WORKS.
APRIL—WHAT IN THE *WORLD* ARE YOU TALKING ABOUT?
THIS, MOM...

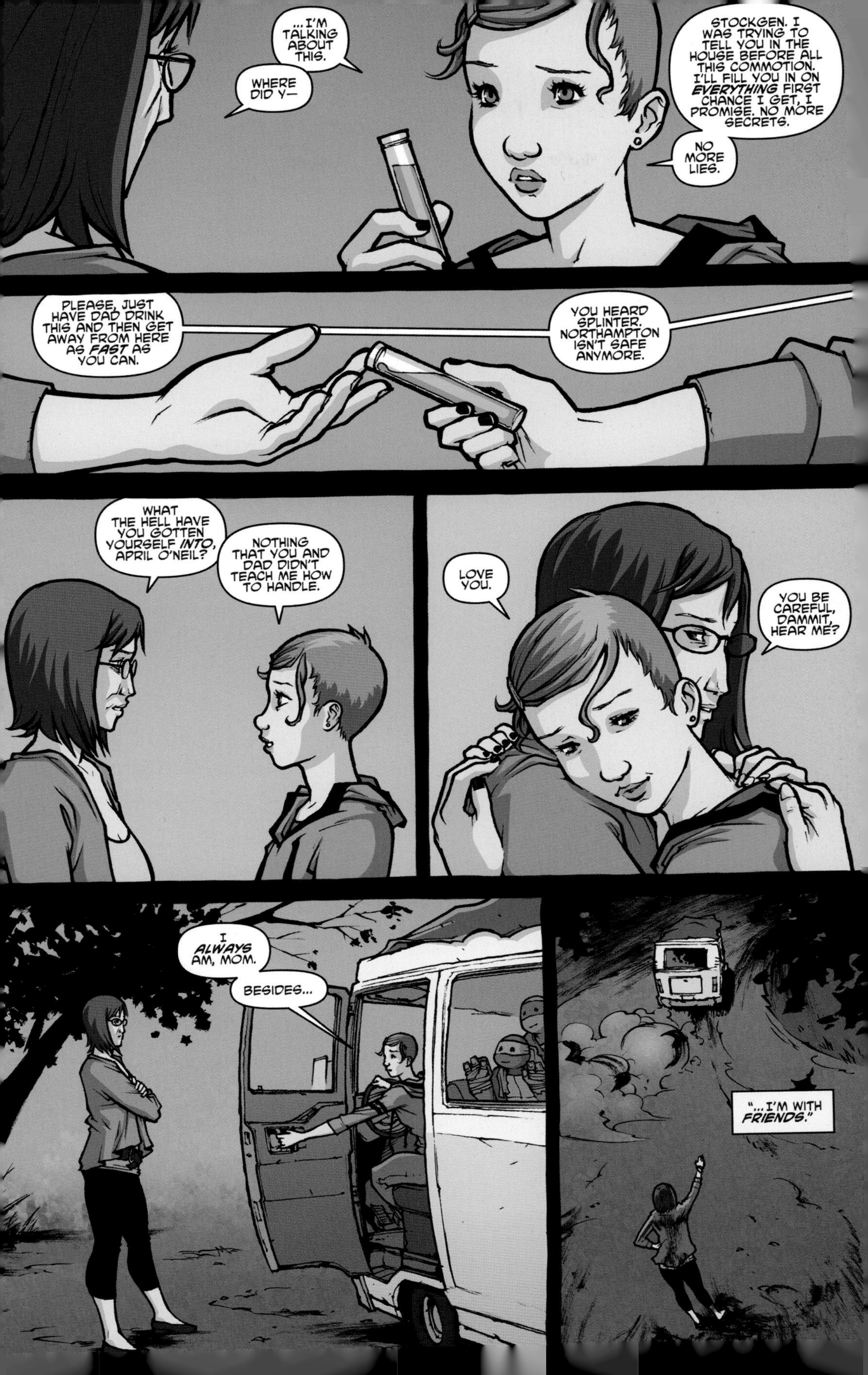
...I'M TALKING ABOUT THIS.
WHERE DID Y—
STOCKGEN. I WAS TRYING TO TELL YOU IN THE HOUSE BEFORE ALL THIS COMMOTION. I'LL FILL YOU IN ON EVERYTHING FIRST CHANCE I GET, I PROMISE. NO MORE SECRETS.
NO MORE LIES.
PLEASE, JUST HAVE DAD DRINK THIS AND THEN GET AWAY FROM HERE AS FAST AS YOU CAN.
YOU HEARD SPLINTER. NORTHAMPTON ISN'T SAFE ANYMORE.
WHAT THE HELL HAVE YOU GOTTEN YOURSELF INTO, APRIL O'NEIL?
NOTHING THAT YOU AND DAD DIDN'T TEACH ME HOW TO HANDLE.
LOVE YOU.
YOU BE CAREFUL, DAMMIT, HEAR ME?
I ALWAYS AM, MOM.
BESIDES...
"...I'M WITH FRIENDS."

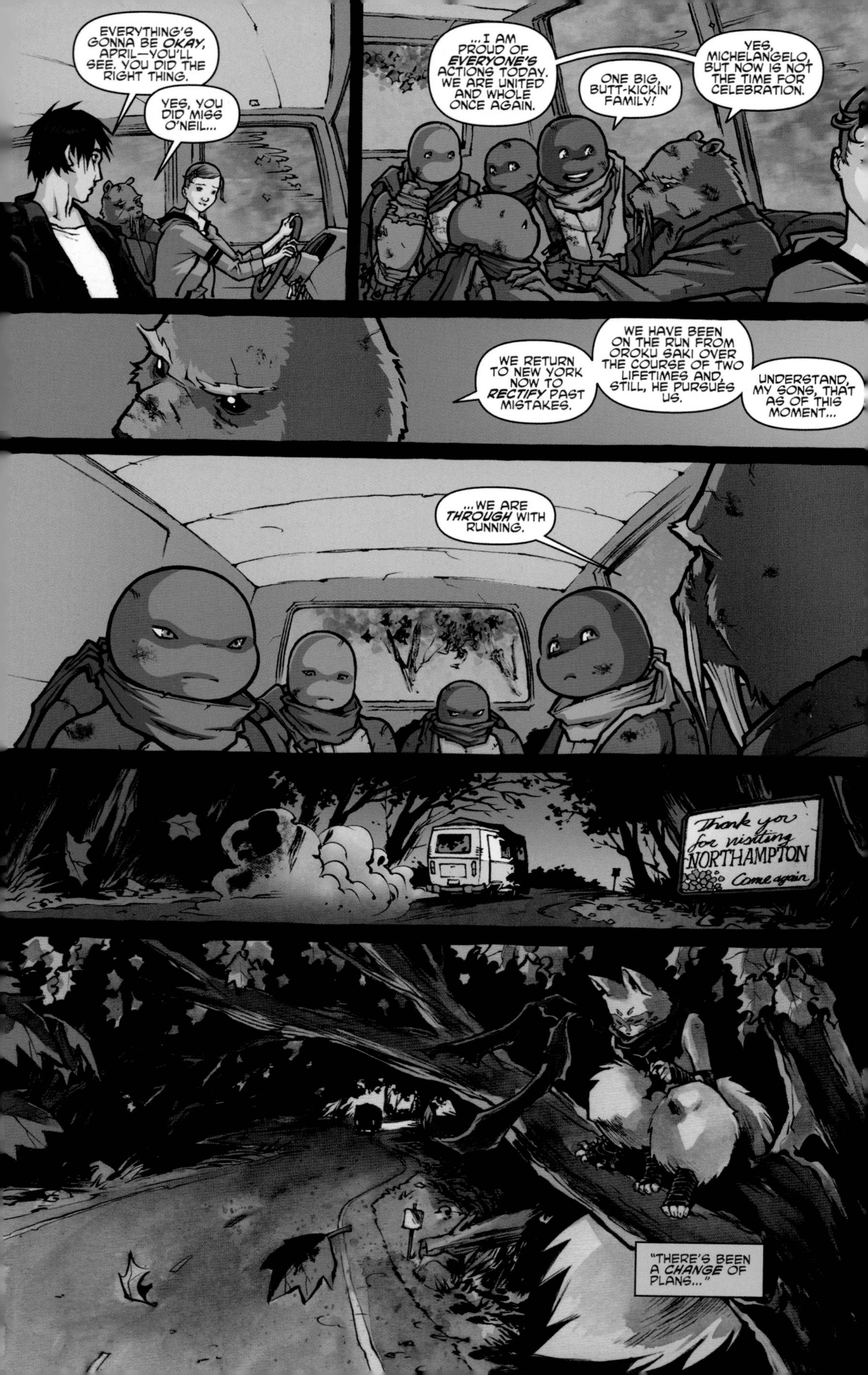
EVERYTHING'S GONNA BE OKAY, APRIL—YOU'LL SEE. YOU DID THE RIGHT THING.
YES, YOU DID MISS O'NEIL...
...I AM PROUD OF EVERYONE'S ACTIONS TODAY. WE ARE UNITED AND WHOLE ONCE AGAIN.
ONE BIG, BUTT-KICKIN' FAMILY!
YES, MICHELANGELO, BUT NOW IS NOT THE TIME FOR CELEBRATION.
WE RETURN TO NEW YORK NOW TO RECTIFY PAST MISTAKES.
WE HAVE BEEN ON THE RUN FROM OROKU SAKI OVER THE COURSE OF TWO LIFETIMES AND, STILL, HE PURSUES US.
UNDERSTAND, MY SONS, THAT AS OF THIS MOMENT...
...WE ARE THROUGH WITH RUNNING.
Thank you for visiting NORTHAMPTON Come again
"THERE'S BEEN A CHANGE OF PLANS..."

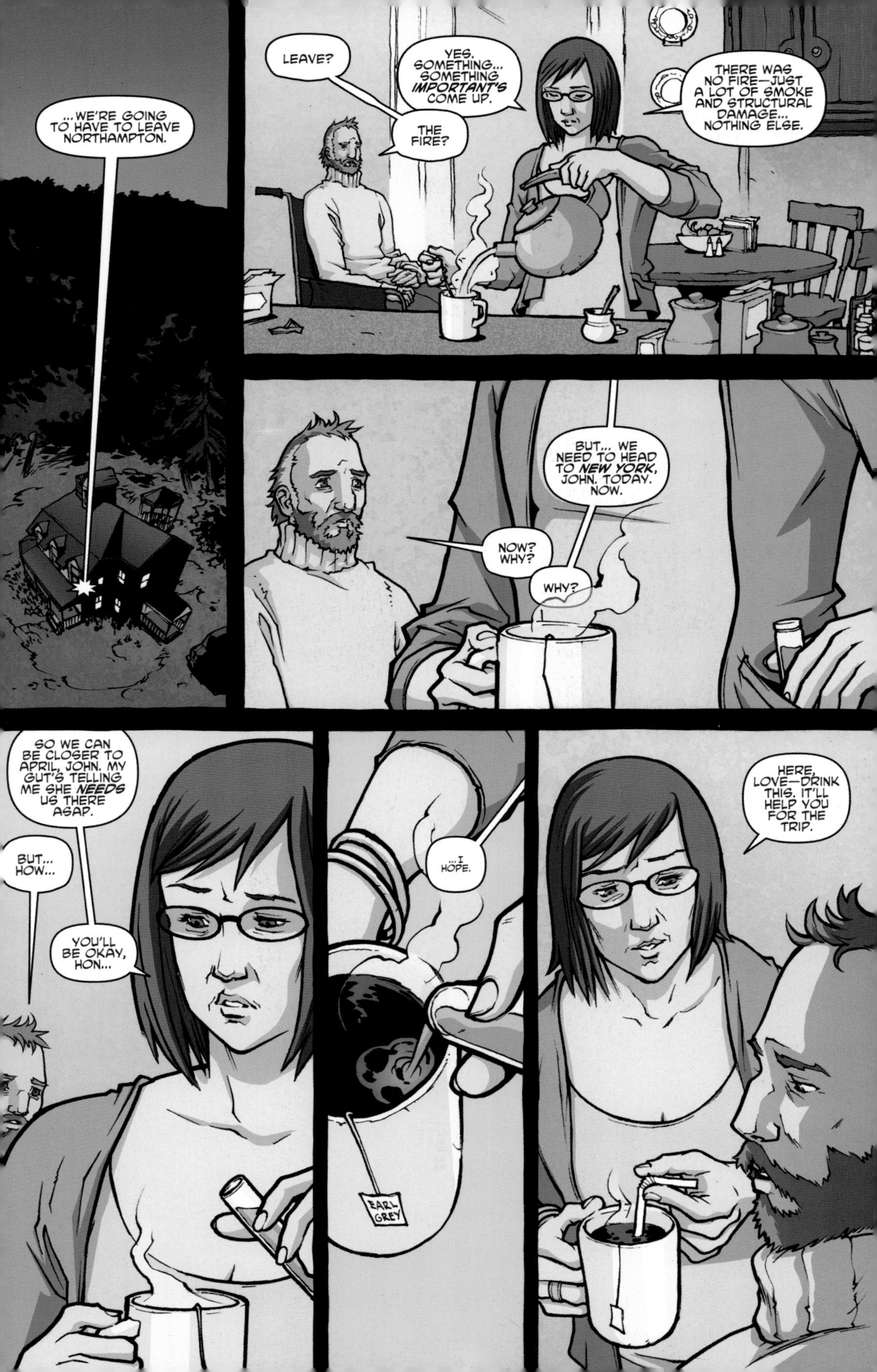
...WE'RE GOING TO HAVE TO LEAVE NORTHAMPTON.
LEAVE?
YES. SOMETHING... SOMETHING *IMPORTANT'S* COME UP.
THE FIRE?
THERE WAS NO FIRE—JUST A LOT OF SMOKE AND STRUCTURAL DAMAGE... NOTHING ELSE.
BUT... WE NEED TO HEAD TO *NEW YORK*, JOHN. TODAY. NOW.
NOW? WHY?
WHY?
SO WE CAN BE CLOSER TO APRIL, JOHN. MY GUT'S TELLING ME SHE *NEEDS* US THERE ASAP.
BUT... HOW...
YOU'LL BE OKAY, HON...
...I HOPE.
EARL GREY
HERE, LOVE—DRINK THIS. IT'LL HELP YOU FOR THE TRIP.

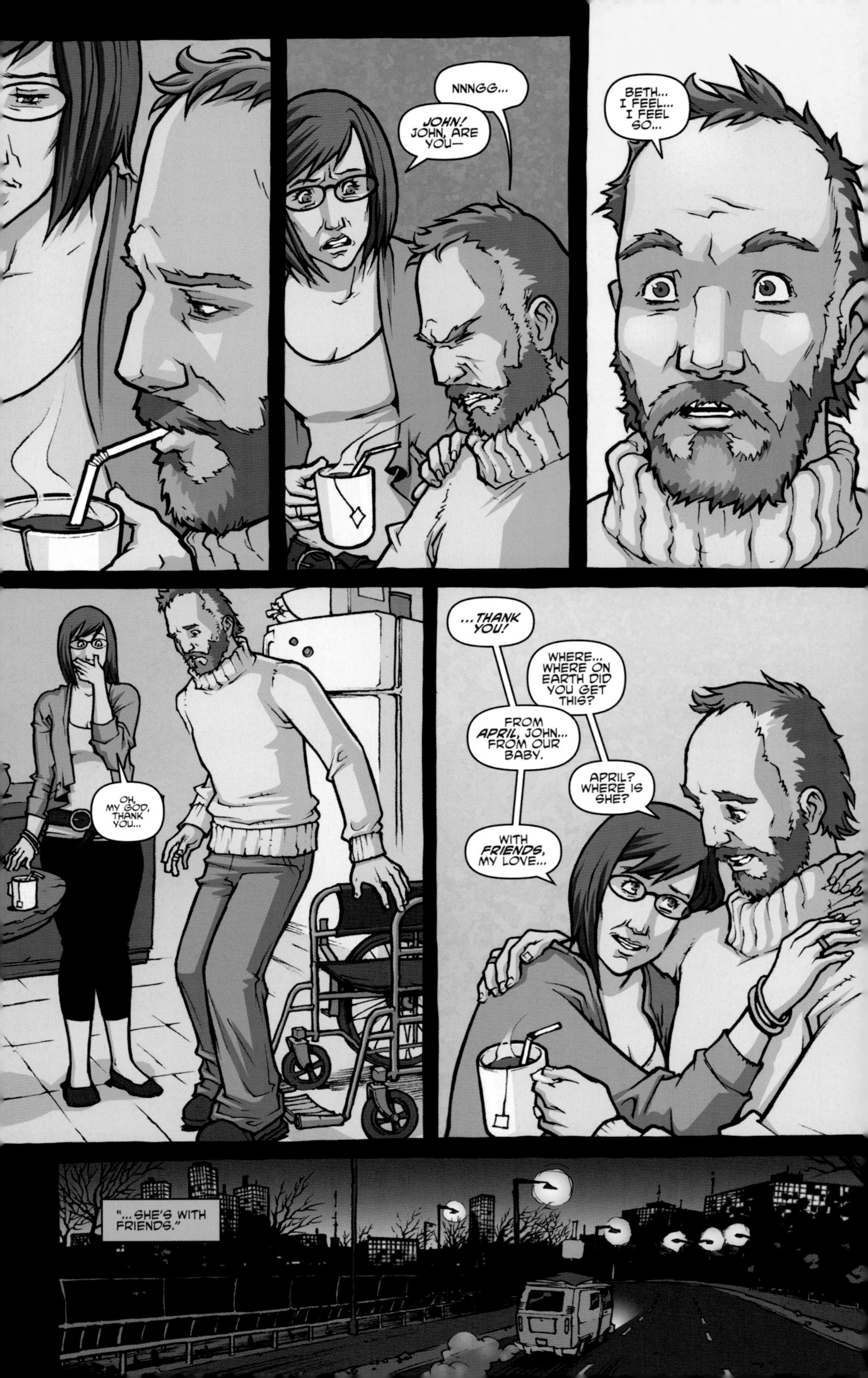
NNNGG...
JOHN! JOHN, ARE YOU—
BETH... I FEEL... I FEEL SO...
OH, MY GOD, THANK YOU...
...THANK YOU!
WHERE... WHERE ON EARTH DID YOU GET THIS?
FROM APRIL, JOHN... FROM OUR BABY.
APRIL? WHERE IS SHE?
WITH FRIENDS, MY LOVE...
"...SHE'S WITH FRIENDS."

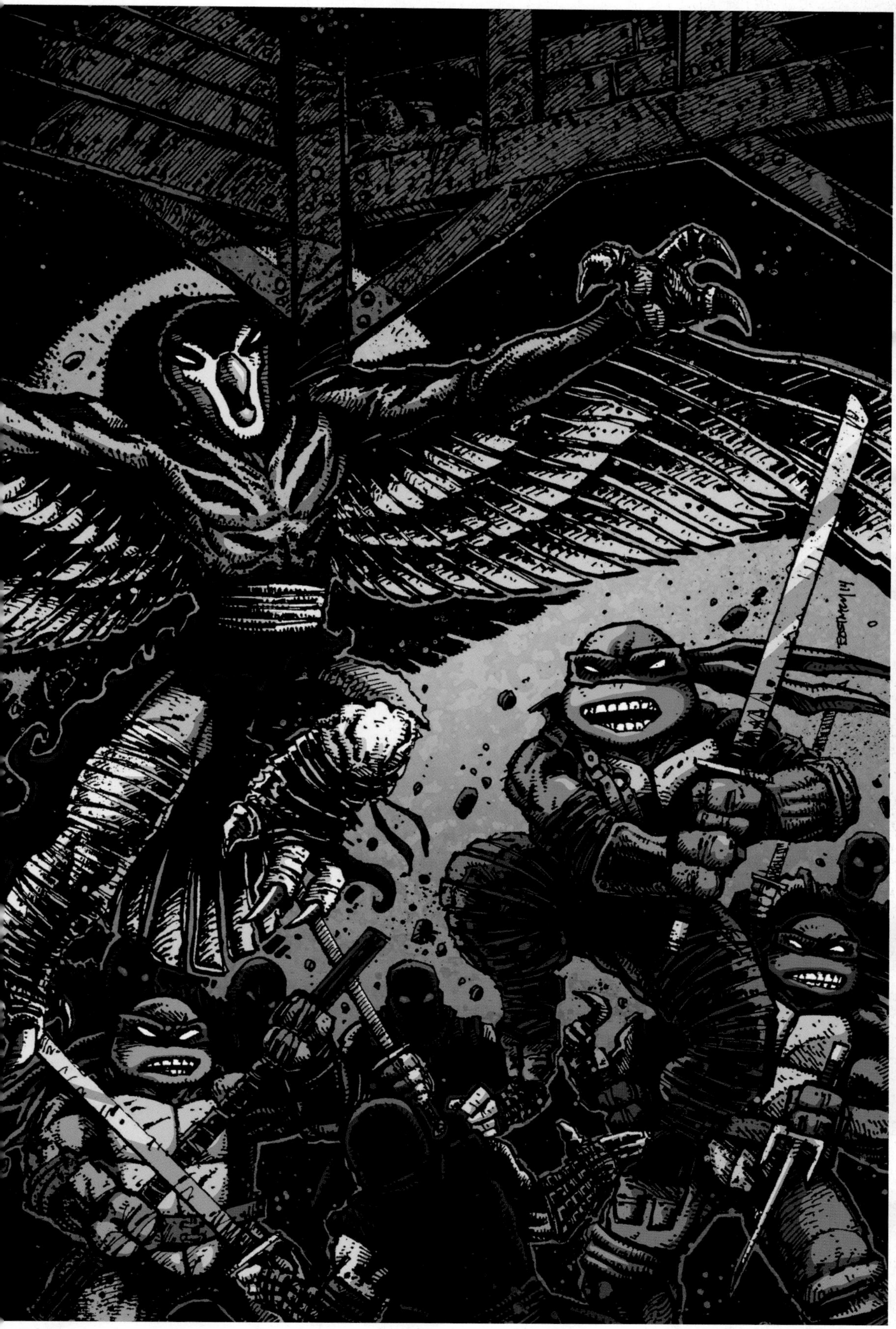

Cover by KEVIN EASTMAN
Colors by RONDA PATTISON

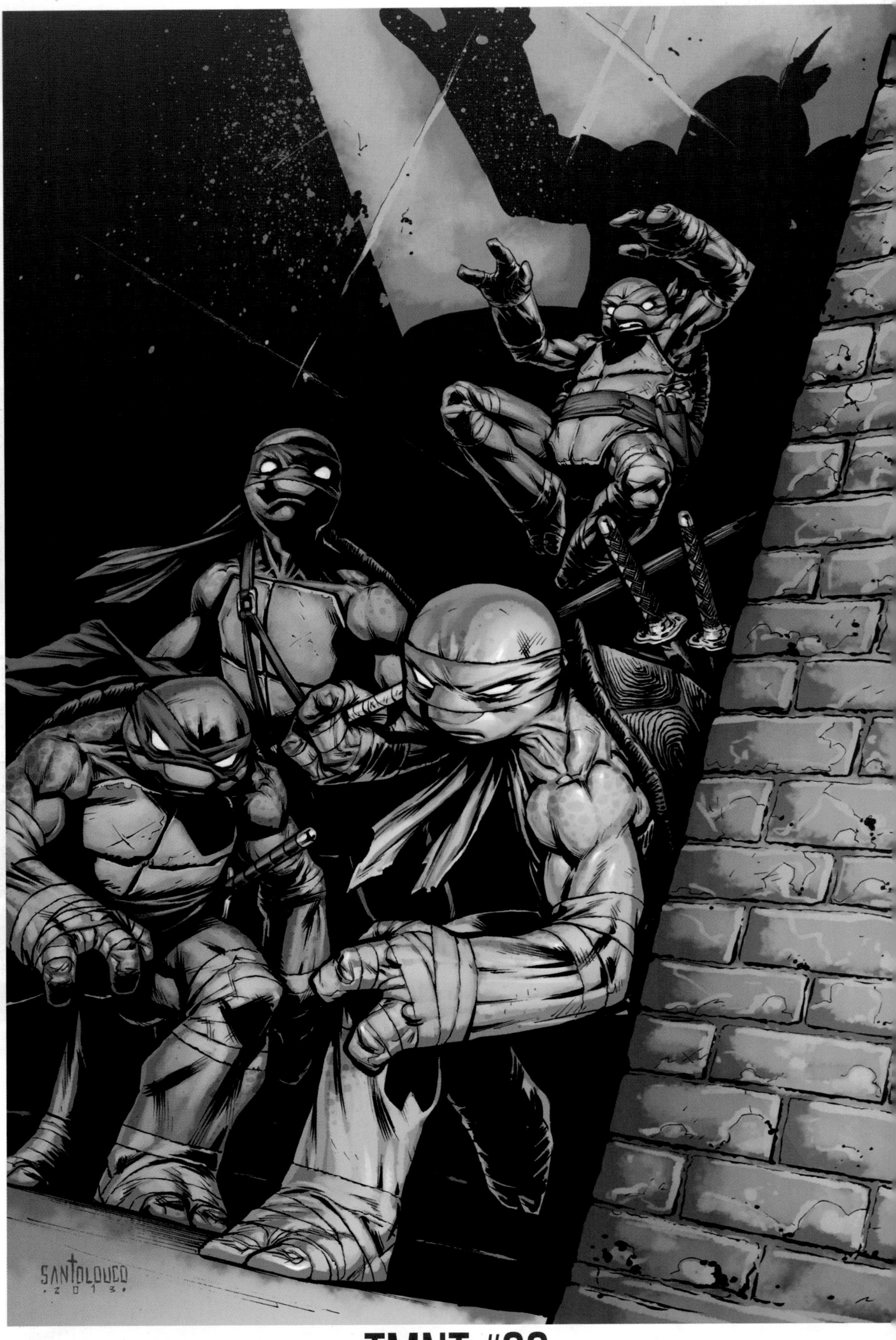
SANTOLOUCO
2013

Cover by MATEUS SANTOLOUCO

TMNT #33

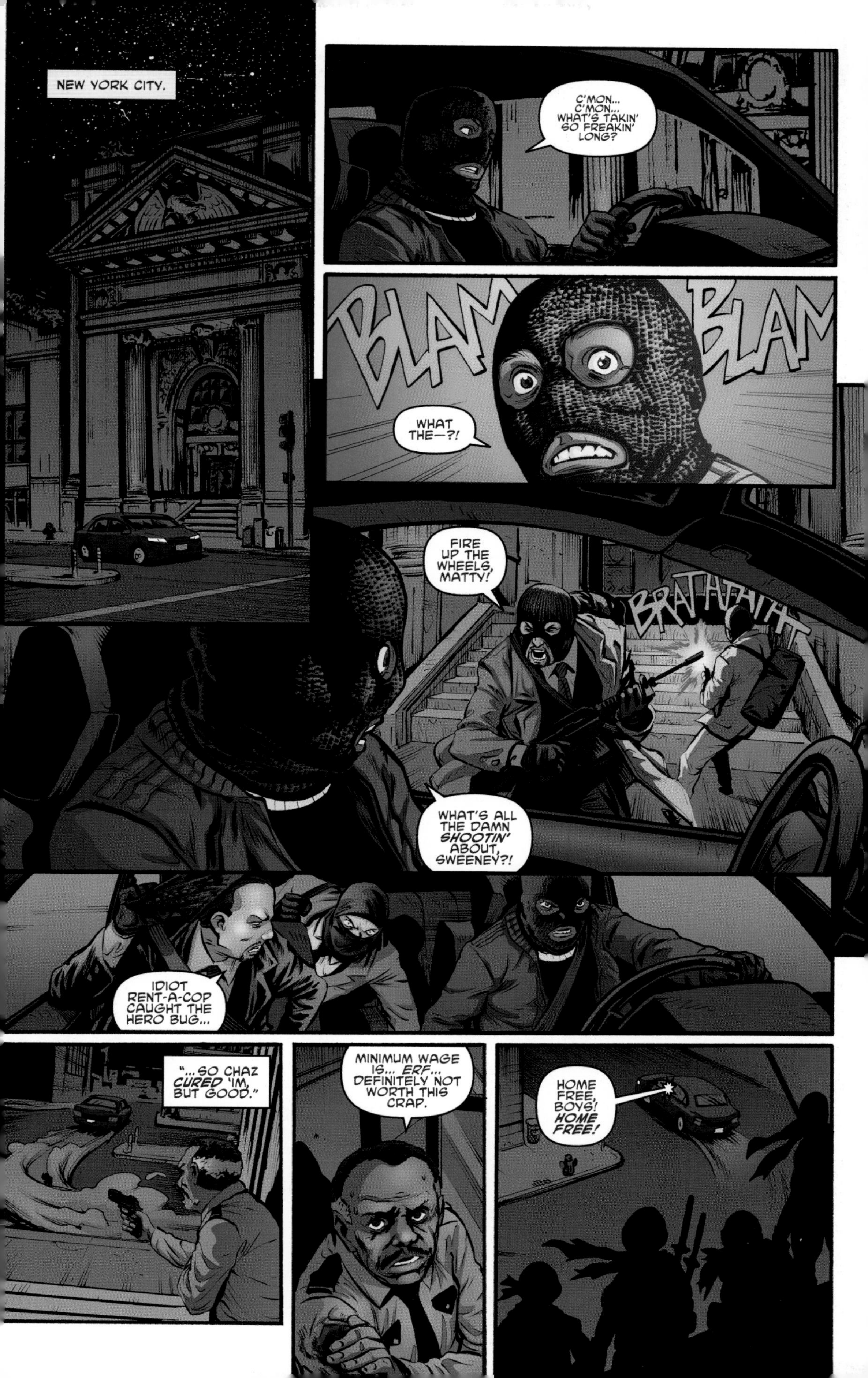
NEW YORK CITY.
C'MON... C'MON... WHAT'S TAKIN' SO FREAKIN' LONG?
BLAM BLAM
WHAT THE—?!
FIRE UP THE WHEELS, MATTY!
BRATATATATT
WHAT'S ALL THE DAMN SHOOTIN' ABOUT, SWEENEY?!
IDIOT RENT-A-COP CAUGHT THE HERO BUG...
"...SO CHAZ CURED 'IM, BUT GOOD."
MINIMUM WAGE IS... ERF... DEFINITELY NOT WORTH THIS CRAP.
HOME FREE, BOYS! HOME FREE!

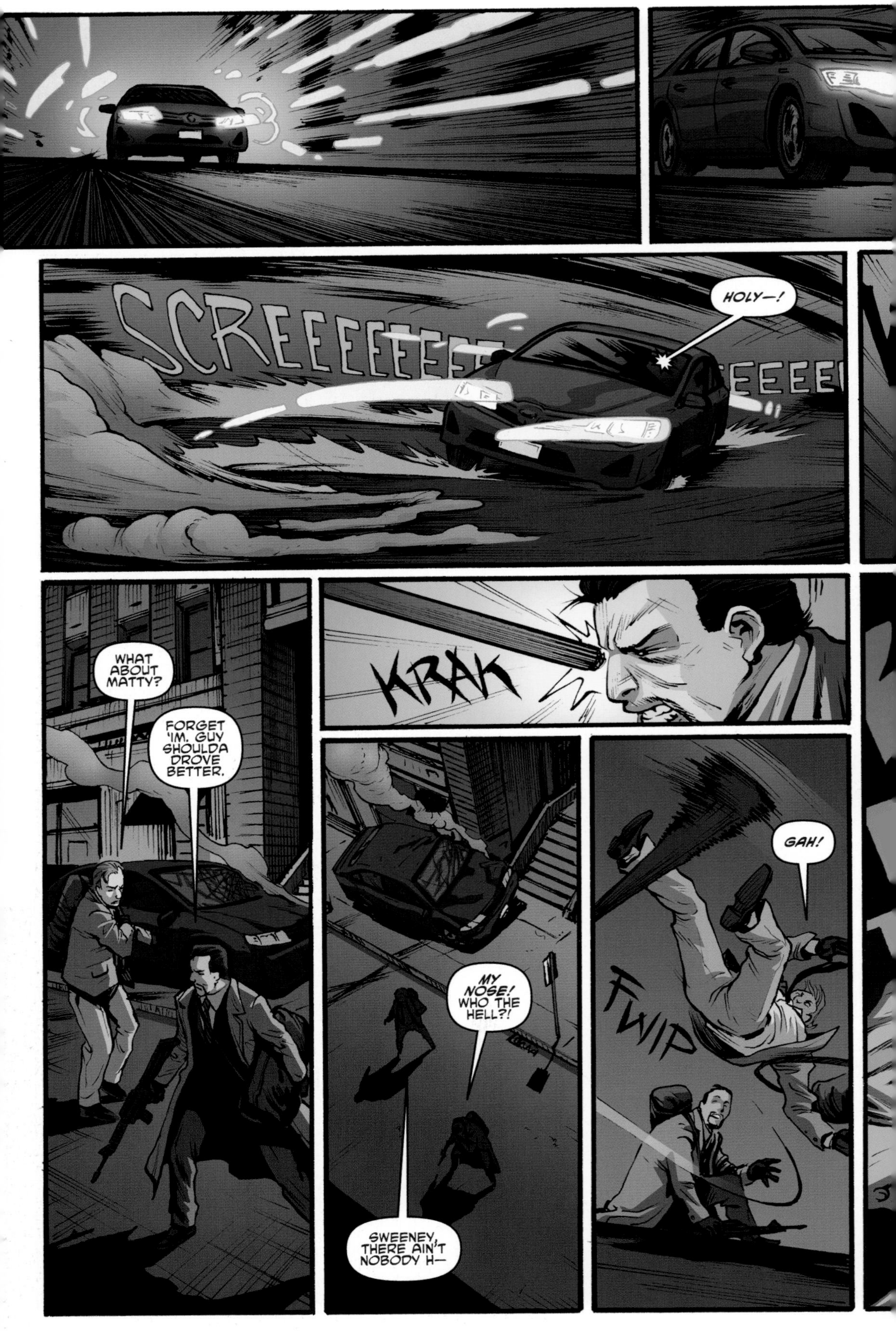
SCREEEEEEEEEEEEEEE
HOLY—!
KRAK
WHAT ABOUT MATTY?
FORGET 'IM. GUY SHOULDA DROVE BETTER.
MY NOSE! WHO THE HELL?!
SWEENEY, THERE AIN'T NOBODY H—
GAH!
FWIP

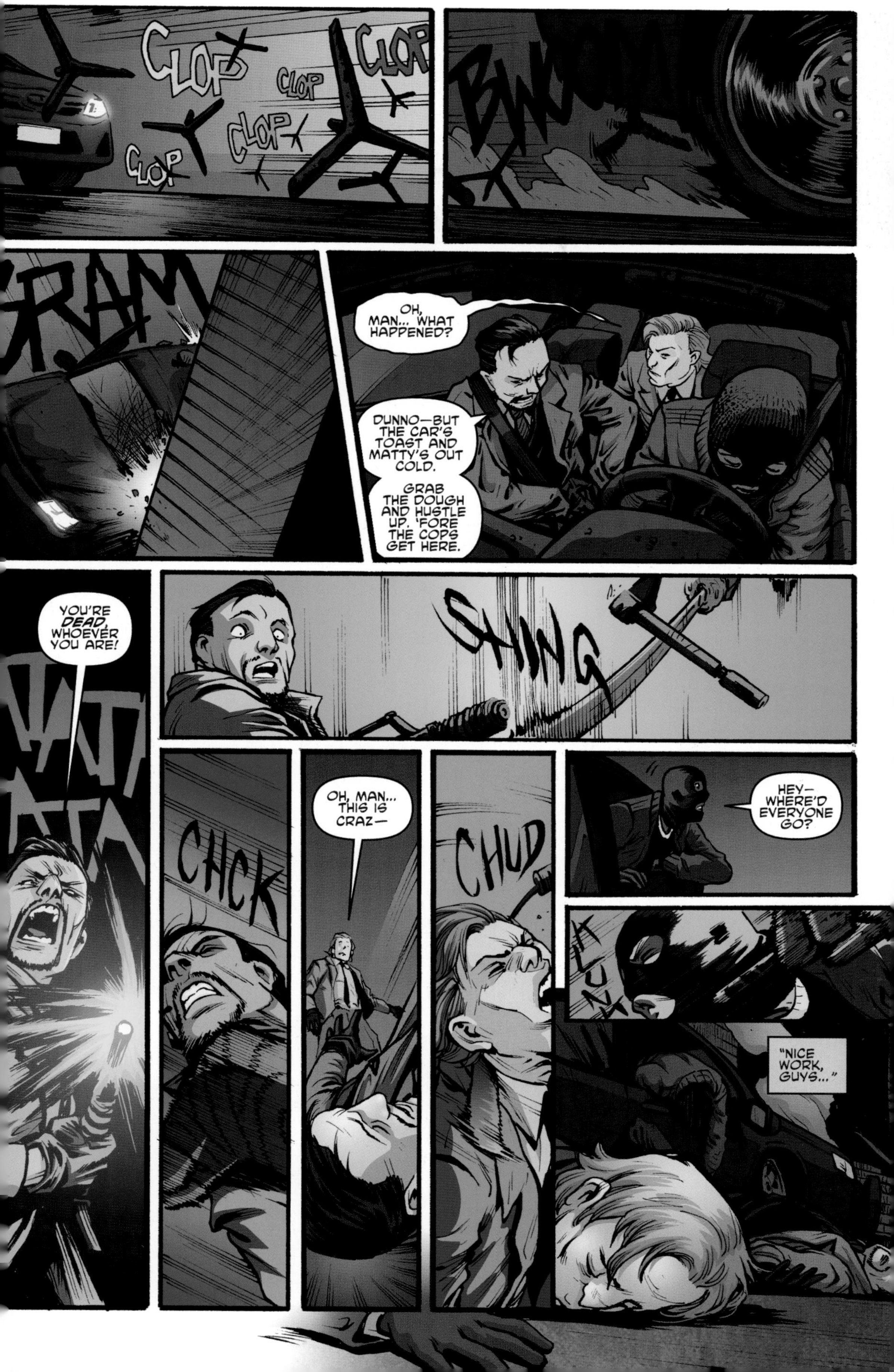
CLOP
CLOP
CLOP
CLOP
CLOP
GRAM
OH, MAN... WHAT HAPPENED?
DUNNO—BUT THE CAR'S TOAST AND MATTY'S OUT COLD.
GRAB THE DOUGH AND HUSTLE UP. 'FORE THE COPS GET HERE.
YOU'RE *DEAD*, WHOEVER YOU ARE!
SHING
CHCK
OH, MAN... THIS IS CRAZ—
CHUD
HEY—WHERE'D EVERYONE GO?
"NICE WORK, GUYS..."

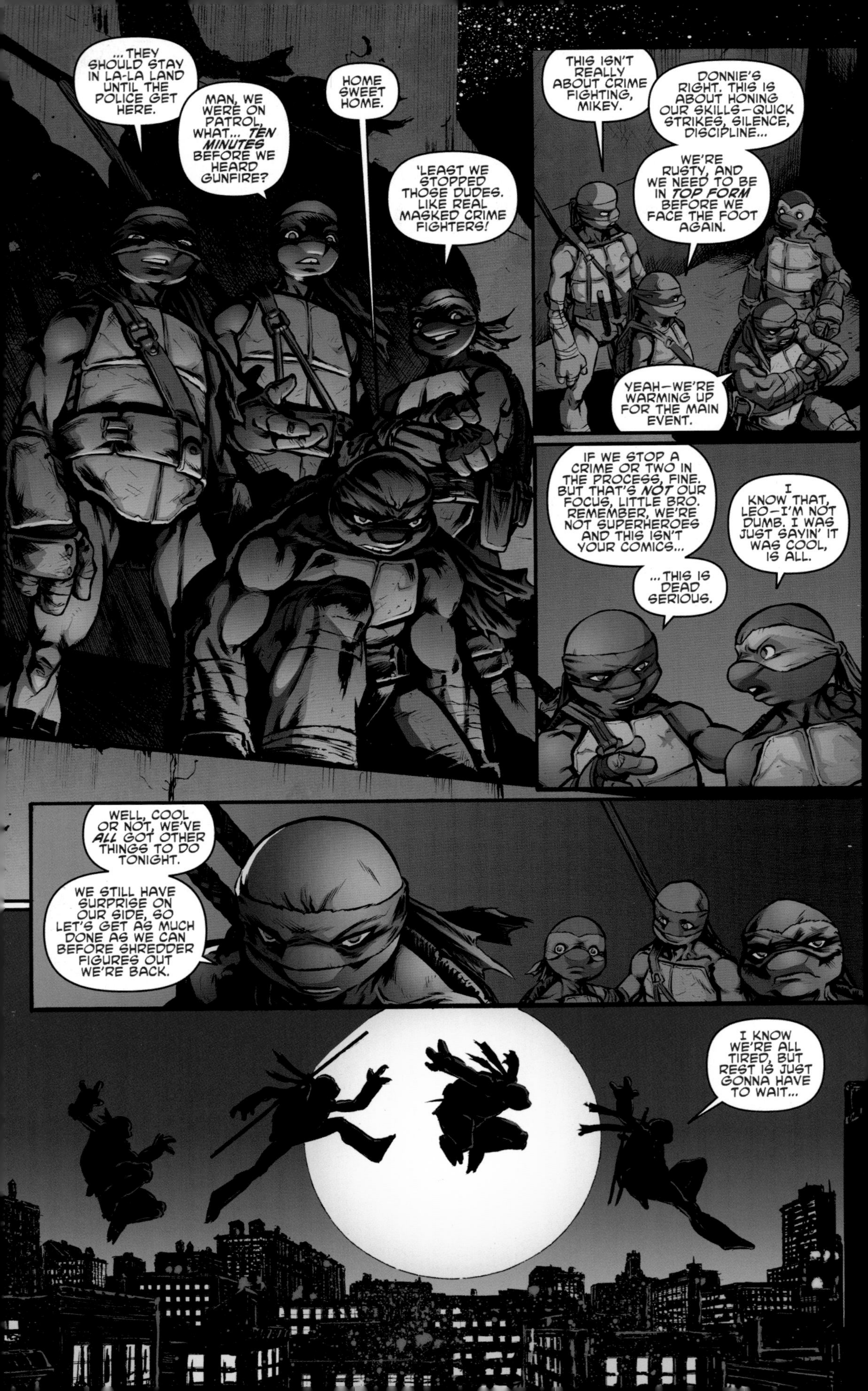
...THEY SHOULD STAY IN LA-LA LAND UNTIL THE POLICE GET HERE.
MAN, WE WERE ON PATROL, WHAT... TEN MINUTES BEFORE WE HEARD GUNFIRE?
HOME SWEET HOME.
'LEAST WE STOPPED THOSE DUDES. LIKE REAL MASKED CRIME FIGHTERS!
THIS ISN'T REALLY ABOUT CRIME FIGHTING, MIKEY.
DONNIE'S RIGHT. THIS IS ABOUT HONING OUR SKILLS—QUICK STRIKES, SILENCE, DISCIPLINE...
WE'RE RUSTY, AND WE NEED TO BE IN TOP FORM BEFORE WE FACE THE FOOT AGAIN.
YEAH—WE'RE WARMING UP FOR THE MAIN EVENT.
IF WE STOP A CRIME OR TWO IN THE PROCESS, FINE. BUT THAT'S NOT OUR FOCUS, LITTLE BRO. REMEMBER, WE'RE NOT SUPERHEROES AND THIS ISN'T YOUR COMICS...
...THIS IS DEAD SERIOUS.
I KNOW THAT, LEO—I'M NOT DUMB. I WAS JUST SAYIN' IT WAS COOL, IS ALL.
WELL, COOL OR NOT, WE'VE ALL GOT OTHER THINGS TO DO TONIGHT.
WE STILL HAVE SURPRISE ON OUR SIDE, SO LET'S GET AS MUCH DONE AS WE CAN BEFORE SHREDDER FIGURES OUT WE'RE BACK.
I KNOW WE'RE ALL TIRED, BUT REST IS JUST GONNA HAVE TO WAIT...

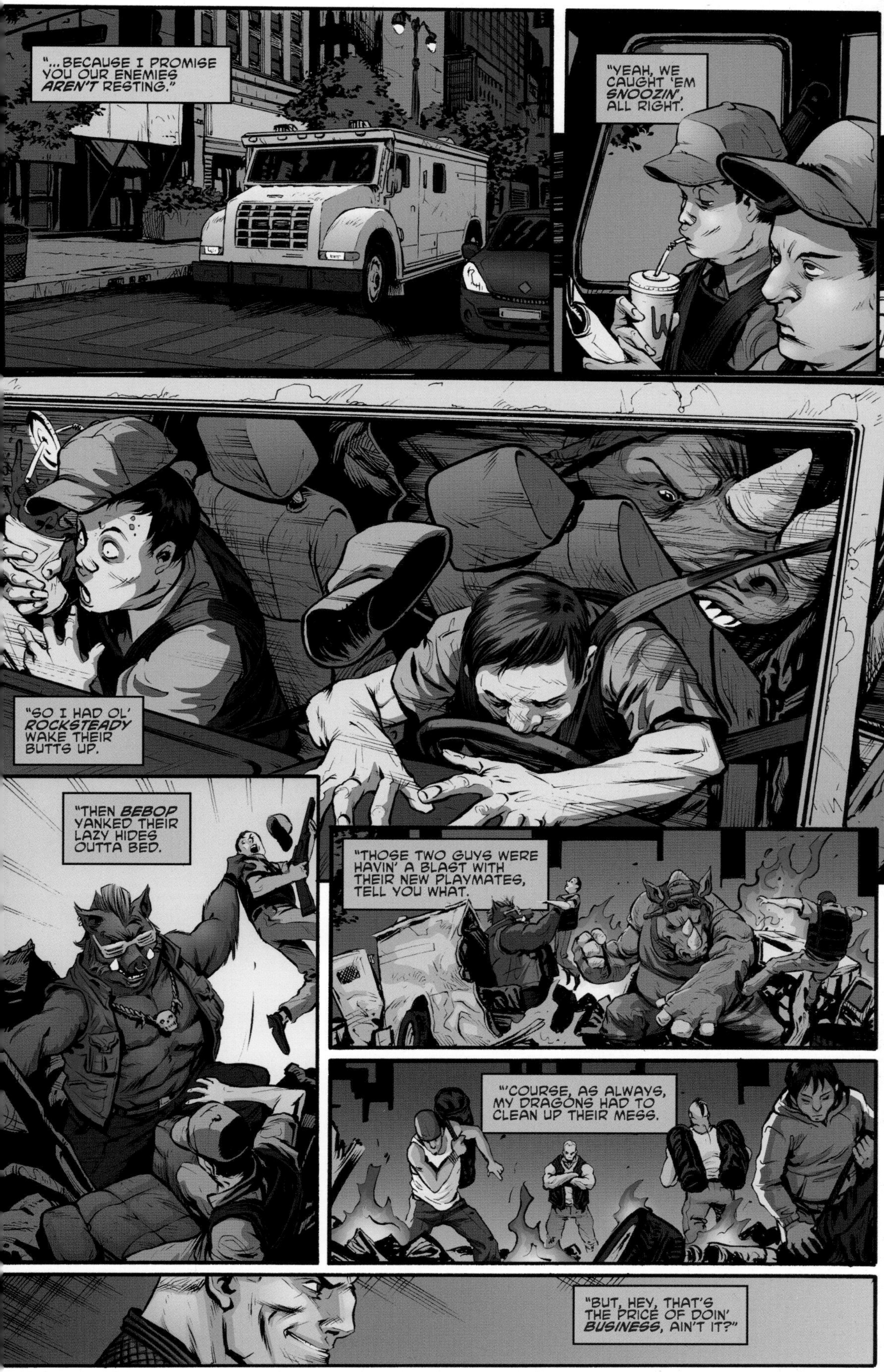
"...BECAUSE I PROMISE YOU OUR ENEMIES *AREN'T* RESTING."
"YEAH, WE CAUGHT 'EM *SNOOZIN'*, ALL RIGHT.
"SO I HAD OL' *ROCKSTEADY* WAKE THEIR BUTTS UP.
"THEN *BEBOP* YANKED THEIR LAZY HIDES OUTTA BED.
"THOSE TWO GUYS WERE HAVIN' A BLAST WITH THEIR NEW PLAYMATES, TELL YOU WHAT.
"'COURSE, AS ALWAYS, MY DRAGONS HAD TO CLEAN UP THEIR MESS.
"BUT, HEY, THAT'S THE PRICE OF DOIN' *BUSINESS*, AIN'T IT?"

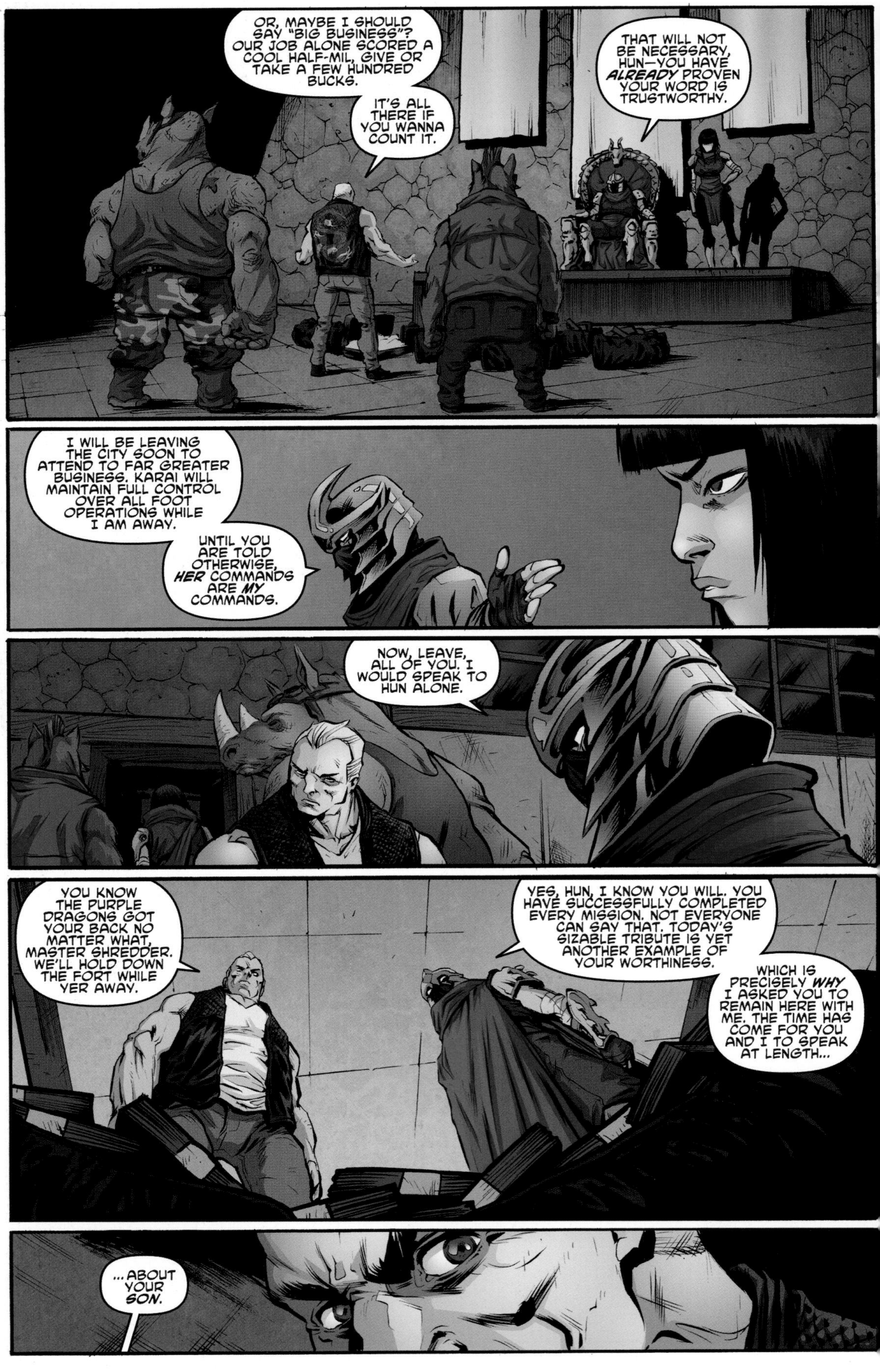
OR, MAYBE I SHOULD SAY "BIG BUSINESS"? OUR JOB ALONE SCORED A COOL HALF-MIL, GIVE OR TAKE A FEW HUNDRED BUCKS.
IT'S ALL THERE IF YOU WANNA COUNT IT.
THAT WILL NOT BE NECESSARY, HUN—YOU HAVE *ALREADY* PROVEN YOUR WORD IS TRUSTWORTHY.
I WILL BE LEAVING THE CITY SOON TO ATTEND TO FAR GREATER BUSINESS. KARAI WILL MAINTAIN FULL CONTROL OVER ALL FOOT OPERATIONS WHILE I AM AWAY.
UNTIL YOU ARE TOLD OTHERWISE, *HER* COMMANDS ARE *MY* COMMANDS.
NOW, LEAVE, ALL OF YOU. I WOULD SPEAK TO HUN ALONE.
YOU KNOW THE PURPLE DRAGONS GOT YOUR BACK NO MATTER WHAT, MASTER SHREDDER. WE'LL HOLD DOWN THE FORT WHILE YER AWAY.
YES, HUN, I KNOW YOU WILL. YOU HAVE SUCCESSFULLY COMPLETED EVERY MISSION. NOT EVERYONE CAN SAY THAT. TODAY'S SIZABLE TRIBUTE IS YET ANOTHER EXAMPLE OF YOUR WORTHINESS.
WHICH IS PRECISELY *WHY* I ASKED YOU TO REMAIN HERE WITH ME. THE TIME HAS COME FOR YOU AND I TO SPEAK AT LENGTH...
...ABOUT YOUR *SON*.

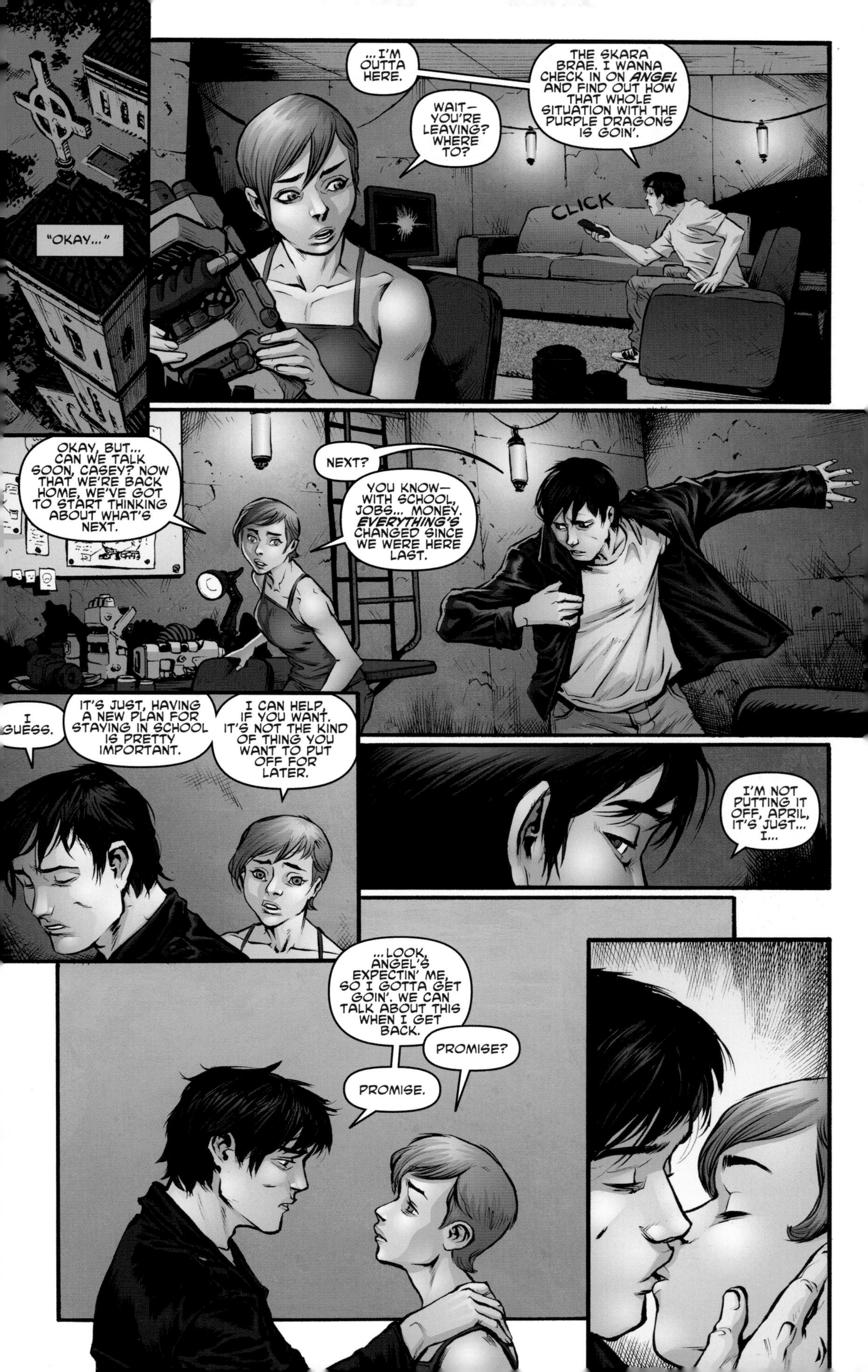
"OKAY..."
...I'M OUTTA HERE.
WAIT— YOU'RE LEAVING? WHERE TO?
THE SKARA BRAE. I WANNA CHECK IN ON ANGEL AND FIND OUT HOW THAT WHOLE SITUATION WITH THE PURPLE DRAGONS IS GOIN'.
CLICK
OKAY, BUT... CAN WE TALK SOON, CASEY? NOW THAT WE'RE BACK HOME, WE'VE GOT TO START THINKING ABOUT WHAT'S NEXT.
NEXT?
YOU KNOW— WITH SCHOOL, JOBS... MONEY. EVERYTHING'S CHANGED SINCE WE WERE HERE LAST.
I GUESS.
IT'S JUST, HAVING A NEW PLAN FOR STAYING IN SCHOOL IS PRETTY IMPORTANT.
I CAN HELP, IF YOU WANT. IT'S NOT THE KIND OF THING YOU WANT TO PUT OFF FOR LATER.
I'M NOT PUTTING IT OFF, APRIL, IT'S JUST... I...
...LOOK, ANGEL'S EXPECTIN' ME, SO I GOTTA GET GOIN'. WE CAN TALK ABOUT THIS WHEN I GET BACK.
PROMISE?
PROMISE.

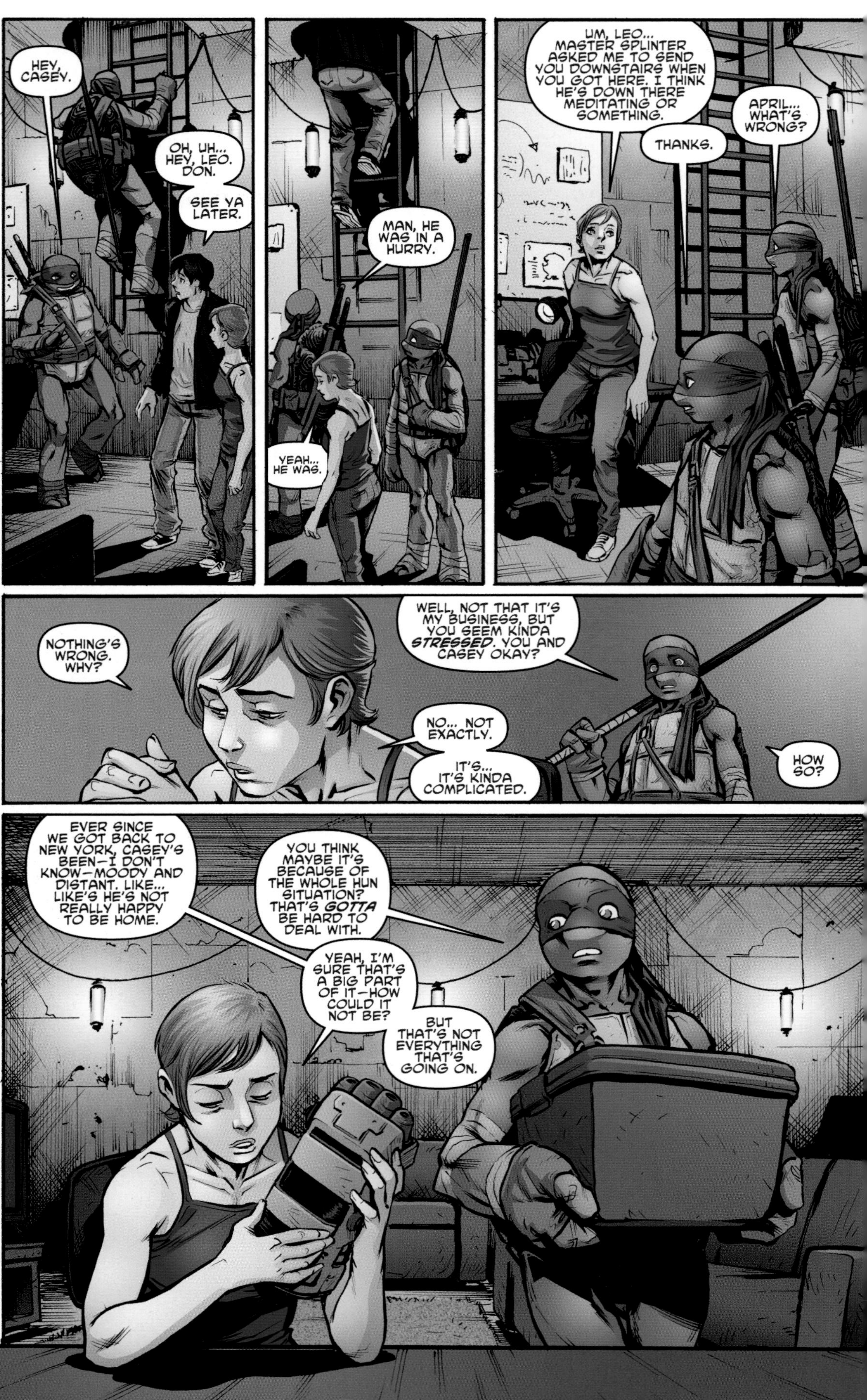
HEY, CASEY.
OH, UH... HEY, LEO. DON.
SEE YA LATER.
MAN, HE WAS IN A HURRY.
YEAH... HE WAS.
UM, LEO... MASTER SPLINTER ASKED ME TO SEND YOU DOWNSTAIRS WHEN YOU GOT HERE. I THINK HE'S DOWN THERE MEDITATING OR SOMETHING.
THANKS.
APRIL... WHAT'S WRONG?
NOTHING'S WRONG. WHY?
WELL, NOT THAT IT'S MY BUSINESS, BUT YOU SEEM KINDA STRESSED. YOU AND CASEY OKAY?
NO... NOT EXACTLY.
IT'S... IT'S KINDA COMPLICATED.
HOW SO?
EVER SINCE WE GOT BACK TO NEW YORK, CASEY'S BEEN—I DON'T KNOW—MOODY AND DISTANT. LIKE... LIKE'S HE'S NOT REALLY HAPPY TO BE HOME.
YOU THINK MAYBE IT'S BECAUSE OF THE WHOLE HUN SITUATION? THAT'S GOTTA BE HARD TO DEAL WITH.
YEAH, I'M SURE THAT'S A BIG PART OF IT—HOW COULD IT NOT BE?
BUT THAT'S NOT EVERYTHING THAT'S GOING ON.

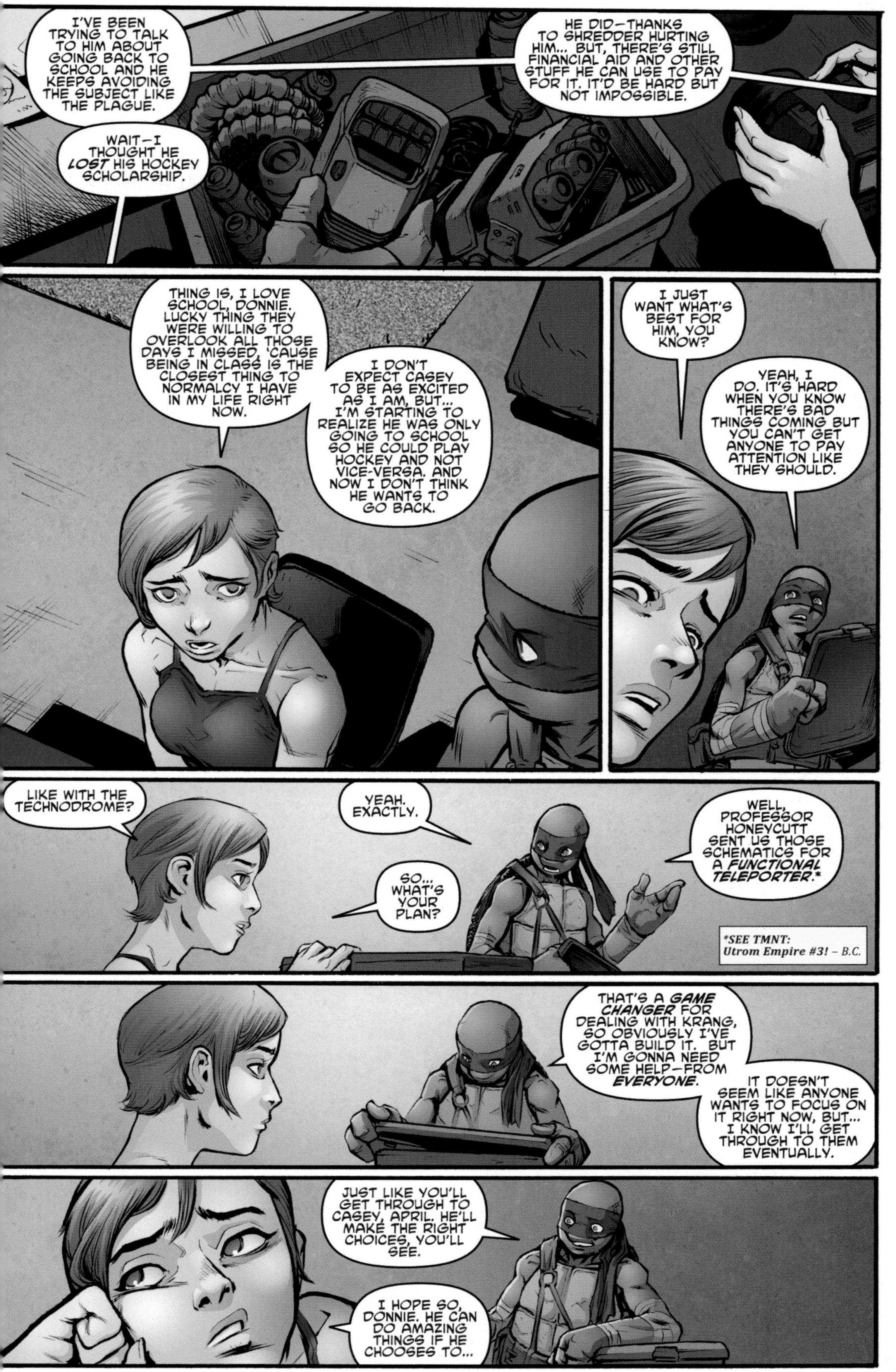
I'VE BEEN TRYING TO TALK TO HIM ABOUT GOING BACK TO SCHOOL AND HE KEEPS AVOIDING THE SUBJECT LIKE THE PLAGUE.
WAIT—I THOUGHT HE *LOST* HIS HOCKEY SCHOLARSHIP.
HE DID—THANKS TO SHREDDER HURTING HIM... BUT, THERE'S STILL FINANCIAL AID AND OTHER STUFF HE CAN USE TO PAY FOR IT. IT'D BE HARD BUT NOT IMPOSSIBLE.
THING IS, I LOVE SCHOOL, DONNIE. LUCKY THING THEY WERE WILLING TO OVERLOOK ALL THOSE DAYS I MISSED, 'CAUSE BEING IN CLASS IS THE CLOSEST THING TO NORMALCY I HAVE IN MY LIFE RIGHT NOW.
I DON'T EXPECT CASEY TO BE AS EXCITED AS I AM, BUT... I'M STARTING TO REALIZE HE WAS ONLY GOING TO SCHOOL SO HE COULD PLAY HOCKEY AND NOT VICE-VERSA. AND NOW I DON'T THINK HE WANTS TO GO BACK.
I JUST WANT WHAT'S BEST FOR HIM, YOU KNOW?
YEAH, I DO. IT'S HARD WHEN YOU KNOW THERE'S BAD THINGS COMING BUT YOU CAN'T GET ANYONE TO PAY ATTENTION LIKE THEY SHOULD.
LIKE WITH THE TECHNODROME?
YEAH. EXACTLY.
SO... WHAT'S YOUR PLAN?
WELL, PROFESSOR HONEYCUTT SENT US THOSE SCHEMATICS FOR A *FUNCTIONAL TELEPORTER*.*
*SEE TMNT: Utrom Empire #3! – B.C.
THAT'S A *GAME CHANGER* FOR DEALING WITH KRANG, SO OBVIOUSLY I'VE GOTTA BUILD IT. BUT I'M GONNA NEED SOME HELP—FROM *EVERYONE*.
IT DOESN'T SEEM LIKE ANYONE WANTS TO FOCUS ON IT RIGHT NOW, BUT... I KNOW I'LL GET THROUGH TO THEM EVENTUALLY.
JUST LIKE YOU'LL GET THROUGH TO CASEY, APRIL. HE'LL MAKE THE RIGHT CHOICES, YOU'LL SEE.
I HOPE SO, DONNIE. HE CAN DO AMAZING THINGS IF HE CHOOSES TO...

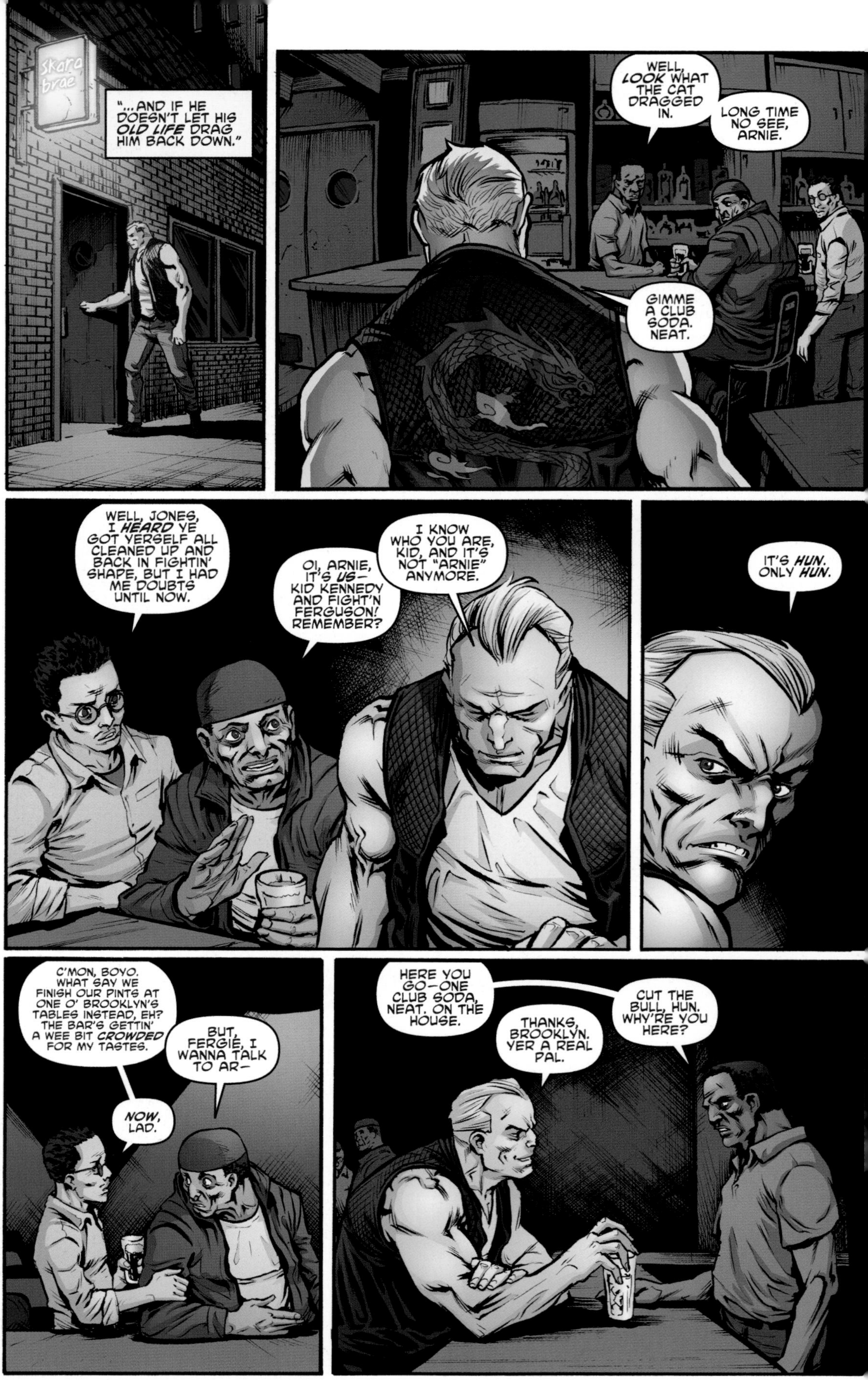

Skara brae
"...AND IF HE DOESN'T LET HIS OLD LIFE DRAG HIM BACK DOWN."
WELL, LOOK WHAT THE CAT DRAGGED IN.
LONG TIME NO SEE, ARNIE.
GIMME A CLUB SODA. NEAT.
WELL, JONES, I HEARD YE GOT CLEANED YERSELF ALL CLEANED UP AND BACK IN FIGHTIN' SHAPE, BUT I HAD ME DOUBTS UNTIL NOW.
OI, ARNIE, IT'S US— KID KENNEDY AND FIGHT'N FERGUSON! REMEMBER?
I KNOW WHO YOU ARE, KID, AND IT'S NOT "ARNIE" ANYMORE.
IT'S HUN. ONLY HUN.
C'MON, BOYO. WHAT SAY WE FINISH OUR PINTS AT ONE O' BROOKLYN'S TABLES INSTEAD, EH? THE BAR'S GETTIN' A WEE BIT CROWDED FOR MY TASTES.
BUT, FERGIE, I WANNA TALK TO AR—
NOW, LAD.
HERE YOU GO—ONE CLUB SODA, NEAT. ON THE HOUSE.
THANKS, BROOKLYN. YER A REAL PAL.
CUT THE BULL, HUN. WHY'RE YOU HERE?

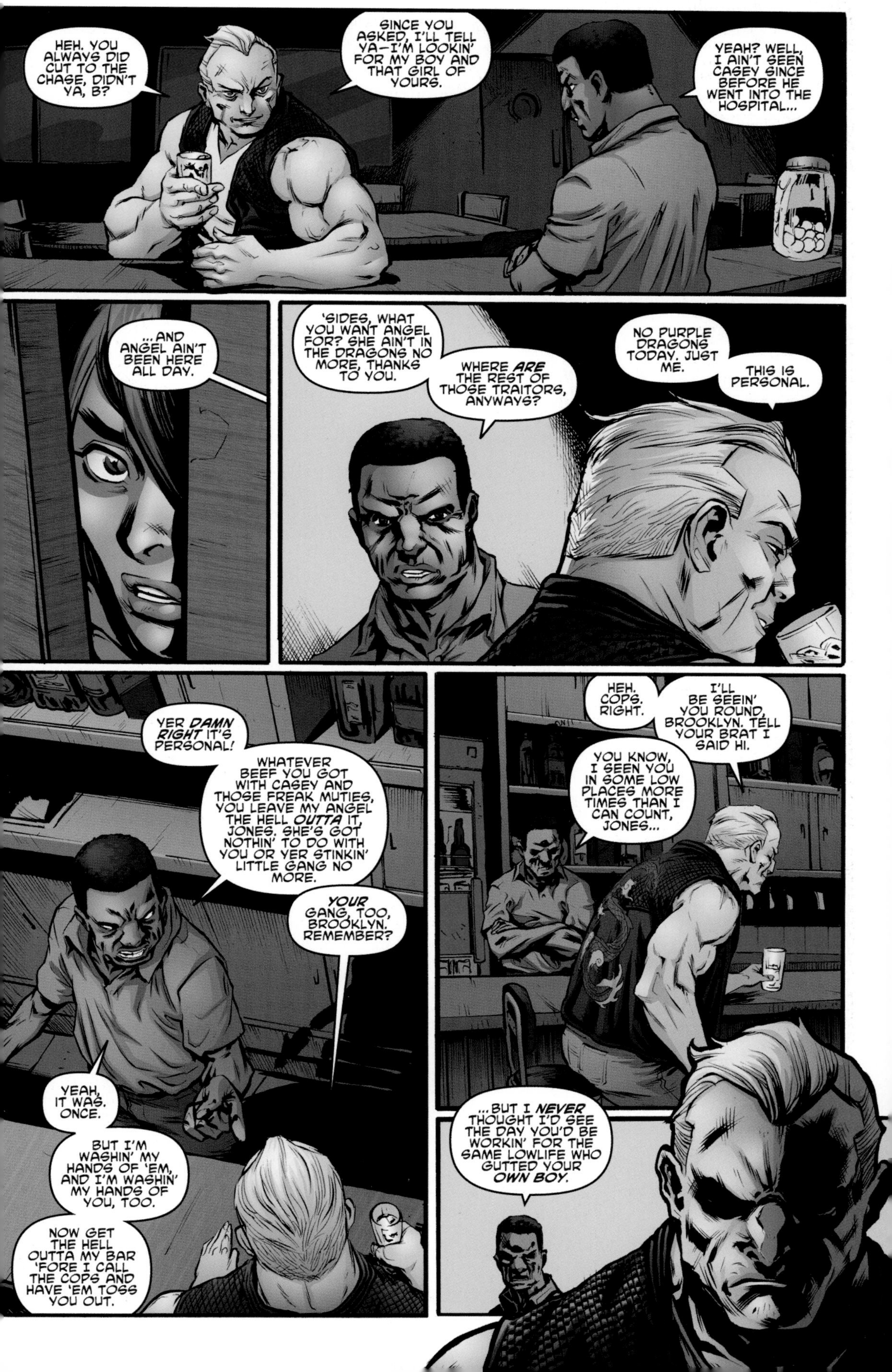
HEH. YOU ALWAYS DID CUT TO THE CHASE, DIDN'T YA, B?
SINCE YOU ASKED, I'LL TELL YA—I'M LOOKIN' FOR MY BOY AND THAT GIRL OF YOURS.
YEAH? WELL, I AIN'T SEEN CASEY SINCE BEFORE HE WENT INTO THE HOSPITAL...
...AND ANGEL AIN'T BEEN HERE ALL DAY.
'SIDES, WHAT YOU WANT ANGEL FOR? SHE AIN'T IN THE DRAGONS NO MORE, THANKS TO YOU.
WHERE ARE THE REST OF THOSE TRAITORS, ANYWAYS?
NO PURPLE DRAGONS TODAY. JUST ME.
THIS IS PERSONAL.
YER DAMN RIGHT IT'S PERSONAL!
WHATEVER BEEF YOU GOT WITH CASEY AND THOSE FREAK MUTIES, YOU LEAVE MY ANGEL THE HELL OUTTA IT, JONES. SHE'S GOT NOTHIN' TO DO WITH YOU OR YER STINKIN' LITTLE GANG NO MORE.
YOUR GANG, TOO, BROOKLYN. REMEMBER?
YEAH, IT WAS. ONCE.
BUT I'M WASHIN' MY HANDS OF 'EM, AND I'M WASHIN' MY HANDS OF YOU, TOO.
NOW GET THE HELL OUTTA MY BAR 'FORE I CALL THE COPS AND HAVE 'EM TOSS YOU OUT.
HEH. COPS. RIGHT.
I'LL BE SEEIN' YOU ROUND, BROOKLYN. TELL YOUR BRAT I SAID HI.
YOU KNOW, I SEEN YOU IN SOME LOW PLACES MORE TIMES THAN I CAN COUNT, JONES...
...BUT I NEVER THOUGHT I'D SEE THE DAY YOU'D BE WORKIN' FOR THE SAME LOWLIFE WHO GUTTED YOUR OWN BOY.

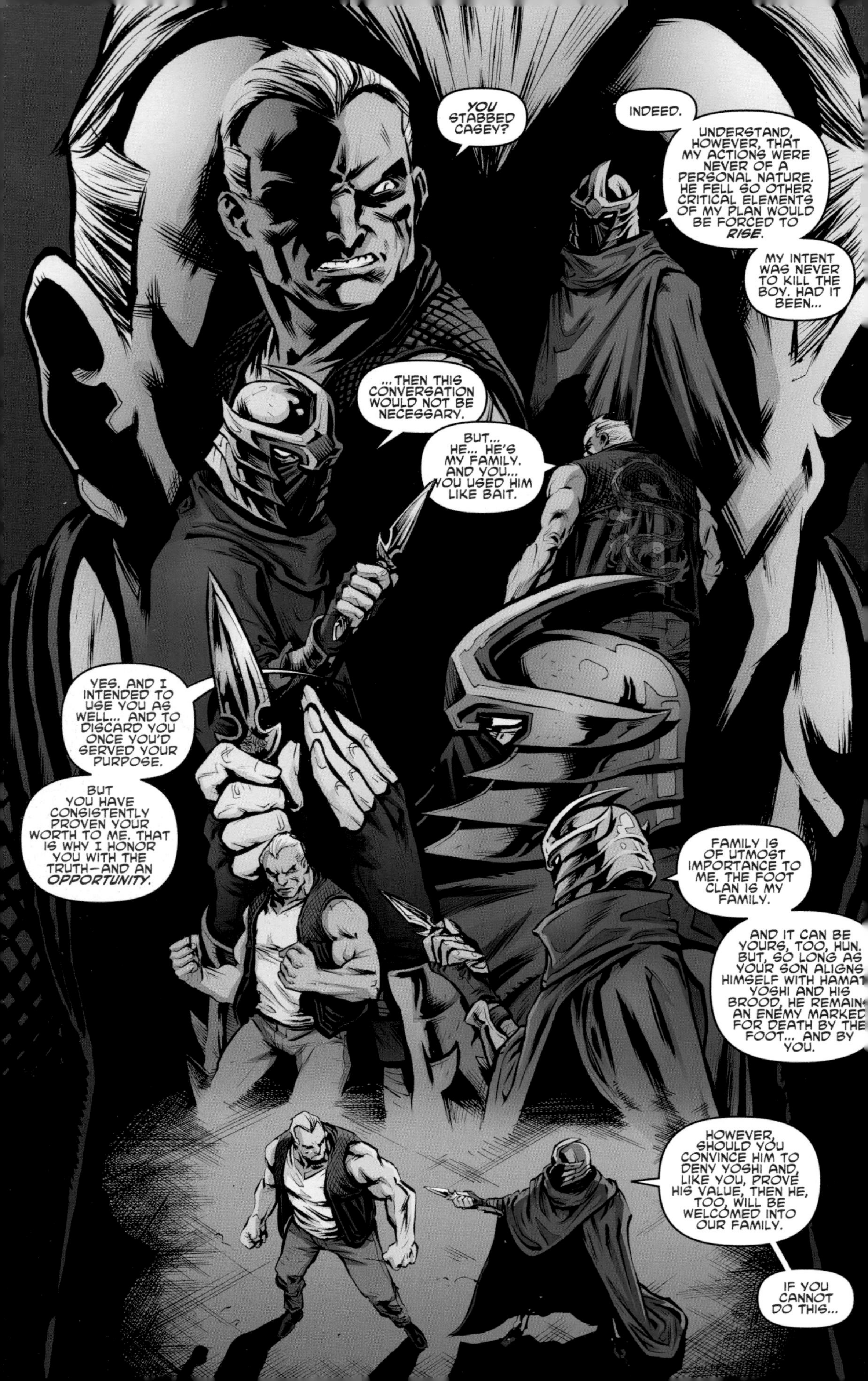
YOU STABBED CASEY?
INDEED.
UNDERSTAND, HOWEVER, THAT MY ACTIONS WERE NEVER OF A PERSONAL NATURE. HE FELL SO OTHER CRITICAL ELEMENTS OF MY PLAN WOULD BE FORCED TO RISE.
MY INTENT WAS NEVER TO KILL THE BOY. HAD IT BEEN...
...THEN THIS CONVERSATION WOULD NOT BE NECESSARY.
BUT... HE... HE'S MY FAMILY. AND YOU... YOU USED HIM LIKE BAIT.
YES. AND I INTENDED TO USE YOU AS WELL... AND TO DISCARD YOU ONCE YOU'D SERVED YOUR PURPOSE.
BUT YOU HAVE CONSISTENTLY PROVEN YOUR WORTH TO ME. THAT IS WHY I HONOR YOU WITH THE TRUTH—AND AN OPPORTUNITY.
FAMILY IS OF UTMOST IMPORTANCE TO ME. THE FOOT CLAN IS MY FAMILY.
AND IT CAN BE YOURS, TOO, HUN. BUT, SO LONG AS YOUR SON ALIGNS HIMSELF WITH HAMATO YOSHI AND HIS BROOD, HE REMAINS AN ENEMY MARKED FOR DEATH BY THE FOOT... AND BY YOU.
HOWEVER, SHOULD YOU CONVINCE HIM TO DENY YOSHI AND, LIKE YOU, PROVE HIS VALUE, THEN HE, TOO, WILL BE WELCOMED INTO OUR FAMILY.
IF YOU CANNOT DO THIS...

"...KNOW THAT YOUR SON HAS *LITTLE* TIME LEFT."

YOU BASTARD, BROOKLYN...

...YOU *THINK* YER SO SMART, DONTCHA?!

FWAM

JUST LIKE THAT *MOUTHY BRAT* O' YOURS.

HUN, LAD, WHAT'S GOT INTO YER *HEAD,* BOYO?!

YEAH, ARNIE— WHY'RE YE BEIN' SO *MEAN* TO BROOKLYN? HE'S YER GOOD MATE!

HUN... ERK... WHA— GLG—HELL... DOIN'?

NO, HE AIN'T—I GOT *NO* FRIENDS HERE.

NOW BACK OFF, BOTH OF YA, OR I'LL SNAP THIS LOUDMOUTH'S NECK LIKE A TWIG.

NO, *YOU* BACK OFF, HUN...

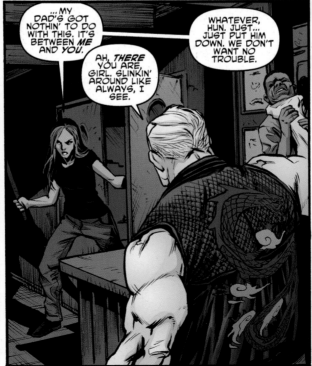

...MY DAD'S GOT NOTHIN' TO DO WITH THIS. IT'S BETWEEN *ME* AND *YOU.*

AH, *THERE* YOU ARE, GIRL. SLINKIN' AROUND LIKE ALWAYS, I SEE.

WHATEVER, HUN. JUST... JUST PUT HIM DOWN. WE DON'T WANT NO TROUBLE.

TROUBLE?

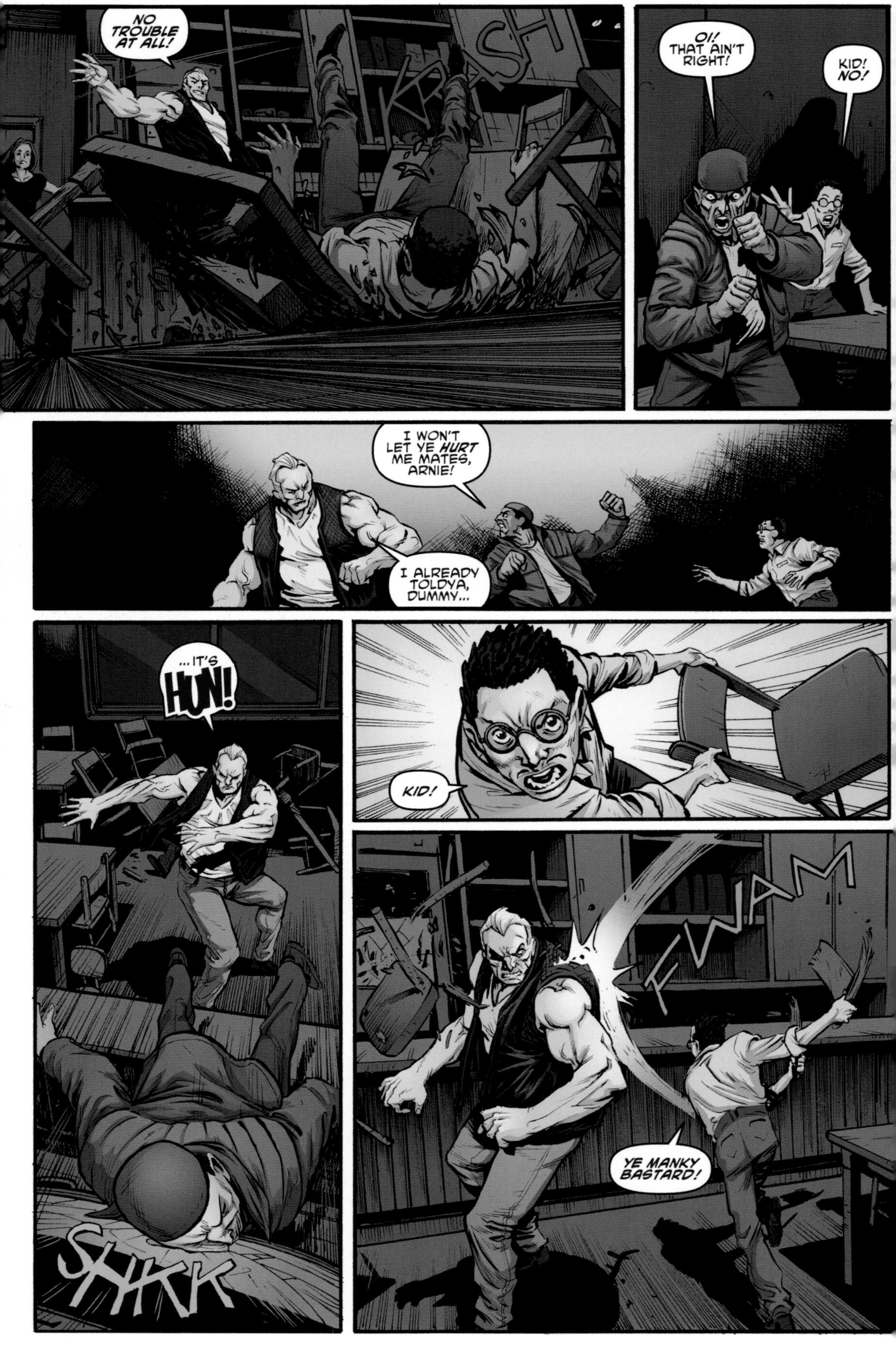
NO TROUBLE AT ALL!
KRASH
OI! THAT AIN'T RIGHT!
KID! NO!
I WON'T LET YE *HURT* ME MATES, ARNIE!
I ALREADY TOLDYA, DUMMY...
...IT'S HUN!
SHKK
KID!
FWAM
YE MANKY BASTARD!

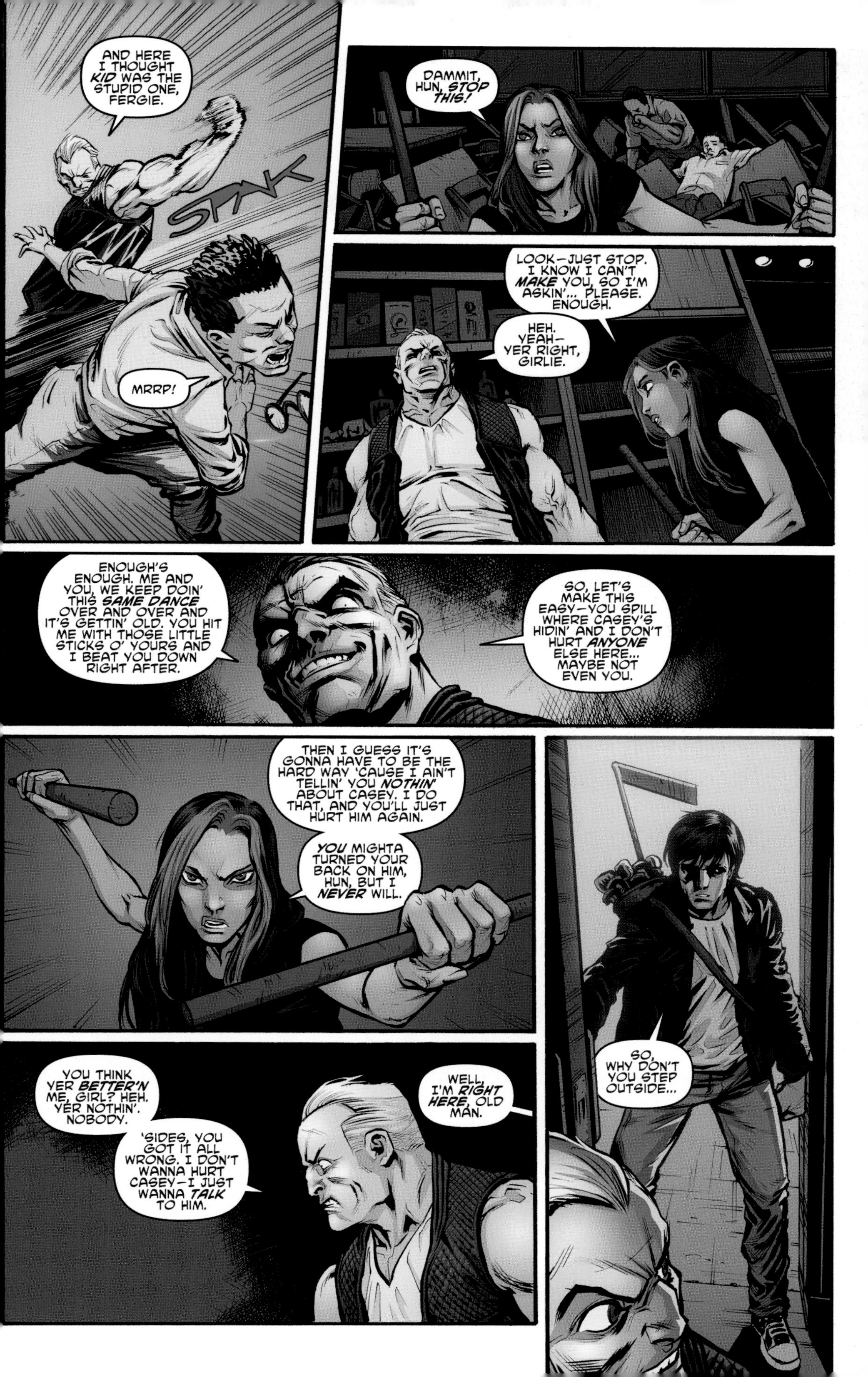
AND HERE I THOUGHT KID WAS THE STUPID ONE, FERGIE.
STAK
MRRP!
DAMMIT, HUN, STOP THIS!
LOOK—JUST STOP. I KNOW I CAN'T MAKE YOU, SO I'M ASKIN'... PLEASE. ENOUGH.
HEH. YEAH—YER RIGHT, GIRLIE.
ENOUGH'S ENOUGH. ME AND YOU, WE KEEP DOIN' THIS SAME DANCE OVER AND OVER AND IT'S GETTIN' OLD. YOU HIT ME WITH THOSE LITTLE STICKS O' YOURS AND I BEAT YOU DOWN RIGHT AFTER.
SO, LET'S MAKE THIS EASY—YOU SPILL WHERE CASEY'S HIDIN' AND I DON'T HURT ANYONE ELSE HERE... MAYBE NOT EVEN YOU.
THEN I GUESS IT'S GONNA HAVE TO BE THE HARD WAY 'CAUSE I AIN'T TELLIN' YOU NOTHIN' ABOUT CASEY. I DO THAT, AND YOU'LL JUST HURT HIM AGAIN.
YOU MIGHTA TURNED YOUR BACK ON HIM, HUN, BUT I NEVER WILL.
YOU THINK YER BETTER'N ME, GIRL? HEH. YER NOTHIN'. NOBODY.
'SIDES, YOU GOT IT ALL WRONG. I DON'T WANNA HURT CASEY—I JUST WANNA TALK TO HIM.
WELL, I'M RIGHT HERE, OLD MAN.
SO, WHY DON'T YOU STEP OUTSIDE...

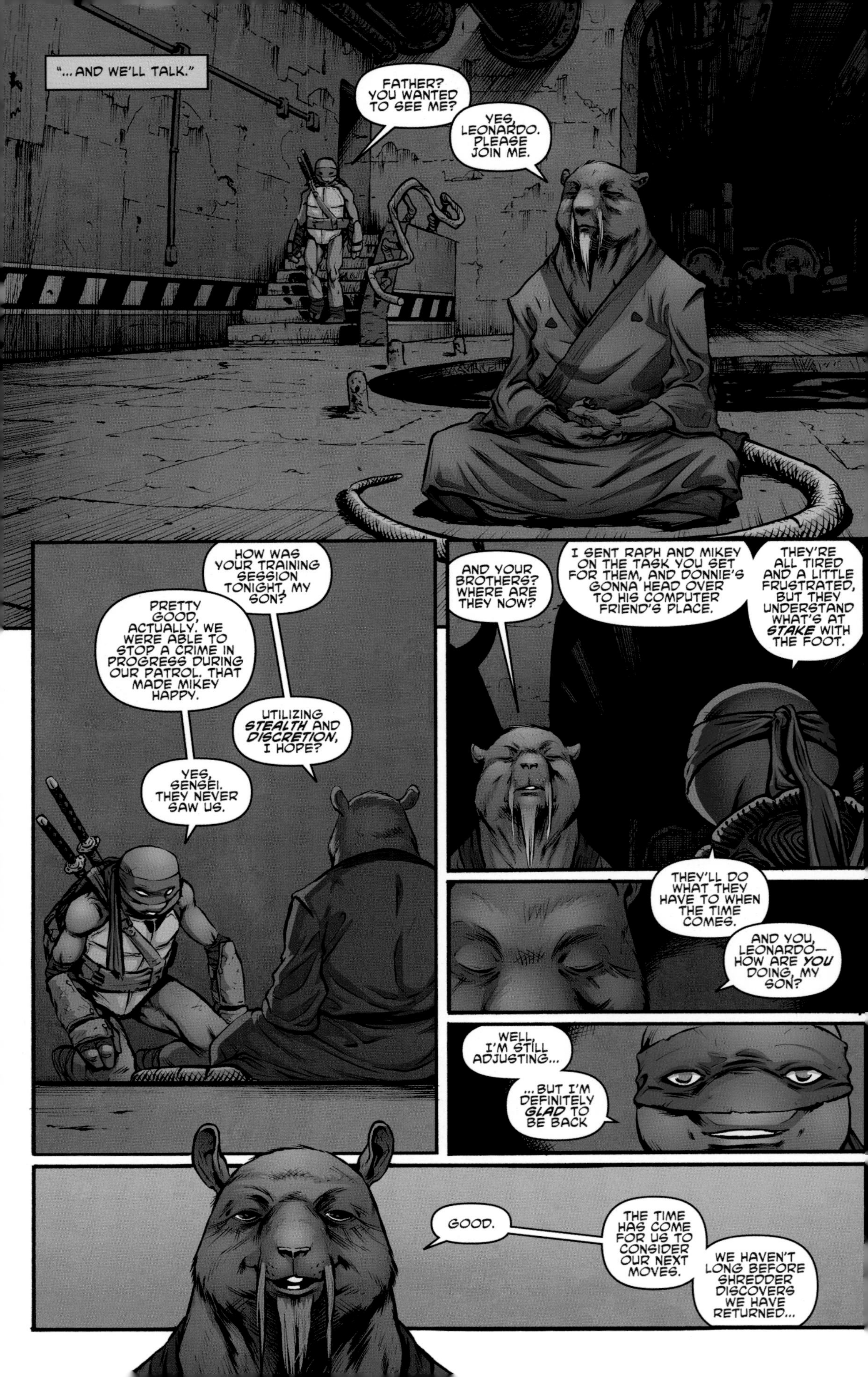
"...AND WE'LL TALK."
FATHER? YOU WANTED TO SEE ME?
YES, LEONARDO. PLEASE JOIN ME.
HOW WAS YOUR TRAINING SESSION TONIGHT, MY SON?
PRETTY GOOD, ACTUALLY. WE WERE ABLE TO STOP A CRIME IN PROGRESS DURING OUR PATROL. THAT MADE MIKEY HAPPY.
UTILIZING *STEALTH* AND *DISCRETION*, I HOPE?
YES, SENSEI. THEY NEVER SAW US.
AND YOUR BROTHERS? WHERE ARE THEY NOW?
I SENT RAPH AND MIKEY ON THE TASK YOU SET FOR THEM, AND DONNIE'S GONNA HEAD OVER TO HIS COMPUTER FRIEND'S PLACE.
THEY'RE ALL TIRED AND A LITTLE FRUSTRATED, BUT THEY UNDERSTAND WHAT'S AT *STAKE* WITH THE FOOT.
THEY'LL DO WHAT THEY HAVE TO WHEN THE TIME COMES.
AND YOU, LEONARDO— HOW ARE *YOU* DOING, MY SON?
WELL, I'M STILL ADJUSTING...
...BUT I'M DEFINITELY *GLAD* TO BE BACK
GOOD.
THE TIME HAS COME FOR US TO CONSIDER OUR NEXT MOVES.
WE HAVEN'T LONG BEFORE SHREDDER DISCOVERS WE HAVE RETURNED...

"...AND WE HAVE *MUCH* TO DISCUSS."

OKAY, YOU *GOT* ME, SO TALK. NOT THAT YOU GOT ANYTHING I WANNA HEAR.

TRUST ME, YOU WANNA HEAR THIS.

LOOK, IT AIN'T NO BIG SECRET THAT THE DRAGONS ARE IN DEEP WITH THE FOOT NOW—SHREDDER RUNS THIS TOWN AND WE GOTTA STAY ON HIS GOOD SIDE.

BUT YOU AND THEM DAMN MUTANT FRIENDS OF YOURS... YOU *CROSSED HIM.* THAT *SAVATE BOSS* FOUND OUT WHAT HAPPENS WHEN YOU CROSS THE MAN—

—THE *WORST* KIND A' *HAIRCUT,* THAT'S WHAT.

BUT ME AND SHREDDER, WE GOT US AN *UNDERSTANDIN',* OKAY? AND HE'S WILLIN' TO RETHINK THINGS WHEN IT COMES TO YOU—TOLD ME SO HIMSELF.

WHAT HE WANTS, CASEY... IT'S REAL SIMPLE. YOU QUIT THEM MUTANTS AND JOIN THE FOOT—JOIN *ME*—AND SHREDDER FORGETS ALL ABOUT BEIN' TICKED OFF AT YOU.

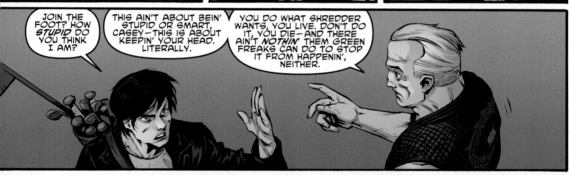

JOIN THE FOOT? HOW *STUPID* DO YOU THINK I AM?

THIS AIN'T ABOUT BEIN' *STUPID* OR SMART, CASEY—THIS IS ABOUT KEEPIN' YOUR HEAD. LITERALLY.

YOU DO WHAT SHREDDER WANTS, YOU LIVE. DON'T DO IT, YOU DIE—AND THERE AIN'T *NOTHIN'* THEM GREEN FREAKS CAN DO TO STOP IT FROM HAPPENIN', NEITHER.

WELL, GUESS I'M DEAD, THEN, 'CAUSE THERE'S *NO WAY IN HELL* I'M GONNA JOIN SHREDDER'S LITTLE PSYCHO SHOW... OR YOURS.

WE'RE DONE HERE.

DAMMIT, CASEY...

...*DON'T* YOU WALK AWAY FROM ME, BOY!

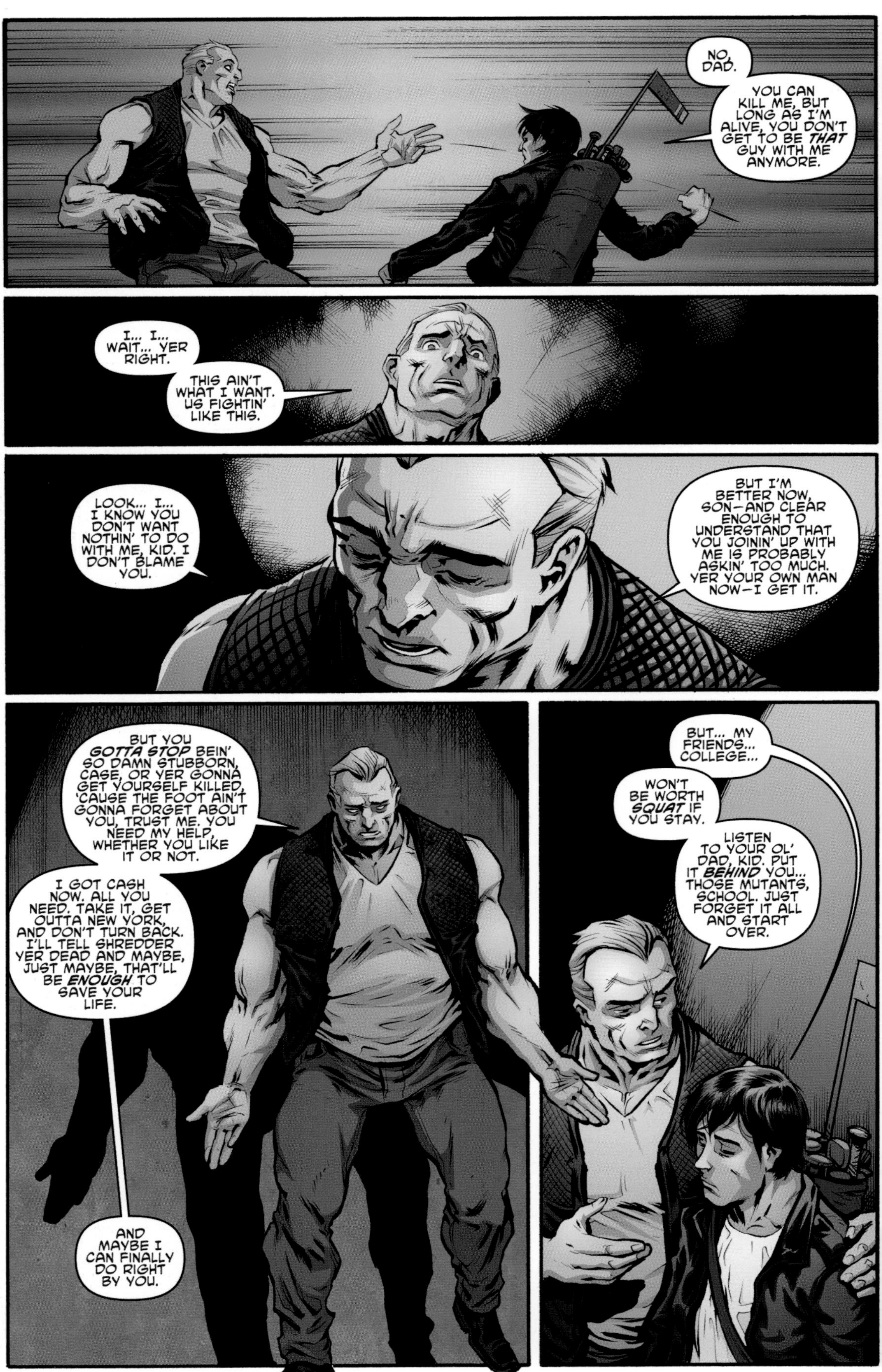
NO, DAD.
YOU CAN KILL ME, BUT LONG AS I'M ALIVE, YOU DON'T GET TO BE *THAT* GUY WITH ME ANYMORE.
I... I... WAIT... YER RIGHT.
THIS AIN'T WHAT I WANT. US FIGHTIN' LIKE THIS.
LOOK... I... I KNOW YOU DON'T WANT NOTHIN' TO DO WITH ME, KID. I DON'T BLAME YOU.
BUT I'M BETTER NOW, SON—AND CLEAR ENOUGH TO UNDERSTAND THAT YOU JOININ' UP WITH ME IS PROBABLY ASKIN' TOO MUCH. YER YOUR OWN MAN NOW—I GET IT.
BUT YOU *GOTTA STOP* BEIN' SO DAMN STUBBORN, CASE, OR YER GONNA GET YOURSELF KILLED, 'CAUSE THE FOOT AIN'T GONNA FORGET ABOUT YOU, TRUST ME. YOU NEED MY HELP, WHETHER YOU LIKE IT OR NOT.
I GOT CASH NOW. ALL YOU NEED. TAKE IT, GET OUTTA NEW YORK, AND DON'T TURN BACK. I'LL TELL SHREDDER YER DEAD AND MAYBE, JUST MAYBE, THAT'LL BE *ENOUGH* TO SAVE YOUR LIFE.
AND MAYBE I CAN FINALLY DO RIGHT BY YOU.
BUT... MY FRIENDS... COLLEGE...
WON'T BE WORTH *SQUAT* IF YOU STAY.
LISTEN TO YOUR OL' DAD, KID. PUT IT *BEHIND* YOU... THOSE MUTANTS, SCHOOL. JUST FORGET IT ALL AND START OVER.

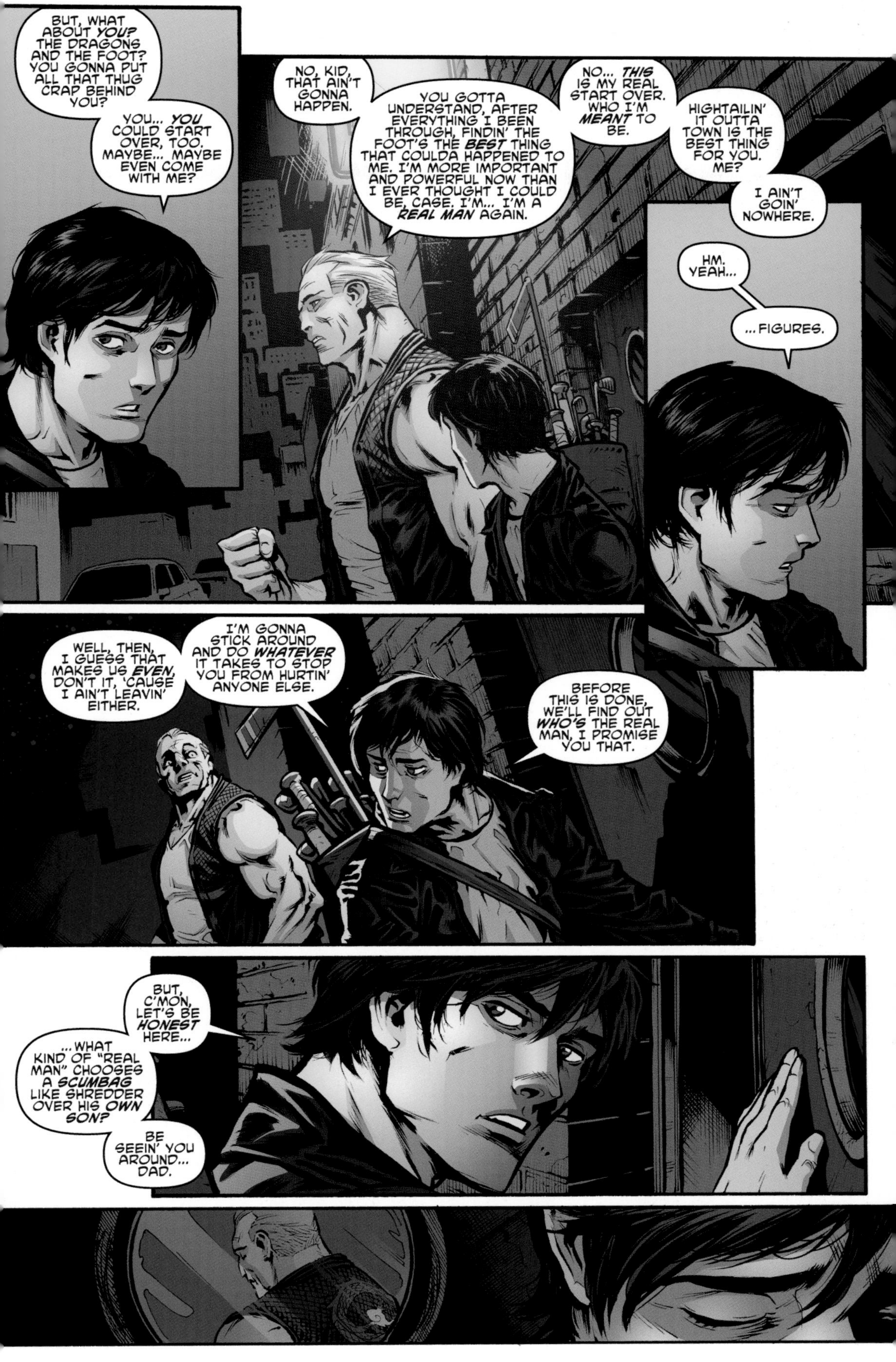
BUT, WHAT ABOUT YOU? THE DRAGONS AND THE FOOT? YOU GONNA PUT ALL THAT THUG CRAP BEHIND YOU?
YOU... YOU COULD START OVER, TOO. MAYBE... MAYBE EVEN COME WITH ME?
NO, KID, THAT AIN'T GONNA HAPPEN.
YOU GOTTA UNDERSTAND, AFTER EVERYTHING I BEEN THROUGH, FINDIN' THE FOOT'S THE BEST THING THAT COULDA HAPPENED TO ME. I'M MORE IMPORTANT AND POWERFUL NOW THAN I EVER THOUGHT I COULD BE, CASE. I'M... I'M A REAL MAN AGAIN.
NO... THIS IS MY REAL START OVER. WHO I'M MEANT TO BE.
HIGHTAILIN' IT OUTTA TOWN IS THE BEST THING FOR YOU. ME?
I AIN'T GOIN' NOWHERE.
HM. YEAH...
...FIGURES.
WELL, THEN, I GUESS THAT MAKES US EVEN, DON'T IT, 'CAUSE I AIN'T LEAVIN' EITHER.
I'M GONNA STICK AROUND AND DO WHATEVER IT TAKES TO STOP YOU FROM HURTIN' ANYONE ELSE.
BEFORE THIS IS DONE, WE'LL FIND OUT WHO'S THE REAL MAN, I PROMISE YOU THAT.
BUT, C'MON, LET'S BE HONEST HERE...
...WHAT KIND OF "REAL MAN" CHOOSES A SCUMBAG LIKE SHREDDER OVER HIS OWN SON?
BE SEEIN' YOU AROUND... DAD.

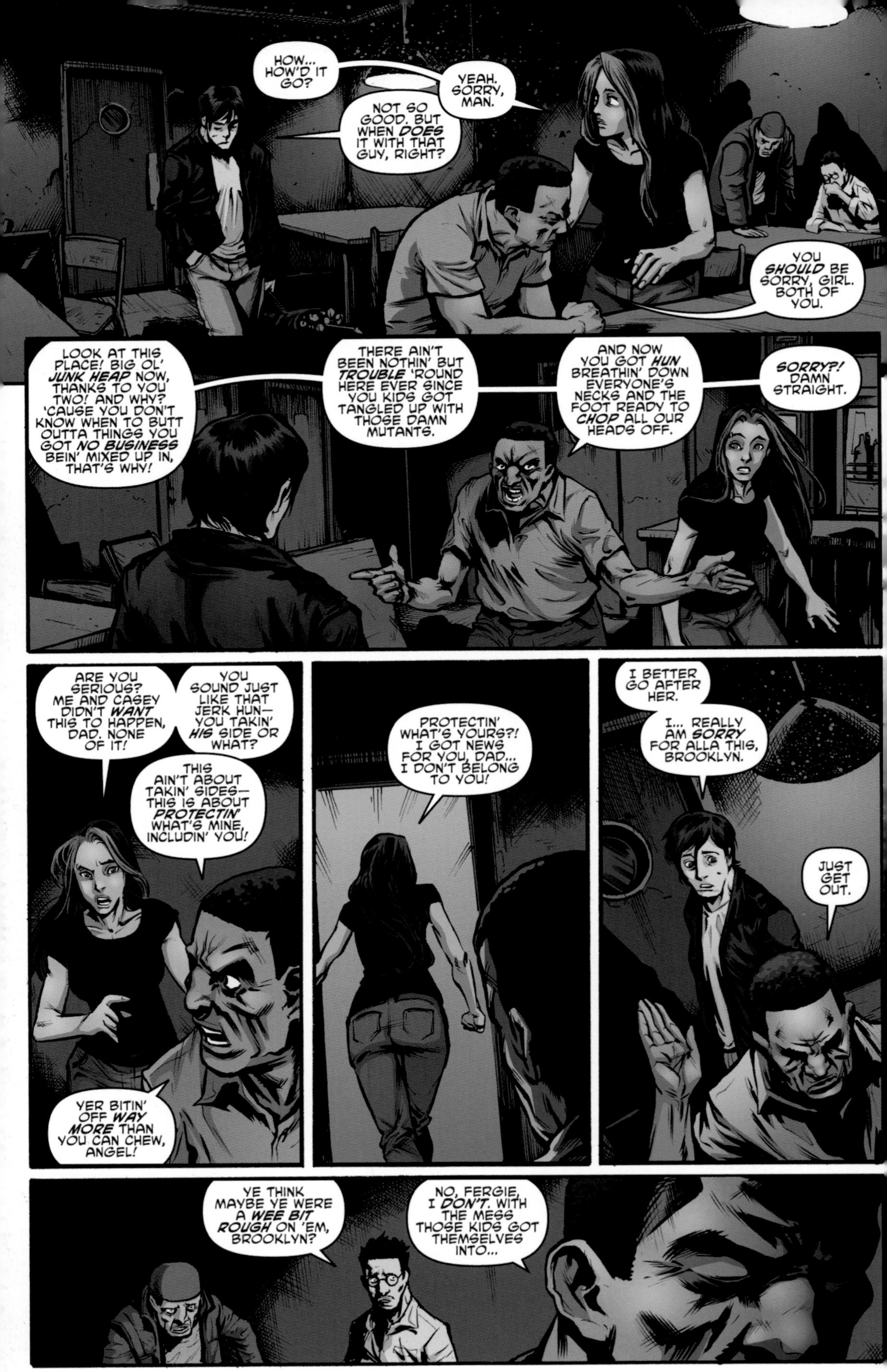
HOW... HOW'D IT GO?
NOT SO GOOD. BUT WHEN *DOES* IT WITH THAT GUY, RIGHT?
YEAH. SORRY, MAN.
YOU *SHOULD* BE SORRY, GIRL. BOTH OF YOU.
LOOK AT THIS PLACE! BIG OL' *JUNK HEAP* NOW, THANKS TO YOU TWO! AND WHY? 'CAUSE YOU DON'T KNOW WHEN TO BUTT OUTTA THINGS YOU GOT *NO BUSINESS* BEIN' MIXED UP IN, THAT'S WHY!
THERE AIN'T BEEN NOTHIN' BUT *TROUBLE* 'ROUND HERE EVER SINCE YOU KIDS GOT TANGLED UP WITH THOSE DAMN MUTANTS.
AND NOW YOU GOT *HUN* BREATHIN' DOWN EVERYONE'S NECKS AND THE FOOT READY TO *CHOP* ALL OUR HEADS OFF.
SORRY?! DAMN STRAIGHT.
ARE YOU SERIOUS? ME AND CASEY DIDN'T *WANT* THIS TO HAPPEN, DAD. NONE OF IT!
YOU SOUND JUST LIKE THAT JERK HUN— YOU TAKIN' *HIS* SIDE OR WHAT?
THIS AIN'T ABOUT TAKIN' SIDES— THIS IS ABOUT *PROTECTIN'* WHAT'S MINE, INCLUDIN' YOU!
YER BITIN' OFF *WAY MORE* THAN YOU CAN CHEW, ANGEL!
PROTECTIN' WHAT'S YOURS?! I GOT NEWS FOR YOU, DAD... I DON'T BELONG TO YOU!
I BETTER GO AFTER HER.
I... REALLY AM *SORRY* FOR ALLA THIS, BROOKLYN.
JUST GET OUT.
YE THINK MAYBE YE WERE A *WEE BIT ROUGH* ON 'EM, BROOKLYN?
NO, FERGIE, I *DON'T*. WITH THE MESS THOSE KIDS GOT THEMSELVES INTO...

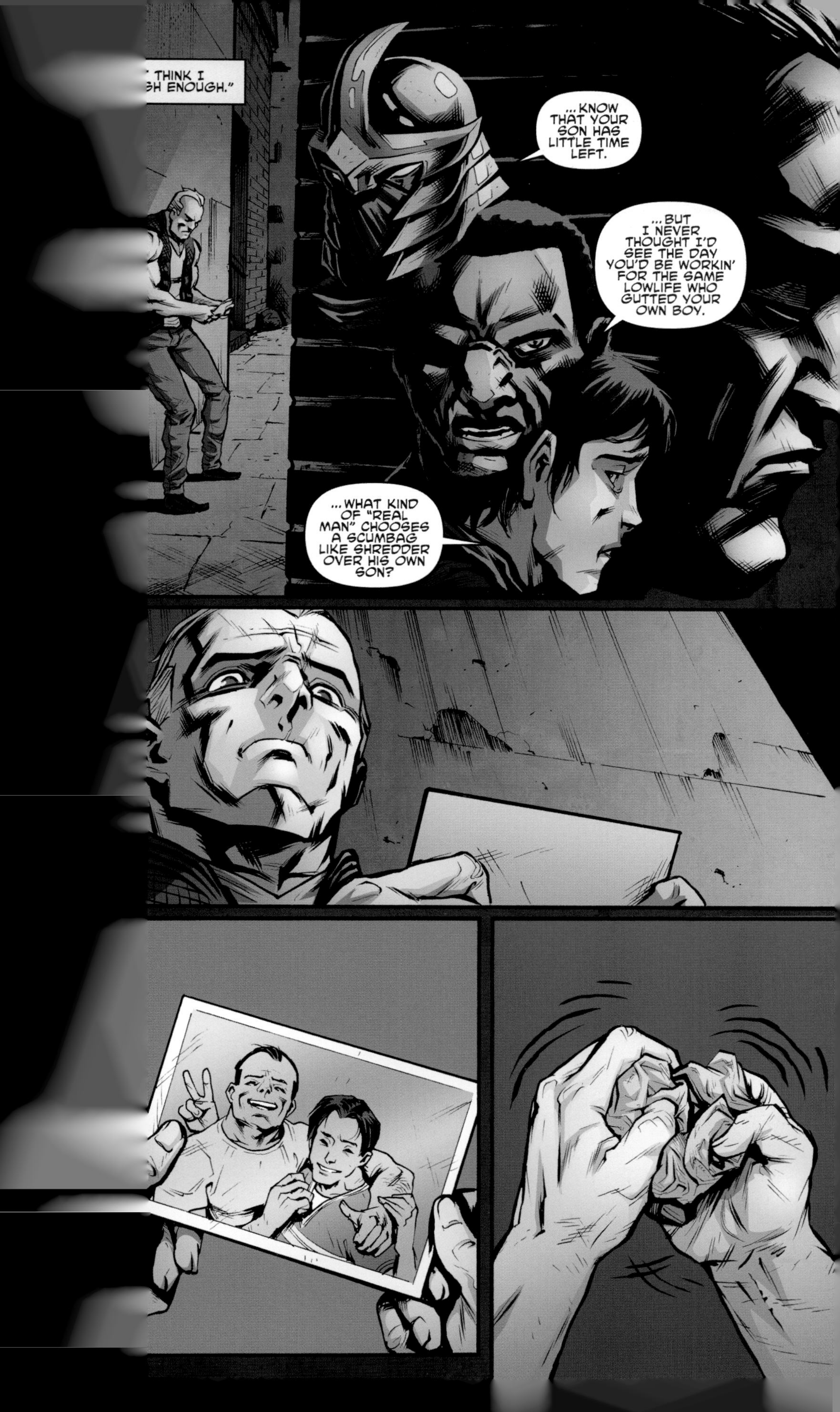

"...THINK I ...GH ENOUGH."
...KNOW THAT YOUR SON HAS LITTLE TIME LEFT.
...BUT I NEVER THOUGHT I'D SEE THE DAY YOU'D BE WORKIN' FOR THE SAME LOWLIFE WHO GUTTED YOUR OWN BOY.
...WHAT KIND OF "REAL MAN" CHOOSES A SCUMBAG LIKE SHREDDER OVER HIS OWN SON?

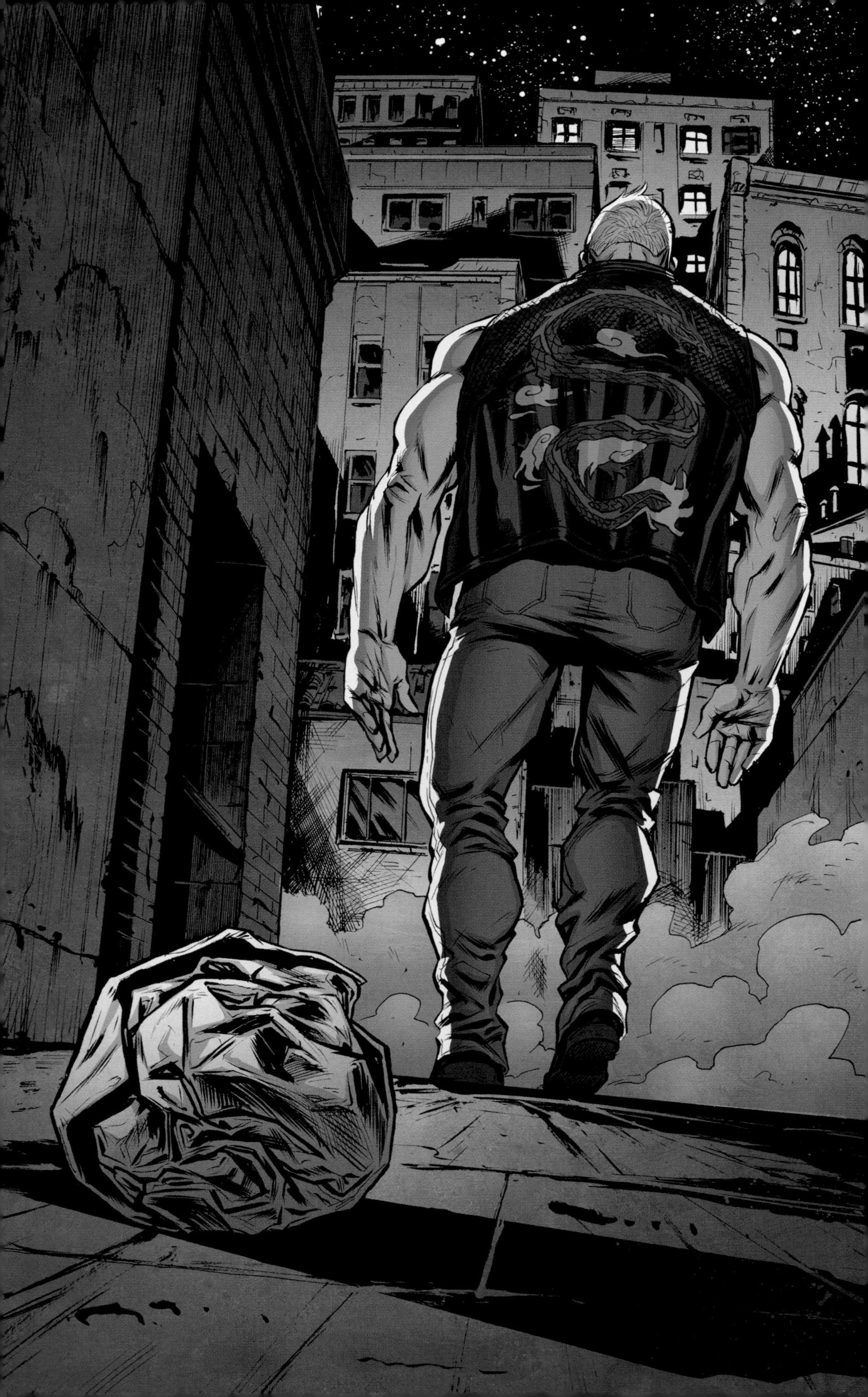

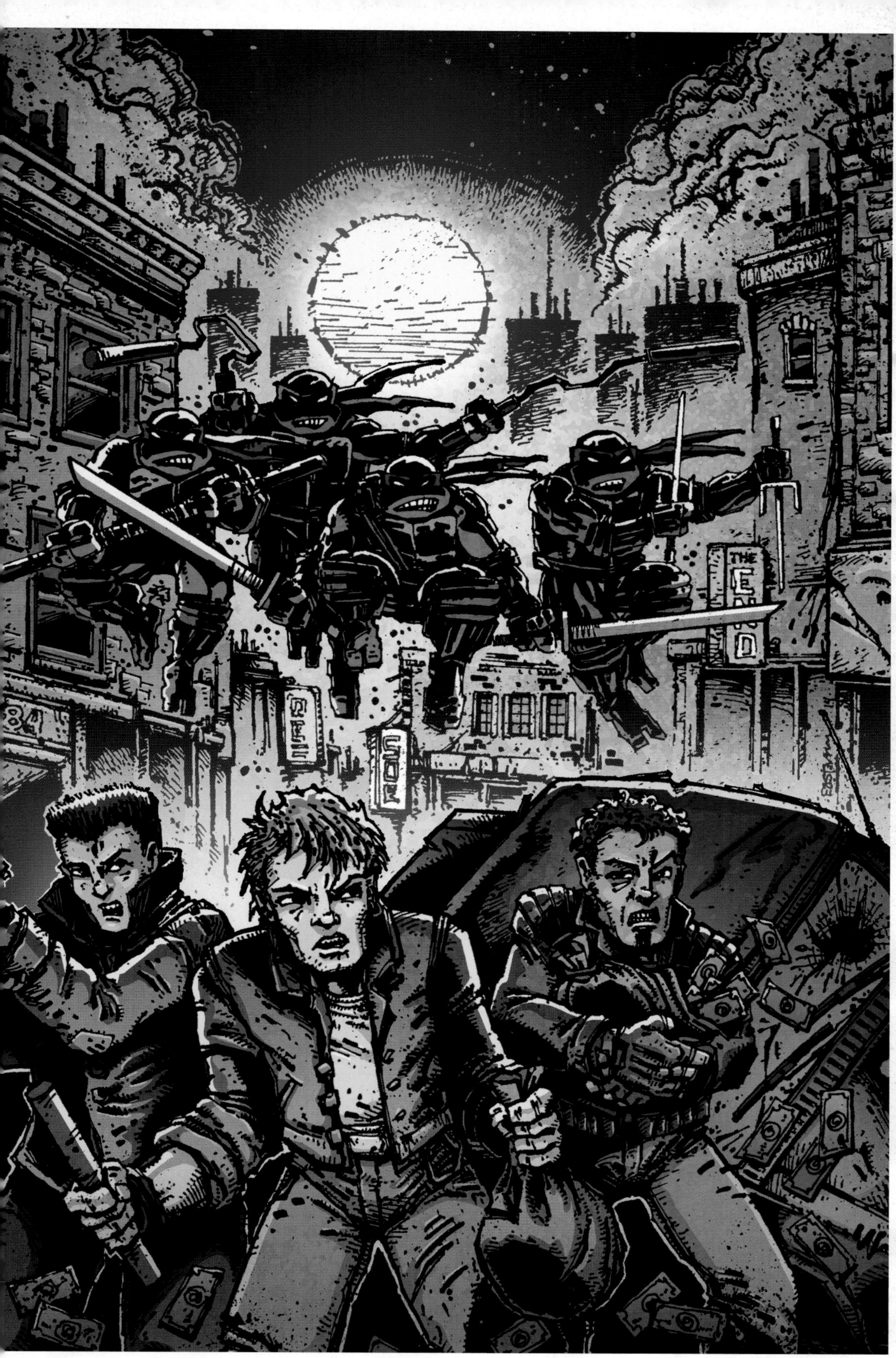

Cover by KEVIN EASTMAN
Colors by RONDA PATTISON

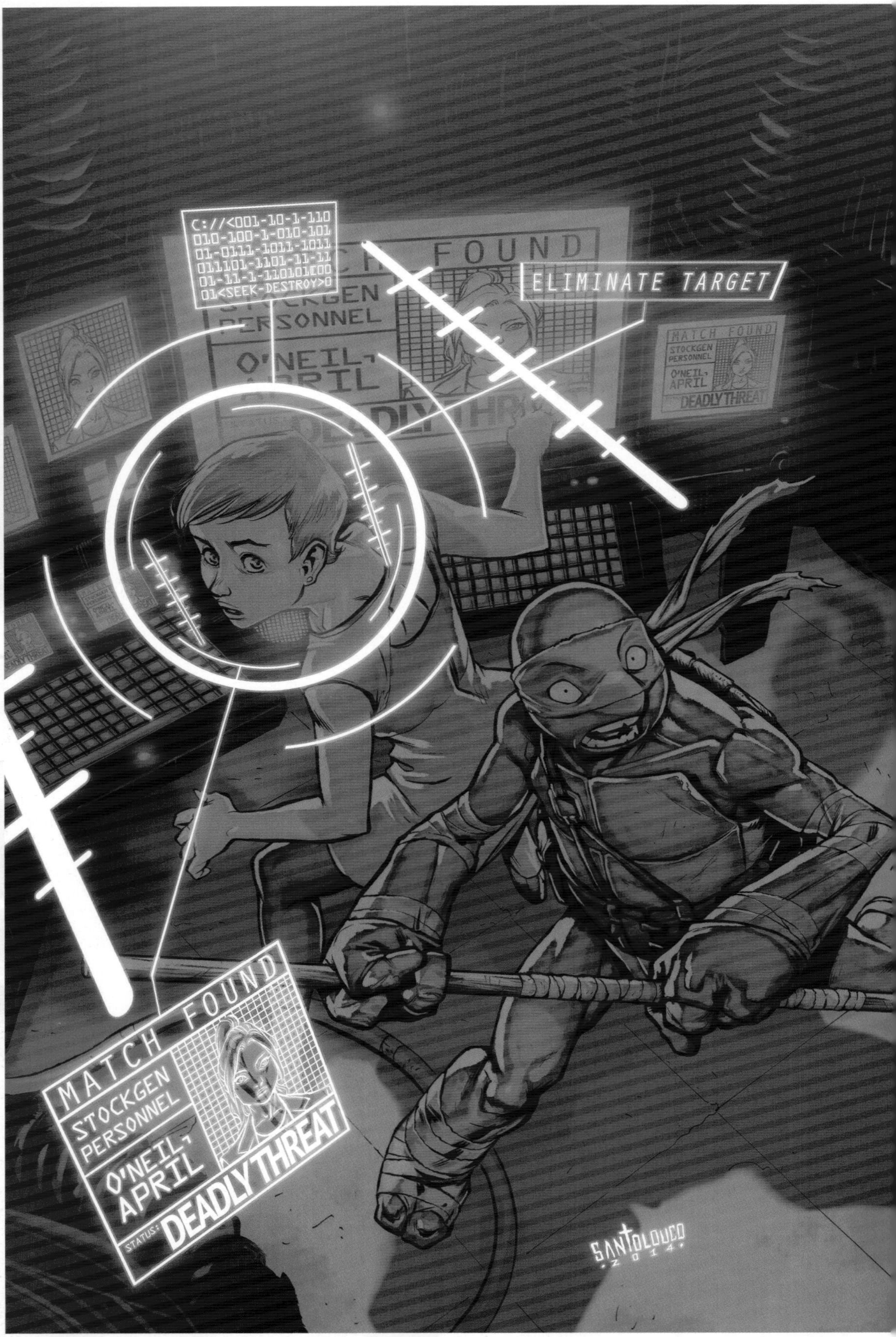

C://<001-10-1-110
010-100-1-010-101
01-0111-1011-1011
011101-1101-11-11
01-11-1-110101100
01<SEEK-DESTROY>0
ELIMINATE TARGET
MATCH FOUND
STOCKGEN PERSONNEL
O'NEIL, APRIL
STATUS: DEADLY THREAT
SANTOLOUCO 2014

Cover by MATEUS SANTOLOUCO

TMNT #34

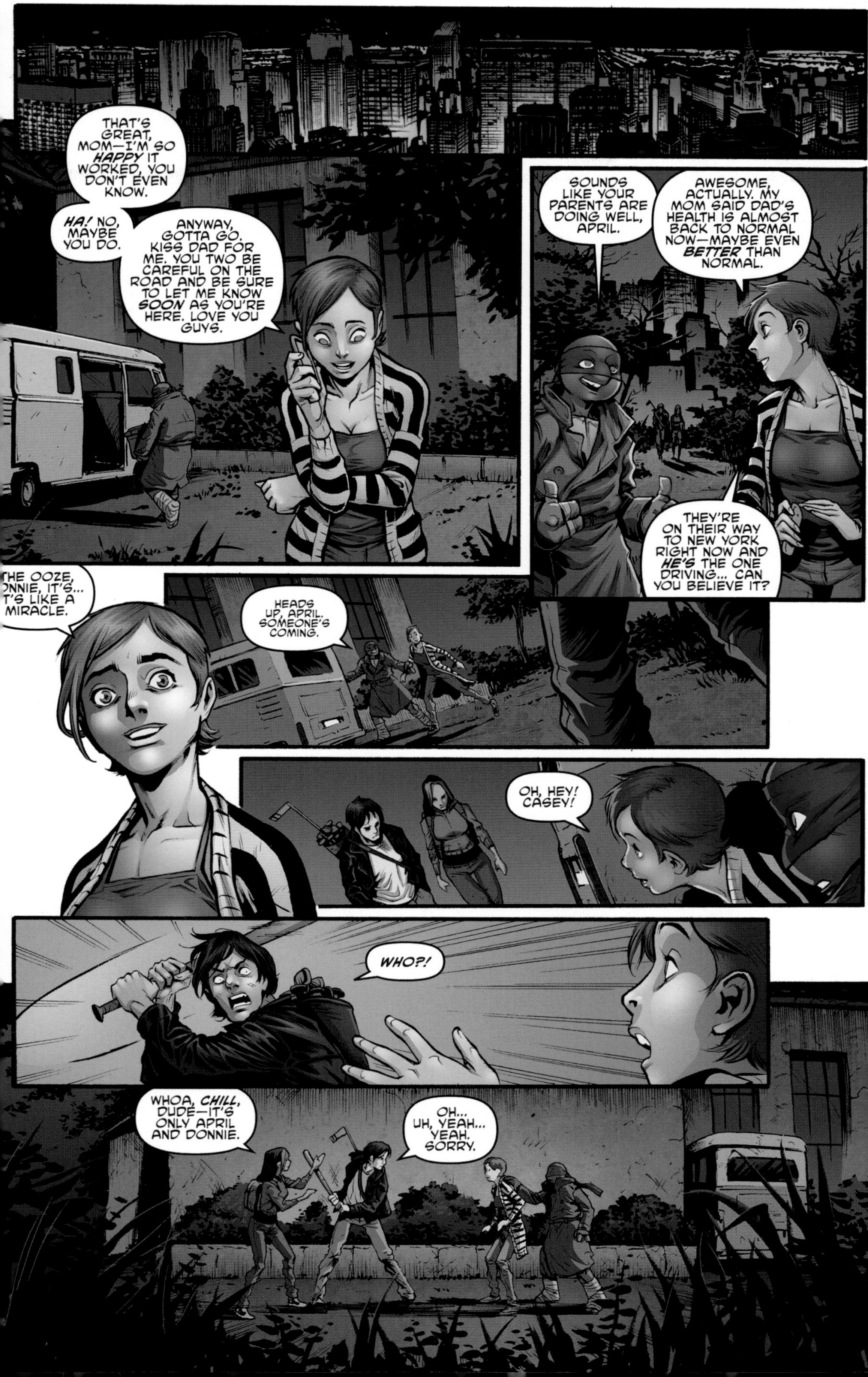

THAT'S GREAT, MOM—I'M SO HAPPY IT WORKED, YOU DON'T EVEN KNOW.
HA! NO, MAYBE YOU DO.
ANYWAY, GOTTA GO. KISS DAD FOR ME. YOU TWO BE CAREFUL ON THE ROAD AND BE SURE TO LET ME KNOW SOON AS YOU'RE HERE. LOVE YOU GUYS.
SOUNDS LIKE YOUR PARENTS ARE DOING WELL, APRIL.
AWESOME, ACTUALLY. MY MOM SAID DAD'S HEALTH IS ALMOST BACK TO NORMAL NOW—MAYBE EVEN BETTER THAN NORMAL.
THEY'RE ON THEIR WAY TO NEW YORK RIGHT NOW AND HE'S THE ONE DRIVING... CAN YOU BELIEVE IT?
HEADS UP, APRIL. SOMEONE'S COMING.
OH, HEY! CASEY!
WHO?!
WHOA, CHILL, DUDE—IT'S ONLY APRIL AND DONNIE.
OH... UH, YEAH... YEAH. SORRY.

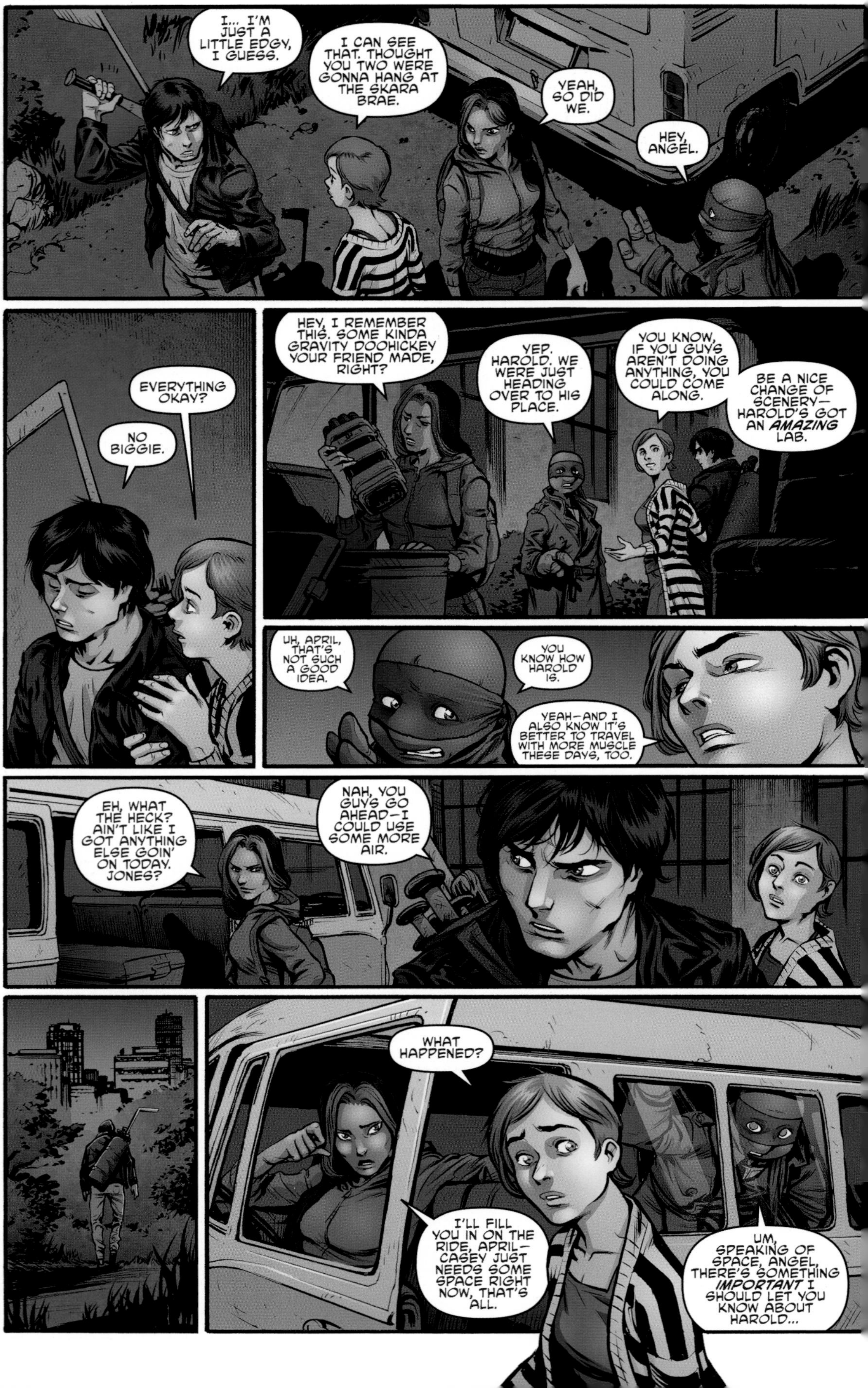
I... I'M JUST A LITTLE EDGY, I GUESS.
I CAN SEE THAT. THOUGHT YOU TWO WERE GONNA HANG AT THE SKARA BRAE.
YEAH, SO DID WE.
HEY, ANGEL.
EVERYTHING OKAY?
NO BIGGIE.
HEY, I REMEMBER THIS. SOME KINDA GRAVITY DOOHICKEY YOUR FRIEND MADE, RIGHT?
YEP. HAROLD. WE WERE JUST HEADING OVER TO HIS PLACE.
YOU KNOW, IF YOU GUYS AREN'T DOING ANYTHING, YOU COULD COME ALONG.
BE A NICE CHANGE OF SCENERY—HAROLD'S GOT AN *AMAZING* LAB.
UH, APRIL, THAT'S NOT SUCH A GOOD IDEA.
YOU KNOW HOW HAROLD IS.
YEAH—AND I ALSO KNOW IT'S BETTER TO TRAVEL WITH MORE MUSCLE THESE DAYS, TOO.
EH, WHAT THE HECK? AIN'T LIKE I GOT ANYTHING ELSE GOIN' ON TODAY. JONES?
NAH, YOU GUYS GO AHEAD—I COULD USE SOME MORE AIR.
WHAT HAPPENED?
I'LL FILL YOU IN ON THE RIDE, APRIL—CASEY JUST NEEDS SOME SPACE RIGHT NOW, THAT'S ALL.
UM, SPEAKING OF SPACE, ANGEL, THERE'S SOMETHING *IMPORTANT* I SHOULD LET YOU KNOW ABOUT HAROLD...

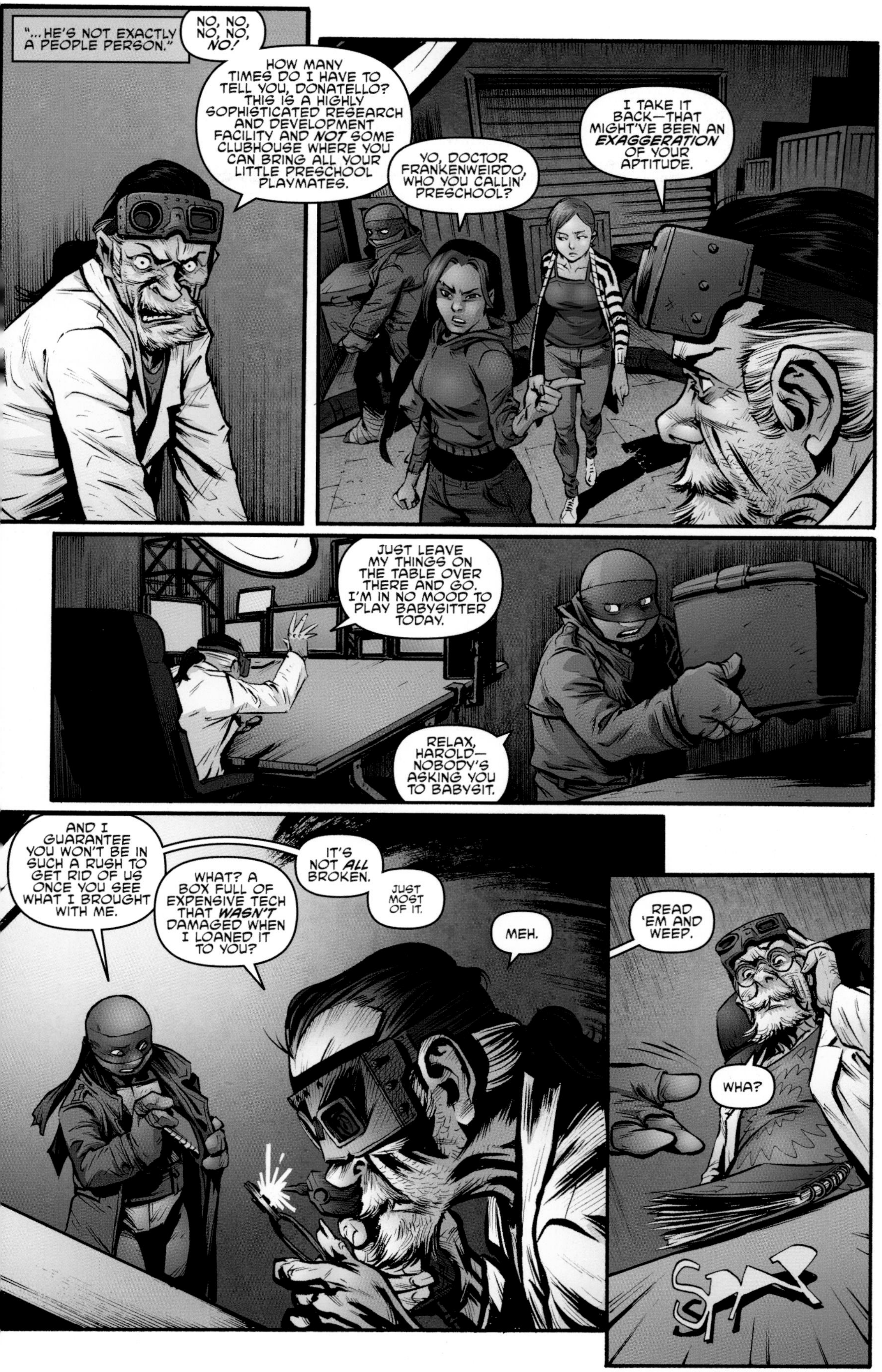
"...HE'S NOT EXACTLY A PEOPLE PERSON."
NO, NO, NO, NO, *NO!*
HOW MANY TIMES DO I HAVE TO TELL YOU, DONATELLO? THIS IS A HIGHLY SOPHISTICATED RESEARCH AND DEVELOPMENT FACILITY AND *NOT* SOME CLUBHOUSE WHERE YOU CAN BRING ALL YOUR LITTLE PRESCHOOL PLAYMATES.
YO, DOCTOR FRANKENWEIRDO, WHO YOU CALLIN' PRESCHOOL?
I TAKE IT BACK—THAT MIGHT'VE BEEN AN *EXAGGERATION* OF YOUR APTITUDE.
JUST LEAVE MY THINGS ON THE TABLE OVER THERE AND GO. I'M IN NO MOOD TO PLAY BABYSITTER TODAY.
RELAX, HAROLD—NOBODY'S ASKING YOU TO BABYSIT.
AND I GUARANTEE YOU WON'T BE IN SUCH A RUSH TO GET RID OF US ONCE YOU SEE WHAT I BROUGHT WITH ME.
WHAT? A BOX FULL OF EXPENSIVE TECH THAT *WASN'T* DAMAGED WHEN I LOANED IT TO YOU?
IT'S NOT *ALL* BROKEN.
JUST MOST OF IT.
MEH.
READ 'EM AND WEEP.
WHA?
SPAT

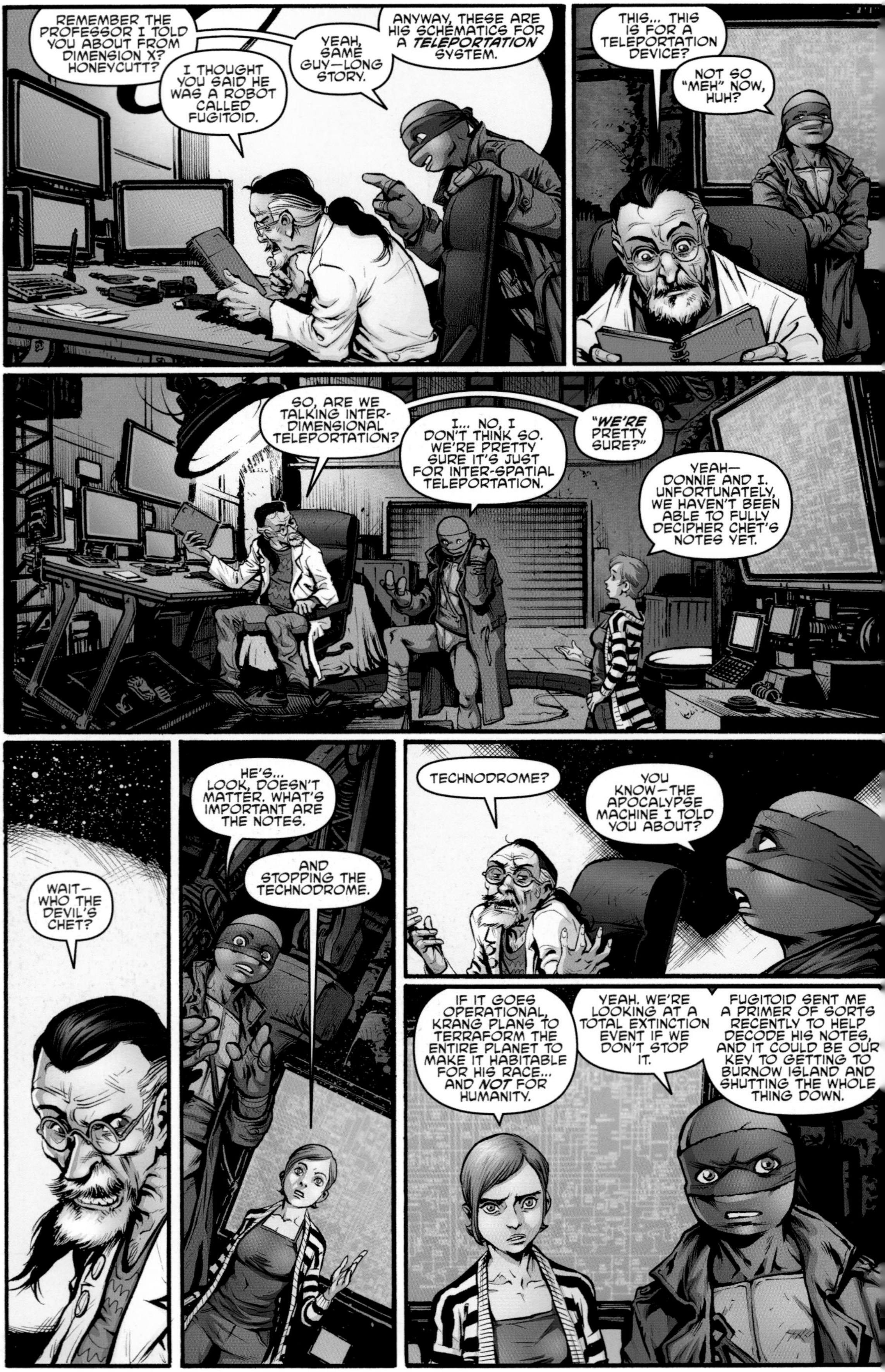
REMEMBER THE PROFESSOR I TOLD YOU ABOUT FROM DIMENSION X? HONEYCUTT?
I THOUGHT YOU SAID HE WAS A ROBOT CALLED FUGITOID.
YEAH, SAME GUY—LONG STORY.
ANYWAY, THESE ARE HIS SCHEMATICS FOR A *TELEPORTATION* SYSTEM.
THIS... THIS IS FOR A TELEPORTATION DEVICE?
NOT SO "MEH" NOW, HUH?
SO, ARE WE TALKING INTER-DIMENSIONAL TELEPORTATION?
I... NO, I DON'T THINK SO. WE'RE PRETTY SURE IT'S JUST FOR INTER-SPATIAL TELEPORTATION.
"*WE'RE* PRETTY SURE?"
YEAH—DONNIE AND I. UNFORTUNATELY, WE HAVEN'T BEEN ABLE TO FULLY DECIPHER CHET'S NOTES YET.
WAIT—WHO THE DEVIL'S CHET?
HE'S... LOOK, DOESN'T MATTER. WHAT'S IMPORTANT ARE THE NOTES.
AND STOPPING THE TECHNODROME.
TECHNODROME?
YOU KNOW—THE APOCALYPSE MACHINE I TOLD YOU ABOUT?
IF IT GOES OPERATIONAL, KRANG PLANS TO TERRAFORM THE ENTIRE PLANET TO MAKE IT HABITABLE FOR HIS RACE... AND *NOT* FOR HUMANITY.
YEAH. WE'RE LOOKING AT A TOTAL EXTINCTION EVENT IF WE DON'T STOP IT.
FUGITOID SENT ME A PRIMER OF SORTS RECENTLY TO HELP DECODE HIS NOTES, AND IT COULD BE OUR KEY TO GETTING TO BURNOW ISLAND AND SHUTTING THE WHOLE THING DOWN.

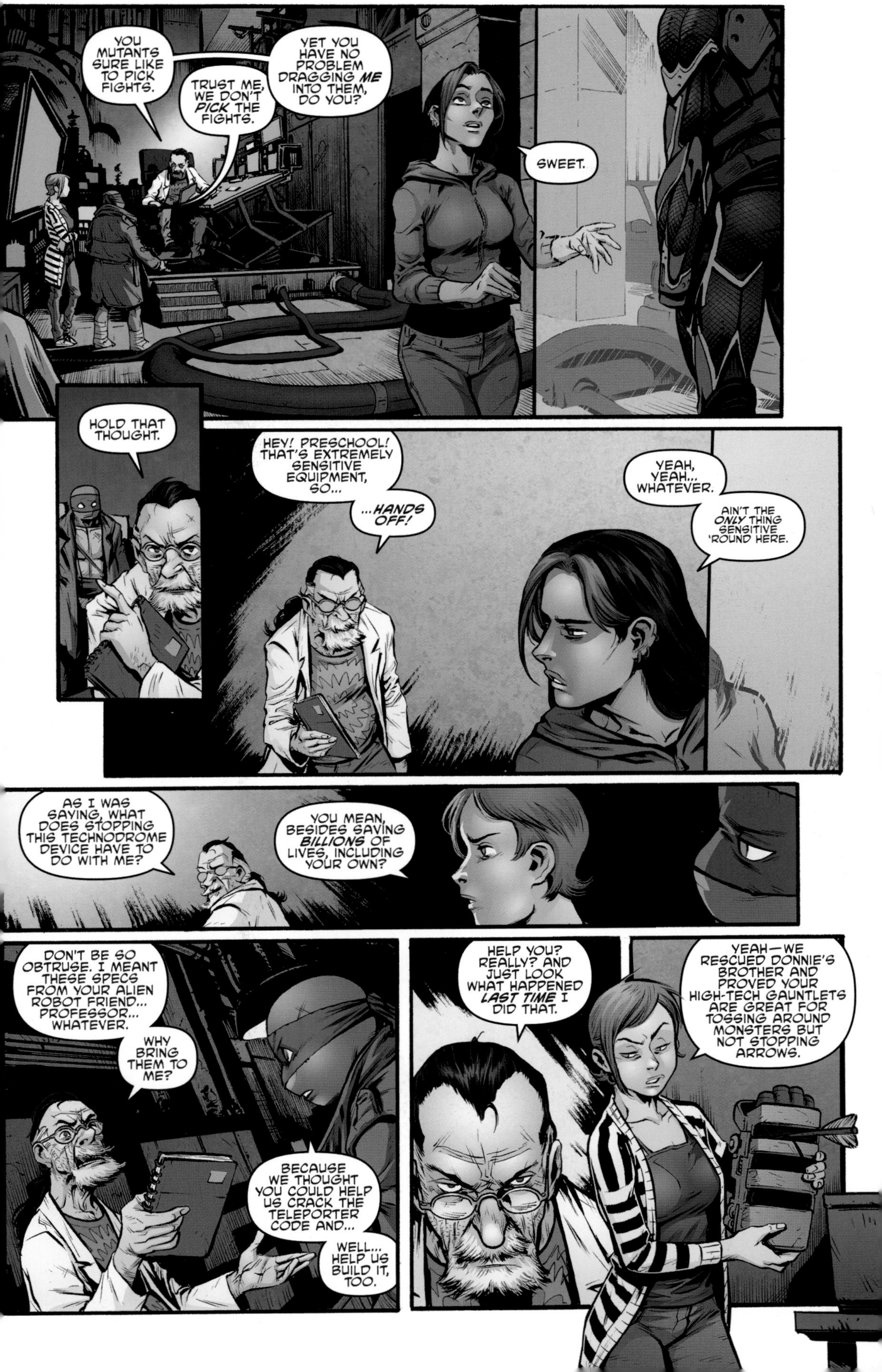
YOU MUTANTS SURE LIKE TO PICK FIGHTS.
TRUST ME, WE DON'T *PICK* THE FIGHTS.
YET YOU HAVE NO PROBLEM DRAGGING *ME* INTO THEM, DO YOU?
SWEET.
HOLD THAT THOUGHT.
HEY! PRESCHOOL! THAT'S EXTREMELY SENSITIVE EQUIPMENT, SO...
...*HANDS OFF!*
YEAH, YEAH... WHATEVER.
AIN'T THE *ONLY* THING SENSITIVE 'ROUND HERE.
AS I WAS SAYING, WHAT DOES STOPPING THIS TECHNODROME DEVICE HAVE TO DO WITH ME?
YOU MEAN, BESIDES SAVING *BILLIONS* OF LIVES, INCLUDING YOUR OWN?
DON'T BE SO OBTRUSE. I MEANT THESE SPECS FROM YOUR ALIEN ROBOT FRIEND... PROFESSOR... WHATEVER.
WHY BRING THEM TO ME?
BECAUSE WE THOUGHT YOU COULD HELP US CRACK THE TELEPORTER CODE AND...
WELL... HELP US BUILD IT, TOO.
HELP YOU? REALLY? AND JUST LOOK WHAT HAPPENED *LAST TIME* I DID THAT.
YEAH—WE RESCUED DONNIE'S BROTHER AND PROVED YOUR HIGH-TECH GAUNTLETS ARE GREAT FOR TOSSING AROUND MONSTERS BUT NOT STOPPING ARROWS.

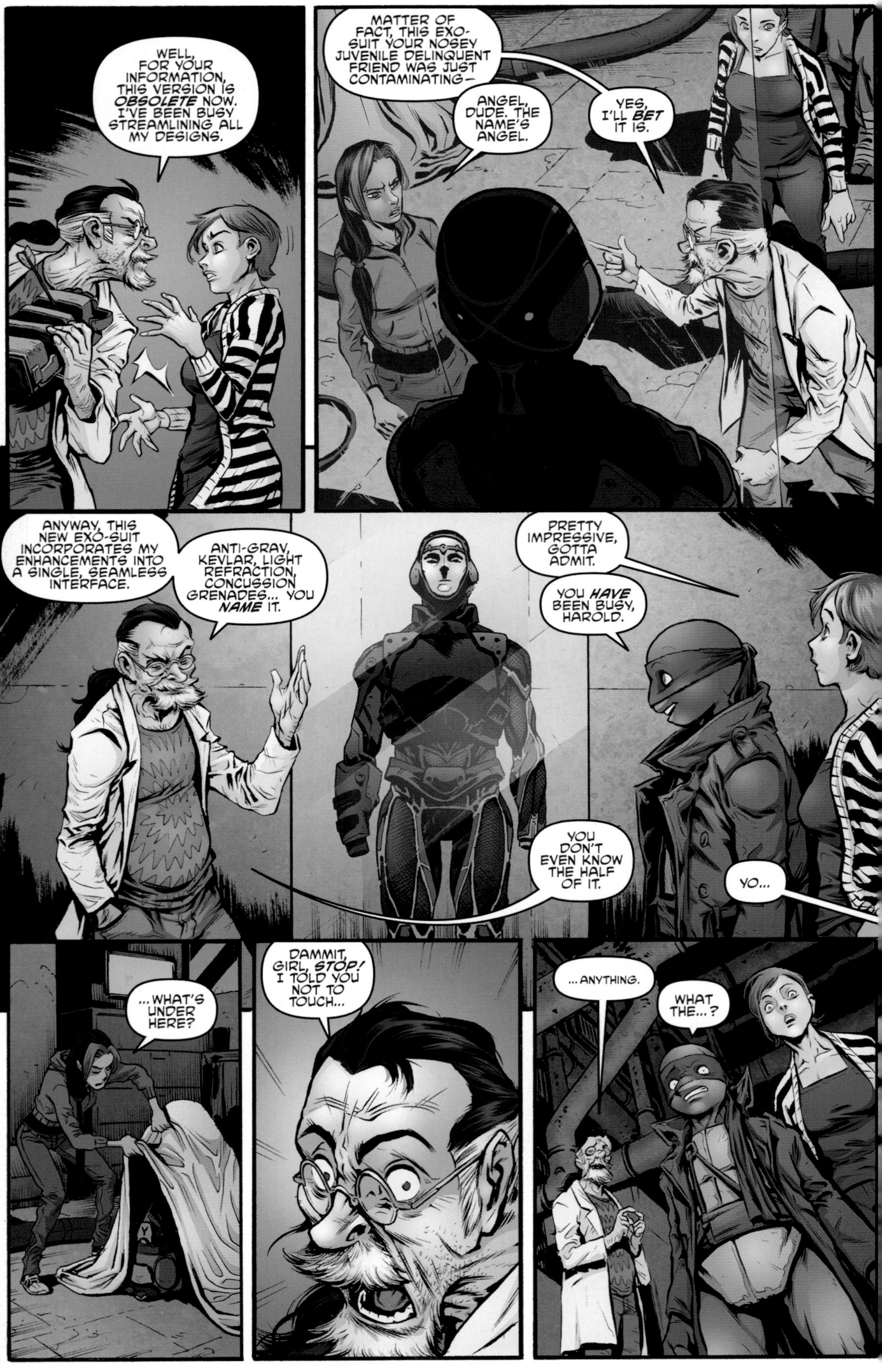
WELL, FOR YOUR INFORMATION, THIS VERSION IS OBSOLETE NOW. I'VE BEEN BUSY STREAMLINING ALL MY DESIGNS.
MATTER OF FACT, THIS EXO-SUIT YOUR NOSEY JUVENILE DELINQUENT FRIEND WAS JUST CONTAMINATING—
ANGEL, DUDE. THE NAME'S ANGEL.
YES, I'LL BET IT IS.
ANYWAY, THIS NEW EXO-SUIT INCORPORATES MY ENHANCEMENTS INTO A SINGLE, SEAMLESS INTERFACE.
ANTI-GRAV, KEVLAR, LIGHT REFRACTION, CONCUSSION GRENADES... YOU NAME IT.
PRETTY IMPRESSIVE, GOTTA ADMIT.
YOU HAVE BEEN BUSY, HAROLD.
YOU DON'T EVEN KNOW THE HALF OF IT.
YO...
...WHAT'S UNDER HERE?
DAMMIT, GIRL, STOP! I TOLD YOU NOT TO TOUCH...
...ANYTHING.
WHAT THE...?

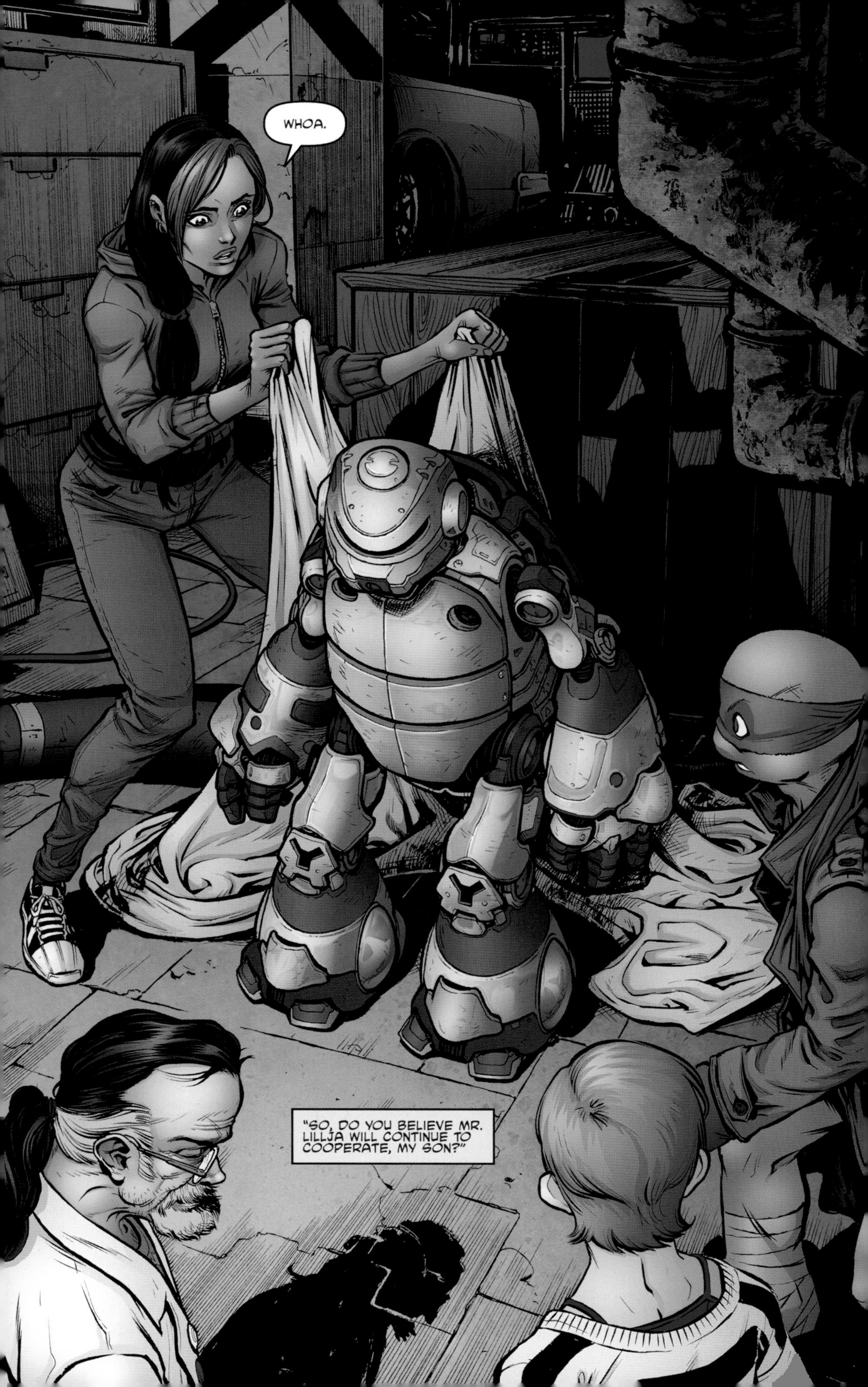
WHOA.
"SO, DO YOU BELIEVE MR. LILLJA WILL CONTINUE TO COOPERATE, MY SON?"

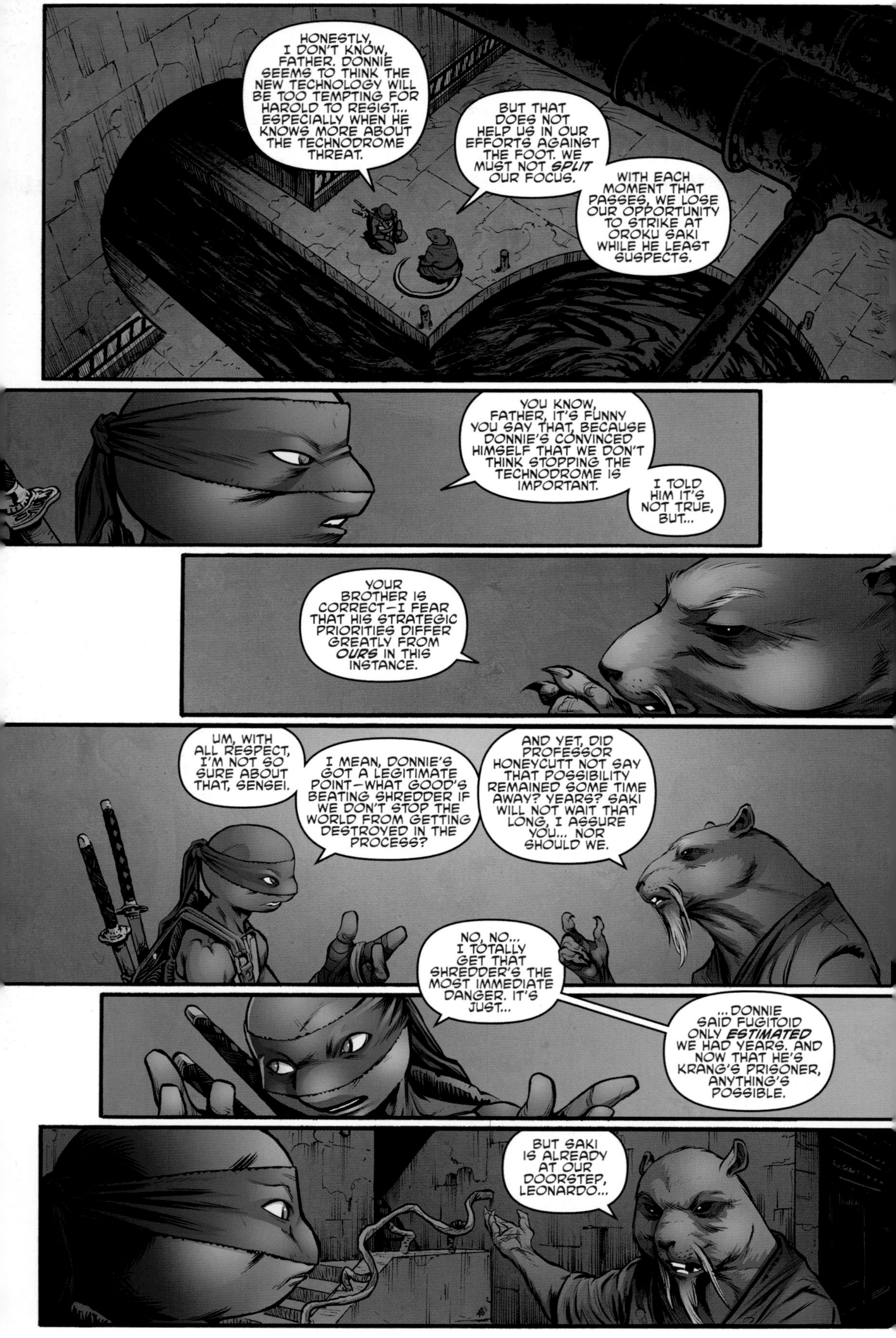
HONESTLY, I DON'T KNOW, FATHER. DONNIE SEEMS TO THINK THE NEW TECHNOLOGY WILL BE TOO TEMPTING FOR HAROLD TO RESIST... ESPECIALLY WHEN HE KNOWS MORE ABOUT THE TECHNODROME THREAT.
BUT THAT DOES NOT HELP US IN OUR EFFORTS AGAINST THE FOOT. WE MUST NOT SPLIT OUR FOCUS.
WITH EACH MOMENT THAT PASSES, WE LOSE OUR OPPORTUNITY TO STRIKE AT OROKU SAKI WHILE HE LEAST SUSPECTS.
YOU KNOW, FATHER, IT'S FUNNY YOU SAY THAT, BECAUSE DONNIE'S CONVINCED HIMSELF THAT WE DON'T THINK STOPPING THE TECHNODROME IS IMPORTANT.
I TOLD HIM IT'S NOT TRUE, BUT...
YOUR BROTHER IS CORRECT—I FEAR THAT HIS STRATEGIC PRIORITIES DIFFER GREATLY FROM OURS IN THIS INSTANCE.
UM, WITH ALL RESPECT, I'M NOT SO SURE ABOUT THAT, SENSEI.
I MEAN, DONNIE'S GOT A LEGITIMATE POINT—WHAT GOOD'S BEATING SHREDDER IF WE DON'T STOP THE WORLD FROM GETTING DESTROYED IN THE PROCESS?
AND YET, DID PROFESSOR HONEYCUTT NOT SAY THAT POSSIBILITY REMAINED SOME TIME AWAY? YEARS? SAKI WILL NOT WAIT THAT LONG, I ASSURE YOU... NOR SHOULD WE.
NO, NO... I TOTALLY GET THAT SHREDDER'S THE MOST IMMEDIATE DANGER. IT'S JUST...
...DONNIE SAID FUGITOID ONLY ESTIMATED WE HAD YEARS. AND NOW THAT HE'S KRANG'S PRISONER, ANYTHING'S POSSIBLE.
BUT SAKI IS ALREADY AT OUR DOORSTEP, LEONARDO...

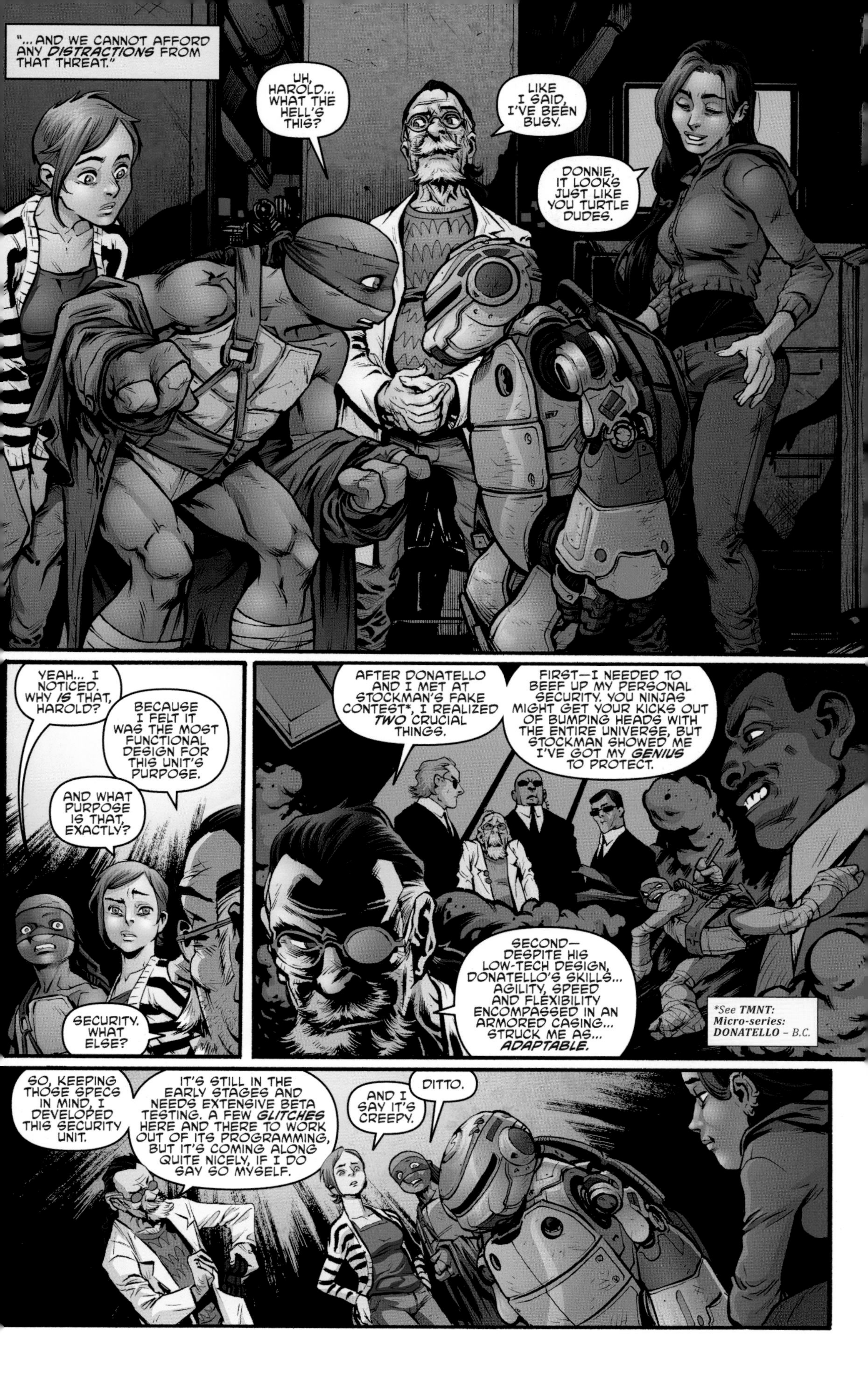
"...AND WE CANNOT AFFORD ANY DISTRACTIONS FROM THAT THREAT."
UH, HAROLD... WHAT THE HELL'S THIS?
LIKE I SAID, I'VE BEEN BUSY.
DONNIE, IT LOOKS JUST LIKE YOU TURTLE DUDES.
YEAH... I NOTICED. WHY IS THAT, HAROLD?
BECAUSE I FELT IT WAS THE MOST FUNCTIONAL DESIGN FOR THIS UNIT'S PURPOSE.
AND WHAT PURPOSE IS THAT, EXACTLY?
SECURITY. WHAT ELSE?
AFTER DONATELLO AND I MET AT STOCKMAN'S FAKE CONTEST*, I REALIZED TWO CRUCIAL THINGS.
FIRST—I NEEDED TO BEEF UP MY PERSONAL SECURITY. YOU NINJAS MIGHT GET YOUR KICKS OUT OF BUMPING HEADS WITH THE ENTIRE UNIVERSE, BUT STOCKMAN SHOWED ME I'VE GOT MY GENIUS TO PROTECT.
SECOND—DESPITE HIS LOW-TECH DESIGN, DONATELLO'S SKILLS... AGILITY, SPEED AND FLEXIBILITY ENCOMPASSED IN AN ARMORED CASING... STRUCK ME AS... ADAPTABLE.
*See TMNT: Micro-series: DONATELLO – B.C.
SO, KEEPING THOSE SPECS IN MIND, I DEVELOPED THIS SECURITY UNIT.
IT'S STILL IN THE EARLY STAGES AND NEEDS EXTENSIVE BETA TESTING. A FEW GLITCHES HERE AND THERE TO WORK OUT OF ITS PROGRAMMING, BUT IT'S COMING ALONG QUITE NICELY, IF I DO SAY SO MYSELF.
AND I SAY IT'S CREEPY.
DITTO.

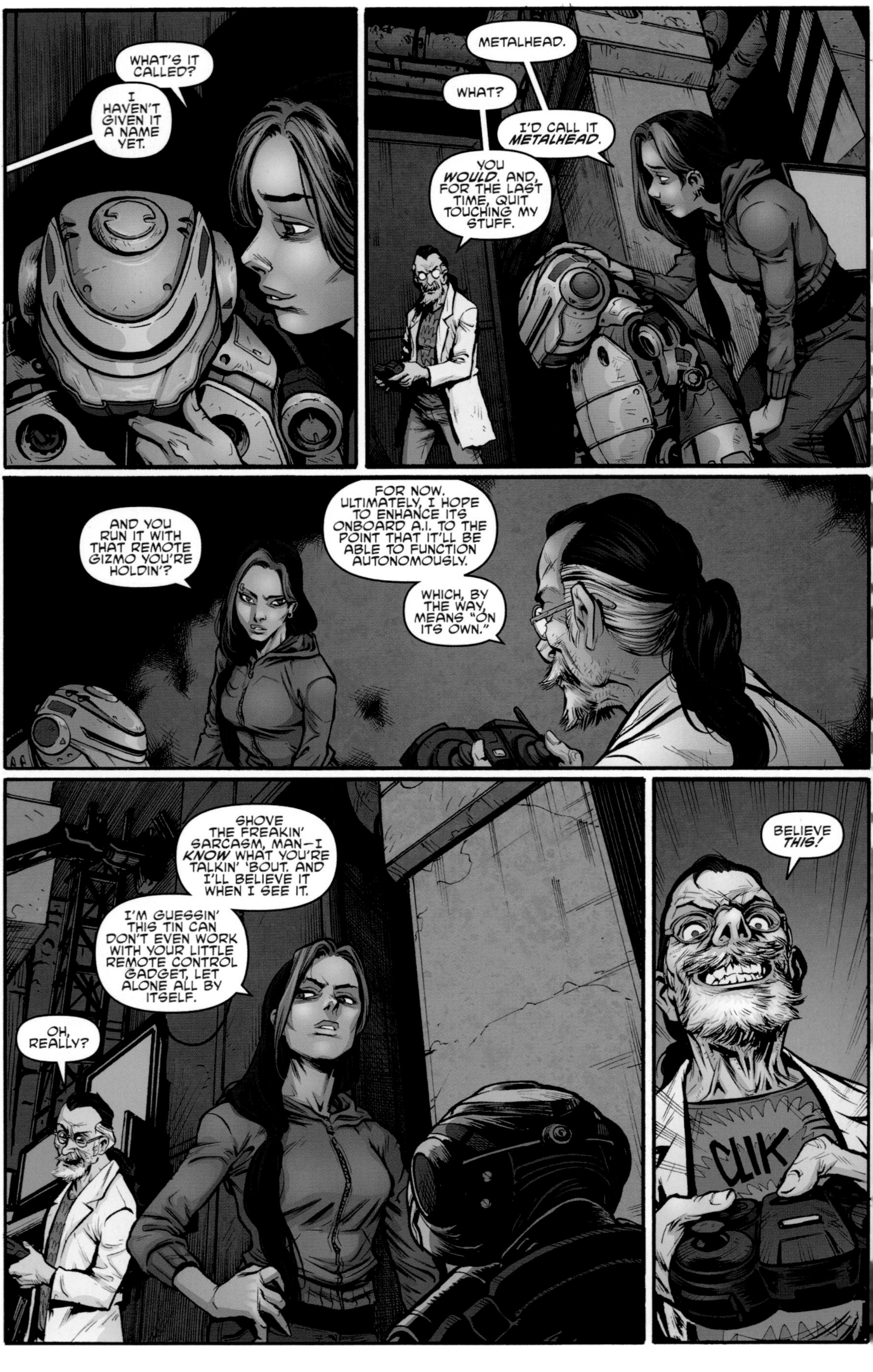
WHAT'S IT CALLED?
I HAVEN'T GIVEN IT A NAME YET.
METALHEAD.
WHAT?
I'D CALL IT *METALHEAD*.
YOU *WOULD*. AND, FOR THE LAST TIME, QUIT TOUCHING MY STUFF.
AND YOU RUN IT WITH THAT REMOTE GIZMO YOU'RE HOLDIN'?
FOR NOW. ULTIMATELY, I HOPE TO ENHANCE ITS ONBOARD A.I. TO THE POINT THAT IT'LL BE ABLE TO FUNCTION AUTONOMOUSLY.
WHICH, BY THE WAY, MEANS "ON ITS OWN."
SHOVE THE FREAKIN' SARCASM, MAN—I *KNOW* WHAT YOU'RE TALKIN' 'BOUT. AND I'LL BELIEVE IT WHEN I SEE IT.
I'M GUESSIN' THIS TIN CAN DON'T EVEN WORK WITH YOUR LITTLE REMOTE CONTROL GADGET, LET ALONE ALL BY ITSELF.
OH, REALLY?
BELIEVE *THIS!*
CLIK

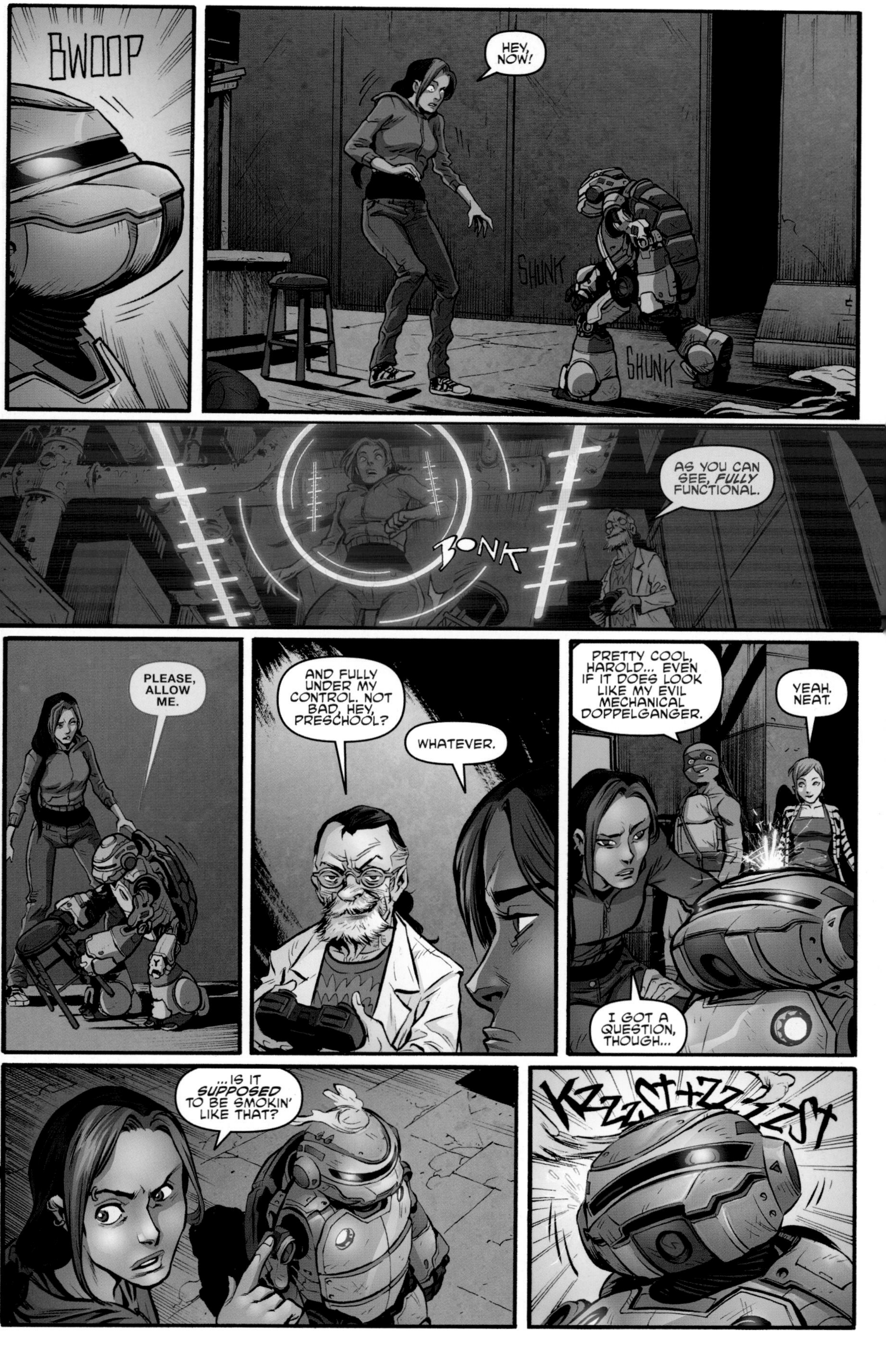
BWOOP
HEY, NOW!
SHUNK
SHUNK
AS YOU CAN SEE, FULLY FUNCTIONAL.
BONK
PLEASE, ALLOW ME.
AND FULLY UNDER MY CONTROL. NOT BAD, HEY, PRESCHOOL?
WHATEVER.
PRETTY COOL, HAROLD... EVEN IF IT DOES LOOK LIKE MY EVIL MECHANICAL DOPPELGANGER.
YEAH. NEAT.
I GOT A QUESTION, THOUGH...
...IS IT SUPPOSED TO BE SMOKIN' LIKE THAT?

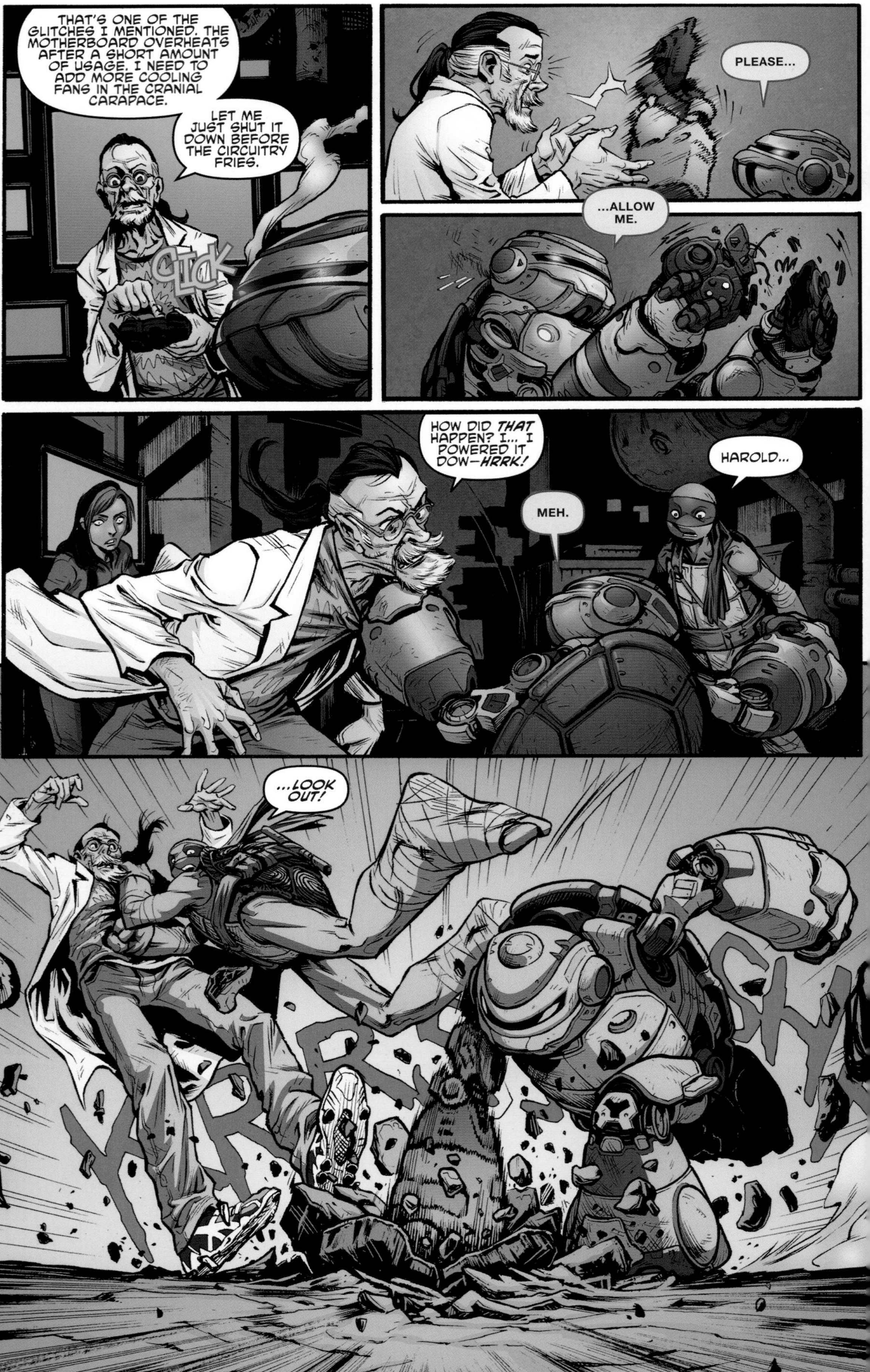

THAT'S ONE OF THE GLITCHES I MENTIONED. THE MOTHERBOARD OVERHEATS AFTER A SHORT AMOUNT OF USAGE. I NEED TO ADD MORE COOLING FANS IN THE CRANIAL CARAPACE.
LET ME JUST SHUT IT DOWN BEFORE THE CIRCUITRY FRIES.
CLICK
PLEASE...
...ALLOW ME.
HOW DID THAT HAPPEN? I... I POWERED IT DOW-HRRK!
HAROLD...
MEH.
...LOOK OUT!

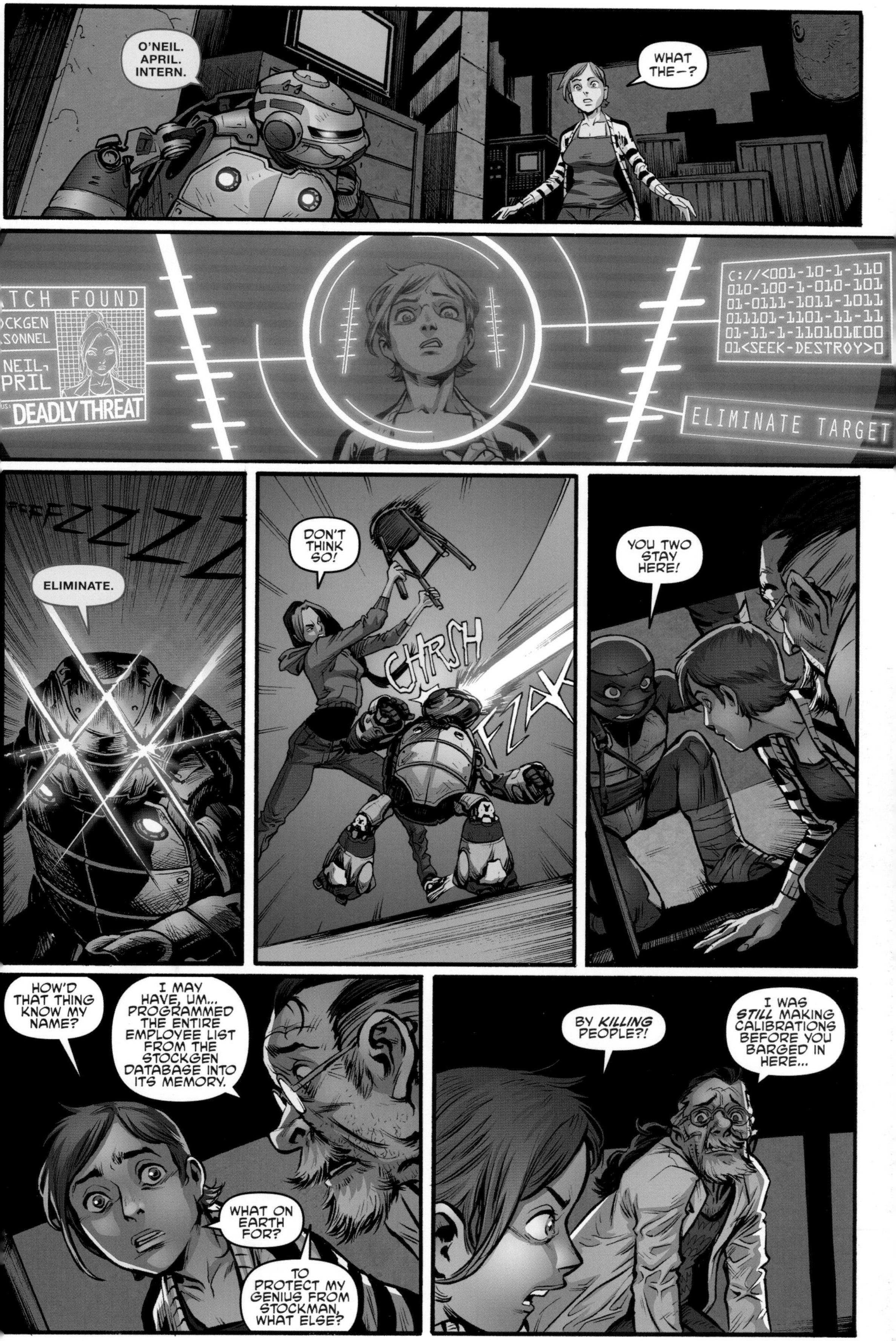
O'NEIL. APRIL. INTERN.
WHAT THE—?
TCH FOUND
OCKGEN
SONNEL
NEIL,
PRIL
DEADLY THREAT
C://<001-10-1-110
010-100-1-010-101
01-0111-1011-1011
011101-1101-11-11
01-11-1-110101C00
01<SEEK-DESTROY>0
ELIMINATE TARGET
FFFZZZZ
ELIMINATE.
DON'T THINK SO!
CHRSH
FZAK
YOU TWO STAY HERE!
HOW'D THAT THING KNOW MY NAME?
I MAY HAVE, UM... PROGRAMMED THE ENTIRE EMPLOYEE LIST FROM THE STOCKGEN DATABASE INTO ITS MEMORY.
WHAT ON EARTH FOR?
TO PROTECT MY GENIUS FROM STOCKMAN, WHAT ELSE?
BY KILLING PEOPLE?!
I WAS STILL MAKING CALIBRATIONS BEFORE YOU BARGED IN HERE...

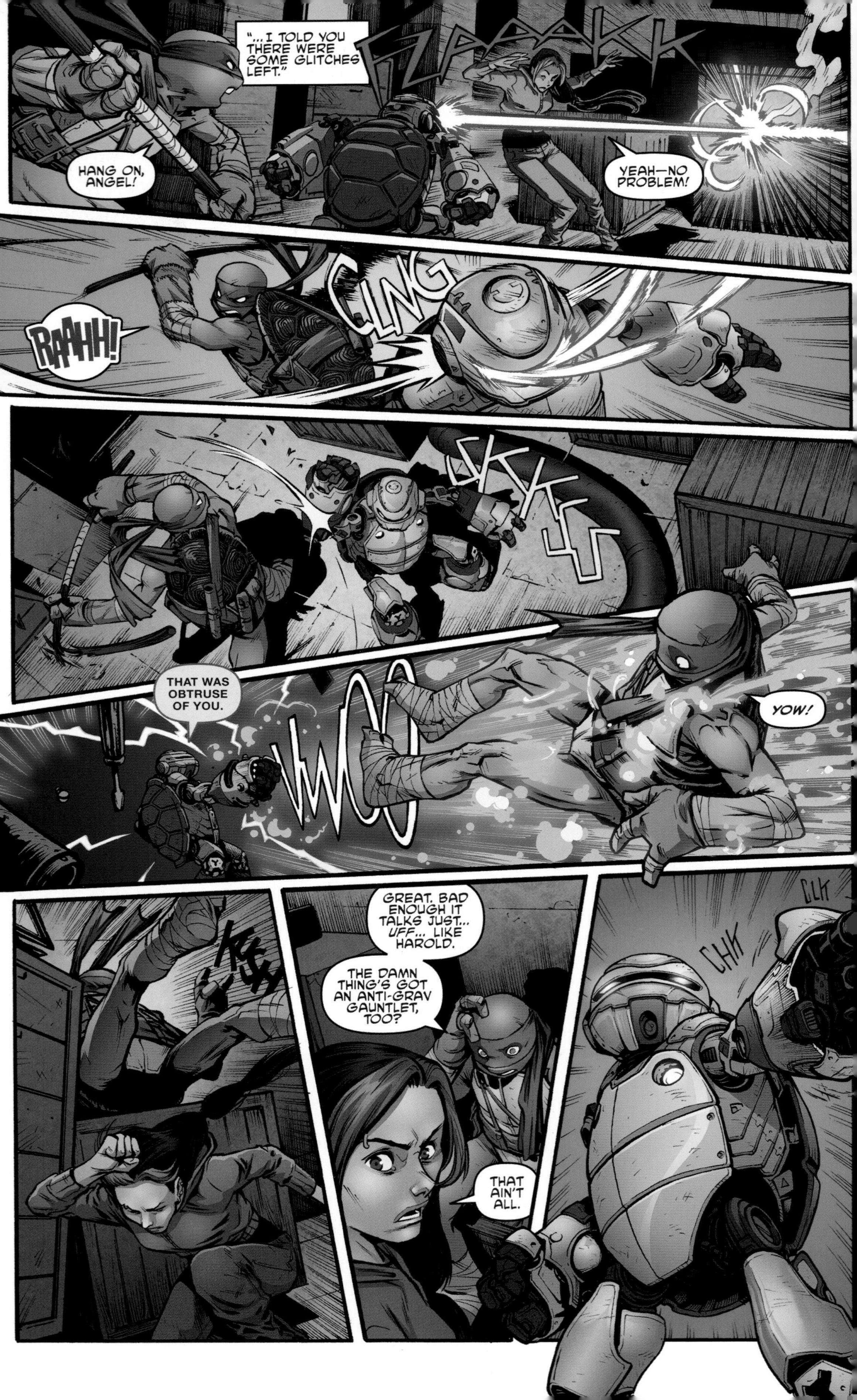
"...I TOLD YOU THERE WERE SOME GLITCHES LEFT."
FZRAAKK
HANG ON, ANGEL!
YEAH—NO PROBLEM!
RAAHH!
CLING
SKKEESS
THAT WAS OBTRUSE OF YOU.
VWOO
YOW!
GREAT. BAD ENOUGH IT TALKS JUST... UFF... LIKE HAROLD.
THE DAMN THING'S GOT AN ANTI-GRAV GAUNTLET, TOO?
THAT AIN'T ALL.
CLK
CHK

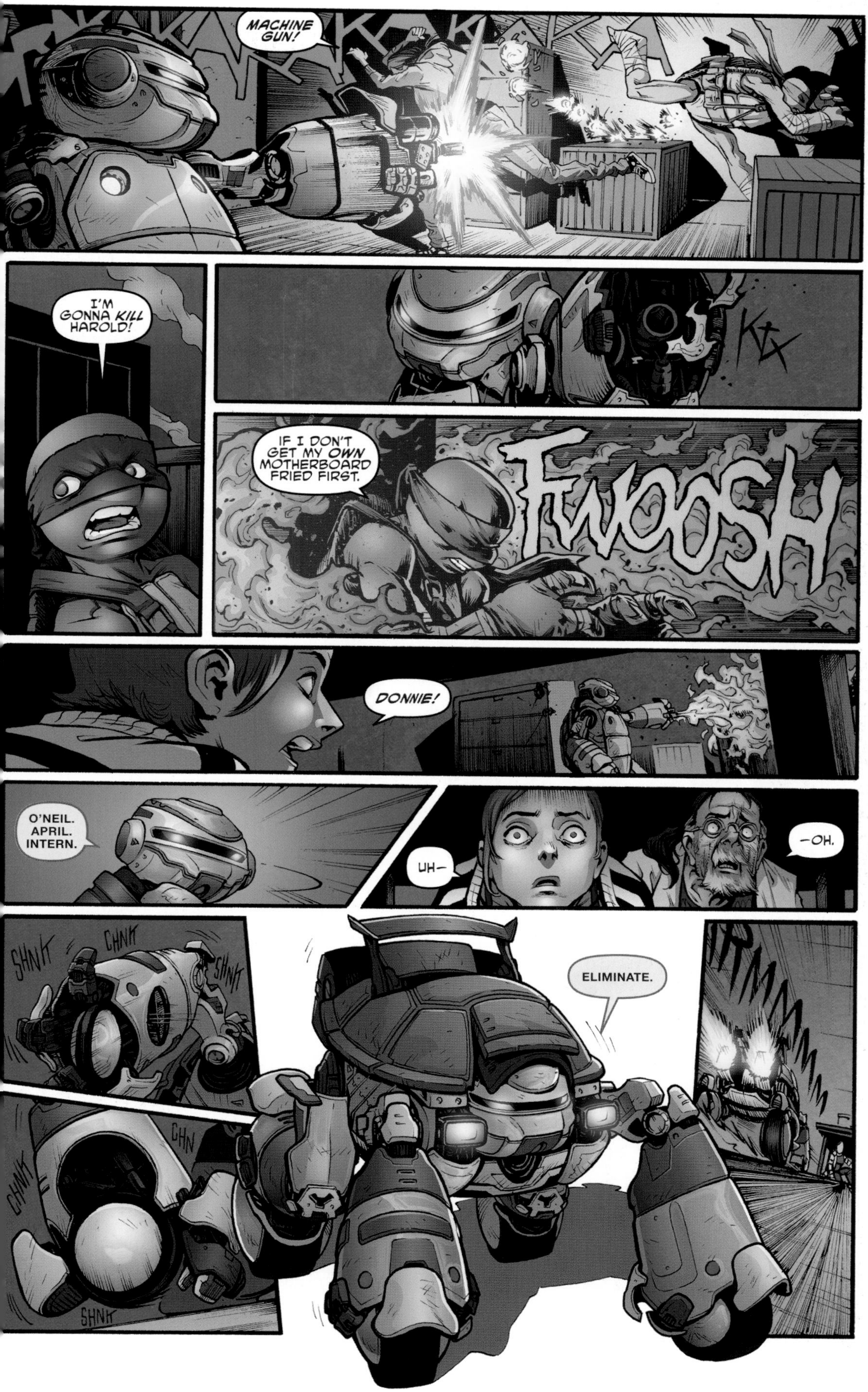
MACHINE GUN!
I'M GONNA KILL HAROLD!
KLIK
IF I DON'T GET MY OWN MOTHERBOARD FRIED FIRST.
FWOOSH
DONNIE!
O'NEIL. APRIL. INTERN.
UH–
–OH.
SHNK
CHNK
SHNK
ELIMINATE.
CHN
CHNK
SHNK

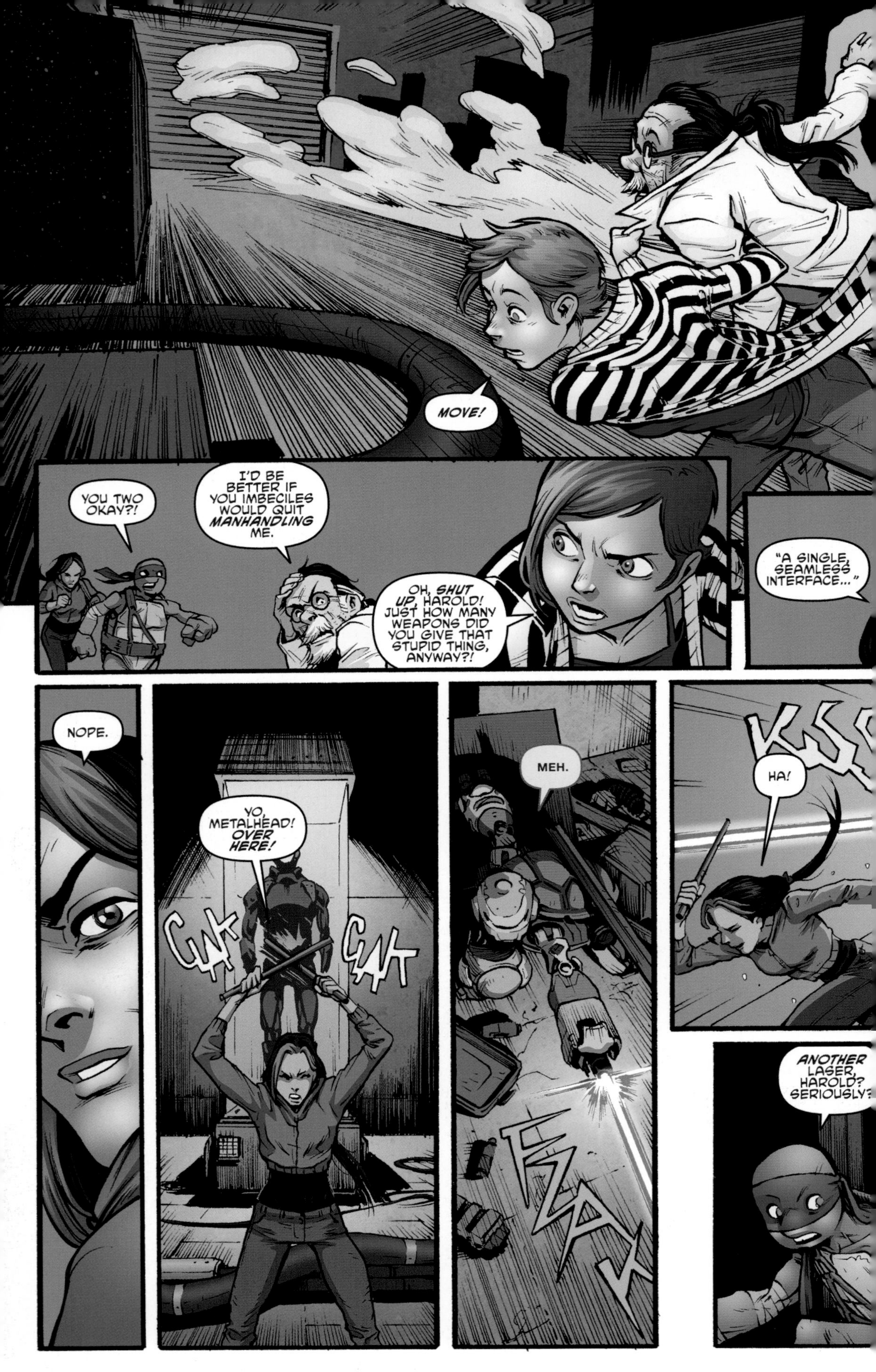
MOVE!
YOU TWO OKAY?!
I'D BE BETTER IF YOU IMBECILES WOULD QUIT MANHANDLING ME.
OH, SHUT UP, HAROLD! JUST HOW MANY WEAPONS DID YOU GIVE THAT STUPID THING, ANYWAY?!
"A SINGLE, SEAMLESS INTERFACE..."
NOPE.
YO, METALHEAD! OVER HERE!
CLAK
CLAK
MEH.
FZZAK
HA!
ANOTHER LASER, HAROLD? SERIOUSLY?

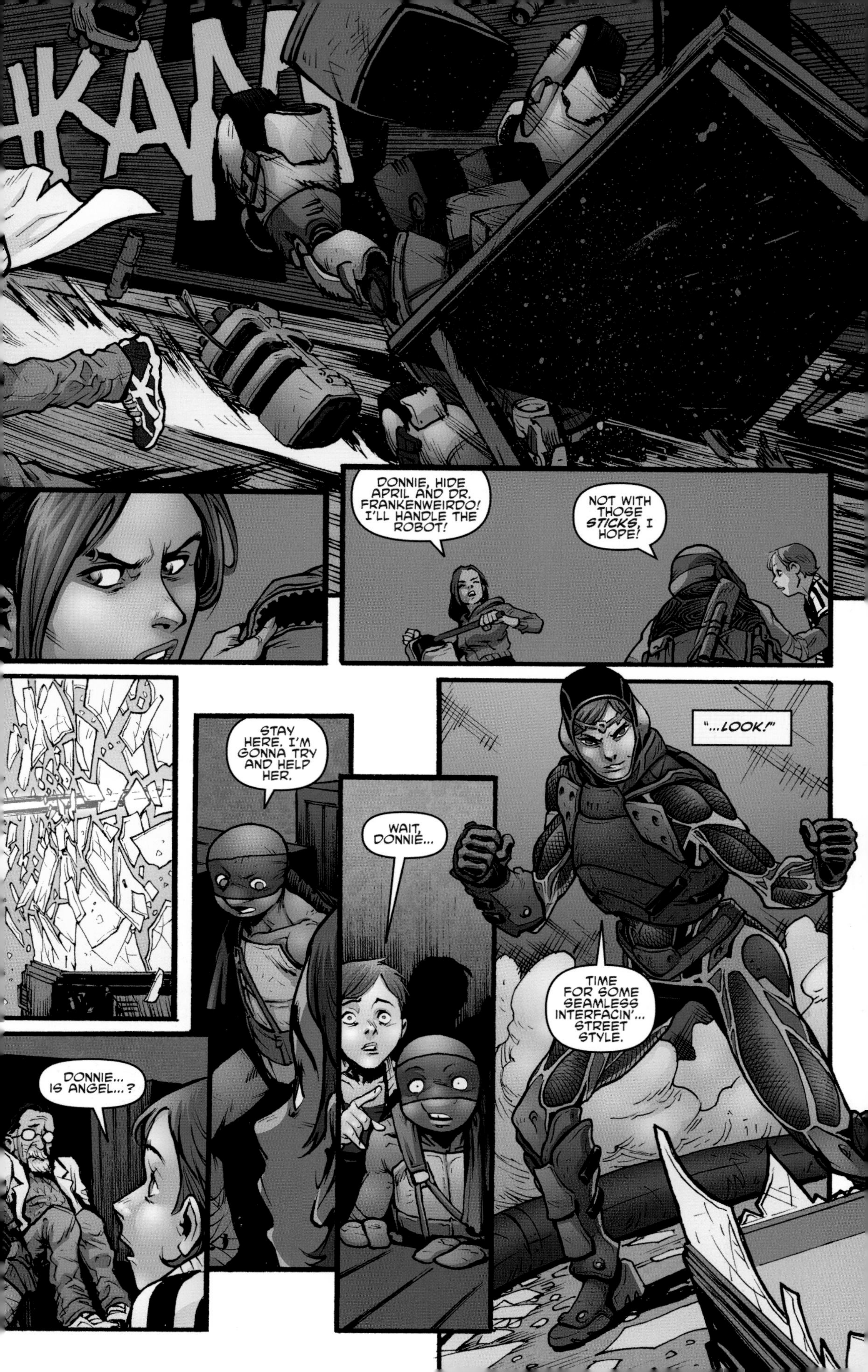
KAM
DONNIE, HIDE APRIL AND DR. FRANKENWEIRDO! I'LL HANDLE THE ROBOT!
NOT WITH THOSE STICKS, I HOPE!
STAY HERE. I'M GONNA TRY AND HELP HER.
WAIT, DONNIE...
"...LOOK!"
TIME FOR SOME SEAMLESS INTERFACIN'... STREET STYLE.
DONNIE... IS ANGEL...?

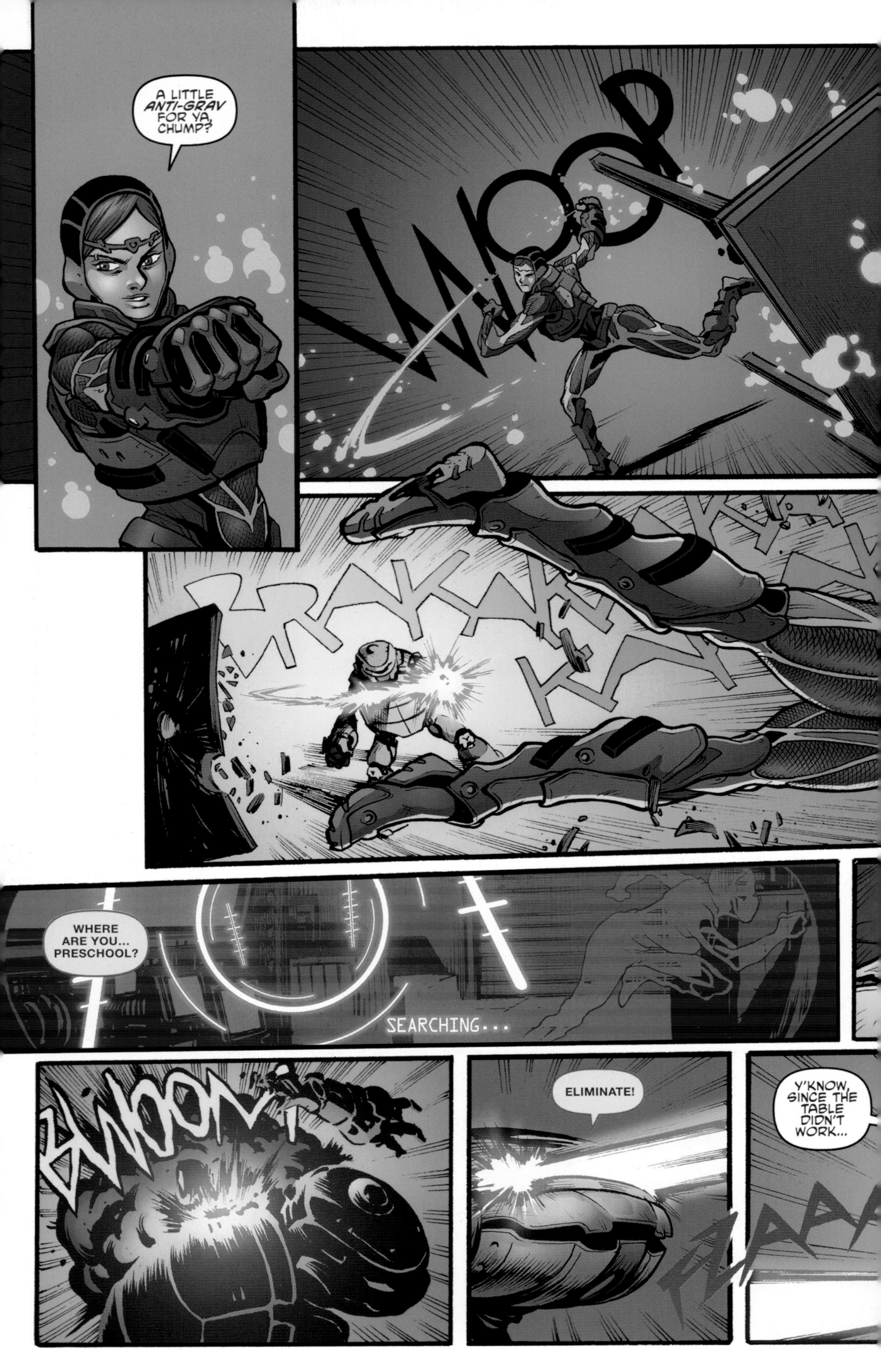
A LITTLE ANTI-GRAV FOR YA, CHUMP?
WHOOP
WHERE ARE YOU... PRESCHOOL?
SEARCHING...
ELIMINATE!
Y'KNOW, SINCE THE TABLE DIDN'T WORK...

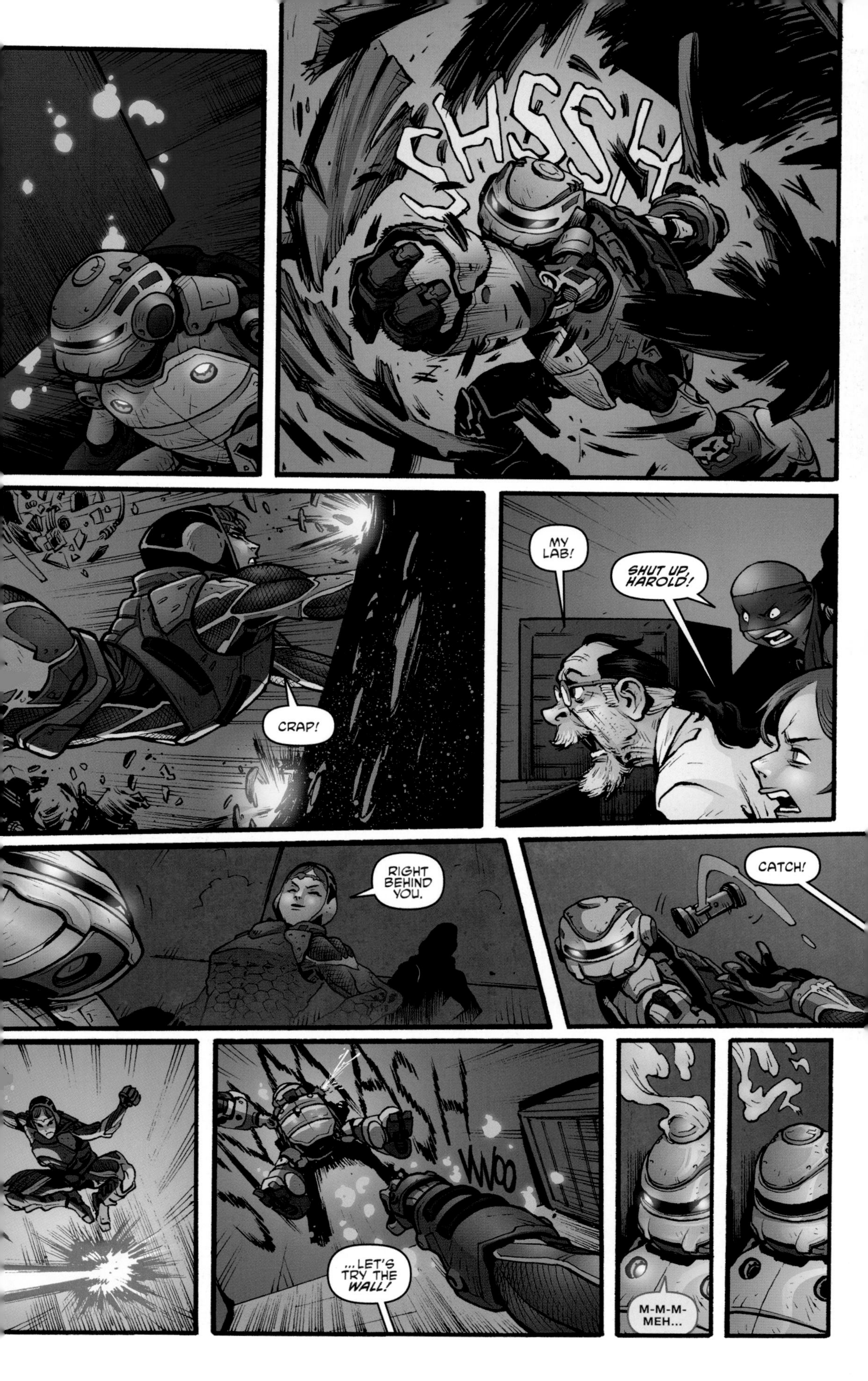
CHSSH
CRAP!
MY LAB!
SHUT UP, HAROLD!
RIGHT BEHIND YOU.
CATCH!
...LET'S TRY THE WALL!
VVVOO
M-M-M-MEH...

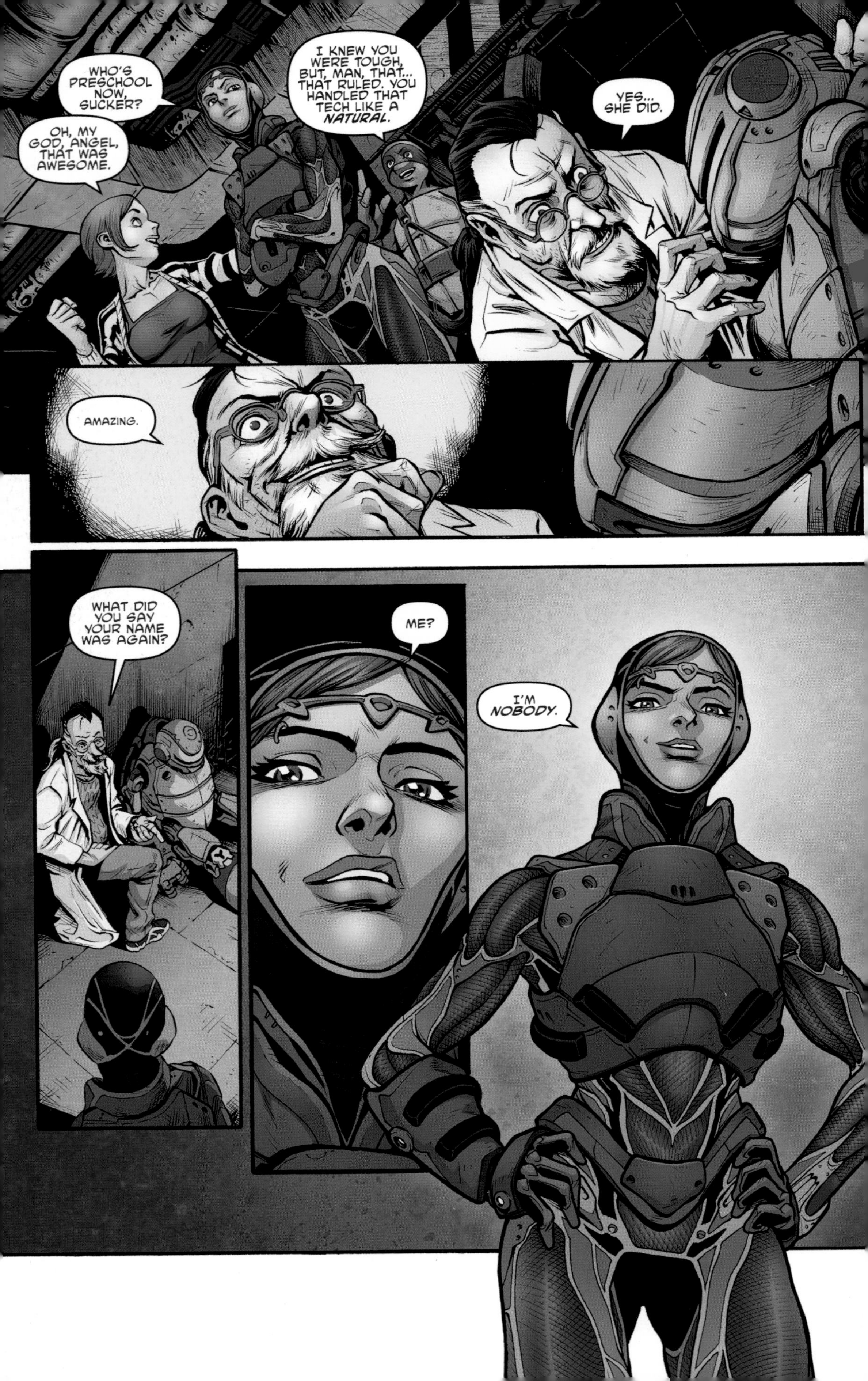
WHO'S PRESCHOOL NOW, SUCKER?
OH, MY GOD, ANGEL, THAT WAS AWESOME.
I KNEW YOU WERE TOUGH, BUT, MAN, THAT... THAT RULED. YOU HANDLED THAT TECH LIKE A *NATURAL*.
YES... SHE DID.
AMAZING.
WHAT DID YOU SAY YOUR NAME WAS AGAIN?
ME?
I'M *NOBODY*.

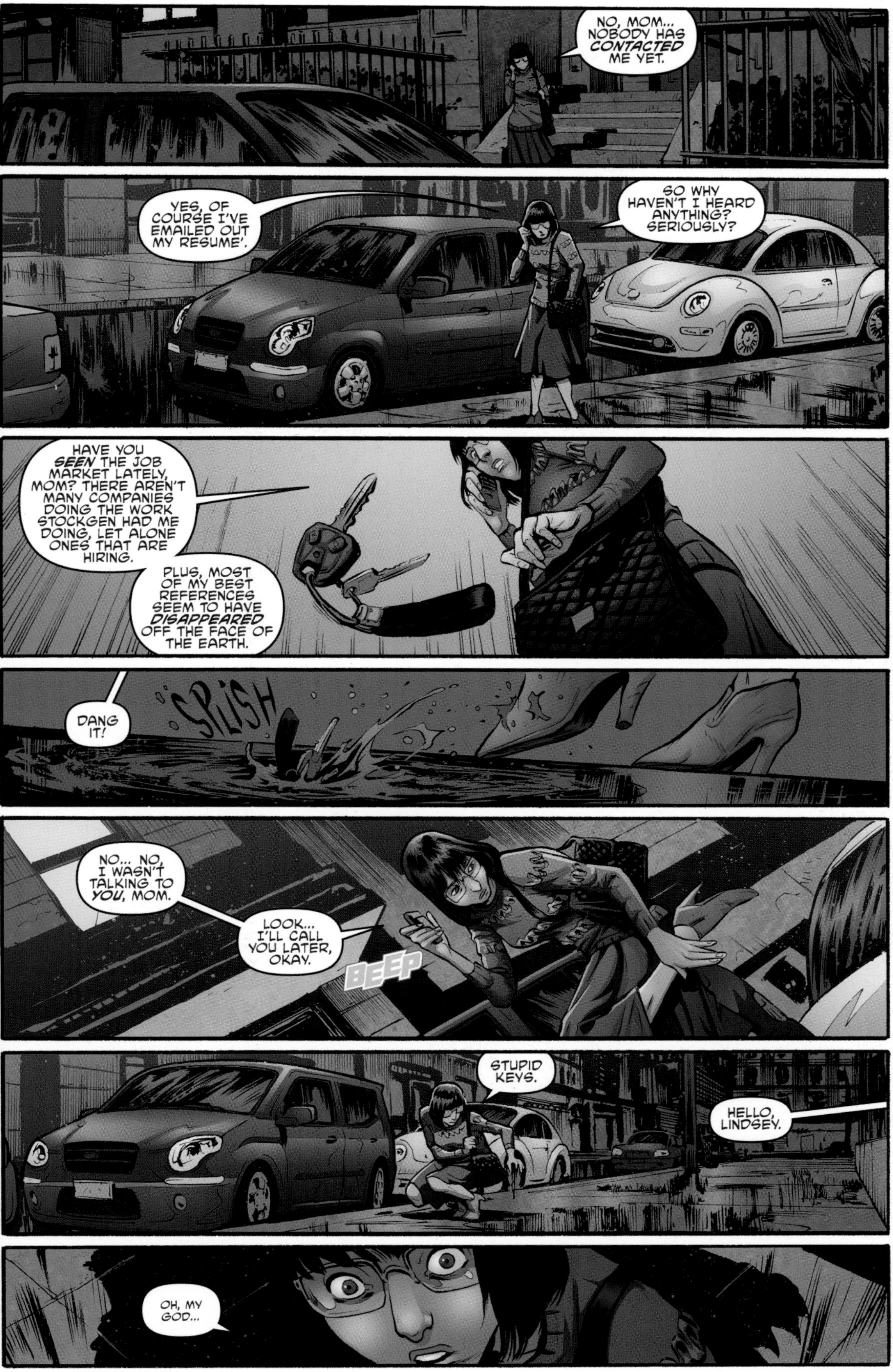
NO, MOM... NOBODY HAS CONTACTED ME YET.
YES, OF COURSE I'VE EMAILED OUT MY RESUME'.
SO WHY HAVEN'T I HEARD ANYTHING? SERIOUSLY?
HAVE YOU SEEN THE JOB MARKET LATELY, MOM? THERE AREN'T MANY COMPANIES DOING THE WORK STOCKGEN HAD ME DOING, LET ALONE ONES THAT ARE HIRING.
PLUS, MOST OF MY BEST REFERENCES SEEM TO HAVE DISAPPEARED OFF THE FACE OF THE EARTH.
DANG IT!
SPLISH
NO... NO, I WASN'T TALKING TO YOU, MOM.
LOOK... I'LL CALL YOU LATER, OKAY.
BEEP
STUPID KEYS.
HELLO, LINDSEY.
OH, MY GOD...

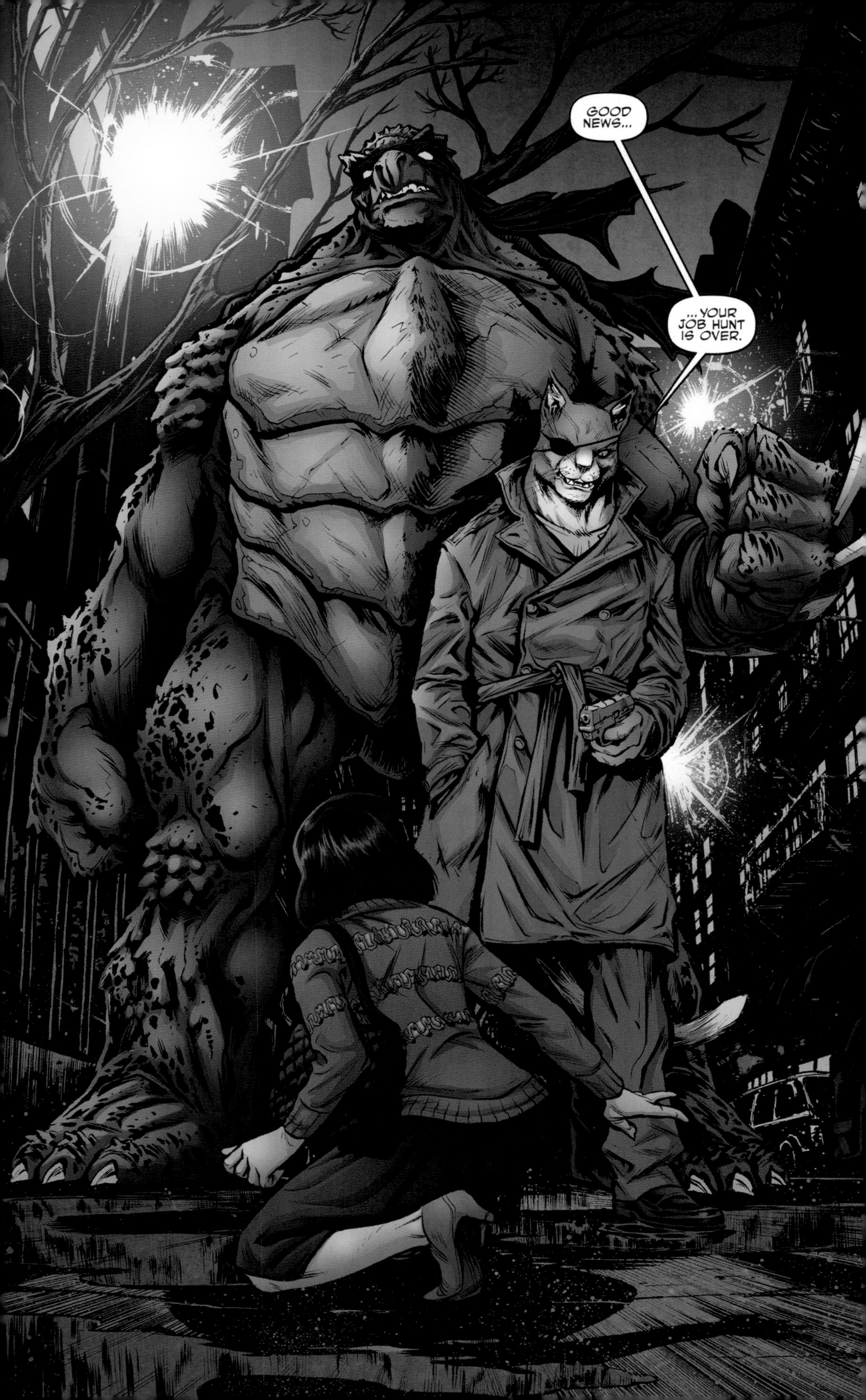
GOOD NEWS...
...YOUR JOB HUNT IS OVER.

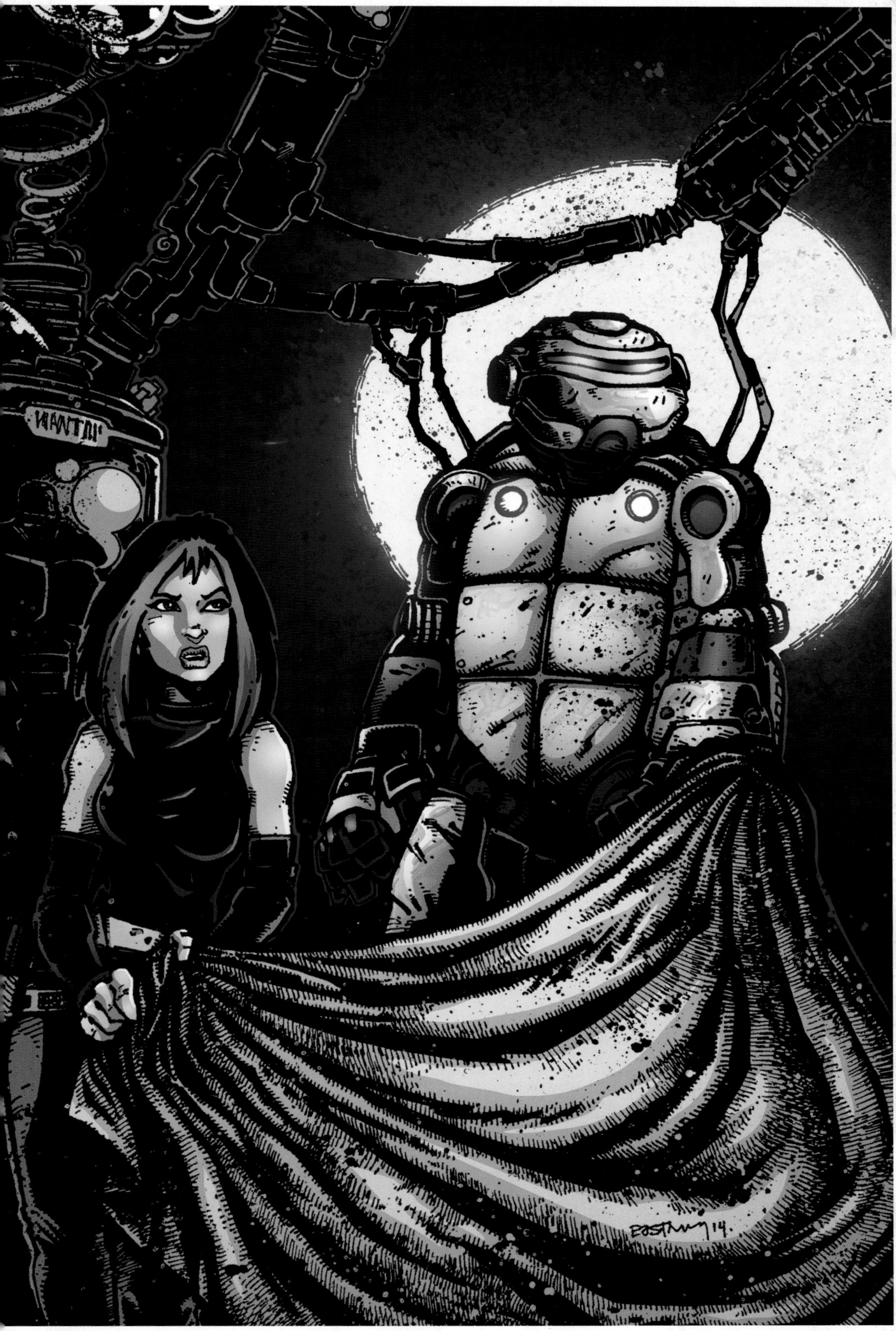

Cover by KEVIN EASTMAN
Colors by RONDA PATTISON

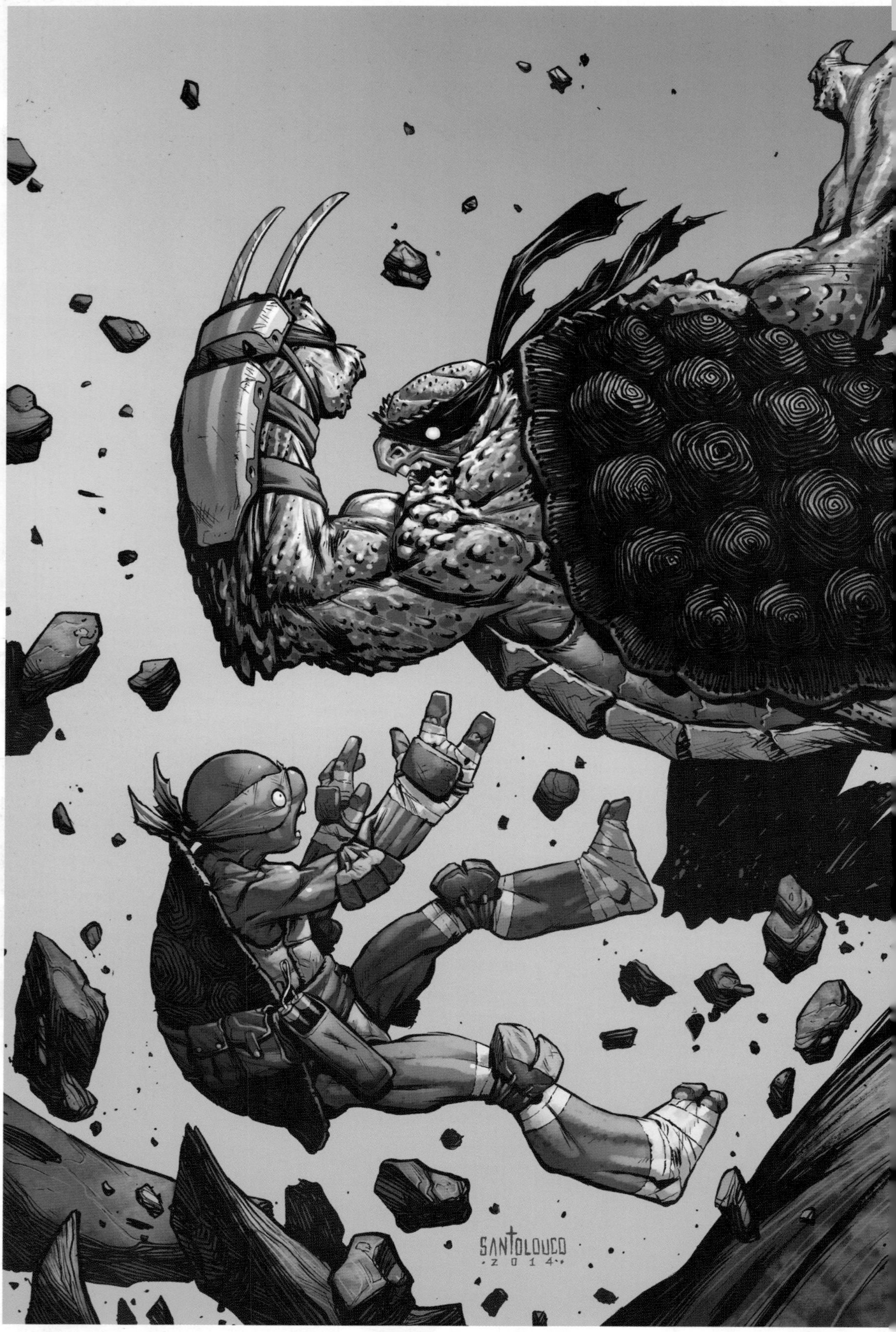
SANTOLOUCO
2014

Cover by MATEUS SANTOLOUCO

TMNT #35

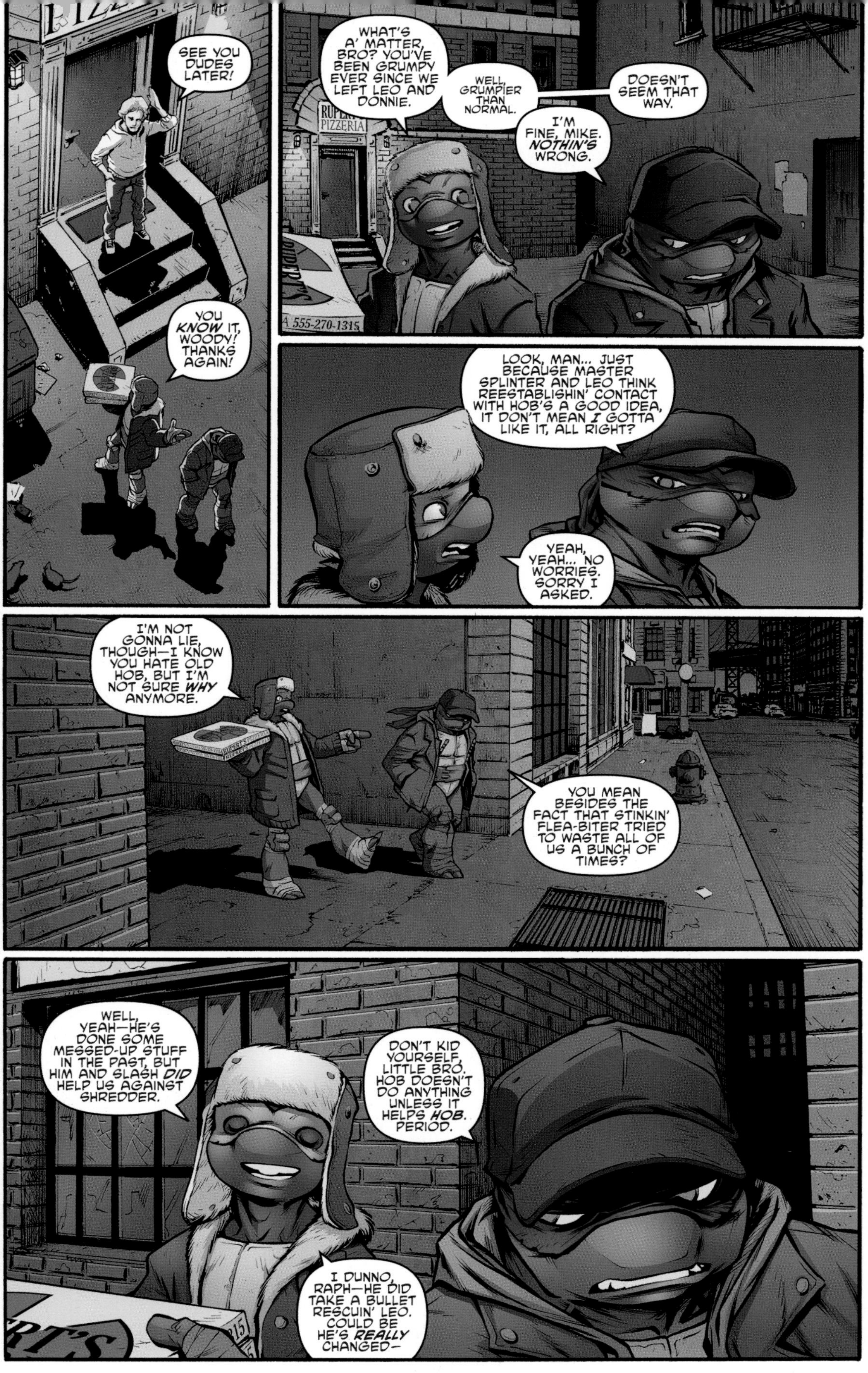
PIZZ
SEE YOU DUDES LATER!
YOU KNOW IT, WOODY! THANKS AGAIN!
RUPERT'S PIZZERIA
WHAT'S A' MATTER, BRO? YOU'VE BEEN GRUMPY EVER SINCE WE LEFT LEO AND DONNIE.
WELL, GRUMPIER THAN NORMAL.
DOESN'T SEEM THAT WAY.
I'M FINE, MIKE. NOTHIN'S WRONG.
A 555-270-1315
LOOK, MAN... JUST BECAUSE MASTER SPLINTER AND LEO THINK REESTABLISHIN' CONTACT WITH HOB'S A GOOD IDEA, IT DON'T MEAN I GOTTA LIKE IT, ALL RIGHT?
YEAH, YEAH... NO WORRIES. SORRY I ASKED.
I'M NOT GONNA LIE, THOUGH—I KNOW YOU HATE OLD HOB, BUT I'M NOT SURE WHY ANYMORE.
YOU MEAN BESIDES THE FACT THAT STINKIN' FLEA-BITER TRIED TO WASTE ALL OF US A BUNCH OF TIMES?
WELL, YEAH—HE'S DONE SOME MESSED-UP STUFF IN THE PAST, BUT HIM AND SLASH DID HELP US AGAINST SHREDDER.
DON'T KID YOURSELF, LITTLE BRO. HOB DOESN'T DO ANYTHING UNLESS IT HELPS HOB. PERIOD.
I DUNNO, RAPH—HE DID TAKE A BULLET RESCUIN' LEO. COULD BE HE'S REALLY CHANGED—

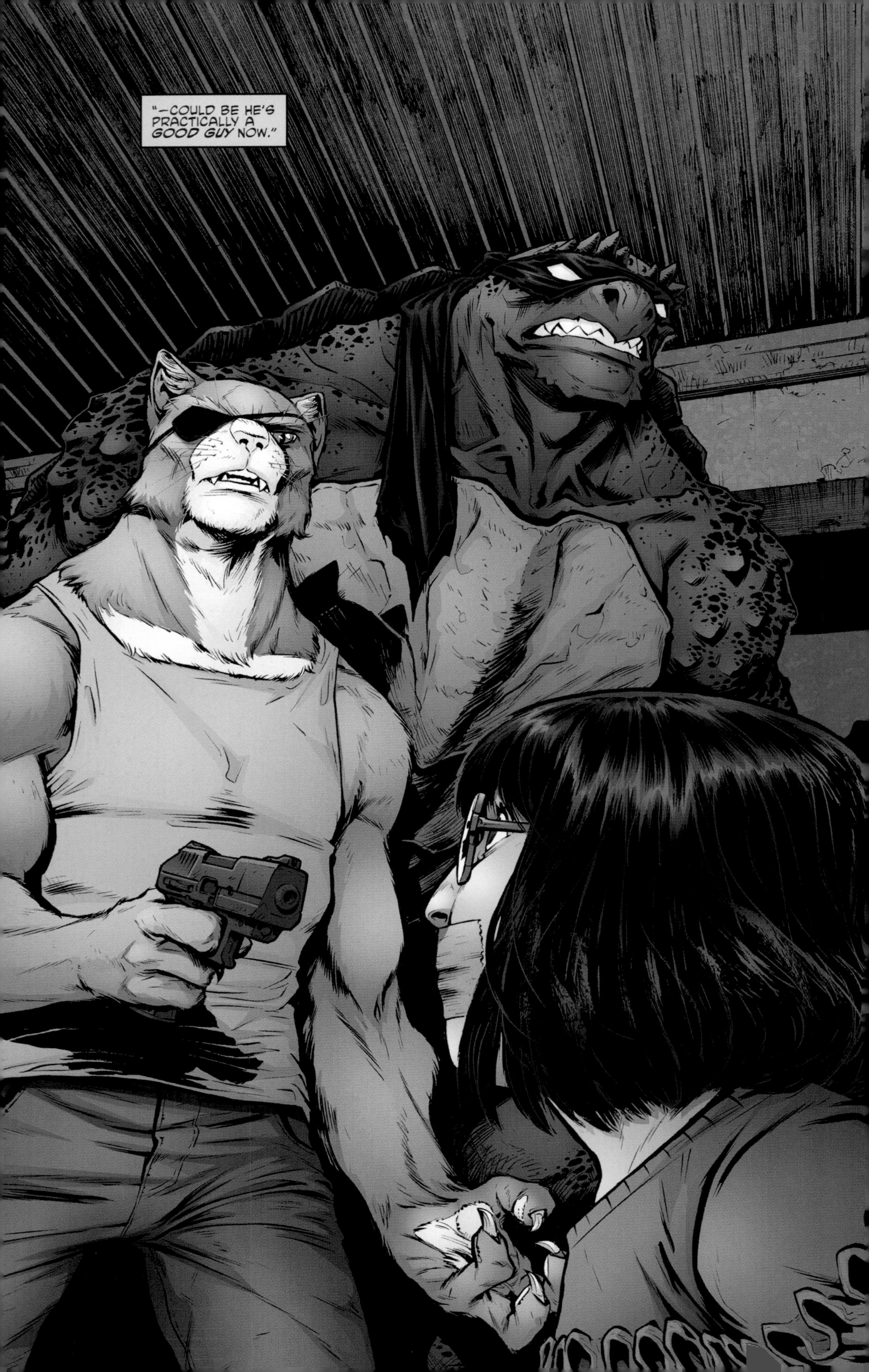
"—COULD BE HE'S PRACTICALLY A *GOOD GUY* NOW."

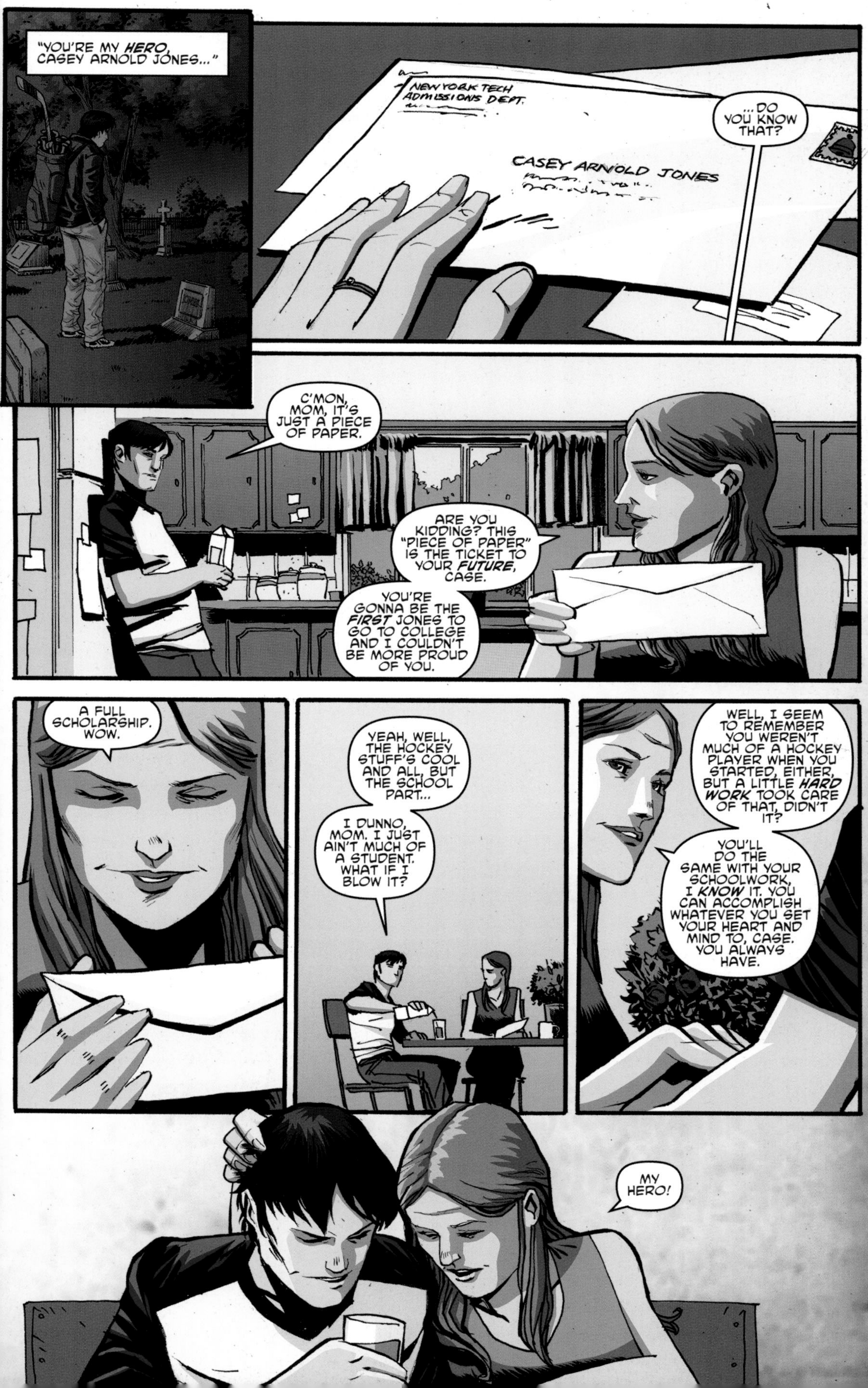
"YOU'RE MY HERO, CASEY ARNOLD JONES..."
NEW YORK TECH ADMISSIONS DEPT.
CASEY ARNOLD JONES
...DO YOU KNOW THAT?
C'MON, MOM, IT'S JUST A PIECE OF PAPER.
ARE YOU KIDDING? THIS "PIECE OF PAPER" IS THE TICKET TO YOUR FUTURE, CASE.
YOU'RE GONNA BE THE FIRST JONES TO GO TO COLLEGE AND I COULDN'T BE MORE PROUD OF YOU.
A FULL SCHOLARSHIP. WOW.
YEAH, WELL, THE HOCKEY STUFF'S COOL AND ALL, BUT THE SCHOOL PART...
I DUNNO, MOM. I JUST AIN'T MUCH OF A STUDENT. WHAT IF I BLOW IT?
WELL, I SEEM TO REMEMBER YOU WEREN'T MUCH OF A HOCKEY PLAYER WHEN YOU STARTED, EITHER, BUT A LITTLE HARD WORK TOOK CARE OF THAT, DIDN'T IT?
YOU'LL DO THE SAME WITH YOUR SCHOOLWORK, I KNOW IT. YOU CAN ACCOMPLISH WHATEVER YOU SET YOUR HEART AND MIND TO, CASE. YOU ALWAYS HAVE.
MY HERO!

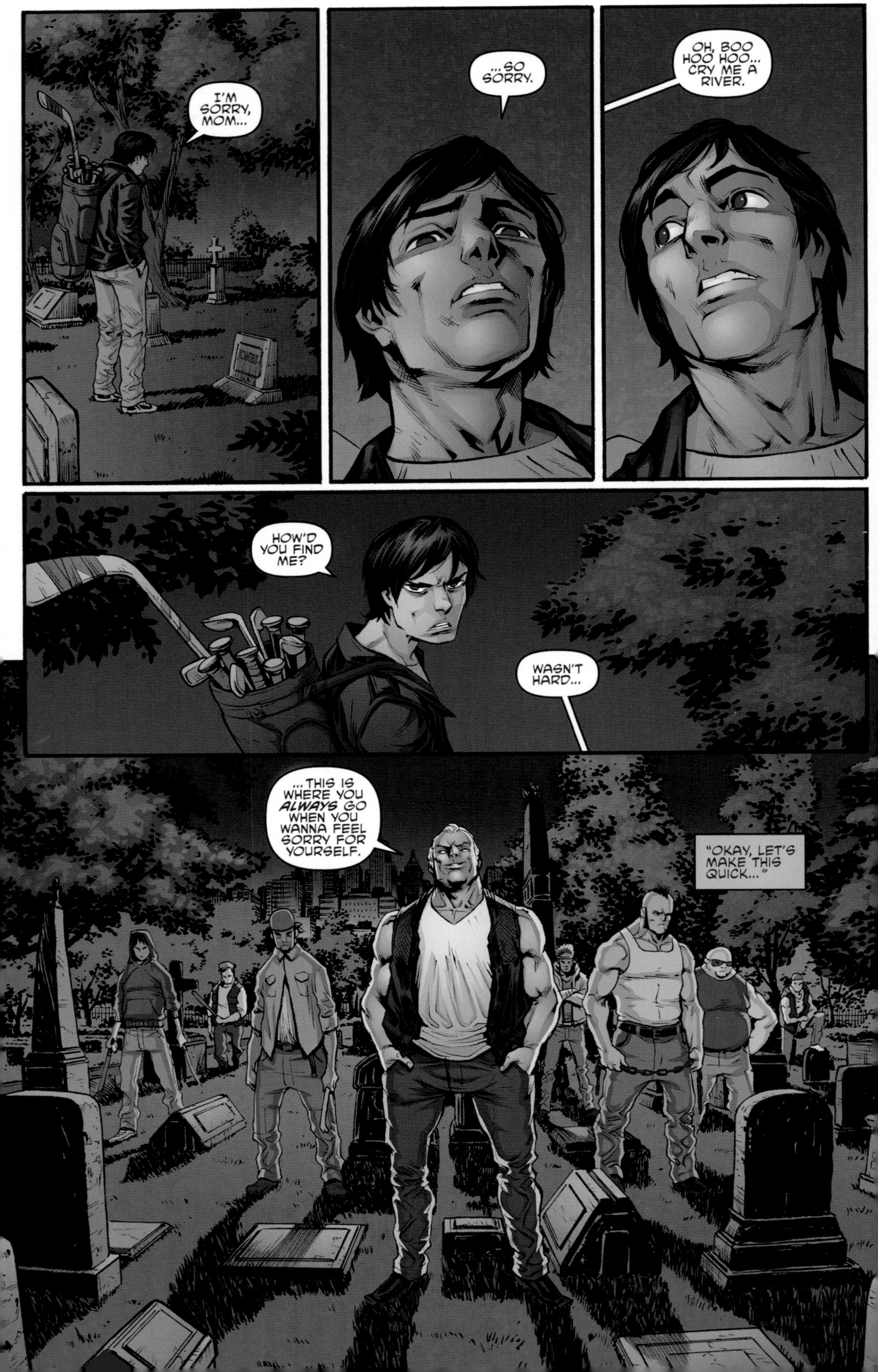
I'M SORRY, MOM...
...SO SORRY.
OH, BOO HOO HOO... CRY ME A RIVER.
HOW'D YOU FIND ME?
WASN'T HARD...
...THIS IS WHERE YOU *ALWAYS* GO WHEN YOU WANNA FEEL SORRY FOR YOURSELF.
"OKAY, LET'S MAKE THIS QUICK..."

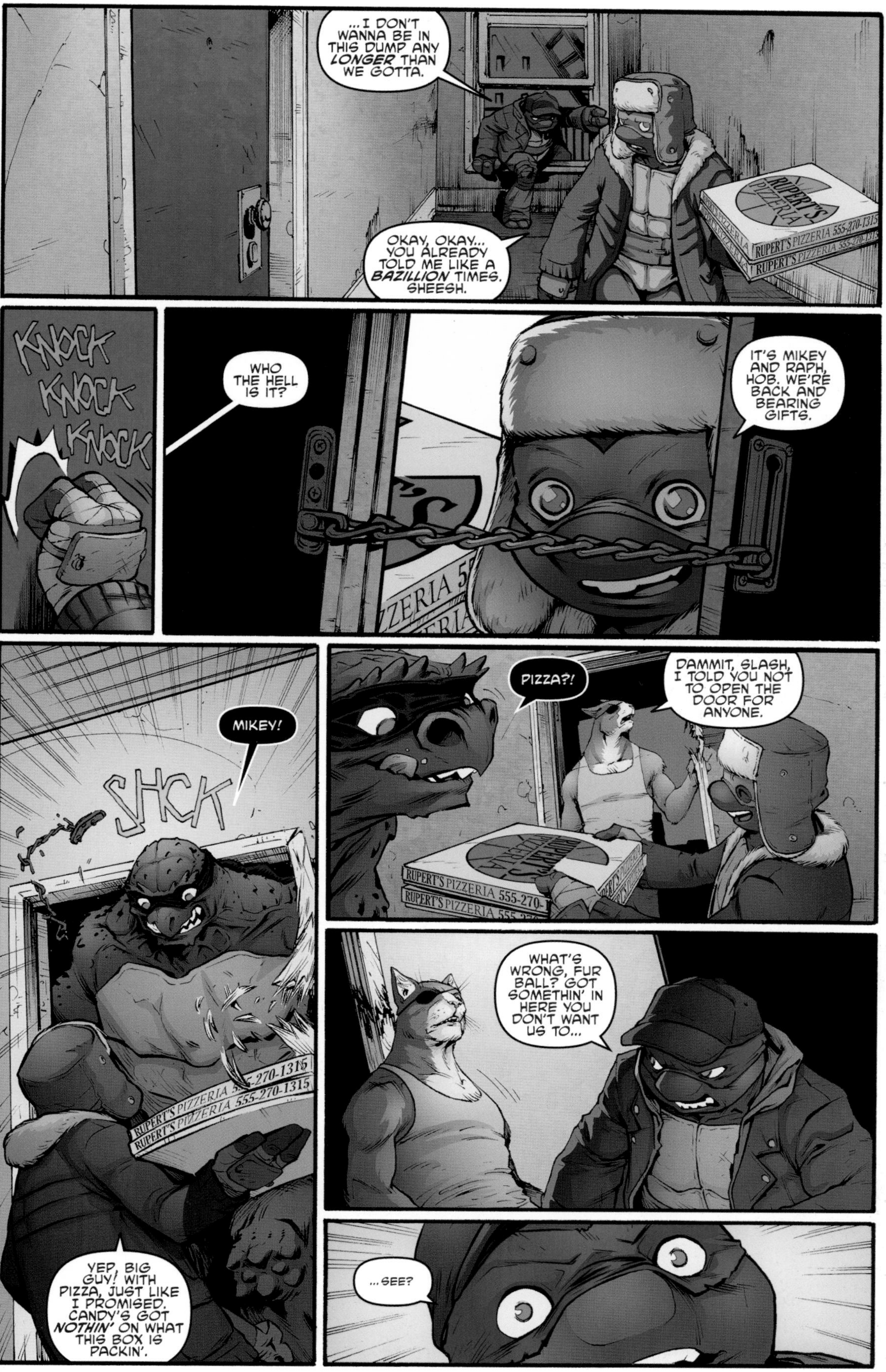
...I DON'T WANNA BE IN THIS DUMP ANY LONGER THAN WE GOTTA.
RUPERT'S PIZZERIA
RUPERT'S PIZZERIA 555-270-1315
OKAY, OKAY... YOU ALREADY TOLD ME LIKE A BAZILLION TIMES. SHEESH.
KNOCK KNOCK KNOCK
WHO THE HELL IS IT?
IT'S MIKEY AND RAPH, HOB. WE'RE BACK AND BEARING GIFTS.
MIKEY!
SHCK
RUPERT'S PIZZERIA 555-270-1315
YEP, BIG GUY! WITH PIZZA, JUST LIKE I PROMISED. CANDY'S GOT NOTHIN' ON WHAT THIS BOX IS PACKIN'.
PIZZA?!
DAMMIT, SLASH, I TOLD YOU NOT TO OPEN THE DOOR FOR ANYONE.
WHAT'S WRONG, FUR BALL? GOT SOMETHIN' IN HERE YOU DON'T WANT US TO...
...SEE?

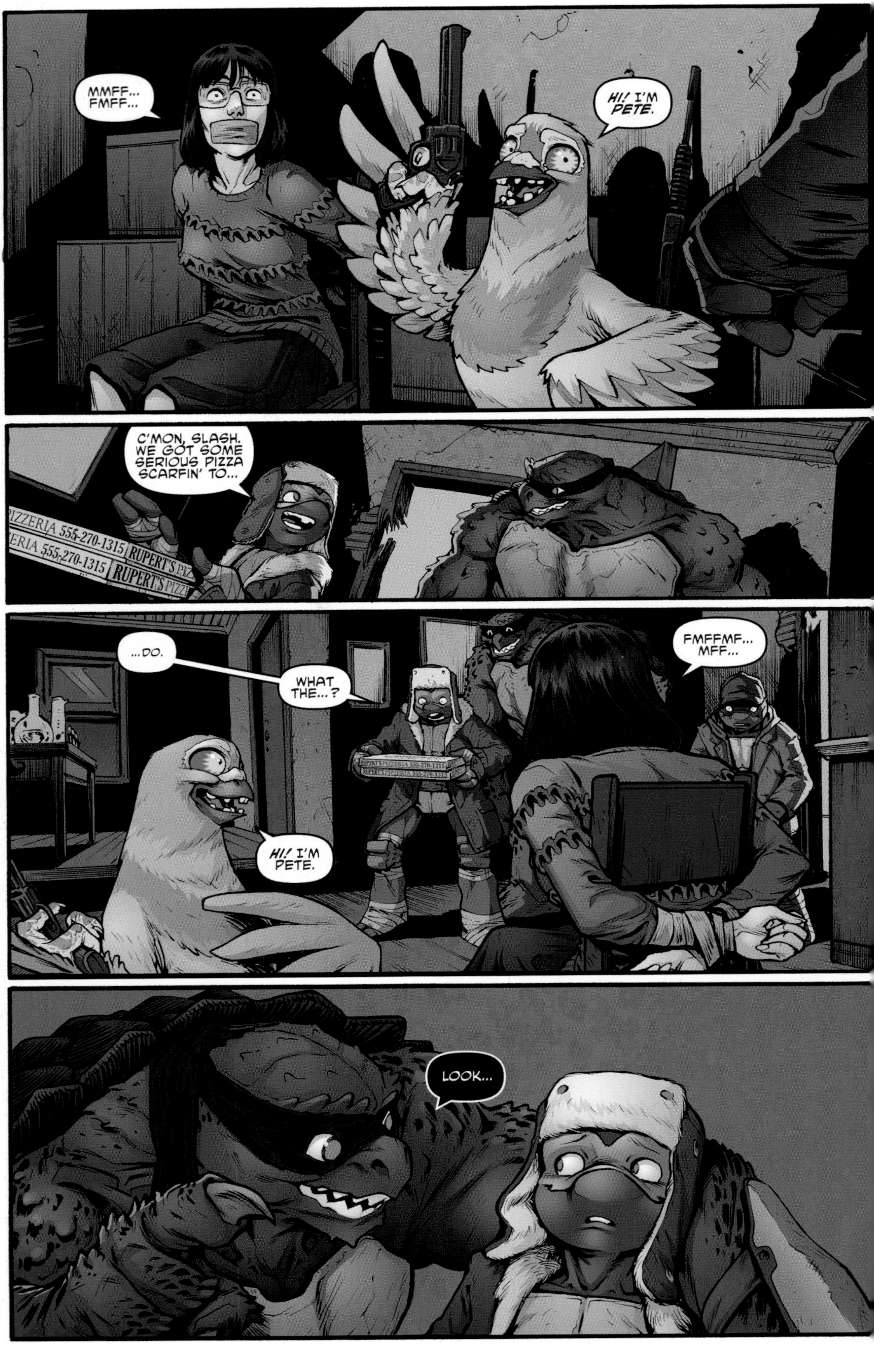
MMFF... FMFF...
HI! I'M PETE.
C'MON, SLASH. WE GOT SOME SERIOUS PIZZA SCARFIN' TO...
RUPERT'S PIZZERIA 555-270-1315
...DO.
WHAT THE...?
FMFFMF... MFF...
HI! I'M PETE.
LOOK...

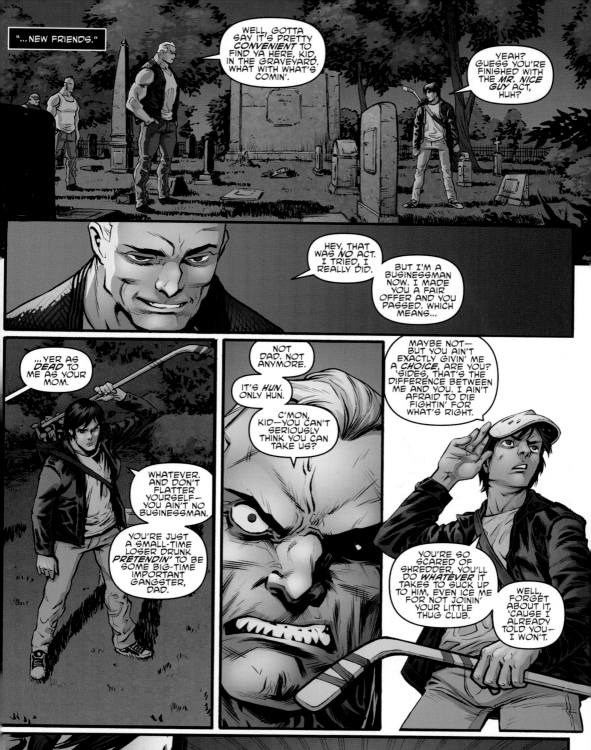

"...NEW FRIENDS."

WELL, GOTTA SAY IT'S PRETTY *CONVENIENT* TO FIND YA HERE, KID, IN THE GRAVEYARD. WHAT WITH WHAT'S COMIN'.

YEAH? GUESS YOU'RE FINISHED WITH THE *MR. NICE GUY* ACT, HUH?

HEY, THAT WAS *NO* ACT. I TRIED, I REALLY DID.

BUT I'M A BUSINESSMAN NOW. I MADE YOU A FAIR OFFER AND YOU PASSED. WHICH MEANS...

...YER AS *DEAD* TO ME AS YOUR MOM.

WHATEVER. AND DON'T FLATTER YOURSELF—YOU AIN'T NO BUSINESSMAN.

YOU'RE JUST A SMALL-TIME LOSER DRUNK *PRETENDIN'* TO BE SOME BIG-TIME IMPORTANT GANGSTER, DAD.

NOT *DAD*. NOT ANYMORE.

IT'S *HUN*. ONLY HUN.

C'MON, KID—YOU CAN'T SERIOUSLY THINK YOU CAN TAKE US?

MAYBE NOT—BUT YOU AIN'T EXACTLY GIVIN' ME A *CHOICE*, ARE YOU? 'SIDES, THAT'S THE DIFFERENCE BETWEEN ME AND YOU. I AIN'T AFRAID TO DIE FIGHTIN' FOR WHAT'S RIGHT.

YOU'RE SO SCARED OF SHREDDER, YOU'LL DO *WHATEVER* IT TAKES TO SUCK UP TO HIM, EVEN ICE ME FOR NOT JOININ' YOUR LITTLE THUG CLUB.

WELL, FORGET ABOUT IT, 'CAUSE I ALREADY TOLD YOU— I WON'T.

SO... HUN... WE GONNA DO THIS, OR WHAT?

YEAH. WE ARE.

WASTE HIM.

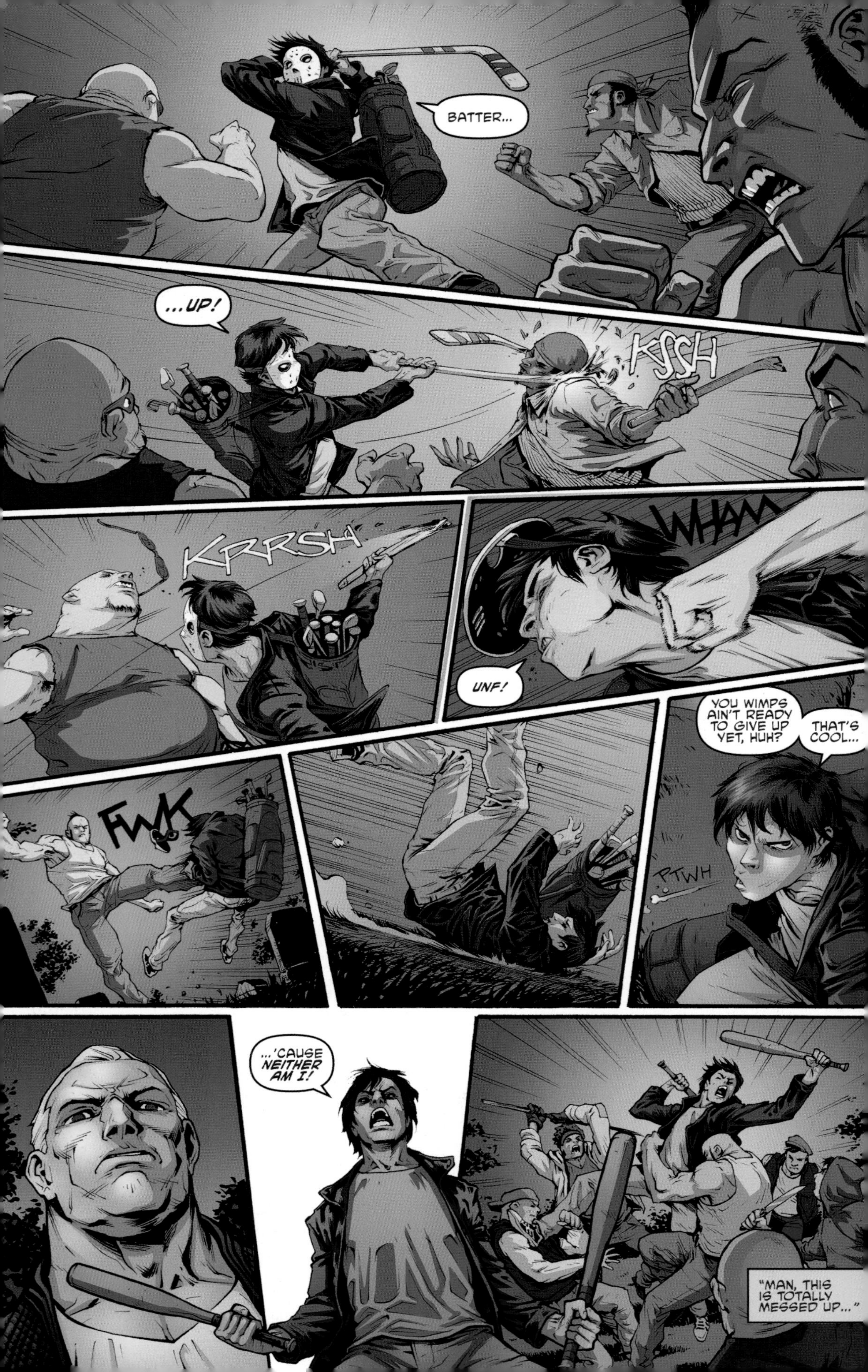
BATTER...
...UP!
KSSH
KRRSH
WHAM
UNF!
FWK
YOU WIMPS AIN'T READY TO GIVE UP YET, HUH?
THAT'S COOL...
PTWH
...'CAUSE NEITHER AM I!
"MAN, THIS IS TOTALLY MESSED UP..."

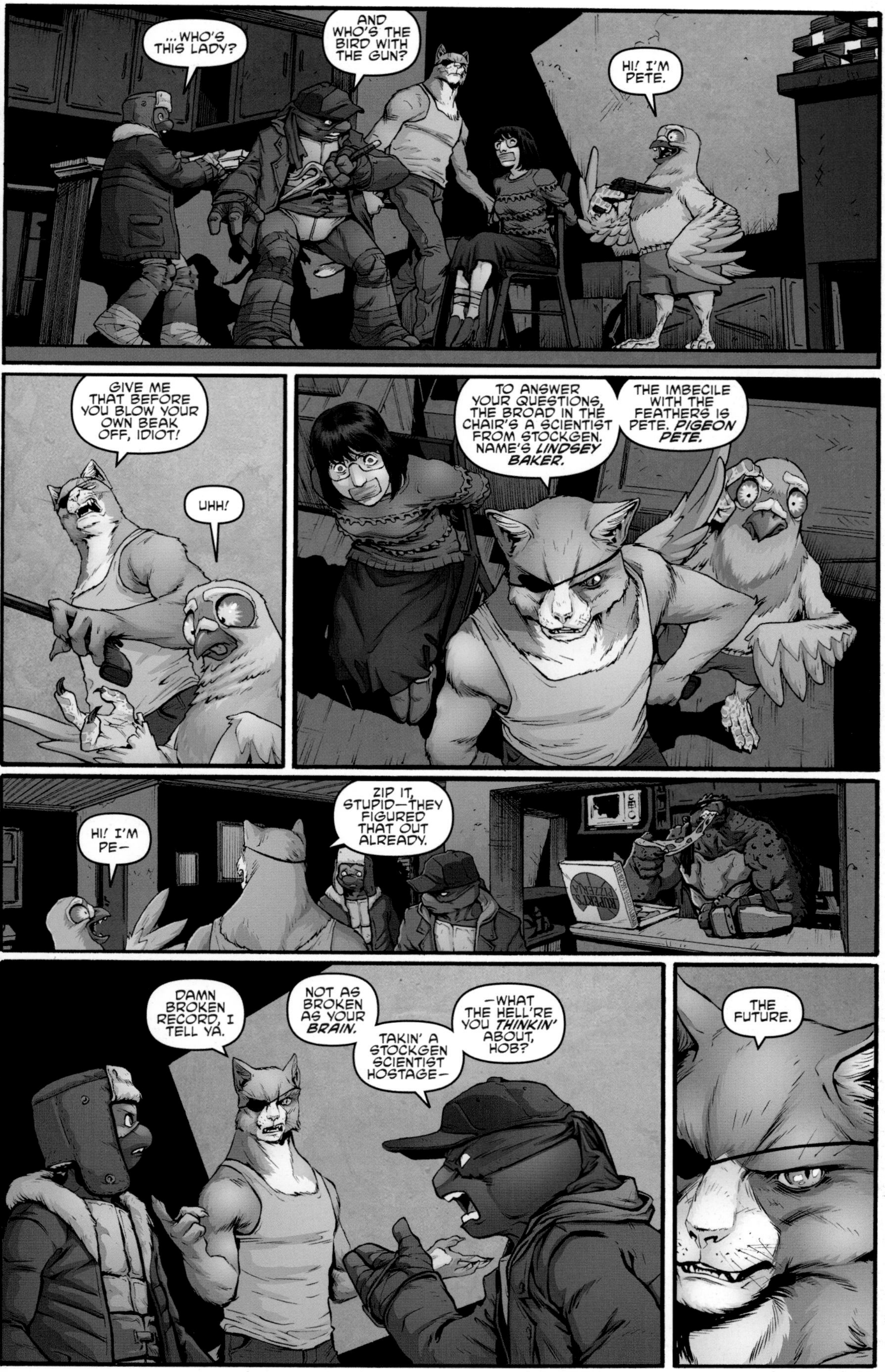
...WHO'S THIS LADY?
AND WHO'S THE BIRD WITH THE GUN?
HI! I'M PETE.
GIVE ME THAT BEFORE YOU BLOW YOUR OWN BEAK OFF, IDIOT!
UHH!
TO ANSWER YOUR QUESTIONS, THE BROAD IN THE CHAIR'S A SCIENTIST FROM STOCKGEN. NAME'S *LINDSEY BAKER.*
THE IMBECILE WITH THE FEATHERS IS PETE. *PIGEON PETE.*
HI! I'M PE—
ZIP IT, STUPID—THEY FIGURED THAT OUT ALREADY.
DAMN BROKEN RECORD, I TELL YA.
NOT AS BROKEN AS YOUR *BRAIN.*
TAKIN' A STOCKGEN SCIENTIST HOSTAGE—
—WHAT THE HELL'RE YOU *THINKIN'* ABOUT, HOB?
THE FUTURE.

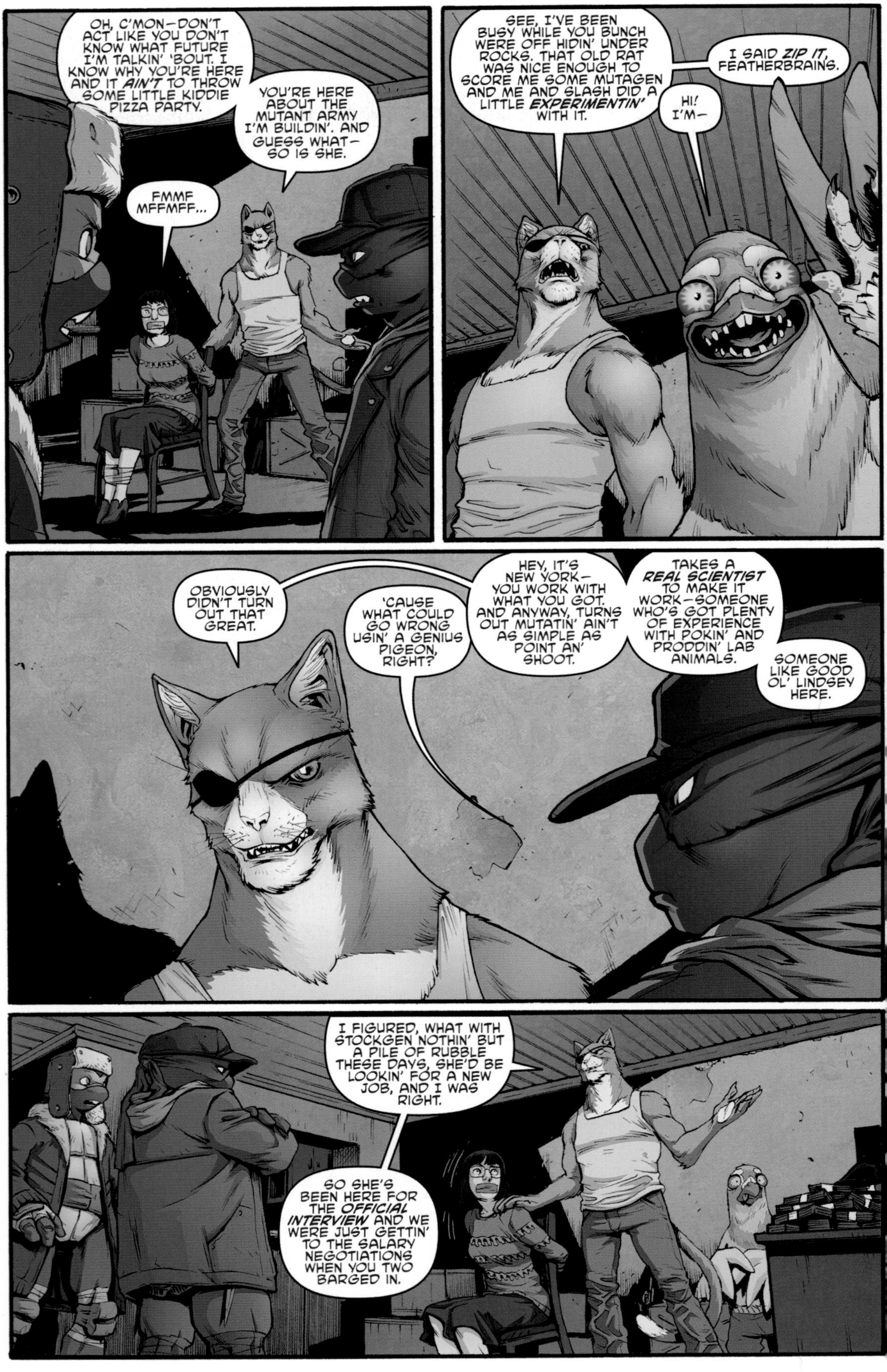
OH, C'MON—DON'T ACT LIKE YOU DON'T KNOW WHAT FUTURE I'M TALKIN' 'BOUT. I KNOW WHY YOU'RE HERE AND IT AIN'T TO THROW SOME LITTLE KIDDIE PIZZA PARTY.
YOU'RE HERE ABOUT THE MUTANT ARMY I'M BUILDIN'. AND GUESS WHAT—SO IS SHE.
FMMF MFFMFF...
SEE, I'VE BEEN BUSY WHILE YOU BUNCH WERE OFF HIDIN' UNDER ROCKS. THAT OLD RAT WAS NICE ENOUGH TO SCORE ME SOME MUTAGEN AND ME AND SLASH DID A LITTLE EXPERIMENTIN' WITH IT.
HI! I'M—
I SAID ZIP IT, FEATHERBRAINS.
OBVIOUSLY DIDN'T TURN OUT THAT GREAT.
'CAUSE WHAT COULD GO WRONG USIN' A GENIUS PIGEON, RIGHT?
HEY, IT'S NEW YORK—YOU WORK WITH WHAT YOU GOT. AND ANYWAY, TURNS OUT MUTATIN' AIN'T AS SIMPLE AS POINT AN' SHOOT.
TAKES A REAL SCIENTIST TO MAKE IT WORK—SOMEONE WHO'S GOT PLENTY OF EXPERIENCE WITH POKIN' AND PRODDIN' LAB ANIMALS.
SOMEONE LIKE GOOD OL' LINDSEY HERE.
I FIGURED, WHAT WITH STOCKGEN NOTHIN' BUT A PILE OF RUBBLE THESE DAYS, SHE'D BE LOOKIN' FOR A NEW JOB, AND I WAS RIGHT.
SO SHE'S BEEN HERE FOR THE OFFICIAL INTERVIEW AND WE WERE JUST GETTIN' TO THE SALARY NEGOTIATIONS WHEN YOU TWO BARGED IN.

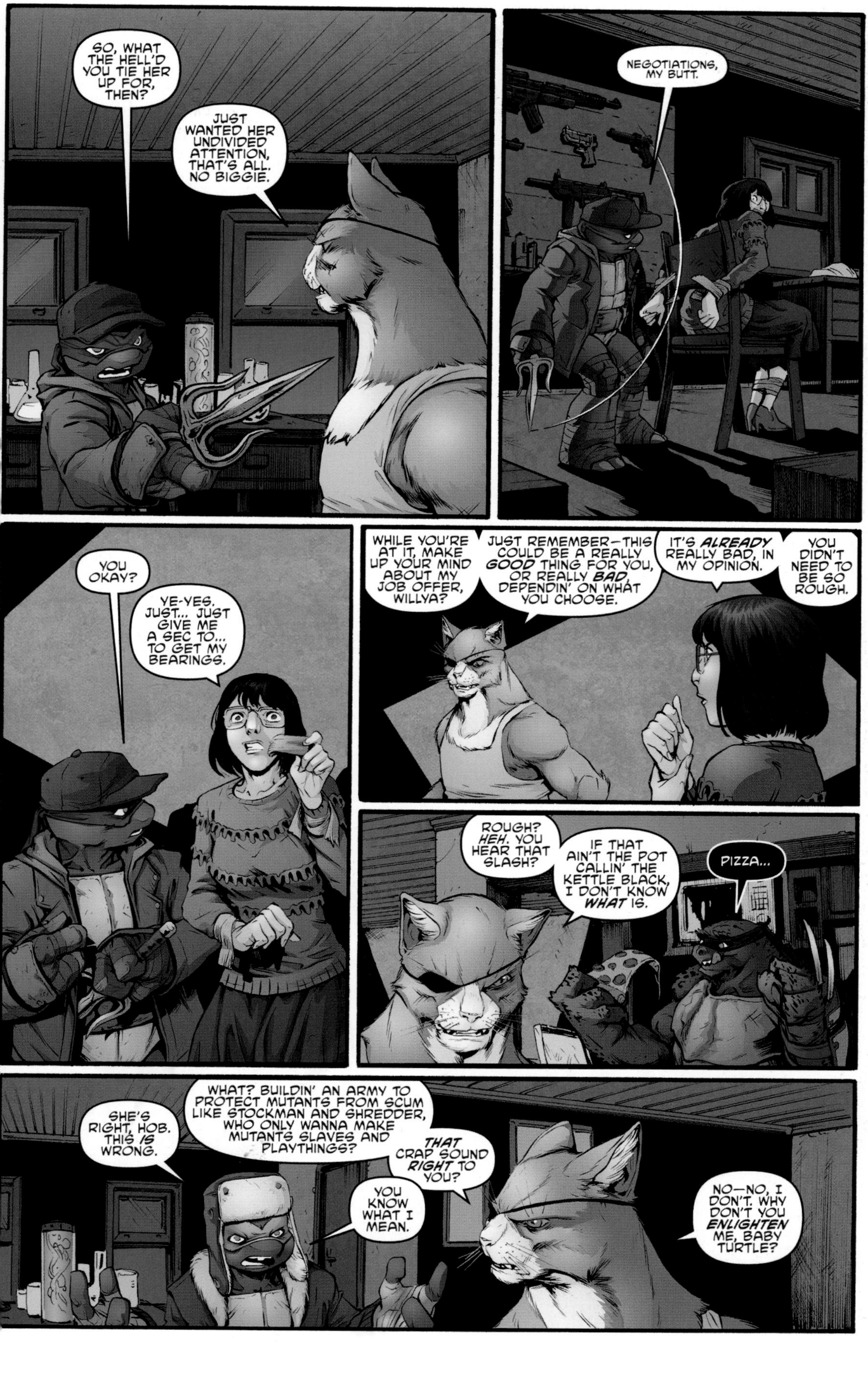
SO, WHAT THE HELL'D YOU TIE HER UP FOR, THEN?
JUST WANTED HER UNDIVIDED ATTENTION, THAT'S ALL. NO BIGGIE.
NEGOTIATIONS, MY BUTT.
YOU OKAY?
YE-YES. JUST... JUST GIVE ME A SEC TO... TO GET MY BEARINGS.
WHILE YOU'RE AT IT, MAKE UP YOUR MIND ABOUT MY JOB OFFER, WILLYA?
JUST REMEMBER—THIS COULD BE A REALLY *GOOD* THING FOR YOU, OR REALLY *BAD*, DEPENDIN' ON WHAT YOU CHOOSE.
IT'S *ALREADY* REALLY BAD, IN MY OPINION.
YOU DIDN'T NEED TO BE SO ROUGH.
ROUGH? *HEH.* YOU HEAR THAT SLASH?
IF THAT AIN'T THE POT CALLIN' THE KETTLE BLACK, I DON'T KNOW *WHAT* IS.
PIZZA...
SHE'S RIGHT, HOB. THIS *IS* WRONG.
WHAT? BUILDIN' AN ARMY TO PROTECT MUTANTS FROM SCUM LIKE STOCKMAN AND SHREDDER, WHO ONLY WANNA MAKE MUTANTS SLAVES AND PLAYTHINGS?
THAT CRAP SOUND *RIGHT* TO YOU?
YOU KNOW WHAT I MEAN.
NO—NO, I DON'T. WHY DON'T YOU *ENLIGHTEN* ME, BABY TURTLE?

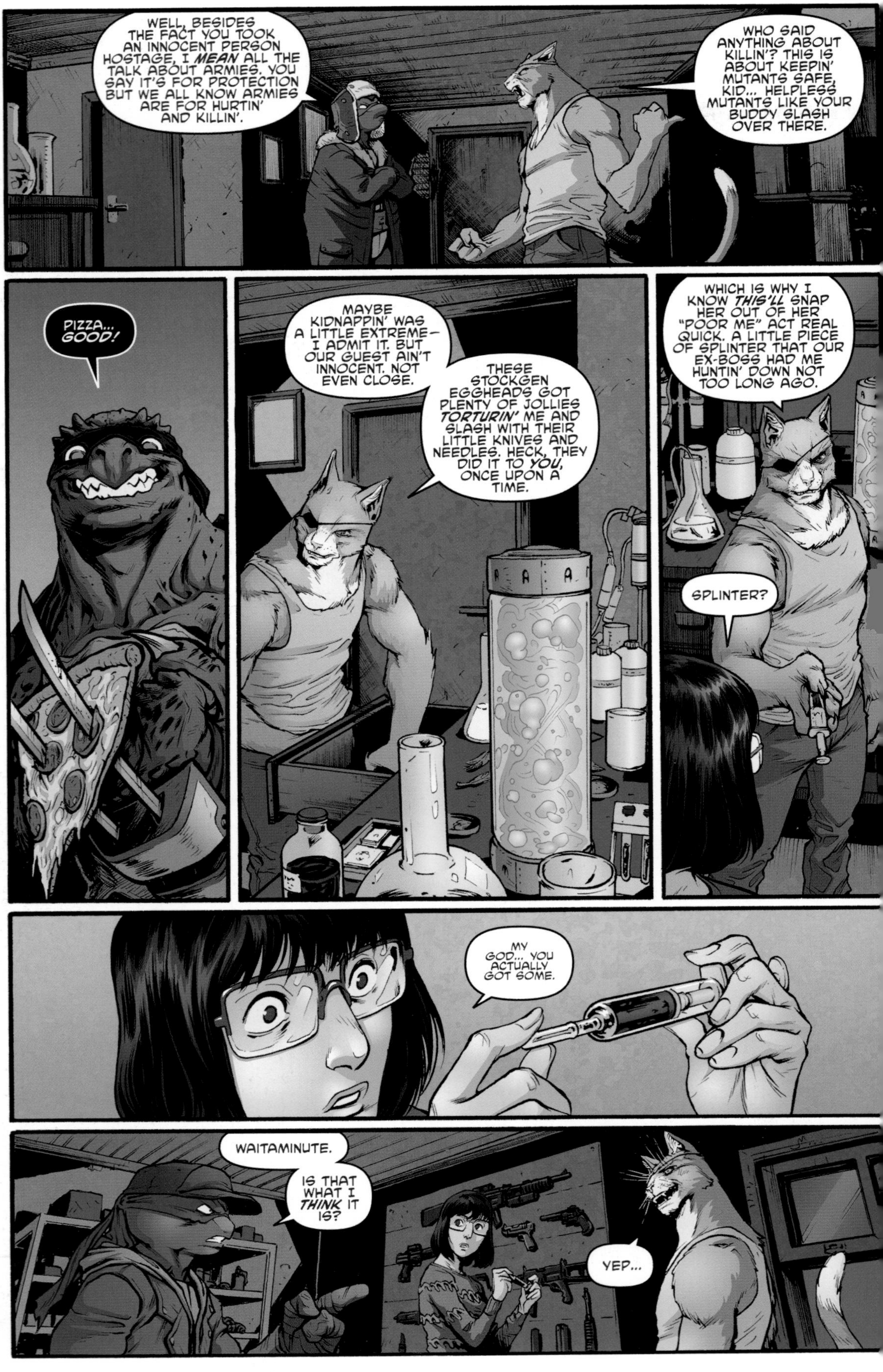
WELL, BESIDES THE FACT YOU TOOK AN INNOCENT PERSON HOSTAGE, I MEAN ALL THE TALK ABOUT ARMIES. YOU SAY IT'S FOR PROTECTION BUT WE ALL KNOW ARMIES ARE FOR HURTIN' AND KILLIN'.
WHO SAID ANYTHING ABOUT KILLIN'? THIS IS ABOUT KEEPIN' MUTANTS SAFE, KID... HELPLESS MUTANTS LIKE YOUR BUDDY SLASH OVER THERE.
PIZZA... GOOD!
MAYBE KIDNAPPIN' WAS A LITTLE EXTREME-- I ADMIT IT. BUT OUR GUEST AIN'T INNOCENT. NOT EVEN CLOSE.
THESE STOCKGEN EGGHEADS GOT PLENTY OF JOLLIES TORTURIN' ME AND SLASH WITH THEIR LITTLE KNIVES AND NEEDLES. HECK, THEY DID IT TO YOU, ONCE UPON A TIME.
WHICH IS WHY I KNOW THIS'LL SNAP HER OUT OF HER "POOR ME" ACT REAL QUICK. A LITTLE PIECE OF SPLINTER THAT OUR EX-BOSS HAD ME HUNTIN' DOWN NOT TOO LONG AGO.
SPLINTER?
MY GOD... YOU ACTUALLY GOT SOME.
WAITAMINUTE.
IS THAT WHAT I THINK IT IS?
YEP...

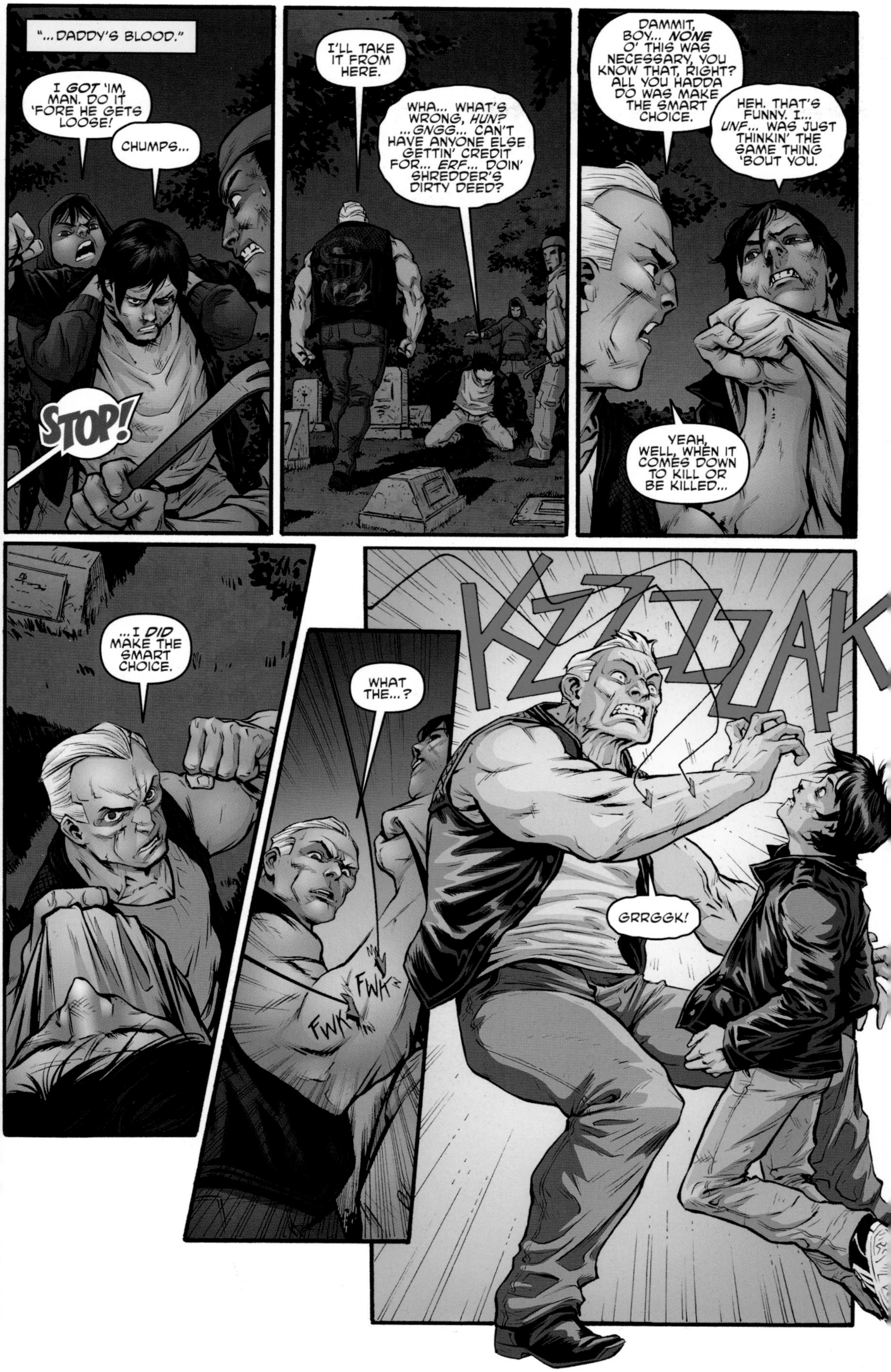
"...DADDY'S BLOOD."
I GOT 'IM, MAN. DO IT 'FORE HE GETS LOOSE!
CHUMPS...
STOP!
I'LL TAKE IT FROM HERE.
WHA... WHAT'S WRONG, HUN? ...GNGG... CAN'T HAVE ANYONE ELSE GETTIN' CREDIT FOR... ERF... DOIN' SHREDDER'S DIRTY DEED?
DAMMIT, BOY... NONE O' THIS WAS NECESSARY, YOU KNOW THAT, RIGHT? ALL YOU HADDA DO WAS MAKE THE SMART CHOICE.
HEH. THAT'S FUNNY. I... UNF... WAS JUST THINKIN' THE SAME THING 'BOUT YOU.
YEAH, WELL, WHEN IT COMES DOWN TO KILL OR BE KILLED...
...I DID MAKE THE SMART CHOICE.
WHAT THE...?
FWK
FWK
KZZZZAK
GRRGGK!

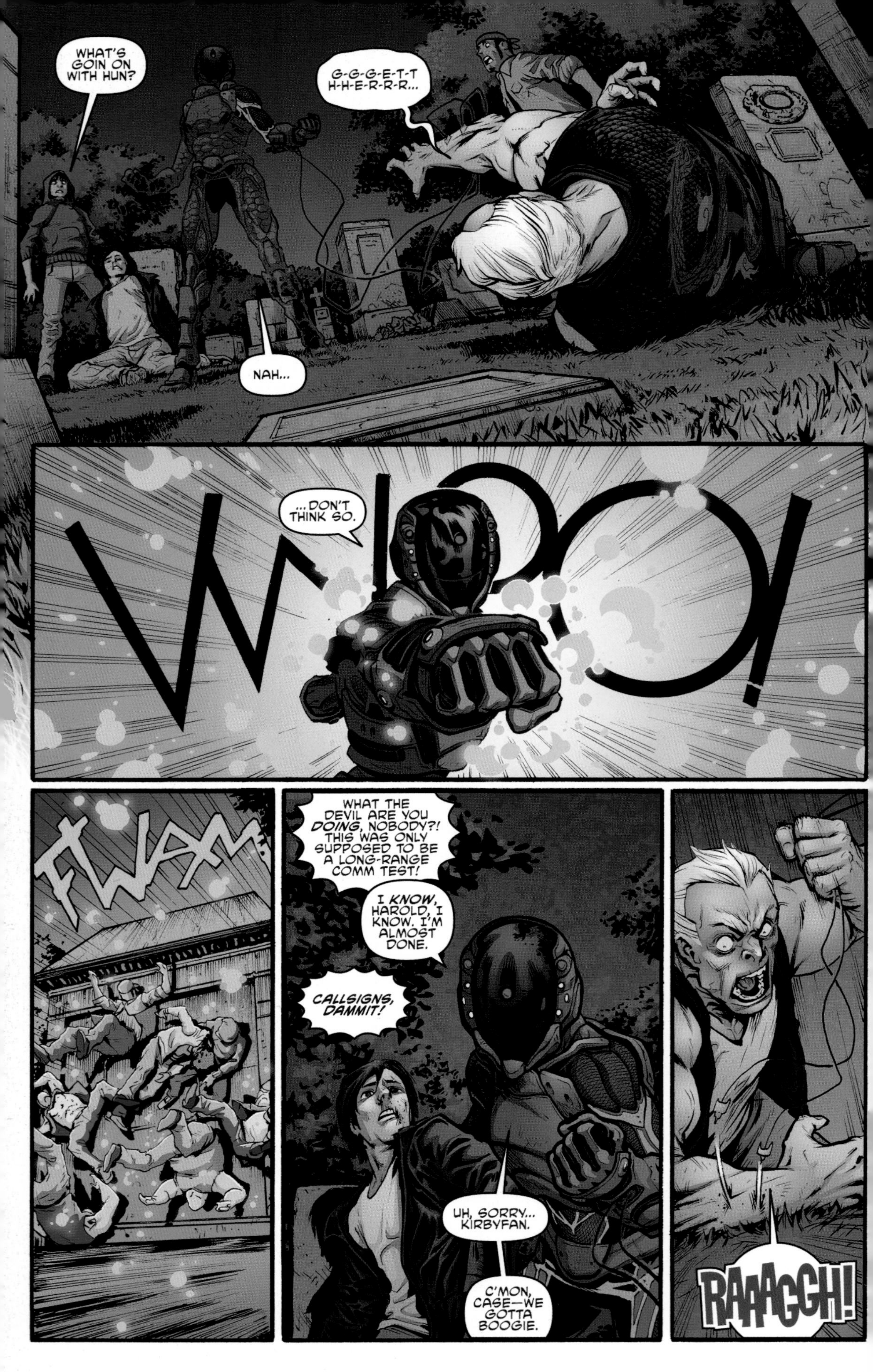
WHAT'S GOIN ON WITH HUN?
G-G-G-E-T-T H-H-E-R-R-R...
NAH...
...DON'T THINK SO.
WHOOM!
FWAM
WHAT THE DEVIL ARE YOU DOING, NOBODY?! THIS WAS ONLY SUPPOSED TO BE A LONG-RANGE COMM TEST!
I KNOW, HAROLD, I KNOW. I'M ALMOST DONE.
CALLSIGNS, DAMMIT!
UH, SORRY... KIRBYFAN.
C'MON, CASE—WE GOTTA BOOGIE.
RAAAGGH!

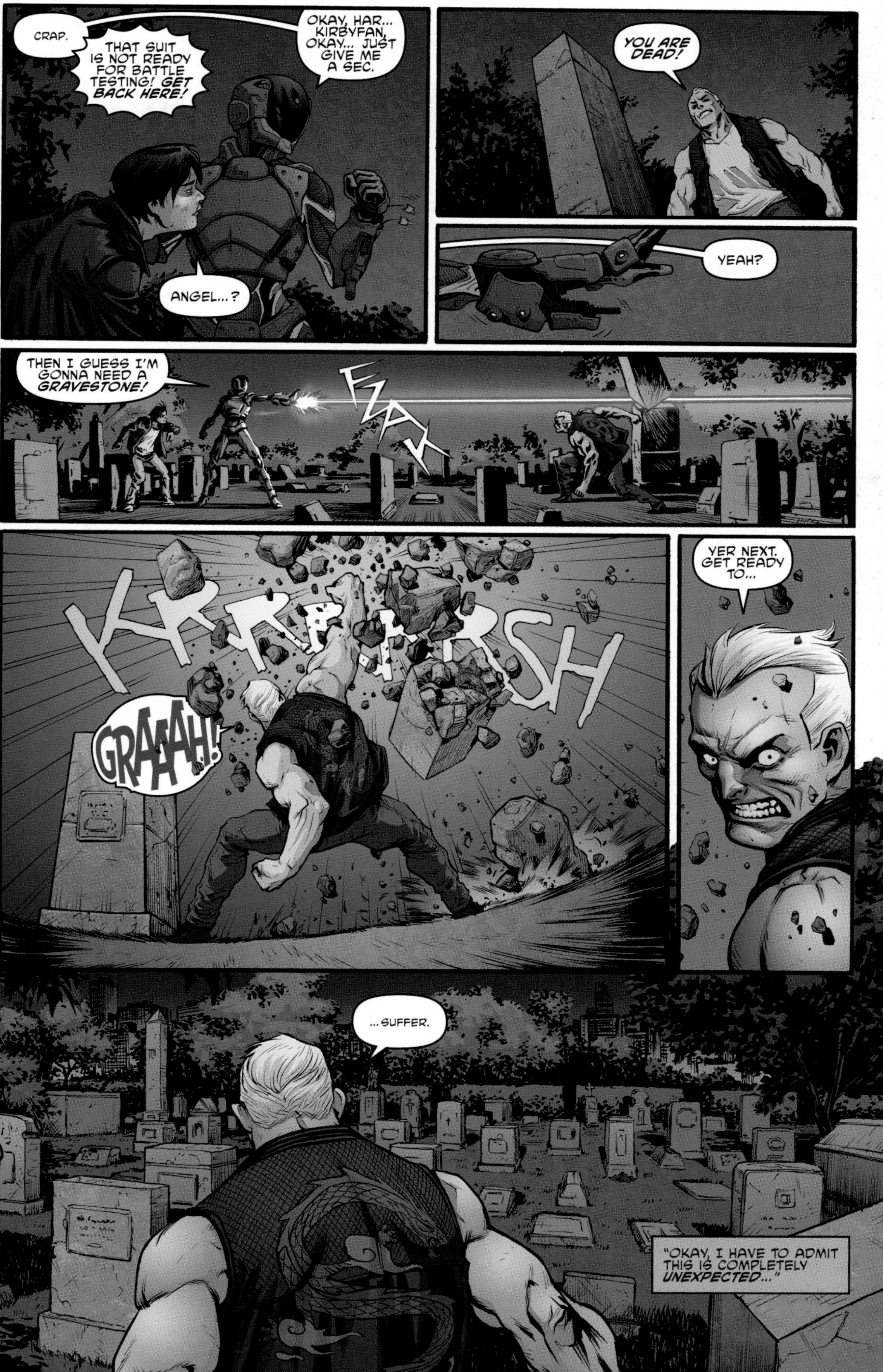
CRAP.
THAT SUIT IS NOT READY FOR BATTLE TESTING! GET BACK HERE!
OKAY, HAR... KIRBYFAN, OKAY... JUST GIVE ME A SEC.
ANGEL...?
YOU ARE DEAD!
YEAH?
THEN I GUESS I'M GONNA NEED A GRAVESTONE!
FZAX
KRRRAASH
GRAAAH!
YER NEXT. GET READY TO...
...SUFFER.
"OKAY, I HAVE TO ADMIT THIS IS COMPLETELY UNEXPECTED..."

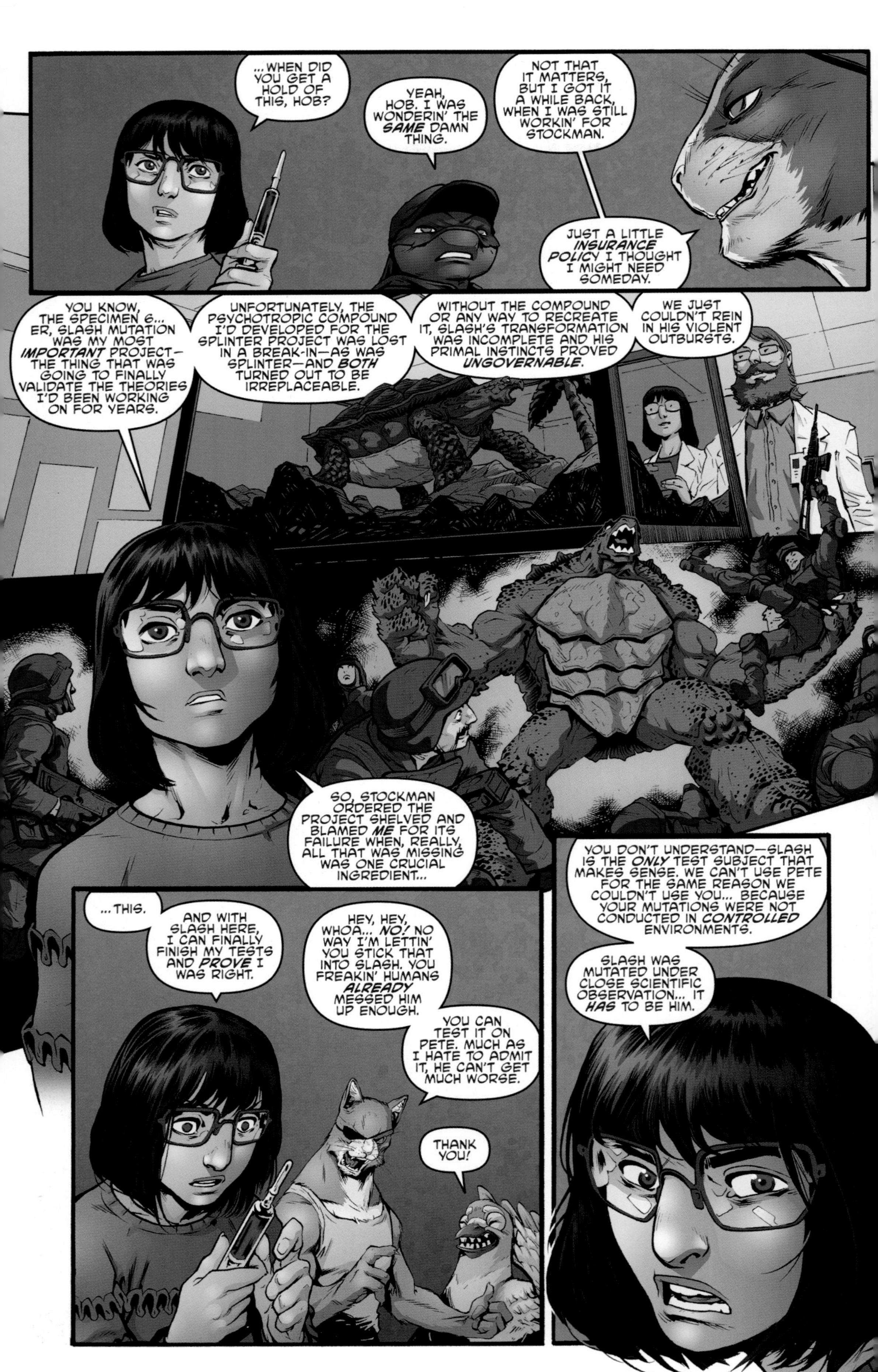
...WHEN DID YOU GET A HOLD OF THIS, HOB?
YEAH, HOB. I WAS WONDERIN' THE SAME DAMN THING.
NOT THAT IT MATTERS, BUT I GOT IT A WHILE BACK, WHEN I WAS STILL WORKIN' FOR STOCKMAN.
JUST A LITTLE INSURANCE POLICY I THOUGHT I MIGHT NEED SOMEDAY.
YOU KNOW, THE SPECIMEN 6... ER, SLASH MUTATION WAS MY MOST IMPORTANT PROJECT—THE THING THAT WAS GOING TO FINALLY VALIDATE THE THEORIES I'D BEEN WORKING ON FOR YEARS.
UNFORTUNATELY, THE PSYCHOTROPIC COMPOUND I'D DEVELOPED FOR THE SPLINTER PROJECT WAS LOST IN A BREAK-IN—AS WAS SPLINTER—AND BOTH TURNED OUT TO BE IRREPLACEABLE.
WITHOUT THE COMPOUND OR ANY WAY TO RECREATE IT, SLASH'S TRANSFORMATION WAS INCOMPLETE AND HIS PRIMAL INSTINCTS PROVED UNGOVERNABLE.
WE JUST COULDN'T REIN IN HIS VIOLENT OUTBURSTS.
SO, STOCKMAN ORDERED THE PROJECT SHELVED AND BLAMED ME FOR ITS FAILURE WHEN, REALLY, ALL THAT WAS MISSING WAS ONE CRUCIAL INGREDIENT...
...THIS.
AND WITH SLASH HERE, I CAN FINALLY FINISH MY TESTS AND PROVE I WAS RIGHT.
HEY, HEY, WHOA... NO! NO WAY I'M LETTIN' YOU STICK THAT INTO SLASH. YOU FREAKIN' HUMANS ALREADY MESSED HIM UP ENOUGH.
YOU CAN TEST IT ON PETE. MUCH AS I HATE TO ADMIT IT, HE CAN'T GET MUCH WORSE.
THANK YOU!
YOU DON'T UNDERSTAND—SLASH IS THE ONLY TEST SUBJECT THAT MAKES SENSE. WE CAN'T USE PETE FOR THE SAME REASON WE COULDN'T USE YOU... BECAUSE YOUR MUTATIONS WERE NOT CONDUCTED IN CONTROLLED ENVIRONMENTS.
SLASH WAS MUTATED UNDER CLOSE SCIENTIFIC OBSERVATION... IT HAS TO BE HIM.

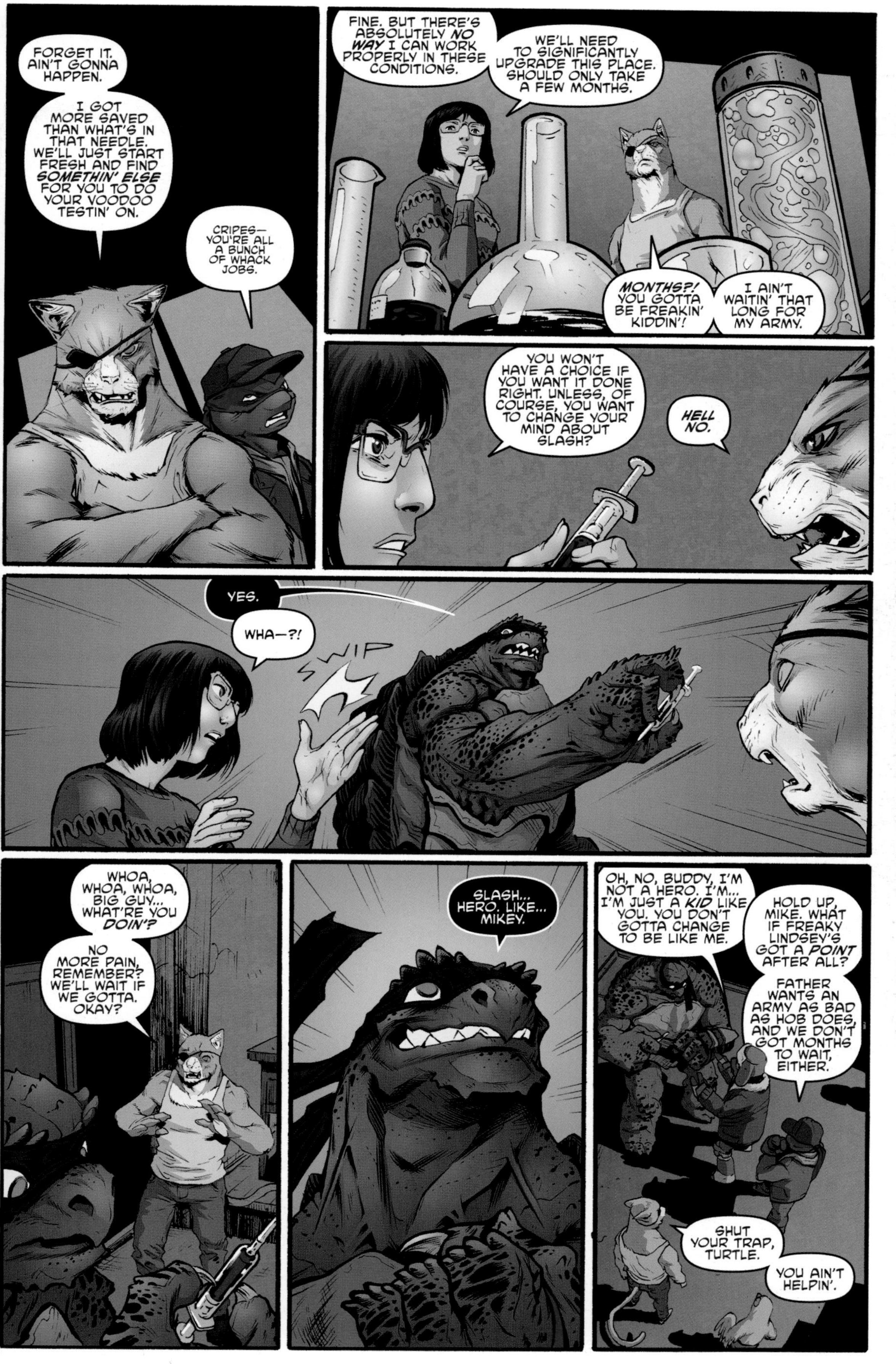
FORGET IT. AIN'T GONNA HAPPEN.
I GOT MORE SAVED THAN WHAT'S IN THAT NEEDLE. WE'LL JUST START FRESH AND FIND SOMETHIN' ELSE FOR YOU TO DO YOUR VOODOO TESTIN' ON.
CRIPES— YOU'RE ALL A BUNCH OF WHACK JOBS.
FINE. BUT THERE'S ABSOLUTELY NO WAY I CAN WORK PROPERLY IN THESE CONDITIONS.
WE'LL NEED TO SIGNIFICANTLY UPGRADE THIS PLACE. SHOULD ONLY TAKE A FEW MONTHS.
MONTHS?! YOU GOTTA BE FREAKIN' KIDDIN'!
I AIN'T WAITIN' THAT LONG FOR MY ARMY.
YOU WON'T HAVE A CHOICE IF YOU WANT IT DONE RIGHT. UNLESS, OF COURSE, YOU WANT TO CHANGE YOUR MIND ABOUT SLASH?
HELL NO.
YES.
WHA—?!
SWIP
WHOA, WHOA, WHOA, BIG GUY... WHAT'RE YOU DOIN'?
NO MORE PAIN, REMEMBER? WE'LL WAIT IF WE GOTTA. OKAY?
SLASH... HERO. LIKE... MIKEY.
OH, NO, BUDDY, I'M NOT A HERO. I'M... I'M JUST A KID LIKE YOU. YOU DON'T GOTTA CHANGE TO BE LIKE ME.
HOLD UP, MIKE. WHAT IF FREAKY LINDSEY'S GOT A POINT AFTER ALL?
FATHER WANTS AN ARMY AS BAD AS HOB DOES, AND WE DON'T GOT MONTHS TO WAIT, EITHER.
SHUT YOUR TRAP, TURTLE.
YOU AIN'T HELPIN'.

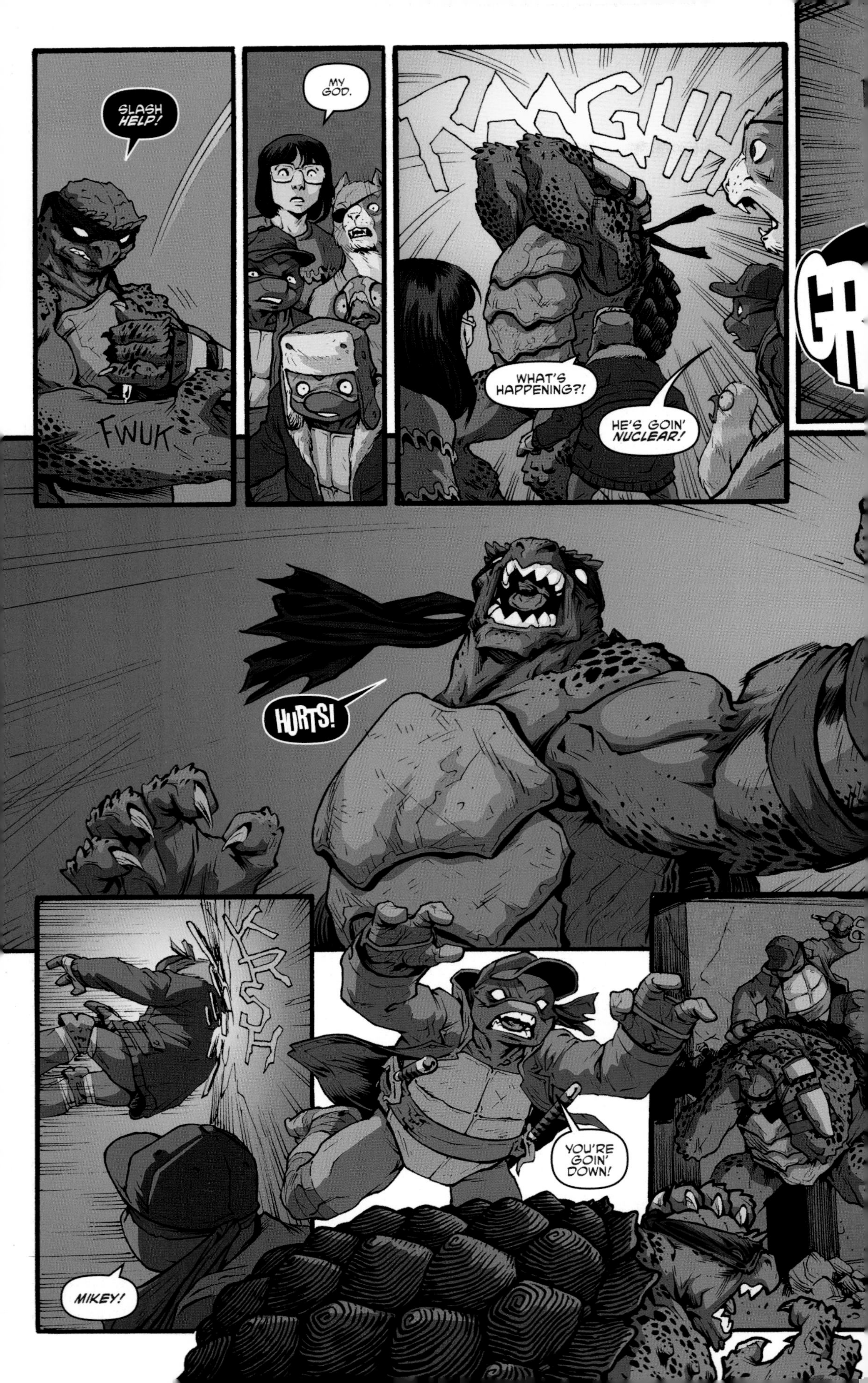
SLASH HELP!
FWUK
MY GOD.
WHAT'S HAPPENING?!
HE'S GOIN' NUCLEAR!
HURTS!
YOU'RE GOIN' DOWN!
MIKEY!

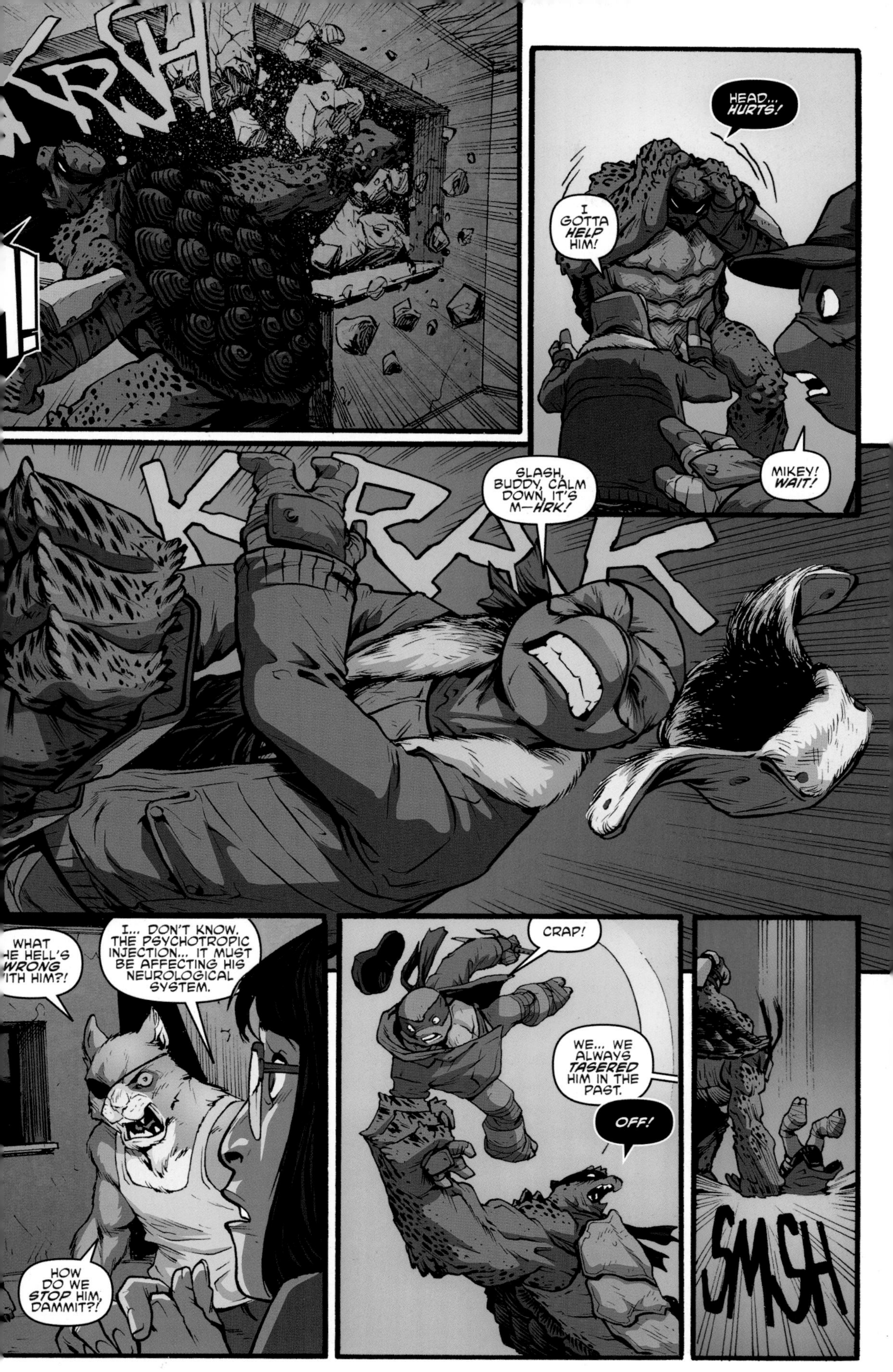

KRRRSH
HEAD... HURTS!
I GOTTA HELP HIM!
MIKEY! WAIT!
SLASH, BUDDY, CALM DOWN, IT'S M—HRK!
KRAK
WHAT THE HELL'S WRONG WITH HIM?!
I... DON'T KNOW. THE PSYCHOTROPIC INJECTION... IT MUST BE AFFECTING HIS NEUROLOGICAL SYSTEM.
HOW DO WE STOP HIM, DAMMIT?!
CRAP!
WE... WE ALWAYS TASERED HIM IN THE PAST.
OFF!
SMASH

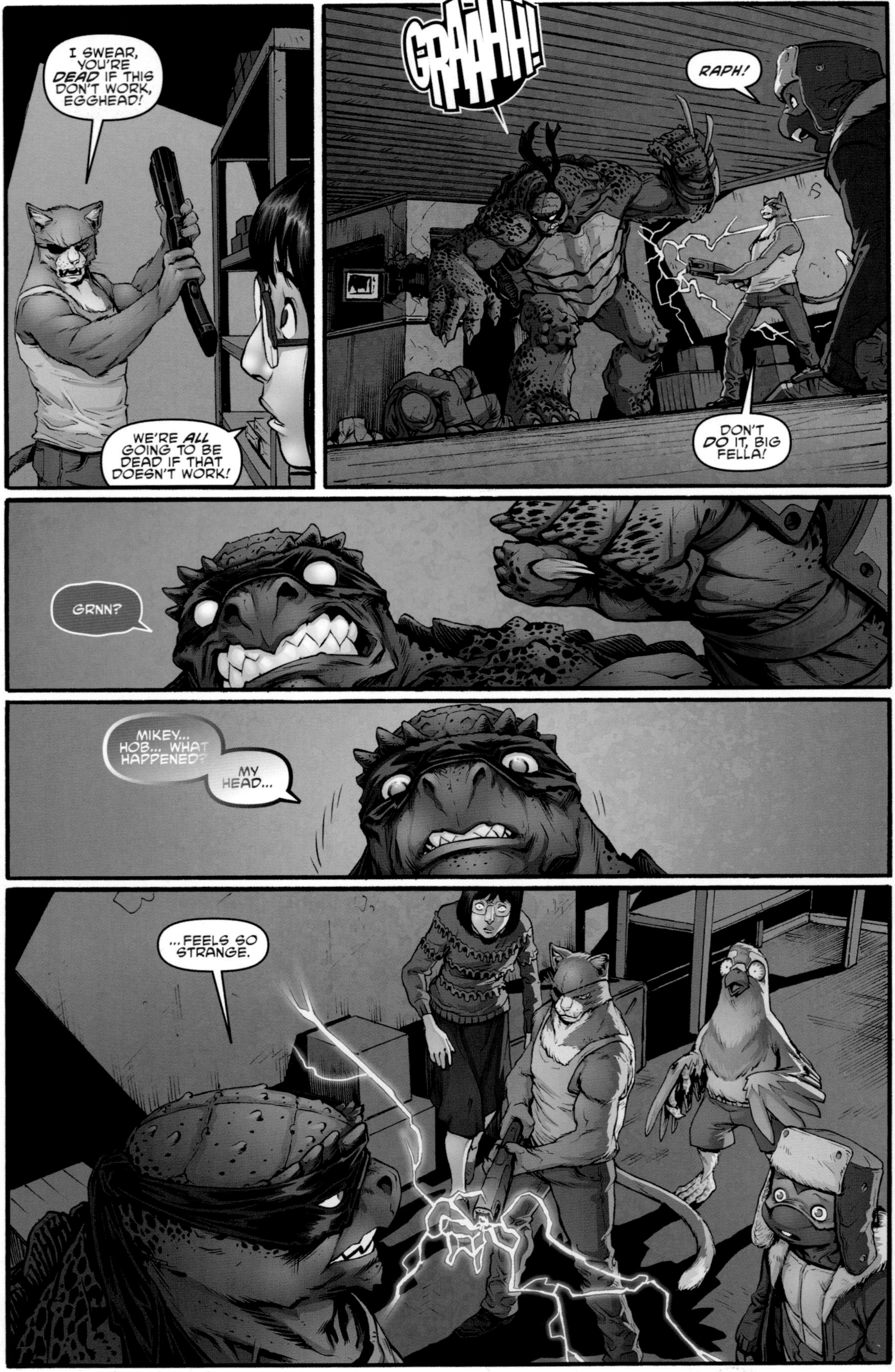
I SWEAR, YOU'RE DEAD IF THIS DON'T WORK, EGGHEAD!
WE'RE ALL GOING TO BE DEAD IF THAT DOESN'T WORK!
GRAAHH!
RAPH!
DON'T DO IT, BIG FELLA!
GRNN?
MIKEY... HOB... WHAT HAPPENED?
MY HEAD...
...FEELS SO STRANGE.

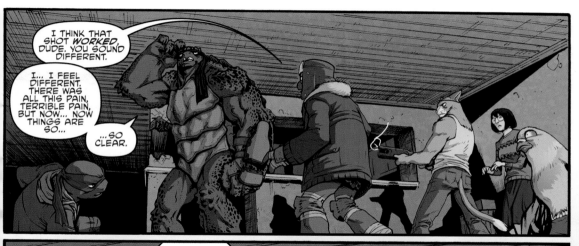

I THINK THAT SHOT *WORKED*, DUDE. YOU SOUND DIFFERENT.

I... I FEEL DIFFERENT. THERE WAS ALL THIS PAIN, TERRIBLE PAIN, BUT NOW... NOW THINGS ARE SO...

...SO CLEAR.

IT'S OKAY, EVERYONE. I'M ALL RIGHT NOW.

YOU CAN LOWER YOUR GUN, HOB. I WON'T *HURT* ANYONE.

WELL, EGGHEAD, GUESS YOU GOT YOUR PROOF. THE RAT'S BLOOD WORKS.

I WAS *RIGHT* ALL ALONG.

GREAT. YOU WERE RIGHT. WHOOP-DEE-DO.

ONLY QUESTION I GOT IS...

...*WHERE* THE HECK DO WE GO FROM HERE?

"YOU'RE *SURE* YOU'RE OKAY?"

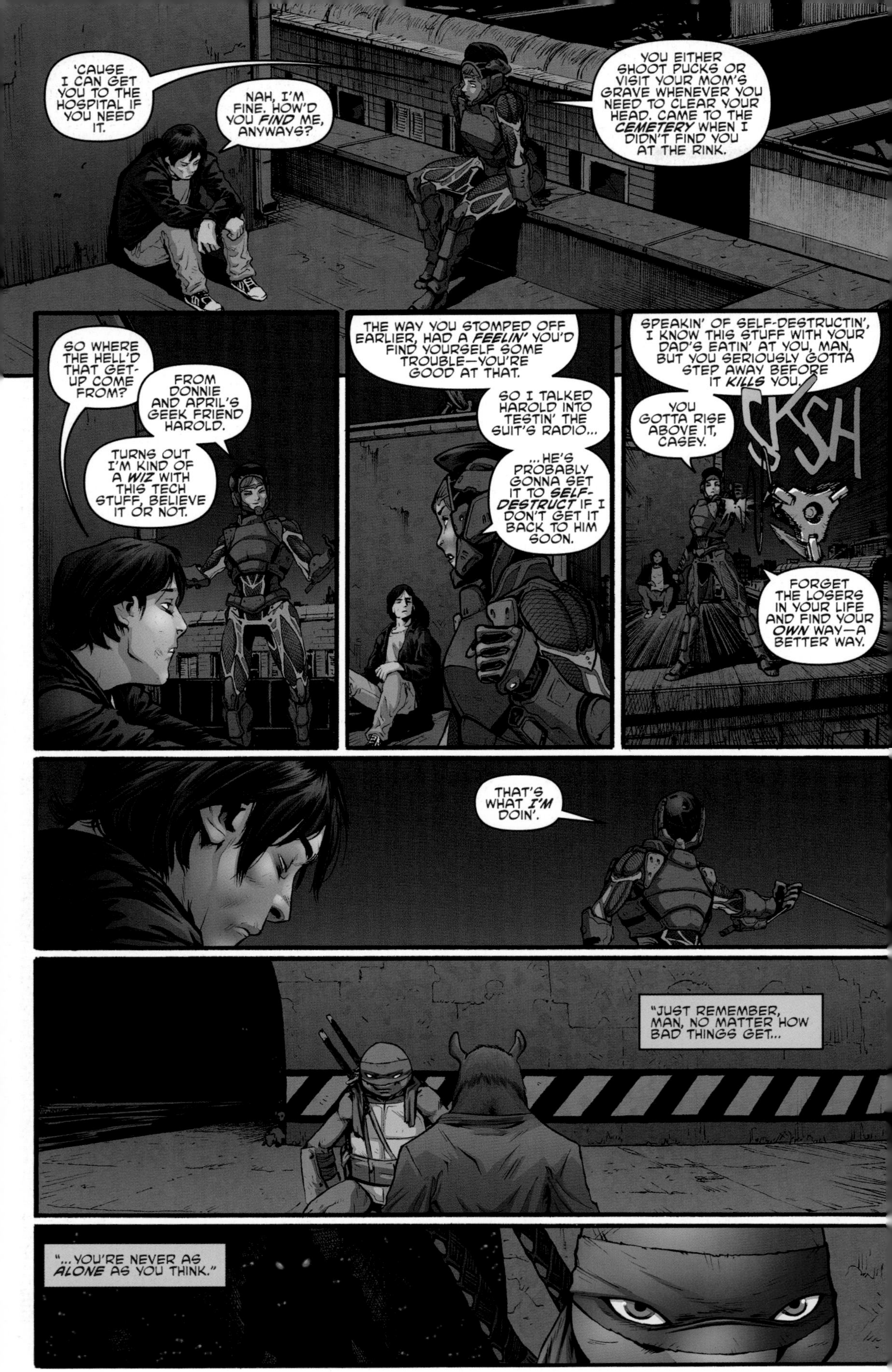
'CAUSE I CAN GET YOU TO THE HOSPITAL IF YOU NEED IT.
NAH, I'M FINE. HOW'D YOU *FIND* ME, ANYWAYS?
YOU EITHER SHOOT PUCKS OR VISIT YOUR MOM'S GRAVE WHENEVER YOU NEED TO CLEAR YOUR HEAD. CAME TO THE *CEMETERY* WHEN I DIDN'T FIND YOU AT THE RINK.
SO WHERE THE HELL'D THAT GET-UP COME FROM?
FROM DONNIE AND APRIL'S GEEK FRIEND HAROLD.
TURNS OUT I'M KIND OF A *WIZ* WITH THIS TECH STUFF, BELIEVE IT OR NOT.
THE WAY YOU STOMPED OFF EARLIER, HAD A *FEELIN'* YOU'D FIND YOURSELF SOME TROUBLE—YOU'RE GOOD AT THAT.
SO I TALKED HAROLD INTO TESTIN' THE SUIT'S RADIO...
...HE'S PROBABLY GONNA SET IT TO *SELF-DESTRUCT* IF I DON'T GET IT BACK TO HIM SOON.
SPEAKIN' OF SELF-DESTRUCTIN', I KNOW THIS STUFF WITH YOUR DAD'S EATIN' AT YOU, MAN, BUT YOU SERIOUSLY GOTTA STEP AWAY BEFORE IT *KILLS* YOU.
YOU GOTTA RISE ABOVE IT, CASEY.
SKSH
FORGET THE LOSERS IN YOUR LIFE AND FIND YOUR *OWN* WAY—A BETTER WAY.
THAT'S WHAT *I'M* DOIN'.
"JUST REMEMBER, MAN, NO MATTER HOW BAD THINGS GET...
"...YOU'RE NEVER AS *ALONE* AS YOU THINK."

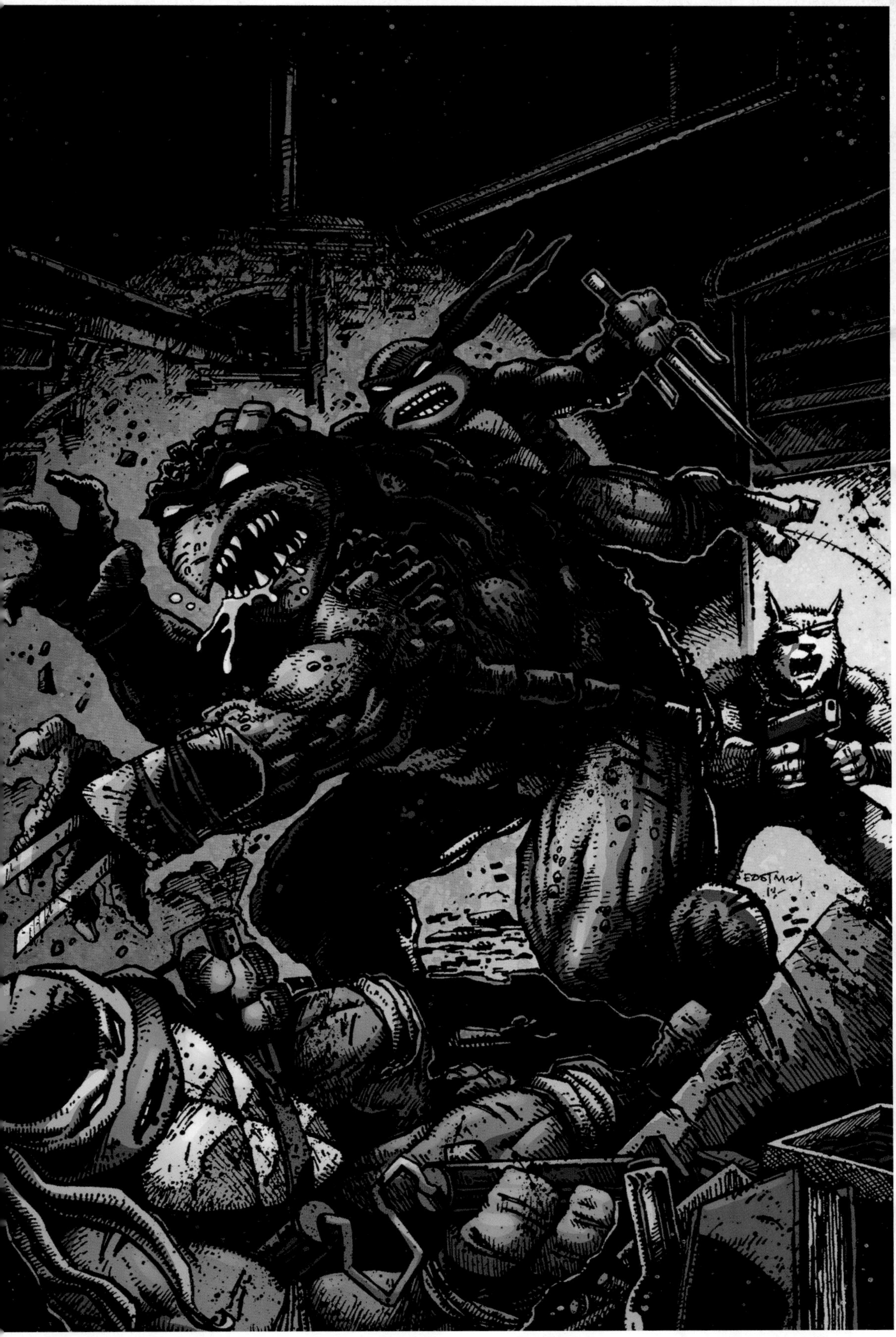

Cover by KEVIN EASTMAN
Colors by RONDA PATTISON

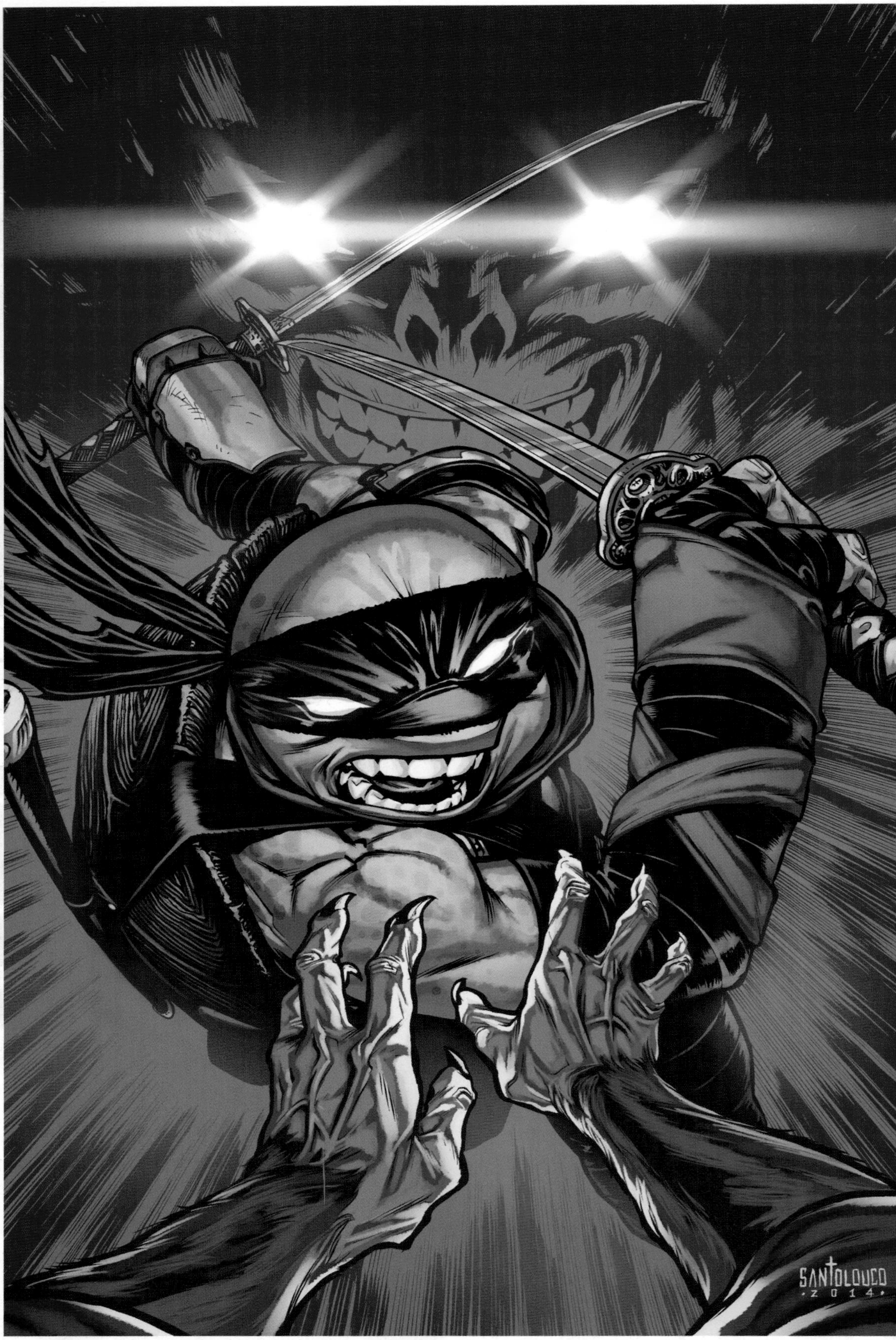
SANTOLOUCO
2014

Cover by MATEUS SANTOLOUCO

TMNT #36

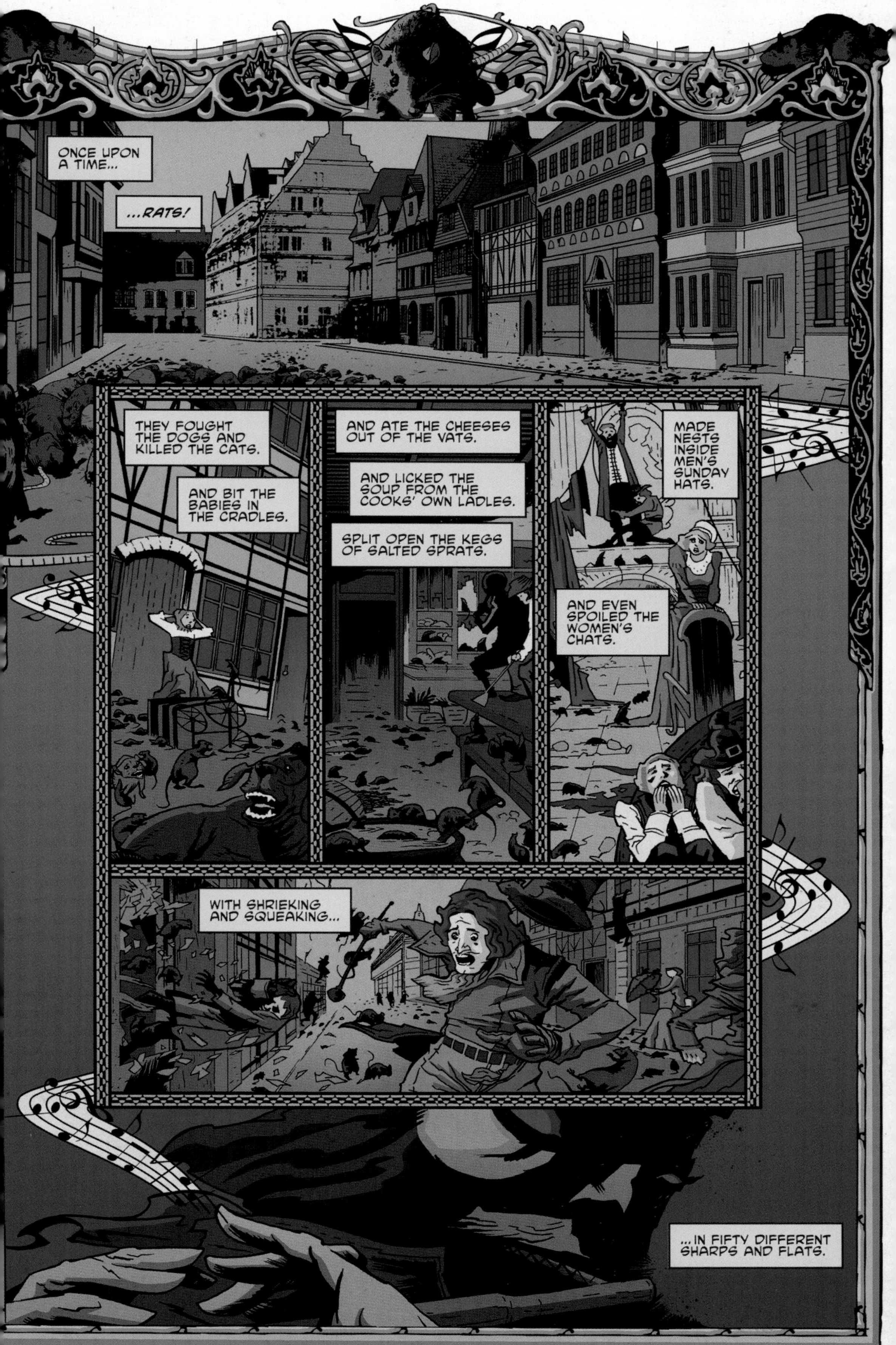
ONCE UPON A TIME...
...RATS!
THEY FOUGHT THE DOGS AND KILLED THE CATS.
AND BIT THE BABIES IN THE CRADLES.
AND ATE THE CHEESES OUT OF THE VATS.
AND LICKED THE SOUP FROM THE COOKS' OWN LADLES.
SPLIT OPEN THE KEGS OF SALTED SPRATS.
MADE NESTS INSIDE MEN'S SUNDAY HATS.
AND EVEN SPOILED THE WOMEN'S CHATS.
WITH SHRIEKING AND SQUEAKING...
...IN FIFTY DIFFERENT SHARPS AND FLATS.

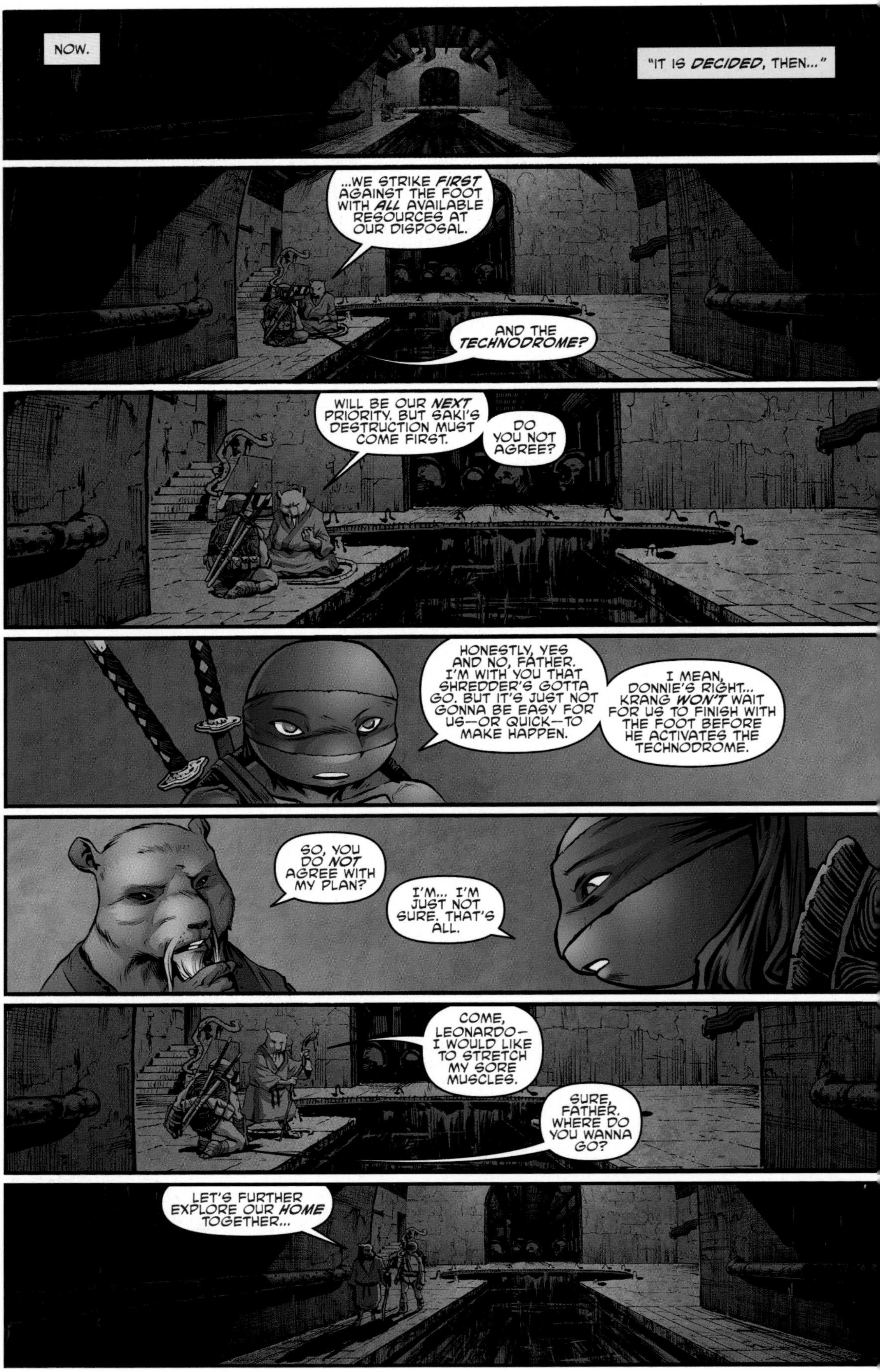
NOW.
"IT IS DECIDED, THEN..."
...WE STRIKE FIRST AGAINST THE FOOT WITH ALL AVAILABLE RESOURCES AT OUR DISPOSAL.
AND THE TECHNODROME?
WILL BE OUR NEXT PRIORITY. BUT SAKI'S DESTRUCTION MUST COME FIRST.
DO YOU NOT AGREE?
HONESTLY, YES AND NO, FATHER. I'M WITH YOU THAT SHREDDER'S GOTTA GO. BUT IT'S JUST NOT GONNA BE EASY FOR US—OR QUICK—TO MAKE HAPPEN.
I MEAN, DONNIE'S RIGHT... KRANG WON'T WAIT FOR US TO FINISH WITH THE FOOT BEFORE HE ACTIVATES THE TECHNODROME.
SO, YOU DO NOT AGREE WITH MY PLAN?
I'M... I'M JUST NOT SURE. THAT'S ALL.
COME, LEONARDO— I WOULD LIKE TO STRETCH MY SORE MUSCLES.
SURE, FATHER. WHERE DO YOU WANNA GO?
LET'S FURTHER EXPLORE OUR HOME TOGETHER...

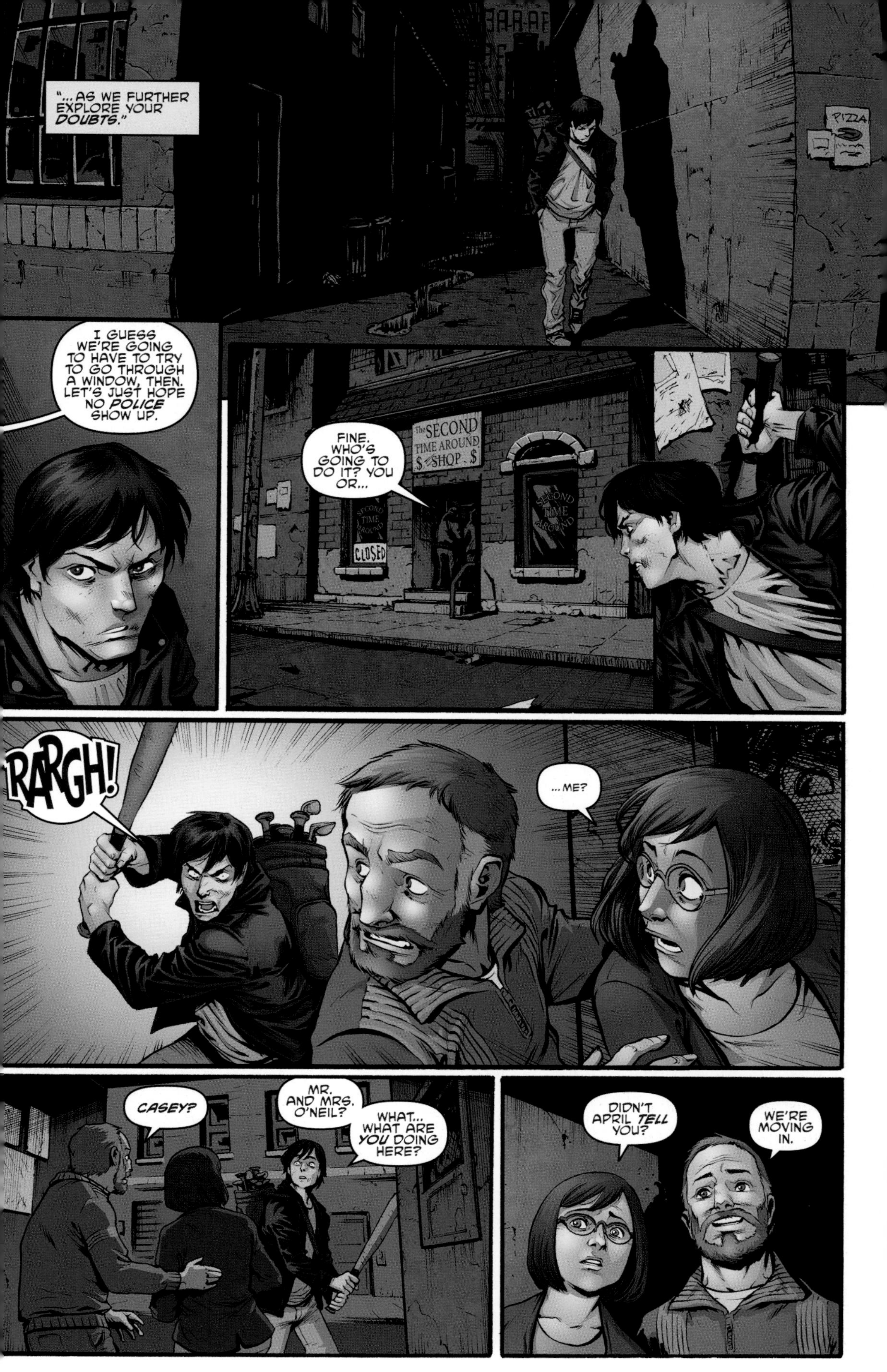
"...AS WE FURTHER EXPLORE YOUR DOUBTS."
I GUESS WE'RE GOING TO HAVE TO TRY TO GO THROUGH A WINDOW, THEN. LET'S JUST HOPE NO POLICE SHOW UP.
The SECOND TIME AROUND $ SHOP $
FINE. WHO'S GOING TO DO IT? YOU OR...
SECOND TIME AROUND
CLOSED
SECOND TIME AROUND
RARGH!
...ME?
CASEY?
MR. AND MRS. O'NEIL?
WHAT... WHAT ARE YOU DOING HERE?
DIDN'T APRIL TELL YOU?
WE'RE MOVING IN.

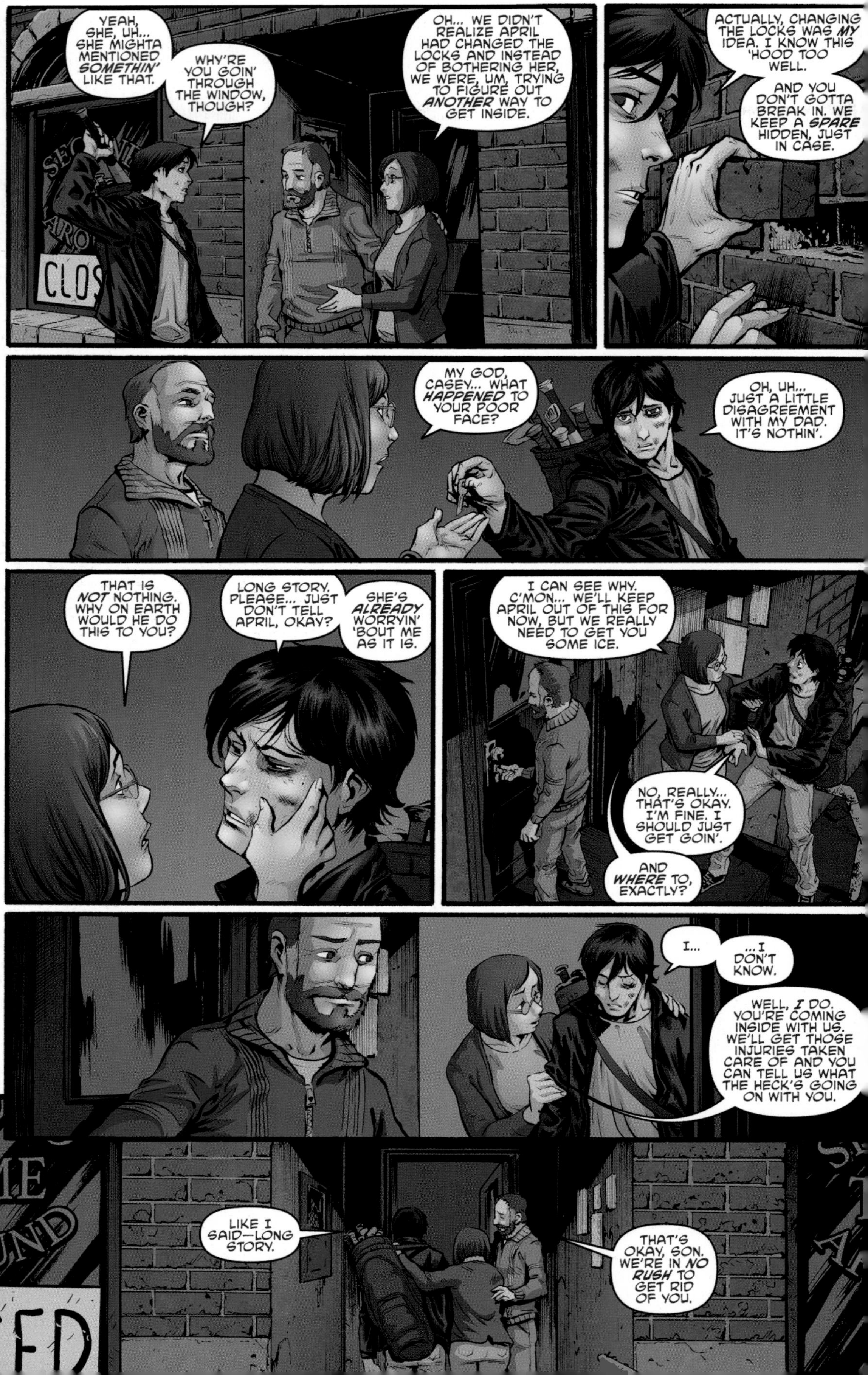
YEAH, SHE, UH... SHE MIGHTA MENTIONED SOMETHIN' LIKE THAT.
WHY'RE YOU GOIN' THROUGH THE WINDOW, THOUGH?
OH... WE DIDN'T REALIZE APRIL HAD CHANGED THE LOCKS AND INSTEAD OF BOTHERING HER, WE WERE, UM, TRYING TO FIGURE OUT ANOTHER WAY TO GET INSIDE.
CLOS
ACTUALLY, CHANGING THE LOCKS WAS MY IDEA. I KNOW THIS 'HOOD TOO WELL.
AND YOU DON'T GOTTA BREAK IN. WE KEEP A SPARE HIDDEN, JUST IN CASE.
MY GOD, CASEY... WHAT HAPPENED TO YOUR POOR FACE?
OH, UH... JUST A LITTLE DISAGREEMENT WITH MY DAD. IT'S NOTHIN'.
THAT IS NOT NOTHING. WHY ON EARTH WOULD HE DO THIS TO YOU?
LONG STORY. PLEASE... JUST DON'T TELL APRIL, OKAY?
SHE'S ALREADY WORRYIN' 'BOUT ME AS IT IS.
I CAN SEE WHY. C'MON... WE'LL KEEP APRIL OUT OF THIS FOR NOW, BUT WE REALLY NEED TO GET YOU SOME ICE.
NO, REALLY... THAT'S OKAY. I'M FINE. I SHOULD JUST GET GOIN'.
AND WHERE TO, EXACTLY?
I...
...I DON'T KNOW.
WELL, I DO. YOU'RE COMING INSIDE WITH US. WE'LL GET THOSE INJURIES TAKEN CARE OF AND YOU CAN TELL US WHAT THE HECK'S GOING ON WITH YOU.
LIKE I SAID—LONG STORY.
THAT'S OKAY, SON. WE'RE IN NO RUSH TO GET RID OF YOU.

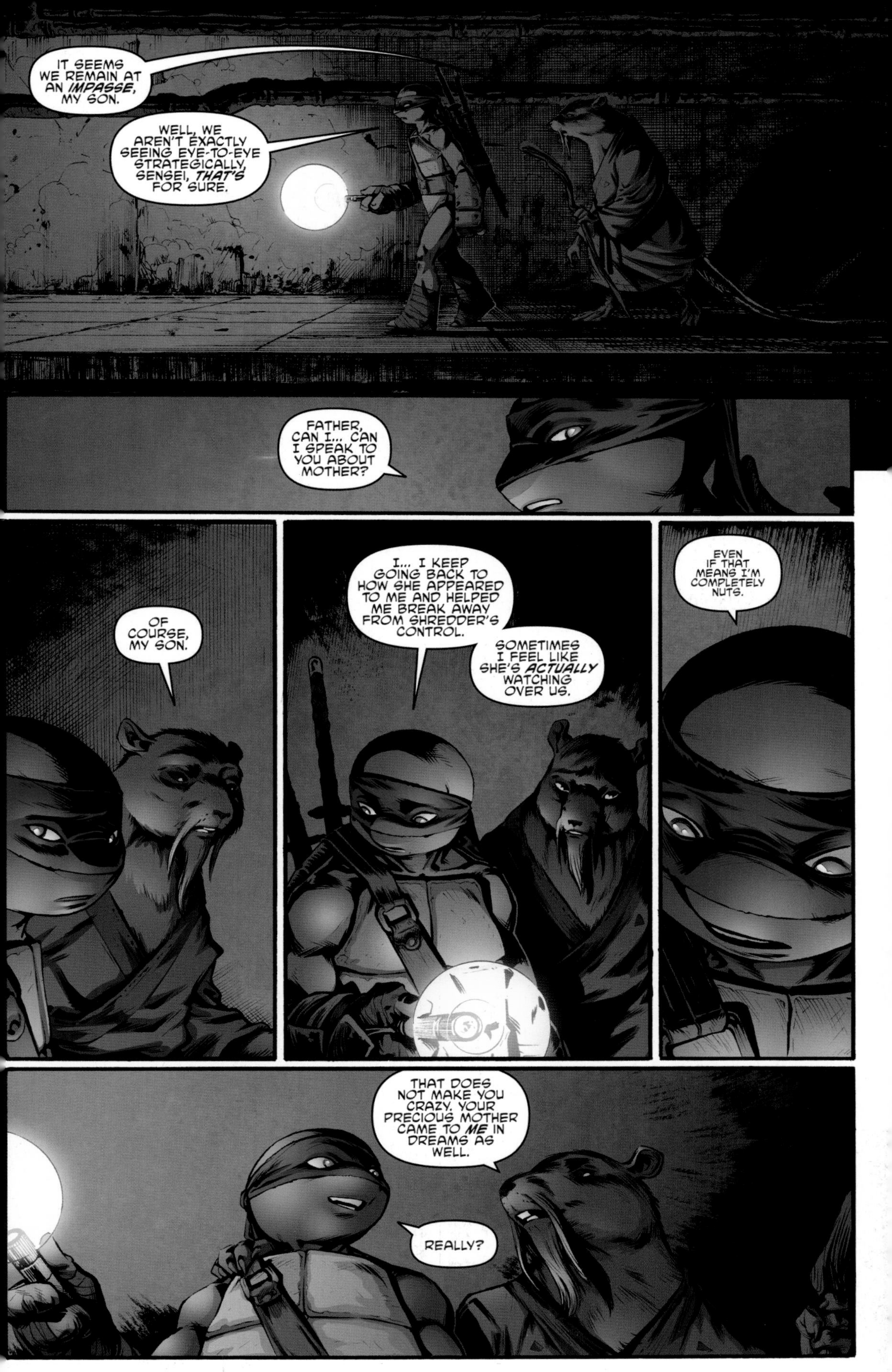
IT SEEMS WE REMAIN AT AN *IMPASSE*, MY SON.
WELL, WE AREN'T EXACTLY SEEING EYE-TO-EYE STRATEGICALLY, SENSEI, *THAT'S* FOR SURE.
FATHER, CAN I... CAN I SPEAK TO YOU ABOUT MOTHER?
OF COURSE, MY SON.
I... I KEEP GOING BACK TO HOW SHE APPEARED TO ME AND HELPED ME BREAK AWAY FROM SHREDDER'S CONTROL.
SOMETIMES I FEEL LIKE SHE'S *ACTUALLY* WATCHING OVER US.
EVEN IF THAT MEANS I'M COMPLETELY NUTS.
THAT DOES NOT MAKE YOU CRAZY. YOUR PRECIOUS MOTHER CAME TO *ME* IN DREAMS AS WELL.
REALLY?

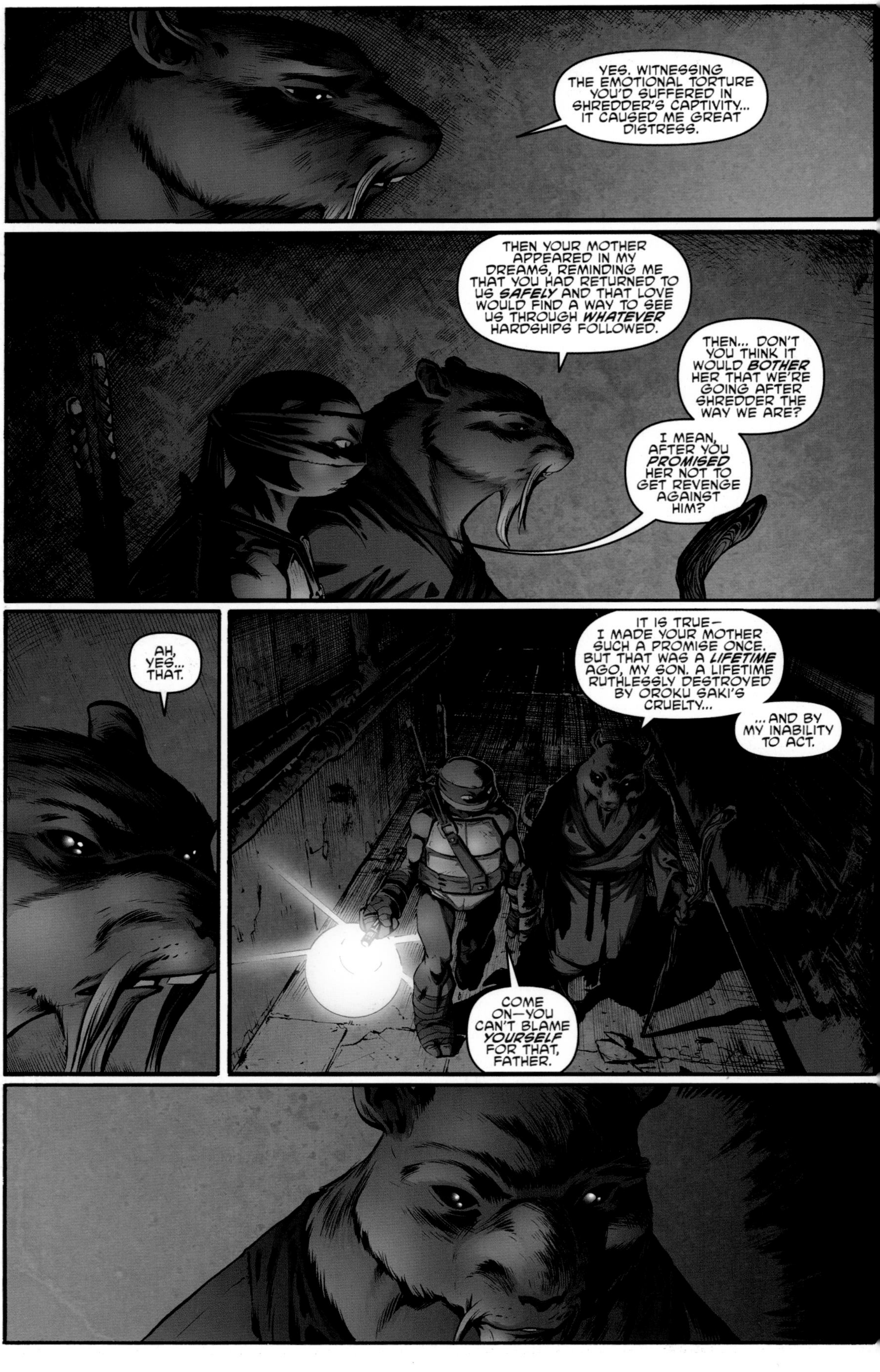
YES. WITNESSING THE EMOTIONAL TORTURE YOU'D SUFFERED IN SHREDDER'S CAPTIVITY... IT CAUSED ME GREAT DISTRESS.
THEN YOUR MOTHER APPEARED IN MY DREAMS, REMINDING ME THAT YOU HAD RETURNED TO US SAFELY AND THAT LOVE WOULD FIND A WAY TO SEE US THROUGH WHATEVER HARDSHIPS FOLLOWED.
THEN... DON'T YOU THINK IT WOULD BOTHER HER THAT WE'RE GOING AFTER SHREDDER THE WAY WE ARE?
I MEAN, AFTER YOU PROMISED HER NOT TO GET REVENGE AGAINST HIM?
AH, YES... THAT.
IT IS TRUE— I MADE YOUR MOTHER SUCH A PROMISE ONCE. BUT THAT WAS A LIFETIME AGO, MY SON. A LIFETIME RUTHLESSLY DESTROYED BY OROKU SAKI'S CRUELTY...
...AND BY MY INABILITY TO ACT.
COME ON—YOU CAN'T BLAME YOURSELF FOR THAT, FATHER.

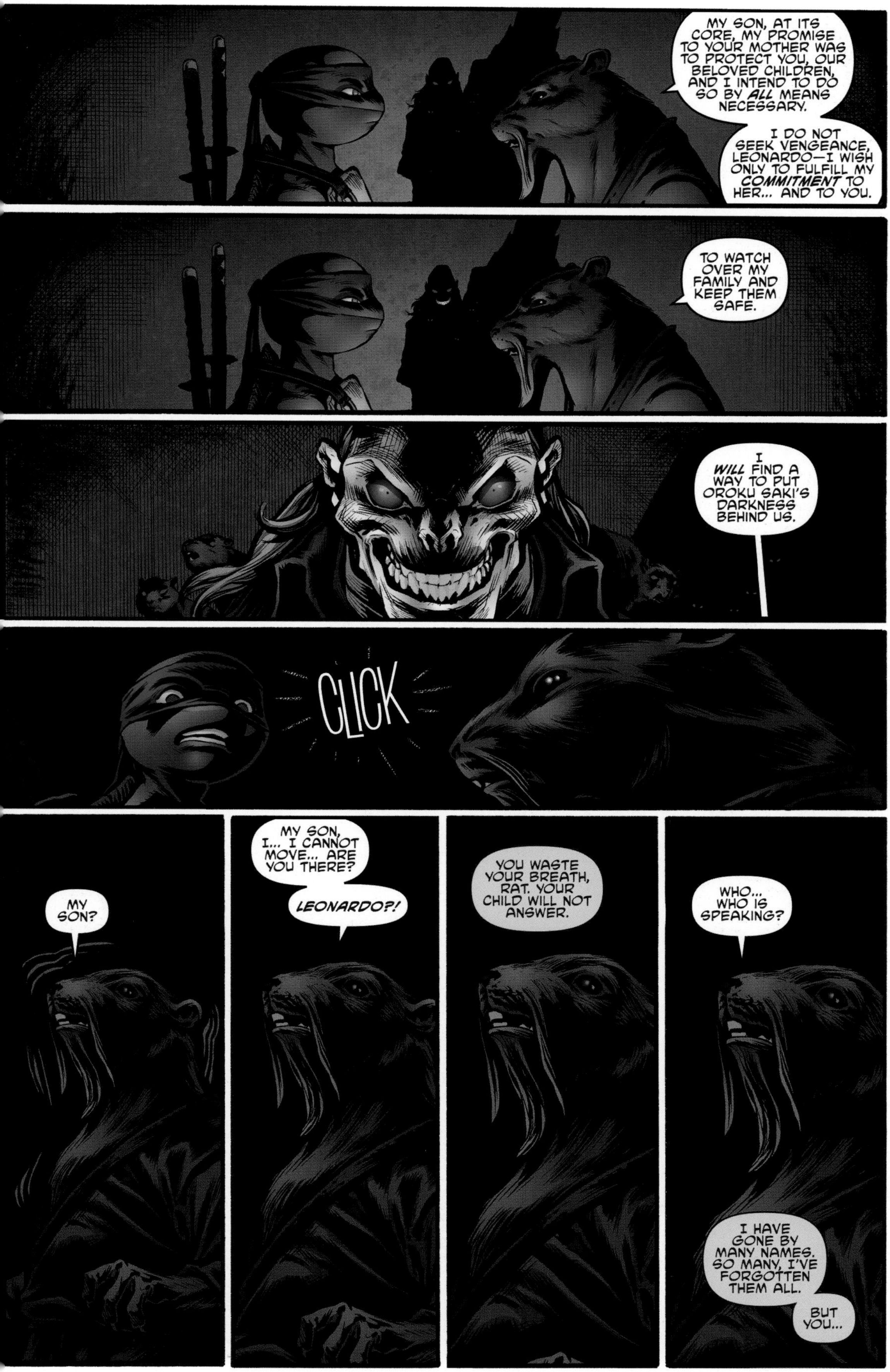
MY SON, AT ITS CORE, MY PROMISE TO YOUR MOTHER WAS TO PROTECT YOU, OUR BELOVED CHILDREN, AND I INTEND TO DO SO BY ALL MEANS NECESSARY.
I DO NOT SEEK VENGEANCE, LEONARDO—I WISH ONLY TO FULFILL MY COMMITMENT TO HER... AND TO YOU.
TO WATCH OVER MY FAMILY AND KEEP THEM SAFE.
I WILL FIND A WAY TO PUT OROKU SAKI'S DARKNESS BEHIND US.
CLICK
MY SON?
MY SON, I... I CANNOT MOVE... ARE YOU THERE?
LEONARDO?!
YOU WASTE YOUR BREATH, RAT. YOUR CHILD WILL NOT ANSWER.
WHO... WHO IS SPEAKING?
I HAVE GONE BY MANY NAMES. SO MANY, I'VE FORGOTTEN THEM ALL.
BUT YOU...

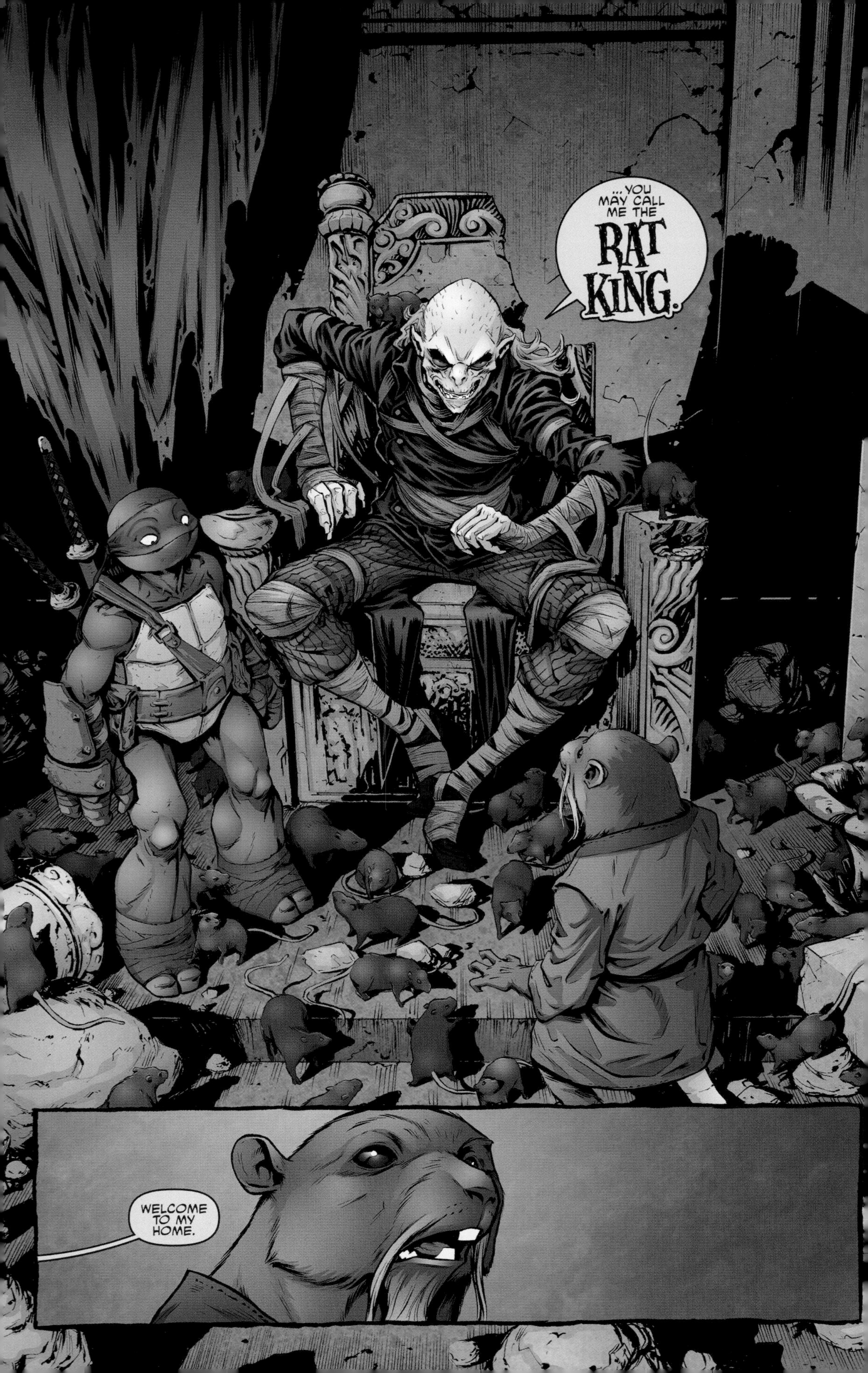
...YOU MAY CALL ME THE RAT KING.
WELCOME TO MY HOME.

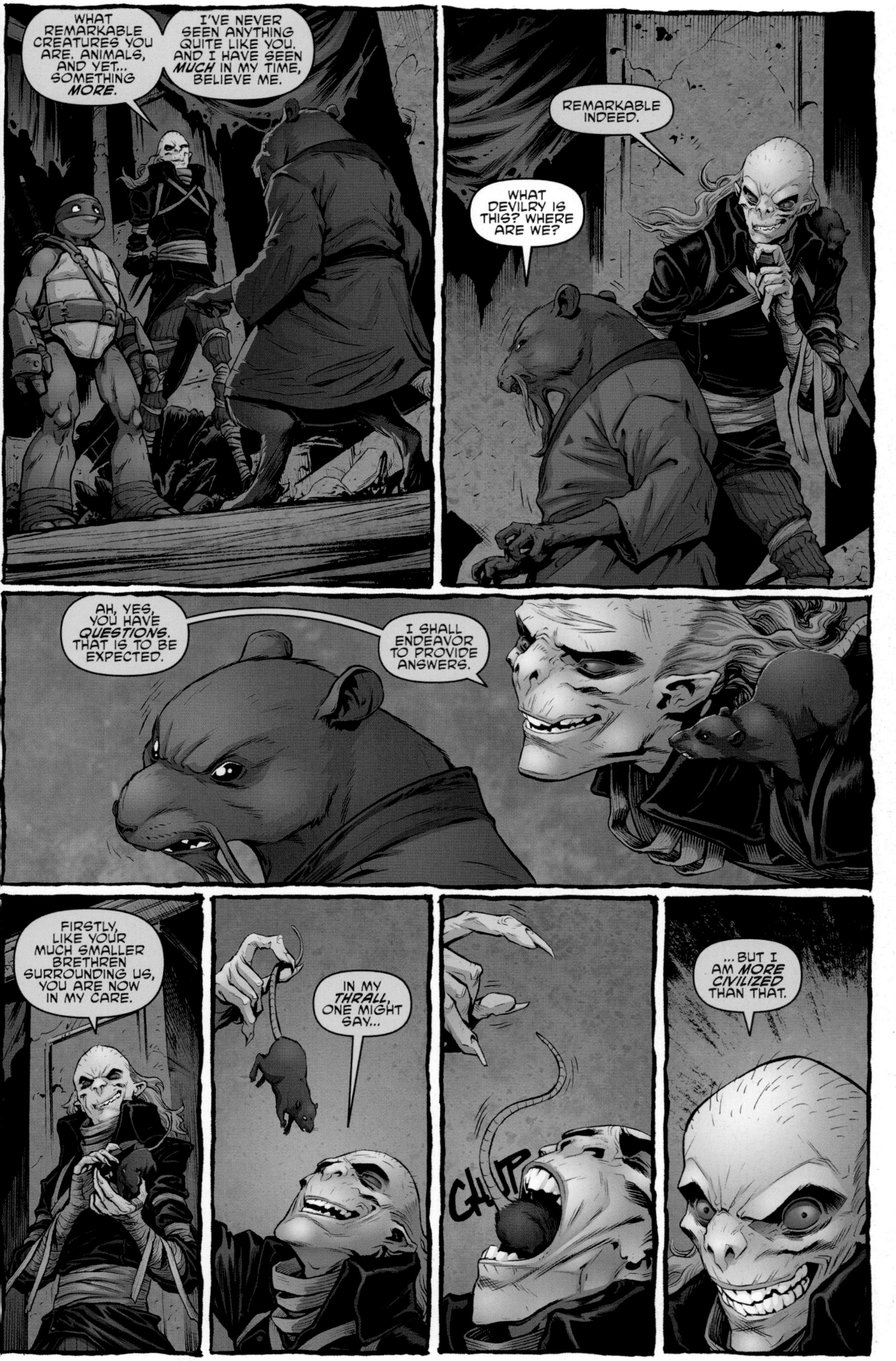
WHAT REMARKABLE CREATURES YOU ARE. ANIMALS, AND YET... SOMETHING MORE.
I'VE NEVER SEEN ANYTHING QUITE LIKE YOU. AND I HAVE SEEN MUCH IN MY TIME, BELIEVE ME.
REMARKABLE INDEED.
WHAT DEVILRY IS THIS? WHERE ARE WE?
AH, YES, YOU HAVE QUESTIONS. THAT IS TO BE EXPECTED.
I SHALL ENDEAVOR TO PROVIDE ANSWERS.
FIRSTLY, LIKE YOUR MUCH SMALLER BRETHREN SURROUNDING US, YOU ARE NOW IN MY CARE.
IN MY THRALL, ONE MIGHT SAY...
CHUP
...BUT I AM MORE CIVILIZED THAN THAT.

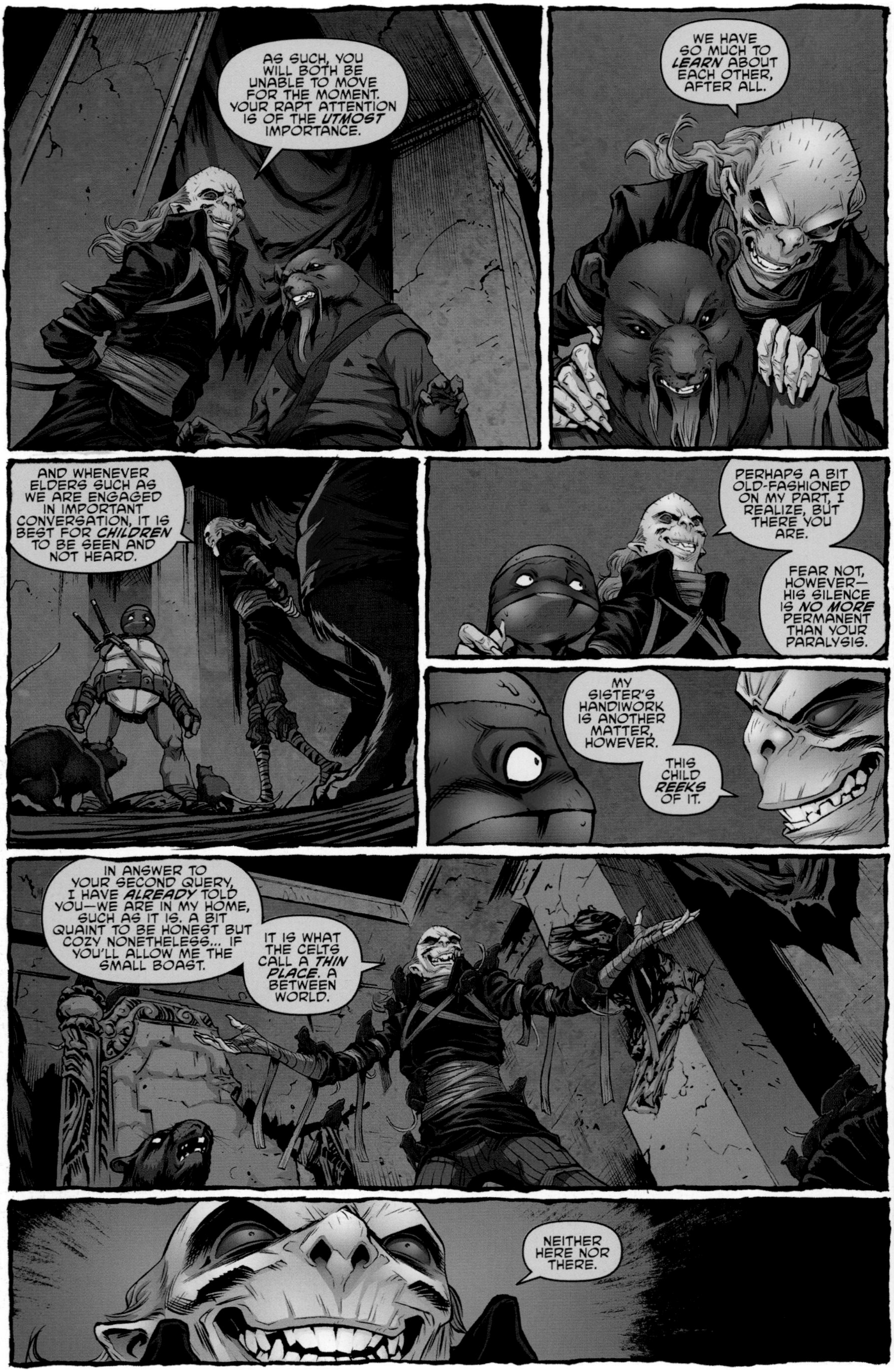
AS SUCH, YOU WILL BOTH BE UNABLE TO MOVE FOR THE MOMENT. YOUR RAPT ATTENTION IS OF THE UTMOST IMPORTANCE.
WE HAVE SO MUCH TO LEARN ABOUT EACH OTHER, AFTER ALL.
AND WHENEVER ELDERS SUCH AS WE ARE ENGAGED IN IMPORTANT CONVERSATION, IT IS BEST FOR CHILDREN TO BE SEEN AND NOT HEARD.
PERHAPS A BIT OLD-FASHIONED ON MY PART, I REALIZE, BUT THERE YOU ARE.
FEAR NOT, HOWEVER— HIS SILENCE IS NO MORE PERMANENT THAN YOUR PARALYSIS.
MY SISTER'S HANDIWORK IS ANOTHER MATTER, HOWEVER.
THIS CHILD REEKS OF IT.
IN ANSWER TO YOUR SECOND QUERY, I HAVE ALREADY TOLD YOU—WE ARE IN MY HOME, SUCH AS IT IS. A BIT QUAINT TO BE HONEST BUT COZY NONETHELESS... IF YOU'LL ALLOW ME THE SMALL BOAST.
IT IS WHAT THE CELTS CALL A THIN PLACE. A BETWEEN WORLD.
NEITHER HERE NOR THERE.

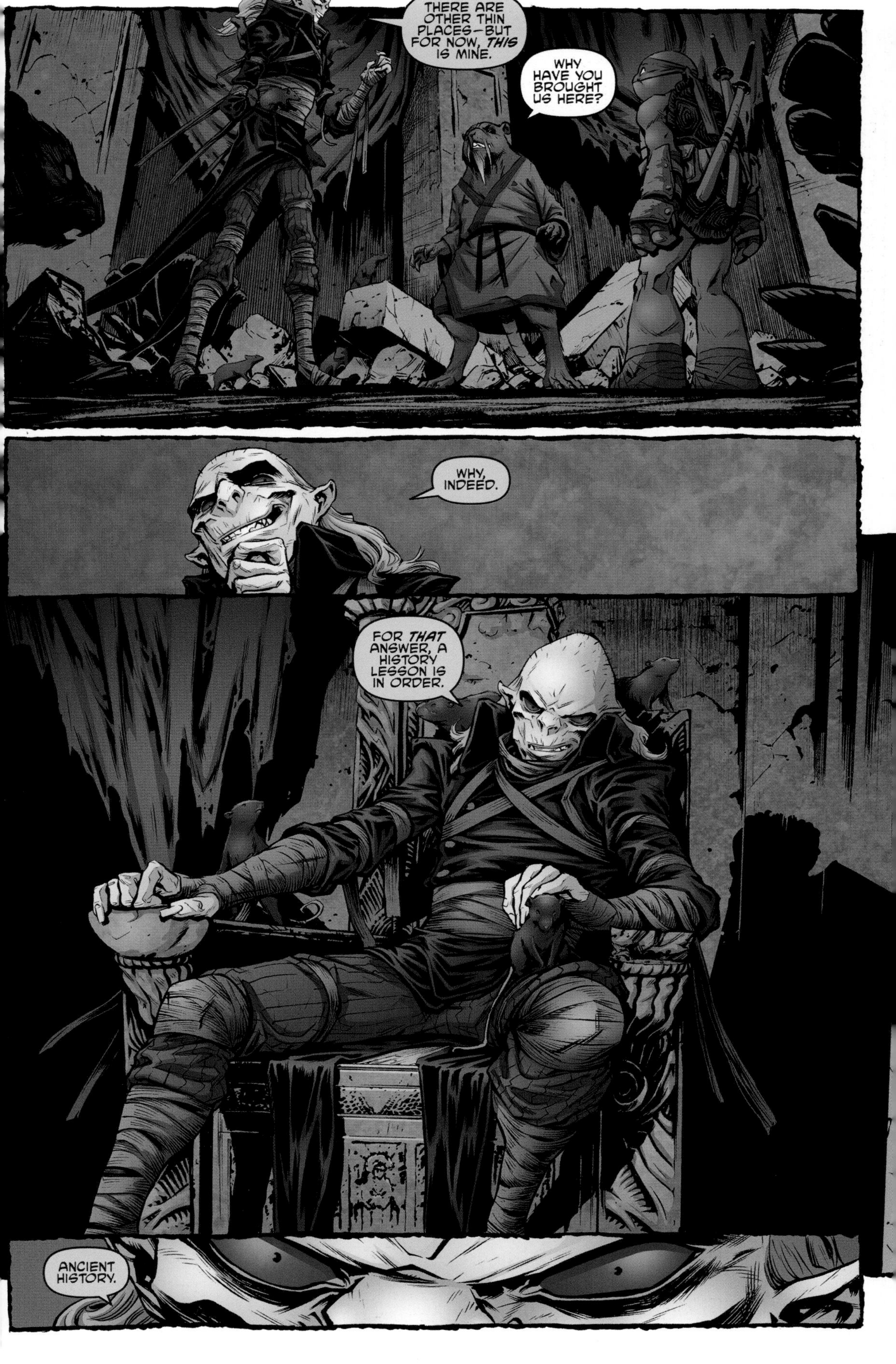
THERE ARE OTHER THIN PLACES—BUT FOR NOW, *THIS* IS MINE.
WHY HAVE YOU BROUGHT US HERE?
WHY, INDEED.
FOR *THAT* ANSWER, A HISTORY LESSON IS IN ORDER.
ANCIENT HISTORY.

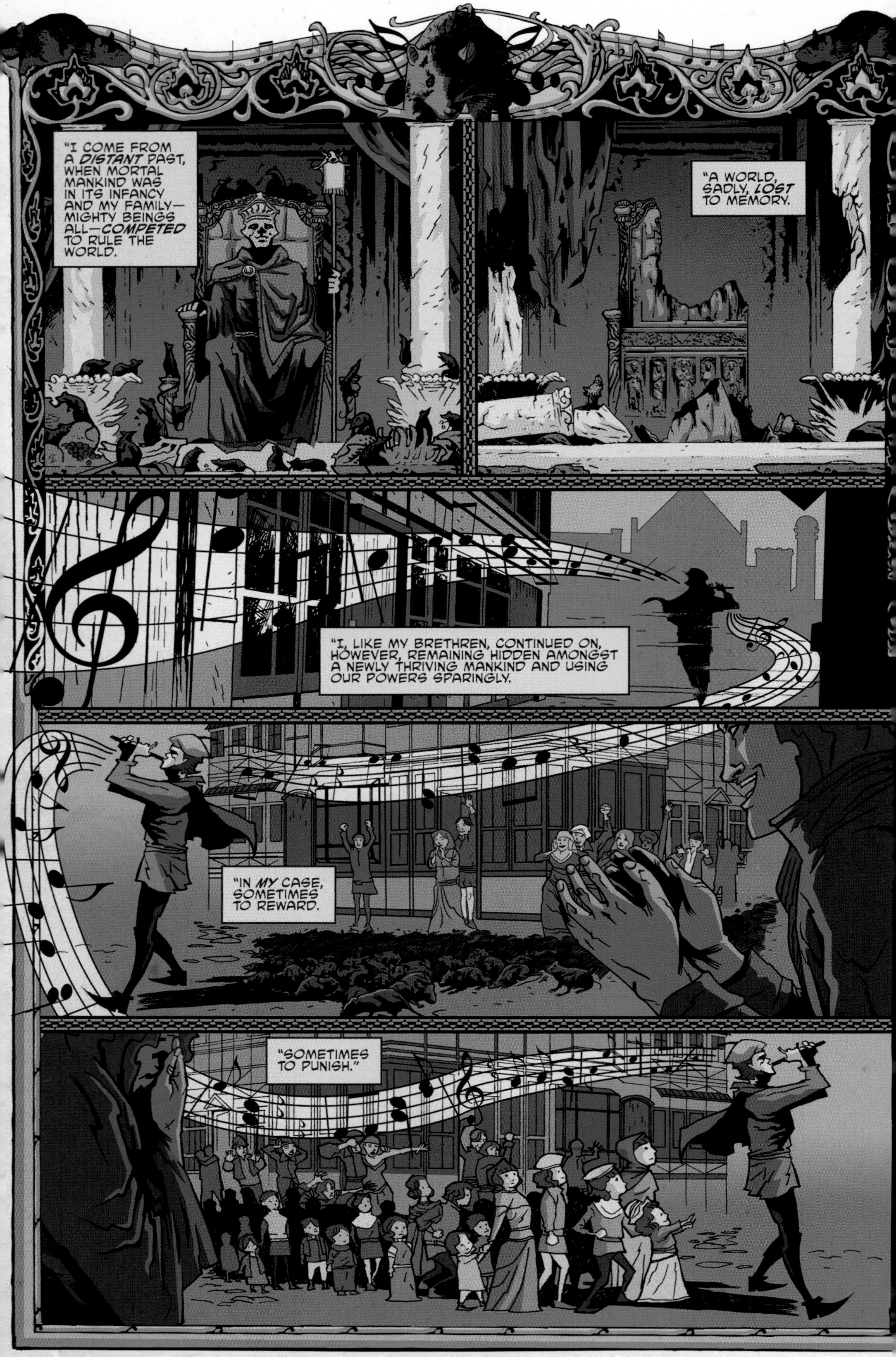
"I COME FROM A DISTANT PAST, WHEN MORTAL MANKIND WAS IN ITS INFANCY AND MY FAMILY—MIGHTY BEINGS ALL—COMPETED TO RULE THE WORLD.
"A WORLD, SADLY, LOST TO MEMORY.
"I, LIKE MY BRETHREN, CONTINUED ON, HOWEVER, REMAINING HIDDEN AMONGST A NEWLY THRIVING MANKIND AND USING OUR POWERS SPARINGLY.
"IN MY CASE, SOMETIMES TO REWARD.
"SOMETIMES TO PUNISH."

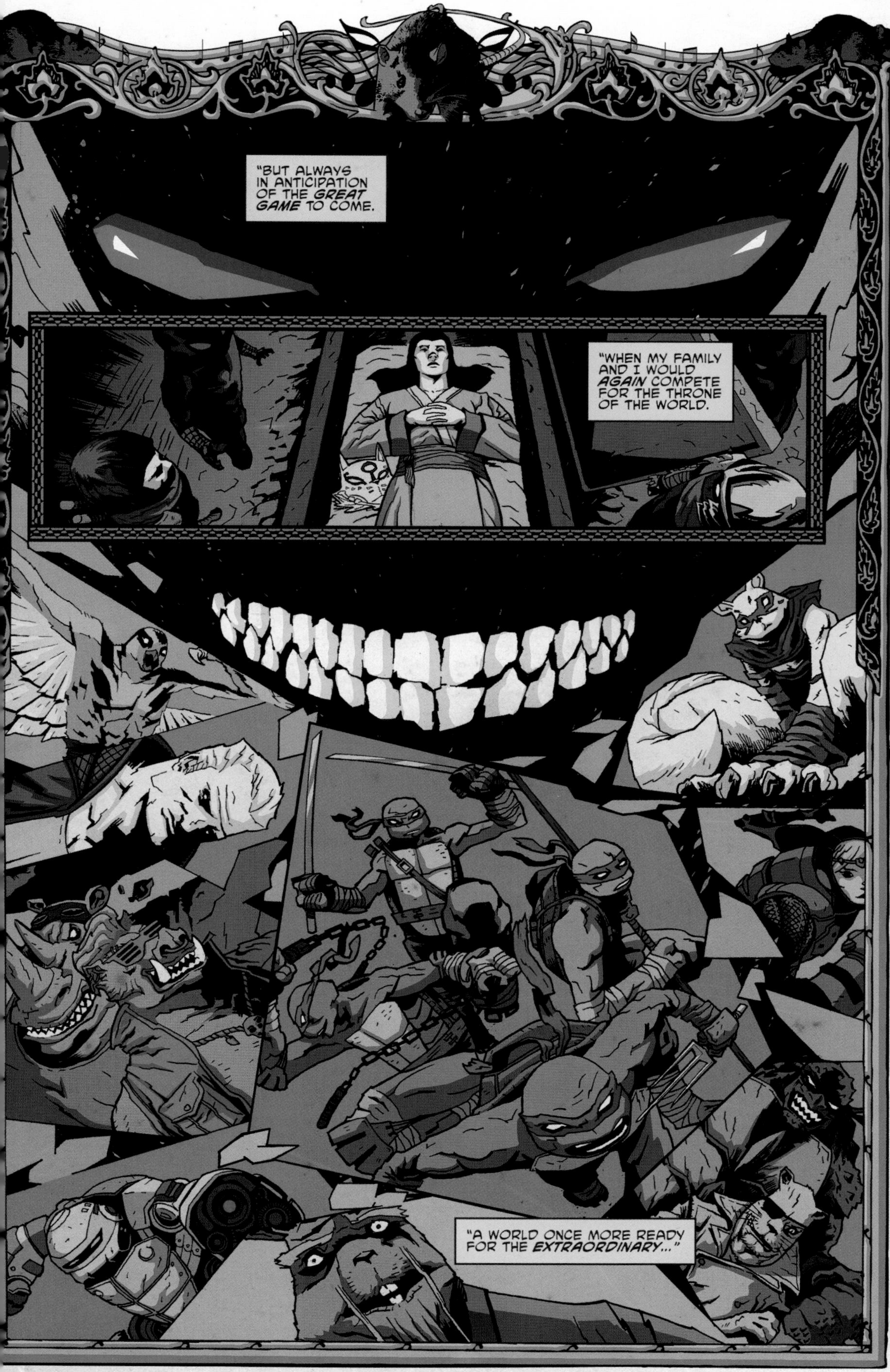
"BUT ALWAYS IN ANTICIPATION OF THE GREAT GAME TO COME.
"WHEN MY FAMILY AND I WOULD AGAIN COMPETE FOR THE THRONE OF THE WORLD.
"A WORLD ONCE MORE READY FOR THE EXTRAORDINARY..."

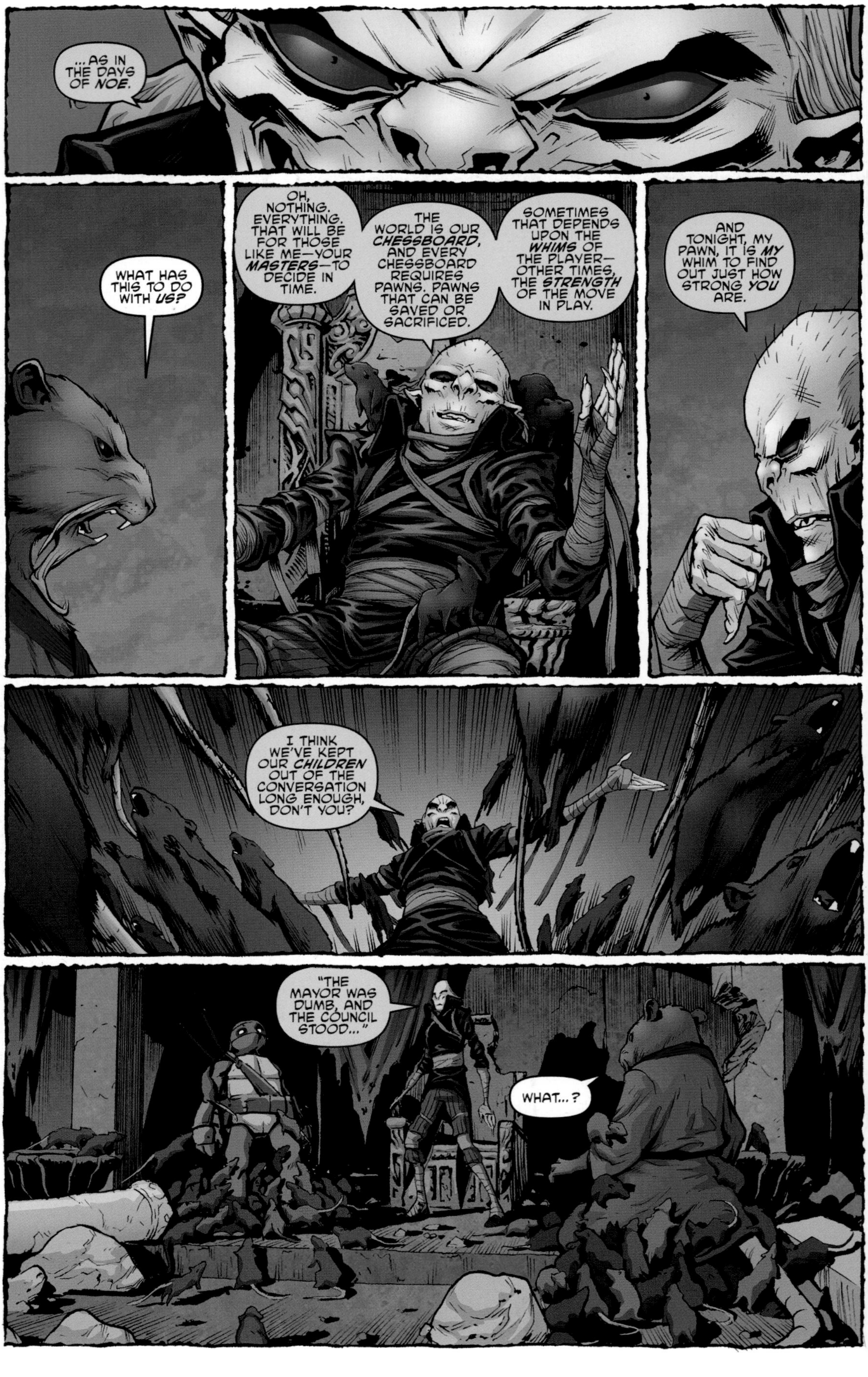
...AS IN THE DAYS OF NOE.
WHAT HAS THIS TO DO WITH US?
OH, NOTHING. EVERYTHING. THAT WILL BE FOR THOSE LIKE ME—YOUR MASTERS—TO DECIDE IN TIME.
THE WORLD IS OUR CHESSBOARD, AND EVERY CHESSBOARD REQUIRES PAWNS. PAWNS THAT CAN BE SAVED OR SACRIFICED.
SOMETIMES THAT DEPENDS UPON THE WHIMS OF THE PLAYER—OTHER TIMES, THE STRENGTH OF THE MOVE IN PLAY.
AND TONIGHT, MY PAWN, IT IS MY WHIM TO FIND OUT JUST HOW STRONG YOU ARE.
I THINK WE'VE KEPT OUR CHILDREN OUT OF THE CONVERSATION LONG ENOUGH, DON'T YOU?
"THE MAYOR WAS DUMB, AND THE COUNCIL STOOD..."
WHAT...?

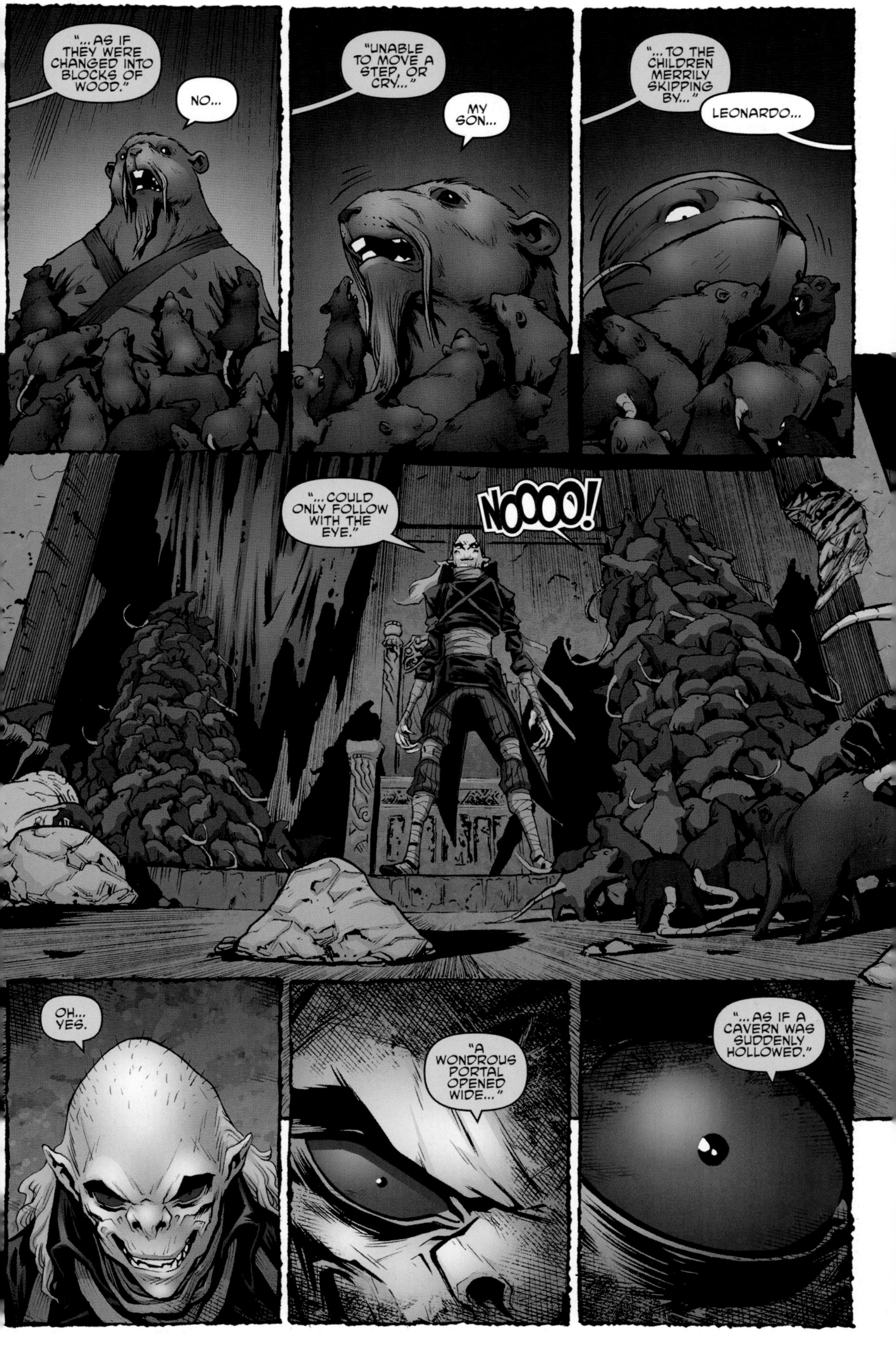
"...AS IF THEY WERE CHANGED INTO BLOCKS OF WOOD."
NO...
"UNABLE TO MOVE A STEP, OR CRY..."
MY SON...
"...TO THE CHILDREN MERRILY SKIPPING BY..."
LEONARDO...
"...COULD ONLY FOLLOW WITH THE EYE."
NOOOO!
OH... YES.
"A WONDROUS PORTAL OPENED WIDE..."
"...AS IF A CAVERN WAS SUDDENLY HOLLOWED."

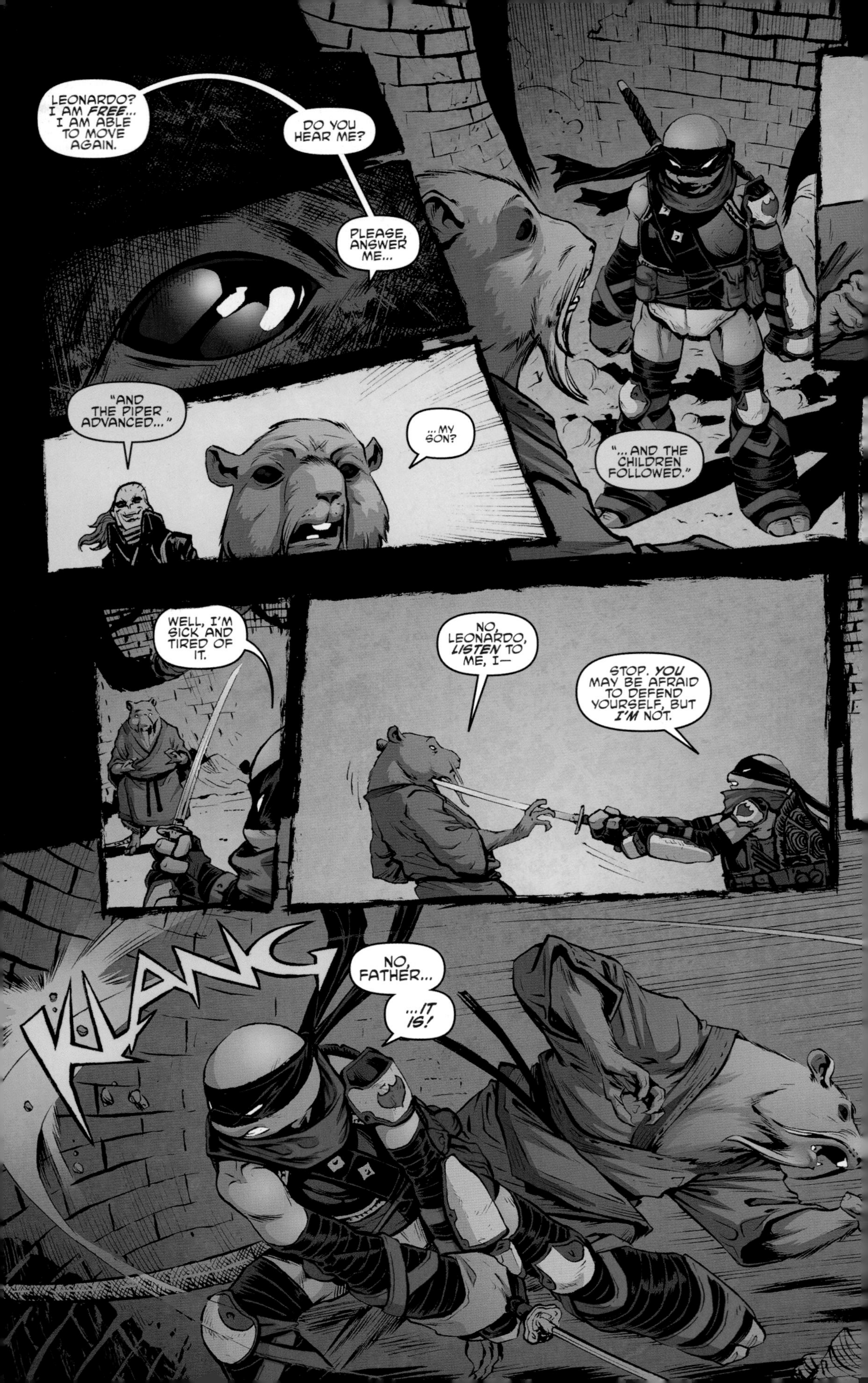
LEONARDO? I AM FREE... I AM ABLE TO MOVE AGAIN.
DO YOU HEAR ME?
PLEASE, ANSWER ME...
"AND THE PIPER ADVANCED..."
...MY SON?
"...AND THE CHILDREN FOLLOWED."
WELL, I'M SICK AND TIRED OF IT.
NO, LEONARDO, LISTEN TO ME, I—
STOP. YOU MAY BE AFRAID TO DEFEND YOURSELF, BUT I'M NOT.
KLANG
NO, FATHER...
...IT IS!

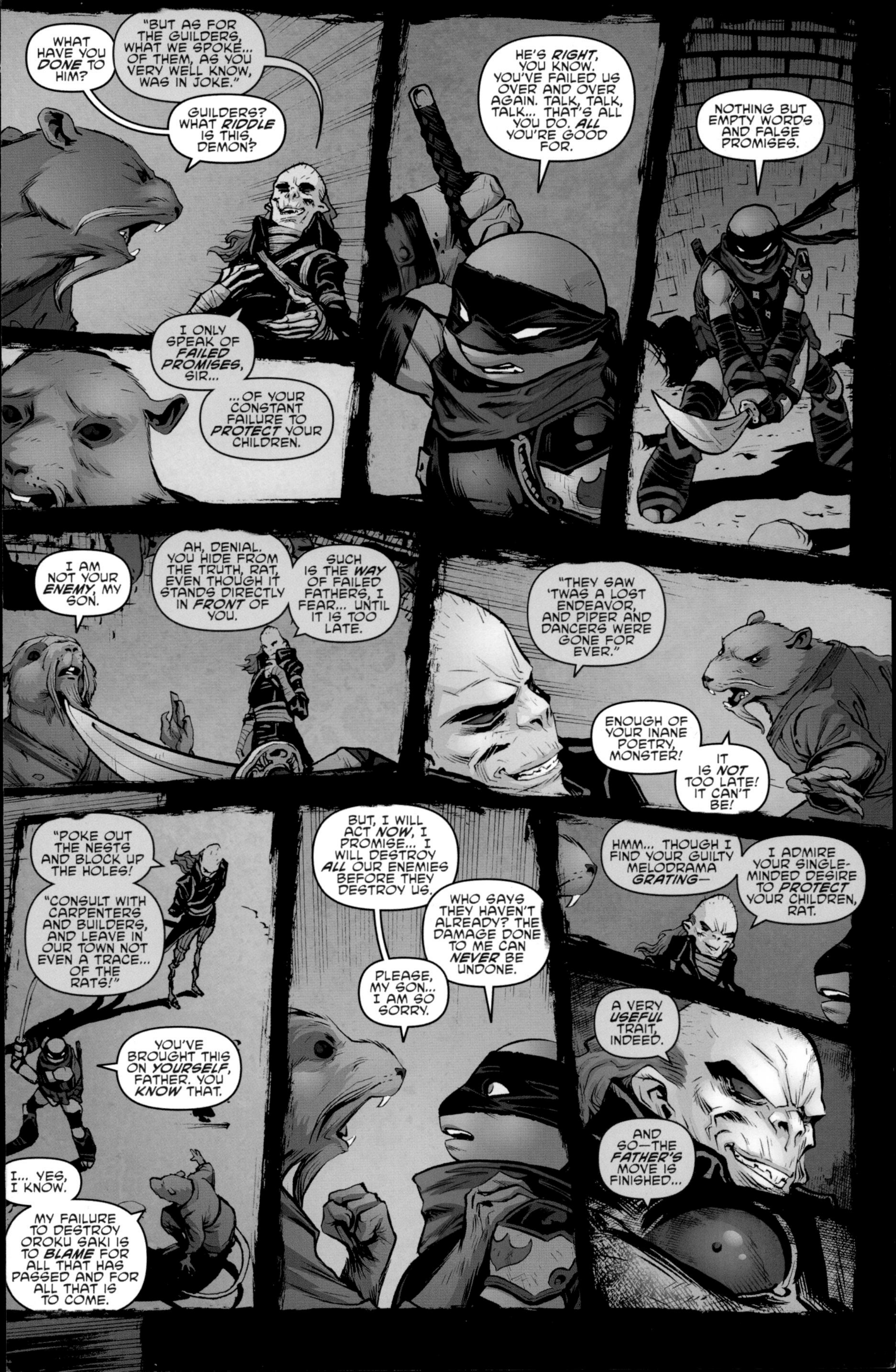
WHAT HAVE YOU DONE TO HIM?
"BUT AS FOR THE GUILDERS, WHAT WE SPOKE... OF THEM, AS YOU VERY WELL KNOW, WAS IN JOKE."
GUILDERS? WHAT RIDDLE IS THIS, DEMON?
I ONLY SPEAK OF FAILED PROMISES, SIR...
...OF YOUR CONSTANT FAILURE TO PROTECT YOUR CHILDREN.
HE'S RIGHT, YOU KNOW. YOU'VE FAILED US OVER AND OVER AGAIN. TALK, TALK, TALK... THAT'S ALL YOU DO. ALL YOU'RE GOOD FOR.
NOTHING BUT EMPTY WORDS AND FALSE PROMISES.
I AM NOT YOUR ENEMY, MY SON.
AH, DENIAL. YOU HIDE FROM THE TRUTH, RAT, EVEN THOUGH IT STANDS DIRECTLY IN FRONT OF YOU.
SUCH IS THE WAY OF FAILED FATHERS, I FEAR... UNTIL IT IS TOO LATE.
"THEY SAW 'TWAS A LOST ENDEAVOR, AND PIPER AND DANCERS WERE GONE FOR EVER."
ENOUGH OF YOUR INANE POETRY, MONSTER!
IT IS NOT TOO LATE! IT CAN'T BE!
"POKE OUT THE NESTS AND BLOCK UP THE HOLES!
"CONSULT WITH CARPENTERS AND BUILDERS, AND LEAVE IN OUR TOWN NOT EVEN A TRACE... OF THE RATS!"
YOU'VE BROUGHT THIS ON YOURSELF, FATHER. YOU KNOW THAT.
I... YES, I KNOW.
MY FAILURE TO DESTROY OROKU SAKI IS TO BLAME FOR ALL THAT HAS PASSED AND FOR ALL THAT IS TO COME.
BUT, I WILL ACT NOW, I PROMISE... I WILL DESTROY ALL OUR ENEMIES BEFORE THEY DESTROY US.
WHO SAYS THEY HAVEN'T ALREADY? THE DAMAGE DONE TO ME CAN NEVER BE UNDONE.
PLEASE, MY SON... I AM SO SORRY.
HMM... THOUGH I FIND YOUR GUILTY MELODRAMA GRATING—
I ADMIRE YOUR SINGLE-MINDED DESIRE TO PROTECT YOUR CHILDREN, RAT.
A VERY USEFUL TRAIT, INDEED.
AND SO—THE FATHER'S MOVE IS FINISHED...

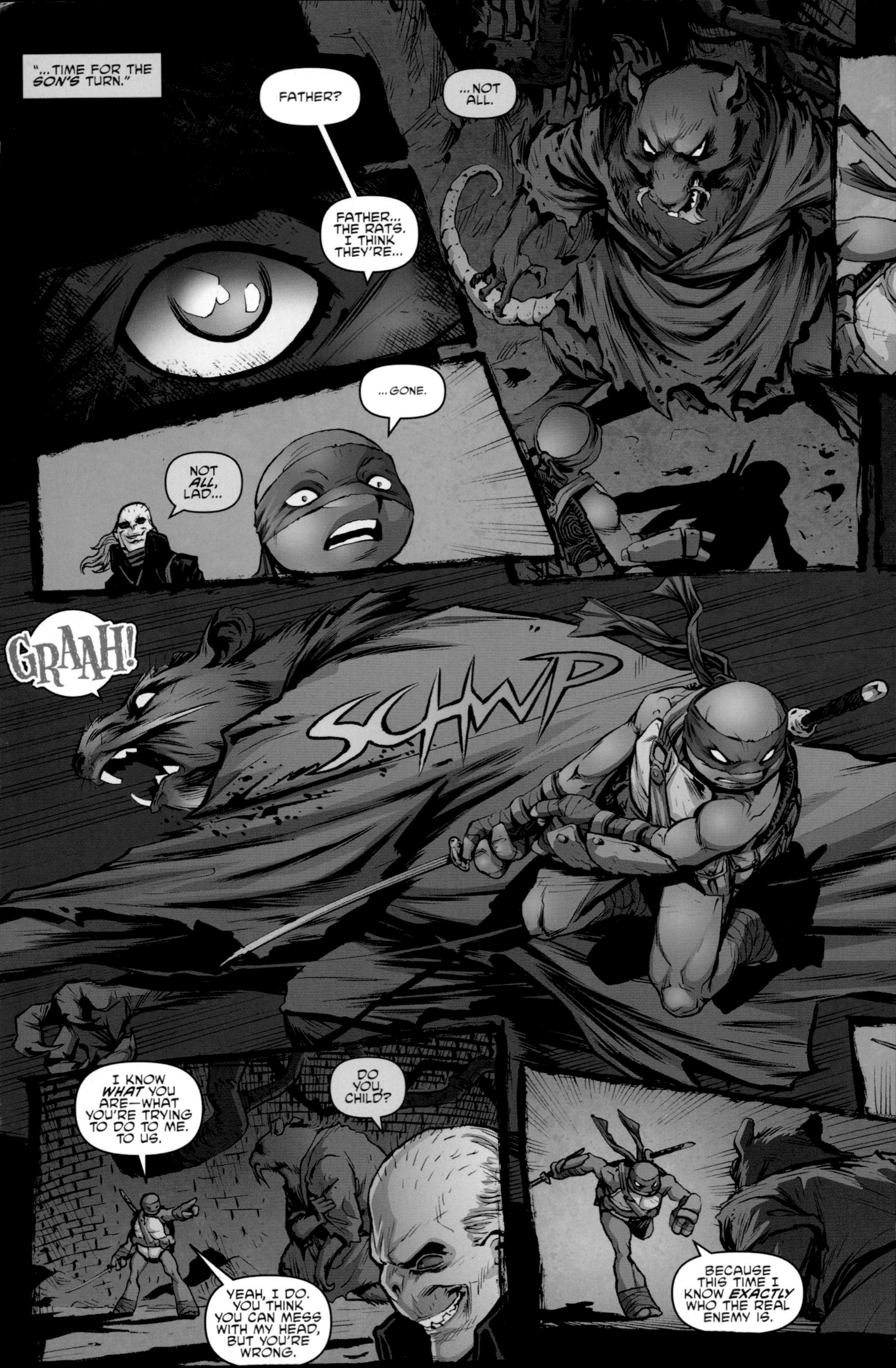
"...TIME FOR THE SON'S TURN."
FATHER?
...NOT ALL.
FATHER... THE RATS. I THINK THEY'RE...
...GONE.
NOT ALL, LAD...
GRAAH!
SCHWP
I KNOW WHAT YOU ARE—WHAT YOU'RE TRYING TO DO TO ME. TO US.
DO YOU, CHILD?
YEAH, I DO. YOU THINK YOU CAN MESS WITH MY HEAD, BUT YOU'RE WRONG.
BECAUSE THIS TIME I KNOW EXACTLY WHO THE REAL ENEMY IS.

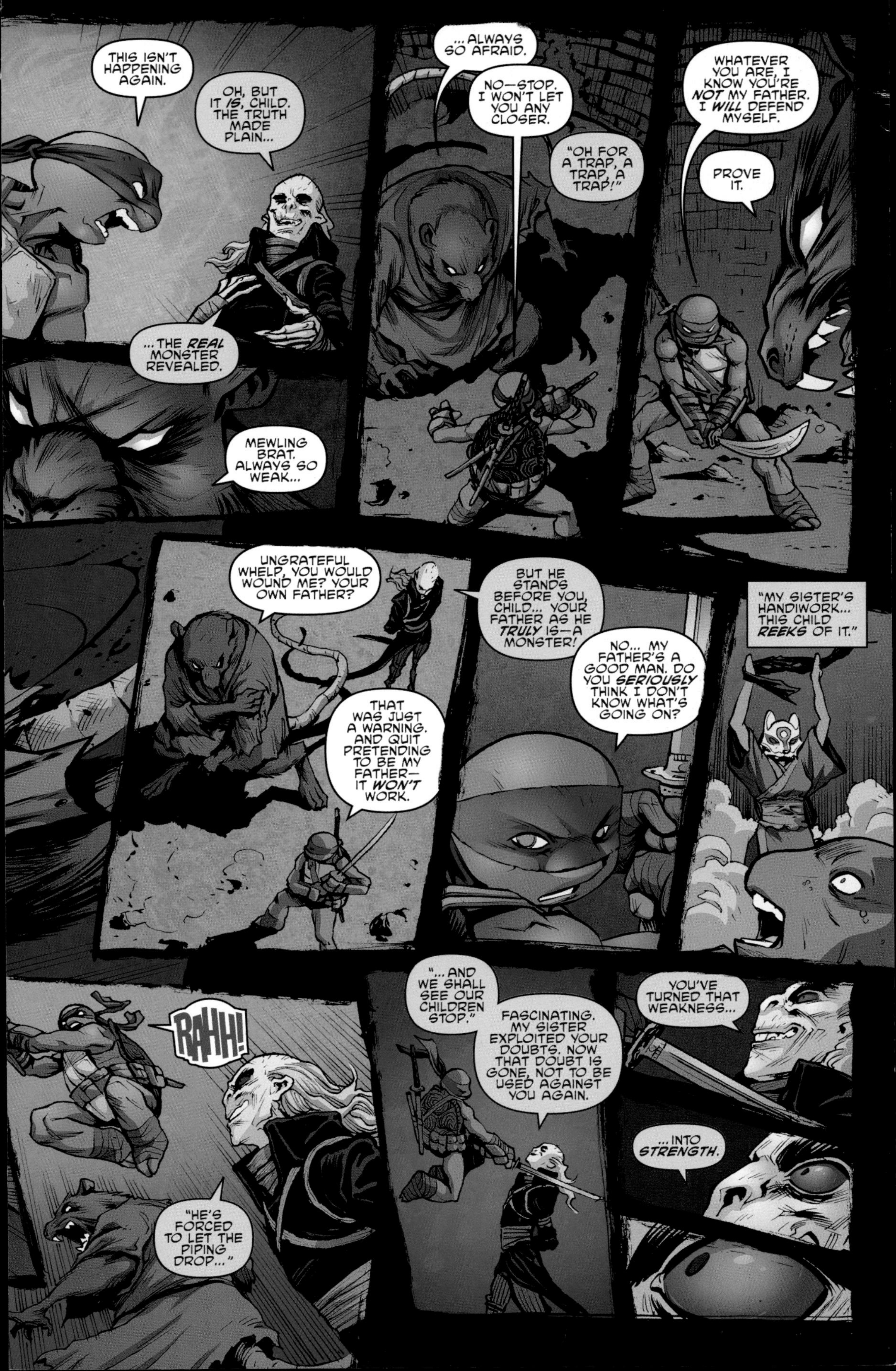
THIS ISN'T HAPPENING AGAIN.
OH, BUT IT *IS*, CHILD. THE TRUTH MADE PLAIN...
...THE *REAL* MONSTER REVEALED.
MEWLING BRAT. ALWAYS SO WEAK...
...ALWAYS SO AFRAID.
NO—STOP. I WON'T LET YOU ANY CLOSER.
"OH FOR A TRAP, A TRAP, A TRAP!"
WHATEVER YOU ARE, I KNOW YOU'RE *NOT* MY FATHER. I *WILL* DEFEND MYSELF.
PROVE IT.
UNGRATEFUL WHELP, YOU WOULD WOUND ME? YOUR OWN FATHER?
THAT WAS JUST A WARNING. AND QUIT PRETENDING TO BE MY FATHER— IT *WON'T* WORK.
BUT HE STANDS BEFORE YOU, CHILD... YOUR FATHER AS HE *TRULY* IS—A MONSTER!
NO... MY FATHER'S A GOOD MAN. DO YOU *SERIOUSLY* THINK I DON'T KNOW WHAT'S GOING ON?
"MY SISTER'S HANDIWORK... THIS CHILD *REEKS* OF IT."
RAHH!
"HE'S FORCED TO LET THE PIPING DROP..."
"...AND WE SHALL SEE OUR CHILDREN STOP."
FASCINATING. MY SISTER EXPLOITED YOUR DOUBTS. NOW THAT DOUBT IS GONE, NOT TO BE USED AGAINST YOU AGAIN.
YOU'VE TURNED THAT WEAKNESS...
...INTO *STRENGTH*.

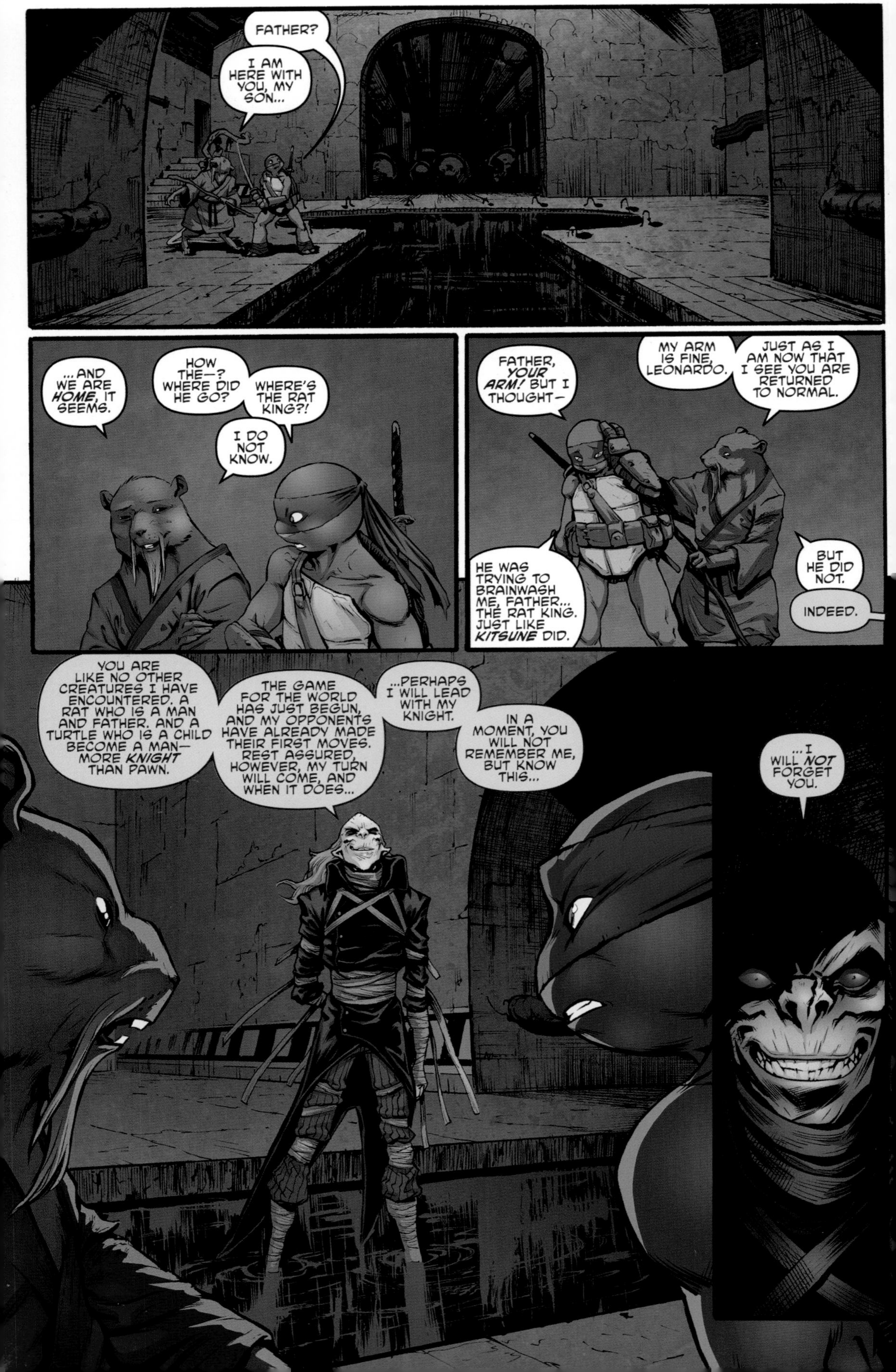
FATHER?
I AM HERE WITH YOU, MY SON...
...AND WE ARE *HOME*, IT SEEMS.
HOW THE—? WHERE DID HE GO?
WHERE'S THE RAT KING?!
I DO NOT KNOW.
FATHER, *YOUR ARM!* BUT I THOUGHT—
MY ARM IS FINE, LEONARDO.
JUST AS I AM NOW THAT I SEE YOU ARE RETURNED TO NORMAL.
HE WAS TRYING TO BRAINWASH ME, FATHER... THE RAT KING. JUST LIKE *KITSUNE* DID.
BUT HE DID NOT.
INDEED.
YOU ARE LIKE NO OTHER CREATURES I HAVE ENCOUNTERED. A RAT WHO IS A MAN AND FATHER. AND A TURTLE WHO IS A CHILD BECOME A MAN—MORE *KNIGHT* THAN PAWN.
THE GAME FOR THE WORLD HAS JUST BEGUN, AND MY OPPONENTS HAVE ALREADY MADE THEIR FIRST MOVES. REST ASSURED, HOWEVER, MY TURN WILL COME, AND WHEN IT DOES...
...PERHAPS I WILL LEAD WITH MY KNIGHT.
IN A MOMENT, YOU WILL NOT REMEMBER ME, BUT KNOW THIS...
...I WILL *NOT* FORGET YOU.

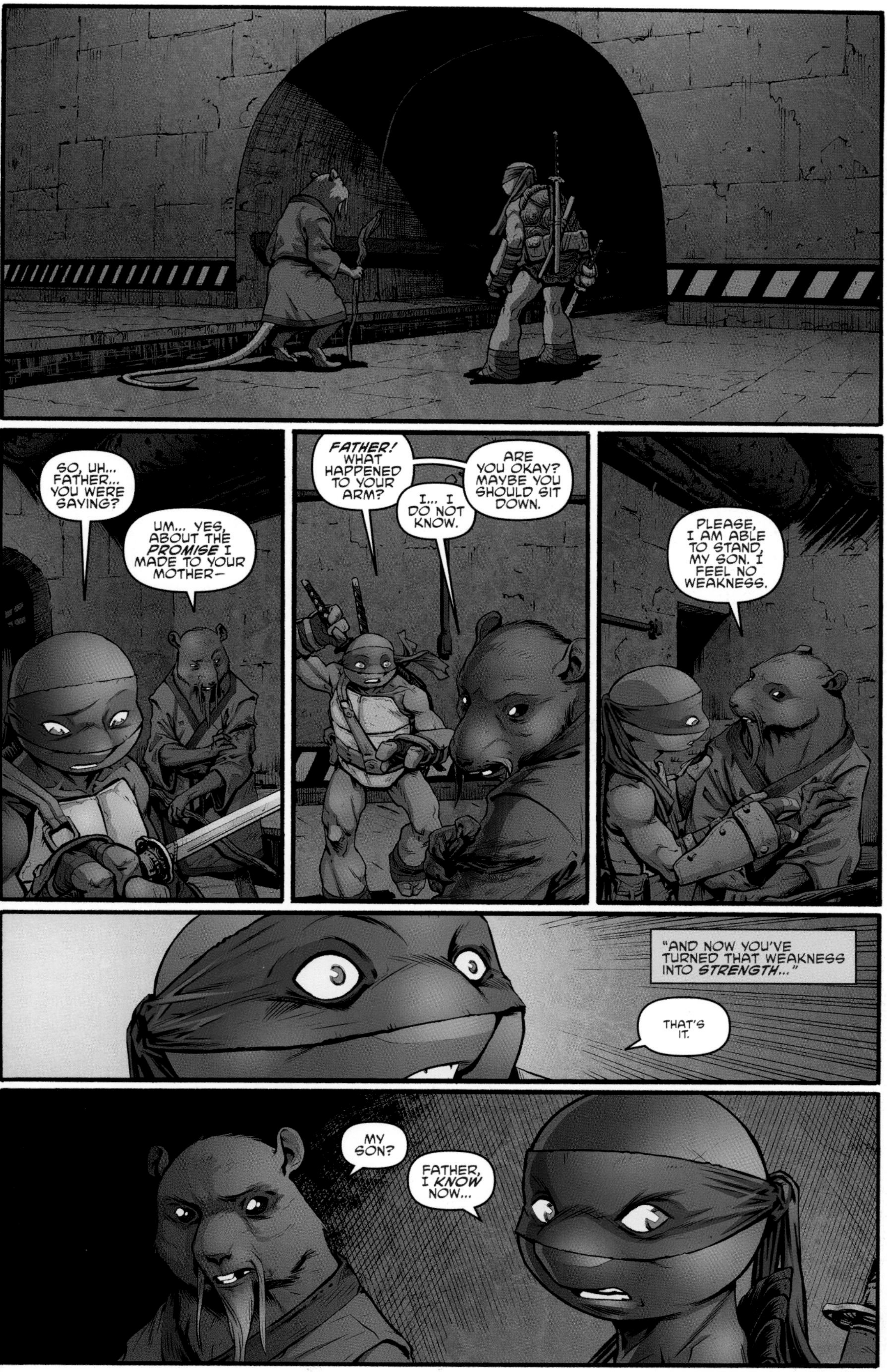
SO, UH... FATHER... YOU WERE SAYING?
UM... YES, ABOUT THE *PROMISE* I MADE TO YOUR MOTHER--
FATHER! WHAT HAPPENED TO YOUR ARM?
I... I DO NOT KNOW.
ARE YOU OKAY? MAYBE YOU SHOULD SIT DOWN.
PLEASE, I AM ABLE TO STAND, MY SON. I FEEL NO WEAKNESS.
"AND NOW YOU'VE TURNED THAT WEAKNESS INTO *STRENGTH...*"
THAT'S IT.
MY SON?
FATHER, I *KNOW* NOW...

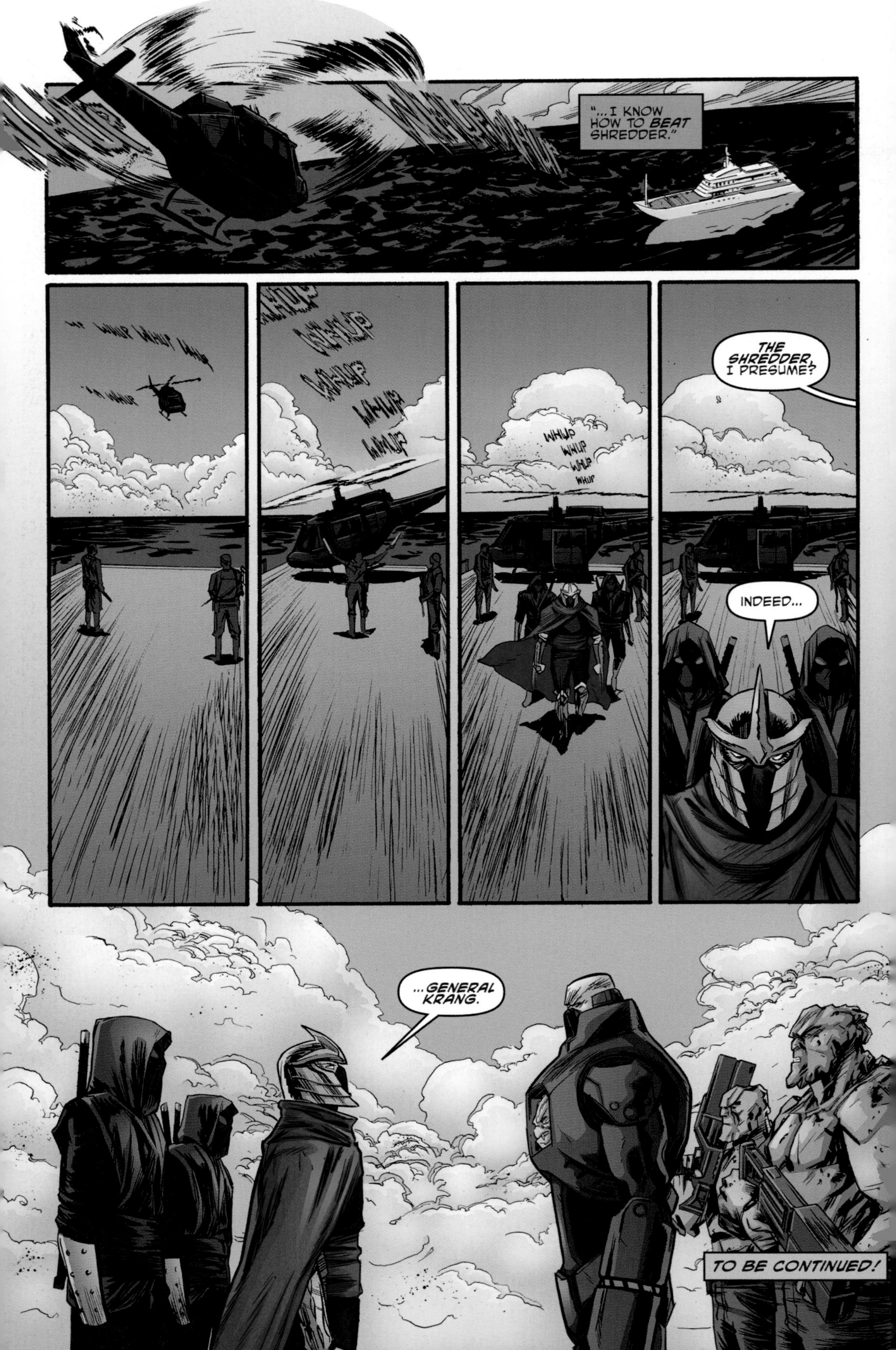
"...I KNOW HOW TO BEAT SHREDDER."
WHUP WHUP WHUP WHUP
THE SHREDDER, I PRESUME?
INDEED...
...GENERAL KRANG.
TO BE CONTINUED!

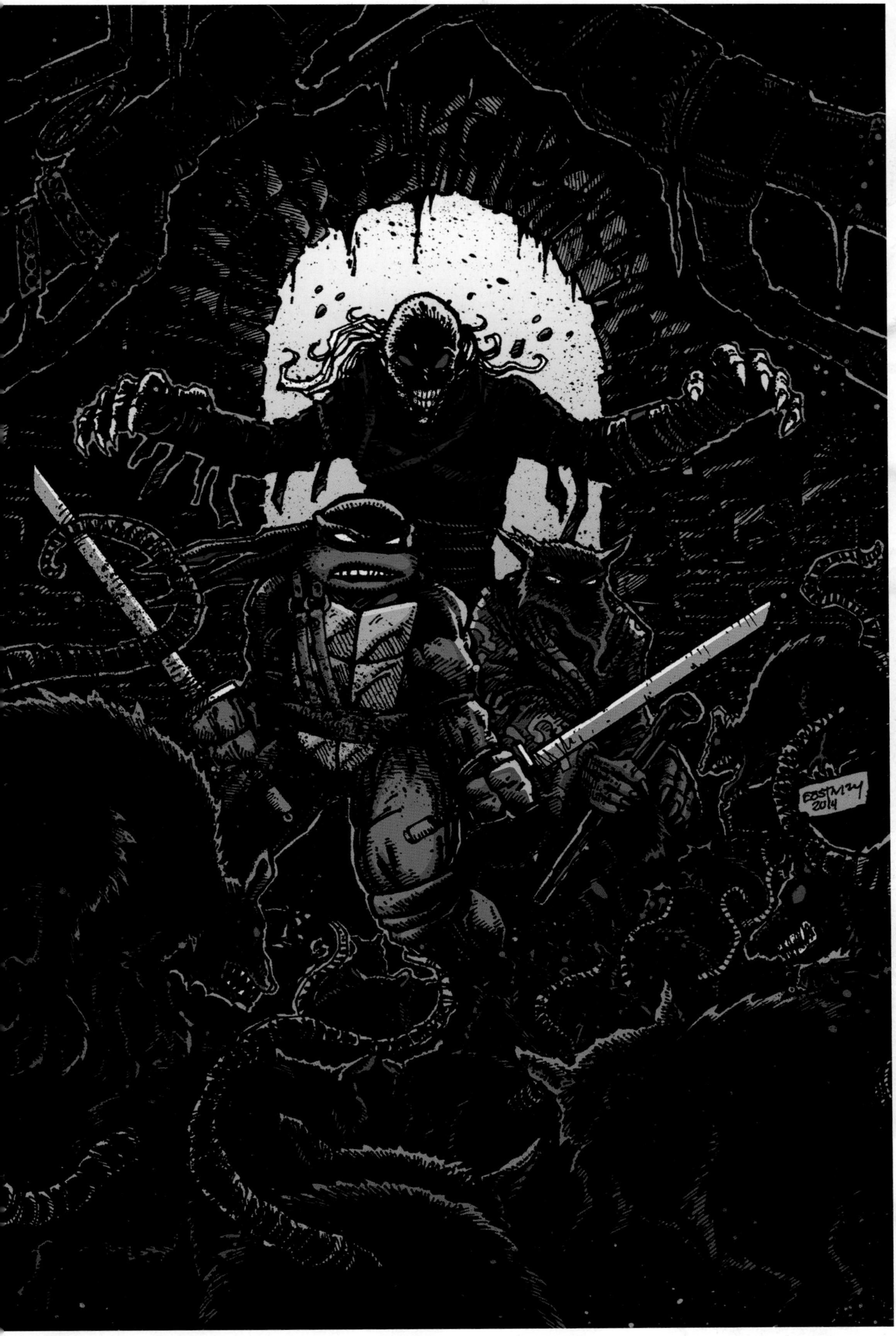
EASTMAN
2014

Cover by KEVIN EASTMAN
Colors by RONDA PATTISON

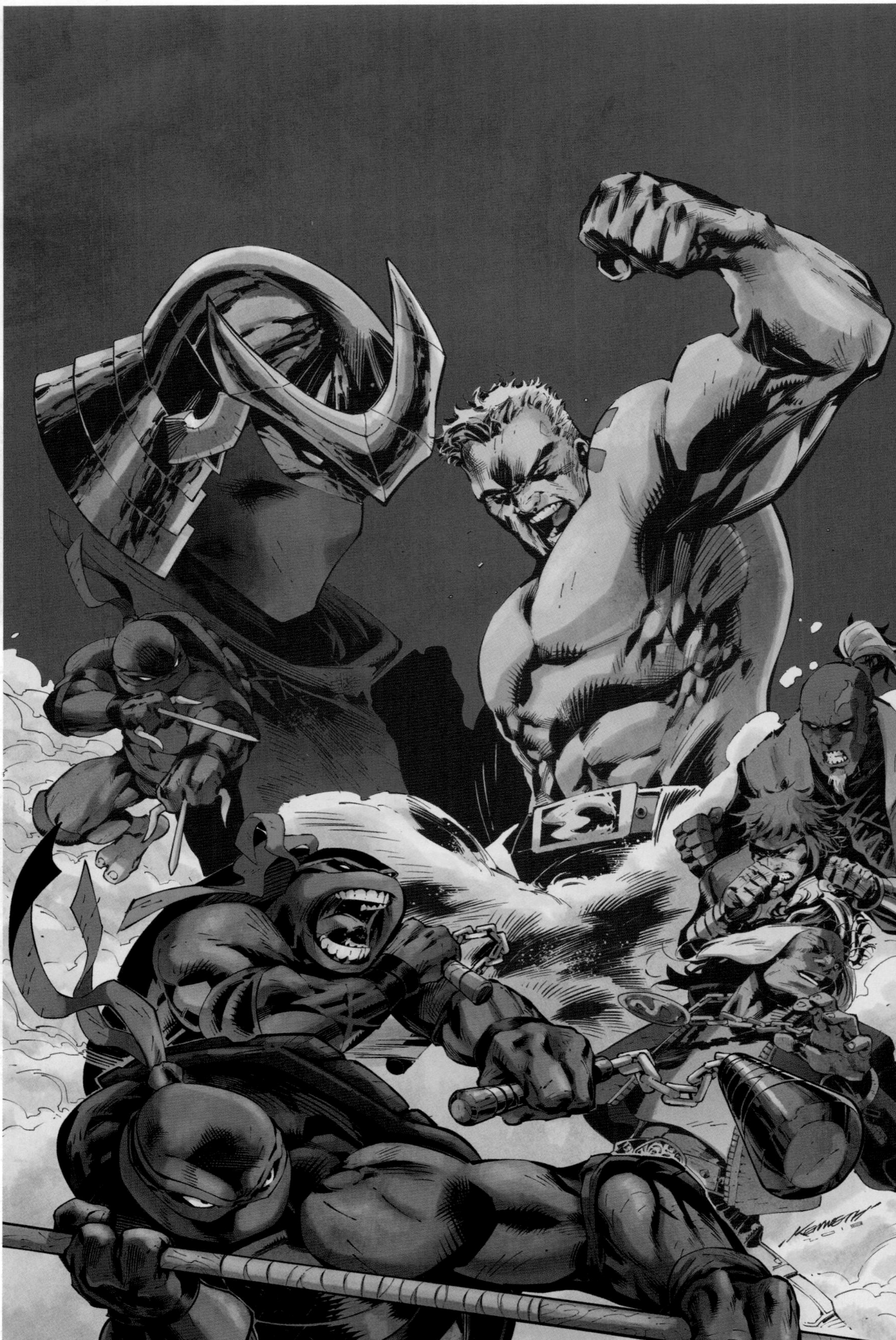

Cover by KENNETH LOH
Colors by IAN HERRING

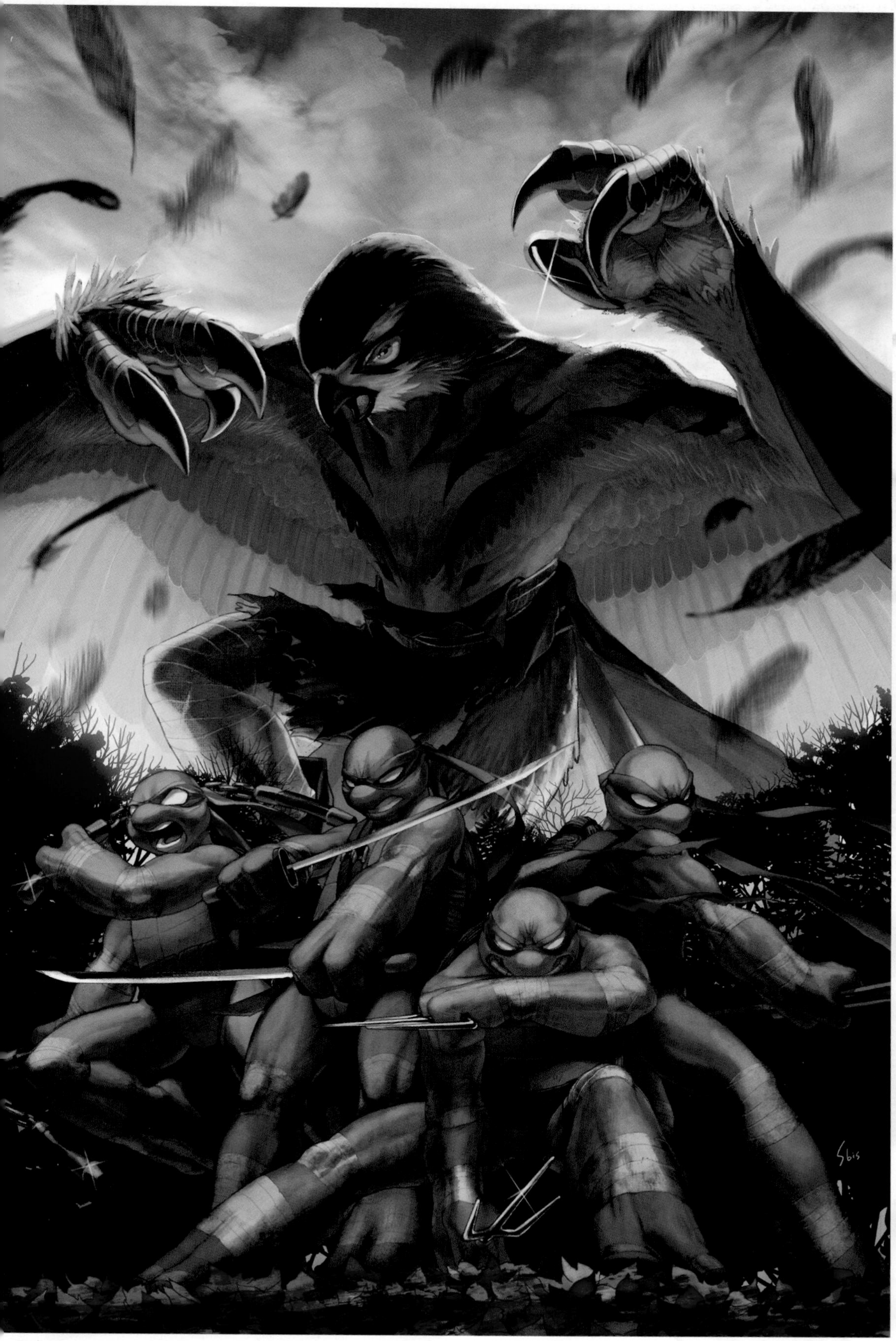
Sbis

Cover by s-bis

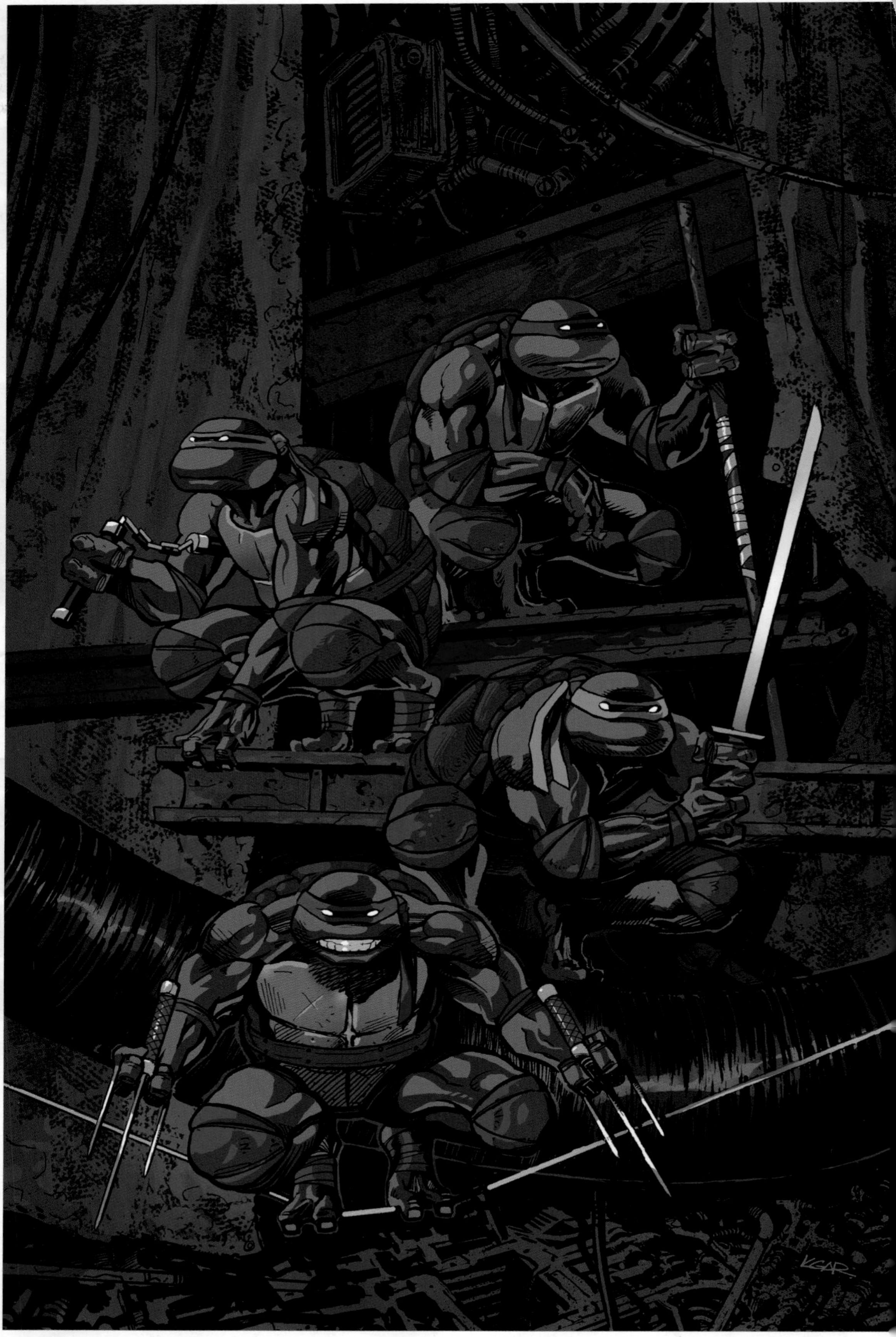
KGAR.

Cover by KEN GARING